Christer Bergström

The Battle of Britain:
AN EPIC CONFLICT REVISITED

Vaktel Förlag Publishing • Casemate Publishers

Copyright © 2014 & 2015 Christer Bergström.
All rights reserved. No part of this book may be reproduced
or transmitted in any form or by any means, electronic or
mechanical, including photocopying, recording, or by any
information storage and retrieval system, without permission
in writing from the author. Requests for permission to make
copies of any part of the work should be mailed to
vaktelforlag@gmail.com

This edition of The Battle of Britain: An Epic Conflict Revisited
first published 2015.
First published in Swedish by Vaktel Förlag 2014.
Original Swedish edition: Slaget om England
© 2014 Christer Bergström
English translation copyright © 2015 Christer Bergström
Translation assistants Donald Bryant, Louise Strömbäck
Cover design: Sarah Ommanney
Colour illustrations: Jim Laurier
Layout: Fredrik Gustafson
Maps: Samuel Svärd, info@samuelsvard.se
Front cover photos: Top: Hawker Hurricane, © The Royal
Aeronautical Society (National Aerospace Library)/Mary Evans
Picture Library. Bottom: Pilots seen running to their aircraft
during the Battle of Britain. © IWM (HU 49253)
Printing: Printon Publishing House, Estonia.
ISBN 978-1-61200-347-4

Casemate UK
10 Hythe Bridge Street, Oxford,
OX1 2EW, United Kingdom
www.casematepublishing.co.uk

Casemate Publishers
908 Darby Road, Havertown,
PA 19083, USA
www.casematepublishers.com

Vaktel förlag
Box 3027
S-630 03 Eskilstuna
Sweden
www.vaktelforlag.se
vaktelforlag@gmail.com

CONTENTS

GLOSSARY AND GUIDE
TO ABBREVIATIONS

A.I. Airborne interception (British) an aircraft on-board interception radar.

AufklObdL Aufklärungsgruppe Oberbefehlshaber der Luftwaffe German reconnaissance aviation group of the commander of the Luftwaffe.

Bf (Bayerische Flugzeugwerke) German aircraft designer; original designation of Messerschmitt 109 and 110. The abbreviations Bf 109/110 or Me 109/110 are both correct.

Bordfunker (German) Radio operator in an aircraft.

DB Daimler-Benz.

DFC Distinguished Flying Cross.

DFM Distinguished Flying Medal.

Do Dornier, German aircraft designer.

DSO Distinguished Service Order.

Ergänzungsgruppe Replacement wing, (German) a training unit that prepared aircrew for operations on a particular type or types of aircraft or roles. The equivalent of the British OTU.

ErprGr Test group, Erprobungsgruppe. German unit assigned to test various aircraft types and methods in combat (compare Lehr/-Geschwader.)

Erprobungs/-Gruppe (German) see ErprGr.

Fernaufklärer (German) long-distance (strategic) reconnaissance aircraft.

F.I.U. Fighter Interception Unit (British), a special interceptor aircraft unit of the RAF, tasked to evaluate technological advances such as airborne interception (A.I.).

Fliegerkorps (German) German aviation corps.

F/O Flying Officer.

Fw Focke Wulf, German aircraft designer.

He Heinkel, German aircraft designer.

Heinkel He 113 A hoax by German propaganda – a non-existent single-engined fighter plane, often erroneously appearing in RAF reports as a confusion with Bf 109s.

Hptm Hauptmann.

Geschwader (German) group, usually consisting of three Gruppe with a total of about 120 aircraft.

Geschwaderkommodore (German) Commander of a Geschwader, not a military rank.

Gruppe (German) Wing, consisting of three Staffel with a total of 40 aircraft.

Gruppenkommandeur (German), commander of a Gruppe.

Heeresaufklärer (German) German Army (tactical) reconnaissance aviation group.

(J) Jagd, German designation for fighter aviation.

Jafü Jagdfliegerführer, fighter leader, the commander of the fighter units within a certain air fleet (Luftflotte).

Jagd (German) German designation for fighter aviation.

JG Jagdgeschwader, fighter group.

Ju Junkers.

Kampf (German) German designation for bomber aviation.

KG (German) Kampfgeschwader, bomber group.

KGr (German) Kampfgruppe, bomber wing.

Knickebein (German) Navigational device through radio beams. The name was taken from the German legend of the bird who could see in the dark.

KüFlGr Küstenfliegergruppe, (German) coastal air unit.

Lehr (-Geschwader) (German) Learn, German unit assigned to test various aircraft types and methods in comnbat (compare Erprobungs-.)

LG Lehrgeschwader, learn group.

Luftflotte (German) air fleet.

Luftwaffe (German) the German Air Force.

Maggiore Italian military rank, equivalent to the RAF's Squadron Leader or the Luftwaffe's Major.

Maresciallo Italian military rank, equivalent to the RAF's Warrant Officer.

Me Messerschmitt, the new designation of Bayerische Flugzeugwerke since this had been overtaken by Willy Messerschmitt.

MG Maschinengewehr, machine gun (German).

Mk. (British) Mark.

NCO Non-commissioned officer, a military officer who has not been given a commission

NJG Nachtjagdgeschwader (German) night fighter group.

Oblt Oberleutnant.

Obstlt Oberstleutnant.

OTU Operational Training Unit (British) a training unit that prepared aircrew for operations on a particular type or types of aircraft or roles. The equivalent of German Ergänzungsgruppe.

P/O Pilot Officer.

RAF Royal Air Force.

RCAF Royal Canadian Air Force.

Reichsmarschall Reich (Realm) Marshal, the rank of the Luftwaffe C-in-C from 19 July 1940.

Rotte (German) A pair of aircraft operating as a team.

Rottenflieger (German) Wingman, No. 2 in a Rotte.

Rottenführer (German) Commander of a Rotte.

(S) Schlacht, battle, (German) assault (ground-attack) aviation.

Schwarm (German) Two Rotte in a formation, called finger-four in the RAF.

Seenotflugkommando (German) Air-sea rescue service.

Sergente Italian military rank, equivalent to the RAF's Sergeant or the Luftwaffe's Feldwebel.

Sergente Maggiore Italian military rank, equivalent to the RAF's Flight Sergeant or the Luftwaffe's Oberfeldwebel.

Sgt Sergeant.

S/Ldr Squadron Leader.

Sottotenente Italian military rank, equivalent to the RAF's Flight Sergeant or the Luftwaffe's Oberfeldwebel.

Sqdn (British) Squadron.

Staffel (German) Squadron, consisting of twelve aircraft in 1940.

Staffelkapitän (German), the commander of a Staffel.

Stuka (German) Abbreviation of Sturzkampf, dive-bomb aviation.

(St) (German) Abbreviation of Sturzkampf, dive-bomb aviation.

StG Sturzkampfgeschwader, dive-bomber group.

WAAF Womens' Auxiliary Air Force (British).

Wekusta Wettererkundungsstaffel, (German) weather reconnaissance squadron.

WNr (German) Werknummer, works number.

Tenente Italian military rank, equivalent to the RAF's Flying Officer or the Luftwaffe's Oberleutnant.

V formation Three-plane formation flying in the form of a 'V'.

Vee formation Three-plane formation flying in the form of a 'V'.

Vic Three-plane formation flying in the form of a 'V'.

X-Gerät (German) X-device, German radio beam aviation navigation system.

(Z) Zerstörer, destroyer, (German) long-range fighter aircraft.

Zerstörer (German) long-range fighter aircraft.

ZG Zerstörergeschwader, (German) long-range fighter aviation group.

AIR UNITS OF THE ROYAL AIR FORCE AND THE LUFTWAFFE IN 1940

Royal Air Force

Section 3 aircraft.

Flight The Flight usually consisted of two Sections, 'Yellow' and 'Red', often with a third Section in reserve, 'Blue''. Commander: Flight Lieutenant (a military rank).

Squadron The Squadron usually consisted of two Flights, 'A' and 'B', usually with 12 aircraft, often with more in reserve. Commander: Squadron Leader (a military rank).

Group Fighter Command was geographically divided into four Groups: 10 Group in southwestern England, 11 Group in southeastern England, 12 Group in central England and 13 Group in the north of the British isles.

Wing During the Battle of Britain the Duxford Wing was a special case – a formation consisting of several of 12 Group's squadrons, but subordinate to 12 Group.

(Note that the RAF's Group roughly is the equivalent of a Wing in the US Air Force, and vice versa.)

Luftwaffe

Rotte 2 aircraft, leader: Rottenführer

Kette As an alternative to the above, 3 aircraft, leader: Kettenführer

Schwarm Two Rotte, leader: Schwarmführer

Staffel Three Schwarm, 12 aircraft, commander: Staffelkapitän

Gruppe Three Staffel plus Stabsschwarm, 40 aircraft, commander: Gruppenkommandeur

Geschwader Two to five Gruppe, plus a Stabsstaffel, commander: Geschwaderkommodore

Fliegerkorps Several Geschwader

Luftflotte Two or more Fliegerkorps

RANK EQUIVALENCY 1940

	Royal Air Force	Luftwaffe
Generals	Marshal of the Royal Air Force	Generalfeldmarschall
	Air Chief Marshal	Generaloberst
	Air Marshal	General der Flieger
	Air Vice-Marshal	Generalleutnant
	Air Commodore	Generalmajor
Officers	Group Captain	Oberst
	Wing Commander	Oberstleutnant
	Squadron Leader	Major
	Flight Lieutenant	Hauptmann
	Flying Officer	Oberleutnant
	Pilot Officer	Leutnant
	Warrant Officer	-
NCOs	Flight Sergeant	Oberfeldwebel
	Sergeant	Feldwebel
	Corporal	Unteroffizier
Enlisted	Leading Aircraftman	
	Aircraftman First Class	Gefreiter
	Aircraftman Second Class	Flieger

The Luftwaffe also had several ranks for officer aspirants, e.g. Fähnrich, Fahnenjunker-Oberfeldwebel and Fahnenjunker-Feldwebel. The highest military rank within the Luftwaffe, Reichsmarschall, was held by a single person, Hermann Göring.

LUFTWAFFE UNIT ABBREVIATIONS

The basic tactical unit of the Luftwaffe was normally the Geschwader. Each Geschwader was identified by a number and had a prefix according to its branch of service, like Jagdgeschwader (JG) = fighter and Kampfgeschwader (KG) = bomber. The normal structure of a Geschwader was as follows:

Stabsstaffel of the Geschwader

I. Gruppe:	II. Gruppe:	III. Gruppe:	(IV. Gruppe:
Stabsschwarm	Stabsschwarm	Stabsschwarm	Staffel
Staffel	Staffel	Staffel	Staffel
Staffel	Staffel	Staffel	Staffel)
Staffel	Staffel	Staffel	

The commander of a Geschwader was the Geschwaderkommodore or Kommodore, which was not a rank in itself. His rank would be Major, Oberstleutnant or Oberst. The commander of a Gruppe was the Gruppenkommandeur or Kommandeur. His rank would be Major or Hauptmann. The commander of a Staffel was the Staffelkapitän. His rank would be Hauptmann, Oberleutnant or Leutnant.

Several Geschwader were organized into a Fliegerkorps (Air Corps, numbered with Roman numerals), or a Flieger-division (Air Division, numbered with Arabic numerals), or a Fliegerführer. The largest tactical organization within the German Air Force of World War II was the Luftflotte or Luftwaffenkommando, which normally comprised of two Fliegerkorps or Fliegerdivisionen or Fliegerführer. The Luftflotte roughly corresponds to a numbered U.S. Army Air Force.

Where an abbreviation stands in brackets, it indicates the aircraft type in the unit in question – this only applies reconnaissance units and so-called Lehrgeschwader:

IV.(St.)/LG 1 = Fourth (Stuka-) Gruppe of Lehrgeschwader 1
V.(Z)/LG l = Fifth (Zerstörer-) Gruppe of Lehrgeschwader 1
1.(F)/120 = First Staffel of (Fern-) Aufklärungsgruppe 120
3.(H)/31 = Third Staffel of (Heeres-) Aufklärungsgruppe 31.

TIME LINE

1939	1 September:	Germany invades Poland.
	3 September:	Britain and France declare war on Germany.
1940	10 May:	Germany launches a major offensive in the West, attacking France, Netherlands, Belgium and Luxembourg. Winston Churchill is appointed Prime Minister.
	4 June:	The British Expeditionary Force is evacuated from France via Dunkirk.
	22 June:	France surrenders.
	30 June:	The German Air Force Commander Hermann Göring issues the 'General Directive for the Air Force's warfare against England'.
	13 July:	Hitler approves the plan for an invasion of England, Operation 'Sea Lion'.
	19 July:	Göring issues instructions for 'Eagle Attack', the air offensive to neutralise the RAF.
	13 August:	'Eagle Day', the 'Eagle Attack' begins with attacks on British airfields, radar stations and aircraft factories.
	25 August:	Nocturnal British air strikes against Berlin.
	7 September:	The German Air Force shifts the priority and starts bombing London instead of the RAF's ground installations.
	15 September:	The 'Battle of Britain Day'. The Luftwaffe has a major defeat inflicted on it in the air over southern England.
	17 September:	Hitler postpones Operation 'Sea Lion' 'indefinitely'.
	20 September:	Göring shifts the bomber offensive against England to mainly the hours of darkness.

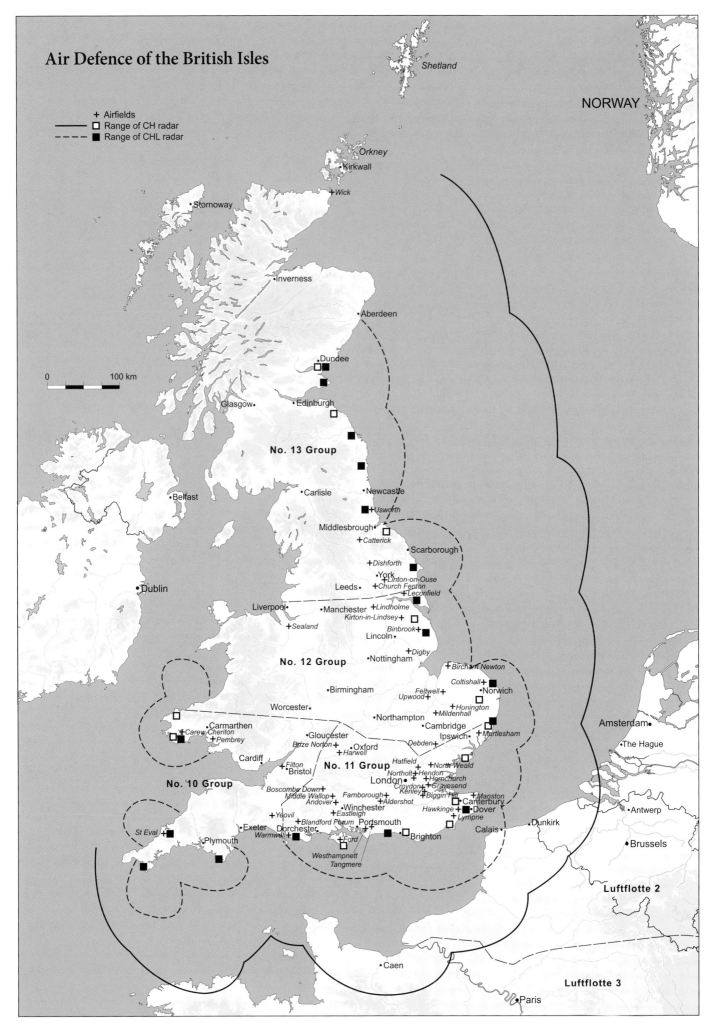

Air Defence of the British Isles

+ Airfields
□ Range of CH radar
■ Range of CHL radar

NORWAY

Shetland

Orkney
•Kirkwall
•Wick

•Stornoway

•Inverness

•Aberdeen

Glasgow•
•Edinburgh
□ Dundee
■

No. 13 Group
■

•Carlisle
•Newcastle
■ •Usworth

Middlesbrough
□
+Catterick
•Scarborough ■

+Dishforth
•York +Linton-on-Ouse
Leeds• +Church Fenton
+Leconfield ■

•Belfast

•Dublin

Liverpool•
•Manchester •Lindholme
Kirton-in-Lindsey+ □
+Sealand +Binbrook ■
Lincoln•

No. 12 Group
+Digby
•Nottingham

•Birmingham
+Bircham Newton
■Coltishall
Feltwell+ •Norwich ■
Worcester• Upwood+ +Honington
•Northampton +Mildenhall

•Cambridge
Gloucester• Ipswich• +Martlesham
Brize Norton+ Debden+ □
+Harwell Hatfield+
Carmarthen +Filton No. 11 Group +North Weald □
+Carew Cheriton •Bristol Northolt+ Hendon+
□■ +Pembrey Croydon+ +Hornchurch
London +Gravesend
Cardiff• Boscombe Down+ Kenley+ +Manston
No. 10 Group Middle Wallop+ Biggin Hill+ Canterbury
Andover+ Farnborough+ Hawkinge+ ■Dover
Winchester +Aldershot +Lympne
+Yeovil Eastleigh+ •Calais
St Eval +Blandford Forum Portsmouth
■ •Exeter Dorchester• •Brighton ■
Plymouth Warmwell• +Ford
■ Westhampnett •Caen
Tangmere

•Amsterdam
•The Hague

•Antwerp

•Dunkirk
•Brussels

Luftflotte 2

•Paris

Luftflotte 3

0   100 km

-14-

PREFACE

'Never in the field of human conflict was so much owed by so many to so few.' These words by the British Prime Minister Winston Churchill, uttered when the Battle of Britain was at its height, are valid even to this day, 75 years later.

No one doubts that the United States and the Soviet Union were the countries that primarily contributed to the defeat of Nazi Germany. But the question is what it would have looked like, had it not been for a few hundred British airmen who alone fought the Battle of Britain in the summer and autumn of 1940. By holding out, they managed to influence the United States and President Roosevelt to gradually abandon their isolationist policy and adopt a more active stance in the war, which eventually resulted in the great invasion of Normandy in June 1944. By dealing Germany its first major defeat of the war, these brave British airmen also set an example for millions of Soviet citizens who certainly had every reason to despair when Hitler's armies in 1941 seemed to be about to grind down the entire Soviet Union. Less than four years later, the Soviet Army stood as the victor in the ruins of Berlin.

Not without reason, the Battle of Britain has been depicted in hundreds – perhaps thousands – of books. Tens of thousands of articles have been written about this epic battle, it has been portrayed in hundreds of documentary films, and a Google search on 'Battle of Britain' gives nearly 59 million hits.

Then one may reasonably ask why yet another book about the Battle of Britain? The simplest answer is that it is precisely due to the great attention that this chapter in the Second World War has received in the historiography. This goes back to the winter of 1940–41, when the British Ministry of Information published its soon classic compilation, *The Battle of Britain August–October 1940*. This small publication of only 32 pages has set the tone for almost all of the following works even to this day. It ends with the following words: 'Future historians may compare [the Battle of Britain] with Marathon, Trafalgar and the Marne.' The fact that this is exactly what has happened is not without reason, but that most of these later depictions have also carried forwarded the tone set by the British Ministry of Information, is less fortunate for history writing.

There is no reason to revise the British ministry's main conclusions in the brochure from 1941. Beyond any doubt, this was a great British victory, achieved by a relatively small number of airmen. But when we go down to the level of details – and hardly any battle during the Second World War has been described in such meticulous detail as the Battle of Britain – many works seem to be characterized more by the enthusiasm to tell this fantastic story rather than a scientific research into primary sources. Other authors have made magnificent efforts to map the battle in great detail, but have been hampered by the inaccessibility of important first-hand information.

It is said that historians stand on the shoulders of giants. One of the 'giants' in the documentation of the Battle of Britain is Francis K. Mason, whose now classic work *Battle over Britain* (1969) took the historiography of the Battle of Britain to a completely new level. In this more than 600-page opus, Mason had the ambition to document every single aircraft loss during the battle. Based on the availability of primary sources at the time he managed exceptionally well. Although new research – not least inspired by Mason's huge pioneering work – has come to refute much of the findings in this book, Francis K. Mason is *the Giant*, as the British would put it, on whose shoulders we all stand.

Unfortunately Francis K. Mason is not among us any longer. He passed away just two weeks before the 70th anniversary of the Battle of Britain Day, 15 September 2010. The present work is dedicated to the memory of Francis K. Mason and his work.

When Mason published his book, the Battle of Britain lay closer in time than the 46 years that have passed since his book came out. In the meantime, much has happened on the research front. Virtually all British documents from the Battle of Britain are now available to the public and are admirably well collected in the gigantic National Archives at Kew, London. But maybe it is precisely the immense amount of material that today causes even more magnificent works in Mason's oeuvre – e.g. the new classic *The Battle of Britain Then and Now* – to have their flaws here and there. But *The Battle of Britain Then and Now* is still a giant on whose shoulders anyone researching the Battle of Britain must stand. By departing from the results presented in that book, it has been possible to penetrate deeper into the Battle of Britain.

A major reason for many gaps in the story of the Battle of Britain is that the German material is far less attainable. German Bundesarchiv certainly has access to a large collection of Second World War documents that were captured by the Western Allies in 1945. In addition, German researchers in recent years have been authorized to copy documents captured by the Soviets during the war. The most important collections are to be found at the Bundesarchiv/Militärarchiv in Freiburg. However, a review of the Bundesarchiv's collections, produces the rather disappointing conclusion that the Germans actually managed to destroy the bulk of their military records right at the end of the war, or during their repeated retreats during the war. Therefore it has been necessary, especially in the case of the German side, to also go searching outside of the official history collections.

Having been in contact with Second World War pilot veterans for more than forty years, I am in the fortunate position to have had many doors opened to me, and this has given access to documents and other materials that are outside the official archives. In fact, and especially on the German side – perhaps because of the politically sensitive nature of the subject – there is a not inconsiderable collection of original documents in private archives, alongside the official collections, and often unbeknown to researchers and historians. No single person has opened such doors to such an extent as Adolf Galland, one of the major aces during Battle of Britain and later Inspector of the German Fighter Aviation. I had the privilege of knowing Galland personally in early age, and my visit to his home in 1974, when I was only 16, took me on a path that resulted in numerous aviation books. The first of these, a book in Swedish dealing with the Battle of Britain, *Luftstrid över Kanalen (Air Combat over the Channel)* was published in 1983. It reflects at best the general state of research at that time; since then my own knowledge on the subject has advanced to a point where the present work could be regarded as an utter refutation of this first approach.

More than forty years of studies of the Battle of Britain have resulted in several new insights. Not least, I have found evidence to refute many of the long-standing beliefs that have remained especially since the Germans themselves in the 1950s began to write the story of the Battle of Britain. Defeated generals rarely are the most reliable sources, and this is perhaps particularly valid regarding the German commanders of the Second World War, who after the war have found it appropriate to blame their own shortcomings on Hitler and – in the case of the air war – Hermann Göring.

Although it has been hard on occasions, the sheer amount of concrete evidence that has emerged has forced me to reconsider many previously unreflective beliefs that actually turned out to be 'inherited' by the simple reading of literature. One example is the perception of Hermann Göring as an incompetent commander, whose unfortunate decisions placed the Luftwaffe in an unnecessarily difficult position. Another common belief is that the German twin-engined fighter Messerschmitt Bf 110 really was not of much value during the Battle of Britain. Both of these perceptions are examples of matters that I have found reason to reconsider, and which are presented in detail in this work.

Another area where ambiguity prevails, is regarding aircraft losses during the Battle of Britain. After years of in-depth studies into not only unit records, but also into small details such as individual pilot log books, I find reason to revise a portion of the previously accepted loss figures. This applies in particular, but not exclusively, to the German side. Regarding the RAF, I have found reason to make some corrections, though not to any dramatic extent. This is an undertaking that I never could have made without the assistance of many, many helpful persons. I am eternally grateful to the people who over the years have put an extensive material from private archives at my disposal. Some of these have wished to remain anonymous in this context, and I wish to hereby express my gratitude to them.

I owe a deep gratitude to the following pilot veterans who have contributed in various ways through interviews, logbooks, other documents, photographs, etc:

RAF:
Group Captain Sir Douglas Robert Steuart Bader
Squadron Leader Cyril Bamberger
Air Commodore Peter Brothers
Air Commodore James Coward
Wing Commander Thomas Dalton-Morgan
Wing Commander John Francis Durham 'Tim' Elkington
Wing Commander John Connell Freeborn
Sam Finlay/Group Captain Donald O. Finlay
Wing Commander Robert Foster
Flight Lieutenant John Peter Bowtell Greenwood
Squadron Leader James C. F. Hayter
Air-Vice Marshal James Edgar Johnson
Jennifer Baker-David &
Sally Ratledge/Flight Lieutenant Norman Taylor
Squadron Leader Douglas Tidy
Wing Commander Robert R. Stanford Tuck

Luftwaffe:
Oberst a.D. Gerhard Baeker
Major a.D. Hans-Ekkehard Bob
Oberleutnant Johannes Broschwitz
Hauptmann Hugo Dahmer
Generalleutnant a.D. Adolf Galland
Oberst a.D. Gordon M. Gollob
Major a.D. Hans Hahn
Oberstleutnant a.D. Hans-Joachim Jabs
Major a.D. Erhard Jähnert
Major a.D. Heinz Lange
Oberleutnant Erwin Leykauf
Hauptmann a.D. Victor Mölders
Leutnant Hermann Neuhoff
Generalleutnant a.D. Günther Rall
Major a.D. Gerhard Schöpfel
General a.D. Johannes Steinhoff
Generalleutnant a.D. Hannes Trautloft

I also am indebted to many other people who in different ways have offered me support and assistance in the work on this book. First of all, I would like to extend my warm and sincere gratitude to my family, Maria, Bambi, Caroline, Albin, Benjamin and Kristoffer. Without their understanding and support this book would never have become a reality.

Until his tragic and untimely death a few years ago, my friend and colleague Günther Rosipal left a collection of material in the form of documents and copies of photos as well as valuable new contacts, the extent of which will put its mark on every work on anything involving the German Air Force that I will do for the rest of my life. Alfons Altmeier and my friend and colleague Manfred Wägenbaur also have provided me with great assistance in gaining access to an invaluable material in the shape of copied original documents and photographs, and they also have been of major importance when it comes to opening important doors.

I would also like to extend my special gratitude to two persons from Sweden's eastern neighbour country: Matti Salonen put his totally amazing research on German aircraft losses at my disposal over the years. Raimo Malkamäki has, in a thousand and one ways given an extremely valuable support to my work. A very big thank you also goes to Donald Caldwell, who has allowed me to use some of his comprehensive historical material.

Besides the pilot veterans and the aforementioned persons, the following people have placed most valuable photographic material at my disposal: Bernd Barbas, Eddie Creek, Brian Cull, Ludwig von Eimannsberger, Mary Farron, Robert Forsyth, Chris Goss, Bas Hanrahan, Barbro Holmbäck, Tony Holmes, James Ivers, Daniel Johansson, Jack Kutzner, Tor Idar Larsen, Ola Laveson, Eric Mombeek, Dr. Jochen Prien, Tomasz Szlagor, John Vasco, Peter Vollmer and Walter Waiss.

I also am greatly indebted to the following individuals for their significant support in various respects: Paul Abbot, Michael Balss, Dénes Bernád, Lennart Berns, Jan Bobek, Steve Brew, Dave Brocklehurst Mbe, Ian J. Brodie, Pawel Burchard, Cynthia Coward, Mrs. D. Dalton-Morgan, Jürgen Grislawski, Fredrik Gustafson, Tomas Jönsson, Tony Kirk, Stefan Kumlien, Jack Kutzner, Ronnie Lamont, Kenneth Lewin, Andy Long, Martin Lundwall, Edward McManus, Meg Marnon, Jan-Olof Nilsson, Doug Norrie, Carina Notzke, Andy Saunders, Klaus Schiffler, Malcolm Smith, Claes Sundin, Hans E. Söder, Peter Taghon, Colonel Raymond F. Toliver, Dariusz Tyminski, John Vasco, Mattias Widén and Stefan Åberg.

Should I have accidentally missed any person above, please accept my implied gratitude.

Eskilstuna, Sweden, 3 April 2015

'HERR REICHSMARSCHALL, I WOULD LIKE AN OUTFIT OF SPITFIRES FOR MY UNIT!'

The small village of Caffiers with a railway station on the line between Boulogne and Calais is located among large fields on the fairly flat agricultural landscape in the French Pas de Calais region, about six miles from the coast opposite the famous white cliffs of Dover. Here the British had constructed a military airfield during the First World War, and it had now been occupied for a month by fighter wing III. Gruppe of fighter group Jagdgeschwader JG 26 'Schlageter'. It was 15 August 1940.

Its commander, the moustache-embellished Major Adolf Galland, was a veteran from the Spanish Civil War. Shortly after General Franco's right-wing revolt against the Spanish left government in 1936, Hitler had decided to assist him with a German volunteer force of mostly aviators, the 'Legion Condor'. Galland was among the first to sign up as a volunteer, and completed 280 combat flights in Spain. In mid-August 1940, he had advanced to the position of the most successful fighter pilots of the Second World War. For two weeks he had carried, not without pride, the Knight's Cross – Germany's highest military award at the time.

The fighter pilots of the Luftwaffe were the darlings of the Air Force commander Hermann Göring. He himself had been a fighter ace in Manfred von Richthofen's – the 'Red Baron' – so-called 'flying circus' during the First World War. Inspired by the romantic view of war that prevailed in those days, von Richthofen developed the air war into a kind of 'sport' where each pilot's number of shot down enemy aircraft were of prime importance. Göring, who put his personal mark on the new Luftwaffe – officially formed by him in 1935 – forwarded this attitude to his young fighter pilots, who enthusiastically took it to heart.

On 14 August Galland had downed his 18th enemy, and his unit reached its 100th aerial victory. When Thursday 15 August dawned, he looked forward to an opportunity to increase his personal tally past the 'magic' 20-level.

The morning was just as grey and dull as the previous days had been, but towards noon the clouds began to disperse, and at 12:20 Galland received an order to immediately take off with his wing.

A tremendous noise broke out as the pilots rushed to their planes while the ground personnel prepared the machines for take-off. Mechanics pulled the starting cranks and the first Daimler Benz engines chugged into life. A deafening roar from dozens of 1,100-hp engines set in. Then the planes taxied out on the runway, bumping on their brittle landing gears on the grass field.

As Galland's Messerschmitts came climbing up towards the clear blue sky, a large air combat could be seen at high altitude right ahead of them, straight above the white cliffs of Dover. A couple of aircraft tumbled downwards, burning and trailing thick black wisps of smoke.

But when Galland and his aviators reached the area, the combat was over. Fighter group JG 51, led by Major Werner Mölders – Galland's closest rival in terms of aerial victories – had driven off the British fighters from the Junkers 87 Stuka dive-bombers. It fell to Galland and his pilot's lot to escort the Ju 87s back across the Channel. This did not suit the hot-blooded Galland, who afterwards said: 'When we had escorted the Stukas back across the Channel, we still had much fuel left in the tanks, so I decided to try my luck with fighter sweeps. It was not long before I spotted a formation of Spitfires at a lower altitude above the Channel. I gave the attack order and attacked at the head of my Gruppe.'

What Galland had spotted were six Spitfires from RAF 54 Squadron, which, following the combat with the dive-bombers, were beset by this mass of Messerschmitts. 'The first Spitfire that I opened fire at,' said Galland, 'caught fire and fell like a comet until it hit the water and disappeared. Shortly afterwards I had another one in my gun sight and scored several hits, but this Spitfire pilot managed to get out of my line of fire through a tight turn. Since I had accumulated quite a high speed because of my diving, I passed the Englishman. When I pulled up from the dive, all the British aircraft had disappeared, so I gave the order to return to base.'

54 Squadron's Sergeant Norman A. Lawrence, who claimed to have shot down three Ju 87s in the previous engagement with the Stukas, bailed out of his burning Spitfire at the last moment and opened his parachute. Shortly afterwards he was picked up from the sea by the British Navy, and was admitted to hospital with severe shock. His aircraft was recorded as Adolf Galland's 19th victory.

Back at Caffiers the elated pilots of III./JG 26 gathered around their Gruppenkommandeur Galland, who lit one of his ubiquitous cigars. The result was summed up: Leutnant 'Jupp' Bürschgens had shot down a Spitfire east of Dover. It was his fifth victory. For this the ground personnel painted a fifth black bar beneath a small British cockade on the rudder of his Messerschmitt Bf 109. Leutnant Heinz Ebeling had shot down a Hurricane at 1,200 metres altitude. This was symbolized by a ninth bar on the rudder of Ebeling's Bf 109, 'Yellow 1'. Oberleutnant Gustav Sprick also brought home his ninth victory. In addition, Oberfeldwebel Heinz Oetteking had shot down a Spitfire. And above all, all pilots had returned safely to base.

For 'Jupp' Bürschgens it was a great relief to have fully shed the loss of his Bf 109, 'White 7', four days earlier, when he had narrowly escaped from a dogfight with the South African ace 'Sailor' Malan of 74 Squadron. But his Bf 109 was not saved. Bürschgens crashed it at Caffiers, with the fuselage breaking in two just behind the cockpit. Galland had not been gracious in his criticism. Some

A formation of Messerschmitt Bf 109 Es on their way in over the English Channel. The aircraft in this image are from Jagdgeschwader JG 2 'Richthofen'. Note the 20mm MG FF automatic cannon. (Photo: Mombeek.)

people reproached him for his harshness with his pilots, but this criticism later subsided, when the men noticed the positive outcome of Galland's tough requirements.

After lunch Galland spent a couple of hours preparing his unit for the Luftwaffe's great operation on this 15 August 1940.

It was a very ambitious plan. The twin-engined Dornier 17 bombers from Oberst Johannes Fink's bomber group KG 2 and Oberst Wolfgang von Chamier-Glisczinski's KG 3 were to be launched at full strength against the airfields at Hornchurch, Gravesend, Eastchurch and Rochester, and against the Short aeroplane works in Rochester.

In defiance of Göring's orders that the fighters must be unrestricted, the German air fleet commander Kesselring decided, in consultation with the air corps staff, to tie 130 Bf 109s from JG 51, JG 52 and JG 54 to the bombers as close escort. This was justified by the simultaneous order to dispatch two fighter groups on 'free hunting' over the target area – JG 3 and JG 26 'Schlageter'. Moreover, the main attack was preceded by a diversionary raid by fast assault aircraft against the airfield at Martlesham Heath near Ipswich, northeast of the Thames Estuary. And after the main attack – when the exhausted British fighter pilots had landed to refuel and replenish ammunition – small groups of Heinkel and Dornier bombers were to be deployed against the radar stations at Dover, Rye and Foreness, and against the ongoing repair work at the Hawkinge air base.

This time, JG 26 was in the lead. But the British fighter controller, who was in direct contact with the radar stations, knew nothing of this when he directed seven fighter squadrons against 'plus fifty bandits' approaching across the Channel. East of Dover Squadron Leader Aeneas MacDonell, commanding Spitfire-equipped 64 Squadron, spotted 'a swarm of about sixty Messerschmitt 109s'. In a letter to his cousin Marsali Bonar ten days earlier, MacDonell had expressed how pleased he was with the pilots in his squadron, 'I have a great squadron, all the men are really first class.' But he also thought they were a bit too eager. 'It's like holding in a team of wild horses to keep them in formation when there are Germans near', he once said. When they caught sight of the enemy, 64 Squadron's hotspurs hurled themselves against the 109s – notwithstanding the fact that they were twelve against sixty!

Adolf Galland, who now saw the opportunity to score his 20th victory, was equally excited. He said: 'Just as we had flown over the coast between Folkestone and Dover, we were attacked from above by twelve Spitfires. There was nothing to complain about the courage of those Englishmen!'

MacDonnell, Pilot Officer James 'Orange' O'Meara and Flight Sergeant Ernest Gilbert fell upon a formation of four 109s at 6,500 metres altitude. This was the leading group in the 7th Staffel of Galland's wing, and it consisted of the squadron leader Oberleutnant Georg Beyer, and Leutnants Josef 'Jupp' Bürschgens, Gerhard Müller-Dühe

A Spitfire from 64 Squadron. During sixteen hectic days of combat, the pilots of 64 Squadron were credited with 39½ victories against own losses of 13 aircraft.

and Walter Blume. All of them had between four and five victories each.

But the British pilots who attacked them also were no greenhorns. Russian-born Aeneas MacDonell was a 26-year old veteran who had served as a pilot in the RAF since 1934 and already had five victories, and O'Meara had chalked up six victories. Only Flight Sergeant Gilbert was less experienced.

MacDonnell and O'Meara swooped down into firing position behind one '109 each, both of which were claimed shot down. In reality, MacDonnell barely had opened fire before he got the '109 piloted by Oberleutnant Georg Beyer on his own tail. Beyer noted how his bullets slammed into the Spitfire, but in an instant Gilbert's Spitfire sat behind himself. The last Beyer saw of MacDonnell's Spitfire was that it disappeared, trailing black smoke. Then he performed a snap half roll and dived with the Messerschmitt fighter's Daimler Benz engine roaring. He managed to escape his pursuer, and in the next second Gilbert's own aircraft shivered under the hits from another Messerschmitt. It was 'Jupp' Bürschgens who had placed himself in a good firing position and now opened up with all guns.

Leaving a white band of leaking coolant behind, Gilbert's Spitfire escaped at full speed. In the heat of combat it seems as though it was also fired upon by Leutnant Walter Blume. Both Bürschgens and Blume claimed one shot down.

By now the air battle was in full swing. 'I managed to sneak up behind one of the Spitfires in the rear of their formation and opened fire from a distance of 100 metres', Galland said, and continued: 'The hits from my cannons and machine guns tore off large chunks of metal from the Spitfire, and as these came flying towards me I had to break off. But the Spitfire already was on fire and went into its final dive.'

Galland immediately attacked his next victim. 'I came in obliquely below and behind a Spitfire and opened fire from a distance of 100 metres', he recalled. 'The Spitfire slowly turned over while I continued to fire, and metal pieces rained from the plane. Flames shot out from the fuselage and wings. I had to swerve because otherwise I had come too close, and then Oberleutnant Schöpfel attacked the Spitfire, which plunged straight into the water.'

Twenty-three-year-old Flying Officer Christopher John Drake Andreae had arrived at 64 Squadron as a newly trained pilot as late as on 23 July 1940. He never managed to get out of his burning Spitfire as it whirled down to finally hit the surface of the English Channel and sink to the bottom.

Meanwhile, Galland's wingman, Oberleutnant Joachim Müncheberg, and Oberleutnant Beyer opened fire against one Spitfire each, recorded as their 13th and 7th victories. It is possible that the impact into the sea of of Andreae's Spitfire – which was probably shot down by Galland – a few minutes later from such a high altitude (6,000 metres) was perceived by different pilots as the aircraft that they just had hit. In actual fact, Andreae's machine was the only Spitfire to go down into the sea in that engagement.

Gilbert managed to force-land his damaged Spitfire at Hawkinge. However, it is conceivable that other British units interfered in this particular combat. No. 151 Squadron recorded a Hurricane damaged west of Dover.

All this was typical of the swirling air combats at these high altitudes and over a limited area. The British had no better idea of the damage they managed to deal their opponent. When they returned to base, MacDonnell, O'Meara and Pilot Officer Adrian Francis Laws reported that they had shot down one Messerschmitt each out there over the Strait of Dover. In reality, not a single German fighter had been lost.

Among all the participating pilots, only Leutnant Gerhard Müller-Dühe of III./JG 26 can with certainty be said to have shot down an enemy aircraft. When he, together with 'Jupp' Bürschgens and Walter Blume, flew back towards the base at Caffiers, they encountered a lone Spitfire. The British pilot, Pilot Officer Ralph Roberts, had set off to the wrong coast – an error considerably more serious than to mistakenly believe to have shot down an enemy aircraft. After a fierce dogfight, Müller-Dühe forced Roberts to belly-land his Spitfire 'SH-W' in a field near Calais. Bürschgens said: 'I met Roberts after we had landed. It was a heavy combat, and Roberts was a very brave and skilled pilot.' Roberts would spend the rest of the war in a German POW camp. He lived until 1994.

When Galland and his airmen turned back for home, they encountered a large formation of twin-engined Dornier 17 bombers that came processing in towards England.

Once again, there was reason for the men at Caffiers to celebrate. Again, all pilots had returned to the airfield safe and sound, and nine victories were reported. In reality, nine British fighters had been shot down, with another four damaged by the German operation across the Strait of Dover in the afternoon of 15 August 1940. But besides Galland and his aviators, several other German fighter pilots claimed their share in the British losses. Werner Mölders' JG 51 was also credited with nine kills.

After just over an hour, at half past five in the evening, Galland and his airmen took off against England again, this time on a regular fighter sweep – i.e. with the task of seeking out and shooting down enemy aircraft to take control of the airspace. This time, however, they saw no British fighters and returned with dwindling fuel reserves in their '109s an hour later. At Caffiers the ground crew was waiting. In haste, the planes were refuelled and replenished with ammunition. To the extent that time permitted, the machines also were looked over. At seven in the evening the pilots were back and entered their cramped cockpits.

At twenty past seven, Galland's III./JG 26 was up above the Channel, along with the group's II. Gruppe and III./JG 54. Again, the task was to perform a fighter sweep.

The mission began in a quite strange way. A lone Spitfire suddenly dived right through the German formation, without opening fire. A couple of '109s pursued the British fighter down to 800 metres, where they shot it on fire. The pilot was seen to bail out.

Shortly afterwards, the Germans spotted a large formation of thirty Spitfires and Hurricanes and attacked, with devastating results. These were the Spitfires of 54 and 266 squadrons and the Hurricanes of 151 Squadron, whose Operations Record Book describes what followed: 'A large formation of ME 109s were again encountered. In this action we fared badly, Pilot Officer [James] Johnson, Sub Lieutenant [Henry] Beggs, Pilot Officer [John] Ellacombe and Pilot Officer [Gustaw] Radwanski being shot down. . . . Squadron Leader[John] Gordon was peppered with shrapnel from a cannon shell and was slightly wounded in the back of the head and leg.'

Sub Lieutenant Henry Beggs' 151 Squadron Hurricane 'DZ-C' crash-landed in this condition after encountering JG 26 on 15 August 1940.

One of the Spitfire pilots, 54 Squadron's Flight Lieutenant 'Al' Deere, was bold enough to pursue a damaged Bf 109 to Pas de Calais in France. It cost him dearly. Oberleutnant Kurt Ebersberger from II./JG 26 chased Deere straight across the Channel – back to the British coast – before he finally managed to shoot down the Spitfire. Deere himself was lucky to escape with only minor injuries.

Here III./JG 26 seems to have underreported its accomplishments: Leutnants Heinz Ebeling, Joseph Haiböck and Wilhelm Fronhöfer were credited with one victory each. In reality, the British lost not only the four Hurricanes from 151 Squadron, but also two Spitfires, with a third crashing with severe combat damage near Maidstone. It can't be excluded that this day's intense combat activity caused the pilots to make errors when they afterwards wrote on which mission they made their claims for shot down enemy aircraft in their reports.

To Adolf Galland and his III./JG 26, 15 August 1940 was a great success, which was celebrated that evening. The unit had not only achieved 18 victories, but their commander Galland had scored three of these, and thus reached a total number of 21. On top of this, not one of the unit's pilots, not a single aircraft, had been lost.

This was one perspective on 15 August 1940, when the Battle of Britain – the Luftwaffe's attempt to wipe out the RAF in preparation for the planned invasion of the British Isles – peaked.

Adolf Galland returning from a mission over southern England, with the classic cigar between his lips. Adolf Galland advanced to become the Inspector of the German Fighter Aviation. Galland passed away on 9 February 1996, at the age of 84. (Photo: Galland.)

Galland and his pilots still knew nothing of the scope of the defeat suffered by the German Air Force. On this day, Hermann Göring's Luftwaffe had made a major effort to crush the British opposition. But despite an apparent numerical inferiority, the British airmen struck back hard. When the day was over, several German air units were in shambles. One of them was the élite unit Erprobungsgruppe 210, which had been cut to pieces by two Hurricane squadrons while other Spitfire and Hurricane pilots kept Galland and his airmen busy during the day's final mission. One of the airmen who failed return was the famous commander of Erprobungsgruppe 210, Hauptmann Walter Rubensdörffer.

While Galland shot down his 20th and 21st enemy aircraft on the afternoon of 15 August, other German units were dealt disastrous losses. Of the fifteen Ju 88 bombers

from bomber group LG 1, only seven returned to base. Fighter unit ZG 76 was hit even harder, losing no less than 19 aircraft and one of its wing commanders.

When the Germans counted their losses of 15 August 1940, they found that no less than 77 own aircraft had been shot down. No one had the big picture clearer to himself than the British Prime Minister Winston Churchill, who commented on the achievements of the British fighter pilots with a few words that would become immortal: 'Never in the field of human conflict was so much owed by so many to so few'.

But most of the young men who participated in the fighting on this historic day saw nothing special about it, more than what they and their closest comrades experienced personally. Each unit lived in a microcosm, and to the airmen who never knew if they would live to see tomorrow, the next mission was what mattered. The mood of the British pilots was marked by exhaustion rather than triumph. At air bases Croydon, Martlesham, Rochester and other places hit by German air attacks, the personnel asked themselves how it all would end. Many of the British fighter pilots also had serious thoughts, like Pilot Officer Robert Doe in 234 Squadron. When he went to bed that evening, he came to realize that he might not survive the summer. He decided that if he saw tracers coming from behind, he would push the control stick forward and dive. This was something he promised himself to think about every night until it would become an automatic reaction.[1]

To the 'aces', the above-average skilled fighter pilots who were far superior to the vast majority of the opponent's airmen, it was even a kind of 'adventurous' war. Their youth and all the encouragement they received from superiors and the media contributed to this attitude. Two of these were Galland and Mölders. Even though they were summoned to Göring's residence Karinhall for a conference about the difficult situation in the Battle of Britain two days later, they retained their youthful frivolity. After the meeting with Göring the two fighter pilots agreed that if Galland was the war's 'Red Baron' – the top ace of First World War, von Richthofen – Mölders was its 'Boelcke', the fighter ace who also contributed to the tactical and technical development of the air force. This perspective also is important to realise in order to understand the Battle of Britain.

Although 15 August 1940 was the climax of the battle, it was just the beginning. Even III./JG 26 would be badly decimated. In the next two weeks, Müller-Dühe would be killed, and both Bürschgens and Blume would end up shot down and in British captivity. By that time, Galland had also grown more serious. When Göring visited him and asked him what he wished for, the answer came quicker than Galland had time to think, 'Herr Reichsmarschall, I would like an outfit of Spitfires for my unit!'

THE BATTLE OF BRITAIN IN COLOUR

A formation of British Hawker Hurricanes. This fighter played the main role in the defence of Britain during the summer and autumn of 1940. All colour photographs are placed on a German so-called Gradnetz-Karte on oilcloth which was used by a Luftwaffe crew during the Battle of Britain. (Via Daniel Johansson.)

A formation of Messerschmitt Bf 109 Es at low altitude over the Dover Strait in the summer of 1940. (Photo: Galland.)

This image, arranged for propaganda purposes with German pilots in both aircraft (a captured Spitfire) shows what air combats could look like between the Spitfire (left) and the Messerschmitt Bf 109 (right) during the Battle of Britain. (Photo: Galland.)

Luftwaffe personnel – so-called 'schwarze Männer' (black men) – crank the engine running on a Junkers Ju 87 dive bomber.

An NCO of the Luftwaffe ground staff is studying the 22 bars on the stabiliser of a Bf 109. Each bar indicates an air victory. This aircraft, Bf 109 E-4 'Yellow 1', was flown by Oberleutnant Josef Priller, the commander of 6./JG 51. The picture was taken on 19 October, 1940, when Priller was awarded the Knight's Cross. (Photo: Trautloft.)

Heinkel He 111 bombers. The twin-engined Heinkel 111 was Germany's most common bomber during the Battle of Britain. (Photo: Waiss.)

A Ju 87 Stuka from 6./StG 77.

A member of the crew of a German twin-engined Junkers
Ju 88 bomber. He wears the thick life vest of the 1939 model.
This was replaced in 1940 by a lighter, inflatable version.

A three-plane 'Kette' of Ju 87s wing-tip to enter a
dive-attack.

A He 111 is getting ready for take-off. (Photo: Waiss.)

Messerschmitt Bf 109s from III./JG 53 'Pik As' (Ace of Spades) at an airfield in France during the Battle of Britain. By this time the unit had, in protest against the Luftwaffe Commander Göring, painted over the swastikas on their aircraft. A member of the ground crew just 'happens' to 'pass by', appropriately enough obscuring this in this German photography. See also page 94. (Photo: Neuhoff.)

General Wolfram Freiherr von Richthofen, the commander of German Fliegerkorps VIII, studies the map along with some airmen from I./StG 1 at the beginning of the Battle of Britain.

Spitfire Mk I

Flown by Flight Lieutenant Alan Deere, 54 Squadron, RAF.

Profile by Jim Laurier.

Spitfire Mk I

Flown by Flight Lieutenant Brian Kingcombe, 92 Squadron, RAF.

Profile by Jim Laurier.

Spitfire Mk I

Flown by Pilot Officer Eric Lock, 41 Squadron, RAF.
This aircraft was shot down when flown by Flying Officer 'Tony' Lovell
on 5 September 1940.

Profile by Jim Laurier.

Spitfire Mk I

Flown by Pilot Officer Richard Hillary, 603 Squadron, RAF.
Hillary was shot down in this aircraft on 3 September 1940.

Profile by Jim Laurier.

Hurricane Mk I

Flown by Squadron Leader Archie McKellar, 605 Squadron, RAF. McKellar shot down three He 111s and damaged a fourth with this aircraft on 15 August 1940, shortly before his own aircraft was damaged by fire from the German bombers.

Profile by Jim Laurier.

Hurricane Mk I

Flown by Squadron Leader Douglas Bader, 242 Squadron, RAF.

Profile by Jim Laurier.

Hurricane Mk I

Flown by Sergeant Josef František, 303 (Polish) Squadron, R.A.F. František was killed during a flight with this aircraft on 8 October 1940. Before that the same aircraft was damaged in combat with Bf 109s on both 5 and 6 September 1940.

Profile by Jim Laurier.

Hurricane Mk I

Flown by Pilot Officer Robert Foster, 605 Squadron, R.A.F.

Profile by Jim Laurier.

Messerschmitt Bf 109 E-4/N

Flown by Oberstleutnant Adolf Galland, Stab/JG 26 'Schlageter'.
Galland achieved his 57th victory with this aircraft on 5 December 1940.
Profile by Jim Laurier.

Messerschmitt Bf 109 E-4

Flown by Major Helmut Wick, Stab/JG 2 'Richthofen'.
Wick was killed after getting shot down in this aircraft
on 28 November 1940.
Profile by Jim Laurier.

Messerschmitt Bf 109 E-4

Flown by Hauptmann Wilhelm Balthasar, III./JG 3.

Profile by Jim Laurier.

Messerschmitt Bf 109 F-1

Flown by Oberstleutnant Werner Mölders, Stab/JG 51.

Profile by Jim Laurier.

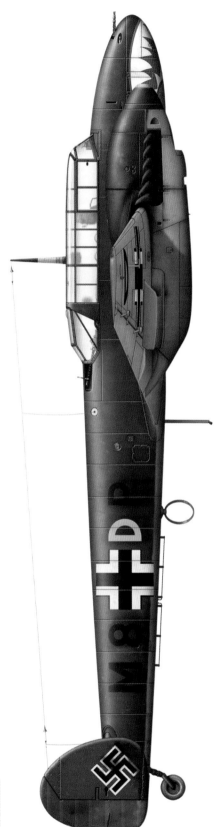

Messerschmitt Bf 110 C

II./'Haifischgruppe'/ZG 76.

Profile by Fernando Estanislau.

Messerschmitt Bf 110 C-2

Flown by Hauptmann Horst Liensberger/Unteroffizier Albert Köpge, V.(Z)/LG 1. Liensberger and Köpge were killed in action over Hailsham in this Bf 110 on 27 September 1940.

Profile by Fernando Estanislau.

Messerschmitt Bf 110 D

Fitted with a 1050-litre auxiliary tank, a so-called 'Dackelbauch', under the belly, I./ZG 76.

Profile by Fernando Estanislau.

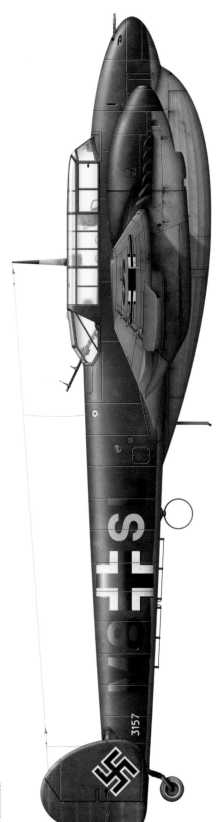

Messerschmitt Bf 110 D-0/B

Flown by Hauptmann Martin Lutz/Unteroffizier Anton Schön, 1./ErprGr 210.

Profile by Fernando Estanislau.

CHAPTER 1
THE LUFTWAFFE VERSUS
THE ROYAL AIR FORCE

Operation 'Seelöwe'

On 4 June 1940, the Battle of Dunkirk was over. The British Expeditionary Force in France had been expelled from the continent by the lightning offensive launched by Hitler in the West on 10 May. Indeed, 338,000 men had been evacuated across the narrow Strait of Dover, but the British Expeditionary Force had lost all its heavy equipment in France.

In the UK, there were exactly 167 anti-tank guns and the heavy military equipment at hand was no more than that normally assigned to two infantry divisions. Almost 1,000 British aircraft had been lost during the Battle of France. [2] On 4 June 1940, RAF Fighter Command mustered no more than 446 operational fighter aircraft, of which only 331 were the single-engined modern types that had any chance to take up the battle with the German fighters – Hawker Hurricane and Vickers Supermarine Spitfire. The words uttered by British Prime Minister, 65-year-old Winston Churchill, in a radio broadcast speech on the same day have become winged:

We shall go on to the end,
we shall fight on the seas and oceans,
we shall fight with growing confidence and growing strength in the air,
we shall defend our Island, whatever the cost may be,
we shall fight on the beaches,
we shall fight on the landing grounds,
we shall fight in the fields and in the streets,
we shall fight in the hills,
we shall never surrender!

At that time, many characterized Churchill as an irresponsible adventurist. But Winston Churchill was not only a 'fighter'; his resolve to fight on was based on deep psychological insights, and – not least – an understanding of the personalities of two most important statesmen, Germany's self-willed dictator Hitler and the President of the United States, Franklin D. Roosevelt. When Roosevelt in August 1940 sent an American military delegation for a conference with the highest military command in Britain, the commander of the British Air Staff Air Chief Marshal Sir Cyril Newall, admitted that the US economic and industrial co-operation was the foundation of the entire British strategy. [3]

Churchill knew that Roosevelt was on his side, but there also was a large isolationist public opinion in the United States who wished the United States to continue to stay out of the war, so it was obvious that Roosevelt could not do much before the presidential elections in November 1940. Thus, everything hung on the British ability to hold out until then. Moreover, Churchill expected that if Britain could hold out until the autumn weather made it impossible to carry out air operations on a large scale, Hitler would lose his patience and turn his attention against Communist Soviet Union, which would be Britain's rescue. Until then, there were four critical factors that would determine whether Britain would sustain the German onslaught: the will to fight on, the Royal Navy, the Royal Air Force, and whether the British would be able to buy themselves time.

Regarding the first, Churchill personally contributed more than anyone else in reinforcing the British will to resist. When Hitler eventually realized that he needed to use force to subdue Britain, he met a people with dogged resolve to resist. The Royal Navy, their powerful fleet, was still the strongest in the world and still ruled the seas. The third and fourth factors – concerning the air force and time – were closely linked to each other. Britain's good fortune was, as so often in history, one of geography – that the country is surrounded by sea. With the Royal Navy's mas-

This British propaganda poster from 1940 clearly illustrates Winston Churchill's prominent role in stoking the British will to resist.

tery at sea and the Germans in possession of the world's most effective air force, it was not hard to figure out that the battle would be decided by the outcome of the air war.

As it would turn out, Churchill in an almost eerie way managed to read the mind of the Nazi dictator. Hitler lived in a world of racist fantasies, and to him it was both unnatural and undesirable to have the two 'white master races' – the German and the British people – in a feud with each other. No one could be less prepared for a war with Great Britain than Adolf Hitler.

On 2 June 1940, he had said that he looked forward to a peace settlement with London so that he 'could finally get his hands free' for his 'great and real task: to deal with Bolshevism'. Since Hitler wished to save his armed forces for the latter purpose, he conveyed to the British that he was prepared to accept a separate peace. According to this, Britain would retain its Empire – with the possible exception of the returning to Germany of the small colonies that Imperial Germany had in 1914 – and also its armed forces intact. The only concession that Hitler demanded was, except of course for an end to the fighting, that Britain would recognize the Third Reich's hegemony in Europe.

While the British were given a few weeks of relative calm, which they used to prop up war production, Hitler showed what can only be described as an apathetic approach towards warfare against Great Britain. On 17 June, a conference at the German Naval Headquarters noted that regarding an invasion of England, 'the Führer still has not uttered any such intentions,' while 'the High Command still has not made any studies or preparation.'[4]

When France surrendered on 22 June 1940, Hitler regarded the war as largely finished. 'The Führer really does not wish to put any pressure on the British', propaganda minister Goebbels noted on 27 June. Hermann Göring, the Luftwaffe's C-in-C, wanted to get started with air operations against England, but was held back by Hitler.[5]

Only on 13 July did Hitler care to take a look at the various draft plans for an invasion of England that had been made by the various branches of the Wehrmacht. But he was still hesitant. 'The Führer', wrote Generalleutnant Franz Halder, Chief of the German Army Staff, 'accepts that it may be necessary to force Britain to make peace, but he is very reluctant to take this step because he believes that if we defeat the British on the battlefield, the British Empire will collapse, and Germany would not benefit from that.'

This operations' plan, originally called 'Löwe' (lion), largely called for an amphibious landing on the English south coast over the course of three days with thirteen army divisions – four between Brighton and the Isle of Wight, six between Ramsgate and Eastbourne, and three at Lyme Bay. Once this first assault force had established bridgeheads to a depth of 10-15 kilometres, another twenty-eight divisions were to follow, in order to develop an offensive from these bridgeheads, aiming to occupy the entire United Kingdom. Hitler made only one remark – he changed the code name from 'Löwe' to 'Seelöwe' (sea lion).

Following Churchill's rejection of Hitler's peace offer on 22 July, Operation 'Seelöwe' advanced to the highest priority, and the Germans began to look for resources for the invasion. Suddenly there was a rush! It was calculated that 'Seelöwe' had to be implemented no later than 15 September 1940, because after that, the autumn weather was assessed to be too uncertain to guarantee the crucial Luftwaffe support of the operation.

Army units were hastily assembled at Pas de Calais, the Seine Estuary and the Cotentin Peninsula. But the German army lacked the necessary sea vessels for an amphibious landing. The kind of landing crafts that the Allies used in the Pacific and during the invasions in Europe in 1943–1944 did not exist. Things had to be improvised. Basically, what the Germans had available for the landing operation was common river barges! In a few weeks, the Rhine and the Dutch channels were cleared of their small coal barges. These took out in their thousands to the North Sea and entered the French and Belgian Channel ports.

Next were the logistical problems. How would half a million combat soldiers be supported on the other side of a sea which would definitely swarm with British battleships, cruisers, destroyers and submarines in the crucial moments? It was obviously out of the question. Therefore, several conditions must be met before a German invasion fleet could be sent across the English Channel. German bombers would have to shield the invasion fleet against British warships. But not least the experience from the air fighting over Dunkirk in late May and early June 1940 had shown that German bombers were relatively easy prey for the RAF fighters. Hence, first of all the RAF had to be neutralised. This too could only be the Luftwaffe's task. The first step was of course to wipe out Fighter Command.

But even if the Germans succeeded in annihilating the RAF and achieving total air supremacy, it was far from certain that the Luftwaffe would be able to hold the powerful British fleet away from the vulnerable invasion craft and transport ships that were to support the invasion army. Nothing but a totally fearless effort by the Royal Navy could be expected. A failure of the invasion of Britain would likely have far-reaching political consequences; it would be a terrible blow against both German military prestige and Hitler's political authority. The Nazi leader feared that such a large failure could jeopardize his main war aim, the invasion of the Soviet Union.

Moreover, the aviation that would bear the main burden of the first phase of the Battle of Britain as the Germans envisioned it, was at the time of the surrender of France in need of recovery. During May and June 1940 alone, 1,428 German aircraft had been lost and another 1,916 badly damaged and in need of repairs (the figures include both combat losses and accidents). Although the aviation industry's output figures roughly kept pace with losses during the Battle of France, the aviation that was so crucial for operations against the British Isles, the bombers, had declined from 1,102 operational aircraft in March 1940 to only 841 in June, thus a reduction of almost a quarter. Another important type of aircraft, transport planes, had been reduced in number by more than a third since the outbreak of war – from 552 to 357. What was expected to be the Luftwaffe's most important and most difficult task of the entire war – to keep the whole Royal Navy at bay during an invasion of the British Isles – would, even in the most favourable scenario, have been carried out by a

*One of the RAF Hurricanes that remained on the continent
following the brief Battle of France in May and June 1940.
(Photo: Trautloft.)*

further decimated German aviation immediately after the
intended final battle with the RAF.

There were no real plans that showed exactly how the
RAF was to be annihilated. It was absolutely clear that the
Luftwaffe would not be able to use its full strength as in the
Blitzkrieg operations; the geographic distances to various
attack targets in and around the British Isles was too large.
The single-engined Ju 87 Stukas and Bf 109s were only able
to reach the southern parts of England. The Germans had
good reason before the war to put the emphasis on the creation a tactical air force, but now they would be forced to
use it for a strategic purpose. To top it all, there was no previous experience of this kind of strategic air offensive. The
Germans had to invent everything by themselves, through
trial and error. No wonder the air operations against England had got off to a very slow start, which was of great
benefit to the British.

Relations of strength

By this time Germany and Great Britain had arguably the
two most modern air forces in the world. But despite the
fact that Germany had begun to expand their armed forces ahead of the UK, the British would surpass their enemy
in combat aircraft output figures in 1940. One of the first
steps made by Churchill when he was appointed Prime
Minister on 10 May 1940, was to make Max Aitken – Lord
Beaverbrook – Minister for Aircraft Production. Owing
to a combination of state bureaucracy and an unhealthy
competition between various private enterprises, British
production of the most important fighters was at that time
only 144 planes a month. If it had remained at that level,
this alone would have been enough to bring the Battle of
Britain to a very different ending.

Lord Beaverbrook moved energetically to alter the
situation. By putting pressure on the factory owners – including harsh crackdowns on factories that hoarded spare
parts and tools, and the expropriation of property that
was required – plus a comprehensive and systematic loot-
ing of non-airworthy aircraft for spare parts, the previous
owner of the Rolls-Royce Automobile Company achieved
a miracle with British aircraft production. In June alone,
446 fighters were manufactured. At the same time bomber production also increased to a record of 407. Between 4
June and 10 July – the period of tranquillity that the British
were given before the real German air offensive begun –
the strength of RAF Fighter Command increased by 68%,
from 446 to 656 serviceable fighters. On top of that, a force
of 467 serviceable bombers exposed Germany and the occupied territories to regular nocturnal attacks.

However, the RAF was opposed by a force that was
more than twice as large. Not only was the Luftwaffe on the
whole superior to the RAF in terms of aircraft quality, but it
also enjoyed a more than satisfactory numerical advantage.
In June 1940 the Luftwaffe had 2,295 operational combat
aircraft at its disposal – 841 bombers, 337 dive-bombers
and assault aircraft, and no less than 1,117 fighters (856 Bf
109s and 261 Bf 110s). [6]

But time was on the side of the British – and this in
more than one respect. The Luftwaffe was indeed more
powerful than the RAF, but British aircraft production already exceeded that of Germany. Hitler's idea of the German people's grandeur frequently led him to decisions that
went counter to the war plans. Such was the case with his
decision not to set the country on a total war footing, but
instead maintain civilian production at a high level.

When the Battle of Britain began, the Luftwaffe really
had too few of the two aircraft that were most critical to
the new strategic air operations over the British Isles – the
bomber Junkers Ju 88 and the fighter plane Messerschmitt
Bf 110. These the two most modern aircraft in the Luftwaffe
inventory were the only ones with a sufficient operational
range to reach every corner of the British Isles. Although
the Ju 88 received the highest priority in German bomber
production, with almost two-thirds of all new bombers in
1940 being Ju 88s, it still only was 1,816 out of a total 2,852,
while at the same time British output was 3,488 bombers,
this in a year when fighter production received the highest
priority!

Of the twin-engined Bf 110 fighters, no more than an
average of 102 a month were manufactured. For this simple
reason, it would be an air offensive against England rather
than Great Britain, which gave the RAF the opportunity to
withdraw worn-out units to tranquil regions further north
in order to rest and refit. Had there been Bf 110s in large
numbers, the RAF would not have had this great advantage. While Germany throughout 1940 produced 3,106 Bf
109 and Bf 110 fighters, the British produced 4,283 fighters.
During the critical four-month period of June-September
1940 alone, output figures from British aviation industry
were 1,743 fighters, while another 1,872 fighter aircraft
were repaired.

Of equal importance for the British as this stunning
production apparatus, was the superiority of their fighter
control system, which to some extent balanced their numerical inferiority.

A glance into 11 Group's Operations Room. On the plotting table immediately below the staff officers' observation balcony, the WAAF plotters place wooden blocks, each representing a friendly or a hostile air unit.

The organisation

In 1940 Great Britain had the world's first radar-directed air defence system. It consisted of two parallel chains of radar stations extending along the southern and eastern coasts, as well as around major industrial centres and ports on the west coast: Chain Home (CH) and Chain Home Low (CHL). Chain Home consisted of twenty-one radar stations – or Radio Direction Finder as they were called at that time. These operated on a wavelength of between 10 and 13.5 metres and the signals from their 110-metre high transmission masts could reach aircraft at high altitudes at a distance of around 190 kilometres. In other words, the British were able to spot German aircraft almost all the way to Rotterdam, Brussels or Paris, provided that they flew high enough. These CH stations were supplemented with thirty Chain Home Low stations (CHL), operating with more sophisticated facilities that were able to detect aircraft at 150 metres' altitude at distance of up to 50 kilometres.

Contrary to a common perception, the British were not ahead of the Germans on in the field of radar. The Germans had their so-called Freya radar operating at 1.2-metre wavelength, i.e. only a tenth of the British CH, providing greater precision. In fact, the first radar-guided fighter interception of the war was when German fighter planes in December 1939 repulsed a British air raid over the German Bight. Even if radar played a key role in the British air defence, its great role was decided by organisation rather than technology. The Germans may have taken the lead in the field of technology, but the British were the first to organise the use of this technology in the most optimal way. Created in 1936 by Air Chief Marshal Hugh Dowding, commander of RAF Fighter Command, it was the first large-scale centralized air defence command and control system in aviation history.

The nerve centre of the system was the so-called Filter Room at Fighter Command's headquarters at Bentley Priory near Stanmore in London's northwestern outskirts. All sightings at radar stations of incoming signals were forwarded to the Filter Room by means of a direct telephone line. The radar was supplemented with the Royal Observer Corps' well-developed network of air observation posts, which were scattered across the UK. Any observation of what could be hostile aircraft was also reported via telephone to Bentley Priory. In the Filter Room at Bentley Priory, all incoming reports were weighed together and evaluated. These also were compared with the reports of all incoming IFF signals. IFF – Identification Friend or Foe – was a device with which all British aircraft were equipped, and which simply identified them as British aircraft by means of a radio device called 'pip-squeak'.

The evaluated reports were forwarded to the adjacent Operations Room, which was dominated by a large table map, called a plotting table. Observed from small balconies above, WAAF plotters placed and moved differently coloured wooden blocks, each representing hostile or friendly aircraft formations, on the map according to the incoming reports. This gave Air Chief Marshal Dowding and General Frederick Pile, the commander of Anti-Air-craft Command, a perfect overview of the whole situation. Based on this overview, reports were forwarded to the various Fighter Groups.

In early July 1940, Fighter Command was regionally and operationally divided into three Groups:

- **11 Group** in the South, with headquarters in Uxbridge, west of London.
- **12 Group** in Central UK, with headquarters in Watnall in Nottingham.
- **13 Group** in the north, with headquarters in Newcastle.

A fourth unit, 10 Group, was about to be formed – with headquarters in Box, northeast of Bristol – to take over operations in the airspace in the southwest. This was declared operational on 8 July, with initially four squadrons assigned from 11 Group – Nos. 87 and 213 squadrons at Exeter, 92 Squadron at Pembrey and 234 Squadron at St Eval.[7]

Each of these Group headquarters also had an Operations Room with a similar plotting table showing the Group's operational area. Next, the information was forwarded to the Group's various Sectors, who organised the various squadrons in each group. Each Sector Base also had such an Operations Room with a plotting table showing the Sector's operational area.

Operational command rested with each Group Headquarters. There, orders went out by telephone to the Sector Bases, where the Sector Controller decided which units were to be alerted. The fighter units in the front line in southern England were divided into nine Sectors, each located at a base that served both as an airfield and an operations command centre: Middle Wallop and Filton in 10 Group; Tangmere, Kenley, Biggin Hill, Hornchurch, Northolt, North Weald and Debden in 11 Group. Each Sector usually divided into between two and four squadrons at the Sector bases and so-called satellite airfields.

While the airborne fighter pilots received instructions via radio from the Sector Base, and the commander of each Group had the overall responsibility for the operational command, Fighter Command's headquarters at Bentley Priory had an overview of the entire airspace and was responsible for air raid warnings, and for alerting the anti-aircraft units and the barrage balloon units.

Owing to this ingenious organisation, Fighter Command was able to operate with a much higher efficiency than the Luftwaffe, which by this time had nothing even remotely reminiscent of the British air defence system. Eventually, the British air defence system was introduced in all other major air forces – although in the German case it was hardly a question of copying the British system, but rather simply the Germans having the same idea.

Another British advantage, albeit not to the same extent as many have assumed, was that they had managed to come across a copy of the German code machine 'Enigma'. British SIS (Secret Intelligence Service) intercepted German radio traffic and decrypted Enigma-coded messages at Bletchley Park. Code-named 'Ultra', this was shrouded in such secrecy that not even the commander of Fighter Command, Air Chief Marshal Dowding, was informed of its existence until 16 October 1940.

One of the most comprehensive books on the Battle of Britain, the more than 800-page fifth edition of *The Battle of Britain Then and Now* (1989), devotes a chapter to Ultra and the Battle of Britain, without having access to more than a fraction of the decoded Ultra messages. Since then, however, most of the Ultra information has been made available at the UK National Archives, and an extensive review shows that Ultra actually was of no substantial benefit to the operational command of Fighter Command during the Battle of Britain. Ultra provided the British with valuable information on German intentions, strategies and unit transfers, etc., but in most cases was not able to help Fighter Command to intercept individual air raids, since the instructions on these went out by telephone line. In his famous book published 30 years after the war, Group Captain Fred Winterbotham, the RAF's chief representative in the SIS and Bletchley Park admits that 'it was due to Dowding's tactics that we survived the onslaught', and describes Ultra as a bonus.'[8]

In 1940, the Luftwaffe's control and command system was more centralised than that of RAF Fighter Command. The selection of the Luftwaffe's main targets was made in Hermann Göring's headquarters, the Oberkommando der Luftwaffe (OKL). From there the directives for the next day's operations went out to the air fleets (Luftflotte). The Luftwaffe forces employed against the British Isles were divided into three air fleets in a crescent-shaped area: Luftflotte 3 in the central and western parts of northern France; Luftflotte 2 in northeastern France, Belgium and the Netherlands; and Luftflotte 5 in Denmark and Norway. The individual Luftflotte headquarters divided the operational orders between the next organisations in the hierarchy – the Fliegerkorps (air corps), Fliegerdivision (air division) or Jagdfliegerführer (fighter unit controller).

There were nine such major organisations in the three air fleets:

Four in Luftflotte 3:
• Fliegerkorps IV (Generaloberst Alfred Keller)
• Fliegerkorps V (General Robert Ritter von Greim)
• Fliegerkorps VIII (General Wolfram Freiherr von Richthofen)
• Jagdfliegerführer 3 (Oberst Werner Junck)

Four in Luftflotte 2:
• Fliegerkorps I (Generaloberst Ulrich Grauert)
• Fliegerkorps II (General Bruno Loerzer)
• 9. Fliegerdivision (General Joachim Coeler)
• Jagdfliegerführer 2 (Oberst Kurt-Bertram von Döring)

In Luftflotte 5:
• Fliegerkorps X (General Hans Geisler)

Besides the above mentioned formations, there was a special strategic aerial reconnaissance unit Aufklärungsgruppe Oberbefehlshaber der Luftwaffe (under Oberstleutnant Theodor Rowehl) plus a couple of weather reconnaissance units under Göring's personal command. The German air force commander had made sure that the Luftwaffe became an independent service branch – unlike the situation in many other countries, where the military aviation was divided between several different staffs, such as army aviation, naval aviation, strategic bombers, etc. However, despite Göring's energetic protests, Admiral Erich Raeder, the commander of the German Navy, had managed to acquire some air units – organised into Seefliegerverbände. In mid-1940, these mustered a total of nearly two hundred operational aircraft and operated according to the German Navy's strategy.

Similar to RAF Fighter Command's Sector Commanders, each Fliegerkorps/Fliegerdivision or Jagdfliegerführer decided which of the subordinated units were to be deployed on the assigned missions. From there orders were submitted to the individual air units – usually a Geschwader, but occasionally (as in the case of Erprobungsgruppe 210) a Gruppe.

The methods

If Fighter Command was superior in terms of command and control, the Luftwaffe had developed far better combat tactics.

'We quickly learned that it was very dangerous to attack the Messerschmitt 109's', said British fighter pilot Cyril Bamberger. 'These flew in such "open" formations that when you dived down behind one of them, it was not long before you had another one of the "yellow noses" on your tail.'[9]

The German fighter tactics, developed by the ace Werner Mölders in the Condor Legion during the Spanish Civil War, were significantly superior to the British. While all other air forces kept their fighters in tight formations (a relic from the First World War, when all communication in the air had to be made with visual signals), the German fighter aircraft operated in open combat formations with large spacing and altitude differences between the small groups of fighters. Mölders dissolved the old, bulky three-plane 'Vee formations' and instead divided the fighter aircraft into Rotte (two aircraft) and Schwarm (two Rotte). The new formation allowed the fighter pilots to cover a larger airspace while it also reduced the risk of visual detection, which made it easier to catch the enemy by surprise. But the greatest advantage was the teamwork that the Rotte method meant: the leader (Rottenführer) was the sword – he was the one who attacked and shot down the enemy – and the wingman (also called Rottenflieger) was the shield that protected the leader. Eventually, this tactic was copied by all other air forces – but not until well into the war by the Luftwaffe's opponents.

The RAF actually proved to be tactically quite unprepared for modern fighter combat. The Royal Air Force Manual of Air Tactics, released two years before the Battle of Britain, expressed the British view of fighter combat: 'Manoeuvre at high speeds in air fighting is not now practicable, because the effect of gravity on the human body during rapid changes of direction at high speed causes a temporary loss of consciousness, deflection shooting becomes difficult and accuracy is hard to obtain.'

Cyril 'Bam' Bamberger in the cockpit of a Spitfire later in the war. Bamberger arrived as a rookie pilot to Spitfire-equipped 610 Squadron on 27 July, 1940. In September 1940 he was transferred to 41 Squadron and scored his first air victory against a Bf 109 on 5 October. In 1941–1943 Bamberger participated in the air fighting over Malta, Tunisia and Sicily, and advanced to the rank of a Flight Lieutenant. Bamberger, who contributed with interviews and footage for this book, passed away on 3 February, 2008, at an age of 88. (Photo: Bamberger.)

Consequently, the RAF entered the war without any elaborate doctrine for fighter combat. This was in itself logical, because the British – as a result of their own dogma that 'the bomber will always get through' – could not imagine the existence of escort fighters. Still less conceivable – before June 1940 – was the possibility that the Germans would be able to take control of France, and thus French airfields. The conservative strategists in the British Air Ministry and the RAF's senior command envisioned nothing but engagements with unescorted Luftwaffe bombers that had flown all the way from Germany. Thus, Fighter Command's combat tactics were adopted solely for bomber interceptions. The so-called Area Fighter Tactics was based on keeping their own fighters in formations of three in tight Vee formations, attacking the bombers from behind and exposing these to a concentrated fire. When the Vee formations were confronted with the German fighter aviation's – the Jagdwaffe's Rotte and Schwarm formations, chaos often broke out on the British side.

Robert Foster, who served as a Pilot Officer with 605 Squadron during the Battle of Britain, analyses the Vee formation: 'It was designed to attack bombers. There was no tactical doctrine for fighter combat. When we attacked the German fighter or when they attacked us, our formations became dispersed and then it was every man for himself. The Germans had a very big advantage that they worked in teams, where one protected the other one's back. In retrospect, one can conclude that had our commanders introduced the "finger four formation" [the British designation of the German Schwarm formation] earlier, we would have avoided many quite unnecessary losses.' [10]

During the Battle of France, the British copied the French tactic of operating in groups of five aircraft – a Vee formation of three fighters and two other aircraft sweeping from side to side above and behind, to cover the Vee formation against enemy fighters who tried to sneak in from above. But instead of placing two planes as top cover, the British reduced it to a single airplane. This mission – where the pilot was called the 'weaver' because of the sweeps from side to side, or 'tail end Charlie' – was justifiably quite unpopular among the pilots, and not even particularly effective. Quite commonly, a squadron returned from what the pilots initially thought was an uneventful mission, only to find after the landing that the 'weaver' had been shot down. New Zealand ace 'Al' Deere called the 'weaver' method 'a costly and stupid practice'.[11]

Even though the German fighter aviation gave ample proof of the superiority of the Rotte/Schwarm tactics during the Battle of France, most units of the Fighter Command continued to stick to the old Vee formation.

This conservatism might possibly in part be explained by the strict British class system which at this time still

Werner Mölders (left) and Adolf Galland, the two most prominent German fighter aces during the Battle of Britain. With 14 victories, Mölders was the most successful ace of the German Condor Legion in the Spanish Civil War. He was appointed Inspector of Fighter Aviation in August 1941 but died in a plane crash on 22 November 1941, and was succeeded by Galland. Mölders and Galland were among the first to be awarded the Third Reich's highest awards. The first to be awarded with the Knight's Cross with Oak Leaves was the Mountain Troop Commander in Norway, Generalleutnant Dietl. Thereafter, Mölders received Oak Leaves No. 2 on 21 September and Galland No. 3 three days later. Galland became the first to receive the higher award, the Swords to the Oak Leaves, on 21 June 1941, and Mölders received Swords as No. 2 the following day. On 15 July 1941, Mölders became the first to receive the even higher level, the Diamonds to the Knight's Cross with Oak Leaves and Swords, an award that Galland became the next person to obtain on 28 January 1942. (Photo: Caldwell.)

weighed down even the new branch of arms. A sharp distinction was made between officers and men, and this took multiple forms. For instance, it was common that strength reports submitted to headquarters only mentioned the officers by name, adding 'and X number of NCOs and men'. For instance, the DFC (Distinguished Flying Cross) – awarded for 'acts of valour, courage or devotion to duty whilst flying in active operations against the enemy' – was exclusively for officers and warrant officers; other ranks were instead awarded the 'Distinguished Flying Medal' (DFM), ranked below the DFC in order of precedence. Officers of the Fighter Command had a far greater influence on the caretaking of their individual aircraft – such as the converging of the machine guns – than lower ranks.

The airmen

The superior combat tactics on the German side were to some extent balanced by often very high motivation among Fighter Command's fighter pilots. The latter's extremely high combat spirits as they fought in the summer and autumn of 1940 to defend their country and society against the German bombers is beyond all doubt. The volunteer pilots from other countries who flew with the RAF during the Battle of Britain were characterized – in contrast to what the Germans believed before the Battle – by the same fighting élan. The glowing hatred felt by the Poles against the Germans, who devastated their country, is well documented. Pilots from other countries occupied by Germany found the same motivation to fight their homeland's occupier. There even was a Belgian volunteer who had fought on the same side as the German Condor Legion in the Spanish Civil War!

Pilots from countries in the British Commonwealth showed the same determination. Among these were to be found a number of New Zealanders. At the time, the ties between New Zealand and the UK were much stronger than today; in the early 1940s, quite a few New Zealanders were first or second generation immigrants from the UK, still emotionally regarded as 'Mother England'. When

Britain called because it was hovering in mortal danger, many a young New Zealander responded with great enthusiasm. Among other volunteers, ideology – the fight against Nazism – played the same important role as it had done for the idealists who flocked to the Spanish Civil War to defend democracy against the unified extreme right dictatorships.

On the German side, there was not nearly the same mental readiness. In general, the German soldier in the Second World War was characterized by a quite high motivation which stemmed not least from the indoctrination of Germany's young men in the Hitler Jugend which skilfully prepared the entire German youth for war. However, after the surrender of France a feeling spread that the war was practically over. That soldiers will be less prone to the self-sacrificing efforts when they feel that the war is approaching a victorious end, is a well-known phenomenon in the history of warfare.

Ernst Kühl, who with the rank of a Major flew with the Stabsstaffel of KG 55 during the Battle of Britain, describes the situation amongst the Luftwaffe air units in occupied France who were flying against England: 'An exhilarated mood, deriving from the knowledge that, following a struggle of life and death, victory was now safe "at hand", dominated. This conviction was reinforced by rumours of demobilizations in the Army . . . Of course, the war was not yet quite over. England still remained. But we imagined that even in the worst case it would be a question of no more than two or three months before the British came to their senses. Both men and officers felt the same.'[12]

Initially, many of these young Germans regarded the stationing in France – in many cases in the vicinity of Paris – as a pure vacation. How could a tedious barrack yard somewhere in Germany be compared with Orly, Villacoublay or Le Bourget in the outskirts of Paris, la Ville Lumière! France . . . ' There were exotic cities, Gothic cathedrals and majestic proud castles', wrote a German aviator; 'there was the magical stillness of a radiant beautiful landscape, there was the wonderful cuisine, the colourful street cafés with wonderful spirits such as Cognac, Armagnac and Calvados and similar magic names, there was the sweet wines and the sparkling champagne; there was a people with whom you quickly could get into good contact with . . . and there was – last not least – the mademoiselles!'

France received a new kind of tourist. Restaurants, cafés, theatres, cinemas and nightclubs were filled and thrived as never before. French refugees returned to their homes and the population soon learned to cohabit with these uniformed intruders. The Germans enjoyed some really happy days. In many cases, the German airmen were completely unprepared for the determined British resistance that they soon would confront.

However, the individual pursuit of aerial victories played an important role in motivating the German fighter pilots. In no air force were the fighter pilots more focused

A group of RAF pilots from 'B' Flight, 32 Squadron, at the air base Hawkinge in July 1940. From left to right: Pilot Officer Rupert Smythe, Pilot Officer Kenneth Gillman, Pilot Officer John Proctor, Pilot Officer Peter Brothers, Pilot Officer Peter Gardner, Pilot Officer Douglas Grice and Pilot Officer Alan Eckford. All survived the war, except Keith Gillman, who was listed as missing after he was shot down on 25 August 1940, possibly by the German ace Adolf Galland. Peter Gardner was recorded with 8.66 air victories, including 5.33 during the Battle of Britain. He died on 23 May 1984. Alan Eckford achieved 12 air victories. He passed away in 1990. Douglas Grice scored eight victories and passed away at the age of 79. Peter Brothers, who contributed with interviews and footage for this book, tallied 16 victories, 10 of them during the Battle of Britain. He passed away on 18 December 2008, at the age of 91. Smythe attained five air victories during the Battle of Britain.

South African Adolphus Gysbert Malan, best known as 'Sailor' Malan, was the top ace of the RAF when he was taken out of active service in 1941. By then he had 32 air victories to his credit. Malan fought against Nazi Germany for ideological reasons. After the war he returned to South Africa where he became chairman of the leftist Springbok Legion, which organised war veterans against apartheid. Malan described this as 'against the police state, government abuse of power, censorship, racism, attempts to deprive the coloured of their voting rights and other oppressive expressions of the ruling Nationalist Party's sly fascism'. Malan spent the last years of his life fighting apartheid and died in 1963, 53 years old. In the film 'Battle of Britain' from 1969, Malan was played by actor Robert Shaw, as 'Squadron Leader Skipper'.

on the individual success of shooting down an enemy aircraft than in the Luftwaffe. This was the result of the mark put by the old fighter ace Hermann Göring on his own creation, the Luftwaffe.

Göring's great idol was the legendary Manfred von Richthofen, 'the Red Baron' who had shot down 80 enemy aircraft – more than any other aviator in the world by this time. Göring had the privilege to fly in von Richthofen's fighter unit, the so-called 'Flying Circus', and after von Richthofen's death Göring was appointed as his successor. The 'Red Baron' had a famous maxim: 'Find your enemy and shoot him down – everything else is unimportant.' This was fully embraced by Göring, and when a few years later he founded his air force, he transferred this attitude to the young fighter pilots – who undoubtedly were Göring's favourites, regardless of what has sometimes been stated after the war.

Quite logically, the Germans had a whole bureaucratic apparatus to assess whether a victory should be confirmed or not. First of all, the pilot who claimed the shooting down had to write a report and fill out an extensive form where all possible details of the shooting down would be described. If there was a witness to the shooting down, it was rather clear that it eventually would be confirmed. The German Rotte system almost automatically created witnesses to the victories of the Rottenführer – several fighter aces maintained that the wingman's main task, of course besides that of covering the Rottenführer from being attacked, was to witness the leader's victories (shootdowns).

When there was a witness to the shooting down, he too would submit a written testimony. In cases where there were no witnesses, the unit commander would interrogate the pilot in question and then submit his judgement on the credibility of the claim. Finally all of this was submitted to a special section in the RLM – the Reichsluftfahrtministerium (National Aviation Ministry) – in Berlin, where the case was subjected to a rigorous examination. The bureaucrats at the RLM made the final decision as to whether the claim would be accepted and confirmed or not. Then an official statement was sent to the relevant unit, where the pilot was informed of the decision. An individual 'victory case' could take up to six months.

The British had no such centralised verification of claims of shot down enemy aircraft. Immediately after a combat, an intelligence officer assessed the pilots' reports as to whether reports of hit enemy aircraft would be decided as a 'certain' (i.e. confirmed) victory, a 'probable' (i.e. an uncertain case) or just a 'damaged' aircraft. Another distinction of the victories in the RAF was that in cases where more than one pilot participated in the shooting down of an enemy aircraft, the victory was divided among all of them. In the Luftwaffe, only one pilot got the full credit.

The German fighter aces received the same attention as today's big stars in sport and music. The greatest fighter aces of the Battle of France were Hauptmann Werner Mölders with 25 and Hauptmann Wilhelm Balthasar with 23 victories. The attention they received because of their

Two Messerschmitt Bf 109 Es over Paris in June/July 1940. These aircraft belonged to the staff of III./JG 51 and the machine to the left was flown by the unit commander, Hauptmann Hannes Trautloft. (Photo: Trautloft.)

victories inspired many a young and eager fighter pilot to seek similar personal successes in air combat.

Mölders and Balthasar had in June 1940 both been awarded with Germany's highest military award – the Knight's Cross of the Iron Cross (Ritterkreuz des Eisernen Kreuzes), which had been instituted by Hitler on the first day of the war. This replaced the Prussian Pour le Mérite that had been awarded only to officers. The Knight's Cross was more 'democratic' in the sense that it could be awarded without any rank distinction. A Knight's Cross holder became a kind of a 'national hero', and it would soon be proved that there was no quicker way to a Knight's Cross than a large number of personal shootdowns by a fighter pilot. This created a phenomenon that even received a sarcastic name in German soldiers' gallows humour – 'sore throat', as if those who fought mainly with the goal of obtaining a Knight's Cross were cured of their 'sore throat' through the the red-white-and-black ribbon around the neck on which the Knight's Cross was carried.

The RAF had a completely different take on the issue of personal success in air combat. 'The term "ace" was frowned upon in the RAF where it was deemed a team effort', said South African Squadron Leader Douglas Tidy. His fellow countryman, Squadron Leader 'Sailor' Malan

– possibly the RAF's most gallant fighter pilot during the Battle of Britain – was famous for never looking for personal successes; he did not care much about how many planes he shot down. On the contrary, he argued that it was better to damage the German aircraft and let them return to base – 'with dead and injured crews as a warning to other Luftwaffe crews'. Such an attitude would have been perceived as 'barbaric' among most German fighter pilots, fostered in Göring's and von Richthofen's spirit to regard air combats as modern knights' tournaments. However, 'Sailor' Malan was least of all a barbarian; he drew his combat motivation from a fervent anti-Nazi conviction, and after the war he continued to fight the emerging apartheid system in his country with the same determination.

Whereas on the one hand it seems as though the RAF pilots had the greatest motivation, the Germans, on the other, had a larger proportion of highly combat-experienced airmen. This was the result of the Condor Legion. This regular Luftwaffe formation's participation in the Spanish Civil War between 1936 and 1939 earned a core of airmen invaluable combat experience. Thus, for instance, Werner Mölders flew around 100 combat missions in Spain, and was credited with 14 aerial victories before the Second World War began.

However, flight training in the RAF and the Luftwaffe were – in contrast to what has often been assumed – more or less equal. 'Tim' Elkington, who served as a pilot officer with No. 1 Squadron during the Battle of Britain, describes his flight training:

'In July 1939 I gained entry into the Royal Air Force College, Cranwell, for Permanent Commision. Originally, the course was intended for three years. But outbreak of war changed that! On 31 October 1939 I started training on Tiger Moth aircraft at No. 9 Elementary Flying Training School, near Coventry. On 12 April 1940, after 75 hours there, I started training on Hawker Harts and Hinds at the RAF College. After 100 hours there, I joined No 1 Squadron, Hawker Hurricanes, at RAF Northolt on 18 July 1940. I had two flights in a Miles Master – which was the first monoplane I ever flew. After only 16 hours on Hurricanes, I made my first operational flight on 27 July 1940, covering the de-beaching of a tanker in the English Channel.'[13]

One month after Elkington was received at the Royal Air Force College in Cranwell, 20-year-old Alfred Grislawski began his flight training at the flight school in Delmenhorst in Germany. After 480 training flights, mostly take-off and landing, with a total of about 80 flight hours, Grislawski was selected to become a fighter pilot and transferred to a fighter aviation school. He flew a Bf 109 for the first time on 25 April 1940. After 34 flight hours on the fighter, half of those on the Bf 109, and half on Avia B 534 and Fw 58, he graduated as a fighter pilot and was transferred to Ergänzungsjagdgruppe Merseburg, where newly trained fighter pilots had their training refined by more experienced fighter pilots. After 456 minutes of flight training on the Bf 109 in Ergänzungsjagdgruppe Merseburg, Grislawski was finally, in early August 1940, transferred to a combat unit, III./JG 52.[14] The British equivalent of the Luftwaffe's Ergänzungsgruppe was the

Operational Training Units, OTU, where the fresh fighter pilots received a fairly comprehensive training on modern fighter types. The newly trained RAF pilots also benefited from the RAF's practice of holding about a quarter of its pilots outside the combat zone, in the northern parts of the British Isles. There they would receive additional training on Spitfires or Hurricanes. Robert Foster, for example, arrived straight from flight school to an OTU in June 1940 and flew a Hurricane for the first time on 6 June 1940. On 8 July he was transferred to a combat unit, No. 605 Squadron, which, however, was stationed at Drem in Scotland, far from the scene of the fighting. When 605 Squadron was transferred to southern England on 7 September, Foster had received between 40 and 50 flight hours on a Hurricane.[15] This actually was more than an average German airman had on a modern fighter when he was transferred from an Ergänzungsgruppe to a combat unit – which in accordance with the practice of the Luftwaffe was in frontline service most of the time.

An important difference between the British and the German fighter pilot training consisted in that the latter received superior gunnery training. The Germans received a fairly extensive training in shooting at flying targets and ground targets from a fighter in the air. Cyril Bamberger, who arrived at his first combat unit, No. 610 Squadron, on 27 July 1940, said: 'I had 100 flight hours, including 25 on a Spitfire. But I barely had any gunnery training. Only once had I fired on sandbags from an airborne Spitfire. Next time I fired the guns was during combat, when I fired against a '109, and I was very scared. During most of the

Luftwaffe commander Hermann Göring, together with the commanders of Luftflotte 3 and 2, Hugo Sperrle (left) and Albert Kesselring (behind Göring).

Battle of Britain, I was shooting out of range, spreading thousands of machine gun bullets across southern England without hitting much.' [16]

'The average shooting skills were not particularly high in Fighter Command' explained James Edgar Johnson, who eventually developed into the RAF's most successful fighter ace. 'Too little time had been devoted to gunnery training, and this was directly reflected at the front units. Each squadron's kills always seemed to end up with three or four pilots, while the other rarely managed to achieve more than an "unconfirmed" or "damaged" because they emptied their guns while turning, they shot at too great a distance and they were unable to calculate deflection shooting.' [17]

Johnson continued: 'When I joined 616 Squadron in August 1940, during the Battle of Britain, I had a total of 200 hours flying, including 12 on Spitfires. I had never fired the guns of a Spitfire at a towed drogue and as a combat pilot I was quite useless until I had flown the Spitfire for at least 30 hours and could handle it well. Fortunately, 616 Squadron was pulled out of the front line on the very day I joined because of heavy casualties, so I had the opportunity to accumulate more hours.' [18]

The commanders

As with aviators, the command of the air operations during the Battle of Britain rested in the hands of quite skilful men on both sides. One man on each side stands out particularly for his very high level of competence, which put its mark on the entire battle. On the British side, this man was Air Vice-Marshal Keith Park, and on the German side the C-in-C of the Luftwaffe, Hermann Göring.

In 1935 Hitler revealed his intention to create a new air force, the Luftwaffe. In fact, the German Air Force has already begun to be created in secret, but when the veil lifted, neither London nor Paris protested. The task of leading the Luftwaffe was assigned to one of Hitler's most brilliant collaborators, the 42-year-old Hermann Göring.

Few men in recent history have been regarded with such scorn and have been so ridiculed as Hermann Göring. Even fewer have been subject to this fate in historiography on such weak grounds. To some extent, he opened himself to criticism by his forthright approach and his often self-mocking humour. Göring was unique among the Third Reich's leaders in terms of jokes around him. The merry Göring even encouraged such good-witted stories. Undoubtedly, Göring was the most popular figure among the Nazi leaders, and the people referred to him simply as 'Hermann' or 'Der Dicke' (Fatty).

Certainly, he was a ruthless Nazi who eventually amassed a huge list of crimes against humanity. However, the widespread image of him as a thoroughly incompetent Air Force Commander needs to be corrected. At the beginning of the Second World War, the Luftwaffe, the most effective air force in the world, was after all Göring's very personal creation. Not everything in the Luftwaffe was due to Göring's accomplishments, but he had the ability to put

The Chief of the British Air Staff, Air Chief Marshal Cyril Newall.

the right man in the right place (although this ability would sometimes let him down during the Battle of Britain, as we shall see), and he was more open to new revolutionary ideas than many of his younger subordinates.

Göring realized early the benefits of new types of combat aviation, such as dive-bombers and long-range fighter escort. As one of the first Air Force commanders in the world he also took the initiative to create a specialised night fighter force. Early in the war, he ordered a couple of fighter units to begin night fighter experiments. The twin-engined Messerschmitt Bf 110 proved to be the aircraft best suited for this task, and in June 1940 Göring decided to redesign the fighter wing I./ZG 1 under Hauptmann Wolfgang Falck to become the first regular night fighter unit, NJG 1.

Göring has been accused of advocating slow-flying close escort to bombers during the Battle of Britain, and he has also been blamed for the fateful decision to cease the successful attacks against the RAF's ground organisation at the crucial moment and instead turn the Luftwaffe against London. In reality, as we shall see, things were exactly the opposite. No one advocated the German fighters to be unleashed on free hunting – where they were most effective – more strongly than Hermann Göring, who also was the fiercest opponent among the German commanders to the idea that London was to be bombed.

Hermann Göring also had a testified inspiring effect on his subordinates. Hans-Jürgen Stumpff, who commanded Luftflotte 5 during the Battle of Britain, described Göring as a man 'with a tremendous strength; he was full of bright ideas. After each meeting with him you felt strongly in-

spired and filled with energy'. [19] Had the Luftwaffe had
another commander during the Battle of Britain – such as
any of those who by that time led the units at the Channel
Front – the RAF would likely have been in a less difficult
situation than that which was now the case. We shall see
more of this later.

Hermann Göring's 'colleague' on the British side was Air
Chief Marshal Cyril Newall, Chief of Air Staff (CAS), and
hence the military commander of the RAF. 54-year-old
Cyril Louis Norton Newall, 1st Baron Newall, had an unusually long career as an aviator. He had learned to fly in
1911, and early on reached a high position in the young
Royal Air Force. Having led the British military aviation in
the Middle East, he was appointed to become CAS in 1937.
Newall caused quite a stir, especially among the Conservative Party MPs and ministers, for his 'insubordination'
when he in May and June 1940 refused to comply with the
political decision to send a large part of Fighter Command
to France. Without a doubt, this gave the British a probably decisive point of departure for the Battle of Britain.
Newall's insubordination, however, was not taken kindly
in certain political strata, and while the Battle of Britain
was raging, political scheming took part behind the scenes
that ultimately – in October 1940 – resulted in his removal
from the command of the RAF.

One difference between the British Air Force commander and his German counterpart (Göring) was that the
former (Newall) did not lead any military operations. And
Fighter Command's C-in-C, 58-year-old Air Chief Marshal Hugh Dowding, hardly led any military operations
either. But, as we have seen, the British air defence system
was his merit, and Dowding stood behind Newall's reluctance to send more British fighter aircraft to France.

Like Göring, Dowding had been a fighter pilot in the
First World War, and he showed the same confidence in his
subordinates as Göring did (until the latter felt that they
did not fulfill his expectations). However, he utterly lacked
Göring's personal charm. Dowding was dutiful and totally
focused in everything he did, but might have needed a tad
of what in modern expression is called social skills. This
gained him the nickname 'Stuffy'. Author Len Deighton
puts it aptly: 'Too often he resorted to caustic comments
when a kind word of advice would have produced the same,
or better, result. . . . He was to confront Churchill in such
a way that he made an enemy of him, and so was deprived
of Churchill's aid at a time when he desperately needed
it.'[20] Moreover, Dowding stood faithfully by Newall's side,
which gained him enemies among senior politicians. The
result was that even Dowding finally had to go. Although it
is debated whether he in any case would have retired then,
he considered himself to be the victim of political intrigue
and never overcame his bitterness about this.

The machinations behind the scenes on the British
side during the Battle of Britain were perhaps an expression of the desperation of the country. In any event, Newall
and Dowding fell, paving the way for the air battle's real
victor – Air Vice-Marshal Keith Park, the commander of
11 Group.

Hugh Dowding, C-in-C of RAF Fighter Command.

Keith Park, the commander of 11 Group, RAF.

Born in New Zealand on 15 June 1892 as the son of Scottish immigrants, Park served as fighter pilot in British 48 Squadron in 1917 and 1918. He fought in the air in the same area and during the same time as Göring, and was credited with 20 victories – just two fewer than the same-aged Göring. In the 1930s, he served as Dowding's chief of staff. Dowding took a fancy to Park's very professional attitude and in April 1940 appointed him to the prestigious post of leading 11 Group – at the time, responsible for the air defence of the whole southern England, including the capital. This seems to have attracted the envy of another of Fighter Command's senior commanders, one who actually was passed by Park – Air Vice-Marshal Trafford Leigh-Mallory, who had served as the commander of 12 Group since 1937. With some justification Leigh-Mallory could consider that according to regular promotion it was he who should have assumed command of 11 Group, but Dowding refused to listen to this. Park and Dowding were very much in agreement, and although Park was not as uncommunicative as his superior, he gained enemies in various senior positions with his sharp forthright manner. To the political intrigues against Newall, where Dowding seems to have ended up on the losing side, was added a growing personal conflict between Park and Leigh-Mallory. This also resulted in negative operational consequences.

In view of the difficulties between Leigh-Mallory and Park, Fighter Command's regional division between the different Groups perhaps was a mistake. In any case, it definitely was a mistake to place two such antagonistic persons like Park and Leigh-Mallory in the command of 11 and 12 Group. A weakness in the air defence system was that the fighters were not authorized to cross the dividing lines between two Groups, unless authority to do so was given from above. Cooperation between 10 and 11 Group went smoothly because the two commanders got on so well. But Leigh-Mallory's aversion to Park turned the dividing line between 11 and 12 Groups into a barrier, and the difficulties between the two commanders worsened because of this division into two Groups. In the handling of this problem, Dowding showed his most arrogant side; in fact he did nothing to solve the problem.

The commander of 10 Group, Air Chief Marshal Sir Quintin Brand, had also been a fighter pilot in the First World War, where he was credited with twelve victories. He had participated in the air defence against German air raids against England already at that time. In the summer and autumn of 1940, Brand watched the conflicts at different levels within the RAF and Fighter Command with quite some distress, but he managed to stay out of it. Historian Stephen Bungay describes him as 'well respected, competent and courageous', and – above all – 'he got on very well with his more dynamic and dominating colleague at 11 Group.'[21]

Although sinister plotting characterized much of what was going on 'behind the scenes' in the RAF and Fighter Command, it was nothing compared to what took place in the senior echelons of the Luftwaffe.

On the German side, besides Air Force Commander Hermann Göring, Erhard Milch played a crucial role in the construction of the new Luftwaffe. Milch had served as a reconnaissance aviator in the First World War, and in the early 1920s, he and fighter ace Gotthard Sachsenberg founded a commercial air line between East Prussia and the Baltic States. When the various German airlines merged into Lufthansa in 1926, Milch became its first executive director. With his right-wing political views, Milch saw to it that the Lufthansa supported the Nazi campaign in 1928, and this gave him access to the corridors of power after Hitler took power five years later. Göring appointed Milch to the Secretary of the newly founded German Air Ministry (RLM), and in that position, he played a key role in the creation of the Luftwaffe. Milch made himself known for his brutality and ruthlessness. He had demonstrated this already in 1918-1919, when he participated in the Free Corps' crushing of the German workers' uprisings. As the Secretary of State in the RLM, he saw to it that the German government first took over the important Junkers firm, and then Milch had the CIO Hugo Junkers arrested. A short time later, the old man, who has been called 'the father of European aviation', died.

Despite his Jewish ancestry Milch was a devoted Nazi right from the 1920s, and enjoyed the special patronage of Göring, who spotted Milch's organisational qualities early on. 'I decide who is a Jew and who is not', Göring said. But Milch's authoritarian and brutal methods also created an unhealthy climate within the RLM. Competition and petty intrigues embossed the RLM's work. Göring tried to fight this without much success, and over time the relations between Göring and Milch deteriorated. Without a doubt, drunk with power, Milch was jealously yearning for Göring's position.

The more good-natured Göring increasingly leaned towards his old pilot compatriot Ernst Udet, who with 62 victories assumed second place among First World War's German flying aces. The Epicurean Udet, with his joviality and enthusiasm for flying, closely resembled Göring. In 1936 Göring appointed Udet to command the technical department of the RLM, and three years later he became the Luftwaffe's Feldzeugmeister – i.e. in charge of the inspection of the technical equipment. Udet played a decisive role in the introduction of the dive-bombers Junkers Ju 87 and Ju 88, and also was of great importance in the selection of the Bf 109 as the main single-engined fighter. Quite naturally, Udet's growing influence attracted the envy of a competitive man like Milch, and the latter's blackening of Udet's image has influenced history writing to this day.

It was in this strange mix of innovation, bitter personal feuds, expertise and cronyism that the generals of the Luftwaffe had to work.

Luftflotte 3 was commanded by General Hugo Sperrle, another pilot veteran from the First World War who later served as the first commander of the Condor Legion in the Spanish Civil War. Albeit no charismatic leader and with quite an austere appearance, Sperrle was a highly experienced and competent aviation commander. When other commanders, some of whom were less experienced in air operations, started arguing later on that it was time to end the offensive against the British airfields and instead attack London, Sperrle opposed them fiercely. As it would turn out, he was right.

General Albert Kesselring – Sperrle's colleague who commanded Luftflotte 2 in northeastern France, Belgium and the Netherlands – didn't have the same flight experience. Kesselring served as an artillery officer in the First World War, and later in the German General Staff. Like Milch, he had participated in the Free Corps' suppression of the revolutionary uprisings in Germany in the winter of 1918-1919, and this brought him in touch with the right-wing circles that soon joined together in the Nazi party. After Hitler's seizure of power in 1933, he was appointed to lead of the Department of Administration that would become the RLM. Largely owing to the growing conflict between Milch and Göring, this man, who really did not know much about aviation, continued his career in the Luftwaffe. Göring's decision to promote Kesselring to Chief of Staff of the Luftwaffe was another element in the Air Force Commander's attempt to reduce Milch's emerging powers. From there it was just a short step to the appointment in 1939 of Kesselring to command Luftflotte 1, and the following year to lead Luftflotte 2. In Kesselring's defence it must be said that his instincts as a former artillery officer were of good use to him when he led his air fleets during the lightning wars against Poland and France, where the Luftwaffe largely served as a kind of 'flying artillery'. But the Battle of Britain with its strategic air operations – which had never before been tried in practice – proved to be a task of a different kind. In the leadership of air operations during the Battle of Britain, Kesselring undoubtedly stands out clearly when compared with his British 'colleagues'. Stephen Bungay puts the difference between them in the spotlight when he notes that Kesselring, the old artillery officer, was 'facing men who had spent the best part of their careers working out how to defeat an attack by an enemy air force.'

In this respect Kesselring was quite similar to the commander of Luftflotte 5 in Norway and Denmark, General Hans-Jürgen Stumpff. He came from the Army, and owing to the good administrative skills that he demonstrated in the German Reichswehr in the 1920s and early 1930s, he was picked by Göring to lead the new Luftwaffe personnel department. Stumpff achieved very good results in the construction of new Luftwaffe officer corps, and was twice selected to become Kesselring's successor; the first time as the Luftwaffe's Chief of Staff, which earned him the enmity of Milch, and the second time as commander of Luftflotte 1. Quite interestingly, he was then appointed to become Milch's successor. Although Göring was concerned about Milch's growing power ambitions and ambushing, he could not ignore his great skills. In 1938 Milch was appointed to become the Luftwaffe's chief inspector. In April 1940, when the Battle of Norway was balanced on a knife-edge, Göring appointed Milch to lead the new Luftflotte 5, in charge of air operations in Norway. Milch performed his new task gallantly, and then returned to his position as the Luftwaffe chief inspector. Next, General Stumpff became the new commander of Luftflotte 5.

In addition to these commanders, one air force general on the German side deserves to be mentioned – Wolfram Freiherr von Richthofen. It is often claimed that he was a cousin of fighter ace Manfred von Richthofen, the 'Red Baron'. This is a misunderstanding, based on the broad concept of the German word Vetter, which sometimes is used in the sense of 'cousin' but often – and in this case – simply means a relative in a broader sense. Wolfram and Manfred were more distantly related, but flew in the same fighter unit during the First World War, with Wolfram achieving eight victories. After the war Wolfram Freiherr von Richthofen studied to become a technical engineer. He was shifted from a position at the head of the Technical Development Department within the RLM to become chief of staff of the Legion Condor. However, owing to controversies between him and his commander, Sperrle, von Richthofen was soon sent home again. But before that, von Richthofen had – along with Adolf Galland, commander of the fighter squadron 3./J 88 – developed and refined the close cooperation between ground-attack aviation and ground forces that was to become the hallmark of the German lightning war. (In contrast, the widespread image of von Richthofen as the father of the Stuka plane is incorrect; it was Ernst Udet who, with Göring's enthusiastic support, gave the Luftwaffe the Stuka concept, while von Richthofen was originally opposed to the idea.) In late 1938, von Richthofen returned to Spain as the Legion Condor's last commander. The lessons learned by von Richthofen in Spain came to be of great use and were further developed during the Second World War's Blitzkrieg campaigns, where he led Fliegerkorps VIII specialised in tactical support. Ironically, von Richthofen was thus intimately was associated with the aircraft that he initially had expressed strong doubts in – the groundbreaking Ju 87 Stuka.

Wolfram von Richthofen's high level of competence as air commander is indisputable; he personally played a very significant role in the air support of countless major ground operations. But it is more doubtful that his abilities were equally suited to the new sort of operations that the Battle of Britain entailed. Von Richthofen may have been among those who following the victory over France regarded the war as more or less over. A perusal of his personal diary shows that he spent a large part of the Battle of Britain on French golf courses, where he learned to play golf. Hitler's grand victory banquet on 19 July 1940 – when the Führer promoted Sperrle, Kesselring and Milch to the rank of Generalfeldmarschall, and von Richthofen to General – helped reinforce the impression that the war was more or less over.

Among these commanders, the German Air Force Commander Göring and Erhard Milch were actually among the youngest – their 47 and 48 years of age respectively put them on a par with the commanders at air corps level: von Richthofen was 45 years old, Leigh-Mallory and Park were of the same age as Milch, and Brand was of the same age as Göring. The youngest of them all was Ernst Udet, at 44. All the other commanders were over fifty – Stumpff 51, Newall 54, Sperrle and Kesselring 55. The oldest of them all was Fighter Command's C.O., Hugh Dowding, who was 58 when the Battle of Britain began.

CHAPTER 2
THE AIRCRAFT

Spitfire versus Messerschmitt Bf 109

The Battle of Britain has come to be symbolised by the duel between two single-engined fighter planes – the British Vickers Supermarine Spitfire and the German Messerschmitt Bf 109.* This is really remarkable, since the single-engined Hawker Hurricane was the British fighter that bore the main brunt of air combat during the Battle of Britain, and the other German fighter plane, the twin-engined Messerschmitt Bf 110 was actually better suited to the conflict.

The Spitfire, which was significantly better and more modern than the Hurricane, entered service in 1938, just one year after the Bf 109. But when the Second World War broke out in September 1939, the RAF only had 306 of this aircraft, while the Germans had over a thousand Bf 109s. On 20 July 1940, RAF Fighter Command mustered 308 operational Hurricanes and 224 Spitfires. Throughout the Battle of Britain the RAF had more than twice as many Hurricanes as Spitfires – the proportion of Hurricanes even increased from 2.3 times more than the number of Spitfires on 20 July to 2.6 times more a month later, and 2.75 times more on 30 October 1940 (399 and 227 respectively).

The question over which of the two fighters, the Spitfire and the Bf 109, was better has been discussed over and over again. The most common versions during the Battle of Britain were the Spitfire Mark I and Bf 109 E. A widely held concept is that the Bf 109 E was faster but less manoeuvrable than the Spitfire Mk I. Both of these beliefs need to be modified.

Although the turning radius of the Spitfire was generally tighter than that of the '109, the difference was no greater than it could be offset by a skilful pilot in the Bf 109. Furthermore, owing to its 'clipped' wing tips the Bf 109 E had a better roll rate, which means that the German plane could initiate a turn faster – although the Spitfire so to speak could turn better 'in the long run'. For instance,

A formation of Spitfire Mk Is from 65 Squadron. The picture was taken in 1939. The aircraft closest to the camera probably is flown by future ace Flying Officer Robert Stanford Tuck. Tuck had reached a total of 29 air victories when he in January 1942 was shot down over France and captured. Tuck, who was of Jewish heritage, became a close friend of Adolf Galland after the war. He passed away on 5 May 1987.

* The abbreviation Bf stands for Bayerische Flugzeugwerke which designed the Messerschmitt 109 and the 110. Willy Messerschmitt's own company, Messerschmitt AG, took over the company in July 1938, but the abbreviation 'Bf' was retained.

A Messerschmitt Bf 109 E-1 from 4./JG 2 'Richthofen'. The Bf 109 E-1 was armed with only four 7.92mm MG 17 machine guns: one in each wing and two on top of the engine. (Photo: Meimberg via Prien.)

German fighter ace Erwin Leykauf, who flew with JG 54 during the Battle of Britain, maintained that the Bf 109 E was both faster and more manoeuvrable than the Spitfire.[22]

The Spitfire had wider wings than the '109, resulting in lesser load per square metre. Its distinctive elliptical wings also gave a superior lifting ability. Another advantage was that with turns that were too tight the Spitfire pilot was alerted to the danger because the wings began to vibrate heavily, while the Bf 109's wings often began to vibrate only when it was too late. Hence, the British pilots dared to 'loosen up' more in combat, whereas it took considerably more experience for the German pilot to do the same.

At altitudes of up to 5,000 metres the Bf 109 was slightly faster in level flight (560 km/h against the Spit's 552 km/h). But at 6,000 metres' altitude – where many of the air combats of the Battle of Britain took place – the Spitfire was considerably faster than its opponent (nearly 570 km/h compared to slightly above 550 km/h). Then the Spitfire was faster up until an altitude of 7,600 metres. The conclusion must be that they were quite evenly matched in speed.

The British, however, had a significant advantage in a more efficient fuel – 100-octane, compared to the German regular 87 octane. Britain gained access to the 100-octane fuel for the first time in June 1939 from the Esso refinery in Aruba in the Caribbean. Irregular supplies continued over the next year, but because of the great importance of 100-octane fuel to fighter aircraft, it was almost exclusively reserved for them. From August 1940 the availability of this high-grade aviation fuel was ensured through regular shipments from the United States. From the spring of 1940, the Rolls-Royce aviation engines were adapted to 100-octane fuel, first for Spitfires, and then also for Hurricanes. The 100-octane fuel allowed a Spitfire to temporarily increase its maximum speed by around 40 km/h at sea level and 55 km/h at an altitude of 3,000 metres.

Owing to the lower quality of German aviation fuel, the German aircraft engines emitted thick and dark smoke when subjected to high stress – which is an important explanation of frequent Allied reports of a shot down Messerschmitt when in fact the enemy pilot had just dived steeply to escape an attack. In the autumn of 1940 a new version of the Bf 109 entered service, the E-4/N, equipped with a 1,200-horsepower DB 601 N-motor adapted for the new 100-octane C 3 special aviation fuel. However, most of the '109s continued to fly on the lower octane fuel, mainly because of the difficulty of acquiring such high-quality fuel.

The British fighters' Rolls-Royce Merlin III was a carburettor engine, while the Bf 109 had an engine with fuel injection – the Daimler-Benz DB 601 A in most versions of the Bf 109 E. Therefore Messerschmitt pilots were often able to avoid a pursuing Spitfire or Hurricane by simply pushing the control stick forward and diving. The British fighter pilot who attempted the same manoeuvre quickly noticed that it was not so simple – his engine simply stopped if the aircraft went into a dive too abruptly. The deceleration caused when the engine stopped and then came afloat again could often be decisive in fighter combat. But as with all advanced technology, it was a matter of compromises and priorities. Tests had shown that if the Spitfire's Rolls-Royce Merlin III engine had been fitted with fuel injection, it would have reduced engine power by about 60 hp, which corresponds to an average speed decrease of about 10 km/h.[23]

German fighter pilot Hermann Neuhoff, who served with JG 53 during the Battle of Britain, had the privilege to test a captured Spitfire in 1940. He was impressed by the quietness of the Rolls-Royce engine in the British fighter. 'The Spitfire purred like a cat', Neumann said, 'while the Daimler-Benz engine, particularly the N-engine, in our Messerschmitt 109s sounded like someone was shovelling coal!'[24] In the German engine's defence it must be said that only a relatively thin bulkhead separated the engine from the cockpit in the Messerschmitt 109; in the Spitfire the engine sound was dampened by the fuel tank which was mounted between the engine and the cockpit.

Concerning the cockpit, the feeling is markedly different when you sit in a '109 or in a Spitfire. In the case of the Messerschmitt 109, you immediately feel that this is a cold war machine, not intended for anything but to bring death and destruction to the enemy. The cockpit is cramped, square and quite tight even for a person of average height. The narrow cockpit made it difficult for the pilot to push the control stick sideways at high speeds, because the small space did not allow much leverage. The '109 also was notorious for being very 'heavy' on the rudders at high speeds. This contributed further to the larger turning radius of the '109.

In comparison, the cockpit of a Spitfire feels luxuriously spacious, almost comfortable. One has plenty of room, and the arched hood of the Spitfire offers a far better rear view than the flat hood of the '109.*

But the Bf 109 pilot had a better view forward and downwards, as German pilot Hermann Neuhoff said: 'When I first sat down in a Spitfire, I was struck by how much of the view downwards was hidden by the wings because the cockpit was positioned much further back than on our '109s. It was an advantage that we had and for which I was glad.'

One advantage held by the Spitfire was that it was larger and therefore considerably more durable than the small '109. This, however, was offset by the heavier armament of the German plane.

Many a British fighter pilot gazed at the Messerschmitt's 20mm cannons with envy. But a fact that has often been lost in historiography on the Battle of Britain, is that a large number of the Bf 109s that served during the Battle of Britain were the early version Bf 109 E-1 – which differed from the later versions, particularly in the armament which consisted of only four 7.92mm MG 17 machine guns: one in each wing and two on top of the engine cowling. As many as 40% of the Bf 109s in the units at the English Channel were of the E-1 version almost throughout the entire Battle of Britain: of 740 serviceable Bf 109s on 31 August 1940, 307 were Bf 109 E-1s, 103 were of the E-3 version, 304 of the E-4 version and 27 of the E-7 version.[25] Although production of the Bf 109 E-1 version was terminated in August 1940, it is a fact that out of 323 Bf 109s delivered to the

units at the English Channel as late as in September 1940, exactly 100 were the version E-1.[26]

The Bf 109 E-1 was gradually exchanged for the Bf 109 E-3, which had the two wing-mounted machine guns replaced with two 20mm cannons of the type MG FF. (Several Bf 109 E-1s were in this way converted to E-3s.) This represented a significantly more powerful armament. But on the minus side was the MG FF's low rate of fire – only nine shells per second, which is only half the rate of fire of the MG 17. In addition, the MG FF had a relatively slow muzzle velocity – 575 metres per second (compared to the 790 m/s of the MG 17) – which of course was a major drawback in fighter combat. This made the trajectory more sensitive to the influence of the manoeuvres of the aircraft itself, impeding deflection shooting from a turn. It also gave the enemy aircraft more time to disappear from the trajectory; if a German pilot opened fire from a distance of 200 metres, it took half a second for the shells to reach the enemy aircraft if this departed with a speed of 500 km/h, and in this time a Spitfire or a Hurricane could perform an evasive manoeuvre.

With the Bf 109 E-4 version – which was introduced in front-line service in the spring of 1940 – the German fighter pilots had access to the improved MG FF/M, loaded with the new high explosive so-called Minengeschoss, an explosive shell with a thin mantle, which increased the amount of explosives in the grenade. One or two hits of 20mm Minengeschoss shells would often suffice to send a Spitfire to the ground. But in the summer of 1940 only a small portion of the Bf 109s were E-4s. These did not appear in large numbers in the German fighter units until later in the Battle of Britain.

Perhaps the largest drawback regarding the fitting of Bf 109s with the MG FF was that the small aircraft only allowed space for 60 shells per wing cannon. This meant that the Bf 109 pilots could not fire for more than seven seconds with their automatic cannons. Besides the two MG FFs, the Bf 109 E had room for only two more guns – the two 7.92mm machine guns that were mounted on top of the engine cowling. Two machine guns were usually was insufficient to achieve any significant damage to an enemy aircraft in aerial combat; to do that required either a very experienced pilot or a good portion of luck for the shooter.

The Spitfire was armed with eight 7.7mm Browning .303 machine guns, four in each wing. Each of these guns had 300 rounds, which gave 16 seconds of firing. Quite often, these British machine guns produced no effect other than a series of small holes in the wings or fuselage of enemy aircraft, particularly if it was a larger bomber. The armour plates that protected the Bf 109 fighter pilots against firing from behind gave perfect protection against these bullets. Contradictory to this a British report in August 1940 noted: 'One very short burst directed against the tanks was sufficient in most cases to destroy the [Bf 109].'[27]

Since Fighter Command's most important targets in the air were German bombers, cannons would have been much more effective, but in this field the British lagged behind. If this had not been the case – had the British had an effective automatic cannon for its fighter aircraft already in 1940 – German bomber losses during the Battle of Britain

---

* The Bf 109 was equipped with 'rear mirrors' on top of the hood, but almost all pilots had these removed because they increased air resistance.

would certainly have been considerably higher. The British were aware of this, but the truth is that by this time they simply had not found any technical solution. They had imported the French Hispano-Suiza HS.404, which also was a 20mm automatic cannon. But the Hispano-Suiza was designed to be installed in a robust engine block, and the Spitfire had not been constructed for cannon armament. The only technical possibility was to place the gun lying on its side, one in each wing of a Spitfire, in order to accommodate the large magazines. It turned out that this did not work at all. Fire stoppages became the rule. During the cannon-equipped Spitfire's baptism of fire – on 16 August 1940 – only one of seven participating pilots reported both guns working during the entire combat. The unit commander's conclusion was quite disappointing: 'In all the engagements so far occurring it is considered that had the unit been equipped with [machine gun] fighters it would have inflicted far more severe losses on the enemy.'[28]

Without a doubt, the Messerschmitt 109 was more difficult to fly than the Spitfire, and certainly more difficult when it came to landing. German pilot Hans-Ekkehard Bob described the machine as 'a diva who must be treated with great caution'. But this was offset by the fact that the German pilots usually had more flight hours on the Bf 109 – in some cases up to three years – than those that the British had on the Spitfire.

The Spitfire Mk I and the Messerschmitt Bf 109 E each had their advantages, but overall they balanced one another. The proponents of the Spitfire often gladly cite the German fighter ace Adolf Galland, who, as we have seen, at one point asked Göring for his Geschwader to be equipped with Spitfires. In several conversations with the author, however, Galland stated that this was not meant literally: 'Actually, I preferred our Messerschmitt 109. You have to view my statement in its context. I was tired and frustrated with our lack of success, and I felt that Göring didn't understand us fighter pilots. But I never really wished to exchange my Messerschmitt 109 for a Spitfire.'[29]

Alan 'Al' Deere, the New Zealand fighter ace who flew Spitfires with No. 54 Squadron during the Battle of Britain, considered the Spitfire to be 'in general superior to the Messerschmitt 109, except for the initial climb rate and in divings'. After a test flight with a Bf 109 E-3, Robert Stanford Tuck, another British ace in the Battle of Britain, described the machine as 'an undoubtedly nice little airplane – although not as manoeuvrable the Spit and not as easily flown at low altitude.'

German ace Werner Mölders described his impression of the Spitfire following a test flight with a Mark I: 'It is easy to fly, easy on the rudders, turns very well and has a performance not far from our Me 109. But regarded as a combat aircraft it is quite bad. A quick push forward of the control stick causes the engine to die.' Undoubtedly, these rather negative opinions of the enemy's aircraft were heavily influenced by the fact that the pilots had flown them as they used to fly their own planes.

Zerstörer, Hurricane and Defiant

The backbone of RAF Fighter Command during the Battle of Britain was made up of the single-engined single-seater Hawker Hurricane. In the 1930s this was the RAF's first monoplane fighter, but in 1940 it was growing increasingly outdated in comparison to more recent aircraft.

Above all, the Hurricane was relatively slow. Top speed was 520 km/h at an altitude of 5,500 metres, which meant that it was about 35-40 km/h slower than the Bf 109. But the Hurricane's larger rudder gave better stability during sharp manoeuvres, making it more manoeuvrable for less experienced pilots, and it could turn much more sharply than both the Bf 109 and Spitfire. In addition, the quite robust construction of the Hurricane made it able to sustain much more damage than both the Spitfire and the Bf 109. Another advantage – especially compared to the Spitfire and the Bf 109 E-1 – was its armament. Similarly to the Spitfire, the Hurricane was equipped with eight 7.7mm Browning .303 machine guns, but these were fitted closer together in the Hurricane, which gave a more concentrated firepower than that of the Spitfire, which had its four guns in each wing more spread out.

In the case of the Hurricane versus the Messerschmitt 109, most pilots agree – the latter was clearly better. Peter Brothers, who flew with Hurricane equipped 32 and 257 squadrons during the Battle of Britain, said: 'As a pilot of a Hurricane you always had a certain respect, and even fear, for the Messerschmitt 109s. Firstly, they could dive faster. If the pilot of a Messerschmitt 109 saw you, he dived down and gave you a burst of fire, whizzed past, pulled the stick and climbed away very rapidly. You had no chance to follow him.' According to 'Al' Deere, the Hurricane was, 'although much more manoeuvrable than both the Spitfire and the Messerschmitt 109, pitifully slow and an extremely lazy climber.'

The second German fighter, the twin-engined two-seater Messerschmitt Bf 110, has been the subject of many myths and misconceptions. A fairly common notion is that it didn't suffice as a day fighter, that it performed poorly in combat, and because of this had to be assigned with fighter escorts of Bf 109s. However, none of this stands up to closer scrutiny.

The Bf 110 was the result of the wargames conducted under Göring's supervision in the winter of 1933/1934. These showed that the by then prevailing view that 'the bombers will always get through' – the notion that regardless of intercepting fighters and air defence a sufficient number of bombers always would get through to their assigned targets, where they were expected to cause enormous damage – was incorrect. In the summer of 1934, the leadership of the still secret Luftwaffe presented a study that suggested what at that time was quite revolutionary – a twin-engined fighter, heavily armed with automatic cannons as well as machine guns, to protect the bombers against enemy fighter interception. The idea was to dispatch these twin-engined fighter aircraft in advance, at a high altitude over the intended bombing target area, to clear the air of enemy fighters before the bombers arrived. Several of the more traditional thinking staff

officers opposed this proposal, but Göring understood how far-sighted this was. Thus the fighter escort doctrine was born – the one that most air forces would adopt, although it would not be until ten years later that the Western Allies understood its benefits. Göring immediately in 1934 assigned the German aviation industry the task of constructing a new aircraft according to these principles. The new aircraft was designated 'Zerstörer' (destroyer). Göring eventually chose a design by the Bayerische Flugzeugwerke, Bf 110. *

It is commonly cited that the Bf 110 could not turn as tightly as the single-engined fighters. Good manoeuvrability was of course a significant factor in the fighter combats of the Second World War, but not to the same extent as in the First World War's so-called 'dogfights' between slow biplanes and triplanes that circled in the same area. The fighter combats of the Second World War more often had the character of a kind of 'Big Bang in miniature': when both sides clashed, their flight formations dissolved explosively, with all the aircraft careering off at high speed in different directions. In such a melee, speed, climb and diving performances were at least as important as manoeuvrability. The tight turn is in itself a defensive feature – it makes it easier to avoid being hit by the fire of a pursuer. But in the offensive, the fighter pilots of the Second World War were able to use more powerful engines.

Hubert 'Dizzy' Allen, who flew a Spitfire with No. 66 Squadron during the Battle of Britain, wrote: 'We were better at dogfighting than the fighter arm of the Luftwaffe, but only because both the Spitfire and Hurricane were more manoeuvrable than the Messerschmitt 109 and 110. In fact,

While the arms mechanic performs weapons care of the machine guns and cannons of a Bf 110, the engine technicians are replacing the radiator on the aeroplane. The heavy nose armament of the Bf 110 was second to none during the Battle of Britain. (Photo: von Eimannsberger.)

dog-fighting ability was not all that important during the war. Fighter attacks were hit-and-run affairs on average. Either you dived with the sun behind you and caught him napping, or he did that to you.'[30]

The Bf 110 was designed to strike down on enemy aircraft like hawks striking doves. With superiority in speed and altitude it could perform an attack effectively, without allowing itself to be drawn into turning combat – in exactly the same way as the Bf 109 pilots later learned to combat the much more manoeuvrable Soviet Polikarpov fighters on the Eastern Front. In these conditions, the Bf 110's at that time unrivalled fire power often was decisive. In terms of flight speed, the Bf 110 models of 1940 were on pair with both the Bf 109 E and the Spitfire Mk I, and were significantly faster than the Hurricane. The Bf 110 was equipped with the same engines as the Bf 109, the DB 601 A, with fuel injection, and thus could outdive any British fighter. It also outclimbed the Hurricane and climbed almost as well as the Spitfire – unless it attacked the British in a quick dive from above; in doing so, the accumulated speed of the '110 made it impossible to follow in pursuit when it rapidly pulled up again.

In these kind of lightning attacks, the Bf 110's armament at that time was unprecedented: two 20mm MG FF cannons and four 7.92 mm MG 17 machine guns concen

---

* The idea of sending out long-range fighter planes in advance to the intended target area, to clear the air of enemy fighters before the bombers reached the target, was a direct predecessor of the fighter tactics that the US Air Force began to use only in 1944, and which spelt the beginning of the end for the German Air Force.

The Hurricane's four .303 Browning machine guns in each wing were placed closely together. This gave a greater fire power than that of the Spitfire. This Hurricane – 'YO-X' from No. 1 RCAF Squadron – ended up as victory number 18 on the track record of German ace Leutnant Gustav Sprick (JG 26) on 17 September 1940. The pilot, Flying Officer Carl Briese, managed to crash-land the aircraft at High Halstow.

trated in the nose. In addition, this aircraft had relatively ample room for ammunition. Its automatic cannons were loaded with 180 shells each, three times more than in a Messerschmitt 109, giving a total firing time of twenty seconds. The firepower of the Bf 110 was something that all RAF pilots soon learned to fear. Since the '110 was twin-seated, it was also equipped with a rear machine gun. This single, flexible 7.92mm MG 15 did not have any greater firepower, but this was often compensated by the extensive gunnery training of the radio operator who manned the machine gun.

The Messerschmitt Bf 110 was not only superior to the '109 regarding armament, but it also had a significantly larger operational range – which was a significant factor in the Luftwaffe operations over the British Isles. There was an important difference in principle between the two Messerschmitt fighters: as we have seen above, the Bf 110 had been developed according to Hermann Göring's 'Zerstörer Concept', and thus was intended for the offensive. The original concept for the Bf 109, however, was defensive; it was meant as an Objektschutzflugzeug, an object cover aircraft, i.e., a short-range interceptor designed to patrol over for example an important industrial area to protect it against air strikes.

The results of the Bf 110's operations during the Battle of Britain show that contrary to common perception it was at least as effective as the Bf 109 when it was used

in free hunting – in other words according to the concept for which it was designed. Hans-Joachim Jabs, who as an Oberleutnant flew a Bf 110 with II./ZG 76 – the famous 'Haifischgruppe' – during the Battle of Britain, described his favourite method with the aircraft: 'With a Messerschmitt 110 on free hunting you could strike down on the British and destroy them with the aircraft's heavy armament. Then we could use the speed accumulated during the diving to climb to a higher altitude again. If we were attacked by British fighters when we had such a high speed, we could easily outclimb them. Then we could use our dive speed for a renewed attack to shoot down another one of them who was not careful enough.'

Mainly through this tactic, Jabs scored nineteen victories with his Bf 110 up until September 1940, and for this he was awarded with the Knight's Cross. By that time, II./ZG 76 was the Luftwaffe's most successful fighter Gruppe in terms of of victories.

Robert Stanford Tuck served as a Flight Lieutenant with 92 and 257 squadrons during the Battle of Britain and developed into one of the RAF's first big fighter aces. He describes the Bf 110 as 'an airplane that was very unpleasant to face, because of its quite heavy armament in the nose'. Tuck continues: 'Rule number one was: Make sure you do not get a 110 on your tail. If that happened, you could be sure to get a whole lot of ammo over yourself, concentrated. In addition, [the Messerschmitt 110] had a rear gunner, and I had a feeling that their rear gunners were quite good at aiming and very determined. They continued to fire at you until the last moment, until your bullets had wounded them fatally.'[31]

Neither did the Bf 110 have such a bad manoeuvrability as has often been claimed. Indeed, it could not make as tight turns as the Hurricane or the Spitfire, but in the hands of a skilled pilot it could turn almost as tight as a Bf 109 at high speed above medium flight altitude. Several combat reports by RAF pilots from the Battle of Britain testify to this. Eric Marrs, who flew a Spitfire with No. 152 Squadron, describes a dogfight with a Bf 110:

'We circled around each other for a bit in tightening circles, each trying to get on the other's tail, but my attention was soon drawn by another '110 . . . I milled around with him for a bit . . . I rolled on my back and pulled out of the melee and went home.'

Major Walter Grabmann, who commanded Bf 110-equipped ZG 76 during the Battle of Britain, flew mock combats with Bf 110s against captured British fighters on several occasions, and came to the following conclusions: 'Concerning the performance of the Bf 110: I myself carried out very many comparison flights with the Bf 109, Bf 110 C against Bf 109 E. Speed equal, Bf 109 somewhat better in a climb, Bf 110 somewhat faster in a shallow dive. Dogfighting: 50:50. It was the same against the Spitfire.'[32]

What mainly made the Bf 110 actually more suited for the special demands of the Battle of Britain than the Bf 109, was its large operating range. From bases in northern France the Bf 110 could reach all the way to Scotland – a longer distance than all German bomber types except the Ju 88. The Bf 109 on the other hand could at best reach to London's northern outskirts, then the fuel in its small tanks began to run out, and the pilot had to hurry home. If the Bf 109s became involved in fighter combat, or if they were assigned to provide the bombers with close escort – which forced the pilots to orbit above and around the slow bomber – the fuel would run out of even earlier. German bomber formations were repeatedly dealt heavy losses over England because the Messerschmitt 109s had been short on fuel and had to leave the bombers, while there were too few Bf 110s. Of the Luftwaffe's fighter planes in the summer of 1940, only about one-fifth consisted of Bf 110s and the rest were Bf 109s. (The 'He 113', frequently mentioned in the British combat reports from this period, was nothing but a German propaganda trick; 'Heinkel 113' never existed – in cases where such an aircraft was mentioned it was merely a case of confusion with Bf 109s.)

The RAF also had a couple of twin-engined fighters, but none of them could be compared with the Bf 110. The most common was the Bristol Blenheim. The Air Ministry's decision to build a heavy fighter version of the Blenheim bomber soon proved to be a mistake. The Bristol Blenheim IF was slow – the top speed was in line with standard medium bomber, even lower than that of the Ju 88. How it compared with the Bf 110 was made clear by the Zerstörer fliers of I./ZG 1 on 10 May 1940, when they shot down five out of six Blenheims from 600 Squadron's 'B' Flight without own losses. One consequence of this was that the Blenheim IF was shifted to mainly night fighter operations.

The other twin-engined British fighter was Westland Whirlwind – quite a small aeroplane (a length of only 9.83 metres, compared with the Bf 110's 12.3 metres). With a top speed of 580 km/h at 4,500 metres' altitude – more than 10 km/h faster than the Bf 109 at that height – and an armament of four automatic cannons in the nose, the Whirlwind might seem to have been a great fighter plane. But its disadvantage was its low speed at high altitudes – which would have been a great disadvantage if it had been deployed during the Battle of Britain. Deliveries of the Whirlwind began slowly during the Battle of Britain, and on 17 August 1940 only five aircraft were at hand. Fighter Command's Dowding decided not to use the aircraft in combat throughout the Battle of Britain – probably a wise decision.*

Another less common British fighter that was used in the Battle of Britain was something as unusual as a single-engined but twin-seated fighter with an armament consisting of four 7.7mm machine guns in an electric-powered dorsal turret – the Boulton Paul Defiant. This machine probably was better than its reputation. Indeed, because of the extra weight of the turret it was relatively slow – the top speed was 490 km/h at 5,200 metres' altitude, whereas the Bf 110 reached 530 km/h and the Bf 109 550 km/h. However, the plane may be considered a 'slugger'. With the right tactics – where the planes flew in a 'Lufbery-circle' – it could take control over a fairly large airspace where it was quite dangerous for any enemy aircraft. But even if the Defiant has received an undeservedly bad reputation because of erroneous tactics, it could not be compared with the two German fighters planes.

The bombers

Another fairly unique aircraft was the German single-engined two-place dive-bomber Junkers Ju 87 Stuka. This had become legendary during the battles of Poland and France, where swarms of Stukas spread death and terror among soldiers on the opposing side. When an aircraft carries out a prolonged dive at a steep angle, the air resistance creates the same howling sound as when the wind blows through a narrow passage between two houses. This sound came to be associated with diving Stuka planes, and the mere sound often sufficed to sow panic among Allied ground troops. The Germans were not slow to notice this, and to further enhance the psychological effect, sirens were mounted under the wings of their Ju 87s.

Using the Ju 87's capacity to dive against its target, the pilot could drop the bombs with an accuracy unsurpassed among all other aircraft types. However, the Ju 87 was also a relatively easy target for enemy fighters; it was relatively slow, not very manoeuvrable, and weakly armed – two forward 7.92mm machine guns and a flexible rear machine gun manned by the radio operator.

In twin-engined bomber aircraft, the RAF and the Luftwaffe were more evenly matched in terms of quality – with one exception, the Junkers Ju 88. This completely new German bomber had entered service as late as in the

_____

* A German fighter pilot reported shooting down a Whirlwind on 27 October 1940, but a comparison with British documents reveals that this was one of two Bristol Beaufort torpedo planes lost by RAF Coastal Command on that day. (National Archive, Kew. CAB/65/9/40).

autumn of 1939. Hermann Göring had ordered the development of this aircraft, which in 1940 was undoubtedly the most effective medium bomber in the world. The crew consisted of four men – the pilot to the left in the cabin, the bombardier in front of and below the pilot, the observer to the right of the pilot, and the radio operator behind the observer, manning the rear-mounted machine guns. The standard armament of a Ju 88 A-1 – the most common version during the Battle of Britain – consisted of four flexible 7.92mm MG 15 machine guns: one mounted through the front windscreen and which could be operated by the pilot or the observer, two in the rear of the cabin hood, operated by the gunner, and one aft-firing machine gun mounted in a small cupola beneath the fuselage, below the cabin.

But the armament was not the Ju 88's greatest advantage – it was its high speed and its ability to drop bombs with great accuracy. The aircraft's two Junkers Jumo 211 B-1 engines were rated at 1,210 horsepower at take-off. They gave the aircraft a top speed of 450 km/h in level flight and 560 km/h when diving. This was faster than any other bomber at that time, and made the Ju 88 hard to catch up even for Hurricane fighters if they were at too great a distance. Furthermore, a Ju 88 carried up to 2,500 kg of bombs, more than most medium bombers at this time. By an order from Göring the Ju 88 also had been designed to dive-bomb – with almost the same precision as the Ju 87.

The Ju 88 would gradually replace the Luftwaffe's oldest medium bombers at that time – the Dornier Do 17 Z-2, called the 'Fliegende Bleistift' (Flying Pencil) because of its long, narrow fuselage. This four-seater was a typical medium bomber, with a top speed around 30 km/h slower than that of the Ju 88, an armament of three to six 7.92 mm machine guns, and a maximum bomb load of 1,000 kg. It can be compared to the British twin-engined Handley-Page Hampden, which was slightly slower than the Do 17, but in return could carry 1,800 kg of bombs. The armament of a Hampden consisted of six .303-inch (7.7mm) Vickers K machine guns. The Do 17 Z-2 was overall better than the British twin-engined Bristol Blenheim Mk IV bomber, which had a payload of only about half of that of the Dornier plane's, without being able to reach a higher top speed.

Germany's standard bomber during the Second World War was, alongside the Ju 88, the 'workhorse' Heinkel He 111. The most common versions during the Battle of Britain were the He 111 P-2, H-2 and H-3. This twin-engined machine excelled, especially in that it was the most rugged German bomber. The most common versions of the airplane during Battle of Britain could carry a bomb load of up to 2,000 kg. The defensive armament ranged between six MG 15s in the He 111 P-2 and five MG 15s in the He 111 H-2. The transition from the P-version to the H-versions was marked by the two Daimler-Benz DB 601 A-1 engines (rated at 1,150 horsepower at take-off) of the former being replaced by a pair of Junkers Jumo 211 D-2 engines, which was slightly stronger (1,200 hp) in the latter. The crew of a He 111 consisted of five men – observer, pilot, bombardier, radio operator and gunner. Unlike in the Ju 88, where the pilot was the crew commander, the observer usually was the crew commander in the He 111.

Immediately after the Battle of Britain the British Ministry of Information published an official account of the battle, The Battle of Britain August–October 1940. In the Swedish edition, Slaget om Storbritannien augusti – oktober 1940, published in 1941, this comparison between the performances of the participating aircraft was reproduced.

The He 111 could be compared to the twin-engined Vickers Wellington on the British side. The Wellington Mk IC had about the same top speed as the He 111, could carry a bomb load of 2,000 kg and was armed with eight 7.7mm (0.303 inch) Browning machine guns.

The RAF had a bomber of a type which the Luftwaffe lacked – a heavy bomber, the twin-engined Armstrong Whitworth Whitley. A Whitley Mk V – which constituted the majority of Whitleys in service in 1940 – could carry a bomb load of more than 3,000 kg to targets in western Germany, and could reach targets all over Germany if the bomb load was reduced. In addition, by this time three new British heavy bomber types were almost ready for series production – the twin-engined Avro Manchester and the four-engined Handley-Page Halifax and Short Stirling. The latter began a whole new era, the four-engined heavy bomber aircraft epoch. Equipped with four Bristol Hercules II engines, each rated for 1,375 hp at take-off, a single Stirling could carry a bomb load as heavy as that of three German bombers – 6,530 kg. This of course meant a considerable strengthening of British Bomber Command, but as we shall see later on, through a bold low-level attack against Short Brothers' aircraft plant at Rochester on 13 August 1940, three German bombers crews managed to prevent the British from bringing the Stirling into operational service in 1940.

The fact that the RAF was far ahead in the development of an offensive, strategic bomber fleet was the result of the defensive military strategy that had characterized British politicians and military leaders throughout the interwar period. The similarities between the defensive strategic thinking in the United States and in the Soviet Union were

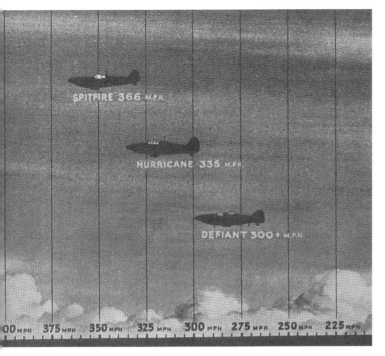

SPITFIRE 366 M.P.H.

HURRICANE 335 M.P.H.

DEFIANT 300+ M.P.H.

00 MPH 375 MPH 350 MPH 325 MPH 300 MPH 275 MPH 250 MPH 225 MPH

striking; the latter country became the first in the world to acquire a large fleet of heavy strategic bombers in the early 1930s. The Cold War's 'Doctrine of Deterrence' in the period after the Second World War goes back to the same idea. The idea behind British and Soviet armadas of heavy strategic bombers was that they would act as a deterrent to an attacker, and in the event of war be sufficient to paralyze the enemy's ability to attack their own country. In the so-called 'Western Air Plan 5' in the late 1930s, the Headquarters of Bomber Command estimated that 3,000 bomber sorties against nineteen power plants and twenty-six plants for the manufacture of synthetic gasoline would suffice to paralyze the entire German war industry in a space of two weeks – all at a cost of fewer than 200 British bombers. [33] This was paired with the maxim 'the bombers always get through'. As a result of the latter idea, the British, the US and the Soviet air forces went to war without an accompanying doctrine of fighter escort for their bombers – which would lead to tragic consequences for British bomber crews in 1939-1940, Soviet bomber crews in 1941, and the Americans two years later.

It has been argued that one crucial mistake made by the Germans during the Second World War was to not build up a strategic bomber fleet. This argument, however, ignores a number of important factors, the most important of which is Germany's major shortage of raw material. Therein lies the material basis for the lightning war – the Germans were simply forced to go for a short and decisive war. Additionally the Luftwaffe high command realized early on that even if a strategic bomber offensive could well have a major impact, it would take much longer than other countries expected.

When Göring a few months after the Nazi takeover in 1933 began the secret construction of the Luftwaffe, he appointed the highly competent General Walther Wever to the Chief of Staff. Wever certainly was no stranger to stra-

tegic bombers – he actually ordered a strategic bomber to be developed – but realized that because of the above, the Luftwaffe's tasks would consist primarily in the establishing of air superiority and direct air support to the army's ground operations, in that order of priority. A strategic bombing of enemy industries came only in third place. Although Wever died in an air accident in 1936, he laid the foundation for the doctrine with which the Luftwaffe went to war three years later.

It is quite clear that without the massive direct air support of the army's ground operations, the German military successes early in the war would hardly have been conceivable. The projected strategic bombers (Do 19 and Ju 89) were removed from the plans in the 1930s because of the weakness of the not yet fully developed German aircraft industry – one must keep in mind that the Versailles Treaty after the First World War prohibited Germany from manufacturing any engine-powered airplanes at all, so Nazi Germany's aviation industry had to beging from scratch to a large extent. In January 1933 there were no more than four thousand trained workers for the German aviation industry.

Given the air industry's limited capacity and the compelling need for the war to be short, the emphasis on medium bombers was optimal. The four-engined heavy bombers Do 19 and Ju 89 would not have been of any great use during the lightning wars against Poland and in the West. In fact, each manufactured Do 19 or Ju 89 would have meant one or two fewer of the more useful medium bombers.

The argument that the Germans could have been more successful during the Battle of Britain if they had had strategic bombers ultimately fails because of the fact that the Luftwaffe bombers actually were equipped for any kind of operation against the British Isles. If the Luftwaffe lacked anything in terms of equipment during the Battle of Britain, it was more long-range escort fighters. But this also was a factor on the British side, one which hampered the RAF to an even greater extent. The first British bomber operations during the Second World War – which were carried out without fighter escort simply because no such fighters had been developed – brutally crushed the thesis that 'the bombers will always get through'. On 14 December 1939, five Wellington bombers were lost from a formation of twelve attempting to attack the German port of Wilhelmshaven, and when 24 Wellingtons were sent out against the same target four days later, half were shot down by German fighters. The shock was so great that Bomber Command immediately switched the bulk of its activities to the hours of darkness – and continued to operate mainly at night for the remainder of the war. At the time, night fighter aviation still was fairly undeveloped, in Germany as in all other countries. In the summer of 1937, Göring had initiated night fighter experiments with and without interaction with anti-aircraft searchlights, but it still was far from what can be described as effective night fighter operations. At the beginning of the Second World War, the darkness of night remained the bomber's best protection.

But darkness also was the greatest obstacle to any effective bombing. At this time, the navigators in the British

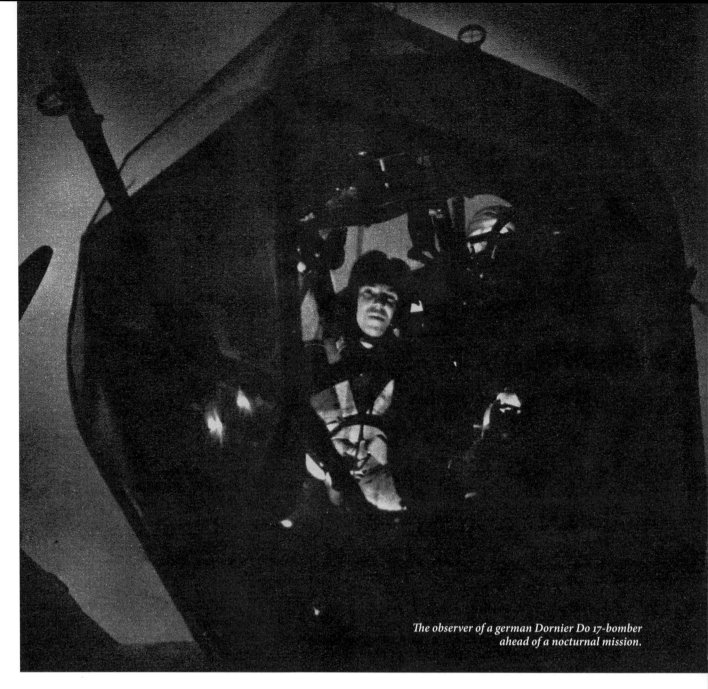

The observer of a german Dornier Do 17-bomber ahead of a nocturnal mission.

bombers were confined to visual navigation – i.e. to what they could see with the naked eye in the darkness – or to try to estimate the wind speed and the aircraft's relative speed and then calculate with the aid of a clock and a ruler on a map.

In this field, the Germans were ahead of the British through a device called 'Knickebein'. Knickebein was a further development of the instrument landing system developed by the electronics company C. Lorenz AG before the war, and which in the 1930s was the standard in civil aviation. This system was based on two radio transmitters that submitted parallel signals that set the course straight to a given airport. If the aircraft deviated to the right (as seen from the transmitter) from this course, the pilot or the navigator heard long Morse signals in their headphones, and if the aircraft deviated from the course to the left (from the transmitter), short Morse signals were heard. The system had a range of about 50 kilometres.

The electronics firm Telefunken further developed this with the Knickebein, a radio beam for military use. The name was taken from the German legend of a bird that was able to see in the dark. The Knickebein system was based on a radio beam that similar to the Lorenz system led the bomber pilots straight towards their target, but this was suppplemented by a crossover radio beam exactly at the target. Thus the crew knew when it was time to drop the bombs. This system had a range of about 400 kilometres.

However, Knickebein could not provide the precision necessary for attacks on what came to be the Luftwaffe's main targets at the beginning of the Battle of Britain – airfields, radar stations, and naval targets. Since the British anti-aircraft artillery at this time was still too weak – both numerically and technically – to constitute a substantial obstacle for German air operations, RAF Fighter Command was crucial to Britain's ability to ward off attacks. This in turn meant that the ability of German fighter aviation to keep the British fighters at bay was crucial for the Luftwaffe's ability to carry out its air raids.

CHAPTER 3
AIR COMBAT OVER THE CHANNEL

A tentative beginning

Although Hitler wanted to wait, Generalfeldmarschall Hermann Göring was not slow in getting to grips with operations against England. Göring was much more energetic than is asserted in most popular accounts. Even David Irving's biography on Göring devotes most attention to how the Luftwaffe Commander ran 'a greedy eye' on art collections at this time, but for some reason doesn't mention the fact that Göring during the days immediately after the surrender of France was already hard at work issuing new orders for attacking Great Britain.[34]

On 26 June, Göring divided the Luftwaffe's operational areas for the war against the British Isles: the line Paris – Le Havre – Portsmouth – the area south of Edinburgh separated the operational areas of Luftflotte 3 in the west and Luftflotte 2 in the east. Additionally, Luftflotte 5 was assigned to carry out operations across northern Britain to the line of Firth of Forth – Glasgow. The next day Göring instructed the strategic reconnaissance aircraft to begin a systematic survey of the airfields in the British Isles.

But there were not many previous experiences to fall back upon. A strategic air war in the true sense of the word had never been carried out before. Although Germany had been at war with Britain for ten months, the Luftwaffe had only appeared on a most limited scale over British Isles. The first actual air strike against targets in Britain took place on 16 October 1939, after nearly seven weeks of war: twelve Ju 88s from I./KG 30 came in over the North Sea and attacked the naval base in the Firth of Forth on the Scottish east coast. The two cruisers Southampton and Edinburgh and destroyer Mohawk were lightly damaged. In return the British shot down two Ju 88s. Already in this first combat between the Luftwaffe and Fighter Command over the British Isles, the new Spitfire Mk I stood well out. Squadron Leader Douglas Farquhar and four other Spitfire pilots from No. 602 Squadron brought home Fighter Command's first two victories of the war.

The next day I./KG 30 attacked the naval base at Scapa Flow with four Ju 88s which severely damaged the old battleship Iron Duke. These air raids, however, were exceptions.

On 20 October 1939, seaplanes from 3./Küstenfliegergruppe 906 under the command of Kapitän zur See Werner Klümper laid half a dozen mines in the water off the Thames Estuary and at the entrance to Harwich. If the Germans learned anything from these relatively few missions, it was that Fighter Command was a serious opponent to be reckoned with. The very next day, on 21 October, Hurricanes and Spitfires from 46 and 72 squadrons engaged a formation of nine He 115 seaplanes from I./Kü-

FlGr 406 off the Humber and shot down four without own losses. Over the next few weeks, German seaplanes laid no more than sixty mines off the shores of England before this activity ultimately ceased completely.

During the remainder of the winter and spring, a few German aircraft occasionally flew in over British airspace, but Hitler had issued strict orders that no bombs were allowed to be dropped on the British mainland.

Then, on 10 May 1940 the German offensive was unleashed in the west. But in the air over England all remained as usual – calm.

Five days later, RAF Bomber Command launched a series of nocturnal raids against cities in western Germany, but even this didn't draw more German aircraft over the 'Channel'. These were by now fully engaged in driving the fleeing enemy armies towards the sea. Only on 4 June 1940, when the victorious Germans stood in the rubble of the former evacuation port of Dunkirk in France, did the name 'England' appear in the operational orders of more German air units. After all, the British coast had suddenly become the front line! Everything was hastily improvised, and two days later some 30 Luftwaffe bombers crossed the British east coast at night and subjected a couple of RAF air bases to small-scale raids. The war had been raging for nine months, but this was the largest formation of enemy planes that had hit England since 1918!

The key word was 'familiarization flights'. Faced with a possible prolonged conflict with Britain, the purpose was to familiarize the flight crews with the conditions above the British Isles. The next mission of this kind took place already in the evening of 6 June, and when the guns on the continent had silenced after the French surrender three weeks later, the frequency in the German 'familiarization flights' increased to up to 70 aircraft per night.

The German airmen who carried out these nocturnal missions felt quite safe because of the protection offered by darkness – not without reason. It is true that the RAF's night fighter force received a major reinforcement when after the disastrous losses in May 1940, the twin-engined Bristol Blenheim IF fighters were shifted to operations at night. But the six squadrons equipped with Blenheim IFs was of course far too small a force to cover the all of the UK. But in the case of night fighting, the British proved their creativity and innovation, and moved ahead of the Germans in terms of radar equipment of night fighter planes. Their first aircraft radar equipment, the A. I. Mark I and II, were quite ineffective, but in the spring of 1940 an improved variant, the Mark III, was brought into service. In April 1940, a special night Fighter Interception Unit (F. I. U.), led by Squadron Leader Peter Chamberlain, was formed to develop night fighter methods with radar-equipped Blenheim IFs.

However, the RAF's first great defensive victory at night over the British Isles was achieved with the 'old-fashioned' night fighter methods that characterized night fighter operations during most of 1940 – fighter pilots attacking enemy aircraft when they were illuminated by anti-aircraft searchlights on the ground. On the night between 18 and 19 June, several He 111s carried out 'familiarization flights' over the British Isles, but this time luck was on the defender's side. The night was cloudless with a bright full moon, and in several places British fighter pilots that had taken to the air managed to catch sight of German bombers. Shortly after midnight, 74 Squadron's Flight Lieutenant Adolphus Gysbert Malan – better known as 'Sailor' Malan – shot down an He 111 from Stab/KG 4 near Chelmsford. Shortly afterwards, a Blenheim of 23 Squadron shot down another He 111 near Sheringham. At a quarter past one in the morning, 'Sailor' Malan downed his second Heinkel. When the last German planes had returned to their bases, it was found that six crews were missing from KG 4. On the other hand the Luftwaffe's ability to bite off had also been displayed during this first nightly air encounter: to shoot down these six German bombers cost the British a loss of four night fighters.

Meanwhile, RAF Bomber Command, led by Air Vice-Marshal Charles Portal, carried out regular attacks against targets in Germany and the occupied countries. In fact, on the same night as KG 4 was inflicted these heavy losses over the British Isles, four British bombers failed to return from operations against Germany.

On 20 June 1940, the British Air Ministry issued new operational directives. For Fighter Command, withdrawn from the continent, the task was clear: Defend the British airspace. Bomber Command was tasked to deploy its heavy bombers against the aviation industry and plants for the production of synthetic fuels in Germany. The medium bombers were to attack Luftwaffe airfields, German coastal shipping and ports, also in the occupied countries, where the build-up of the German fleet intended for the invasion of the British Isles was supposed to take place.

With the exception of certain operations against the latter target category, the British bomber offensive of 1940 was rather ineffective in terms of the material destruction it inflicted. (The fact that the psychological effect on the other hand was of great importance, will be discussed later on.) The German fighter force compelled them to operate at night, and at that time both navigational devices and bomb sights were thoroughly inadequate for operations in darkness. When three specially selected crews from No. 83 Squadron on 2 July 1940 dropped the first 2,000-lb. armour-piercing bombs against the German battleship Scharnhorst in Kiel's harbour, no bomb hit closer to its target than a mile.

Meanwhile, the war in France came to an end. On 22 June, a French delegation arrived at the Compiègne Forest near Paris in order to sign the document of surrender. On 25 June 1940 at 01:35 at night, hostilities in France ceased. 'The war in the West is over', Hitler proclaimed. It would prove to be a premature statement.

Exactly twenty-four hours later several British fighters again managed to intercept German aircraft on 'familiarization missions', and again they reported six German bombers shot down. Churchill was heard speaking on British radio:

'The Battle of France is over. The Battle of Britain is about to begin!'

The German Junkers Ju 88 was developed with the personal support of Hermann Göring. During the Battle of Britain it was the world's fastest medium bomber. Top speed was 450 km/h in level flight and 560 km/h when diving. The aircraft could be used for both horizontal bombing and dive bombing. The picture shows a Ju 88 from KG 51.

Ehre

den

Siegern

Beförderungen in der Luftwaffe

Im letzten Heft des „Adler" haben wir begonnen, Bilder von Offizieren der Luftwaffe zu veröffentlichen, die vom Führer und Obersten Befehlshaber der Wehrmacht wegen besonderer Kriegsverdienste befördert wurden. Wir setzen diese Reihe jetzt fort und werden auch in den nächsten Heften noch Aufnahmen von beförderten Offizieren bringen

General der Flieger Loerzer

General der Flieger Freiherr von Richthofen

Aufn. Scherl Bilderdienst (1)

This article from the Luftwaffe magazine Der Adler shows two of the most important German commanders at the English Channel, Bruno Loerzer and Wolfram Freiherr von Richthofen. Both participated as fighter pilots in the First World War, where Loerzer scored 44 and von Richthofen 8 aerial victories. It is a common misconception that Wolfram 'Wulf' von Richthofen was the cousin of the famous ace Manfred von Richthofen, 'the Red Baron'. In fact, they were fourth cousins. However 'Wulf' served in Manfred von Richthofen's fighter unit and flew his first mission on the day when the famous airman died. 'The Red Baron's' brother Lothar – also a successful ace – died in a plane crash in 1922. Therefore, 'Wulf' was the only survivor among the three famous von Richthofens when the Second World War began. Wolfram Freiherr von Richthofen died in July 1945, 59 years old. Loerzer died in 1960, at the age of 69.

The 'Channel Offensive' begins

On 30 June, Göring issued his 'General Directive for the Air Force's warfare against England'. As we have seen, several of his air units were quite worn out after the Battle of France. The Luftwaffe was in need of a period of rest and recuperation. Göring's idea was to allow most of his units to rest and replenish its losses in France, while initiating an air campaign with smaller forces that would carry out raids across the English Channel in order to familiarize the crews with the weaknesses and strengths of the British air defence. 'Pinprick attacks' with only one or two bombers at a time were to be carried out against British industrial targets and air bases. The largest operations were conducted against British coastal shipping, and the operational objective was to 'close the Channel for all British naval traffic'.[35] This allowed the Luftwaffe to rebuild the strength of many of its units, while the opponent on the other side of the Channel was not given much time to rest.

Due to political considerations, any attack against civilian targets was still strictly prohibited. Hajo Herrmann, who at the time served as an Oberleutnant and pilot in III./KG 4, experienced this one day when he returned to his base after a 'pinprick attack' against the Vickers-Armstrong aircraft works in Newcastle. No sooner had he landed than he was called for questioning by a court martial judge. He informed Herrmann that according to the Führer Headquarters German aircraft had accidentally dropped a few bombs on civilian homes in Newcastle, and the commander of Fliegerkorps X had been ordered to identify and

put those responsible on trial. However, it proved impossible to determine who the guilty party was.[36]

Generalleutnant Bruno Loerzer and Generalmajor Wolfram Freiherr von Richthofen, the commanders of Fliegerkorps II from Luftflotte 2 and Fliegerkorps VIII from Luftflotte 3 respectively, were given the task of organising the so-called 'Channel Offensive'.

Thirty-nine-year old Loerzer was an old pilot mate of Göring from the First World War. Loerzer delegated the operational command to Oberst Johannes Fink, commander of the Do 17-equipped Do KG 2 'Holzhammer' ('wooden hammer'). Appointed as 'Kanalkampfführer' – Channel Combat Leader (which German airmen jokingly interpreted as 'cesspool combat leader') – Fink deployed not less than 150 serviceable combat aircraft, divided between:

Stab, I., II. and **III./KG 2** with 52 operational
Do 17 bombers.
III./StG 51 and **IV.(St)/LG 1** with Ju 87 dive-bombers.
Stab, II. and **III./JG 51,** plus **I.(J)/LG 2** with 76 operational
Bf 109 fighters.

The fighter operations were led by Oberst Theo Osterkamp. The German Lehrgeschwader – LG 1 and LG 2 – were originally élite units formed with the aim of testing operational methods with different aircraft types. By this time, LG 1 was the Luftwaffe's only Geschwader with five Gruppen. The first three Gruppen were equipped with the new Ju 88 bomber. IV.(St)/LG 1, equipped with Ju 87s, was commanded by Hauptmann Bernd von Brauchitsch, the son of the German Army's chief of staff, Generalfeldmarschall Walther von Brauchitsch. In early July, yet another fighter unit arrived at Alençon to participate in the Channel Offensive in the sector assigned to Fliegerkorps VIII. This was the fifth Gruppe from Lehrgeschwader 1, V.(Z)/LG 1, equipped with Messerschmitt Bf 110s.

The main units of Generalmajor Wolfram 'Wulf' von Richthofen's Fliegerkorps VIII were StG 1, StG 2 'Immelmann' – named after a famous German fighter pilot during the First World War – and StG 77. These Ju 87-equipped units were installed at the former French military air bases on the Cotentin Peninsula and in Normandy. A unit of ground personnel also began preparing the airstrip on the Channel Island of Guernsey, which had been occupied on 1 July.

On the night between 3 and 4 July, British convoy O. A. 178 – fourteen merchant ships bound for the Atlantic, escorted by a corvette – departed from Southend on the Thames Estuary's northern side, setting course on the English Channel. At dawn the vessels approached the Strait of Dover, when suddenly a Do 17 from II./KG 2 popped out of the clouds and dropped its bombs. A direct hit set the Dutch merchant ship *Britsum* (5,255 GRT) on fire. The captain beached her on a sandbank at Deal – in vain, however, since the ship was shortly afterwards destroyed in a storm.

The spotting of this convoy was exactly what Fink and von Richthofen had been waiting for. On the airfields at Saint-Malo and Lannion, 90 Junkers 87 Stukas took off. It was not more than slightly after eight o' clock. As they flew out over the sea while climbing to reach altitude, they split up into two formations. Meanwhile, the Bf 110s of V.(Z)/LG 1 took off from Cherbourg, to where they had flown from Alençon to be fuelled, and set off over the Channel in the hope of giving Fighter Command a good thrashing.

To the despair of the ship's crews there were no British fighter around when sixty planes from I. and II. /StG 2 'Immelmann' reached the convoy. The Ju 87s formed a circle a few thousand metres above the ships, and then, one by one, they dropped down towards carefully selected targets. The convoy had no chance of escape. The air became filled with the protracted screaming sound from the diving planes. The same omnious sounds that had made the blood freeze in the veins of Allied troops and civilians in Poland, Norway and France, now filled the British sailors with terror.

The first bombs fell and soon plumes of water rose everywhere around the convoy. A large puff of flame and smoke suddenly showed that a ship had been hit. Almost simultaneously another was hit, and then another and another. Smoke, fire and explosions were seen in several places. All the time new Stukas came howling from above. More and more bombs rained down on the British ships.

The RAF had been alerted too late. Eight Hurricanes were scrambled at the air base Hawkinge, just west of Dover. But these came in only to be attacked by a formation of Messerschmitt Bf 109s from II./JG 51. Hauptmann Horst Tietzen, commanding 5./JG 51, sent Sergeant Harry Cartwright's Hurricane burning down to the Channel, and the other British fighters were driven off.

Without having seen anything of the fighter escort, and with new Stukas constantly emerging, the commander of the convoy decided to order the ships to seek refuge in Portland's harbour. By that time, in addition to *Britsum*, *Dallas City* (4,952 GRT), *Kolga* (3,526 GRT) and *Deucalion* (1,796 GRT) had been sunk, and five other ships were

Junkers Ju 87 Stuka constituted the backbone of the so-called 'Channel offensive' in July 1940, and due to its ability to drop bombs accurately it inflicted heavy losses on British shipping.

seriously damaged. And not a single German aircraft had been lost!

But not even Portland's harbour could offer the ships full protection. While the 'Immelmann' airmen turned for home, III./StG 51 took over. Its 33 Stukas spread out fan-shaped over Portland's waterfront. The attacks were concentrated against the port's 'jewel', the anti-aircraft ship *Foyle Bank* – equipped with radar and automatic targeting for its eight 102 mm pieces, eight 40mm and four 20mm Oerlikon-automatic guns. Two Stukas were hit by the concentrated fire from *Foyle Bank*. One of them dived straight into the water. Meanwhile the first bombs exploded on the anti-aircraft ship's deck. The attack was over in four minutes. *Foyle Bank* continued to burn and eventually sank, dragging down 176 of its crewmen. Another ship was sunk and three more damaged by bomb hits in the port. This airstrike hadn't either encountered any resistance from the RAF either.

The criticism of Fighter Command from the British Navy was not long in coming. Where were the British fighters? Churchill was upset. He turned to the Admiralty and asked for a report on what actually had been done to protect the Channel convoys, and added:

'I would like to know whether the Air Force is in control of the situation.'

The immediate result of the German success on 4 July was that the British Atlantic convoys to and from London were routed around Scotland instead of taking the shorter route through the English Channel. This of course meant a considerable setback in the British supply situation, since the longer time the convoys thus needed, also meant that the monthly tonnage that reached the British Isles dropped slightly relative to what could have been the case if the vessels had been able to go through the Channel.

But Churchill refused to cease the shipping in the English Channel entirely. From 6 July so-called 'CW convoys' laden with coal were regularly sent from Southend. Some of these went to Great Yarmouth in the north, but many were routed through the Strait of Dover and on to the Southwest of England. Under the circumstances it would have been easier to transport the coal by rail. But to Churchill, shipping through the Channel had an important symbolic value: 'They show that it still is our Channel', he said. The first among these convoys, CW.1, went to Great Yarmouth in the north on 6 July and reached port without incident.

Churchill contacted Dowding and requested that he provide each convoy in the English Channel with a constant cover of at least one Flight, i.e., six fighters.

Across the Channel, Oberst Osterkamp, commanding the fighter units in the Pas de Calais sector, was reinforced with III./ZG 26 'Horst Wessel', which began operations over the British Isles on 7 July. III./ZG 26, equipped with Bf 110s, had already gained fame, not least through German propaganda. The unit carried the honorary name of 'Horst Wessel', after a Nazi 'martyr' from the time before Hitler came to power. Under the leadership of Hauptmann Johannes Schalk, III./ZG 26 was listed for 79 victories against only eight own combat losses during the Battle of France.

On the afternoon of 7 July, after two days of bad flying weather, German fighter pilots on a free hunting mission

Two aces in 54 Squadron, 'Al' Deere (left) and Colin Gray, both New Zealanders. Colin Gray was New Zealand's premier ace during The Second World War, with 27½ air victories. His twin brother, Flying Officer Kenneth Gray also was a pilot in the RAF, but was killed in a plane crash with a Whitley bomber from RAF 102 Squadron on 1 May 1940. Alan Deere achieved 22 confirmed and 10 probable victories. Gray died in August 1995, 80 years old. The following month Deere died, at 77 years of age. A Spitfire dropped his ashes over the Thames.

over the Dover Strait managed to draw half a dozen of Spitfires into combat. The fact that III./ZG 26 took part with its twin-engined Bf 110s contributed to this. The inexperienced servicemen of the Royal Observer Corps failed to identify the German fighter planes – otherwise the British fighter pilots had strict orders to avoid allowing themselves to become unnecessarily drawn into fighter combat. But with a new coastal convoy on its way through the Channel, the British dared not take any risks. 'B' Flight of No. 54 Squadron turned towards the Bf 110s, but was surprised by eighteen Bf 109s from III./JG 51 that came diving out of the sun. [37] In rapid succession, three of the six Spitfires were shot down. Alan 'Al' Deere, who served as a Flight Lieutenant with 54 Squadron at the time, commented: 'This was a most unfortunate first engagement over our own soil and it proved that the Luftwaffe pilots had lost none of their cunning and aggressiveness and, worse still, that the lessons of the Dunkirk air fighting had not been fully digested by our pilots.' [38]

That evening a formation of seven Spitfires from 65 Squadron suffered the same fate. They were jumped by II./JG 51 and lost all three planes in Green Section. With the results on 7 July, Osterkamp's JG 51 had so far during the 'Channel Offensive' been credited with 18 victories without any own losses. But Oberst Fink was not pleased. While Osterkamp's 'kids' had been tangling with some of the British fighters, other Spitfires had been able to attack the Do 17s that had been dispatched against a convoy in the Strait of Dover, shooting down two bombers.

An irritated Fink rang up Osterkamp and asked him to hold his fighters near the bombers in so-called 'close escort'. Osterkamp protested energetically – in this case, the Messerschmitt's trump card, speed and height advantage, would come to nothing. But Fink refused to give in. In the end, they agreed that III./ZG 26 would provide the bombers with close escort while Osterkamp's Bf 109s were to continue their unbound free hunting.[39] By all indications, Generalmajor von Richthofen at Fliegerkorps VIII took a similar decision concerning V.(Z)/LG 1.

The Bf 110's lack of fitness for close escort missions has been discussed previously. The aircraft was more effective on free hunting missions – which was underlined by the fighter sweep undertaken by six Bf 110 crews from V.(Z)/LG 1 early on 9 July. They clashed with three Hurricanes from 43 Squadron, and the outcome was almost inevitable from the beginning. One of those who had his Hurricane shot to pieces by the heavy nose armament of the Zerstörer planes in this combat was 43 Squadron's Squadron Leader Charles Lott, a 33-year-old veteran who had served as a fighter pilot since 1928. Lott survived with serious injuries and was later decorated with the Distinguished Service Order. The report for the award described his last combat:

'As leader of a section of Hurricanes, he pressed home an attack in adverse weather conditions against six Messerschmitt 110s. During the combat Squadron Leader Lott's aircraft was badly hit but, displaying great skill, despite an injury which eventually necessitated the removal of an eye, he brought his aircraft to within 3 miles of the base before he was compelled to abandon it.'

Both sides claimed to have shot down three enemy aircraft in the fray. In reality, two Hurricanes were lost while all Bf 110s returned safe and sound to the base.

A few hours later, III./ZG 26 carried out its first close escort mission across the English Channel, being deployed in conjunction with III./KG 2 against a British convoy in the Strait of Dover. Here the Zerstörer used a tactic called 'Angriffskreis' – 'Attack Circle'. This speciality of the Zerstörer has often been confused with the purely defensive so-called 'Lufbery-circle', which meant that the planes formed a circle where each aircraft was covered by the one behind. Aviation historians John Vasco and Peter D. Cornwell explain: 'It also allowed a formation to effectively take possession of an extensive area of sky which they could occupy and defend for as long as necessary – when covering the approach or withdrawal of another formation. Used in this way it lured enemy fighters to attack at disadvantage a potentially lethal formation.'[40]

This gave the bombers such an effective fighter cover that they managed to hit four ships with their bombs without own losses. The air combat resulted in a Hurricane and a Bf 110 getting shot down.

Ahead of the air war over the Channel the Luftwaffe had created an effective air-rescue service with Heinkel 59 seaplanes. Although these were painted white and marked with red crosses, one of them was shot down by three Spitfires of 72 Squadron on 1 July, as it was out searching for the crew of a He 115 that had ditched in the sea off Whitby during a mine laying mission on the night before. This aroused a great deal of bitterness on the German side.

When German Seenotflugkommando 1 in the afternoon on 9 July dispatched a He 59 to search for the downed airmen, an entire Staffel of Bf 109s, 4./JG 51, was assigned to escorted the floatplane. Flight Lieutenant 'Al' Deere led the Spitfires of No. 54 Squadron's 'B' Flight in a climb seven or eight kilometres east of the Deal, and at first was puzzled when he saw the He 59: 'A seaplane painted silver ... civilian registration letters painted on the upper surface of the wing ... What to do about this unexpected discovery?' Deere asked himself, but immediately afterward he heard Pilot Officer Johnnie Allen's voice in the radio, 'Red Leader, there are about a dozen 109s flying in loose formation, well behind and slightly above the seaplane!'[41] It was enough to convince Deere that the He 59 was hostile, Red Cross markings or not. He led his pilots in a turn that placed them in a position with the Bf 109s ahead and below. Then he gave the attack order.

Oberleutnant Josef Fözö, who led the Messerschmitt formation, was already an old hand in the Luftwaffe. He belonged to the group of Austrian airmen who joined the German Luftwaffe when Hitler annexed Austria in March 1938. Shortly afterwards he volunteered to fly combat missions in the Spanish Civil War, and between July 1938 and March 1939, he carried out 147 combat flights with 3./J 88 in Spain, attaining three victories. When the 'Channel Offensive' began in July 1940, 'Joschko' Fözö was among Oberst Osterkamp's most experienced aviators. When he saw the six Spitfires come diving to attack from above and behind, he waited until exactly the right moment, and then he ordered his pilots to split into two groups – one that climbed steeply to the right and one that climbed sharply to the left. This immediately turned the tables. Having lost their initial advantage, the British had to disperse their formation.

'No fool this leader, that's a smart move', Deere thought, and afterwards commented 'I remembered this manoeuvre later on when the RAF was on the offensive, and used it with telling effect against the defending German fighters.'[42]

The Spitfire formation was scattered like fireworks, and in the next moment the sky was filled with fighters that chased each other. In the jumble of diving and turning fighters, 'Al' Deere suddenly found himself on a collision course with a Messerschmitt. Afterwards, the result was recorded in No. 54 Squadron's Operations Record Book: 'Deere had an amazing experience in a head-on attack when neither 109 nor Spitfire would give way and a collision resulted, the 109 striking the Spitfire's propeller and cockpit hood. Deere, with engine stopped, managed to force land at Manston whereupon his aircraft caught fire. He broke his way out, uninjured save for slight burns on his hands.'[43]

Oberfeldwebel Johann Illner, the German pilot who collided with Deere, also made it back to his base, where he force-landed. Unlike Deere, he had his enemy aircraft acknowledged as a victory. His comrades shot down two Spitfires and two British pilots were killed. But 54 Squadron was not wholly without compensation. Flying Officer John Allen was able to take advantage of the confusion in the air combat to attack the He 59. Hit by a volley from

Allen's machine guns the German pilot put down the Heinkel in an emergency landing on the water.

Further to the west, six Spitfires of 609 Squadron's 'B' Flight were dispatched on a patrol mission over Portland at 18:35.[44] It was already dark when Flying Officer Peter Drummond-Hay, leading the three Spitfires in Green Section, caught sight of a formation of Ju 87s that came diving out from a black cloud. These were 27 aircraft from I./StG 77 that had been sent to attack Portland's harbor. Drummond-Hay called out an attack order, but he failed to notice the German fighter escort – Bf 110s of V.(Z)/LG 1, positioned higher up. One of his pilots, Pilot Officer David Crook, recalled:

'I settled down to enjoy a little slaughter of a few Ju 87s, as they are rather helpless machines. I was flying last on the line, and we were now travelling at high speed and rapidly approaching the enemy, when I happened to look round behind. To my intense surprise and dismay, I saw at least nine Messerschmitt 110s about 2,000 feet above us. They were just starting to dive on us when I saw them, and as they were diving they were overtaking us rapidly. This completely altered the situation.'

Crook realised that 'if we were not jolly quick we should all be dead in a few seconds'.

'Look out behind, Messerschmitts behind!' he cried over the radio and banked to the left and dived into a layer of clouds.

Flying Officer Appleby managed to escape the attacking Bf 110s by hurling his Spitfire into a spin down to the clouds – prompting Oberleutnant Joachim Glienke, who led the Bf 110 formation, to report this as a Spitfire shot down. Drummond-Hay was not as lucky; he perished in his burning Spitfire, 'PR-Q', which was shot down by Feldwebel Hans Datz of 13.(Z)/LG 1. Emerging from the clouds, Crook saw a Bf 110 above: 'I pulled up into a steep climb and fired at him, but without result. He turned away immediately, and I lost him.'

Crook continues his account: 'I turned back for the coast, and started to call up Peter and Michael on the R.T. But there was no response, and as far as Peter was concerned, I was already calling into the void. A moment later I saw another Spitfire flying home on a very erratic course, obviously keeping a very good look behind. I joined up with it, and recognized Michael, and together we bolted for the English coast like a couple of startled rabbits. I made a perfectly bloody landing on the aerodrome and overshot so badly that I nearly turned the Spitfire on her nose in my efforts to pull up before hitting the hedge. I got out to talk to Michael and found to my surprise that my hand was quite shaky and even my voice was unsteady. . .'

V.(Z)/LG 1 made it without any own losses, but on the return flight Oberleutnant Glienke discovered that the engines on his plane didn't work properly. Shortly afterwards, he was forced to make an emergency landing in the Channel. Both he and his radio operator were quickly rescued by a He 59. However, the air-sea rescue failed to find I./StG 77's commander, Hauptmann Friedrich-Karl Freiherr von Dalwigk zu Lichtenfels, who was last seen taking refuge in a cloud when the British fighters attacked. He and his radio operator disappeared forever over the English Channel.

Meanwhile, the He 59 that had previously been damaged by Flying Officer Allen sat with its pontoons bogged in a sand bank. The tide was at an ebb at that moment. The British sent out a lifeboat which towed the plane and the crew to land. The pilot's logbook revealed that the British had been right when they assumed that the air-sea-rescue aircraft also were used to search for British convoys. Four days later, British Air Ministry issued Bulletin No. 1254 that instructed the RAF airmen to regard even German aircraft marked with red crosses as legitimate targets.

While the 'Channel Offensive' was carried out by the Luftwaffe, Blenheim bombers of RAF Bomber Command's 2 Group flew attacks against German airfields. According to the directive from the headquarters of the Bomber Command of 6 July 1940, these attacks were also to be carried out in daylight, 'when suitable weather conditions exist which will give adequate security through cloud cover areas of operation.'[45] These attacks were never more than what amounted to 'pinprick attacks'; rarely were there more than a handful of Blenheims at a time carrying out these attacks, and the damage they caused was minimal. But on 4 July twenty-four Blenheims attacked, which resulted in two German planes being knocked out at the air base of Brussels-Everes.[46] Four days later twenty-four Blenheims again attacked and put at least one bomber from KG 3 out of commission at the airfield at Laon. Encouraged by these successes, 2 Group dispatched 12 Blenheim bombers from 21 and 57 squadrons to strike the airport of Stavanger Sola in Norway on 9 July. Since the RAF's meteorologists predicted heavy showers over Norway, the British hoped that they would be able to avoid detection. But when they approached the Norwegian coast, the weather cleared up. The bombers managed to reach the Sola base without being attacked by German fighters, and dropped eighteen bombs, which knocked out three of the new twin-engined Do 215s from AufklObdL.[47] But on the return flight, the Blenheims were overtaken by three Bf 110s from I /ZG 76 and twenty Bf 109s from II./JG 77. In the ensuing combat, seven Blenheims and one Bf 109 were shot down, and none of the remaining Blenheims escaped without any sort of damage. While the Bf 110s of I./ZG 76 pursued the fleeing Blenheims out over the North Sea, the Zerstörer pilots came across two of Coastal Command's aircraft. Both of these – a Lockheed Hudson and a four-engined flying boat of the type Short Sunderland – were shot down.[48]

Unfortunately, the headquarters of Bomber Command failed to learn from this setback. The very next day, 10 July, six Blenheim crews from 107 Squadron were tasked with bombing the German air base at Amiens, 70 kilometres inside France. Without any fighter escort, they flew low to try to avoid detection. But this did not succeed. In a fierce engagement with Bf 109s from III./JG 3, five of the six British bombers were shot down, all without German losses. This time the Germans were able to repel the British raid completely.[49] Unlike Bomber Command, however, the headquarters of Fighter Command had drawn an important conclusion from the fighting in the early July days: Dowding and Park realized that the fighter formations that they had hitherto sent into the air had been inadequately

THE AEROPLANE   *Advertisements*   DECEMBER 15, 193

BRITAIN'S STRENGTH IN THE SKIES

"Bristol" aircraft have always occupied a premier position in British military aviation. The "Bristol" Blenheim, combining great structural strength with exceptional speed, range and manœuvrability, is now an increasingly vital factor in the strength of Britain's air arm, and has already performed valuable service with the Royal Air Force. For high-speed long-range bombing, fighting and reconnaissance.

★ The "Bristol" Blenheim is fitted with two 920 b.h.p. "Bristol" Mercury engines, and is an all-metal mid-wing cantilever monoplane, with a monocoque "stressed-skin" fuselage. It was the first aircraft constructed entirely of metal to go into quantity production for the Royal Air Force, and is now standard equipment. The Blenheim was chosen for large scale production under the Aircraft Shadow Industry Scheme.

"Bristol"

BLENHEIM

THE BRISTOL AEROPLANE COMPANY LIMITED, FILTON HOUSE, BRISTOL.

The British Bristol Blenheim was not quite as effective as this wartime ad from the British aircraft manufacturer Blenheim wants to make out. Its top speed was only 428 km/h and the maximum bomb load was a modest 540 kg.

small. For obvious reasons, both fighter leaders were eager to save their forces as much as possible, so they were still quite unwilling to deploy any major forces. But the serious losses on 7 and 9 July made a strong impression – they were mainly the result of too few British fighters being sent up against too many German planes. It was determined that a larger number of fighter interceptors would be scrambled each time.

10–13 July: 'The most glorious days in the history of the RAF'

10 July 1940 was the start of four days of violent and dramatic air fighting. That is why this date is officially counted in the UK as the beginning of the Battle of Britain – which the battered pilots of 54 Squadron perhaps were not inclined to agree upon. On that day, the following entry was made in the unit's war diary: 'After the first phase of the Battle of Britain, all that remains of the squadron is eight aircraft and thirteen pilots.'[50]

As Wednesday 10 July dawned, a full eight different coastal convoys were at sea in or near the English Channel. When a Do 17 with the escort of ten Bf 109s appeared over Convoy 'Bread', which sailed ballast from the Thames Estuary, No. 74 Squadron was scrambled from Manston airfield. John Freeborn, who served as a Pilot Officer with 74 Squadron, described the following events: 'A convoy was travelling round the North Foreland on its way to Dover on the English Channel. It was an overcast day, but quite clear visibility. "A" Flight was ordered to scramble, as a Do 215 escorted by about 20 Me 109s was taking photos of the convoy and reporting back to base. I was leading the six aircraft of "A" Flight and intercepted the enemy. Somehow the Do 215 got away and we attacked the '109s. I was so close to the leader of the '109s. I opened fire at about 50 yards away. I saw my bullets hitting the '109 and the force of eight guns hitting the target. I saw it move sideways before it turned over and then went down vertically into the sea. I then looked back and saw another '109 coming up towards me. But since my No. 2 was behind it, I would not have had any trouble with this aircraft. I then saw the flashes of the guns of my No. 2, and my aircraft was hit. The top petrol tank was severely damaged and I was getting soaked with petrol. I immediately switched off the engine and all electrical appliances and glided back into Manston airfield.'[51]

Besides Freeborn, Sergeant 'Tony' Mould had his Spitfire damaged and had to force-land. On the German side, Leutnant Erich Hohagen and Feldwebel Heinz Tornow reported one victory each while Unteroffizier Wolfgang Stocker was killed.

The convoy that had been spotted by the German reconnaissance crew, was the largest Channel convoy hitherto noticed by the Germans, and Oberst Fink decided to strike it this when it entered the Strait of Dover. In Cambrai and St. Léger I. and II./KG 2 received directives for the attack. 47 Do 17s took off at 13:45 (German time – which was one hour ahead of British, i.e. Greenwich meridian time). Hauptmann Schalk had the task of organizing the close escort, and for this purpose 18 Bf 110s joined the slow bombers at an altitude of between 1,000 and 2,000 metres. Another 2,000 metres higher, 14 Bf 109s from III./JG 51 carried out so-called free hunting in the target area.

An hour later – 13:50 British time – radar stations in southeastern England reported echoes from a major German aircraft formation over Pas de Calais. From Fighter Command's headquarters at Bentley Priory the information was forwarded to 11 Group's Headquarters in Uxbridge, which ordered up five squadrons. 30 Spitfires and Hurricanes took to the air to cover the ships. This time the Admiralty would not have any reason to complain!

The German radio surveillance post that had been installed at Wissant to intercept the British radio traffic noted that the RAF's ground control gave their airborne units instructions on the approaching German formations before these could reasonably be within sight of England. This made the Germans realize that the British conducted their fighter operations with the aid of radar. So this hardly was a secret to the Germans – which sometimes has been assumed.

When the German formation swept out towards the coast, it was not long until the pilots saw the amount of British escort fighters. For combat-hungry Messerschmitt pilots who longed for British planes to shoot down, it was a little too much of a good thing.

'The whole air seemed to be filled with British fighters', the commander of III./JG 51, Hauptmann Hannes Trautloft, wrote in his diary that evening.[52] A combat equally violent as confused broke out.

Hauptmann Schalk's slowly flying Bf 110s bore the brunt of the British fighter attack – 25 Spitfires and Hurricanes. Sub-Lieutenant Francis Dawson-Paul, an ace from the Fleet Air Arm who currently flew a Spitfire in 64 Squadron, shot down two Bf 110s in quick succession. Pilot Officer Peter 'Paddy' Stevenson from 74 Squadron charged the 'Attack Circle' of the Bf 110s, but had his Spitfire so badly damaged that he had to break off before he got shot down into the sea. Pilot Officer Edward 'Jumbo' Gracie from 56 Squadron also received a few hits from a Bf 110's 20mm cannons in his Spitfire and crash-landed at Manston.

Meanwhile, 11 Hurricanes from 111 Squadron jumped the Dornier bombers. Nine Hurricanes concentrated on a single Do 17 that was completely shot to pieces, and while the Hurricanes spread fan-like after the attack, the Do-17 crew prepared to bail out. At that moment, Trautloft's fourteen Bf 109s came diving down amongst the British fighters. Oberleutnant Walter Oesau, one of Trautloft's best pilots, hit a Hurricane with a well-aimed burst of fire. Apparently unable to control his damaged Hurricane, the British pilot – 111 Squadron's Flying Officer Thomas Higgs – crashed into the Do 17 of Hauptmann Walter Krieger, the Staffelkapitän of 3./KG 2. Both aircraft went down. Higgs and two Germans bailed out. The British vessels managed to save the two Germans from the sea, but Higgs perished.

This time there were enough British fighters to keep the German fighters at bay while others attacked the bombers. Ira Jones' story of 74 Squadron notes: '[Flying Officer]

A Hurricane formation from 87 Squadron, based at Exeter. The unit commander, Squadron Leader John Dewar, was credited with the shooting down of two Bf 110s – one of which may have been the one flown by Hermann Göring's cousin Oberleutnant Hans-Joachim Göring. Thereby Dewar reached a total of 5½ air victories. Later he was promoted to wing commander and led the Exeter Wing. On 11 September 1940, Dewar failed to return from an 'unofficial' combat mission. His body was washed ashore at Kingston Gorse in Sussex on 30 September 1940. In error, the date of Dewar's death was registered as 12 September 1940. (Photo: Goss.)

Peter St. John badly damaged a '109, and [Flight Lieutenant] William Measures, in a hectic ten minutes, badly damaged a Dornier and two Messerschmitts.'[53] Flying Officer John Colin Mungo-Park, one of the best pilots in 74 'Tiger' Squadron, sent another Do 17 burning down towards the Channel with a three second burst. Yet another Do 17 was reportedly shot down by three interacting pilots from 32 Squadron.

The Messerschmitt pilots fought desperately to repel the British fighter attacks. Oberfeldwebel Arthur Dau of 7. Staffel in JG 51 had just hit a Spitfire with his guns when he came up on a collision course with Pilot Officer Geoffrey Page's Hurricane from 56 Squadron. In a split second both the German and the British opened fire. A number of powerful explosions occurred just in front of the cockpit of Dau's plane. Then Messerschmitt and Hurricane flashed past each other with just a few inches apart. 'The German shot a bit too low', said Page, 'but I think I hit him.' When Dau pulled out in a turn towards the French coast, he noticed that something was wrong with the speed. The engine was hit! Something came loose from one of the wings and flew off, and soon white smoke emitted from the radiator. A glance at the radiator temperature: 120 degrees! There was no choice. Dau decided to continue straight ahead, away from the scene of combat. Luckily, no 'Tommy' seemed to have noticed his vulnerable situation.

He switched on the R/T transmitter button and dutifully reported: 'I'm hit. . . have to make an emergency landing!'

Trautloft answered and a couple of '109s disengaged to escort their comrade back to the coast.

'The entire cabin smelled of burnt wires' Dau continued his account. 'Then the engine stopped and I glided in over the beach. Down! I made a violent belly-landing just outside Boulogne. When I jumped out of the cart, it al-ready was in flames. A few seconds later the fuel blew up along with all the remaining ammo.'

Among the pilots of III./ZG 26, Oberleutnant Sophus Baagoe and Leutnant Erich von Bergen reported two victories each. The greatest individual success however was claimed by Oberleutnant Oesau of III./JG 51. He had shot down Higgs' Hurricane already in his first attack. Several other British fighters tried to attack Oesau, but they were driven off by Oesau's wingman, Unteroffizier Robert Fuchs, who reportedly shot one of them down.[54] During the subsequent combat, Oesau finally managed to get into position behind another Spitfire. Badly damaged by Oesau's fire, this Spitfire – according to the testimony of Fuchs – descended vertically down into the Channel. After fifteen minutes of fierce dogfighting, Oesau came up behind a new British fighter, which he pursued inland over southern England before he was able to report it as shot down. Most likely this was the Hurricane flown by Henry Ferris. No. 111 Squadron's Operations Record Book explains: 'Flying Officer H. M. Ferris drove a 109 into the sea and was in turn attacked by three others who shot away an aileron control; he was persistently attacked for about twenty minutes but managed to avoid further damage.'[55]

Overall, the British maintained the initiative throughout the air combat. One measure of this perhaps is the heavily exaggerated German victory claims – they claimed to have shot down no fewer than seventeen British fighters, while actual British losses were confined to one destroyed aircraft (Higgs' Hurricane, which collided with a Do 17) and four damaged. Somewhat more difficult to understand is the success credited to KG 2 – its pilots were reported to have sunk a cruiser (with no cruiser even being nearby!) and four merchant ships totaling 14,000 GRT, and to have damaged another cruiser (!) and three merchant ships with a total of 19,000 GRT.[56] But the reality was quite different.

A Do 17 Z-2 drops its bomb load. The Dornier Do 17 Z-2, called the 'Flying Pencil' because of its sleek appearance, could carry 1,000 kg bombs and was armed with three to six 7.92mm machine guns.

Through their fighter interception the British managed both to disturb the bombing – with the result that nothing but a small sloop of merely 466 tonnes was hit – and to shoot down three Do 17s and three Bf 110s. In addition, they damaged five other German planes so severely that they barely managed to limp back to France. A Do 17 from I./KG 2 returned with 190 bullet holes and one man dead and one injured crewmember aboard. Two bleeding crew members from another Dornier were lifted after landing at Cambrai. The Zerstörer commander Hauptmann Schalk found that besides the three crews and aircraft that he had to remove from the rolls, two Bf 110s returned with battle damage. In one of them the radio operator was missing; he had panicked when a Spitfire riddled the '110 with machine gun bullets, and immediately took to his parachute. The Zerstörer unit's own claims of seven Spitfires and Hurricanes shot down gave the Germans a completely inaccurate impression of the combat. One can only speculate how they would have reacted, had they known that their only result was confined to two damaged British fighters!

'For this victory, we must thank the radar in which placed us in readiness and allowed us to send our fighter squadrons out to meet them', was Air Chief Marshal Dowding's comment to the combat on 10 July. One might add that it also was a result of the decision to meet the Germans with larger fighter forces than before.

The Germans tend to call the weeks that followed the 'Contact Phase', the period of air fighting that preceded the really heavy air operations of the Battle. However, for some units it already was sufficiently 'heavy'.

Fighter Command had one main priority: to maintain its strength in spite of losses. As in so much else, propaganda played an important role here too. Lord Beaverbrook, the British minister of aircraft production, proved to have the same ability as Churchill in coining punchy slogans. On 11 July 1940, he made an appeal to British housewives: 'Give us your aluminum and we will turn your pots and pans into Spitfires and Hurricanes, Blenheims and Wel-

lingtons!' It was an instant success. In just a few days, hundreds of tonnes of household utensils made of aluminum were collected. In addition to the courage displayed by the pilots of the RAF every day and every night, this is a clear measure of the British determination to fight on.

Meanwhile more and more German air units arrived at the 'Channel Front' – which the British were able to follow in detail due to 'Ultra', the decrypting of the German 'Enigma'-ciphered messages.[57] In Paris, General Hugo Sperrle, head of Luftflotte 3, took charge of the operations across the western part of the English Channel. Just as Oberst Fink had done in the east, Sperrle decided that the task of providing his bombers and dive-bombers with close escort would mainly be left to the twin-engined Bf 110s. This established an unfortunate rule for the Zerstörer units.

For 11 July Sperrle planned a whole series of air operations against British shipping in the Channel. It started badly for the British. No. 501 Squadron had three Hurricanes out on convoy escort off Portland, and only two of them returned – the third became the victim of a surprise attack by eight Bf 109s from III./JG 27. When ten Ju 87s from IV.(St)/LG 1 simultaneously approached the convoy, the alarm went to Warmwell near Portland. Six Spitfires from 609 Squadron took off rapidly and set off out over the coast. But these did not fare any better. Just as the Spitfire pilots prepared to engage the Stukas, Bf 109s emerged from the clouds and shot down Flight Lieutenant Barran and Pilot Officer Mitchell. The Ju 87 that 609 Squadron's pilots managed to shoot down was a small consolation for the four surviving British pilots.

Shortly afterwards, 10 Group alerted five of its squadrons. A 'Fifty Plus raid' – i.e. involving more than fifty German aircraft – was reported approaching across the Channel. These were 44 Ju 87s from StG 2 'Immelmann', escorted by Bf 110s from III./ZG 76. The Stukas managed to sink *Warrior*, a 530-ton steamer, before the British fighters appeared and attacked. The Zerstörer fliers had been ordered to stay close to the dive-bombers and protect these 'at any price'. So they did, and managed to keep the Hurricane fighters from Nos. 87, 238 and 601 squadrons from shooting down more than a single Ju 87. But it cost the Zerstörer unit a loss of four crews, including Oberleutnant Hans-Joachim Göring, the Luftwaffe commander's cousin. Afterwards, the RAF reported eight 'certain' shootdowns of Bf 110s, plus an additional eight Bf 110s and a Ju 87 'probably shot down'. The Zerstörer fliers had not expected such high losses, but those who survived immediately prepared for the next mission. John Vasco and Peter D. Cornwell, who interviewed several of the pilots from III./ZG 76, wrote: 'Back at Laval the airfield was a hive of activity as ground-crews and technicians swarmed over damaged aircraft trying to ready them for the next sortie. Officer-pilots with Staff responsibilities were given no time to relax after such a gruelling fight. Leutnant Florenz, Gruppe Signals Officer, summoned all the Bordfunkers together for a de-briefing while Leutnant Marchfelder, the Technical Officer, rushed around supervising repairs. Hauptmann Dickoré reported to HQ while his Adjutant, Leutnant Dieter Nülle began the onerous task of filing casualty reports and drafting letters to next-of-kin.'[58]

III./ZG 76's next task was to escort a bomber raid against the harbour at Portsmouth. In preparation for this, the Stukas of II./StG 2 were supposed to carry out an attack against a British air base – at Yeovil, north of Portland, something which was unusual at that time. This mission was also assigned with close-escort by Bf 110s, this time from V.(Z)/LG 1.

Erhard Jähnert, who served as a pilot with the rank of an Unteroffizier with II./StG 2, recalled: 'It would be our first mission against England, and we noticed that special preparations were made. Early in the morning our Ju 87 were loaded with 500-kg bombs and we flew from our regular base Angers, located far inland, to Dinard on the north Breton coast, just south of the British Channel Islands. There we were received by the commander of Fliegerkorps IV, General Alfred Keller. He gave a speech to embolden us.'[59] Exactly at 12:00 hours, the Stukas took off and climbed towards the Channel.[60] But nothing could be seen of the promised escort. 'While our Ju 87 crept across the sky over the Channel, approaching the British Isles, we became increasingly nervous,' remembers Jähnert. 'Where the hell were the escort fighters?' In fact, the men of V.(Z)/LG 1 had not been able to find the 87s among the thick clouds, and simply turned back home again. The dive bomber crews had every reason to be worried; on the other side of the Channel the German aircraft were detected well in advance by the radar. The Germans had not even reached the British coast when Hurricanes from 601 Squadron pounced on them. Jähnert recalled: 'Our commander gave orders to cancel the mission and return home again. I dived desperately towards a layer of clouds a bit below, and was saved from being attacked by British fighters. When I came out of the clouds again, I discovered that I was right above Portland. We were three Ju 87s, and no British fighters in sight, so we decided to attack. We dropped our bombs over the port facilities and ships, and then we set off at full speed in a low-level flight across the Channel.'[61]

With this rapid escape, the Stukas were able to avoid any losses of their own, but of the raid there was nothing more than Jähnert's and his two comrades' bombing of Portland.

Towards the evening Sperrle dispatched twelve He 111s from I./KG 55 against Portsmouth, escorted by an equal number of Bf 110s from III./ZG 76. The Heinkels reached Portsmouth and dropped their bombs, which set the city's gasworks on fire. They were then intercepted by Hurricanes from 145 and 601 squadrons. This time the result of the fighter combat was the exact opposite of the morning's clash: Hauptmann Rolf Kaldrack, commander of 7./ZG 76, and Oberleutnant Günther Tonne of 9./ZG 76 – two future aces in the Zerstörer aviation – shot down two Hurricanes without a single Bf 110 being lost. But while the Zerstörer acted offensively, they were less successful in protecting the bombers.

When 601 Squadron's Flight Sergeant 'Bill' Pond saw clouds of smoke rise from Portsmouth, he was seized with rage and raced at full speed towards a He 111. He shot, saw the aircraft's both engines start to smoke, but continued riddling the Heinkel with his bullets until it suddenly blew up in an explosion so violent that it also swept down the bomber flying next to it. The entire crew of Feldwebel Herbert Aleith's He 111 was killed while Oberleutnant Siegfried Schweinhagen and two men from his aircraft were able to bail out into captivity. A third He 111 limped back across the Channel with such severe damage that it crashed in France and was totally destroyed.[62]

No. 601 Squadron was credited with four He 111s and a Bf 110 confirmed shot down and four He 111s as 'probables', while 145 Squadron recorded three He 111s and a Bf 110 confirmed shot down. Just as with the Germans on the previous day, these exaggerated claims are likely an expression of the heavy pressure the British fighter pilots had been under in the combat. No. 145 Squadron had undoubtedly taken the heaviest beating. One Hurricane returned with severe combat damage, and the aircraft that was shot down was the one flown by the unit commander, Squadron Leader John Peel. He though, made it through an emergency landing on the water. When the crew of the British lifeboat that was assigned to out to rescue him refused to go so close to enemy-controlled France where Peel gone down, the pilots of 145 Squadron simply told them that if the boat returned without Peel, they would take off with their Hurricanes and shoot the boat to pieces. The result was that Peel was saved – apparently at the last moment. 'When you arrived', he said, 'I had almost given up hope. I don't think that I would have made it many minutes more.' It took six days before he could return to combat service.

The question of how to provide the bombers with fighter escort came to occupy the Germans during the remainder of the Battle. Obviously without considering the fate of the unescorted British bombers on 9 and 10 July, Generalfeldmarschall Kesslering dispatched 40 Do 17s from II./KG 2 and He 111s from III./KG 53 without any fighter cover on 12 July. Their target was the convoy 'Booty' in the fairwaters of the British east coast off Suffolk, which was beyond the limited range of the Bf 109s. It would be a costly experiment.

At around eight o'clock, six Hurricanes of No. 17 Squadrons took off from the wet runway on the airfield at Martlesham and climbed into the air setting course for 'Booty'. Almost simultaneously, the Dover radar detected a large incoming formation of German aircraft. The six British pilots were still in a climb to reach the ordered patrol altitude when the ground controller called and ordered them to intercept the German raid. Meanwhile reinforcements were brought in from several airfields – in total more than thirty British fighters. The Germans and the British clashed straight above the convoy. Divided into three-plane formations, No. 17 Squadron's pilots attacked a formation of twelve Heinkels at 2,500 metres altitude. Pilot Officer Kenneth Manger emptied his guns in one long burst against the closest Heinkel. After him followed Sergeant Glyn Griffiths, who fired a nine-second burst at the He 111, until it – in Griffith's words – 'literally blew apart' in mid-air. Griffiths swung past the debris that tumbled in the air, passed some too low-lying German tracer bullets and finished his remaining ammunition against a straggling He 111; this one reared up as if it had flown into a wall and plunged towards the water with both engines in flames.

Suddenly three Spitfires appeared from another direction. These were Red Section of 74 'Tiger' Squadron and they were led by the ruthless South African Flight Lieutenant 'Sailor' Malan. All three fell upon a single He 111. Malan opened up with his eight machine guns at a distance of 300 metres, closed in and then let his two companions take over.

'Tighten formations!' the German commanders desperately urged their pilots.

Over the British radio 'Sailor' Malan's calm but firm voice was heard: 'Let 'em have it!'

Far below the sailors on the ship decks cheered and threw their caps high in the air in wild delight. A third bomber came tottering down, belching thick smoke. It splashed into the water right next to a trawler, which picked up three survivors from the crew. The Do 17 of Hauptmann Erich Machetzki, commanding 4./KG 2, was attacked by two British fighters. The British attacked again and again, from the front, from the rear and and from both sides. Bit by bit the bomber was shot to pieces, until it finally went into his final dive. None of the four crew members survived.

Eventually the Germans managed to bring their combat formations into order again. It paid off. A short break had occurred when the British gathered for a concentrated attack, and when Squadron Leader Edward Donaldson's 151 Squadron dived down towards the Germans again, the Hurricanes were met with intense crossfire from dozens of rapid-firing machine guns. The engine of a Hurricane was hit and exploded. The plane whirled down in a shower of debris. Close by, New Zealander Flying Officer John Allen tried to regain control of his badly crippled Hurricane which was trailing black smoke. That was the last anyone

Pilot Officer John Freeborn served as a fighter pilot in 74 'Tiger' Squadron from 1938, when he was only 19 years old. In late 1940, he had 11 individual and 2 shared victories on his account. Freeborn passed away on 28 August 2010, 90 years old.

saw of him. Several other British fighters left the scene with severe damage to wings and fuselage.

But the Germans had taken the heaviest punishment. They lost five bombers and a sixth later crashed in Holland. Six planes gone meant a loss of more than one in ten Heinkels or Dorniers out of the entire force! Thus the Germans had discovered another of their own weaknesses in the air war against Britain – which of course was the purpose of the 'contact phase'. It would be some time before they sent out a large formation of bombers without any fighter escort again.

The next ill-fated German experiments affected V.(Z)/LG 1. On 13 July Sperrle decided to load the unit's Bf 110s with bombs and send them against a convoy south of Portland. The Germans failed to find the convoy, but were

A formation of Bf 110s from ZG 26 'Horst Wessel'. III./ZG 26, which initiated operations over the English Channel in early July 1940, was recorded as having 79 air victories against only 8 own combat losses during the Battle of France. The Gruppe contained several aces that had great success during the Battle of Britain also. Two of its most successful pilots, Leutnant Walter Manhart with 13 and Feldwebel Walter Scherer with 10 air victories, were shot down and captured in September 1940. Major Johann (Hans) Schalk and Hauptmann Rolf Kaldrack had 11 each, and Hauptmann Wilhelm Spies and Wilhelm Makrocki 9 victories each.

A formation of Spitfires from 610 Squadron. 'DW-Q' in the middle was flown by Sergeant Sydney Ireland, who was killed in a plane crash on 13 July 1940.

themselves attacked by Hurricanes and Spitfires from Nos. 238 and 609 squadrons. Slow due to their heavy bomb load and caught by surprise, the Bf 110 pilots had no choice but to jettison their bombs and form a defensive circle. Four Bf 110s were hit by British gunfire, and three of those crashed on the French coast. Next in turn were the dive bombers and 109s.

When coal convoy CW.5 a couple of hours later left the port of Dover, the Germans immediately dispatched a formation of Ju 87s. But the convoy was escorted by eighteen Spitfires from 54 and 64 squadrons, which prevented the Germans from carrying out their bombing with precision. Still, the destroyer Vanessa was badly damaged by a bomb that exploded just aft of the vessel. Then the Spitfires were tied up in a dogfight with the ten escorting Bf 109s from III./JG 51, which cost each side one aircraft.[63]

An hour later the Germans launched a new raid against CW.5, this time with 12 Ju 87s from II./StG 1, escorted by 19 Bf 109s from II./JG 51. But once again, the Germans were unable to carry out their attack properly. A formation of Hurricanes from 56 Squadron pounced on the dive-bombers, which immediately jettisoned their bombs and dived to escape at the lowest possible altitude. Instantly the Bf 109s fell upon the British fighters. 'The British made the mistake of placing themselves between the dive-bombers and our Me 109s', said Oberleutnant Josef Fözö, commander of 4./JG 51: 'We attacked, and three Hurricanes immediately broke formation.' Manning a Bf 109 E-4 with a large Mickey Mouse painted beneath the

cockpit, 'Joschko' Fözö and his wingman Unteroffizier Ernst Buder turned to follow those three Hurricanes.

Flight Lieutenant John 'Nine Gun' Coghlan was an ace with five German aircraft on his account. Leading 'B' Flight of 56 Squadron, he just had time to blast away a volley against a Ju 87 which began to smoke, when he saw the two '109s, causing him to break.[64] A fierce dogfight broke out between Fözö's Rotte and the three Hurricanes of Coghlan's Red Section. Shortly afterwards, the German ace Hauptmann Horst Tietzen and his wingman also got in on the action. During one of the tight curves Coghlan managed to get onto the tail of one of the '109s, which he believed he had hit with his bullets. In fact the German escaped unhurt, and in the next moment bullets slammed into Coghlan's cockpit. Fözö and Buder hit one Hurricane each simultaneously, and shortly afterwards Tietzen recorded hits on a third. 'Two descended and the third slid towards the water, leaving behind thick smoke,' said Fözö. But he was unable to stick around to see the effect of his fire. 'At that moment', he said, 'I saw a Stuka diving towards the French coast. The dive-bomber was pursued by a Hurricane. Behind this Hurricane sat a Me 109, and behind this there was a second Hurricane. Each of the planes opened fired simultaneously on the aircraft in front. It was a dangerous situation, and I decided to take action, so I dived for the line of aircraft. Now there were five aircraft diving in a long row. The Stuka had been badly damaged and the two crew members appeared to be wounded. It crashed on the shore near Wissant.'

But twenty-year-old Sergeant James Cowsill would not get the opportunity to celebrate the shooting down of this Ju 87. Feldwebel Hans John, the pilot of the Bf 109 that sat behind him, scored a direct hit. Cowsill remained in the cockpit when the machine plunged into the English Channel. 'One of its wings stuck up out of the water like a shark fin before it finally sank', Fözö recalled. Sergeant James Whitfield, who took aim on Feldwebel Hans John, seemed not to have noticed that he had Fözö's 'White 1' behind himself. Fözö opened fire and saw how the Hurricane 'dropped like a stone and splashed into the water beside the plane that John had shot down.'

As if by a stroke of magic, the sky suddenly seemed to be void of aircraft – a common phenomenon in fighter combats that ended just as suddenly as they had begun. Fözö swept in over the French coast at Boulogne and landed a few minutes later at the makeshift airfield on a grass field near Desvres. At the air base North Weald north of London, Coghlan's damaged Hurricane stopped after rolling down the runway. Coghlan was bleeding from several small cuts caused by shrapnel in the face.

Three of 56 Squadron's aircraft were missing. One of them had made an emergency landing at Rodmersham, just outside Canterbury. In return, the British claimed to have shot down seven Ju 87s (of which, however, only two were confirmed) and two '109s. Actual German losses were confined to two crash-landed Ju 87s, both of which could be repaired.

Although the British, just like the Germans, exaggerated their successes, the statistics were in favour of the RAF. Between 10 and 13 July 1940, 40 German aircraft and 29 British fighters were shot down. Of the latter, ten could be repaired.

When Winston Churchill that evening received Dowding at his residence Chequers, the British Prime Minister declared that 'the previous four days had been the most glorious in the history of the RAF'.

19–20 July: Fighter Command is strengthened

But the battle had only begun. On 14 July, the Luftwaffe would finally settle accounts with the elusive convoy CW.5. The entire IV.(St)/LG 1 with forty Ju 87s was dispatched. The vessel *Island Queen* (779 GRT) was sunk while *Mons* and *Balder* were damaged. Afterwards, the German escort fighters, from III./JG 3 and II./JG 51, returned to their airfields after a well accomplished task. They had prevented three squadrons of British fighter from shooting down more than a single Ju 87.

It was obvious that Fighter Command's force in the south needed reinforcements. Therefore, in the morning of 19 July, No. 141 Squadron was transferred to the air base Hawkinge. This unit, which had previously been based at Turnhouse in Scotland, was equipped with Boulton Paul Defiant – the single-engined but two-place fighter whose armament consisted of four machine guns in an electrically powered dorsal turret. The latter had caught the Germans unaware when the aircraft entered combat over Dunkirk. On 29 May 1940, No. 264 Squadron, the 141's 'sister unit' which in October 1939 became the first to be equipped with this unconventional fighter, flew two missions over Dunkirk and claimed to have shot down 38 German aircraft without own losses. Although the actual German losses were nine aircraft, it still was an impressive achievment.

But since then, the Luftwaffe had learned to distinguish the Defiant from other British fighters, and the clash between the Bf 109s and Defiants from 141 Squadron on 19 July 1940 has become a classic.

At 12:15 on 19 July, 15 Ju 87s, escorted by 15 Bf 109s from Hauptmann Hannes Trautloft's III./JG 51, crossed the Strait of Dover. Telephones in alert shacks on British arifields rang, and 141 Squadron, a squadron of Hurricanes and a Spitfire squadron were scrambled. Of the twelve Defiants, only nine were able to take off. Due to technical errors, three were left on the ground. But before the British fighters reached the German planes, the dive-bombing attack was carried out. In and just outside of Dover's port the British destroyers *Griffin* and *Beagle* were hit by bombs, and the Ju 87s returned at full strength to their bases.

Although the mission was accomplished with total success, the German fighter pilots were not happy. 'We felt very frustrated because it looked as if we would return home without any victories', said Leutnant Werner Pichon-Kalau vom Hofe, technical officer of III./JG 51: 'When we had brought the Stukas back to the French coast, the commander climbed to a higher altitude, and we followed suit. Up ahead, we saw the English landscape spread out.' [65]

Suddenly an excited voice was heard over the German radio: 'To the right, low – over the coast – several aircraft!' It was the nine Defiant planes that came climbing from Hawkinge. 'I immediately recognized them as Defiants', Trautloft wrote in his diary.

This time it was the Germans who adapted their tactics to the Defiant's in contrast with the less experienced fliers of 141 Squadron. The British analysis of the combat describes how the Defiants became completely outmanoeuvred:

'The enemy aircraft dived from out of the sun on to the Defiants and made their attacks from dead astern, preventing the rear gunners from firing. The Me 109s then pulled out in steep turns but their greatly superior speed and the fact that usually our aircraft were pulling out on opposite turns, again prevented our air gunners from firing. After the initial dive many attacks were delivered from below.' [66]

Leutnant Pichon described it from his point of view: 'We dive steeply. My commander attacks the closest aircraft. Then everything happens at the speed of lightning. I fire a short burst. The Tommy emits a white stream of leaking fuel. Then it slowly turns over the right wing and descends vertically. I turn around quickly only to see Oberleutnant Otto Kaht and Leutnant Herbert Wehnelt finish off one enemy aircraft each. These too turn slowly over their vertical axis and then descend. I swing in behind the British on the far right and open fire from a distance

The two-place, single-engined British fighter Boulton Paul Defiant entered service in December 1939, and achieved good results during the air battle over Dunkirk in May–June 1940.

of 20 metres. My tracer disappears into the fuselage and wings. I give only a short burst. The same thing is repeated again: first, a white stream, and then the plane turns over. *Abschuss!* – I got him! By this time we have shot down four and still the British cling to their closed formation and rely on their rearward firepower.'[67]

While the Defiants, divided into Sections, continued to fly in column, several German pilots attacked from below after the initial strike. 'I place myself behind the next airplane', said Leutnant Pichon, 'and again fire a short burst. After my second burst this machine drops like a stone. Ten metres next to me, another Messerschmitt is shelling a Defiant from the next group of three. I see the burst hit one of the enemy's wings, and the next moment the aircraft is torn to pieces in a huge fireball.'

Finally, only one Section of three Defiants remained. Close to each other, these swung narrowly to the left and tried to reach the English coast. Pichon turned to follow them. 'Now we had to be careful with the ammunition,' he said. 'I selected the plane that flew to the far right. Meanwhile we had gone down from 3,000 to 1,000 metres. I blast away with all my guns, but he doesn't fall. This is it! I fire with large deflection while turning, and see the tracers hit the fuselage and wings. Finally, he goes down. A yellowish-white streak marks his descent, which ends in a frothy water fountain in the Channel not far from the English coast.'

These were Pichon's first three victories. The report from No. 141 Squadron reads: 'Six aircraft are shot down or disabled, 4 dive into the sea. P/O Gardner, pilot and P/O Farnes A/gunner are picked up by seacraft. P/O Gardner is taken to hospital at Canterbury. P/O Farnes is uninjured. Pilot Officers Kemp, Kidson and Howley are presumed lost. 5 air gunners are also presumed lost. F/Lieutenant Loudon crashes owing to engine cut out, 200 yards from aerodrome at Hawkinge and is injured. He is also taken to Canterbury hospital. His air gunner had baled out and is safe. F/Lieutenant Donald crashed at Dover and was killed, his air gunner P/O Hamilton who baled out is missing. 3 aircraft land at Hawkinge at 13.00 hrs. P/O MacDougal is 'shot up' but returns to base. His air gunner, however, baled out and is now missing. Total losses are 4 pilots killed or missing, six air gunners missing. Squadron is now released from operations for short period.'[68]

In return, the Defiant gunners managed to shoot down no more than a single Bf 109. This incident has led to quite exaggerated conclusions regarding the Defiant – and this also applies to the leadership of Fighter Command. But 141 Squadron, which had been equipped with Defiants quite late, had not taken note of the special combat tactics developed by No. 264 Squadron: This unit often, and not without success, used the tactic of entering a so called 'Lufbery-circle' where each aircraft is covered by the one in front of it, while the enemy could be fired at. Thus, this formed a kind of 'airborne fortress'.[69] As we shall see, later in the battle the 'sister unit' 264 Squadron also was significantly more successful than No. 141.

On the afternoon of 19 July the British were dealt yet another setback when the Germans dispatched the Bf 110 assault planes from Erprobungsgruppe 210 against the port of Dover. Erprobungsgruppe 210 was a fresh assault unit that specialized in fast precision raids. Among the unit's Bf 110s were some of the C-6 version which was equipped with a 30mm automatic cannon against ground targets or ships. The attack on ships in the port of Dover was carried out with devastating precision. The oil tanker War Sepoy received a direct bomb hit and sank while violently burning. Destroyer *Griffin* and two other ships also were damaged. Without having suffered any own losses, the airmen of Erprobungsgruppe 210 returned to base to celebrate this success.

The next day, 20 July, was also marked by heavy air fighting over the Channel in connection with German air operations against British shipping. As British convoy CW.7 sailed through the Channel, the Germans waited for the right moment to strike while their aerial reconnaissance kept the ships under surveillance. Early in the morning, a Do 17 from III./KG 2 on armed reconnaissance was shot down by Spitfires from 54 Squadron. A short while later, 603 Squadron shot down a Ju 88 of 4.(F)/122.[70]

The next Do 17s of KG 2 on armed reconnaissance were provided with an escort by Bf 109s from I./JG 27. A couple of clashes with Hurricanes and Spitfires of Nos. 43, 152, 238 and 501 squadrons during the afternoon cost I./JG 27 a loss of three planes and as many pilots – including the unit commander, Hauptmann Helmut Riegel. No. 501 Squadron's Sergeant James 'Ginger' Lacey added two of these Bf 109s to the five victories he had achieved during the Battle of France.

As the convoy approached the Strait of Dover towards late afternoon, Park extended the fighter escort to 24 fighters from four squadrons. During the air combat that followed, when the Germans dispatched II./StG 1 (III./StG 51 had been renumbered II./StG 1 on 9 July), provided with a strong fighter escort, to attack the convoy, Fighter Command would reap yet another numerical success. The British pilots, who were alerted in advance owing to the radar observations, dived down with the sun in their back.

'Squadron Leader John Worrall led eight aircraft of 32 Squadron straight through the '109s to shoot down two and cripple four of the dive-bombers below. As the escorting Bf 109s broke they were engaged by eleven Hurricanes of 615 Squadron (who shot down three) and nine Spitfires of 610 Squadron.'[71]

However, this did not deter the Stuka pilots of Haupmann Anton Keil's II./StG 1. Despite the fierce fighter assault, the remaining dive-bombers carried out their mission and sank the destroyer *Brazen* and the coal freighter *Pulborough I*.

'We shall not stop fighting till freedom, for ourselves and others, is secure!'

Eventually it began to dawn on Hitler that the British apparently were not interested in making peace with Nazi Germany. On 16 July 1940 he issued a directive to the High Command of the Armed Forces, declaring that he now regarded it as necessary to bring down Britain by force of arms: 'Since England, despite her hopeless military situation has not yet shown any signs of readiness for a deal, I have decided to prepare, and if necessary also carry out, a landing operation against this country . . . the operation aims to eliminate the English motherland as a base from which the war against Germany can be waged, and if necessary, to occupy the entire country.'

On 19 July, he summoned the supreme commanders of the German armed forces to the Reichstag in Berlin for a slightly delayed celebration of the victory over France. There, the Führer had twelve generals – including the commanders of Luftflotte 2 and 3, Kesselring and Sperrle, promoted to field marshals. For the Luftwaffe commander Göring, he invented a new senior military rank, Reichsmarschall. Then Hitler held a speech in which he gave his view of the situation: 'Mister Churchill,' he said, 'has repeated the declaration that he wants war. About six weeks ago now, he launched this war in an arena in which he apparently believes he is quite strong: namely, in the air war against the civilian population, albeit beneath the deceptive slogan of a so-called war against military objectives. Ever since Freiburg, these objectives have turned out to be open cities, markets, villages, residential housing, hospitals, schools, kindergartens, and whatever else happens to be hit.'

At this time, the British nocturnal bombing raids against Germany were relatively small and inefficient. Interestingly, Hitler used the bombing of Freiburg as the prime example of British bombings of civilian targets. The bombs that fell over central Freiburg on 10 May 1940 killed 57 of the city's population and injured a further 81. The German propaganda made a big fuss out of this. What, however, was not mentioned was the fact that the bombs

were German – dropped by He 111 pilots from III./KG 51 who in error believed that they were attacking Dijon in France![72]

'Up to now I have given little by way of response,' Hitler continued, 'but this is not intended to signal, however, that this is the only response possible or that it shall remain this way! I am fully aware that with our response, which one day will come, will also come the nameless suffering and misfortune of many men. [. . .] And Mr. Churchill should make an exception and place trust in me when as a prophet I now proclaim: A great world empire will be destroyed.'

Hoping to appear magnanimous Hitler added yet another plea for a British surrender to his demands: 'In this hour I feel compelled, standing before my conscience, to direct yet another appeal to reason in England. I believe I can do this as I am not asking for something as the vanquished, but rather, as the victor! I am speaking in the name of reason!'

Two days later, Hitler held a conference with representatives of the three branches of the armed forces – Admiral Raeder for the navy, army commander Generalfeldmarschall Walther von Brauchitsch and Luftwaffe chief of staff, General Hans Jeschonnek. But even if Hitler mentioned that he considered it 'stupid' by the British not to negotiate, he was mainly occupied with thoughts of a future invasion of the Soviet Union.

While Hitler dreamed of destroying the Soviet Union, Göring was focused on the war against the immediate enemy – the United Kingdom. On the same day that Hitler held his meeting in Berlin, Göring summoned his air force generals to a conference at his estate Karinhall. There, the Luftwaffe commander instructed his generals that although attacks against ships would continue to be

The Bristol Blenheim IF fighter aircraft was shifted mainly to the role of a night fighter in 1940. Seen in the image are Blenheim IFs from No. 24 Operational Training Unit (OUT), RAF.

a priority for some time, they were to prepare their forces for what he called the 'Eagle Attack' (Adlerangriff), which could soon become a reality. 'Eagle Attack' was the name Göring gave his plan for a massive air offensive aimed at eliminating the RAF. Apparently concerned by reports on the severe losses sustained by some fighter units during close escort missions, Göring sharply underscored the importance of using the Messerschmitt 109s and 110s on fast fighter sweeps ahead of the bombers. For Göring, himself an old fighter pilot, this was obvious.

'The fighters must be must be used offensively', he said. 'If they are tied to the bombers, they can't be used to their full potential and will only suffer heavy losses themselves. Should the worst happen, the bombers have to rely on their formation flight and the coordinated fire of their gunners.'[73]

The events of the next few weeks were to confirm the correctness of Göring's directives. The British, however, had the good fortune that his commanders did not fully adhere to these instructions. Two of those responsible for the fateful decision to deploy the Zerstörer planes – the Luftwaffe's greatest offensive weapon against the RAF – on close escort were Oberst Theo Osterkamp, JG 51's commander, and the Kanalkampfführer Oberst Fink. Perhaps Hermann Göring's biggest mistake during the Battle of Britain was that he himself was not present all the time at the English Channel to lead the operations. Instead, he trusted his men, as he had always done. At this time he could not imagine that they would simply ignore such important parts of his directives. One of those in which he had the greatest confidence was his old war comrade Osterkamp.

To streamline the offensive operations of the fighter aircraft of Luftflotte 2, Göring divided the operational command between two Jagdfliegerführer, fighter commanders, instead of – as previously – only one: Oberst Karl-Bertram von Döring had to accept that half the fighter units under his Jafü 2 were siphoned off to the newly appointed Jafü 1, Oberst Osterkamp. Thus several of Luftflotte 2's fighter units – Jagdgruppen and Zerstörergruppen – were placed under a man who favoured the Bf 109 units at the expense of the Zerstörer.

Göring gave his commanders four days to give their opinions on attack targets and tactics during 'Eagle Attack'. All of this, including the code name for the invasion plan, 'Sea Lion', was revealed to the British through 'Ultra'– the decrypting of the German Enigma-ciphered messages. [74]

By that time, the three German air fleets assigned to prepare the air offensive against Britain mustered a considerable force. On 20 July, they reported a combined strength of 2,194 operational aircraft, including 864 bombers, 248 dive-bombers and 925 fighters (725 Bf 109s and 200 Bf 110s). All that Fighter Command was able to field against this armada on 20 July was 605 serviceable fighters. In reality, the number was not even that large. To begin with, the only aircraft capable of challenging the Germans in aerial combat were Spitfires and Hurricanes, and of these, only 532 were in operational order on 20 July (224 Spitfires and 308 Hurricanes). But not even that number shows the real

balance of forces; while the Germans were able to launch virtually all of their aircraft against southern England, the five hundred serviceable Spitfires and Hurricanes were spread across the British Isles. Only about three hundred could on short notice be deployed in southern England. This gave the Germans a potential air superiority of more than six to one.

But the British had no intention of giving in. On 22 July, Churchill asked Lord Halifax to give the British response to Hitler's offer of a separate peace: 'In every part of Britain there is only one spirit, a spirit of indomitable resolution. . . We shall not stop fighting till freedom, for ourselves and others, is secure!' This pretty well summed up the mood on the British side. This determination was something the Luftwaffe's airmen would notice during the following days. On the night of 23 July, German bombers attacked a number of targets in the British Isles, including the Maldon district of Essex, Edinburgh, Falmouth, Plymouth, Bristol and the Manston air base. At eleven that evening, Flying Officer Glynn 'Tubby' Ashfield took off with a Blenheim IF from the special night fighter unit F. I. U. (Fighter Interception Unit). This night fighter was equipped with an A. I. Mark III radar. After a short time the crew received information that the radar station at Poling had picked up an echo from an enemy aircraft. The air controller on the ground vectored them to a point about 10 miles south of Selsey Bill, where the air crew's radar operator, Sergeant Reginald Leyland, caught in the echo from the German aircraft on his radar screen. The distance was approximately 8,000 feet. After a few minutes, the Blenheim's observer, Pilot Officer Geoffrey Morris, made visual contact with the enemy – a Do 17 from I./KG 3. It did not take long before Ashfield had shot the bomber down in flames. The first radar guided night fighter shootdown was a reality. The same night, Whitley bombers of RAF Bomber Command's 4 Group attacked the Fieseler aircraft plants in Kassel with such good results that production was temporarily paralyzed. All the participating British bombers returned to base after the raid.

The following night the German night fighters scored. With Bomber Command dispatching 35 Wellingtons against an aircraft plant in Gotha and an oil refinery in Gelsenkirchen, two pilots of II./NJG 2 reported to have shot down one Wellington each. In fact, only one British bomber was lost that night – a Blenheim from 110 Squadron, which crashed into the North Sea off the Dutch coast.

24–29 july: The battle hardens

For the Germans, 24 July is what 10 July is for the British – the beginning of the Battle of Britain.

On that day, Oberst Fink was furnished with the latest technology in the shape of a radar installation of the model Freya, which was installed at Cap Blanc Nez on the French Channel coast at the Strait of Dover. With this, the Germans were able to detect British ships in the Channel in good time to launch an air attack. This was the beginning of an intensification of the attacks against British shipping in the Channel. It began in the morning on 24 July, when II./KG 2 attacked and sank two minesweepers in the Strait of Dover, and then returned to base without having sustained any own losses.

However, when fifteen Do 17s of I./KG 2 returned to bomb ships in the Thames Estuary a couple of hours later, the British were better prepared. When radar caught the echoes of a large force of German aircraft that was being assembled 'beyond Calais', Park decided to scramble several squadrons. Fighters took to the air from Rochford, Manston and Biggin Hill. These were No. 54 Squadron with twelve aircraft, 610 Squadron with eighteen, divided into two groups, and 65 Squadron with its 'A' Flight. [75]

The Germans also mobilised a large force of fighters, but things did not go as planned. A leading force of ten Bf 109s from II./JG 26, led by Hauptmann Erich Noack, was tasked to 'clear the skies' of British fighters. This became a total failure. When they came in over the English coast, Hauptmann Noack spotted of what he estimated as 'thirty Spitfires' above. [76] In actual fact, it was nine Spitfires from 610 Squadron, but this sufficed for Noack to lose his nerve and order his pilots to abort and return to base. When he was about to land at Marquise shortly afterwards, the excited Hauptmann Noack crashed his aircraft and was killed.

Next, fifteen Do 17s from I./KG 2 came lumbering forward. These were provided with an overwhelming fighter cover, in total about seventy Bf 109s, half of which had been assigned as close escort. The latter belonged to III./JG 52 under Hauptmann Wolf-Heinrich von Houwald. 'We crawled and slid at a speed of merely 250-300 km/h, and had a tough job keeping our planes flying at that low speed,' remembered Edmund Rossmann, who served as an Unteroffizier with III./JG 52. [77]

The first British fighters on the scene were from 54 Squadron's 'B' Flight, led by Pilot Officer Colin Gray.

'Tally Ho, Red Leader, a large formation of enemy just south of Dover', Gray yelled belligerently in the radio, and without waiting for further instructions hurled his six Spitfires straight at the Messerschmitt 109s.

'Probably no one even had time to shout a warning' remembered Günther Rall, by then an Oberleutnant with III./JG 52. 'Suddenly a flock of Spitfires were on us like hawks on a bunch of chickens.' [78]

Flight Lieutenant 'Al' Deere, who led 54 Squadron in the air, was so upset by the sight of such a large amount of German aircraft that he failed to notice that Gray's Flight disappeared to attack the Germans. Deere felt that 'an attack against such numbers was a frightening prospect', but he knew that the convoy needed all the help it could get, so he called Gray:

'Blue Leader, you cover with your flight while we try to get at the bombers.'

By that time, Gray had already dispatched one of the '109s, and the reply he gave was anything but what Deere had expected: 'What the hell do you mean, Red Leader, we are already stuck into the fighters!'

'You clot', Deere yelled back, 'you're after the wrong formation! I told you to follow me!' [79]

While the British officers argued in the radio, the pilots of III./JG 52 fought desperately for their lives. Günther Rall

recalled: 'I saw Lothar Ehrlich, who led the first Schwarm in front of me, turn towards the enemy, but then I was fully occupied defending myself. In a fraction of a second my Schwarm formation was split.' [80]

Pilot Officer Gray's self-indulgent act could have led to disciplinary action – had it not been for the fact that his quick initiative resulted in such disastrous consequences for the Germans. 'The biggest and most successful day since Dunkirk', was noted afterwards in 54 Squadron's Operations Record Book, which called it 'the Battle of the Thames Estuary'. [81] Nos. 65 and 610 squadrons soon joined the combat, which degenerated into a pure cat-and-mouse game with the German fighter pilots who fled back to France.

In this situation, the next German fighter unit appeared on the scene. This was III./JG 26, acting as 'extended escort' – which meant that the fighters were placed 2,000 to 3,000 metres higher. This enabled them to gain great surplus speed as they dived down on the British fighters. III./JG 26 was commanded by the renowned Major Adolf Galland, who had flown assault planes in the Spanish Civil War and was credited with 14 victories during the Battle of France.

'At the head of the staff unit I attacked two three-plane formations of Spitfires that we were able to catch by surprise from a favourable altitude', said Galland. 'I picked the aircraft that was positioned to the far left, and from a right turn, I gave it a long burst of fire. The Englishman turned over one wing and descended almost vertically.'

But the pilot of the bullet-riddled Spitfire was quite experienced. It was 54 Squadron's Flying Officer Johnnie Allen, an ace with seven victories to his credit. For this, he had been awarded with the Distinguished Flying Cross (DFC). A few weeks earlier, in a report on his experience in the air battles over Dunkirk, Allen had expressed his opinion on the German airmen: 'I don't think that most of the Hun pilots are very good. I have come across a few who seem to enjoy fighting, but the bulk of them don't. They simply don't know their stuff.' [82] It was an irony of fate that he would come across one of the Luftwaffe's most skilled pilots in this way. Now the 24-year-old Londoner Allen was fighting for his life.

Galland failed to notice, but at low altitude over the Thames Estuary, Allen was able to regain control of his aircraft, and reported over the radio that he was trying to reach the air base Manston. Allen was able to start the damaged engine, then it stopped, he managed to bring it afloat again, but when it stopped for a second time, the Spitfire stalled and fell out of control. The aircraft crashed into the fashionable neighborhood of Omer Avenue in Cliftonville, just a few hundred metres southwest of the CHL radar station on Foreness Point. It caught fire on impact. Some of the local people tried in vain to save the pilot, who at that point was still alive, but he remained stuck in the flames. Today he is buried in Margate cemetery.

But Allen's Spitfire was the only British aircraft lost in this battle. In return, the RAF pilots claimed to have shot down 14 Bf 109s. 'This little "shindy" [combat] has eased the browned off feeling and put our tails up and at least there will be a few Huns unserviceable for some time.' [83]

No. 87 Squadron, based at Exeter, was one of the first units of the RAF to be specialised in night fighter operations, but successes on these missions were scarce in 1940. On the night of 26 July 1940, Pilot Officer John Cock however managed to shoot down a He 111 from I./KG 4 which was out on a mine-laying mission over the Bristol Channel. The image shows the Hurricane of Flying Officer Rafael Watson from 87 Squadron. The aircraft has been blocked up to set the correct angle of the machine guns. (Photo: Goss.)

Meanwhile, No. 610 Squadron was credited with the shooting down of three Bf 109s.

The RAF fighters had indeed dealt their opponents a hard blow, even though the actual German losses were not quite as high as the British believed: six Bf 109s and their pilots. Major Galland was most concerned. After returning to the base he assembled his men and seriously lectured them for their apparent reluctance to engage the Spitfires.

On the airfield at Coquelles, the base of III./JG 52, the mood was absolutely miserable. Among the missing pilots were the unit commander, Hauptmann von Houwald, and the commanders of the 7. and 8. Staffel, Oberleutnant Herbert Fermer and Oberleutnant Lothar Ehrlich. Günther Rall described his thoughts:

'Flying close escort as close to the bombers as possible was totally wrong. This led to extremely unpleasant consequences, especially when we escorted Ju 87s and had to keep a low speed that was absolutely suicidal. One might just as well have set fire to our fighters on the ground!' [84]

Unteroffizier Edmund Rossmann of the same unit saw it from a different perspective: 'Our officers lost their nerves. Only I and [Unteroffizier Josef] "Jupp" Zwernemann shot down one Spitfire each in the combat, but my superiors refused to confirm my victory.' [85]

Although the British fighters had been tied up by the German fighter escort, the mere sight of such a large number of RAF fighters sufficed to frighten the German bomber crews to the extent that that they failed to hit more than a small trawler of 356 tonnes.

The battle continued with unabated intensity the next day, 25 July, focused on British convoy CW.8, whose twenty-one transport ships and two escort ships prepared to leave the port of Dover to sail west through the Channel. The Germans began by ordering a Stuka Gruppe to attack the port of Dover. Once again, III./JG 52 was assigned the mission of providing close escort, and its fighter pilots took off at 13:05. [86] They managed to keep the attacking 65 Squadron busy so that the Ju 87s could carry out their mission – at a cost of one of the German fighter pilots. But this was only the beginning. Two and a half hours later, Hauptmann Keil's II./StG 1 was brought against the convoy.

This time the Germans made use of a primitive but very effective escort method that later came to characterize their air operations over England: Brute force. Five full Jagdgruppen – II. and III./JG 26, I. and II./JG 51 and III./JG 52 – formed an effective shield around the Stuka planes. Around twenty British fighters – from 54, 65 and 610 squadrons – that appeared to defend the ships were attacked by III./JG 26 with Major Adolf Galland at the head, and several Bf 109s from JG 51. One of the pilots of 54 Squadron panicked and turned back towards base. [87] But without considering the odds the others tried to break through to the Ju 87s, even if it meant that they had to run the gauntlet of dozens of Bf 109s. 54 Squadron's Pilot Officer Douglas

◄ *Left: Werner Mölders, the greman top ace in the beginning of the Second World War.*

▼ *Below: A Schwarm of Bf 109s. The German Schwarm-Rotte tactic proved to be superior to the British three-plane Vee formation, which often led to individual pilots having to fight without the same opportunities for interaction which the German tactic gave. (Photo: Mombeek.)*

Turley-George recalled 'the '109s coming at us from above as we still struggled for height, [Flight Lieutenant Basil Hugh Way being hit and falling away out of sight.'

'Damn and blast this bloody war, they've got "Wonky"', Pilot Officer George Gribble was heard sobbing over the R/T.[88]

While 'Wonky' Way fell to his death, Turley-George was attacked by an obviously very skilled Messerschmitt pilot who came in from the left. Turley-George was trying to turn left to get out of the Bf 109's bullet trajectory, but the German pilot reacted swiftly and caught the Spitfire with a perfect deflection shot. 'Even through the pounding fear that I felt, I admired his marksmanship', said Turley-George – who was lucky to survive the German attack.

Squadron Leader Andrew Smith, leading No. 610 Squadron, had his Spitfire 'DW-A' badly shot up and dis-

engaged. The aircraft stalled at Hawkinge and crashed, killing the pilot. One of Andrew's pilots, Pilot Officer Frederick Gardiner, escaped with a bullet in an arm.

The combat cost the British a loss of five planes, but they managed to bring down two Ju 87s and two Bf 109s – including one from the already depleted III./JG 52. (thus 7./JG 52 lost its second commander in two days, Oberleutnant Willi Bielefeld). But the British fighter pilots were too few to be in a position to repel the attack against the ships. The Stukas split up into three groups, which attacked in close succession. It was an effective tactic; the attack became more drawn out, which made it difficult for the British to hold their ships together so that they could meet attackers with a concentrated defensive fire.

The result was devastating. Between dozens of water fountains from the explosions, smoke and blazing fire-lights from bomb hits appeared again and again. Here the

The Stukas dived with the setting sun at their back. The water boiled from the first explosions. Two heavy bombs crashed down on the bridge of *Boreas*, two others shredded the stern of *Brilliant*.

In the air high above the burning destroyers, pilots from 56, 64 and 610 squadrons fought desperately to reach the Stukas, but were kept at bay by III./JG 52, which shot down two Spitfires. One of these was flown by Sub-Lieutenant Francis Dawson-Paul, a naval aviator who served with 64 Squadron, where he was credited with eight victories. German sea rescue picked up Dawson-Paul, heavily afflicted by the Channel's cold water, but he died five days later from the after effects of his injury. It has been assumed that Adolf Galland shot down Dawson-Paul, but a close comparison between British and German sources shows that Galland does not come into the frame. Interestingly, it is possible that 7./JG 52's Edmund Rossmann – an Unteroffizier who was in constant conflict with his superiors, not least because he surpassed them all in terms of combat skills – shot down both Dawson-Paul and, on the previous day, 54 Squadron's Flying Officer Allen. 'But, as usual, my superiors refused to acknowledge and confirm my victory', Rossmann commented laconically. [89] III./JG 52 achieved this defensive success on the evening of 25 July at the price of two planes with both pilots lost. One of these was Oberleutnant Wilhelm Keidel, the newly appointed commander of 7. /JG 52. No. 610 Squadron, which had participated in the bloodletting of III./JG 52 on the day before, returned from this engagement with reports of seven Bf 109s shot down without own losses. Six of these claims were confirmed, and two ended up on the account of Flight Lieutenant John Ellis – who thus reached a total of eight victories.

At that point, both III./JG 52 and No. 54 Squadron were fairly badly mauled, and shortly afterwards they were withdrawn from the front line to recover their strength in quieter corners of their home countries. 'The loss of six pilots in three days, including two of our most experienced leaders, coupled with the strain of long hours at readiness and repeated combats against overwhelming numbers, was having a depressing effect on the more inexperienced squadron pilots', said 'Al' Deere from 54 Squadron. [90] The difference between these two units, however, was pretty great in one respect: while 54 Squadron shot down quite a few German aircraft during the month that the unit was on duty at the Channel, III./JG 52 lost eight pilots in two days without being able to deal the enemy any significant losses.

Convoy CW.8 was in an even worse condition. Eight transport vessels had been sunk. Five others returned to Dover to repair their bomb damage.

On 27 July Ju 88s wiped out the remnants of the 4th Destroyer Flotilla by sinking flotilla leader *Codrington* and damaging the destroyer *Walpole* and the sloop *Sandhurst* in the port of Dover. This forced the British Admiralty to abandon Dover as a base for the invasion defence. The fleet units were withdrawn north, to Harwich and Sheerness, but on the same day as *Codrington* and *Walpole* were put out of action in Dover, He 111s struck another naval unit off the Suffolk coast, sank destroyer *Wren* and damaged *Montrose*. As the demands on Fighter Command to cover

ugly, crow-like Stuka really came into its own. No other aircraft could drop bombs with such a deadly accuracy. When the churning sea had subsided and the last Junkers began to head home, the convoy was in a miserable state. The vessels lay in all directions. Smoke and fires were everywhere. The water was covered with wreckage, desperately swimming sailors and badly mangled corpses held up by their life jackets. Four transport vessels had been sunk or were going down.

Shortly afterwards a group of the German Navy's minesweepers returning from a mission were engaged by British patrol boats and the destroyers *Brilliant* and *Boreas* from the Royal Navy's 4th Flotilla that went out from Dover.

The Luftwaffe was immediately called in. In a rush, 24 bomb-laden Ju 87s took off from the airfield at Tramecourt in Pas de Calais. At Coquelles, III./JG 52 was ordered to cover them, and its remaining '109s took to the sky at 19:32.

the naval units increased, the battle hardened – a fact not lost on the German fighter pilots either.

When 48-year-old Oberst Theo Osterkamp took over as Jagdfliegerführer 1 (Jafü 1) on 27 July, his position as the commander of JG 51 was assumed by 27-year-old Major Werner Mölders. It was Reichsmarschall Göring's idea that young and 'hungry' fighter pilots as unit commanders would galvanise fighter operations. He decided to start with Mölders.

At 15:00 (German time) on 28 July, Mölders took off from the airfield at St Inglevert to lead his Geschwader on a fighter sweep over southeastern England. [91] At Caffiers, only some ten kilometres away, Major Adolf Galland and the Messerschmitts of his III./JG 26 also took off.

Ten minutes earlier twelve Spitfires from 74 'Tiger' Squadron had been sent up on patrol. They were at 1,800 metres above the rooftops of Dover when the radar stations at Dover, Rye and Pevensey noted that the German formations that had been spotted near Calais had begun to move in the direction of Dover.

Ground control called 74 Squadron and issued directives: Intercept plus sixty Heinkels and forty Messerschmitts spotted by air surveillance just off the coast at Dover! The Spitfires climbed in a wide turn to the left. They had reached 5,500 metres when Sergeant Anthony Mould's Spitfire suddenly shook under the impact of 20mm shells. Almost immediately the plane was in flames, and the pilot bailed out. Adolf Galland and his III./JG 26 had been lurking at 6,000 metres, and when the Spitfires came climbing up from below, he had positioned himself in the sharp July sun.

The He 111s had only been a decoy, and now they turned back to their bases. While Galland announced his seventeenth victory (which, however, was not confirmed), his companion Oberleutnant Joachim Müncheberg attacked a formation of Hurricanes from 257 Squadron. Mould's Spitfire had not reached the ground before Sergeant Ronald Forward's Hurricane was shot down by Müncheberg. In that moment, two other formations of fighters appeared, the Messerschmitts from JG 51 and the Spitfires from 41 Squadron. The latter had been ordered up with eleven machines from Hornchurch at 14:25. The 92's Squadron Leader Hilary Richard Hood was above and in front of the others with three other pilots when he heard a warning over the radio.

Mölders said: 'I flew with my adjutant, Oberleutnant Erich Kircheis. Just north of Dover we met a lower flying group of three Spitfires, and behind that more aircraft appeared out of the haze. We attacked the leading formation.' [93]

A lower flying Spitfire trembled in Mölders' gunsight. The German ace fired his cannons. Parts blown off from the Spitfire came flying towards Mölders, and the British plane began to smoke. But although the Spifire pilot, Flight Lieutenant Anthony Lovell was injured in his hip, he managed to evade further attacks. He steered his damaged machine down towards the base at Manston which was in sight, and after just a few minutes he was able to land and was immediately lifted into an ambulance.

Meanwhile, one of the Spitfire pilots in 74 Squadron had discovered 41 Squadron's exposed position. This was something of the counterpart of Mölders within the RAF, the 30-year-old South African Flight Lieutenant Adolphus Gysbert Malan. Flying Officer John Colin Mungo-Park, second to Malan the main ace of 74 Squadron, said: 'What I like about Sailor is his quiet, firm manner and his cold courage. He is gifted with uncanny eyesight and is a natural fighter pilot. When he calls over the R/T, "Let 'em have it!", there's no messing. The b—s are for it, particularly the one he has in his own reflector sight.' [94] Now Malan attacked in the lead of Red Section. He said: 'Met up with six or nine Me 109s at 18,000 feet coming from the sun towards Dover to attack some Hurricanes. Turned on to the tails without being observed and led Red Section into attack. Gave one enemy aircraft about five two seconds' bursts from 250 yards, closing in to 100 yards. He attempted no evasion tactics except gentle right-hand turns and decreasing speed, by which I concluded he had at least had his controls hit.' [95]

It has long been assumed that Mölders was the pilot of this Bf 109, but it was more likely a machine from I./JG 51. Mölders saw a Spitfire attack a Messerschmitt. He manoeuvred into position behind the British fighter, but this made a sudden and surprisingly tight turn and came up behind Mölders! An examination of existing documents indicates that this Spitfire was piloted by 41 Squadron's Pilot Officer John Terence 'Terry' Webster. Afterwards, he wrote in his combat report: 'I was passed by another enemy aircraft. I fired short bursts closing from 100 to 50 yards. I then saw black smoke coming from the cowling over the windscreen.'

'It rattled violently in my machine', said Mölders. 'The radiator and fuel tank were shot up, and for me there was nothing left but to leave at full speed. I got a whole mass of Spitfires after me. '

In that moment a grey-green Messerschmitt '109 swooped down into position behind Webster's Spitfire. In the '109's tight cockpit sat the ace Oberleutnant Richard Leppla. Just as Leppla took his plane up and pressed the firing buttons, Webster shoved his throttle over the catch. Owing to the Spitfire's ability to temporarily increase the maximum speed by 40–50 km/h he managed to escape his pursuer.

Mölders also escaped and turned back towards his airfield. 'Fortunately the engine held to the French coast', he said. 'Only then did it start to run badly. Then when I was about to land, the landing gear would not deploy. I had to make a belly-landing. As I climbed out of the plane, my legs felt strangely weak, and on closer inspection I discovered large blood stains. The medical examination found three pieces of shrapnel in my thigh, one in the knee and one in my left foot. In the heat of battle I had not noticed any of these wounds.'

Not only did Mölders' wounds render him unable to fly for a few weeks – his own plane was so badly damaged that it had to be scrapped. Even worse, one of the newcomers in JG 51, Gefreiter Martin Gebhart, fell in that battle. Furthermore, Unteroffizier Erwin Fleig had to force-land his damaged '109 on the French Channel coast. The three victories claimed by Mölders and his pilots could not outweigh this. For Werner Mölders it was clear that it would be a tough time at the English Channel. His colleague Major Galland was considerably more positive when he visited Mölders by his bedside; Galland's III./JG 26 had scooped three victories without any losses of their own.

On the British side, 41 and 257 squadrons had had an aircraft each shot down while 74 Squadron had three Spitfires shot down and one damaged. The British presumed that they had destroyed five '109s – all by 74 Squadron.

But even if the RAF fighters performed better than many had expected, Fighter Command was not able to offer the British ships full protection. On 28 July the freighter *Orlock Head* (1,563 GRT) was sunk by German bombers off the British North Sea coast. The next day was a crucial date in the 'Channel Offensive'.

It all began in the morning of 29 July when the port of Dover was attacked by IV.(St)/LG 1 and II./StG 1. The Stukas succeeded in sinking the command ship in CW. 8, *Grønland*, which had been damaged on 25 July, and severed the oil pipeline to the harbour. In a raging air combat five Ju 87s and three Bf 109s were shot down (of which, however, a Ju 87 and a Bf 109 made it back to the French coast, where they crashed). The British reported ten shot down, of which Squadron Leader Hood of 41 Squadron and Squadron Leader Donald Aeneas MacDonell and Pilot Officer James O'Meara (the last two from 64 Squadron) were credited with two each. In return the British lost two fighters, with another two crashing with severe combat damage. The Germans reported six kills, of which Oberleutnant Hermann-Friedrich Joppien from I./JG 51 contributed three.

In the afternoon on 29 July the convoy 'Cat' off Harwich, north of the Thames Estuary, was subjected to a lightning attack by eleven Bf 110 assault planes from Erprobungsgruppe 210. Unlike the unit's operation against Dover ten days earlier, the Germans were intercepted this time – by Hurricanes from 151 Squadron. But the Bf 110s of Oberleutnant Karl-Heinz Mayer's 8./ZG 26 were able to to save the assault unit from sustaining any losses. In a classic Zerstörer attack from above, Oberleutnant Mayer, Oberleutnant Sophus Baagoe and Unteroffizier Walter Scherer reported three Hurricanes shot down. According to British records, two Hurricanes made emergency-landings in England. 'No. 151 Squadron were extremely lucky to have avoided more serious loss, the presence of 8./ZG 26 only being recognised at the very last moment. Had the Zerstörers followed up their attacks the Hurricanes would have been at a serious disadvantage.'[96]

A couple of hours later, Luftflotte 3 was deployed against a British convoy off Portland. A terrible explosion occurred midships on the destroyer Delight, which broke in half and disappeared in the depths within a few minutes. Just a few hours later the British Admiralty seemed compelled to expand their previously introduced restrictions to prohibit all British navy operations in the English Channel during daylight, provided it did not concern the warding off of an invasion.

Without a doubt the Germans came off as victorious from the 'Channel Offensive'. Göring had reason to be pleased when he studied the German statistics for the Luftwaffe's operations over and around the British Isles during July.

In all the Germans had performed 5,376 sorties during the 'Channel Offensive', dropping 1,474 tonnes of bombs. 47 British merchant vessels had been sunk by bombs or mines during July 1940. Moreover, the Royal Navy lost 14 naval vessels, including four destroyers, through aerial attacks.

Regarding the battle in the air, things looked somewhat different, however. The RAF's actual combat losses during July amounted to 88 fighters and 72 bombers. Meanwhile combat operations cost the Luftwaffe a loss of 186 aircraft. These German losses were actually surprisingly high – surprising for the Germans themselves. One of the German fighter pilots, formerly Oberleutnant Johannes Steinhoff, wrote in a letter to the author: 'After the German Wehrmacht's easy victories in Poland, Norway and France, the Luftwaffe here met an equal opponent for the first time. The pilots of the Spitfires and Hurricane were not only skilled and fair, they also fought with great courage.'[97]

There was every reason for the Germans to look seriously at the battles that August would bring. They definitely would have been even more cautious if they had known the British aircraft industry's strong uplift under Lord Beaverbrook's command. Even though 213 British fighters had been destroyed or badly damaged (including both combat losses and accidents), 496 new fighters had been manufactured. The same applied to the output of pilots from the flight schools. Fighter Command's number of pilots had actually increased – from 1,200 by the end of June to more than 1,400 a month later.

By contrast however, in terms of losses of experienced pilots and unit commanders, it looked bad. During July Fighter Command had lost eighty squadron leaders and flight lieutenants. And lost aces such as Allen and Dawson-Paul were simply irreplaceable.

For Dowding the near future meant a nerve-racking race against time: would Fighter Command's qualitative level last during the next period? The next two months would undoubtedly be crucial. Mathematically, the RAF needed to shoot down an average of two to three German planes for each British fighter that was lost. It had succeeded so far, but what would it be like when Göring let loose his Luftwaffe in full force against the British Isles?

*A Bf 110 from V.(Z)/LG 1 crossing the English Channel.
This aircraft, 'L1+AK', was piloted by Feldwebel Gottlob Fritz,
with Obergefreiter Karl Dopfer as radio operator.
(Photo: von Eimannsberger.)*

CHAPTER 4
THE GREAT BATTLE

The first hot August days were marked by an impatient wait on both sides of the English Channel. After a few days of inactivity, the Whitley bombers of RAF Bomber Command's 4 Group were sent out towards an oil refinery in Düsseldorf on the night of 1 August. But then an unpleasant surprise awaited them. During the British return flight, a group of Do 17s from KG 2 crept into their formation. When the runway lighting was on at the large bomber base at York, the Germans struck. Their bombs destroyed four hangars, the repair stations and several other buildings. The next day other Bomber Command formations were sent out against German airfields both on the Cotentin Peninsula and in the Netherlands. It cost them a loss of four Blenheims in combat with German fighters, without accomplishing any notable damage on their targets.

Generalfeldmarschall Kesselring spent 1 August visiting JG 26 at Caffiers to award Major Galland with the Knight's Cross. During the ceremony itself, two fighters flew by at a high altitude. When Kesselring found out that they were Spitfires, he laughed and said: 'The first congratulations!'

Meanwhile, Reichsmarschall Göring proceeded with the preparations for 'Eagle Attack'. After the conference with the Luftwaffe Commander on 21 July, the German air force commanders had submitted their analysis on 25 July. Four days later Göring sent them his complementary analysis, and on 1 August he received their comments. On 2 August, Göring issued the final directives for Eagle Attack: As soon as the weather allowed for it, Luftflotte 2 and 3 would be employed in full strength against the airfields and radar stations in southern England. The objective was to deal a quick death blow against RAF Fighter Command.[98] 'Identified British radar stations shall be attacked by special units in the first wave', read the directives concerning the British radar. The attack was to be carried out during three consecutive days, as soon as the weather permitted.

8 August 1940

On Thursday 8 August, Göring submitted his orders for Eagle Day: 'From Reichsmarschall Göring to all units of Luftflotten 2, 3 and 5. Operation Eagle. In a short time you will annihilate the British Air Force. Heil Hitler.' The date was set as Saturday 10 August.

But the great battle would begin before that. In the evening of 7 August, convoy CW.9, also called Peewit, set to sea from Scotland. With 20 cargo vessels it was the largest Channel convoy to date. The ships passed the thirty kilometre narrow Strait of Dover in the hope that the

darkness of the night would protect them from being discovered, but they were spotted by the German Freya radar at Wissant. All too soon in the early hours of 8 August, the first attacks against the convoy were carried out, with motor torpedo boats sinking three vessels and damaging a further three.

The Luftwaffe made a real show of force with the dual aim of annihilating the convoy and pulling Fighter Command into a large air battle. The first attack was carried out by Luftflotte 2 with Stukas from II./StG 1, escorted by JG 26 and JG 51. Park had no choice but to order up three squadrons. They managed to hold the dive bombers away from the vessels, but at the price of four Spitfires while two Bf 109s were shot down.

Next came Luftflotte 3's turn, which at noon dispatched 57 Ju 87 dive-bombers, escorted by 30 Bf 109s from JG 27 and 20 Bf 110s from V.(Z)/LG 1.

The German formation of more than 100 planes was spotted by the radar station at Ventnor on Isle of Wight when it was a quarter of the way along a route from the French coast. At that point 18 Hurricanes were escorting the convoy. More airborne fighters were immediately called for. Squadron Leader Horace 'George' Darley in 609 Squadron wrote afterwards: 'B Flight was ordered to patrol Peewit at 10000ft. After taking off I climbed through cloud from 1 – 4000 ft., and after climbing to 7000 ft I could not see the objective owing to a layer of cloud at 4000 ft. I informed controller and went below cloud to 3500 ft north of the convoy.'[99]

The convoy just had passed St Catherine's Point on the Isle of Wight and was within sight of the island, at a distance of less than four nautical miles. The vessels left small white streaks of foam behind them, and in the air above was a cluster of gas-filled barrage balloons. Around these, the Spitfires and Hurricanes were orbiting, trying to locate the best possible position before the German attack. The British pilots peered nervously in every direction and waited.

'They're coming!' Out of the haze down in the south, tiny, silvery dots emerged. At first only a few appeared. But then more and more popped out and when those in the front were distinguishable as aircraft with wings and fuselages, the approaching formation had expanded to enormous dimensions.

Flight Lieutenant Noel Hall was first to lead his formation – nine Hurricanes from 257 Aquadron – to attack.

'Achtung! Hurricane!' The cry sounded over the German radio. In the next moment other Hurricanes and Spitfires flashed out of the sun and quickly dived past the startled Messerschmitt pilots. These were from 145, 238 and 609 squadrons. With roaring engines they hurtled on down towards the Stuka groups in the front. The air rang

with the rattle of rapid-firing Browning machine guns. Smoke trails from the bullets drew long lines. The first Ju 87 shook from the hits. Oberleutnant Martin Müller's plane (belonging to I./StG 3) fell in an uncontrollable spin, immediately followed by two other violently burning Stukas. Three cascades in the water marked as many dive-bombers' downfall.

The next moment the Messerschmitts were 'down' and attacked the British fighters. 257 Squadron's war diary noted: 'We were involved in a big contact off St. Catherine's Point. F/Lt Hall, F/O D'Arcy Irvine and Sgt Smith were lost in this combat and were posted missing.'[100]

V.(Z)/LG 1 was responsible for ten of the twenty German victory claims in that engagement. Oberleutnant Helmut Müller from V.(Z)/LG 1 was recorded as having shot down three Hurricanes, and Oberleutnant Joachim Glienke from the same formation claimed two. I./ZG 2 contributed with another two. The actual British losses were limited to six fighters. The intervention of the German fighters however had been enough to avert the British from the attacks on the Stukas, which now took on the convoy. 'They came along in V formation, and then flicked into the old familiar "line ahead" position for the attack', said Captain William Dawson on the 500-ton ship *John M*.[101] 'Down they came. I could hear the scream from the leader's flight above the rattle of my guns, which had already opened up. I saw the bombs leave and hurtle downwards. The first salvo hit a Norwegian ship on my starboard side ... Down came more bombs, flinging up great columns of water nearly one hundred feet high, which plunged over the ship and drenched all of us. I saw one water column, green between me and the sun, smash over the forecastle head and sweep the two gunners off their feet. Ahead to the port I saw a bomb hit the commodore's ship and set it on fire. Down came more stuff, and at one time at least twenty bombs struck on either side.'

Within ten minutes eleven merchant vessels were hit by bombs, four of which sank.

A break followed while the Germans sent out air-sea rescue planes to pick up their own shot down airmen. On the British side Squadron Leader Harold Fenton of 238 Squadron took off to search for two of his pilots that were missing after the air combat over the Channel. Fenton clashed with one of the He 59s, but this did not end as usual in such circumstances – the gunner in the air-sea rescue plane managed to hit the Spitfire's engine badly enough to force Fenton to perform an emergency landing in the water next to the trawler Basset, which resulted in the British pilot being badly injured. Shortly afterwards, Captain William Dawson on *John M* caught sight of what he hoped least to see: 'Halfway to the shore, more Junkers appeared in the distance, even more than had attacked us the first time . . .' This time it was no less than 80 Stukas, escorted by nearly 70 Bf 109s and '110s. Just as the dive-bombers started diving towards their targets, a warning was heard over the radio: 'Puma! Watch out for enemy fighters from above! They are diving with you!'

It was Squadron Leader John Peel who led his Hurricanes from 145 Squadron to attack. He said: 'We climbed to 16,000 feet, and looking down, saw a large formation of

A formation of Hurricane fighters above the clouds.

Ju 87s approaching from the South with Me 109s stepped up behind to 20,000 feet. We approached unobserved out of the sun and went in to attack the rear Ju 87s before the enemy fighters could interfere. I gave a five-second burst to one bomber and broke off to engage two Me 109s. There was a dog-fight. The enemy fighters, which were painted silver, were half rolling, diving and zooming in climbing turns. I fired two five-second bursts at one and saw it dive into the sea. Then I followed another up in a zoom and got him as he stalled.'

The German fighter escort struggled to keep the British away from the Ju 87s and took some severe losses in doing so. Among several downed '109s was the one piloted by the commander of II./JG 27, Major Werner Andres. He did, however, bail out and was later picked up by a He 59.

More British fighters, from 43 and 152 Squadron, soon joined the game. Captain Dawson, who followed the course of action onboard *John M*, wrote: 'More Spitfires came out from the land, and a terrific fight took place over our heads. At one time I counted nearly two hundred aircraft in action. In a quarter of an hour's progress towards the land, I saw twelve machines coming down in flames . . .'

43 Squadron's Flight Lieutenant Thomas Dalton-Morgan had already destroyed a Junkers 87 when he and another Hurricane swept in against the '109 formation and daubed a Messerschmitt with bullets. Unteroffizier Heinz Uebe extricated himself at the last moment out of his burning 109 and had to spend some time in the cold water. Feldwebel Erich Krenzke, also of 5./JG 27, suddenly found that instead of his wingman he had two British fighters behind him. The strike of the bullets banged all over the inside of the cabin when the bullets hit and the engine began to emit smoke. At an altitude of no more than 500 metres, Krenzke ejected the canopy and bailed out. He received a violent blow when he bumped against the stabilizer, but – almost paralyzed by pain – kept his consciousness and pulled the parachute chord. He spent the next two hours in the freezing water of the Channel before a German lifeboat discovered him.

A Spitfire Mk I from 609 Squadron over the English south coast. With 97 air victories against 14 own losses, Squadron Leader Horace Darley's 609 Squadron became the most successful RAF unit during the Battle of Britain. The aircraft seen in the image, L1065, 'PR-E' was reported damaged in a taxiing accident at Middle Wallop on 16 August 1940. (Photo: Goss.)

For JG 27, 8 August meant a severe depletion – 10 Bf 109s and four pilots were lost, against 13 victories. The Zerstörer units performed far better. V.(Z)/LG 1 attained 11 victories against four losses of their own, and I./ZG and II./ZG 2 reported two Spitfires each shot down without any losses. In addition, a pilot from I./ZG 2 shot down a Blenheim from Coastal Command's 59 Squadron.

But they had not been able to save the Stuka formations from sustaining severe losses – in all 11 Ju 87s. Worst affected was II./StG 77, where a pilot said: 'After an hour, our Staffelkapitän returned. He looked serious: "The commander still is missing, as well as Hauptmann Horst-Hennig Schmack and Unteroffizier Pitroff!" We could hardly believe our ears. No one had seen the commander go down. After the attack, he flew off with his Stabskette. Nobody knows what happened. A few weeks later we learned that he was in British captivity . . . '

The commander of II./StG 77, Major Waldemar Plewig, was shot down, took to the parachute and ended up in captivity. Plewig was shortly afterwards awarded with the Knight's Cross, which after German requests took place during a military ceremony at POW Camp Shap Wells Hotel near Carlisle.

Without doubt, the British fighters had shown their ability even in larger air battles. That day's most successful unit was 145 Squadron, which claimed to have shot down 21 Germans against own losses of five pilots. Flight Lieutenant Adrian Boyd, leading 145 Squadron's 'B' Flight, was responsible for the destruction of two Bf 109s, two Bf 110s, and a Ju 87 alone.

Of the coal convoy CW.9 merely four vessels remained which hauled themselves in to Swanage harbour that evening.

It is noteworthy that the British allowed themselves to be drawn into such a large air battle just days before Eagle attack. 10 Group had been forced to make 116 sorties.[102] It cost a loss of 19 British fighters and 17 pilots. The fact is that through 'Ultra', the British had intercepted and decoded Göring's instructions about Eagle Day, which would be launched two days later.

When the weather forecasts however predicted deteriorating weather, Göring decided to postpone Eagle Attack. But this message was not sent over the radio, and the British failed to intercept the counter-order. Therefore, according to the plan, Bomber Command was dispatched in a series of smaller attacks against German airfields in France, Belgium and the Netherlands, intended to disrupt Eagle Attack. But the result was meagre. At the airfield at Cherbourg, a Bf 109 from JG 27 was damaged, and at Amsterdam-Schiphol in the Netherlands, a He 111 from KGr 126 was damaged.[103]

'GESCHWADER ACE OF SPADES' – A NON-NAZI LUFTWAFFE UNIT?

On 8 August, yet another Jagdgeschwader, JG 53 'Pik As', made its debut in the war over the Channel, and the unit's first victory in the Battle of Britain was claimed by Hauptmann Günther Freiherr von Maltzahn, the charismatic commander of II. Gruppe. JG 53 was not just any fighter unit. It was one of the most successful German fighter units in the Battle of France, and was greatly influenced by Werner Mölders – who had commanded III./JG 53 until he was shot down and captured by the French on 5 June 1940. JG 53 'Pik As' (Ace of Spades) wore their unit badge, the ace of spades, on the engine cowlings of their Bf 109s with pride. The shock among the men of the 'Ace of Spades Geschwader' was great when the unit was instructed to paint over their ace of spades and replace them with a 25 centimetres wide red band around the nose of the aircraft. 'We were disgusted,' said Hermann Neuhoff, who served as a Feldwebel with III./JG 53 under the command of Mölders and achieved eight victories during The Battle of France. 'The explanation we got was that the British knew of the existence of our Pik As Geschwader and that we were to remove our ace of spades so as to not facilitate for their intelligence service. But none of us believed in it. We knew that it was a thorn in Göring and other Nazi bigwigs that our Geschwaderkommodore, Oberstleutnant Hans-Jürgen von Cramon, had married a so-called "non-Aryan" woman. But he refused to divorce her, and all his subordinates stood behind our Kommodore. Therefore, we had to replace our ace of spades with a "red ring of shame".' [1]

Whether this was really the case has never been clarified, but the fact is that Mölders' old III./JG 53 rebelled against Göring for the reasons Neuhoff states, and the lack of confidence was mutual. It started when Hauptmann Wolf-Dietrich Wilcke, who had served as Gruppenkommandeur under Mölders and followed his example in more than one way, took over as Gruppenkommandeur on 12 August. Neuhoff said: 'We never called Wilcke anything other than "Fürst" [the Prince], which was an expression of the respect we felt for him. He was not only a good flier but a great man in every way. He was always loyal to his men - subordinates as well as superiors. If someone had made a mistake Wilcke used to ensure that it got mildest possible repercussions. After the war, it was popular to say that so and so was not a Nazi, but Wilcke really was hostile to the Nazis. He stood up for our Geschwaderkommodore to the utmost, and because there was an order from above to paint over our ace of spades, Wilcke's response was to have the swastikas on the tail fins on all aircraft in our Gruppe painted over.'

1. Interview with Hermann Neuhoff.

A Bf 109 from 6./JG 53 'Pik As' with the red ring – called the 'shame ring' by the men in the unit – which replaced the unit's Ace of Spades emblem. (Photo: Prien.)

Leutnant Erich Schmidt, one of the top aces of III./JG 53 'Pik As', demonstrates how he shot down an RAF plane during the Battle of Britain. His Bf 109 in the background has had the swastika painted over – an action in solidarity with the unit's Geschwaderkommodore, Oberstleutnant von Cramon. Schmidt achieved a total of 47 air victories before he was killed on the Eastern Front in August 1941. (Photo: Neuhoff.)

Pilot Officer Leonard Walter Stevens was one of three pilots from 17 Squadron who had their Hurricanes shot down or badly damaged by Bf 110s of ZG 2 on 11 August 1940. This image shows the replacement aircraft that Stevens received after this, embellished with his personal emblem – a winged Popeye.

11 August 1940

Sunday 11 August dawned with clear weather, but the meteorologists could not guarantee three days in a row of such weather. So Göring decided to wait with Eagle Attack, which however did not prevent the Germans from taking advantage of the beautiful day to soften up the defence on the other side of the Channel.

It was a quarter to ten, British time, when the radar station at Ventnor on Isle of Wight's southern point spotted the first echoes from a large formation of aircraft over the Cotentin Peninsula on the French Channel coast. The commanders of Fighter Command's 10 and 11 Group quickly agreed that it was probably the beginning of a major German raid.

In Warmwell, Squadron Leader Horace Darley was ordered to take off with his 609 Squadron. At 11:07, three radar stations estimated the formation of Germans aircraft at 'plus one hundred'. That did it. In Middle Wallop the twelve Hurricanes that remained in 238 Squadron took off. From Tangmere eleven other Hurricanes joined in. At Exeter and Westhampnett other Hurricanes rolled out to take off. Almost the entire 10 Group was scrambled – only 93 and 234 squadrons were kept on the ground as a reserve. In addition to 10 Group's five airborne squadrons, 11 Group dispatched 1 and 145 squadrons. A total of seventy-four British fighters flew to the south to intercept Luftflotte 2.

The Hurricane pilots of 87 and and 238 Squadrons clashed with the leading formation of Bf 109s in a combat that cost a loss of six British and two German fighters. These Messerschmitt 109s came from I./JG 2 'Richthofen', one of the Luftwaffe's most successful Jagdgruppen. One of

its pilots – the commander of the 3. Staffel, Oberleutnant Helmut Wick – would soon make his name. In this engagement he claimed to have shot down three British fighters, bringing his total to 17 victories.

Squadron Leader Darley's twelve Spitfires from 609 Squadron performed significantly better than these Hurricane units. Owing to the radar observations, the British air controller could lead 609 Squadron, which had taken off first among all of 10 Group's units, to a position with the sun in the back high above the German main formation. This consisted of 38 Ju 88s from I. and II./KG 54 – the notorious 'Geschwader Totenkopf', whose skull-embellished Ju 88s were responsible for the destruction of Rotterdam in May 1940. Now they flew against the Royal Navy bases at Portland and Weymouth. Above them orbited sixty-one Bf 110s from Oberstleutnant Friedrich Vollbracht's ZG 2, and it was against these that 609 Squadron directed its first attack. In the first surprise strike from above, Flight Lieutenant James 'Butch' McArthur, Flying Officer John Dundas, and Pilot Officers David Crook, John 'Bishop' Bisdee and the Belgian Noel Le Chevalier Agazarian claimed to have shot down one Bf 110 each. Among the pilots lost by the Germans in this first attack was Major Ernst Ott, the commander of I./ZG 2. But the Zerstörer pilots quickly recovered. Flying Officer Dundas had his Spitfire badly damaged and only barely managed to bring it back to Warmwell. As the remaining British fighter units appeared, they became entangled in bitter fighting with ZG 2. In these engagements, the Zerstörer pilots accounted for a shooting down of 17 Hurricanes and Spitfires against only two additional losses of their own. 'I flew on the left side of the Kommodore's machine', said Wilhelm Schaefer, who with the rank of an Oberleutnant flew as the adjutant of ZG 2.

Ju 88s above the clouds. The Junkers 88 was so fast that the British Hurricane fighter would often have a hard time catching up with it, especially if the Ju 88 went into a dive.

'A Hurricane from the right got into position behind him. I got into a good firing position and, with smoking engine, he dived steeply downwards.' [104]

Although Oberstleutnant Vollbracht's Zerstörer pilots performed quite well, ZG 2's success reports were exaggerated – which often is the case in aerial combats involving such large numbers of aircraft. 601 Squadron, which mainly fought the Bf 110s, lost four Hurricanes without being able to attain any successes other than than a few unconfirmed victories. 145 Squadron achieved an equally meagre result in the engagement with the Messerschmitts, with four of the unit's Hurricanes getting shot down. Although two of these could be repaired after emergency landings, two pilots were killed.

III./JG 2 and JG 53 were tasked to cover the Zerstörer planes as these returned back to their base after running out of ammunition. The Bf 109 pilots also reported a large number of British fighters downed, including three Spitfires by the commander of III./JG 53, Hauptmann Harro Harder. III./JG 2 was credited with seven kills but lost four Bf 109s and two pilots, including the adjutant, Leutnant Adolf Steidle. In total, this mission cost JG 2 'Richthofen' a loss of eight Bf 109s.

Meanwhile, the 'Totenkopf' bombers attacked their targets, where they managed to damage two freighters and a destroyer and set the oil tanks at Weymouth Bay ablaze. But when the German bombers turned homeward, they were intercepted by some late arriving Hurricanes that had managed to escape the Messerschmitts' attention. These attacked fifteen kilometres off the coast. Five Ju 88s tumbled down in flames, crashing into the grey waves. With one of them, II./KG 54 lost its commander, Major Kurt Leonhardy.

Afterwards the RAF made a more realistic estimation of the losses inflicted upon their enemy than their German counterparts. When the RAF units added their results, they arrived at a total of 32 confirmed victories. This was not that far from the actual German losses – 17 fighters (11 Bf 109s and 6 Bf 110s) and 5 Ju 88s. The price for this was 16 destroyed British fighters and 10 damaged ones. What weighed even heavier was that 15 of Fighter Command's pilots had been killed and several others wounded. And not only had the German bombing raids been completely successful – 10 Group actually had lost one-sixth of its serviceable fighters in a single battle. In total, 10 Group's units made 143 sorties on 11 August. [105]

Just as the fighting near Portland began to peter out, the focus shifted to the east, where Kesselring dispatched four Bf 110s from Erprobungsgruppe 210 and a handful of Do 17s from II./KG 2 against a convoy off Harwich. The main aim was to pull Fighter Command into combat. [106] Bf 110s of I./ZG 26 'Horst Wessel' lay in wait higher up, ready to strike down on the British fighters. But owing to bad coordination, the German plan misfired. Hauptmann Hans Kogler, the Staffelkapitän of 1./ZG 26, recalled: 'I./ZG 26 had to meet up with a fast bomber formation of Bf 110s over Gravelines and to escort them towards the Thames Estuary. Due to confusion during the planning (the Gruppenkommandeur, Hptm Wilhelm Mackrocki was absent on this day and I was his deputy), we arrived three or four minutes late at the Gravelines assembly point where we found no aircraft to escort. I was of the opinion that the fighter-bombers had already flown towards the target so I decided to head that way.'[107]

The four Messerschmitt assault planes managed to damage the two destroyers Esk and Windsor – the latter so badly that the repair work lasted until October – but it cost them dearly. With no fighter escort in sight, they came under attack by a large number of Hurricanes and Spitfires from 17, 74 and 85 squadrons. The heavy Bf 110s of the C-6 version, equipped with a 30mm automatic cannon under the belly, had no chance. Two were shot down in quick succession and the others barely managed to escape. When the Zerstörer pilots appeared, the British were prepared.

'Somewhere west of Ispwich/Harwich, still without the fighter-bombers, we were attacked by Spitfires', said Kogler. A fierce fighter combat broke out. Oberleutnant Wilhelm Spies banked left, thereby avoiding the British fighter attack and was soon in position behind a Spitfire which he set on fire with a short volley from his machine guns and cannons. 74 Squadron's Pilot Officer Donald Cobden was killed when his Spitfire was shot down by a Bf 110 on this his 26th birthday. Meanwhile five British fighters came up behind Hauptmann Kogler's Bf 110. With several hits on the aircraft, Kogler pushed the control stick forward and managed to escape his opponents in a steep dive, while his rear gunner, Unteroffizier Adolf Bauer, kept the British at arm's length with his machine gun. But the aircraft could not be saved. Kogler made an emergency landing in the sea. At the last moment Bauer managed to get the airplane's inflatable rescue boat out, and the two airmen climbed in.* The downing of their Bf 110 was credited to 74 Squadron's Warrant Officer Ernest Mayne and Sergeant Wilfred Skinner. But their comrade, Pilot Officer Denis Smith, was shot down and killed by another Bf 110.

85 Squadron's Sergeant Harold Allgood attacked a Bf 110 and claimed to have shot it down, but had to disengage after half the fin of his Hurricane had been shot off. Exercising all his skills, he managed to bring the badly damaged plane back to base. Flying Officer David Hanson and Pilot Officer Leonard Stevens from 17 Squadron also had their Hurricanes shot to pieces by the Bf 110s, and the same

---

* Quite incredibly, the crew of Kogler and Bauer returned to base a couple of days later. Having spent nearly one hundred hours in the rubber dinghy – without either food or water – they were discovered and saved by two German MTBs near Nieuport. (Kohl, *Volltreffer*, p. 107.)

ZG 2 claimed to have shot down 17 British fighters on 11 August. With one of these, a Hurricane, Leutnant Hans Schmid from 4./ZG 2 scored his eighth victory. The image shows Schmid's Bf 110, 'A2+JK' before the eighth victory bar had been painted onto the rudder. This number would increase to 15 over the next few months. From October 1940, Schmid flew as night fighter pilot and claimed another 13 kills. ZG 2 had an average of five air victories for each own loss during the first main battle days of the Battle of Britain.

unit's Pilot Officer Kenneth Manger, who carried the DFC, was killed when a Bf 110 shot down his Hurricane.

All in all, I./ZG 26 recorded nine victories against two of its own aircraft missing. A third Bf 110 was so badly damaged that it was later written off after an emergency landing in France. The British lost five of their own planes shot down and two badly damaged in this scrap with I./ZG 26.

Less than two hours later, the alarm went off again on the airfield at Manston, and the pilots of 74 'Tiger' Squadron were scrambled. Along with Hurricanes of 111 Squadron, they were vectored towards the area northeast of Margate, where a German aircraft formation was reported. This was II./StG 1 with 30 Ju 87s, and the escort – a dozen Bf 109s of Hauptmann Horst Tietzen's 5./JG 51. 'Sailor' Malan led his eight Spitfires, divided into two sections of four in each, through the thick clouds. At 5,000 metres, he came out of the clouds and saw the Germans – 700 metres higher, and about a kilometre behind the Spitfire formation. Malan wrote in his combat report: 'On sighting us, the bombers dived towards a gap in the clouds whilst the Me 109s closed their range with the bombers. I ordered Freeborn's Blue Section to attack the bombers whilst I attacked the fighters with Red Section. I closed the range with the fighters and attacked an Me 109 as he dived through a gap. I opened up at 30 degrees deflection at 200 yards and closed to 100 yards dead astern. After the

third two-second burst he burst into flames and went into the sea approximately off Margate. I immediately climbed towards the cloud and then dived towards another group of four Me 109s and delivered 30 degree deflection bursts of about three seconds at about 200 yards. I saw no results. As my ammunition was now expended, I returned to Manston.' [108]

For 111 Squadron the combat was a disaster. Within only a few minutes, five of its Hurricanes were shot down. Haupmann Tietzen accounted for two of them. The German losses were confined to a Ju 87 and a Bf 109.

When Dowding went through the day's reports, he felt a rising concern. The reports of the battles on 11 August showed 28 British fighter losses – plus another six seriously damaged – and 25 pilots killed. Two great battle days – 8 and 11 August – thus had already cost nearly ten per cent of the serviceable fighters in Fighter Command. Such losses were absolutely unsustainable in the long run.

The Germans, on the other hand, were more optimistic. According to their estimations, 90 British fighters had been shot own against 38 own losses on 11 August. In reality, the figthing between 8 and 11 August cost a loss of 74 German planes and 52 British fighters.

The buoyant Germans, however, suffered a setback during an air raid by II./KG 27 and III./KG 55 against the docks in the port of Bristol on the night of 11 August. During the return flight a He 111 H-3, '1G+AC' from II./ KG

A formation of He 111s from II./KG 27 'Boelcke'. (Photo: Waiss.)

Bf 110s from Erprobungsgruppe 210. (Photo: Vasco.)

27, was attacked and shot down by a Hurricane from 87 Squadron. The bomber crew escaped by bailing out and landed in British captivity. It turned out that among them was Major Friedrich-Karl Schlichting, the commander of II./KG 27, and Major Hans-Jürgen Brehmer, adjutant of the Luftwaffe General Staff. An excellent catch for British intelligence!

12 August 1940

Monday 12 August 1940 seemed to promise just as clear weather as on the previous day. At the airfield at Épinoy the Do 17 bombers of I./KG 2 began to taxi out on the runway at 08:30. While the Dorniers climbed to the assigned altitude to form up, bomb-loaded Bf 109s and Bf 110s of Erprobungsgruppe 210 began taking off from Calais-Marck. At 08:53, III./JG 54 took off from the airfield at Guines.[109] This unit constituted only a small part of the large number of Messerschmitt 109s assigned to escort the bomb-carrying aircraft. 'Big mission over England. Nowadays we never fly in small formations', was noted in the war diary of 9./JG 54.[110]

First out over the Channel were scores of Messerschmitts at high altitude. They hade been spotted immediately by the British radar stations on take-off, and as they approached the British coast, the air surveillance reported that they were only Messerschmitts. Again Park decided to wait and keep his units on the ground.

The Messerschmitt assault planes from Erprobungsgruppe 210 came in fast and at low altitude.
Hauptmann Walter Rubensdörffer switched on his radio to broadcast and called out: 'Achtung! Third Staffel: Break out. Good hunting!'

Oberleutnant Otto Hintze, commanding the 3. Staffel, equipped with Bf 109 fighter-bombers, replied: 'Viktor – understood!'

Rubensdörffer and the twelve Messerschmitt 110s in the first and second Staffeln turned to the left and disappeared in the direction of Hawkinge, flying parallel with the coast.

Oberleutnant Hintze's eight Bf 109 E-4s continued straight ahead, towards Dover. This time, neither ships nor port facilities were the target. This time the English radar would be knocked out. By intercepting radio communications between the British air controllers and airborne RAF pilots, the Germans were clear about the essential role played by the radar for the British fighter defence. In theory the task of wiping out the radar stations might not have seemed that difficult. But the German airmen knew better. Firstly, the targets were relatively small, and secondly the raids on radio stations such as in Poland, Norway and France had showed that the buildings could be destroyed, but what was most difficult to get repaired – the transmitter masts – almost always remained unscathed.

The various attacks took place in close succession. Oberleutnant Hintze's Messerschmitt 109s attacked the radar station at Dover. Two minutes later Leutnant Rössiger's 2. Staffel hurtled down on the station at Rye near Hastings, and immediately afterwards 1. Staffel under Oberleutnant Lutz struck Pevensey's facilities. Finally, Hauptmann Rubensdörffer's own Schwarm attacked the radar at Dunkirk near Canterbury. Although almost all of the bombs fell within the station area, the radar unit survived. But in Dover, Rye and Pevensey the destruction was almost complete – the high transmitter masts excluded. A breach of 160 km had been opened in the defence's radar chain.

Around now, the Dornier bombers from I./KG 2 came rumbling in over England, escorted by JG 54. It was only now that Park scrambled his units. Flight Lieutenant Alan Deere of 54 Squadron –which just had returned after replenishing its strength in a quieter corner of the British Isles for ten days – describes the scene at Manston's airfield: 'We had just settled down to the inevitable game of cards in our dispersal hut at Manston when the telephone shrilled warningly. How we hated the dispersal telephone; its very note was abnormal and the unexpectedness with which it rang had the immediate effect of producing an awful sick feeling in the pit of one's tummy. A pin could have been heard to drop as, with cards poised and eyes turned expectantly towards the orderly as he reached for the receiver, we strained to hear the message from the now faintly urgent voice which came over the wire. "Hornet squadron, scramble." There was no need to hear more . . .'[111]

The pilots rushed out and jumped into their Spitfires which stood ready. The engines rapidly came afloat, and the small fighters bounced off across the field and took off to climb in the direction ordered by the air controller over the radio. But they never reached the Dornier bombers. 'Break – now!', Squadron Leader James 'Prof' Leathart screamed over the radio when the Bf 109s came diving, sun rays reflecting their canopies making it appear as if they had already opened fire.

'The early morning sky over Dover, or "Hell's Corner", as it was now known, was patterned with weaving and darting Spitfires and Me 109s while the bombers thrust on towards their target unmolested', wrote Deere.[112] From an altitude of 4,800 metres, ninety SC 50 bombs fell over Lympne. As these exploded in long lines, the Do 17 planes turned home and landed three quarters of an hour later – without having sustained any losses. Without radar, Fighter Command had been unable to find the bombers. Instead its airmen became embroiled in fighter combats that Dowding and Park wished to avoid. However, the RAF pilots once again proved that they were not the 'easy pickings' that the German fighter pilots had hoped for.

610 Squadron took off from Biggin Hill with twelve Spitfires. This unit was led by Squadron Leader John Ellis, who would develop into something of 'JG 52's slayer'. He was credited with five victories during the Battle of France and on 24 July he shot down a Bf 109 from III./JG 52, followed by two more from the same unit the next day. As he led his pilots to attack the closest formation of Bf 109s, it happened to be nine planes from II./JG 52 – which was out on its first mission over England. Two of the Bf 109s were downed in 610 Squadron's first surprise attack – one by Ellis and one by Pilot Officer Constantine Pegge.

Then clusters of German fighters came diving down on the valiant British fighter pilots, who had to fight hard to defend themselves. Leutnant Max-Hellmuth Ostermann, a pilot in 7./JG 54 who participated in the battle, afterwards wrote the following critical lines about the German pilots: 'Our entire Gruppe was whirling around in the sky. There was hardly any single coherent Rotte. The Spitfires proved to be very manoeuvrable. They gave us a real flight show with their loops and barrell-rolls. They shot out of climbing rolls and amazed us with their manoeuvres. There was a good deal of shooting, but not much was hit.' [113]

Pilot Officer Edward Smith was one of the most aggressive fighter pilots in 610 Squadron. He had shot down a He 111 during the Battle of France, and a Bf 109 each day on 24 and 25 July 1940. But when he now pulled up behind a '109, Ostermann managed to place his Bf 109 E-4, 'White 5', on the tail of Smith's Spitfire. 'Suddenly', Ostermann continued his account, 'the Tommy opened fire and the

Messerschmitt dived away. I had also squeezed the firing button, but not until I took careful aim. I opened fire at the Spitfire from a slight left turn and already my first burst hit him.' Pilot Officer Smith felt two powerful explosions when 20mm shells from Ostermann's automatic cannons hit his cockpit and fuel tank. The next moment his Spitfire (L1044, 'DW-H') was burning. 'The British plane immediately caught fire, and leaving a long, grey smoke column it fell into the sea just off the coast. A large water fountain indicated the impact ', wrote Ostermann.[114]

Smith only just made it out of his burning plane and pulled the parachute chord. He was picked out of the Channel by a British trawler, and to his amazement discovered that the captain of the ship was an old school friend. Two weeks later, Smith was awarded the DFC.

This combat cost 610 Squadron two Spitfires, with three more damaged, but the losses could have been worse if the Germans had coordinated their attacks better. In the excitement, the participating German fighter pilots claimed to have shot down three times as many British fighters. In return, 610 Squadron was credited with the shooting down of five Bf 109s, of which Squadron Leader Ellis and Pilot Officer Pegge took two each. The next day Ellis was awarded the DFC.

Half an hour past noon (British time, i.e.one hour after German time) fifteen Hurricanes from 151 and 501 squadrons came down on a formation of twenty-two Ju 87s. These were from IV.(St)/LG 1, and had just attacked a convoy in the fairwaters north of Margate. The British managed to shoot down a Stuka before Major Galland's III./JG 26 intervened. In the confused battle the British reported six Ju 87s shot down, while actual German losses were confined to a single plane. This cost the British a loss of two Hurricanes, with two more damaged. III./JG 26 reported four downed Hurricanes, one of which was credited to Major Galland and two ending up on Leutnant Heinz Ebeling's tally.

Meanwhile, Sperrle dispatched his Luftflotte 3 for a new major attack against 10 Group's area. KG 51 took off with 63 Ju 88s, of which most were directed against Portsmouth – where the battleship Queen Elizabeth, the cruiser Manchester and the French battleship Courbet were anchored. Twenty specially selected Ju 88 crews were commissioned to knock out the radar station at Ventnor on the Isle of Wight's southern tip. In addition to causing as much damage as possible to the targets, an additional goal for the operation was to once again draw as many British fighters as possible into combat. As with the previous day the Zerstörer planes played the lead role in covering Luftflotte 3's bombers against British fighters until the target was reached. ZG 2 and II. and III./ZG 76 dispatched 120 Bf 110s. 25 Bf 109s of JG 53 'Pik As' were positioned high above the twin-engined aircraft. JG 2 and JG 27 set further Bf 109s in readiness to follow up when the Zerstörer planes had exhausted their ammunition.

The long approach flight proceeded without any intervention from Fighter Command. In fact, Sperrle's formations were not spotted by radar until at 12:45. The first spottings were telephoned from the station at Poling, 'neighbour' with the dead Pevensey facilities. But only when hundreds of

The airfield at Guines in early August 1940. Five pilots from III./JG 54 in full combat gear. From the left: Unteroffizier Wilhelm Braatz, Leutnant Max-Hellmuth Ostermann, Leutnant Friedrich-Wilhelm Behrens, Feldwebel Erwin Leykauf and Feldwebel Fritz Oeltjen. Two months later, Braatz was dead, Behrens was missing and Oeltjen was injured. (Photo: Leykauf.)

German aircraft began flying in over the Isle of Wight, did the British commanders realize what was happening. From Middle Wallop, Tangmere, Warmwell and Exeter nearly 60 Spitfires and Hurricanes took off in a great rush.

Meanwhile twenty Junkers crews dived down on the radar station at Ventnor and dropped their 500-kg bombs in a tremendous concentration. All that was left of the target was a heap of smoldering scrap; it would take the British three days of intensive repair work before operations could resume at Ventnor.

As the second, larger formation of Junkers bombers approached Portsmouth, it was met with 50 ascending barrage balloons. They still managed to get through, and over the next fifteen minutes they attacked the naval port in both the horizontal and diving attacks. Docks in the harbour, warehouses, the railway station, oil tanks, fuel storages and ships were hit by the bombs. Fires spread and raged for several hours before the fire brigade managed to get them under control. All this was achieved despite intensive fire from anti-aircraft artillery both on the ground and on the ships in the harbour. This was described as the

heaviest anti-aircraft fire the pilots in KG 51 had yet experienced, and several Ju 88s were hit, of which at least one crashed.

Although the British interceptors arrived too late to prevent the bombing, 10 Group had learned from the previous day's mistakes. In order to avoid attention from the German fighters, the air controllers sent in the Hurricanes and Spitfires in small groups, one after another. Most of these British fighter pilots also focused on the Junker planes as these flew out from the target area at low altitude after their dive-bombings. In that way, the Ju 88 '9K + AA', flown by KG 51's Geschwaderkommodore, Oberst Johannes Fisser, was shot down by five Spitfires and Hurricanes.

While Junkers after Junkers was hit, the German escort continued to orbit 3,000 metres above, waiting for the main force of the British fighters to show up. The Junkers crews defended themselves as best they could, and owing to their good training in the interaction between gunners and pilots they managed to ward off several fighter attacks on their own. The gunners in Major Walter Marienfeld's

A Hurricane from 151 Squadron. This machine was flown by the American volunteer pilot John Haviland. He was the only one of eleven American volunteer pilots in the Battle of Britain who survived the war.

(commander of III./KG 51) and Oberleutnant Lange's (9./KG 51) Ju 88s shot down two of 152 Squadron's Spitfires. But when the fighters started attacking from several directions simultaneously, it was soon no longer possible to avoid the Browning machine gun bursts. Shortly afterwards the next Ju 88 fell with burning engines.

It was only when every tenth Ju 88 had been shot down and large gaps had been torn everywhere in the bomber formations that the German escort became aware of the British tactic and rushed to save what was left of KG 51. In the air battle that followed, it was almost inevitable that both sides greatly overestimated their opponent's losses; nearly three hundred fighters twisted around, in and out of the clouds. The Germans reported 27 victories, of which the Zerstörer units accounted for the majority: ZG 2 bagged thirteen against four of its own lost, and ZG 76 eight against a single own loss. The Bf 109 units contributed with another six victories against two own losses.

In reality, thirteen British fighters were shot down and four were damaged. Eight RAF pilots paid with their lives in that combat. Among the German pilots killed was the commander of III./JG 53, Hauptmann Harro Harder, an ace with 17 victories. 'We heard him over the radio, announcing that he had shot down two Spitfires. Then he was gone', said Hermann Neuhoff.[115]

The five Bf 110s and two Bf 109s lost by the Germans were more than tripled in the British optimistic reports – to claims for nineteen Bf 110s and six Bf 109s. 609 Squadron's Pilot Officer Noel Agazarian was credited with three,

and pilot officers David Crook and Charles 'Teeny' Overton with two each.

At two in the afternoon (British time) the airmen of Erprobungsgruppe 210 were out over the Strait of Dover again. This time, their target was the airfield at Manston. When Rubensdörffer's twenty bomb-carrying Messerschmitts came hurtling down over the Manston base, the fliers could see for themselves the result of the morning's attack on the British radar: all the Spitfire planes stood parked in their revetments. The British were completely taken by surprise. Rubensdörffer's men riddled the field with their machine guns and dropped every bomb with precision. Twelve 500-kg demolition bombs and four 250-kg incendiary bombs hit the hangars and other buildings. A group of Spitfires that attempted to take off in the midst of the hail of of bullets and bombs, was destroyed by a salvoe of two thousand kilograms of bombs. 'Four Hurricanes and five other aircraft destroyed on the ground', reported Erprobungsgruppe 210.

Hauptmann Rubensdörffer's '109s and '110s had barely left the scene when I./KG 2 came in, this time with 18 Do 17s, and dropped 150 bombs over the burning air base. These hit all of the repair shops and two hangars. The airfield at Manston was declared out of action for more than a day. Fighter Command's 54, 65 and 501 squadrons pursued the German planes as these returned to the coast, but failed to shoot down more than one of the attackers.

No sooner had the Dorniers from I./KG 2 landed on their airfield when they were prepared for the next operation. KG 2 and elements of KG 3 took off to attack the airfields at Canterbury, Hawkinge and Lympne.

56 Squadron's Hurricanes were vectored against a formation of German bombers that was believed to be heading towards Manston again. This was II./KG 2, led by Oberst Johannes Fink, aiming for Canterbury's airfield, about 20 kilometres further inland. Two entire Gruppen of Bf 109s – I. and III./JG 54 – had been assigned to escort II./KG 2, but from their position high above, where they orbited to keep pace with the slow bombers, the German fighter pilots failed to detect the green- and brown-camouflaged Hurricanes that came climbing up against the Dorniers. The bombers had to defend themselves, which they actually did brilliantly this time – much owing to some unconventional means of defence. Oberfeldwebel Kurt Wolff, one of the pilots of II./KG 2, said: 'Over the target the British attack us in small formations, but with great skill. Despite our perfect combat formation, individual enemy fighters manage to get quite close to our bombers. My Do 17 receives eight hits. A bullet destroys one of the left aileron brackets. For the first time, we use hand grenades, confetti and toilet paper to defend ourselves! In this way we manage to confuse the attacking fighter pilots so that they abandon their attacks. Our Staffel shoots down two Spitfires, and from one of them the pilot bails out.' [116]

56 Squadron's Pilot Officer Geoffrey Page felt how his Hurricane – 'US-X', nick-named 'Little Willie' – shook under the hits of a Dornier's counter-fire. When he looked out to the side, he saw a big hole that had been torn in the right wing. Next moment there was a violent explosion and flames entered the cockpit. The fuel tank right in front of the cockpit had been hit! At the last possible moment Page managed to abandon his almost completely burning aircraft, and landed in his parachute in the sea off Margate.

Meanwhile the air battle raged on, now mainly between the fighter pilots on both sides. II./JG 52 lost yet another Bf 109 – its third loss on that day. Oberleutnant Albrecht Dressl of the Stabsschwarm in III./JG 54 was shot down and belly-landed his Bf 109 near Margate, where he was taken prisoner. It is possible that he was the victim of 32 Squadron's Flight Lieutenant Michael Crossley, who recorded two Bf 109s shot down in that combat, increasing his victory tally to 11. Crossley belonged to the élite of Fighter Command. He had been a fighter pilot since 1936 and was credited with seven victories during the Battle of France, which earned him the DFC on 21 June 1940. In 32 Squadron, he became known as 'The Red Knight'.

The RAF pilots pursued the withdrawing Germans out over the Channel, firing wildly. A Bf 109 from 7./JG 54 was hit and splashed into the sea. Pilot Officer 'Art' Donahue, an American volunteer in the 64 Squadron, was chasing a Bf 109 that tried to escape in low flight over the crests. He was just about to open fire when his own Spitfire shook from the hits of another '109s automatic cannons. Donahue recalled: 'The din and confusion were awful inside the cockpit. I remember seeing some of the instrument panel breaking up, and holes dotting the gas tank in front of me. Smoke trails of tracer bullets appeared right inside the

cockpit. Bullets were going between my legs, and I remember seeing a bright flash of an incendiary bullet going past my leg and into the gas tank.' [117]

When the British fighter pilots finally turned back, they had seen several German planes limp away with smoking engines. Two Do 17s crashed in France, and Leutnant Josef Eberle from 9./JG 54 barely managed to bring his badly damaged 109 to the French Channel coast, where he crash-landed.

At the airfield at Peupelingues, southwest of Calais, the pilots of II./JG 52 were in a dismal mood. Their first combat day at the English Channel had cost three losses against only one victory. I./JG 26, which also experienced its first combat day at the Channel, had fared only moderately better – three victories against two own losses. 'We learned that we had a very tough opponent, one who also could shoot well,' commented Leutnant Ostermann.[118]

Both sides could endorse this statement. Geoffrey Page was picked up from the Channel with severe burns. It would take until 1943 before he was sufficiently recovered to return to service.

From the air base at Manston, Alan Deere wrote: '54 Squadron landed at Manston again later that afternoon, after a second engagement, to be met by a very shaken body of airmen and a no less frightened gathering of 600 Squadron pilots. The airfield was a shambles of gutted hangars and smouldering dispersal buildings all of which were immersed in a thin film of white chalk dust which drifted across the airfield and settled on men, buildings and parked aircraft with the manner and appearance of a light snow storm.'[119]

On the airfield at Hawkinge, seven hangars and several other buildings lay in ruins. In Westhampnett, Squadron Leader John Peel removed three more names from the rolls. In only three main battle days – 8, 11, and 12 August – 145 Squadron had lost ten of its twenty-one pilots. Of the 217 British fighters that saw combat on 12 August, 18 were lost. Including the airplanes that crash-landed so that they could eventually be repaired, 27 had been shot down. In fact, it could have been even worse, had more German fighter pilots been able to contact the enemy. On this day, the top ace Major Werner Mölders flew his first three combat missions since being wounded in late July, but in none of them did he see any British aircraft.[120]

The attacks on the radar stations were preparations for Eagle Attack, and on 12 August Göring sent out a radio message that gave the order to launch Eagle Attack the following day. The British, who learned of this through 'Ultra', managed to put four of the five attacked radar stations into service again during the following night. Thereby the gap in the radar chain was filled when Eagle Day dawned.

While this was taking place on the British Isles, Bomber Command was in action over Germany at night. Five Handley-Page Hampdens from 49 and 83 squadrons were dispatched in a low-level precision attack against an aqueduct in the Dortmund-Ems Canal – a major hub for the transportation of German barges to the invasion fleet in the English Channel. The first four Hampdens missed the target – two were shot down by anti-aircraft fire. But the pilot of the last aircraft, 49 Squadron's Flight Lieutenant Roderick Learoyd, defied the intense AAA and managed to place his bombs with such effect that the canal was blocked for ten days. For this feat Learoyd was awarded with the finest British award, the Victoria Cross.

13 August 1940: Eagle Day

Oberst Fink's KG 2 was to open the Eagle Attack, and between 05:50 and 06:10 on 13 August seventy-four of its Do 17 took off. In order not to be detected by radar, their approach flight was made at an altitude of only 500 metres. The twin-engined Dorniers split up into two major formations. Major Martin Gutzmann's I./KG 2 was assigned to attack the airfield at Eastchurch, while the remainder of KG 2 flew against Sheerness. Everything seemed to go as planned.

But one thing misfired: German weather reconnaissance planes had reported that a storm front was moving in. This observation was immediately transmitted to Göring, who ordered Eagle Attack to be postponed. All units were to be immediately informed about this, but KG 2 already was airborne. A radio message was sent to the airborne crews: 'AB! AB!' – *abbrechen*, the signal to abort. But this

was in the infancy of the aircraft radio. Only the so-called 'staff aircraft' – those flown by Geschwader and Gruppe commanders – were equipped with long-wave radios able to receive signals from the base. Major Gutzmann received the message and turned back to the airfield at Epinoy with his entire I./KG 2. But the other units from KG 2, which had taken off from other airfields, continued on without knowing what had happened. Oberst Fink personally led the Dornier planes from the Stabsstaffel and III./KG 2, which had taken off from Arras. Afterwards it turned out that long-wave radio in Fink's Do 17 was not working. And in the Do 17 flown by the commander of II./KG 2, Oberstleutnant Paul Weitkus, the radio operator simply did not notice the message!

Oberstleutnant Joachim Huth, the one-legged commander of ZG 26 'Horst Wessel', which was supposed to have escorted KG 2, sent out his Zerstörer to attempt to use visual signals to make the bomber crews realize that the operation was called off. Oberst Fink had been irritated when the escort had failed to turn up at the appointed rendezvous place, and he now became quite upset at what he regarded as 'undisciplined flying' by the Bf 110 pilots. 'There must be limits to how high fighting spirits can be expressed,' muttered the 50-year-old Luftwaffe colonel. His astonishment turned into anger when the 'wild escort' suddenly just left his bomber and disappeared.

A formation of Do 17 bombers. The Dornier 17 was developed according to the 'fast bomber' concept and entered service in 1937. In a flight competition that same year, the machine proved to be faster than the participating foreign fighter planes. But with the arrival of new monoplane fighters, the Do 17 lost this advantage and quickly became outdated. Erhard Milch, the Luftwaffe general inspector, wanted to develop the Do 17 further, but Hermann Göring decided to stop production of this aircraft and instead focus on the more modern Ju 88, which was faster, could take a bomb load twice as large, and also was capable of dive-bombing. When Do 17 production ceased in July 1940, 537 Do 17 Zs had been manufactured.

On the other side of the English Channel, five squadrons were scrambled. Only the thick cloud cover that piled up over the area enabled Oberst Fink and the Dornier planes in his formation to attack Eastchurch unimpeded. The over 200 bombs that were dropped hit barracks and all the hangars, destroying the whole ammunition dump in a series of huge explosions, plus six aircraft on the ground. But then the defence struck back. Just south of the burning airfield Fink's formation ran into 151 Squadron's Hurricanes. Flight Lieutenant Roddick Smith flew the first Hurricane to be equipped with two automatic cannons, and with this he managed to set a Do 17 ablaze. 'Flight Lieutenant Milne shot down two, one of which broke up in the air and the other crashing in the vicinity of Christchurch.' [121]

Immediately afterwards Spitfires from 74 'Tiger' Squadron emerged. Squadron Leader 'Sailor' Malan, now commanding this unit, said, 'Whilst leading the squadron into attack against enemy bombers, Do 17s, in the Estuary, they came across in a vic formation on my beam. I closed to within 100 yards and raked them with machine gun fire. I then swung into line astern and fired at No. 3 of the formation. I fired at 150 yards, using 4 x 2 second bursts. This machine burst into flames in mid-air and was last seen heading for the sea.' [122]

After ten minutes, five Dorniers had gone down, and just as many had been damaged. 74 Squadron claimed six 'certain' victories, three 'probables' and two damaged, and 151 Squadron added three 'certain' and a 'probable'. A massacre of this dimension probably would have occurred, had the Germans not been able to seek cover in among the thick clouds.

Göring's orders to postpone the major attack had also not reached Generalfeldmarschall Sperrle's Luftflotte 3.[123]

While the Do 17s of KG 2 were chased by 74 and 111 Squadron over the Thames Estuary, the first attack force from Luftflotte 3 was on its way towards the air bases Odiham and Farnborough – 20 Ju 88s from I./KG 54 and 18 from II./KG 54, escorted by JG 2 and V.(Z)/LG 1. The British alerted 43, 64, 87 and 601 squadrons. At Tangmere 43 Squadron took off with twelve Hurricanes at 06:25.[124] One of these Hurricane pilots was Flight Lieutenant Thomas Dalton Morgan, who had been in bed when the alarm went off, and therefore had no time to change from his pyjamas. For forty minutes the British fighters repeatedly attacked the German planes between Brighton and Guildford. Oberleutnant Kurt Erdmann's Ju 88 of Stab/KG 54 was shot down at Farnborough. Flight Lieutenant Dalton Morgan was in an attack position behind one of the German bombers and shot up the German's rudder and engine, but in the next moment his own Hurricane shook under hits from German bullets. Afterwards, Dalton Morgan believed that he had been hit by the German bomber's machine guns, but it is also possible that he fell prey to an assault by Unteroffizier Walter Gerigk from V.(Z)/LG 1. Both Ju 88 and Hurricane crashed, and the British and three Germans bailed out. When they hit the ground all of them were captured by a 'Bobby'. Wearing pyjamas, Dalton Morgan had great difficulty in convincing the police officer that he did not belong to the German bomber crew; the policeman simply couldn't imagine an RAF officer flying in such an obnoxious outfit! [125]

This operation cost KG 54 a loss of five Ju 88, with several others sustaining severe damage. The British fighter units returned to their bases in triumph and reported ten German bombers shot down against only three own losses.

According to the plan for Eagle Attack, Luftflotte 3 would carry out the next operation after midday. At 12:10, Hauptmann Horst Liensberger allocated 23 Bf 110s from his V.(Z)/LG 1 to escort the bombers. StG 77 was intended to strike against 10 Group's airfields, whereafter the Ju 87s and Ju 88s of II./StG 2, KG 54 and LG 1 would attack the ports of Portland and Southampton and the airbase Middle Wallop.[126] But in the midst of this the message that Eagle Attack was postponed finally reached Luftflotte 3. For some reason Hauptmann Liensberger however decided to allow his Bf 110s to continue out over the Channel.

While everything went like clockwork on the British side, most things misfired for the Germans. British radar stations picked up the echo from the '110s even before these flew out over the English Channel. Alerted in good time, the commanders at Tangmere and Middle Wallop scrambled Nos. 213, 238 and 601 squadrons. Owing to the early warning from the radar, the air controllers were able lead all of these fighters into a surprise attack from above and behind. For once the British held both an altitude superiority and a numerical advantage.

Hauptmann Liensberger ordered his pilots to form a circle. This time it was not an 'Angriffskreis', but rather the kind of defensive circle that the Luftwaffe pilots' gallows humour named the 'Angstkreis', 'anxiety circle'. Australian Pilot Officer Clive Mayers followed Flight Lieutenant Sir Archibald Hope, leader of 601 Squadron's 'A' Flight, when he ordered his pilots to form a column with their Hurricanes and attack the circling '110s. Mayer boldly attacked one of the Zerstörer planes head-on, but without any visible effect. Then he attacked another '110 from behind and held the firing button down for eight long seconds, while the Browning machine guns sprayed the twin-engined Messerschmitt with more than one thousand bullets. At a distance of 50 metres, Mayer broke off. In that moment one of the Messerschmitt's rudders was torn off and the German plane went into spin. Mayer barely had time to register it when his own Hurricane shuddered under the hits from the nose cannon of a Messerschmitt 110 behind him, and he felt a burning pain in one of his legs. He attempted to turn out of the fire, but discovered that the rudder of his own aircraft was badly damaged, so he quickly bailed out. While Mayer floated down in his parachute, a Messerschmitt 110 with an apparently vindictive pilot came diving down and opened fire on the defenceless pilot. Fortunately for the young Australian, the German missed. Shortly afterwards Mayers hit the water just outside Portland. He was rescued by a motor torpedo boat and was taken to hospital, where some minor shrapnel wounds were found in his right leg. Mayers was back in action again just a few days later.

Five Bf 110s were shot down in that combat. In addition to the shooting down of Mayer's Hurricane, the Zerstörer pilots only managed to damage two Hurricanes.

Scramble! Pilots from 601 Squadron rush to their aircraft.

When Göring received the report on Hauptmann Liensberger's 'solo venture' over the Channel, he was furious. 'The incident involving V./LG 1 shows that some unit leaders still haven't understood the importance of following clear instructions', he told Generalfeldmarschall Sperrle.[127]

Despite counter-orders, several among Eagle Attack's planned operations were launched in an uncoordinated way. While V.(Z)/LG 1 was fighting 601 Squadron over the Channel to the west, the same Geschwader's Stukagruppe, IV.(St)/LG 1, crossed the Strait of Dover with nine Ju 87. Their attack on the airfield at Hawkinge was however disrupted by British fighter attacks, and did not result in any appreciable damage.[128]

What is less known is that twelve Blenheims from RAF Bomber Command's 82 Squadron at midday that day attacked the airfield at Aalborg in Denmark, where II./JG 77 had arrived the day before. Eight Bf 109s were able to take off and intercept the British bombers before these reached the airfield. In a fierce air combat the Germans reported 15 victories, including four by Oberfeldwebel Robert Menge. Of the twelve Blenheims, only one returned to base. 82 Squadron was credited with the shooting down of eleven Bf

109.[129] But in fact not a single German aircraft was lost, and no bombs hit Aalborg's airfield.

Whether this attack affected Göring is not known, but the fact is that at about that time he changed his mind and gave the order to execute the plan for Eagle Attack, albeit delayed.

At 15:30 (German time), Hauptmann Walter Enneccerus' II./StG 2 took off from Lannion.[130] Erhard Jähnert, who served as a Feldwebel and pilot in II./StG 2, recalled this day: 'It is remarkable that pilots often have a kind of a sixth sense. Several times I had that experience of comrades who were able to predict their own death. Shortly before take-off on this day, I heard Oberfeldwebel Erich Maak talk to his mechanic. He said that he felt that this mission would be his last, and he gave the mechanic a letter which he asked to be sent to his young bride. When I heard this, I was quite dismayed and offered to talk to the commander and request that Maak did not fly this day. "No", said Maak decidedly. "I shall fly and you are not going to go the boss!"'[131]

Off the French coast the fighter escort joined II./StG 2 – Bf 109s from II./JG 53 'Pik As'. Overall, about 250 German aircraft set off across the English Channel: 52 Ju

87s from I./StG 1 and II./StG 2 escorted by JG 53, and 39 Ju 88s from I. and II./LG 1 escorted by ZG 2 and ZG 76. When these formations approached the English coast, almost 80 British fighters were either airborne or about to take off from their bases in Exeter, Warmwell, Tangmere and Middle Wallop. Nos. 152, 213, 238, 257 and 601 squadrons attempted to reach the Ju 88s, but became involved in difficult fights with the German fighter escort. Leutnant Wolfgang Münchmeyer of I./ZG 2 recalled: 'The bombers were diving and disappearing in the clouds to seek their target. So, we were free to look for possible adversaries and by chance, we found them in the form of Hurricanes flying at a lower altitude. I was flying as rearguard of our formation as we dived on them with increasing speed.' [132]

'The next thing I knew', said 257 Squadron's Pilot Officer Kenneth Gundry, 'was a ruddy great earthquake in my A/C and my control column was almost solid. On my left another Hurricane was floating about over a complete network of smoke trails left by cannon shells and incendiary. We had been attacked by another unseen bunch of Me 110s.' [133] Gundry was lucky to escape with the stabilizer on his Hurricane shot to rags and the right aileron badly damaged. In the confused air combat between the

Bf 110s and British fighters that dived in and out among the thick clouds, both sides again made greatly exaggerated claims. The British reported nine Bf 110s shot down – two each by Flight Lieutenant Derek Boitell-Gill of 152 Squadron, Pilot Officer Joseph Laricheliere of 213 Squadron and Flying Officer Patrick Hughes of 238 Squadron. The Zerstörer pilots claimed to have shot down twelve Hurricanes. The actual losses were limited to three British fighters and four Bf 110s. However, the Zerstörer pilots managed to prevent their opponents from shooting down any of the Ju 88s – a task which was also facilitated by the the dense cloud cover. The latter, however, was not only a blessing for the bomber pilots; it also prevented them from locating their target – the airfields Boscombe Down and Worthy Down.

The second German formation – the Ju 87s and their Bf 109 escorts – was met by a single squadron, but this would prove to be quite enough. Due to radar observations, the Spitfires in Squadron Leader Horace Darley's 609 Squadron could head straight for this formation. Erhard Jähnert of II./StG 2 recalls what the scene looked like, 'They looked like a swarm of flies, but I knew it was something else. *"Achtung, Jäger!"* I shouted into the microphone. Three Spitfires took aim on the Kette where Maak flew. Their

The pilots from 609 Squadron are still wearing their so-called 'Mae West' life vests as they line up for a group photo after the successful combat against II./StG 2 and II./JG 53 on the afternoon of 13 August 1940.

machine guns were spitting fire and in the next moment all three Ju 87s went down, one of them flown by Maak. It was absolutely terrible! I couldn't believe my eyes. Maak's forebodings were confirmed! We formed a defensive circle, but it was of little help. One after another our aircraft went down in flames.' [134]

The fighter escort from II./JG 53 was not of much help, since it had to fight to defend itself against the Spitfire pilots who attacked from their superior altitude. 'We circled above them and Green 1 dived to attack', said Flying Officer Tadeusz Nowierski, a Polish volunteer in 609 Squadron. Pilot Officer Michael Appleby sent down two '109s, and Pilot Officer David Crook attacked and shot down a third. 'At that moment,' Nowierski continues his account, 'I saw one Me 109 above me and ahead. I climbed up behind him and fired three bursts at fairly close range and dead astern. White smoke appeared from his fuselage and he turned over and started to dive. Some large object, probably the cockpit door or roof flew away and the pilot got out and opened his parachute.' [135]

Without being able to claim more than one British fighter shot down, II./JG 53 lost four Bf 109s. The fact that I./JG 53 claimed to have shot down a Hurricane as well did not alter the situation. II./StG 2, which the Bf 109s were tasked to protect, met with disaster. The Spitfires concentrated their attack on 5./StG 2 at the rear of the German formation, and shot down six of its nine Ju 87 within ten minutes. One of three surviving pilots from 5./StG 2 gave this account: 'The enemy fighters came out of nowhere. The cockard-marked aircraft dive almost vertically against us and we make sharp evasive manoeuvres and close our formation even tighter in order to allow the radio operators/rear gunners to give more concentrated fire. They form a dense barrage, which the attackers must pass through. Amidst the cacophony of clattering machine guns, I suddenly hear a shrill cry: "Fighters below!" I turn around quickly and see Spitfires in a steep climb. And what is even worse: I see that my radio operator is badly wounded. His machine gun is hanging unattended. He clenches his teeth, trying to control himself. Through the internal communication, he informs me about each attacking Spitfire. And the attacks seem to never end . . . This time the Tommies are numerically superior. One after the other breaks through our barrage of machine gun bullets and fly straight into our formation. There a Stuka breaks out from our formation and disappears downwards. Large flames emerge from its hit tank. Shortly afterwards two parachutes blossom in the sky. Good luck, comrades!

'More automatically than consciously, I control the rudders and we begin the descent towards the airfield. The diving has a calming effect on us. We focus only on our target. From 4,000 metres' altitude our aircraft bolt at lightning speed towards the target. The Spitfires have no chance to follow suit. Only now do we discover that the anti-aircraft fire is not moderate at all, but this doesn't bother us now. We are caught by the strange magic of flying in a steep dive. Our bombs explode in a series of bright flashes. Thick smoke is rising from several hangars. Apparently a fuel storage has

A shot down Blenheim.
(Photo: Leykauf.)

also been hit. A later conducted reconnaissance flight mission confirms our assumptions.

'When we fly back at low altitude above the sea, our Staffel is positioned in the rear of the formation. And suddenly the planes with the peacock eyes under the wings are among us again! The British seem to be completely consumed by combat excitement. A Spitfire that manages to approach quite close to me despite all my evasive manoeuvres, recovers from the dive too late, hits the water surface and is torn to pieces. But several others soon have taken its place. Two Spitfires take turns to attack me. The pilots of both these planes seem to have realized that my radio operator is "neutralised". I try every trick in the book to get rid of my pursuers. Sharp turns is the only thing left available to me. As I perform these desperate turns, I involuntarily touch the water surface several times. For ten long minutes we are mercilessly chased and my aircraft becomes severely damaged. I also am hit, although I didn't notice that until much later, when my agitated state slackened a bit.

'Eventually our own fighters arrive and put an end to the wild fight. Despite the enemy's numerical superiority, some of our fighter pilots managed to fight their way out and rush to our aid. And the Spitfires, which by that time must have used up most of their ammunition, leave. Finally we can breathe!'[136]

The radio operator in the same Ju 87 gave his view: 'As is well known, the radio operator of a Stuka sits with his back against the pilot. He may indeed turn around and peek for-ward, but his main attention is directed to the rear. Consequently, he can't see much of what goes on in front of the propeller . . . It all started during the second phase of this attack on the coast of England. We had dropped our bombs and I had just received my first scratch, when suddenly the sky was full of fighters that pounced on us, firing their guns wildly. . . There – a Spitfire behind us! It just has to hit us. Despite my injuries I manage to pull myself together and blast away with my machine gun. What are the odds – my single machine gun against the enemy's eight! Soon his bullets start slamming into our cart. But none of the aircraft's vital parts appear to have been hit. A twin-engined fighter opens up against us, but his bullets pass far below us. When this last Englishman breaks off after his attack, he finds himself in the bullet trajectory of a Ju 87. I see the Bristol Blenheimen get hit. I see fire, and – hooray! – he plunges into the "creek" [Channel]!'

'But I soon forget my initial joy: there is a Hurricane behind our fin. In that position I am unable to shoot back – a problem that he absolutely doesn't seem to bemoan. Once again bullets slam into our plane, and suddenly I notice that our faithful old Jolanthe is descending. My pilot has been hit! A bullet has caused a scratch wound in his head. But to my great relief he soon regains control of the cart and we continue homewards. I had almost began to feel safe again, when a Spitfire re-appeared. This opponent is in no hurry, but calmly takes aim at us. Almost half consciousless I make desperate attempts to move the damaged gun carriage, but in vain. We are totally unarmed! At that moment the Englishman opens fire. He hits, and he hits me – over and over again! Blood drips from my hands and from my face, but the enemy shows no mercy and keeps sending his hailstorms of bullets against us. His bullets whip the wings of our aircraft. I hope the engine keeps running, I only hope the engine keeps running – that's all I think of. We've only got one! And indeed our engine keeps buzzing on! Finally the Spitfire breaks off and leaves for England.

'I tear up a first-aid bag and am about to care for my hands. Then I see blood seeping through my flight suit: four small holes are visible at the shoulder. But I can't feel anything. No – do not say that I've been hit there too! Trembling, I quickly tear down the flight suit and the shirt. And there I see the wounds. Two bullets have penetrated into my shoulder and two more have scratched me. I try to stop the blood flow, but to little avail. Soon I was covered in blood. "How much longer?" I ask my pilot. "Fifteen minutes!"

'Those are the longest fifteen minutes of my life. All the time I lose more blood. At last we reach our base. We turn and attempt to make a gentle landing. Yet the touchdown is quite violent. It is obvious that both tyres have been shot through. The plane spins around its axis a few times and then halts. I try to climb out, but find that I am unable to do so. I am too weak from loss of blood and my head is completely dizzy. One arm has been paralyzed and I can't push the cockpit hood back. After several failed attempts, it is torn loose. "Oh my God, what happened?" my comrades exclaim. Half conscious, I reply: "Why?"

'At the hospital I discover that I look like a clumsy butcher immediately after slaughter. As the blood washed away from my body, I can see my injuries. Two bullets have gone straight through the body, nine others have scratched me, and my face is completely cut by shattered glass.' [137]

The pilots of 609 Squadron returned in triumph to their base. They had scored 13 victories – including nine shot down Ju 87s – without any own losses other than a slightly damaged Spitfire.

While this took place, 11 Group was alerted by new incoming raids. JG 3, JG 26 'Schlageter ' and the Bf 110s of II./ ZG 76 'Haifischgruppe' flew ahead in order to clear the air of British fighters for the German bomb-carrying aircraft. Then followed Erprobungsgruppe 210 and II./StG 1 with the aim of delivering a combined attack against the air bases at Rochester and Rochford. I./ZG 26 was tasked to fly close escort. By that time, the clouds had grown thicker, and the cloud cover now reached an altitude of 3,000 metres.[138]

II./JG 26, now led by Hauptmann Karl Ebbighausen since its last Gruppenkommandeur had been killed on the unit's first combat flight across the Channel, lost contact with the other elements of JG 26. Instead, they were attacked by 65 Squadron, whose pilots subsequently reported the German pilots as 'apparently inexperienced; they made no attempts to evade our attacks.' [138]

Upon its return to base, 65 Squadron was given credit for a Bf 109 confirmed shot down, plus three unconfirmed, one 'probably' shot down and three damaged – without any own losses.[139] II./JG 26 reported one pilot lost, but there is no information on how many of its aircraft limped back

Pilot Officer David Crook's Spitfire, 'PR-L' of 609 Squadron, at Warmwell immediately after the combat on the afternoon of 13 August 1940. Just a few minutes before this photograph was taken, Crook had used this Spitfire to shoot down Unteroffizier Wilhelm Hohenfeld from 5./JG 53, who bailed out and was taken prisoner.

with battle damage. According to Don Caldwell who wrote the chronicle on JG 26, it was rumoured among the unit's pilots that a dozen Bf 109 from II./JG 26 'lost their orientation' among the clouds and crashed on the French coast.[140]

It is possible that II./JG 26 was stunted by a lack of experience in both the pilots' skill and tactical management. In fact, this Jagdgruppe at this time had no pilot listed for more than five victories. One of the officers in this unit told the author about quite bad relations between the unit's officers and those subalterns who happened to be more successful than their superiors.

In these respects, the Zerstörer units that were out on a free hunting mission at the same time were the opposite of II./JG 26. II./ZG 76 'Haifischgruppe' was undoubtedly one of the Luftwaffe's best fighter units. Near Rochford the Messerschmitt 110s with shark jaws painted on their noses bounced 56 Squadron's Hurricane pilots – who, judging by the description in the unit's war diary were so upset by the sudden fighter attack that they confused several Bf 110s with He 111s: 'the Squadron went to Rochford and while on patrol there they engaged 12 Heinkel 111s with escort of about 30 Me 110s near Rochford. In the combat F/O [Peter] Weaver, P/O [Fraser] Sutton and P/O [Maurice] Mounsdon destroyed a Me 110 and F/O Weaver och F/L [Edward] Gracie damaged another. P/O [Charles] Joubert, F/O [Peter] Davies and Sgt [Peter] Hillwood were all shot down and baled out, the former being slightly injured and F/O Davies fairly severely burnt. Sgt Hillwood was practically uninjured having delayed his jump from 12,000 to 6,000 feet and swimming 2½ miles to land. F/O [Robert] Brookers' machine was wrecked when he force-landed at Hawkinge.'[141]

For only the loss of a single Bf 110, the Messerschmitts managed to keep the British fighters away from the bomb-carrying aircraft. These, however, had trouble with the thick cloud cover. Erprobungsgruppe 210 did not find its target, dropped its bombs at random and returned to base. II./StG 1 failed to locate Rochford, but when a gap in the clouds showed the airfield of Detling near Maidstone on the other side of the Thames Estuary, the dive-bomber commander decided to attack that target. The Stukas could not have struck at a more fateful moment. In Britain it was a few minutes past five, and the air base messes were filled with hungry men in uniform. The heavy bombs rained down on the buildings, installations and parked aircraft. All hangars, three messes and the staff building were destroyed. 67 men were killed – including station commander, Group Captain Davis – and 22 aircraft were turned into burning wrecks. But Detling did not belong to Fighter Command, and the 40 bombs that fell there did not inflict any damage on Dowding's fighter force.

Eagle Day 13 August 1940 has gone down in history as a great British victory. But where aircraft losses are concerned, the ratio was not as uneven as it often is portrayed. The British fighter losses on this day are normally set at 13, which also is the figure given by the War Cabinet at its meeting on 14 August. But a review of the participating British fighter units' loss reports shows that the actual loss figure was three more aircraft. In addition, the raid against

Australian Clive Mayers was 30 years old when he flew as a pilot officer with 601 Squadron in the Battle of Britain. When he was killed in aerial combat in North Africa on 20 July 1942, he had been credited with 11 air victories. (Photo: Riddle via Ivers.)

Aalborg cost Bomber Command 12 planes, and 23 were destroyed on the ground. Including Bomber Command's 7 losses at night on 13 August, the RAF lost 58 aircraft in combat on Eagle Day. Moreover, 7 other British fighters barely made it to emergency landings after they had been shot down, and 9 others returned to base with serious damage.

The Luftwaffe's losses were certainly high, 42 aircraft, but they were in fact lower than the British. The German Air Force Commander Göring took the losses seriously, but he did not despair. As he saw things, his Air Force simply suffered from bad luck on 13 August.

When Göring studied the reports received from Eagle Day the next morning, he was not as unhappy as it is sometimes claimed. His fighter pilots had made optimistic claims for 42 shot down RAF fighters on 13 August – 32 by the Zerstörer (against 6 own losses) and 10 by the Bf 109 units (against 9 own losses), to which 15 Blenheims claimed by II./JG 77 during the British Aalborg raid should be added. 'These results, achieved under most difficult weather and operative conditions, are noteworthy', Oberst Werner Junck, Jafü 3, wrote in his report, and added: 'Such achievements have already contributed considerably to the defeat of the English fighter activity.'[142]

According to German intelligence, 311 British aircraft - most of them fighters – were supposed to have been shot down between 8 and 13 August, and over 50 aircraft were expected to have been destroyed on the ground. Göring's conclusion of the hard resistance the Luftwaffe had met on 13 August was that Dowding probably had taken some of his last units in the north to reinforce 10 and 11 Group in the south.

Actually, 13 August was one of the most important days during the Battle of Britain – but not in the way that the Germans had hoped. Although the RAF had taken heavy casualties, the British had in fact won one of their most significant victories so far during the war.

The Germans made a major overestimation of the damage inflicted upon the RAF. Above all they underestimated the miracle accomplished by Lord Beaverbrook with British aircraft production. Certainly Fighter Command had sustained a severe blow during the four main battle days, 8-13 August. 10 and 11 Group had lost the equivalent of more than a quarter of the number of serviceable Spitfires and Hurricanes that had been at hand at the beginning of the month. Fighter Command's numerical strength had decreased, but not nearly to the extent that the Germans thought. The serviceable Spitfires and Hurricanes in Fighter Command decreased from 627 on 8 August to 561 six days later, but as we shall see, it was still a viable force. Contrary to sacrificing the strength in the north for the needs in the south, Dowding actually moved units from the south to the north. 145 Squadron was transferred to 13 Group, while 238 Squadron was sent to an even quieter area further north.

Moreover, the fighter pilots and their commanders gained much valuable experience that they now could use to strike harder and with greater efficiency than ever against the enemy. Above all, the four main battle days proved that Fighter Command was able to strike hard against the Luftwaffe's boasted Messerschmitt fighters. When General Sir Frederick Pile, Commanding-in-Chief of the British Anti-Aircraft Command, met Dowding on the morning after Eagle Day, he found him 'more animated than he had ever known him'.

Bomber Command also made a valuable contribution. The British bombers always came in small groups. Mostly the attacks were of limited military value – such as the attack against Aalborg – but their psychological impact was greater, not least for the British population, which felt a grim satisfaction that Germany was also receiving its share of suffering. During the night of 13 August, Bomber Command extended its small-scale air offensive by dispatching 36 Whitley bombers from 4 Group all the way to Turin in northern Italy, where the Fiat aircraft plants were the target.

The next day the BBC triumphantly announced the outcome of the Eagle Day's battles such as the British perceived them: 78 German aircraft had been shot down against a loss of only 13 British fighters, of which 10 pilots survived.

Churchill's strategy consisted, as previously mentioned, in holding out until the United States realized that it was worth supporting the vulnerable little country. His steely determination and the pilots' dogged fighting spirits started to have results in this respect.

On 14 August 1940, US President Roosevelt decided to donate fifty destroyers to Britain in exchange for access to certain British bases, especially in the Caribbean Sea. This was mainly the result of the British pilots' indomitable struggle.

Churchill thought he could see the light at the end of the tunnel, but he knew that much hard fighting remained. The battle had just begun.

Walter Grabmann, the commander of ZG 76 (left) with Oberleutnant Helmut Müller, the commander of 14.(Z)/LG 1 (middle) and Hauptmann Horst Liensberger, the commander of V.(Z)/LG 1. (Photo: von Eimannsberger.)

CHAPTER 5
A STRUGGLE OF LIFE AND DEATH

14 August 1940

Major Adolf Galland and the young pilots in his III./JG 26 'Schlageter' were utterly convinced that the war would soon be over as they walked after lunch on 14 August towards their Messerschmitt 109s on the small airfield at Caffiers. The cloud cover which concealed the sky in the morning had started to break up and from a piece of blue sky the sun shone down on the parked Bf 109s.

'Hals und Beinbruch, Herr Major!' – Good luck – said the first mechanic, Unteroffizier Gerhard Meyer, who helped Galland up into the cockpit. 'Thank you, Meyer', Galland replied merrily. 'Let's see if I can bring anything home.' He was referring to the possibility that he might shoot down yet another enemy aircraft – which in that case would bring his total to 18.

This was before Galland would describe this period as 'a struggle of life and death'.

Shortly afterwards, Galland was at the front of his III. Gruppe high above the Channel. The entire JG 26 'Schlageter' and elements of JG 51 were out over the Channel, along with eighty Ju 87s from II./StG 1 and IV.(St)/LG 1. The latter were surrounded by thirty Bf 109s from II./JG 52, which flew as close escort. Oberleutnant Johannes Steinhoff, commanding 4./JG 52, was not as enthusiastic as Galland and his aviators. He remembered: 'Our mission was close escort. "Stay with the bombers at any price, do not pursue the Spitfires", read our directives: "do not be tempted to attack even if you are in an ideal position." This was just too much for us young and eager fighter pilots. We glided rather than flew alongside our protégés, who crept forward at what seemed to be walking pace.'[143]

It was an impressive mass of Luftwaffe planes. The target for the Stukas was the airfield at Lympne, but because of the overcast they were unable locate it and instead chose to strike Hawkinge and Dover. However, the Germans succeeded in attracting the attention of Fighter Command's air controllers. Park ordered the sector bases Biggin Hill, Kenley and Hornchurch to scramble their fighters. Forty-two of them – Hurricanes from 32 and 615 squadrons, and Spitfires from 65 to 610 squadrons – climbed to intercept the raiders.

The Stukas dived against Dover and the nearby airfield at Hawkinge while some of the Bf 109 pilots amused themselves by shooting barrage balloons on fire. Suddenly the British fighters appeared. 'The British had formed a reception committee and they came in right above us', said Steinhoff.

Guided by the air controller, the British fighters struck down like raptors on the Stukas with their close escort. Pilot Officer Smythe opened fire against a '109, which caught fire and plunged towards the sea. Oberfeldwebel Heinz

Weiss, one of the pilots of Steinhoff's 4./JG 52, fought desperately to pull up the descending plane. At less than a hundred metres' altitude he succeeded, and the Messerschmitt performed an emergency landing on the water. Meanwhile the pilots of 610 and 615 squadrons shot down one Ju 87 and badly damaged another.

One of the pilots in II./JG 52 opened fire on a Spitfire that attempted to attack a Ju 87, and saw the British plane leave with thick smoke billowing from the engine. Adolf Galland was on the same case. 'I picked out a Hurricane which "hung" in position behind a Ju 87', he said, 'and soon I had him in my gunsight. Usually I opened fire only at close range, when the enemy was so close that it filled the entire windscreen in my plane, but this time I had to open fire at a large distance for fear that he might hit the Ju 87 first. When the Englishman saw my tracer, he broke off and took up the nose of his plane. In that moment, I hit him. I couldn't see the impact, because I myself was attacked by

An apparently satisfied Adolf Galland is helped to take off his life vest following a mission over the English Channel. He wears the typical so-called 'Channel trousers' and boots fitted with flare cartridges for the Mauser flare pistol. (Photo: Caldwell.)

Ground personnel at Warmwell airbase posing in front of Spitfire 'PR-H', N3024, belonging to 609 Squadron. On 14 August 1940, Flying Officer Henry MacDonald Goodwin was shot down in this Spitfire. A few days later, his body washed ashore on the English south coast. (Photo: Goss.)

a Hurricane and had to take evasive action. Müncheberg took care of my pursuer.' [144]

When Oberleutnant Joachim Müncheberg sent a Hurricane burning towards the Channel's grey waves, this young pilot in Galland's Stabsschwarm had scored his 12th victory. The 21-year-old Müncheberg served as adjutant in III./JG 26 and was one of Galland's favourites. He came to develop into one of the Luftwaffe's most prominent fighter pilots, and felt that this was largely due to what he had learned from Galland during the first period at the English Channel.

At 13:14 the Bf 109s of Hauptmann Hannes Trautloft's III./JG 51 took off from St. Omer.[145] They set off on a free hunting mission across the county of Kent. Northwest of Dover, the Germans spotted a formation of Hurricanes heading inland. This was 32 Squadron, which was returning home after the combat over the Channel. Walter Oesau, recently promoted to Hauptmann, brought his 7./JG 51 into the attack. Less than a minute later a Hurricane fell to the ground, marking Oesau's 14th kill. Pilot Officer Rupert Smythe managed to crash-land his bullet-riddled Hurricane and escaped with no more than a few bruises. Two more Hurricanes from 32 Squadron made emergency-landings with combat damage.

This was only a German diversion. Escorted by I./JG 52, the Bf 110 assault planes from Erprobungsgruppe 210 came buzzing just above the waves, passed the cliffs of Dover and shortly afterwards dived down on the airfield at Manston. The British had had no time to bring any air-

borne fighters to Manston, but the defence was warned by the air surveillance posts at Dover. The anti-aircraft gunners waited with their gun barrels in position. There were men from the Royal Artillery with 40mm Bofors cannons and personnel from 600 Squadron manning anti-aircraft machine guns. They met the Messerschmitts, which came racing from the south, with a hailstorm of fire. Everything happened with incredible speed. The bombs fell over the air base's facilities, and then the '110s came back to spray the airfield with their machine guns. Four hangars were blown out by the bombs, three Blenheims caught fire on the ground and the runway was littered with bomb craters. But one of the Bf 110s had been hit. It climbed, trailing black smoke. One crew member bailed out and unfurled his parachute just before he hit the ground at a dangerously high speed. It proved to be the radio operator, Gefreiter Ewald Schank, and he was seriously injured by the heavy impact. The pilot, who remained in the burning plane, failed to keep his Messerschmitt upright. It turned over one wing, descended – and crashed into another '110 passing underneath. Both planes dissolved in a cloud of flaming gasoline.

When both sides withdrew to either lick their wounds or celebrate their successes, a few hours of tranquility ensued. At Manston's air base the injured and dazed Gefreiter Schank was interrogated. 'Big things are about to happen soon, very soon', he told the British.

Later in the afternoon it was time again. Perhaps as a compensation for the close escort at midday, II./JG 52 was sent out on a fighter sweep over the county of Kent. But this was not II./JG 52's lucky day. In the vicinity of Canterbury, the unit was attacked by Hurricanes of 151 Squadron. Although the British fought from a numerical disadvantage, Squadron Leader John Gordon and Sub-Lieutenant Henry Beggs (a pilot on commission from Fleet Air Arm) managed to knock down two Bf 109s without own losses. One of the two pilots lost by II./JG 52 in that engagement belonged to Steinhoff's 4. Staffel. Heinz Weiss, who had been shot down during the earlier mission that day was never seen again. A few days later, his body washed ashore on a beach at Joss Bay in England.

To keep defenders on tenterhooks while the next day's major air operation was being prepared, the Germans took advantage of cloudy weather to dispatch a stream of bombers in small groups for nuisance raids during the rest of 14 August. Shortly after five in the afternoon (British time) several small bomber groups from Luftflotte 3 struck simultaneously against 10 Group's airfield at MiddleWallop, the airfield at Andover, 10 km further to the northeast, the port of Southampton, 30 km southwest of Middle Wallop, and Portland, 60 km further to the west along the coast. Only minor damage was caused at Andover and Portland, but in Southampton the main railway line was blocked. The greatest damage however was caused through a combined attack against Middle Wallop, although it cost the Germans dearly.

A single Ju 88 piloted by Oberleutnant Wilhelm Henrici of I./LG 1 was supposed to initiate the raid on Middle Wallop, carrying out a surprise dive-attack from out of the clouds above, thus drawing the attention of the anti-aircraft guns, while three He 111s of KG 55's Geschwader Stabskette would come in to perform a level attack.

The German tactic did indeed succeed in catching the British unawares. Henrici's Ju 88 dropped out of the clouds and scored a direct hit on Hangar No. 5 with his bombs. 609 Squadron's American volunteer, Pilot Officer Eugene Tobin had arrived at Middle Wallop six days earlier. He had not yet flown any combat mission, and now he had a grim introduction into the realities of war. He was knocked to the ground by the bomb blast, and when he came back to his senses he saw what he afterwards described as 'a carnage . . . I saw one overalled person with his foot and half a leg blown off, another had a great red patch on his chest with a load of mess hanging from it, another was rolling in agony with one of his arms missing. The door of the hangar was only half closed and inside I could see the bodies of four overalled men on the ground with one seemingly splattered against the edge of the door.' [146]

But one Spitfire, flown by 609's Sergeant Alan Feary was airborne even before Henrici struck. He now caught sight of Oberleutnant Henrici's Ju 88 as it climbed towards the clouds. Feary already had four German planes to his account, and now he got the pale blue belly of the Junkers 88 into his gun sight. He delivered a long burst, raking the bomber with bullets from nose to tail. Badly damaged, the twin-engined Junkers disappeared into the low clouds, but twenty kilometres further to the southwest, Oberleutnant Henrici had to take it down in a belly landing. This failed; the Ju 88 exploded on impact on the heath southeast of North Charford, killing all the crew

members except the observer, Gefreiter Eugen Sauer, who was captured.

Meanwhile several Spitfires had taken off through the smoke and dust created by the exploding bombs. They now fell upon the three He 111s of KG 55's Geschwader Stabskette. The leading Heinkel was commanded by the unit commander, Oberst Alois Stoeckl. He was a former combat pilot from the First World War and an old-time Nazi who had participated in the Beer Hall Putsch in 1923. He had flown in Spain, and had been awarded with the Knight's Cross for his feats during the Battle of France. The pilot was Oberleutnant Bruno Brossler, also a highly seasoned pilot who served as KG 55's navigation officer. Also on board the airplane on this mission was Oberst Walter Frank, the Chief of Staff of Fliegerkorps V, who had demanded to fly with Stoeckl to experience one combat mission over England.

Feary's two squadron mates, Flight Lieutenant David Crook and Flying Officer John Dundas, overtook Stoeckl's and Brossler's G1+AA as it fled southwestwards after dropping its bombs, and promptly shot it down. The He 111 crashed into a Royal Navy ammunitions dump at Dean Hill, which exploded. By a miracle, two men survived, albeit badly wounded, and ended up in British captivity. But the Geschwaderkommodore Oberst Stoeckl, the pilot and Oberst Frank were found dead among the wreckage.

This was a heavy blow against KG 55 and Fliegerkorps V. The fact that another He 111 managed to ward off the fighter interception by shooting down an intercepting Spitfire was poor consolation. [147] (The pilot, 609 Squadron's Flying Officer Henry MacDonald Goodwin, was killed.) The loss of Stoeckl –who was an old friend of Göring – and Oberst Frank and Brossler prompted an enraged Luftwaffe commander to issue an order that no more than one officer was allowed to fly in an aircraft, and that Geschwaderkommodores could not take part in such bad-weather operations with single bombers or small groups.

While LG 1 and KG 55 attacked Middle Wallop, eighteen He 111 crews from I./KG 27 fared better in their missions against the airfields at Little Rissington, Hullavington, Upavon, Netheravon, Boscombe Down, and Minchinhampton. Only one of these Heinkel bombers met any fighter interception, and escaped with minor damages. But III./KG 27, which sent out twenty-five crews against the airfields at Yeovil, Blandford Forum, Filton and Sealand, faced heavier opposition.

A Kette of three He 111s from 9./KG 27, heading for the airfield at Chester, had the misfortune of running into three Spitfires from No. 92 Squadron over the Bristol Channel. Led by Flight Lieutenant Robert Stanford Tuck, these had taken off from Pembrey in southwestern Wales at 17.15. [148]

Tuck was one of the most successful aces in the RAF. He had shot down nine Germans during the Battle of France, but found the patrol flights in this 'quiet' corner of the UK quite frustrating. His excitement rose as the fighter controller now directed them towards the incoming enemy.

'Jäger!' – Fighters! - the cry shrilled over the intercom in the Heinkels. Crippled by the bursts from Sergeant Havercroft's Spitfire, which was first to attack in a steep

This wartime ad from Armstrong Whitworth Aircraft Ltd. expresses the importance of RAF Bomber Command for British morale. The twin-engined Whitley bomber (named after the Coventry suburb where this aircraft was manufactured) entered service in 1937. Whitley was Bomber Command's heaviest bomber when the Second World War broke out. The machine could reach targets all over Germany. When Whitley was taken out of service in 1942 and replaced by more modern four-engined bombers, it had conducted close to 9,000 combat sorties and dropped almost 10,000 tonnes of bombs, in the course of which 269 aircraft were lost.

dive from above, Hauptmann Josef Riedl's He 111 plummeted vertically into the Bristol Channel. The crew had no chance of escaping.

But then the Heinkel gunners were ready and managed to ward off the next fighter attacks. After several failed attempts from astern and from the sides, Tuck squeaked through. Together with Havercroft, he made a daring head-on attack against the tight bomber formation. By the time the two formations had passed each other, one aircraft from each side went down. While Ralph Havercroft - swearing in the radio 'like a drunken trooper', according to Tuck – nursed his damaged Spitfire down to a smooth engineless forced-landing in Wales, Oberleutnant Ernst Oehlenschläger turned his crippled He 111 to the south. But the fact that his gunner, Unteroffizier Kurt Kupsch, had shot down a Spitfire, was of little help. After 20 kilometres, Oehlenschläger had to take the bomber down in a forced landing. The whole crew was captured.

Meanwhile the two remaining Spitfire pilots made a new head-on attack on the last Heinkel, and managed to shoot down this too. The crew bailed out and was captured.

In historiography, 14 August 1940 is counted as one of the quietest days during the Battle of Britain. But for the men of 9./KG 27 it was the worst day during the entire battle, just as this day symbolizes the fight of life and death during the Battle of Britain for the pilots of 4./JG 52. They had only been in combat at the Channel for three days, and six of their number – half the unit – had already been lost. 'Our morale was low', said Johannes Steinhoff. In consequence, a few days later II./JG 52 was taken out of front line service and transferred to Jever at the German Bight. Thereby the unit followed the wing's third Gruppe, which was relocated to Berlin-Zerbst on 1 August to lick their wounds.[149] Thus, Fighter Command had in a short time inflicted JG 52 quite serious losses – 14 pilots. (That this fighter wing during the course of the following years would evolve into the war's most successful fighter unit, no one could have guessed at that point.)

At Middle Wallop 14 August 1940 was definitely remembered as the hardest day of the Battle of Britain. The air fighting on 14 August cost RAF Fighter Command a loss of eight aircraft, from which only three pilots could be saved.[150]

While these battles took place, Sperrle, Kesselring and Loerzer were in Karinhall east of Berlin, where they had been summoned to discuss the next major assault against the British Isles. Since meteorologists had predicted cloudy weather, a few quiet days were expected. Before they departed for their meeting with Göring, they had instructed their units to carry out the kind of nuisance raids as we have just seen, and they did not pay much heed to the reports from the so-called 'Channel Front' that arrived on the evening of the 14th.

The Reichsmarschall was particularly concerned about the proven vulnerability of the Ju 87s. Therefore he demanded a reinforced escort of Stukas: From now on, each Stukagruppe would be provided with an escort of three fighter Gruppen: one that flew out overthe target zone in advance to draw the British fighters into combat, one that would fly along with these Stukas when these attacked, and one as top cover.[151]

Göring also realized that the organised resistance met by his his airmen on 13 August was a result of the British having been able to repair their bombed radar stations in a short time. He asked himself if it really was profitable to continue attacking the radar stations. Historian Alfred Price agrees. He wrote: 'Some commentators have suggested that had the Luftwaffe continued its attack on the radar stations along the south coast of England, these vital installations could have been knocked out and Fighter Command deprived of the early warning necessary for its squadrons to go into action effectively. But the radar stations were small pinpoint targets and, as we have seen, they were extremely difficult to hit from the air. Damage to the radar stations could usually be repaired quickly, and where it could not, Fighter Command possessed mobile reserve equipments that could plug the gaps in the radar cover. Although several radar stations were attacked and damaged, only one (at Ventnor) remained out of action for more than a few hours.'[152]

The RAF's nightly bombing raids also were the subject of discussion at the conference in Karinhall. Although these were of relatively limited extent, they had a psychological effect – on both the British and the Germans. 'Each night', complained the war diary of 9. / JG 54, based at the airfield Guines in the Pas de Calais area, 'we are visited by English bombers, and each night the German anti-aircraft artillery opens fire and produces a terrible noise while the searchlight turn night into day. But never ever are they able to shoot down even a single British aircraft!'[153]

Although the raid against Aalborg on 13 August was averted, it showed the British determination to fight back. The bombing of Turin the following night suggested an extension of Bomber Command's operations. The message to the Italian dictator Mussolini was clear: Hitler has failed to neutralise the RAF! Therefore, Göring decided that when Luftflotte 5 was dispatched to test the strength of Fighter Command's 13 Group in the north, the attack targets would be the airfields in northern and central England, from where Bomber Command's 4 Group carried out the raid against Italy. A new attack with nine Whitleys against the Caproni aviation works on the night of 14 August served to reinforce Göring's determination on the issue. The next day, 15 August, his Luftwaffe would make its strongest effort so far to neutralise the RAF.

15 August 1940

Göring and his senior officers stayed up late into the wee hours of 15 August. Meanwhile, the weather across the British Isles improved – contrary to what it looked like the day before. Soon the sky was almost cloudless and the wind had dropped to barely one metre per second. Weather reconnaissance flights reported the same fine weather from central France to the British west coast. It was ideal weather for large air operations!

But by that time, Göring and his commanders were unreachable. Göring had given strict orders to the members of his staff that under no condition must he be disturbed. When the meeting was finished and the men withdrew for rest, this order had not been changed.

The detailed – but postponed – instructions for the major onslaught lay on the tables in the headquarters of the air fleets. They clearly stated: Fliegerkorps II shall initiate the attack – its two Stukagruppen's first targets are the airfields at Hawkinge and Lympne. These were the furthest forward British fighter airfields, located only a few miles from the south coast near Folkestone. Now if only the air corps commander, General Loerzer, had been in place at his headquarters in Ghent, he would have been able to submit the take-off orders to his units.

But the main assault still came to fruition. The man who put the whole thing in motion was Oberst Paul Diechmann, Loerzer's chief of staff and a highly capable officer. At noon on 15 August, he lost patience and gave the attack order of his own accord – to Hauptmann Bernd von Brauchitsch and his IV.(St)/LG 1, to Hauptmann Keil and his II./StG 1. Then Diechmann went to Kesselring's command post and met with his IA (operations officer), Major Herbert Rieckhoff.

Rieckhoff was dismayed when he heard of the liberties taken by his colleague. Upset, he called Karinhall, but when he got through all he learnt was that Göring had ordered that the meeting was not to be disturbed under any circumstances. Stunned, the major put down the receiver. Immediately afterwards the air above was filled with a deafening roar. Hauptmann von Brauchitsch's 25 Junkers 87s flew past on their way out over the Channel – towards the RAF base at Hawkinge. Paul Diechmann glanced at the duty-conscious major. A few minutes later the Messerschmitt units under Jafü 2 also received their take-off orders. A chain reaction started, and soon the whole operation was rolling. At 12:20 Major Mölders took to the air in order to lead his entire JG 51 on a fighter sweep over the target area.[154]

On the British side the Germans again were spotted by radar even before they crossed the French coast. The alarm went off at sector bases Kenley and Biggin Hill. The commander at Kenley, Wing Commander Tom Prickman, sent up six Hurricanes from 615 Squadron. The commander at Biggin Hill, Wing Commander Grice, had several units to choose from. He ordered up 610 Squadron from Biggin Hill. Then he called two coastal airfields – Manston, where 54 Squadron took off with twelve Spitfires, and Hawkinge, where 501 Squadron was scrambled. First up was the latter squadron, whose twelve Hurricanes left the ground at 11:08 (British time).[155] They were the vanguard of a total of more than forty British fighters.

The order was: 'Patrol behind Dover'. The British pilots climbed as fast as they could, but were still at a too low altitude when they saw von Brauchitsch's 25 Stukas marching forward in neat three-plane groups. Higher up the sky seemed to be full of Messerschmitts, and this time they came from all directions. The British fighter pilots immediately turned towards the Ju 87s in the hope of shooting down as many Stukas as possible before the whole horde of Messerschmitts descended. 501 Squadron's Sergeant Paul Farnes, who had knocked down a Ju 87 three days earlier, flew right into the mass of Junkers planes. The first one he

A so-called 'Kette' – three-plane formation – of Ju 87 Stukas.

aimed at dropped like a stone, and he quickly turned to attack another, which he destroyed with a long burst of fire. Hauptmann Münchenhagen's Ju 87 descended vertically until it struck the water. The pilot escaped by bailing out and was captured, but the rear gunner followed the plane in its last dive.

Flight Lieutenant John Gibson, one of the most experienced pilots of 501 Squadron, managed to score a number of decisive hits on a Ju 87 before he was attacked by a whole bunch of Messerschmitts. These were from 5./JG 51, whose Staffelkapitän, Hauptmann Horst Tietzen, claimed to have shot down two Hurricanes in this engagement. However, Gibson engaged the Messerschmitts and sent one of them burning to the ground. Feldwebel Otto Steigenberger of 5./JG 51 accompanied his burning Messerschmitt to the impact in the sea. This was Gibson's fifth victory, and he turned towards the Ju 87s again. But a burst of fire from a Stuka's rear machine gun hit his Hurricane so badly that it immediately caught fire. When Gibson looked down, he saw that he was right above Folkestone. So instead of immediately abandoning his plane and risking it falling down among the buildings, he steered it away from the town area and was down at 300 metres altitude before he took to the parachute.

No. 87 Squadron's Flight Lieutenant Ian 'Widge' Gleed in the cockpit of his Hurricane. On 15 August 1940, Gleed added two victories to the three individual and three shared victories that he had scored during the Battle of France. Gleed attained a total of 16 air victories before he on 16 April 1943 was shot down and killed by German fighter ace Ernst Wilhelm Reinert. (Photo: Goss.)

In a combat of this magnitude and intensity, it was quite natural that both sides misjudged the results. The Germans reported eight British fighters shot down – twice as many as the actual losses. IV.(St)/LG 1 lost only two Ju 87s.[156]

Owing to their large numbers, the Messerschmitts finally managed to rid the Ju 87s of the fighter attacks. This was the result of Göring's new directive on Stukas escort. 'It was an impressive yet frustrating sight as the dive bombers, in perfect echelon formation, swept towards the airfield and peeled off to attack', recollected one of Spitfire pilots who in vain attempted to break through the Bf 109 screen around the Ju 87s.[157]

Several Bf 109s followed the Stuka planes as these dived – quite a difficult manoeuvre since the Bf 109, unlike the Ju 87, lacked dive breaks; consequently the '109s reached speeds of up to 750 km/h in a diving, and overtook the Junkers planes which 'only' dived at 450 km/h.[158]

Hawkinge was badly damaged. A direct hit from a 500-kilo bomb completely destroyed one of the hangars. Other bombs caused damage to the barracks and runways, and cut the cables that supplied the radar stations in Dover, Foreness and Rye with electricity.

Hauptmann Anton Keil's II./StG 1, which owing to the protective screen of the Bf 109s was largely saved from British fighter attacks, managed even better: its 26 Stukas struck Lympne's facilities with such devastating effect that it took two days of intensive repair work before the airfield could be brought into action again. Fortunately for the British, there had been no any aircraft at the aifield when the Germans attacked.

At Biggin Hill, sector commander Wing Commander Richard Grice had barely been notified of the two attacks on Hawkinge and Lympne when a message came in from the ill-fated coastal base at Manston: low-level attacks with machine gun fire and bombings by Me 110s. Two Spitfires destroyed.

Meanwhile, things began to happen up in the northeast. From 13 Group's radar station in Anstruther, more and more detailed reports of a large German approach over the North Sea began to come in.

Generaloberst Stumpff had launched his Luftflotte 5. Neither he nor his pilots expected to meet any serious resistance from the supposedly weak 13 Group.

From the Norwegian Stavanger Sola base came 72 He 111s of KG 26, each with 1,500 kilos of bombs intended for the airfields at Dishforth and Usworth. The Heinkel bombers were accompanied by I./ZG 76 with 21 Bf 110 Ds, each with a 1,050-litre auxiliary tank of wood under the belly. Immediately after the Heinkel bombers' attack, 50 Ju 88s from KG 30, based at Aalborg, Denmark, would strike at the air bases Church Fenton and Leconfield further south on the English east coast.

But 12 and 13 Group were now far from being as weak as the Germans believed – which Stumpff and, not least, his flying personnel would learn in a most painful way.

A Bf 110 from I./ZG 76 with the large 1,050-litre auxiliary tank – the so-called 'Dackelbauch' (dachshund belly) – under the belly. (Photo: Vasco.)

That said, 13 Group's radar operators lacked the experience of their colleagues in southern England, interpreting the echo from over 90 Heinkels and Messerschmitts as nothing more than 'plus 30 bandits'. Hence, 13 Group decided to dispatch no more than one squadron, No. 72.

Flight Lieutenant Edward Graham found himself at the head of eleven Spitfires from 72 Squadron at 5,500 metres altitude out over the North Sea, searching for some thirty Germans, when he suddenly saw not 30 – but almost 100!

Graham took his formation in a wide half circle to a position in the sun. Then they dived down against the Zerstörer planes. Due to a technical error, the German Zerstörer pilots were not able to drop their giant auxiliary tanks – the so-called 'Dackelbauch' ('dachshund bellies'). The result was a disaster. Not only did the bulky tanks make the Messerschmitts slow and cumbersome, turning them into flying targets for the fast Spitfires, but also by the time the British attacked, the Bf 110 pilots had used up much of the fuel in the auxiliary tanks, which thus held large amounts of gasoline vapours that would explode if a single bullet struck and caused a spark.

Flying Officer Desmond Sheen from 72 Squadron describes what followed: 'I attacked a formation of what I thought were Ju 88s with bombs underneath. I went for the leader when they went into a defensive circle and the Me110 (which it was, with a fuel tank, not a bomb underneath) blew up. I flew through the bits and pieces and after pulling up attacked another Me110, which was diving

down at me. I opened fire head on and he just missed me, passing overhead with the port engine on fire.' [159]

During the first attack two Bf 110s were hit in their auxiliary tanks and exploded. With one of them, the commander of I./ZG 76, Hauptmann Werner Restemeyer, was killed. Then the Spitfires proceeded towards the He 111s, which fled into the thick clouds. Rudi Schmidt, who served as an Oberleutnant in KG 26, said: 'For obvious reasons our formation dissolved in the clouds, and we had great trouble in finding each other when we finally came out of the clouds. The closer we got to the coast, the more spread out between the clouds we became.' From Catterick, Acklington and Drem – from the north, the south and the west – British fighters – Spitfires and Hurricanse from 41, 79 and 605 squadrons – came racing. A total of 42 Spitfires and Hurricanes took off to join the slaughter of KG 26 and I./ZG 76. Rudi Schmidt continues his description: 'When we passed the coast we could see the target. By then our unit had formed a tight formation and attacked. All the time we were attacked by Spitfires. They came from below and from above, and during each attack they tried to shoot down one of us. Our defensive fire was not of much use when these "bees" fell upon us, firing wildly. Before we had time to take aim, they were gone. Our Zerstörers fought hard to protect the bomber formation, but not even they could accomplish much against the large amount of British fighters.' [160]

When the combat was over, seven He 111s and just as many Zerstörers had been downed. It was a great victory

Spitfires from 616 Squadron, which claimed eight victories in the battle against KG 30 on 15 August 1940. During the Battle of Britain 616 Squadron was credited with 28 air victories against 14 own losses.

for the defenders, particularly since the participating RAF fighter units did not lose more than one of their own fighters, with another three damaged.

KG 30's operation, carried out shortly afterwards, met with greater success than that of KG 26. Without any escort, the 50 Ju 88s crossed the coast at Flamborough Head, utilizing the cloud cover as protection against 18 intercepting British fighters. The dive-bombing of 4 Groups' large base at Driffield was absolutely devastating: four hangars and nine Whitleys were knocked out in the space of a few minutes. But this still could not offset the price paid by the raiders. Nos. 73 and 616 squadrons attacked the Ju 88s, and managed to shoot down down six Junkers and damage two so badly that these were forced to emergency-land in Denmark and the Netherlands. The British pilots returned to base in a jubilant mood, claiming to have knocked down fifteen Ju 88s, while all the Ju 88s had managed to achieve with their defensive fire was to hit one of the British fighters with a total of two machine gun bullets! [161]

While Generaloberst Stumpff's badly mauled units fled back across the North Sea, Luftflotte 2's hitherto largest operation began. The Do 17 bombers from Oberst Johannes Fink's KG 2 'Holzhammer' and Oberst Wolfgang von Chamier-Glisczinski's KG 3 'Blitz' ('lightning') were dispatched at full strength against the airfields of Hornchurch, Gravesend, Eastchurch and Rochester, and the Short aircraft works in Rochester. It was a very ambitious operation, and it was supported by a fighter sweep over the target area by JG 3 and JG 26 'Schlageter' as well as a di-

versionary raid on the airfield at Martlesham Heath near Ipswich, far northeast of the Thames Estuary. Additionally, 130 Bf 109s from JG 51, JG 52 and JG 54 were assigned as direct escort to the bombers. After the main raid – when the exhausted British fighter pilots landed to refuel and replenish ammo – small groups of Heinkel and Dornier bombers were supposed to attack the radar stations in Dover, Rye and Foreness, and to disrupt the repair work at the Hawkinge base.

Hauptmann Walter Rubensdörffer's Erprobungsgruppe 210 flashed past the English south-east coast, heading north with sixteen Bf 110s and nine Bf 109s, escorted by II./JG 51 and Major Schalk's III./ZG 26. But in Foreness, the radar screens were black; the radar station was still unusable since Hauptmann von Brauchitsch's Stukas had cut the power from Hawkinge.

The personnel at Martlesham were completely surprised by the sudden attack, and Rubensdörffer's pilots conducted the raid with their usual speed and precision. The thirty bombs that were dropped littered the runways with deep craters and destroyed two hangars, several workshops and an airplane, and all telephone lines were cut off. Thus, one more of Fighter Command's bases was out of action for at least two days. The Hurricanes of Nos. 1, 17 and 32 squadrons which were deployed against the invaders found themselves attacked from above by the escort fighters. Five Hurricanes were shot down and a sixth had to make an an emergency landing, with the Germans losing only a single aircraft, a Bf 109 from II./JG 51.

In the meantime, however, Park managed to thwart the German plans on a powerful fighter sweep over the target area through repeated attacks against the Bf 109s of JG 26. Major Galland's III./JG 26 was attacked by twelve Spitfires from 64 Squadron and shot down three of them – with Galland claiming his 20th and 21st victories, bringing his total for the day to three. But soon the pilots of JG 26 had used up their ammunition and had to cancel the mission.

This coincided with the Do 17 bombers of KG 2 flying out over the Strait of Dover on the way towards England. These were the airmen who had seen so many of their comrades get shot down during the disastrous operation on the morning of Eagle Day two days earlier, and when they saw a whole gaggle of Bf 109s return to France, their spirits dropped. Shortly afterwards they saw what was even worse – several British fighters heading towards the bombers. Oberst Fink must have had a sense of deja-vu and immediately gave orders to cancel the operation against Hornchurch, Eastchurch and Gravesend. KG 2's airmen hastily dropped their bombs over the 'reserve target' Dover, and quickly turned back to France. Fink would not expose his unit to a repetition of the massacre of Eagle Day!

The men in the Do 17 planes of the neighbouring unit KG 3 were startled to meet the entire KG 2 heading for home. It is quite possible that the fighters that the frightened airmen of KG 2 believed to be RAF planes, were actually Bf 109s. In fact, the powerful array of Messerschmitt fighters managed to keep most British fighters away from the bombers. Park had scrambled eight squadrons, but half of them had already been spent in combat with III./ZG 26, JG 26 and JG 51, and the four squadrons that remained

Apparently quite relaxed, Oberleutnant Hans-Ekkehard Bob of 9./JG 54 prepares for a combat flight over England. In late 1940, Bob had amassed 19 aerial victories, and in March 1941 he was awarded with the Knight's Cross. When the war ended, Bob had increased his tally to 60 air victories. Hans-Ekkehard Bob, who gave an invaluable contribution in the form of interviews, photos and first-hand material to this book, passed away on 12 August 2013, at the age of 96. Bob continued to fly throughout his life and by the time of his death he was Germany's oldest active pilot. (Photo by Bob.)

made their attacks piecemeal and were unable to do much harm. A Do 17 pilot recalled: 'Just before we reached the target I witnessed a dogfight between one of our Zerstörer and three British fighters. Suddenly the three "brothers" attacked us, leaving the Zerstörer. A short but intense combat broke out between our Do 17, an Me 110 and three Spitfires. But luckily the British lost. Two of them fell in flames and the third one peeled off, with the Zerstörer on its heels. That was the last I saw of them.' [162]

Near Faversham the Do 17 formations split into two groups. While Stab, I. and II./KG 3 continued towards Rochester, III. Gruppe turned to the northeast and dropped its bombs against the air base at Eastchurch on the island of Sheppey in the Thames Estuary. A few minutes later bombs began to rain down over Rochester's airport as well. Leading the three Do 17s of his Stabskette, Hauptmann Otto Pilger, II./KG 3's commander, conducted a low-level attack against the Short Brothers' factory facilities at one end of the airfield, and caused such widespread devastation there that the entire aircraft plant was put out of action for a long time to come. As a result, the production of the new four-engined Stirling bomber – the latest British bomber – was paralyzed for more than three months.[163] Only in January 1941 were the British able to commence operations with their most modern bomber, which had the capacity to carry just over six tonnes of bombs – more than twice as much as the Whitley.

The price for all of this was relatively low – three Do 17s shot down. A fourth – with the commanders of I./KG 3, Oberstleutnant Carl Freiherr von Wechmar, and 2./KG 3, Oberleutnant Otto Köhnke, aboard – was badly damaged but made it back to France, where, however, it had to be written off.

When KG 3 landed at their bases the defence was in a serious situation, at least in 11 Group's sector. Since noon, six air bases and a large aircraft plant had been either severely damaged or completely eliminated. Moreover, three radar stations had their power supplies cut. The price paid by Luftflotte 2 for all of this was limited to four Do 17s, two Ju 87s, and three Bf 109s.

According to the German plans, Luftflotte 3 would deliver the next big blow – against four British airfields – immediately afterwards. I. and II./LG 1 were tasked to attack Andover and Worthy Down, while Warmwell was to be targeted by I./StG 1 and Yeovil by II./StG 2. However, the 27 Ju 88s from LG 1 that were supposed to initiate this operation failed to take off until at a quarter to five in the afternoon. Then it took additional time to form up in combat formations before they could start flying out over the Channel, where they joined up with their close escort, sixteen Bf 110s from Hauptmann Erich Groth's II./ZG 76 'Haifischgruppe'. Shortly afterwards, 47 Ju 87s from I./StG 1 and II./StG 2 took off from Lannion, further to the west. These were escorted by 60 Bf 109s from JG 27 and JG 53 and 40 Bf 110s from III./ZG 76 and V.(Z)/LG 1. While III./

When Erprobungsgruppe 210 struck against Martlesham Heath on 15 August, Nos. 17 and 25 squadrons were located at the air base. The image shows a pair of 25 Squadron Blenheim Mk IF night fighters. The aircraft closest to the camera is equipped with AI Mk III radar.

ZG 76 flew close escort, V.(Z)/LG 1 was detached for free hunting.

In fact, the British had learned of this German operation through Ultra decrypts on the previous day, and Fighter Command ordered nine squadrons into the air. A new large air battle developed. Pilot Officer Eric Marrs from 152 Squadron gave the following account of the combat: 'I was nearly head-on to them and opening fire at a fairly long range. I plastered a Vee of three '87s but did not manage to put the coup-de-grace to any of them. I nipped under them at the last minute and went down in a dive. I then met up with another '110. I couldn't help it, there were so many of them. We circled around each other for a bit in tightening circles, each trying to get on the other's tail, but my attention was soon drawn by another '110. Down underneath him I went and pulled up

Three Bf 110s from Erprobungsgruppe 210. The aircraft in the middle, 'S9+CK', was flown by Oberleutnant Alfred Habisch with Unteroffizier Ernst Elfner as radio operator. They were shot down and captured on 15 August 1940. (Photo: Vasco.)

Heinz Nacke was among the most successful pilots of II./ZG 76 'Haifischgruppe'. He was a veteran of the Spanish Civil War and on 2 November 1940 he was awarded with the Knight's Cross for 12 victories. Nacke passed away on 16 September 1984, at the age of 74.

giving him a long burst into the belly. Nothing seemed to happen. I was then occupied by yet another '110. I milled around with him for a bit, but when I wanted to get in a shot, I found I had run out of ammunition. I rolled on my back and pulled out of the melee and went home. I had unfortunately shot down nothing but as I came home I saw a Hurricane. Reinforcements had come up and were having their turn at the enemy.'[164]

The Stukas managed to get through, but over the target area they were met by more British fighters. 'Luckily we had the Me 110s as fighter escort', remembered Feldwebel Erhard Jähnert from II./StG 2. 'But the British would not give up. They attacked us all the time, and we had to form a defensive circle. I got the idea of trying to shoot down a

Spitfire, so when a Spitfire broke off after an attack against us, I tried to follow suit. But of course my Ju 87 was too slow. In the next moment two Me 110 flashed past in front of me. Both were chasing the Spitfire, but the Zerstörer pilots were a bit too eager to shoot down the Englishman. In the next moment the Me 110s collided, only a hundred metres in front of me. The one that came from the left flew straight into the other one. Both Messerschmitts fell in a cloud of debris. I saw no parachutes.'[165]

Meanwhile, during their approach flight, the Ju 88s from LG 1 and their escorts from II./ZG 76 were shadowed by three Spitfires which flew high above the German planes. 'Yet', said Unteroffizier Maz Guschweski from 6. / ZG 76, 'the attack against the airfield seems to have caught the British by surprise, as it was only when the LG 1 passed the target from the north to the south, without dropping any bombs, that the Spitfires began to take off – and this in all directions in a most chaotic manner.'[166]

A German war correspondent who had taken the radio operator's place in the Messerschmitt 110 flown by Hauptmann Heinz Nacke, the commander of 6./ZG 76, afterwards described what immediately followed: '*The British fighter units are taking off now, and about 1,000 metres below the 6. Staffel their tight formations start climbing in spirals. Our 6. Staffel is getting ready to tackle them. Hauptmann Nacke radioes his instructions to the individual aircrews. The enemy unit consists of about twenty aircraft, thus outnumbering us. Suddenly, while all eyes were directed towards the climbing enemy below, a lone fighter appears unexpectedly out of a cloud and dives towards our Staffel commander. I notice that the aircraft is painted in grey-green with a light blue underside. Our Hauptmann hesitates for a moment, and that is enough for the other aircraft to get close. Small red flames are dancing along the leading edge of his wings and the tracer bullets' small "white mice" scurry past the cabin. "Damn! It's a Hurricane!" Our Staffelkapitän reacts swiftly. The Zerstörer's automatic cannons bang and the Hurricane is hit at a range of no more than approximately 50 metres just as it breaks off, and for a fraction of a second is exposing its vulnerable belly. It is a decisive hit, and at the same time we see other tracers that whiz past to the left of our cabin; our wingman also opens fire against the British plane. The badly damaged Hurricane disappears beneath our right wing. I notice a large hole in its right wing, and flames emerge from the bullet-riddled fuel tanks. The British aircraft descends in flames.*'[167]

But what the Germans initially perceived as aimlessness on the British side, was in fact a well-organised fighter attack in several consecutive waves. 'Suddenly, a tight formation of about 70 British fighters dived to attack from 6,000 metres' altitude, with the sun in their back', said Hauptmann Joachim Helbig, who flew in the rear of the German formation with the seven Ju 88s of his 4./LG 1. The war correspondent aboard Hauptmann Nacke's Bf 110 continues his story: '*All aircraft in our Staffel are embroiled in individual air combats, and the air above Worthy Down becomes the scene of a fierce dogfight. Two aircraft from our Staffel dive against a formation of three Hurricanes. The combat takes place just below us. For a short while, the black crosses and the cockards sparkle in the sunlight, then the aircraft disappear in the haze. Our Staffel has lost two aircraft ...'*

Max Guschweski, radio operator in Feldwebel Jakob Birndorfer's Bf 110 'M8+BP', remembered: *'The aircraft of 4. and 5. /ZG 76 remained with LG 1, which finally dropped the bombs and sought refuge behind a giant cumulus cloud in the south. The dogs always bite the last one, but 6./ZG 76 had no choice but to stay and fight it out with an enemy that constantly increased in numbers. I began to fear that our time had come. In the beginning, Feldwebel Birndorfer faithfully fulfilled his duty to protect our Staffelkapitän. But when three Spitfires – soon to be joined by a fourth – took up position behind our Messerschmitt, he had to fight for our lives. We both realized that only a miracle could save us. While he tried his hand at all sorts of manoeuvres – he hurled our plane up and down and went into incredibly tight turns to evade his pursuers – I emptied one magazine after another from our MG 15, but without any noticeable results. By that time we had lost sight of our Staffelkapitän and couldn't see Leutnant Jabs' Rotte or Oberleutnant [Wilhelm] Herget's covering Schwarm either.'* [168]

Leutnant Hans-Joachim Jabs was one of the best pilots in 6./ZG 76. He reacted quickly when he heard the cry from his radio operator: 'Six enemy fighters behind!' Using all his flying skills, Jabs managed to turn his Bf 110 so tightly that he got the last of the Hurricanes in his sights. He opened fire with all his nose guns. 'The Hurricane shook violently, while parts of it flew off, and then one of its wings dropped, the aircraft turned around its own axis and plummeted downwards in wide spirals', reads the German report. The war correspondent in Nacke's Bf 110 said: *'The air combat continues with unabated fury. The bombers have already departed over the Channel, escorted by the comrades of the other Staffels, with our 6. Staffel acting as the rearguard. Again, tightly closed formations of enemy fight-ers pop up. [Leutnant Jabs] suddenly discovers a Hurricane that gets into position behind a German fighter and prepares to open fire. He turns and dives against the enemy aircraft, which is torn to pieces already by his first burst of fire. Debris swirls down through the air, and a parachute unfurls. The land breeze carries the British pilot out to sea.*

'Meanwhile, our Staffelkapitän has dived against a formation of three Hurricanes. The closest aircraft attempts to evade the devastating cannon shells through incessant right and left turns. Meanwhile, the two other Englishmen do whatever they can to save their comrade. We find ourselves surrounded by a network of glowing tracers. But the Zerstörer's guns have already hit their target, and once again an enemy aircraft spins down. On the blue water surface, a small white spot of foaming water is visible for a brief moment.'

The German war correspondent's perspective probably would have been different, had he not flown together with an ace such as Hauptmann Nacke. For the crews Feldwebel Franz Wagner/Unteroffizier Fritz Spörl and Feldwebel Jacob Birndorfer/Unteroffizier Max Guschweski, who became separated from the formation, things did not look as bright. Guschewski said: *'Suddenly I felt a hard slap in the face. The thick edges of my flight goggles had been shattered by shrapnel that hit my temple on the left side. Blood ran down my chin and onto the life jacket. This burst of fire had crashed through the plexiglass hood of the cockpit and hit the left engine, which began to emit white and black smoke. Soon flames could be seen, and these spread out over the wing. The propeller of the burning engine stopped and Jakob trimmed the aircraft and continued south towards the Channel. The Spitfires chased us in a long column and closed in to just five metres before they opened fire. I could easily make out the pilots' facial features, and when they pressed their firing buttons, the bullets from their eight machine guns struck our aircraft as a hail storm. Even today, so many years later, I can hear that terrible sound.*

During the battle on 15 August 1940, 601 Squadron was credited with the shooting down of four Ju 88s. The swastika on the fin of one of them was nailed up as a souvenir in the alert hut at the air base at Tangmere. (Photo: Riddle via Ivers.)

'Soon I had finished the last of my ten magazines, and all that remained was to wait. By that time, our aircraft was so badly shot up that all the paint had disappeared and the metal wings looked like a sieve, but still we kept flying! When we reached the Solent, I began to hope that we would manage to escape. But my optimism was shattered when the Spitfires changed tactics. Now they began to attack us head on. Just as Jakob had jettisoned the canopy and we both had unstrapped and were preparing to bail out, a new burst of fire slammed into the cabin, hitting both of us, with the result that I passed out.'

At that point Birndorfer chose to perform an emergency landing. It cost him his own life, but saved Guschweski. The crew Wagner/Spörl was never seen again. A third Bf 110 from 6./ZG 76 crashed in the Channel, where the two airmen were picked up by a Do 18 air boat. It was a hard blow, but in return, 6./ZG 76 was credited with six confirmed victories – two by Hauptmann Nacke (his victories Nos. 10 and 11), three by Leutnant Jabs (Nos. 7-9) and one by the latter's rear gunner, Stabsfeldwebel Alfred Kühne.

5./ZG 76 fared better; its airmen reported seven victories against one own loss. With two kills each on this mission, Feldwebel Karl Langberg scored his fourth and fifth, and Feldwebel Max Leschnig his third and fourth victories in total. 4. Staffel brought home two victories against one own loss. Hauptmann Groth's Stabsschwarm of II./ZG 76, on the other hand, was almost obliterated: one of its four aircraft was shot down and two others crashed on their return to France. It was only Hauptmann Groth himself who escaped. Leutnant Siegfried Hahn and his rear gunner Unteroffizier Willy Lehner managed to shoot down a Spitfire each before their own aircraft was so badly hit that it crashed on its return to France. Both airmen were wounded.

While the Zerstörer fliers were busy defending themselves, they had no chance of offering the Ju 88s any particularly effective protection. The Spitfires and Hurricanes of 32, 43, 601 and 609 squadrons focused primarily on the seven Ju 88s in Hauptmann Helbig's 4./LG 1, which lay at the rear of the German formation. Helbig flew at the front of the formation with his 'Anton Marta' ('L1+AM'). Having seen the same scene before, during the air battle over Dunkirk, he watched the British manoeuvres closely and urged his pilots to close the formation even tighter. It paid off – at least initially. The first fighter attack was averted by the combined fire from 21 German machine guns.

But the British soon returned for a new attack, this time using a new tactic. They took on the rearmost Kette, attacking simultaneously from several directions. Defying the desperate machine gun fire from the Junkers, the RAF pilots made one attack after another, and finally caused the pilot of one of the Ju 88s to lose his nerves. To avoid one of the attacks, he banked his aircraft to the side, and the German three-plane formation dissolved.

The Spitfires and Hurricanes immediately attacked the separate Ju 88 crews, which fled in panic towards the Channel. Most of them became easy prey. The Hurricane pilots of 601 Squadron were especially successful with co-ordinated attacks, resulting in four Ju 88s claimed shot

The crew in the cabin of a Ju 88. It was Göring's idea to have the bomber constructed so that the crew was placed close together, which was considered to be good for cohesion and cooperation in combat.

down. One of these was recorded as the American volunteer Flying Officer Carl Davis' fifth victory.

Hauptmann Helbig was himself pursued and had his 'Anton Marta' badly mangled by several Spitfires and Hurricanes. One of the RAF pilots – 601 Squadron's Pilot Officer Gordon 'Mouse' Cleaver, a youngster who four days earlier had shot down two Bf 110s outside of Portland – especially gunned for the green-painted 'L1+AM'. Cleaver fired burst after burst into the apparently already doomed bomber. The aircraft shook violently. Row after row of bullet holes appeared on the green and blue wings. Some bullets tore off the port engine's plates and caused the Jumo motor to seize.

Ahead, Helbig saw a city with a high cathedral or something similar. It must be Winchester on the railway towards Southampton, he thought. Then some fifty kilometres still remained to the coast, and the Hurricane was preparing for yet another attack!

With the sweat pouring all over his body, Helbig heard the radio operator Oberfeldwebel Schlund in the radio phone. The previous Saturday they had all been celebrating Franz Schlund's twenty-seventh birthday in Orléans. Now he sat concentrating intensely behind his MG 81 machine gun with his back against Helbig, calculating the distance

Hauptmann Joachim Helbig (second from the right). Next to Helbig, leaning over the map, stands Leutnant Hans Sauer, another pilot from 4./LG 1. Besides Sauer, Franz Schlund is visible. Joachim Helbig was one of the most successful German bomber pilots during the Second World War. He was awarded with the Knight's Cross on 24 October 1940, after 75 bomber missions. In January 1942, following 210 combat sorties, he was awarded with the Oak Leaves to the Knight's Cross. On 28 September 1942, he received the Swords to the Knight's Cross with Oak Leaves, one of only a handful of bomber pilots to do so. By that time, Helbig had flown 330 combat missions in the West, over the British Isles, and in the Mediterranean area. When the war ended, he had participated in 480 bombing missions. After the war, Helbig became director of the Berliner-Kindl-Schultheiss brewery. Helbig contributed interviews, footage and miscellaneous documents for this book. On 3 October 1985 he was involved in a car accident in Spain and died two days later. (Photo: Helbig.)

to the enemy fighter. This he did with a calm and mono-tone voice that annoyed the upset pilot: 'Here he is again . . . 400 metres . . . 300 . . . 250 . . . 200 . . .' Inside the Hurricane-machine's relatively spacious cabin, it smelled of exhaust fumes, oil, carbide, and sweat. The sun shone in from the right and the cockpit frames created shadow lines that fell over the lone pilot and moved in the opposite direction as the plane turned. Pilot Officer Gordon Cleaver leaned forward, towards the windshield. He had removed his goggles and squinted through the reflector gunsight, which showed a thin haircross. The distance to the Junker was still too large. A little further . . . Cleaver pressed the rudder pedals up and down and with both hands on the control stick he turned his fighting machine towards the target. He had only one thing in mind – to destroy that flying German monster, to shoot it to pieces, to make it finally fall from the sky in a cloud of smoke and fire. His thumbs were already rested on the firing mechanism.

'One hundred fifty metres', Schlund said with restraint. Instinctively Joachim Helbig put his head down

and crouched in what resembled a foetal position in front of the dashboard. At once the cabin filled with noise. It slammed and crunched. Pieces of plexiglass, wood and metal flew in all directions. A stream of cold air hit Helbig in the face with such force that it felt like a punch.

In the midst of this chaos he perceived a cry of jubilation, 'I got him!' Franz Schlund shouted triumphantly and clapped his hands with excitement. And indeed: Behind them the 'Tommy' fell, trailing smoke, and disappeared out of sight. Schlund had scored the crucial hit with the last of his ammunition.

Inside of Cleaver's cockpit a hellfire raged. With flames licking his body and face, Cleaver fought desperately to free himself from his harnesses and get out of his blazing, tumbling machine. With a final effort, he pushed himself up and was flung out of the flaming wreckage. The icy wind blast stung like needles in the young pilot's badly scorched face. He pulled the chord to the parachute and a painful jerk in his whole body told him that it had unfolded. Cleaver closed his eyes and allowed himself be carried down by the broad parachute cloth. At a speed of five metres per second he touched down on the outskirts of Winchester and was hurriedly brought to the city hospital.

But the four Germans in the bullet-riddled Ju 88 were not allowed much room to think of the downed enemy's fate. Their own machine was badly shot up, and both the observer and the ventral gunner had been hit by bullets and shrapnel. While Franz Schlund carried out makeshift first aid on their wounds, Helbig had to exercise his entire physical strength to keep the battered plane in a single-engine flight to the south.

The danger was far from over. This was no more than an occasional pause in the combat. New British fighters could emerge at any moment, and nowhere could any of the much-needed Messerschmitts be seen. But after some quiet minutes the four Germans started to relax a bit. It seemed as though the RAF had withdrawn to its bases after the violent combat. Small villages, churches and fields passed below and Helbig's nervousness gave way to an excited optimism. To his immense relief, he finally flew out over the Channel's sunlit water. He almost had forgotten about the British fighters and began to think of the long journey across the water.

Then, what the quartet in 'Anton Marta' least of all needed, happened. To the right the outlines of a lone aircraft could be seen, and as it came closer it proved to be a Spitfire!

The British pilot spotted the 'easy meat' at several miles distance and followed it at full speed. 'Spitfire!' yelled Oberfeldwebel Schlund. But this time, his voice sounded resigned. As before he was in position behind his guns and gave his pilot instructions. But with empty ammunition drums, this was all he could do.

Helbig desperately attempted to slip out of the net through evasive manoeuvres, but it was an attempt doomed to fail with such a badly damaged bomber. The nimble little Spitfire fighter followed the slow turns with great ease. Joachim Helbig had been in trouble many times before without losing his mind, but this time he was really, in his own words, 'damned frightened'. It was really only now that the German bomber ace – with experience from dozens of fights with the weather, air defence and fighters over Warsaw, Belgium, Calais, Dunkirk, Somme and the English Channel – learned what real fear is.

With throbbing hearts, Helbig and his comrades waited for the death blow. But nothing happened. Instead, the Spitfire pilot swept in close to the German plane and curiously peered into the Ju 88's bullet-riddled cabin. He spared them, and contented himself with studying Germany's best bomber from a few metres' distance. The German airmen hardly dared to believe it was true!

Thus they flew on quietly, mile after mile, escorted by an enemy fighter pilot who probably valued a so-called 'honest war' more than an easy kill. Only when the French coast came in sight, did RAF pilot leave. He put one hand up in a salute and set off secure in the knowledge that the damaged Ju 88 would bring the four frightened Germans the last few kilometres to the mainland.

Joachim Helbig never found out who this pilot was. It might have been 234 Squadron's Pilot Officer Richard Hardy. He lost his comrades somewhere between Swanage and the Isle of Wight at around half past four and flew out

This Spitfire, flown by 234 Squadron's Pilot Officer Richard Hardy, crashed in Cherbourg in German-occupied France on 15 August 1940. Hardy spent the rest of the war in a German prisoner-of-war camp. Richard Hardy passed away in September 1997.

alone over the English Channel with his Spitfire ('AZ-H'). According to British records, however, he took a little too long turn to the south, and was forced by a German fighter to land in a field near Cherbourg. He spent the rest of the war in a German Stalag Luft POW camp.

For II./LG 1, 15 August meant a disaster. Of the 15 Ju 88s that had taken off, only seven returned to base. Hauptmann Helbig's 'L1+AM' landed with more than 180 bullet holes in the fuselage and wings and two crew members wounded. For II./ZG 76 'Haifischgruppe' it was just as bad – it lost half its 16 Bf 110s, but in return claimed 18 victories. III./ZG 76 lost four Bf 110s and its Gruppenkommandeur, Hauptmann Friedrich-Karl Dickoré, against only two victories. This was in stark contrast to V.(Z)/ LG 1, which on its free hunting mission claimed eleven victories against a single aircraft lost: Feldwebel Gerhard Jecke crashed his badly damaged Bf 110 at the airport Cherbourg-west. Owing to the Zerstörers' effective fighter screen, I./StG 1 and II./StG 2 escaped with a loss of only four of the 47 participating Ju 87s.

Both sides made grossly inflated claims for the number of shot down enemy aircraft.

39 victories reported by the German fighter and Zerstörer fliers actually equated to RAF losses of ten Spitfires and Hurricanes. In addition, seven British fighters had to emergency-land or were severely damaged, but could be repaired. Undoubtedly the Bf 110s bore the main burden of the German fighter combat; due to the large distance from their bases, the Bf 109s of JG 27 and JG 53 could not contribute more than five reported victories all told.

On the other side of the Channel the pilots of 213 Squadron celebrated a magnificent success – 19 victories against two losses of its own. The Belgian volunteer pilot Pilot Officer Jacques Phillipart and Sergeant Reginald Llewellyn contributed with three Bf 110s each. For the latter, this meant that he thereby reached a total number of eight victories. 87 Squadron was credited with 13 victories, of which Pilot Officer Jay Dudley accounted for three and Flight Lieutenant Ian Gleed for two. However, this unit also lost three aircraft and two pilots, including the unit commander, Squadron Leader John Lovell Gregg.

In total the RAF units that were in action against Luftflotte 3 in the afternoon of 15 August were credited with 61 confirmed victories – two and a half times more than the actual German losses.

Victories were succeeded by defeats. Yet another round remained in the battle before the curtain finally went down on this bloody Thursday. The time had come for Luftflotte 2 again, and its third major operation on this 15 August was organised in the same way as the previous one. The main attack was to be carried out by I. and III. Gruppen of the next Do 17 Geschwader, KG 76, with the sector base Biggin Hill as the main objective. The British fighters would be held down or diverted by free hunting missions and a new blitz by Hauptmann Walter Rubensdörffer's Erprobungsgruppe 210.

When Park was informed of the approaching Luftwaffe formations – reported as 'four rows of plus 70 aircraft' – he ordered up seven squadrons. Once again he made the mistake of committing his fighters in too small groups. When such a small formation arrived and saw the amassed groups of Bf 109s, the pilots did not really know what to do. Oberleutnant Hans-Ekkehard Bob flew along with III./JG 54 when a lone Spitfire suddenly dived straight through the German formation without opening fire. Obviously shocked to discover his precarious situation, the Spitfire pilot immediately afterwards began a series of wild manoeuvres which the experienced Bob was able to follow without any difficulty. Bob chased the British fighter down to 800 metres, where his bullets set it on fire.[169] The unfortunate pilot was Pilot Officer Francis Cale, a 25-year-old Australian volunteer in 266 Squadron. He managed to bail out, but came down in Medway River where he drowned.

At the same time Erprobungsgruppe 210 flew towards the RAF base Croydon, south of London. But this time the assault planes did not have the escort of the veterans of III./ ZG 26 'Horst Wessel', but II./JG 52's demoralized Bf 109 pilots instead, who had lost a fifth of their peers in just two days of battle. During the approach flight over southern England, the fighters from II./JG 52 suddenly disappeared, turning back to the English Channel without any explanation, leaving the bomb-laden planes in Erprobungsgruppe 210 alone.

At 20:05 (German time), the bombs fell among hangars and repair shops at Croydon. It was a typical Erprobungsgruppe 210 raid – swift and with deadly precision. 280 men of the base personnel were killed or wounded, 40 training aircraft were knocked out, the H.E. Rollason Aircraft Plant was completely destroyed, and British NSF Factory (manufacturer of electronic components) was badly damaged, and sixty civilian deaths were claimed. The airfield was left out of commission for four days. Triumphantly, Rubensdörffer led his Gruppe home to add a new great success in the unit's war diary. But he never got that far. Above Rotherfield the Messerschmitts' line of retreat was intercepted by Squadron Leader John Thompson's 111 Squadron, followed by 32 Squadron, led on this mission by Flight Lieutenant Michael Crossley. Eventually, 501 Squadron would also join in the game.

Hauptmann Rubensdörffer and his Stabskette, comprising three Messerschmitt 110 Ds, was chased through an aperture in the clouds by John Thompson and three of his pilots. Oberleutnant Horst Fiedeler, the adjutant in Erprobungsgruppe 210, was killed by Sergeant John Craig's bullets. To the left of him fell Leutnant Karl-Heinz Koch, responsible for the unit's technical equipment. Finally Hauptmann Walter Rubensdörffer's 'S9+AB' descended in flames, and crashed on a field near Rotherfield. The 30-year-old fighter-bomber veteran died along with his radio operator, Obergefreiter Ludwig Kretzer.

While three squadrons pursued the aircraft of Erprobungsgruppe 210 south of London, III./JG 26 tangled with 151 Squadron's Hurricanes near Dover, far to the southeast. This cost 151 Squadron a loss of four planes, but through this effort no German fighters could rescue Erprobungsgruppe 210, which was destroyed one aircraft at a time. A total of seven of the unit's Messerschmitts were shot down before the remaining managed to escape out over the Channel.

Thanks to the overwhelming German fighter escort KG 76 succeeded in getting through without any losses. Because of reduced visibility as the sun went down, the formation however got lost. West Malling airfield was attacked instead of the important Biggin Hill sector station. At that time West Malling was only a reserve airfield for the RAF.

When the Germans compiled the losses of 15 August 1940 they found that as many as 77 of their own aircraft had been shot down, and of these one third were Bf 110s. Above all the losses suffered by Luftflotte 5 were a very unpleasant surprise. But Göring didn't give up, and in fact, 15 August 1940 – sometimes called 'the Luftwaffe's Black Thursday' – also involved a series of very hard blows to the RAF. Six air bases – Lympne, Hawkinge, Martlesham, Rochester, Croydon and 4 Group's base at Driffield – had suffered heavy damage, in some cases being knocked out of action for some time. In addition, a number of important industrial plants had been seriously hit; of these Short's aircraft works in Rochester was the most important. A side effect of the attacks on the airfields was that several British radar stations lost their power supply. Göring's new orders for the fighter escort of the Stukas had proven to be very effective. Furthermore, the Messerschmitt fighter pilots achieved good results in free hunting fighter sweeps.

But the commanders of the German air fleets were not satisfied. Luftflotte 3's Generalfeldmarschall Sperrle was concerned about the severe losses that the bombers of LG 1 suffered, and he angrily described the free hunting that V.(Z)/LG 1 had allowed itself as insubordination. Experience should have told him that the Bf 110 in particular with its relatively poor acceleration was highly inappropriate for the close escort missions that the bomber units demanded. The nineteen aircraft that ZG 76 lost on just such assignments on 15 August – I. Gruppe over the North Sea and the other two Gruppen across the English Channel – should have served as a serious warning to the German commanders but the commanders of the three air fleets were obviously too shaken by their bomber losses to realize this.

It was worse for Luftflotte 5: more than 10 per cent of the Fifth Air Fleet's total strength had already been expended on the first mission against the supposedly 'emptied' Northern RAF fighter Groups! The daylight offensive against England by Luftflotte 5 came to an abrupt halt. Some of the units were transferred to Luftflotte 2 and 3 in France, so that from there they would be able to continue their operations over the British Isles. What was left in Norway and Denmark continued the operations launched in the autumn of 1939: the air war against the Royal Navy in the North Sea. More missions like those of 15 August 1940 were out of the question for the Fifth Air Fleet.

Kesselring, the commander of Luftflotte 2, may not have liked the report on how some of his units broke off their missions without valid reason: this concerned KG 2 and II./JG 52. The loss of the popular Hauptmann Rubensdörffer also hit him very hard. As a final gesture of honour to Rubensdörffer, he awarded him with the Knight's Cross posthumously. The conclusion drawn by the air fleet commanders from the fighting on 15 August was – contrary to Göring's instructions – that more close escort was needed.

On the other side Channel, British Prime Minister Churchill was euphoric. He had spent the day in Fighter Command's headquarters in Bentley Priory, where the evening's total showed an astonishing 182 victories against 34 own losses. In other words, according to British reports, nearly five German losses for each British. Churchill thought he discerned a marked turnaround compared to just a few days before. With such a gap between the losses of both sides – which would suggest a reassuring British qualitative superiority – it seemed highly unlikely that the Luftwaffe would win.

Churchill was overwhelmed when he and Lord Ismay left Fighter Command's headquarters that evening. 'Don't say a word', he said. Only a good while later, when they were sitting in the staff car that would bring them to the Prime Minister's residence at Chequers, did he begin to speak.

'Never in the field of human conflict was so much owed by so many to so few' he said. Later he would repeat these words in a famous radio speech.

That evening he phoned his predecessor, Neville Chamberlain, and proclaimed 15 August 1940 as 'one of the greatest days in history'.

The British were not alone in exaggerating their successes. Luftwaffe intelligence estimated that half a month of battle had cost the RAF a loss of 770 fighters. Production during the same period was estimated at about 300 fighter planes. This meant that there should be no more than about 430 British fighters left, of which an estimated 300 were in serviceable condition.

Actual figures for Fighter Command during the above mentioned period were almost exactly the reverse of what the Germans estimated: 290 fighter aircraft had been lost and 750 manufactured – thus an increase rather than, as OKL thought, a decrease of 500 planes!

16 August 1940

The fighting on 16 August began straightaway in the morning, as hundreds of aircraft from Kesselring's air fleet began to fly in, wave after wave. The whole of 11 Group was scrambled, and from all sides Spitfires and Hurricanes converged. When they made contact with the enemy they found he had divided his forces into a variety of smaller formations, each of which flew towards its chosen goal. For several hours the skies above Kent were torn apart by dozens of small combats which were all, in fact, part of one huge air battle. Between the columns of smoke from downed aircraft, the fires from the bombed RAF installations glowed. During one of the wild air combat a Hurricane from 111 Squadron collided with a Ju 88 from III./KG 76. Neither of the pilots involved survived. The Englishman, Flight Lieutenant Henry Ferris, was one of Fighter Command's most successful fighter pilots at that time; he had 11 victories to his credit.

At about the same time the pilots of 266 Squadron fought an unequal combat with 50 Bf 109s from two Jagdgruppen, II./JG 3 and II./JG 26. They managed to shoot

A Rotte of Bf 109s from II./JG 3 is sweeping by Dover's famous limestone cliffs. This fighter unit began its operations over England on 14 August 1940. The first two weeks were very difficult, and the unit sustained 16 combat losses against 24 air victories during this period. (Via Prien.)

down three of the German fighters. In one of them II./JG 26 lost its Gruppenkommander, Hauptmann Karl Ebbighausen. It was the second time in just over three weeks this unit had lost its commander. In another of the Bf 109s that 266 Squadron shot down, Hauptmann Alfred Müller, the commander of 4./JG 3, fell. The combat cost the bold RAF airmen three Spitfires and two pilots, including Squadron Leader Rodney Wilkinson.

As a result of the savage combat the aircraft of 266 Squadron spread out over a large area, and apparently, while he was looking for his comrades, one of the Spitfire pilots – twenty-two year old Sub-Lieutenant Henry Lafone Greenshields – caught sight of another formation of Bf 109s on its way back across the Channel. It was 9./JG 54, the so-called 'Teufelstaffel' – the Devil's Squadron. Inconspicuously Greenshields placed himself behind the Germans and followed them out over the Strait of Dover. Above Calais, he boldly attacked and shot down a Bf 109 but it cost him dearly. The next moment he was himself attacked by Oberleutnant Hans-Ekkehard Bob. Although his Spitfire was shot to pieces by bursts from Bob's Bf 109, Greenshields refused to bail out – this would have meant that his aircraft would have crashed among the houses of Calais. Instead, he steered away and crashed into a canal

outside the town, which cost him his life. Bob and the other airmen in 9./JG 54 afterwards went to the crash site and formed a guard of honour for the brave enemy pilot. His final resting place is Calais Southern Cemetrey. The German pilot he shot down, Unteroffizier Gustav Kuhlmann, died from his injuries twelve days later.

Towards the early afternoon, when the confused battles over southeast England began to show signs of abating, the British radar screens farther west caught a new major formation approaching across the Channel from Luftflotte 3's base area. Sperrle had dispatched 54 Ju 87s of I. and III./StG 2 to strike a heavy blow against Tangmere airfield. This was to be complemented by an attack of Stab and III./StG 1 against the navy airfield at Lee-on-Solent and Ventnor's radar station (which had come back into operation the day before after bomb damage on 12 August), as well as by 23 Ju 87s from I./StG 3 hitting Gosport airfield. An array of no less than 268 Bf 109s and Bf 110s were deployed to protect the Stukas; it was obvious that 609 Squadron's massacre of II./StG 2 and its fighter escort the day before had taught Sperrle a useful lesson.

But once again, the teleprinted operations order had been intercepted and decrypted by British 'Ultra' in advance. As the nearly four hundred German aircraft ap-

John 'Tim' Elkington, born on 23 December, 1920, is one of a few remaining veterans of the Battle of Britain. He arrived as a rookie pilot to No. 1 Squadron, RAF, in July 1940. The following year he was among the RAF pilots who were transferred to Murmansk to fight alongside the Russians. (Photo: Elkington.)

proached the British coastline, Fighter Command had eight squadrons in the air waiting for them. The Germans split up into four groups. Five of the RAF squadrons engaged the majority of the Luftwaffe fighter escort just off the coast. East of Portsmouth, the ace of I./JG 2, 'Richthofen', Oberleutnant Helmut Wick, attacked a lone Hurricane that he immediately shot down in flames. The pilot, 1 Squadron's Pilot Officer 'Tim' Elkington, escaped by bailing out.[170] By pure coincidence this took place in the air above Elkington's parents' house on Hayling Island, and his mother happened to witness the event. According to the official report, he was shot down by British anti-aircraft fire, which Elkington himself finds unlikely.

He says: 'This happened at 13:40 hours (I seem to remember checking the time as I tried for the second time to leave the aircraft). I was flying there all alone, after 'losing' the squadron – careless! Although the official record shows that I was hit by our own AA, I cannot see how anyone could have assessed that. I saw no flak that day and it seems unlikely that they would have been firing at a fighter squadron. Also, what anti-aircraft guns? 4-inch batteries on Hayling Island? Bofors from elsewhere? At 10-12,000 feet? And which would give me six separte wounds in the legs? It is a can of worms! I only have my Mother's account to go on – saying that she saw these three aircraft, and the first being hit. Thirty minutes later she was called by the Ambulance to say that I had been shot down. I landed in my parachute at West Wittering and my aircraft crashed at Chidham, near Thorney Island.'[171]

The Canadian ace of 213 Squadron, Flying Officer Joseph Laricheliere, was killed in combat with JG 27. He had a strangely uniform combat record: during the battle over Portland on 13 August he shot down two Bf 110s and a Bf 109, again above Portland, on the 15 August he bought down two more Bf 110s and a Ju 87.

Hurricane-equipped 249 Squadron, which had joined the battle just two days earlier, was taken by surprise by the Bf 110s which dived to attack from out of the sun and shot down three Hurricanes in the first engagement.[172] Squadron Leader Eric King managed to disengage and land his damaged machine at Boscombe Down. His namesake, Pilot Officer Martyn King, bailed out of his Hurricane when it caught fire. Ira Jones described Flight Lieutenant James B. Nicolson's fate: 'As he climbed to rejoin his squadron he was "jumped" by an Me 110, who poured four cannon shells into his Hurricane. There was a hell of a clatter in his

Pilot Officer John Elkington's Hurricane from 1 Squadron. (Photo: Elkington.)

601 Squadron's American pilot volunteer Flight Lieutenant Carl Davis shot this Ju 87 of 3./StG 2 completely to pieces during the battle on 16 August. The German dive-bomber crashed with two crew members, pilot Oberfeldwebel Witt and radio operator Feldwebel Röcktäschel, mortally wounded.

cockpit. One shell hit his spare petrol tank and caused a fire. Another crashed into the cockpit, tearing away part of his trouser leg. A third wounded him in the left heel. The fourth completed his discomfiture when it burst through the cockpit hood, sending splinters into his left eye and almost severing the eyelid.' [173]

Half-blinded by the blood pouring down his face, Nicolson still fired on a Messerschmitt. He then turned his already doomed Hurricane ('GN-A') over on its back and fell out, badly burned on the face and hands. Both he and Pilot Officer King drifted down under their parachutes, and while Nicolson hung helpless under the big dome he saw a Bf 110 circling him in a suspicious manner. Nicolson feared that he would be shot at and played dead. It is possible that this saved his life. Martyn King didn't survive. He fell to the ground at high speed even though his parachute had opened. According to the 249 Squadron Operations Record Book his death was caused by his parachute having been shredded by a 20mm shell. James Nicolson was about to meet the same fate – but by what is called 'friendly fire'. While he was on his way down, he was shot at from the ground. Down below an overzealous Home Guard soldier tried to hit him with his shotgun in the belief that he was German. Nicolson was wounded by two lead pellets before he hit the ground. A civilian who witnessed this assaulted the Home Guardsman, and had it not been for a policeman who turned up, the Home Guardsman might have been killed. Nicolson's first combat flight of the war ended in an intensive care unit at Southampton's Royal Hospital. He

was later awarded the Victoria Cross, the highest British award for gallantry, the first and only pilot of Fighter Command to receive this honour.

While these British airmen self-sacrificingly kept the German fighters busy, the Hurricane and Spitfire pilots from 43, 601 and 602 squadrons could attack the unprotected Ju 87 dive-bombers from I. and III./ StG 2 'Immelmann' as these dived to attack the Tangmere base. When the scrap was over, nine Ju 87s had crashed in the fields around Tangmere. Six others were more or less badly damaged and Hauptmann Heinrich Brücker, the commander of III./StG 2, was among those who came back to France bleeding from bullet wounds. The pilots of 43 Squadron accounted for the majority of 'Geschwader Immelmann's' losses, and optimistically reported 17 shot down. Squadron Leader John Badger, Flying Officer Hamilton Charles Upton and Sergeant James Hallowes were each credited with three downed Ju 87s.

Despite everything twenty or so bombs fell on Tangmere airfield and hit all of the hangars and knocked out seven Hurricanes, six Blenheims and a Miles Magister. It is easy to imagine what the result could have been without the intervention of the British fighter aircraft – if all 54 Ju 87s had been able to attack the airfield.

While this carnage was played out on the ground and in the air above Tangmere, the Ju 87s in Stab and III./StG 1 achieved complete success. Without suffering any losses they managed to put Ventnor's radar station out of action for another week, and at the marine air base Lee-on-

Solent three hangars and half a dozen aircraft of the Fleet Air Arm were destroyed.

KG 2 mounted the next operation against the British Isles. Its third Gruppe, which took such a beating on 13 August, was permitted to rest and recover its strength, but I./KG 2 took off at 16:40 to attack the Hornchurch sector station with 27 Do 17s. Park sent up six squadrons and the British fighters met the Germans even before they crossed the British coast. Spitfires from 54 and 610 squadrons delivered the first attack, directed against the flank of the bomber formation. The German fighter escort promptly attacked the British formation, and Hauptmann Walter Oesau from III./JG 51 shot down two of the Spitfires. 54 Squadron's Pilot Officer Colin Gray chased Unteroffizier Ernst Buder's Bf 109 from 7,000 metres altitude down to treetop height before he finally shot him down. Afterwards, he told his friend 'Al' Deere: 'The Hun pilot tried everything he knew to shake me off his tail, and this made him a damn difficult target, but he wasn't losing me. Eventually I put his engine out of action and he made a forced landing in a field. I was amused to see that as soon as he got clear of his aircraft the first thing he did was to take off his helmet, throw it on the ground and jump on it. He was obviously peeved at being shot down.'[174]

While the fighter combat was raging, four squadrons crept up behind the Dornier bombers. All the Do 17s of the rear three-plane formation were hit. Oberfeldwebel Heinz Gerlach, the pilot of one of these aircraft, said: 'We were 2000 metres above the cloud cover over England when suddenly a large number of British fighters appeared out of a cloud bank and attacked our rear Kette. Before we were able to defend ourselves, they had shot down the two other planes in our Kette, and then the bullets started hitting us

too. Then there was dead silence. In the seat behind me the radio operator Günter Krakow hung with his face covered in blood. The flight engineer Alex Holle had one arm torn by bullets and he slowly collapsed.'[175]

No. 1 Squadron hit the German bombers hardest and claimed to have shot down five, of which Flying Officer Arthur Victor 'Darky' Clowes accounted for two – his eighth and ninth victories.

The fighter attack was so dramatic that the entire I./KG 2 jettisoned their bombs and turned back towards the Channel. During the pursuit towards the French coast three British fighters were shot down by JG 51 and JG 54, but even if the combat cost the British more losses than the Germans, it was of course a remarkable achievement to have averted the attack against Hornchurch.

Two Ju 88 crews managed to establish a kind of 'balance' when they shortly afterwards attacked the airfield at Brize Norton, west of Oxford. By first lowering their landing gears and pretending to be British bombers coming in to land, they tricked the base's defences into lowering their guard. They were then able to drop their bombs right on target. In one hangar no less than 46 aircraft were destroyed by fire, and in another hangar seven Hurricanes were damaged.

Kesselring had also sent eight Bf 109s from I./JG 52 for a low-level attack on the airfield at Manston, and this was described in the war diary of I./JG 52: 'A radio message had been intercepted, revealing that a bomber unit had landed

Sergeant Arthur 'Darky' Clowes climbs into his Hurricane for a combat mission. Clowes had 5½ air victories when the Battle of Britain began. When it ended, the number had risen to 11. Clowes survived the war but died in 1949.

One of the RAF pilots who were killed during the defensive fight against the Stuka raid on Tangmere on 16 August 1940, was American volunteer Pilot Officer William Fiske from 601 Squadron. Fiske, who was double Olympic champion in bobsled, had his Hurricane shot in flames by a Ju 87's rear gunner. Although his aircraft was on fire, Fiske brought it back to the base and landed. Severely burned, he was rushed to the Royal West Sussex Hospital, Chichester, but died two days later. (Photo: Riddles via Ivers.)

from there, that it was because the evacuation of one of the major airfields was considered a moral victory to the enemy. If this was so, it is difficult to understand the reasoning behind it.' [177]

Both sides sustained heavy losses in the fighting on 16 August. The RAF lost no less than 90 aircraft – 22 fighters and 7 bombers in the air – as well as 61 aircraft of all types on the ground. On the German side the fighting on 16 August cost 38 aircraft, including 13 Bf 109s and 6 Bf 110s. As regards the balance of strength between the forces, Fighter Command, for the second day in a row, had clearly managed to hold up better than the Luftwaffe. No. 266 Squadron's courageous noon combat against the fivefold superiority in numbers of two full Jagdgruppen on 16 August captures the situation in a nutshell. In fact, the Luftwaffe fielded more aircraft on 16 August than it had done during the main attack on the 15th, and of over seventeen hundred individual German sorties more than thirteen hundred were carried out by the Messerschmitt fighters. Fighter Command, however, only put up half as many fighters, considerably fewer than the day before. Against this background, the results of the German fighters undeniably appear pretty mediocre. In addition, they had failed to offer the Ju 87s full protection – with disastrous results for StG 2 'Immelmann'.

The following night Bomber Command made its biggest effort so far and sent 150 bombers to the Zeiss works in Jena, the Messerschmitt works in Augsburg and a power station in Bohlen. It cost them seven aircraft without managing to inflict any significant damage. The psychological effect of having raided Germany, however, had great significance, not only for the hard-pressed British themselves. The population of Germany began asking increasingly difficult questions about when those annoying nocturnal air-raid alerts would actually cease.

18 August 1940

Despite clear weather on 17 August, it was quiet in the air over the British Isles. Reichsmarschall Göring sent new attack orders to his commanders. He gave them 24 hours to prepare the next major operation against the British Isles, and in the meantime called two of his favourites, fighter aces majors Galland and Mölders, to his hunting lodge Karinhall in the forests east of Berlin. Göring got straight to the point and told them that the losses had so far been worse than expected, especially among Stuka units. He stated bluntly that in his opinion, the German fighters had not been used aggressively enough. However, this did not reflect on Galland and Mölders. He had not ordered them to Karinhall to criticize them – on the contrary, as the old fighter pilot that he was, he wanted to use their young belligerence to improve fighter operations over the Channel. His decision to make Major Mölders, who was only 27 years old, commander of the whole of JG 51 had proven very successful. Since Mölders took over JG 51 had developed into the most successful Bf 109 unit under Jafü 2's command. Now Göring wanted to forge ahead and do the

at Manston to refuel before the next night attack against Germany. Under Hauptmann Ewald's command, 2. Staffel took off at 18:38 to attack Manston. The weather was very hazy with an overcast at about 1,500 metres. The attack and the return flight were carried out in an exemplary manner. A great success was achieved. Five Bristol Blenheims, two Spitfires, a tanker, a fuel storage and two crew barracks were set on fire or severely damaged.' [176] It is obvious that I./JG 52 at this time was of an entirely different standard than the other two Gruppen in JG 52.

The coastal airfield at Manston was one of the most exposed of the forward bases that Fighter Command's leaders insisted on keeping operational, even though it was so vulnerable to surprise attack. British pilots who took off from airfields so near the coast often found themselves attacked from above while they were climbing after take-off. After the war 'Al' Deere from 54 Squadron, which operated from Manston during most of August, sharply criticised the decision to keep units on the coastal airfields: 'there seemed no tactical advantage in continuing to use an airfield so far forward, especially when it had such a damaging effect on the morale of the pilots and ground crews to say nothing of the aircraft lost on the ground. At the time it was generally believed by the pilots, who had the misfortune to operate same with the other Bf 109 units, and he was going to start with Galland – who, besides Mölders, was also a favourite of Göring's.

'Galland', said Göring, 'you shall take over JG 26!' 'I did not like the idea, because I wanted to lead my unit in combat', said Adolf Galland. 'Göring tried to reassure me that his idea was to have fighting Geschwaderkommodores.' Mölders disagreed with Göring, but he did undoubtedly have unusual organisational and management skills. 'I still could not reconcile myself to the idea of being a Geschwaderkommodore.'[178]

Major Martin Mettig, who was replaced as Geschwaderkommodore JG 54 by 28-year-old Major Hannes Trautloft on 25 August considered that this reform was basically sensible: 'the replacing of five Geschwaderkommodores in the fighter aviation came about because the heavy combat demanded a rejuvenation at senior command level. With my 37 years I was the fighter aviation's second-youngest Geschwaderkommodore at that time. The new aim was that our Staffelkapitäns would be less than 27 years, our Gruppenkommandeurs under 30 years, and our Geschwaderkommodores under 32 years of age. I maintain that it was a correct measure.'[179]

Göring also found cause for optimism in a new report which he received from the Luftwaffe's Intelligence Chief, Oberst 'Beppo' Schmid, which again stated that all that remained of the RAF was 'the last 300 Spitfires'. In reality, thanks to the 24-hour reprieve, the number of serviceable aircraft in Fighter Command increased from 631 at dawn on 17 August to 706 twenty-four hours later. This gain came in handy when Göring's plan of attack came into force on 18 August. The first goal was to once and for all wipe out the 11 Group sector stations Kenley and Biggin Hill, and to do that the Germans had a sophisicated plan of attack.

Sunday 18 August dawned with beautiful weather. On the German airfields in France the unit commanders assembled their men for briefings. This time the RAF would be decisively defeated, the unit commanders explained.

On the other side of the Channel the British felt increasingly nervous. The sun shone from an almost cloudless sky and it was a warm and lovely summer day, but except for a few reconnaissance aircraft it was completely quiet in the air over England. Would there be a two day reprieve? What were the Germans up to?

Naturally, it was just the calm before the storm. Shortly before lunch Park was notified that the Dover radar station had picked up radar echoes suggesting the largest gathering of German aircraft ever. In the air above the Pas de Calais 110 He 111s from KG 1 formed up together with Do 17s and Ju 88s from KG 76. These were joined by nearly five hundred Messerschmitts from JG 3, JG 26, JG 51, JG 52, JG 54 and ZG 26. Major Martin Mettig, still the commander of JG 54, said: 'of our five Jagdgeschwaders, two were tasked to fly close escort. We climbed to the flight altitude we had been ordered above Cap Gris Nez.'[180]

When the first fifty or so German aircraft began to fly over the Strait of Dover, at high altitude, Park might have been able to guess but could not know that these were the Bf 109s going out first on a free hunting mission. In any event, the commander of 11 Group had no choice but to alert his fighter units. He decided to send up five squadrons to shield the southeast coast. Nos. 17, 54, 56, 65 and 501 squadrons were tasked with patroling the Canterbury area.

In this situation to send up twelve Hurricanes from the coastal Hawkinge airfield, outside Folkestone, was not very well-advised. They took off just as the Bf 109s left the French coast at Wissant, just five minutes flying time away. Oberleutnant Gerhard Schöpfel from III./JG 26 spotted them, dived immediately and shot down four of them in rapid succession.

The remaining pilots of No. 501 Squadron dived to escape. It was the signal for the entire III./JG 26 to go after them. The Germans did not catch up with 501 Squadron, but instead ran into another group of Hurricanes, No. 17 Squadron. When its pilots saw the whole gaggle of '109s coming down, they turned and tried to dive away from danger. The Germans shot down three Hurricanes before they broke off the pursuit in order to not lose too much height. One of the downed Hurricanes from 17 Squadron crashed near Dover, but the pilots of the other two managed to land their machines so that they could be repaired.

While this was going on, nine Do 17s from 9./KG 76 under Hauptmann Joachim Roth were about to cross the Channel at wave-top height. The German plan was that twelve Ju 88s from II./KG 76 would begin by dive bombing Kenley air base, after which the nine Do 17s from 9./KG 76 would take advantage of the confusion among the defenders to carry out a low-level attack on the same target. Meanwhile, KG 1 carried out a high altitude attack against the Biggin Hill airfield using sixty He 111s.

But the German plan failed. The purpose of Hauptmann Roth's formation flying so low was to avoid detection by the British radar stations. This was successful, but when the nine planes surprisingly came thundering in over the coast at Beachy Head, it had a different effect than the Germans expected. The report from the British air observers worried Park, who had take-off orders sent to Kenley and Biggin Hill, where the Hurricanes and Spitfires from 32, 64, 610 and 615 squadrons were scrambled. Thus a second wave of British fighters was airborne further inland, as yet unaffected by the Bf 109s' intrusion.

To top it all, the high-altitude and dive bombers were very late. The morning's clear weather had been replaced by increasing rain, which made the other German bombers lose a lot of time climbing above the clouds before they could assemble in combat formations. The crews on board the low-flying Dornier planes were never informed of this, so they therefore became the first attack wave.

Hauptmann Roth's nine Do 17s followed the Brighton – London railway northwards. The tracks would lead them right to their target – Kenley airfield. At Croydon, near Kenley, but on the other side of the railway, 111 Squadron was alerted. Twelve Hurricanes went up and were ordered to circle 100 feet above Kenley, which unit commander Squadron Leader John Thompson thought was 'insane'. He soon had reason to change his mind – when the nine Dornier bombers broke out of the haze in the direction of Reigate. While the bombers fanned out towards the four

German war correspondent Rolf von Pebal flew with one of the Do 17 bombers during the operation against Kenley air base on 18 August 1940. He took this picture of the Do 17 planes as they swept low over Channel, crossing the English coast at Beachy Head.

large hangars, fuel depot and operations room, Thompson ordered his fighters out of the target area to get around behind the bombers.

The airfield's air defences hastily launched their PAC – 'Parachute and Cable', a countermeasure against low-level attacks consisting of a 500-foot steel cable that was fired up to its full length in the air and then sank down under a parachute. The nine bombers flew straight into the maze of steel cables that popped up like a snake-charmer's snakes in front of them, and dropped their bombs. Chaos broke out on the ground and in the air. Oberleutnant Rudolf Lamberty, the pilot of Roth's 'F1+ DT', had no chance to turn away but ran into one of the wires. Anti-aircraft machine guns also opened fire furiously, hitting Roth's plane and setting it on fire. The entire crew survived – albeit as prisoners of war. The crew of 'F1+HT' were not that lucky; it perished when their plane crashed in a field just outside the airfield. Oberleutnant Magin, the pilot of another Do 17 from 9./KG 76, collapsed in his seat mortally wounded and involuntarily pushed the control column forward. His observer, Oberfeldwebel Wilhelm Friedrich Illg, threw himself forward and grabbed the control column, and at the last moment succeeded – just ten metres above the ground – in pulling the plane out of its dive. In addition, according to the German report, he succeeded in dropping the remaining eight bombs.

While bomb explosions spread across Kenley airfield, Squadron Leader Thompson's Hurricanes got themselves into attack position behind the remaining Dorniers, which attempted to climb away to the right, where they hoped to meet their own fighters. Several of the German bombers were damaged by collisions with PAC wires or by gunfire from the ground, and now they met the RAF pilots' fury. But it was no easy fight for 111 Squadron, which lost three Hurricanes to the Dornier gunner's fire.

On the other hand, not one of the Dorniers of 9./KG 76 escaped being hit by British fire. Two crashed into the Channel and two others crashed on the French coast with dead or wounded crew members onboard. Miraculously, it was the Do 17 manned by Oberfeldwebel Illg on this his first flight that fared best. Illg even managed to bring the aircraft and crew back to France, to Norrent-Fontes airfield! For this feat he was awarded the Knight's Cross.

By then a gigantic air battle had developed over a large area south of London. At 6,500 metres altitude No. 615 Squadron, which had also been ordered to Kenley, clashed with the Bf 109s of III./JG 3, which had joined Schöpfel's unit on a fighter sweep. Four Hurricanes and a Bf 109 fell to the ground like flaming torches. Two thousand metres below I. and II./KG 76 came in with twenty-seven 'fresh' Do 17s and twelve Ju 88s to finish the planned annihilation of Kenley sector station. This was the fomation that should have carried out their attack before Roth's group. Now they were met by an alerted and vindictive British fighter force. A gigantic cloud of smoke, visible for miles around, rose from the devastation of the Kenley station, and this spurred the British pilots to fight with even greater determination.

Twelve Hurricane pilots from 32 Squadron were already present in the air above the airfield. This unit was now led by Michael Crossley, promoted to Squadron Leader, who had, in the last few days, trained his pilots for frontal attacks. Now it was time for a baptism by fire! 'Tally Ho!' shouted 'Red Knight' Crossley over the radio and the dozen Hurricanes turned on a collision course with the twin-engined Luftwaffe planes.

Twenty Bf 110s from ZG 26 had been assigned as close escort to these Dornier planes, and the Zerstörer airmen turned and dived to attack the first formation of Hurricanes from behind. 'Flight Lieutenant [Humphrey] "Humph" Russell [of 32 Squadron] was surprised to be hit by extremely accurate and concentrated return fire from the Bf 110s and was forced to bale out over Edenbridge wounded in the left arm and right leg. First blood to the Zerstörer!'[181]

But because they flew with the bombers, the Bf 110s were far too slow, and when they attempted to get speed up by diving, they also ended up at a height disadvantage. At that moment eight of 64 Squadron's Spitfires plummeted from 7,000 metres, straight towards the Zerstörers. Squadron Leader Aeneas MacDonell hit the Bf 110 flown by Oberleutnant Rüdiger Proske, adjutant of I./ZG 26, and the pilot and the radio operator had to bail out. While they drifted down to imminent captivity under their parachutes, the

German formation dispersed as the terrified bomber pilots swerved to avoid fighter attacks. Their bombs were scattered widely and caused no great harm.

The Dorniers and Junkers then fled back towards the coast as fast as they could. For the airmen in the Bf 110 fighters, who were forced to stay close to the bombers, it became a frustratingly slow journey back over hostile territory – while they were easy targets for the nimble Spitfire and Hurricane fighters which constantly harrased them from above. Several fresh British fighter units joined the combat. The German return track soon became marked by the wreckages of crashed Bf 110s, Do 17s and Ju 88s.

Even Flight Lieutenant Robert Stanford Tuck – who belonged to 92 Squadron, which was not in the front line – joined the battle. He was temporarily visiting Northolt airfield and, without waiting for orders, took off alone as soon as he heard about the severe fighting. Tuck, with 11 kills on his tally, pursued two German aircraft over the sea. Tuck identified them as Do 17s or Ju 88s,[182] but it is more likely that they were a couple of fleeing Bf 110s. One of them may have been the plane flown by Oberleutnant Hans-Jürgen Kirchhoff, head of 3./ZG 26. He was killed along with his radio operator when they crashed into the sea.[183] After a long chase, Tuck managed to shoot down one of the German aircraft into the water, but immediately afterwards Tuck's own Spitfire was hit by cannon fire.[184] Judging by

German war correspondent Rolf von Pebal took this picture of a 64 Squadron Spitfire in its revetment during the raid against Kenley air base on 18 August 1940.

Tuck's own description, it seems that he was attacked from behind by another Bf 110 – which he never saw. Tuck abandoned his burning Spitfire and bailed out over land.

The sixty He 111s from KG 1 were meanwhile lucky to avoid serious fighter attacks. 'We flew zig-zagging with the He 111s', said Major Mettig from JG 54. 'Because of their bad formation flight, the He 111 formation became widely scattered. I estimate the distance to 35 km between the first and the last airplane. We knew that the British would concentrate their attacks against stragglers, so this placed great demands on us in the fighter escort. By the time we reached the target, the fuel reserve allowed us no more than ten minutes to spare. But we were replaced by two other Jagdgeschwaders and then flew straight back to our bases, where many landed with standing propellers.'

The attack against Biggin Hill became a total failure. All that was accomplished was a small number of bomb craters and some unexploded bombs on the runways.

Sometime after two o'clock the fighting died down. It had caused terrible losses on both sides. The German had lost 22 aircraft – nine Do 17s from KG 76, one He 111 from KG 1, eight Bf 110s and four Bf 109s. In return, their fighter pilots claimed to have shot down 34 British planes – of which ZG 26 'Horst Wessel' took half. The difference in results between Messerschmitts on close escort and those who had been out free hunting was striking. 6./ZG 26, which flew as close escort, suffered half of the eight Zerstörer losses. Three more had been shot down from I./ZG 26, which had also been tied to the bombers in this way. In contrast, Major Johannes Schalk's III./ZG 26 – which was free hunting – was the Messerschmitt Gruppe which succeeded best during this mission – 15 victories against one own loss. Oberleutnant Sophus Baagoe from 8./ZG 26 contributed two victories and thereby increased his total to nine. But the most successful German fighter pilot on this mission was clearly Oberleutnant Gerhard Schöpfel from III./JG 26, who had knocked down four.

The German victory claims were exaggerated, but the British units had still suffered severe attrition. A total of 16 Spitfires and Hurricanes were shot down and completely destroyed, and another nine were so badly damaged that they were out of action for some time to come. Worst affected however was Kenley sector station, where ten hangars and the Operations Room were in ruins, and all telephone lines were broken. For the first time the Germans had managed to neutralise one of Fighter Command's nine 'nerve centres'. In addition 17 British planes had been knocked out on the ground.

At half past two I./JG 52 made a new low-level attack against Manston airfield, similar to the attack the unit had made with such success two days before. The War Diary of I./JG 52 reads: 'A radio message was intercepted, revealing that a fighter unit had landed at Manston to refuel. This time too, we carried out the attack with great success. 10-11 Spitfires, three Bristol Blenheims and a hangar were seriously damaged or set burning.'[185] According to British records, two of 266 Squadron's Spitfires were completely destroyed on the ground at Manston.

The next blow was dealt by Luftflotte 3. Twenty-five Ju 88s from I. and II./KG 54 'Totenkopf' subjected the naval air base in Gosport to a devastating new attack. They were escorted by eighteen Bf 110s from ZG 76, and all German aircraft returned safe and sound to their bases. The main force of Ju 87s attacked the airfield at Thorney Island and Poling radar station further east, but there things went quite differently.

10 and 11 Group sent up five squadrons against the Stuka formations and their fighter escorts. Although the 85 Ju 87s from StG 77 had been given virtually the entire strength of Bf 109s at Jafü 3's disposal – more than 200 Bf 109s from JG 2, JG 27 and JG 53 – and thus were many times stronger than the relatively limited number of RAF fighters, the British succeeded in tearing the Stuka formations to pieces. Twelve Hurricanes from 43 Squadron were the first ones there and attacked the Stukas just as they pulled out of their dives after dropping their bombs. From their position 5,000 metres higher the Bf 109 pilots saw how suddenly one Ju 87 after another erupted in flames far below them. When they, shocked, dived as fast as they could to rescue their protectees, they were themselves attacked.

Shouting wildly, No. 234 Squadron's Spitfire pilots threw themselves into the mass of Bf 109s and created utter confusion among them. Flying Officer Paterson Clarence Hughes shot down two of the German fighters. So did Sergeant Alan Harker, and other '109s were downed by Pilot Officers Robert Doe and Edward Mortimer-Rose. Most of the Messerschmitt pilots were forced to fight to save themselves, and meanwhile even 152, 601 and 602 squadrons appeared to complete the massacre of the Stukas.

In the space of a few minutes, the British fighter pilots shot down 16 Stukas. No. 43 Squadron was credited with 8 downed Ju 87s, 152 Squadron was credited with 9, and 601 and 602 Squadron, 6 each. Sergeant James Hallowes from 43 Squadron once again shot down three Ju 87s – thus repeating his feat from 16 August – and reached a combined total of 16 victories. In 601 Squadron Flight Lieutenant Carl Davis and Flying Officer Tom Grier were credited with two victories each in the Stuka massacre. In addition, Davis shot down one of the Bf 109s which had managed to escape 234 Squadron and was trying to rescue the embattled Stukas.

In addition to the 16 Ju 87s which remained in England, two more crashed on their return to France because of severe battle damage. Among the missing crew members was Hauptmann Herbert Meisel, commander of I./StG 77. It was an unmitigated disaster for Stukageschwader 77, which was immediately withdrawn from combat. The scattered and disordered remnants of the fighter escort returned to base at irregular intervals with utterly demoralised pilots. Their unit commanders were completely unable to explain what had happened. They themselves had lost 8 Bf 109s – in combat with an enemy where they had not only had the advantage of height but also a fourfold superiority in numbers! It was a first class defeat.

The price of this amazing success to the participating RAF formations was confined to three destroyed and eight damaged aircraft. The only drawback for the British was that two pilots of 601 Squadron had been killed, and that

43 Squadron's top ace, Flight Lieutenant Frank Carey (11½ victories), was badly wounded.

Air fighting on 18 August ended that evening when Kesselring sent a hundred or so bombers and more than 150 fighters across the Channel.

58 Do 17s from I. and II./KG 2, with a close escort consisting of 25 Bf 109s from III./JG 51, had factories and railway stations on the outskirts of London as their main objectives. North Weald airfield was the target for 51 He 111s from II. and III./KG 53, with 20 Bf 110s from I. and II./ZG 26 as close escort.

A hundred Bf 109s from all the Jagdgeschwaders in Luftflotte 2 went out free hunting ahead of them. Once again the Bf 110s from III./ZG 26 flew on free hunting. No less than 143 Spitfires and Hurricanes went up to repel the invaders. Even Wing Commander Victor Beamish, the almost forty-year-old commander of North Weald sector-airfield, took off with one of the 151 Squadron Hurricanes. The Irishman Beamish was a fierce fighter. 'We have to kill all the Germans in the air', he said.

In a cruel repeat of the previous day's mission, 4./ZG 26 – which was the close escort for KG 53 – bore the brunt of the British fighter attack . 'We had strict orders to fly close escort, and that was the cause of the disaster that followed', said Unteroffizier Theo Rutter, rear-gunner of one of the Bf 110s downed in the air combat. This Staffel was attacked by at least three squadrons, and of four Zerstörers that were lost during the mission, three belonged to 4./ZG 26. The German Bf 109 units fared little better. III./JG 51 was admittedly credited with three victories and no own losses. Hauptmann Walter Oesau accounted for two of these and this raised his personal score to twenty. But three Bf 109 aces were lost in the engagement, and in all cases Polish airmen were involved. II./JG 51 lost two Bf 109s without managing to shoot down a single British plane (at least none that was confirmed). Pilot Officer Pawel Zenker, a Polish pilot in 501 Squadron, explained how he shot down Hauptmann Horst Tietzen, the ace with 20 victories who commanded 5./JG 51: 'With Green 1 I went straight to the the fighters and engaged one of them. He turned back towards France and I chased him as he climbed firing from 300 [feet] and closer ranges and about 10 miles over the sea I saw smoke and fire come from the fuselage and he rapidly lost height. The Me 109 did not adopt evasive action but flew straight on until it crashed into the water somewhere near the North Goodwin Lightship.'[186] Tietzen's dead body later washed ashore near Calais. Flying Officer Stefan Witorzenc, another Pole in 501 Squadron, shot down another of the pilots of 5./JG 51, Leutnant Hans-Otto Lessing, who was killed.

III./JG 26 was credited with two victories – which was slight consolation for the loss of two of the unit's most important aces: Leutnant Gerhard Müller-Dühe dived to attack a Hurricane, eager to record his sixth victory. It was a mistake that would cost him dearly. Peter Brothers, who then served as a Pilot Officer in 32 Squadron, explained what happened: 'I turned sharply right, on to the tail of an Me 109 as he overtook me. I gave a quick glance behind to ensure that there was not another one on my tail, laid my sight on him and fired a short burst. I hit him, another short burst and he caught fire and his dive steepened. I followed him down, he went into a field at a steep angle and a cloud of flame and black smoke erupted.'[187]

By all accounts Müller-Dühe was then fired upon by the Polish Pilot Officer Boleslaw Wlasnowolski, who described how he followed the Bf 109 down towards the ground: 'I followed, firing several short bursts, he dived into the ground and went up in flames.'[188]

Pilot Officer Peter Brothers contributed one of No. 32 Squadron's 16 confirmed victories on 18 August 1940. When 32 Squadron was withdrawn from combat on 3 September 1940, Brothers was transferred to 257 Squadron, and on the same day he was promoted to Flight Lieutenant. (Photo: Cull.)

Müller-Dühe did not survive. His comrade from III./JG 26, Leutnant Walter Blume – also credited with five victories – had slightly better luck. Blume had a Hurricane in his sights when suddenly a tracer passing his cockpit made him look upwards and back. To his horror he found that he was staring right into the eight fire-spitting muzzles of a diving Hurricane. Blume turned as he dived, but could not get away from the Hurricane pilot – 32 Squadron's Pilot Officer Karol Pniak. The latter's commander, Squadron Leader Michael Crossley, and Pilot Officer Alan Eckford

601 Squadron's Flying Officer Carl Davis flew Hurricane 'UF-K' in the massacres on Stukas on 16 and 18 August 1940. (Photo: Riddle via Ivers.)

also raced after Blumes steeply diving Messerschmitt 109. Blume crash landed his 109 near Canterbury; he was seriously injured, but was still alive.

Despite the mediocre performance of the Bf 109s only four German bombers were shot down – all from KG 53. This was mainly due to the free hunting Bf 110s from ZG 26 'Horst Wessel'. They accounted for most of the 12 British fighters shot down in this combat – nine of which were completely destroyed.[189] When Squadron Leader Peter Townsend intervened with 13 Hurricanes from his 85 Squadron, he found that the Bf 110s made it almost impossible to reach the bombers. 'A general engagement was now taking place, enemy aircraft consisting chiefly of Me 110's', said Townsend.[190] Among the British pilots shot down by Bf 110s was Squadron Leader Gordon, commander of No. 151 Squadron. It was the second time in three days he had been shot down, but this time Gordon was badly burned. Another RAF pilot to be shot down – possibly also by a pilot from III./ZG 26 – was an ace with 15 victories, albeit an unusual one. His name was Rodolphe de Hemricourt de Grunne, and he was a Belgian nobleman who had fought side by side with several Luftwaffe veterans as a volunteer fighter pilot in Franco's Air Force during the Spanish Civil War. There he had been credited with 14 victories. Now, he served as a pilot officer with 32 Squadron. Badly burned, Count de Hemricourt de Grunne bailed out of his blazing Hurricane and spent six months in hospital.

Even Wing Commander Beamish came close to being shot down, but was fortunate to escape with his Hurricane badly damaged. When Flight Lieutenant George Stoney was shot down and killed by a Bf 110 over the Thames estuary at 18:45 (German time), 501 Squadron had lost six Hurricanes and four pilots during the day.

Upon its return to France, Oberleutnant Theodor Rossiwall's 5./ZG 26 – which had been free hunting with III./ZG 26 – counted four victories without own losses. Major Johannes Schalk's III./ZG 26 'Horst Wessel' was as usual the most successful, with 11 new victories – this time without any own losses. In Oberleutnant Ernst Matthes' 7./ZG 26, Leutnant Kuno Konopka and Feldwebel Franz Sander were credited with two victories each; in the latter case it was the pilot's third victory that day. With the Spitfire Oberfeldwebel Joseph Bracun reported shot down at 18:58, 7./ZG 26 reached its 30th victory – achieved against only one own combat loss since the war had started.

Typically, both sides proclaimed themselves as victors in the air battles on 18 August. Fighter Command reported 126 German aircraft downed. Of these, 54 Squadron claimed 14, with no own losses. That evening 54 Squadron received a telegram from Lord Newall, Chief of the Air Staff: 'Well done 54 Squadron. In your hard fighting this is the way to deal with the enemy.'

The German High Command announced that 124 British aircraft had been shot down. With 51 victories ZG 26 'Horst Wessel' claimed the lion's share of this result, which gained the unit a special mention in the OKW communiqué. According to German estimates the RAF had lost 732 aircraft in the previous eight days.

Flight Lieutenant Frank Carey stood out as one of the most daring pilots in 43 Squadron. He scored seven victories during the Battle of France, but was himself shot down and wounded. He shot down a Bf 109 on 19 July, but on 8 August he was wounded in combat with a Bf 110. Back in service on 12 August he managed to add another three and a half air victories to his tally before he on 18 August was once again shot down and injured. He did not return to front-line service until in December 1941, when he was transferred to a fighter unit in Burma. When the war ended Carey had 28 air victories. He passed away on 6 December 2004, at 92 years of age.

tively small force of RAF fighters had been able to beat up a mass formation of 200 Bf 109s and inflict a defeat of historic proportions on his dive-bombers. Göring had long been aware of the vulnerability of the Ju 87, and he had watched the losses among the Stuka units mount with growing concern. On 8 August, ten Ju 87s were lost, on the 13th six, on the 15th seven and on the 16th nine. But not even in his worst nightmares could the Reichsmarshall have imagined what happened on 18 August. Perhaps the worst thing was that it took place under the eyes of Jafü 3's entire fighter force! The Luftwaffe's total combat losses amounted to nearly 350 aircraft since large scale attacks had started on 8 August. Göring was not the only one to conclude that the air offensive against England was not going as planned. The RAF was proving a far harder nut to crack than the Germans expected.

Not only in Britain, but throughout the world, the British airmen's stubborn fight against the vastly stronger Luftwaffe was looked on with amazement and admiration. After Poland, Norway and France people had come to regard Hitler's new Germany as invincible, but on this tiny island, led by its irrepressible prime minister, the people continued to offer resistance. In particular this made a big impression in the USA. Winston Churchill's speech in the British Parliament on 20 August was full of admiration for the pilots in the RAF, and some of the words he uttered have become legendary: 'The gratitude of every home in our Island, in our Empire, and indeed throughout the world, except in the abodes of the guilty, goes out to the British airmen who, undaunted by odds, unwearied in their constant challenge and mortal danger, are turning the tide of the World War by their prowess and by their devotion. Never in the field of human conflict was so much owed by so many to so few. All hearts go out to the fighter pilots, whose brilliant actions we see with our own eyes day after day.' Then he added: 'but we must never forget that all the time, night after night, month after month, our bomber squadrons travel far into Germany, find their targets in the darkness by the highest navigational skill, aim their attacks, often under the heaviest fire, often with serious loss, with deliberate careful discrimination, and inflict shattering blows upon the whole of the technical and war-making structure of the Nazi power.'

Only days later the British bomber pilots – whose contribution to the Battle of Britain is often underestimated – would make a vital contribution that helped change the course of the battle.

The actual combat losses on 18 August were 71 German aircraft and 30 fighters from Fighter Command. In addition, 10 RAF fighters crashed or emergency-landed with combat damage in England, and as many again had landed with moderate damage. For Dowding and Park the British loss figures were enough to prevent themselves from getting carried away by the victory communiqués. Without a doubt more hard air fighting that would grind down already beleaguered units lay ahead. 501 Squadron's Operations Record Book for 18 August gives a clear picture of the pressure the fighters on both sides were under: 'Squadron 15-mins Available from dawn to 8.30 when aircraft took off from Hawkinge. Combat near Canterbury in broken cloud and haze. P/O [Kenneth] Lee wounded in the leg, P/O [Franciszek] Kozlowski seriously injured, Sgt [Donald] McKay slight burns, P/O [John] Bland killed. Squadron returned to Gravesend. All aircraft scrambled – vectored to Biggin Hill which was under attack.P /O [Robert] Dafforn [shot down and] baled out. 7 Hurricanes took off for Hawkinge patrol at 16.50. Met 50 bombers and fighters. Red section attacked. 2 Me 110 shot down. F/L [George] Stoney killed in that combat.'[191]

The mood was even more sombre on the German side. Göring was utterly shocked by the reports he received that night. In particular he could not understand how a rela-

CHAPTER 6
'THE CRITICAL PERIOD'

New directives

Monday 19 August, the commander of Fighter Command's 11 Group, Air Vice-Marshal Keith Park, summoned his sector commanders and their air controllers to an 'emergency meeting'. Nowhere on the British side was the crisis more evident than within the leadership of 11 Group, which was under the heaviest pressure from Göring's air armada. Unit after unit had been sent up against the relentless enemy bomber formations and fighter units, the British had achieved impressive results, but they still had not been able to quell the violence of the German storm. The heavy air strikes against Kenley, Lympne, Hawkinge, Manston, Martlesham, Rochester and Croydon showed weaknesses in the defence.

'Now that Göring knows that he can penetrate our inland airfields, there will be no stopping him from continuing', said Park.

On top of that the air fighting had developed into a war of attrition, and even despite exaggerated victory claims, Fighter Command's leadership realized that at the present rate the RAF would not last long. The outlook had not, as we have seen, been particularly favourable when the first great battle took place on 8 August. Since then, the RAF had lost 211 single-engined fighters and 154 experienced fighter pilots. In the same period, total replacements were no more than 170 new aircraft and 63 newly trained pilots!

'In a months' time, how many pilots and aircraft will I have at my disposal?' Hugh Dowding asked himself.

It was obvious that Fighter Command had made many tactical mistakes. One of the most serious was that the fighter pilots often let themselves be drawn into 'unnecessary' battles with the German Messerschmitts instead of concentrating on the bombers. Fighter pilots in all air forces often tended to prefer classical fighter combat, which appealed to adrenaline-filled young hotheads. Attacks against bomber formations, however, were not as popular – 'they also shoot rearwards', complained fighter pilots of all nations. The men of Fighter Command were no exception. But fighter-versus-fighter combat cost Fighter Command high losses while the German bombers broke through to their targets. This was something that Park tackled when he issued his Directive No. 4:

• Use fighter aircraft to attack the large enemy formations over land or close enough to land for our own fighters to be able to glide to the coast if they are damaged. For the next two or three weeks, we cannot afford to lose pilots through ditching in the sea.

One of the German aircraft that was shot down during the 'calm' period between 18 and 24 August, was a Bf 110 of Erprobungsgruppe 210 that was destroyed on 20 August by the Spitfire pilots of 66 Squadron's 'A' Flight. Seen in this image is one of them, Pilot Officer Hugh Kennard, the leader of 'Yellow' Section. (Photo: Vasco.)

- Avoid sending fighters out over the sea to hunt reconnaissance aircraft or small formations of enemy fighters.
- Dedicate a couple of fighters to tackle occasional reconnaissance aircraft that come in over the land. If it is cloudy, keep a patrol of one or two fighters up over any airfield that the enemy can approach through the clouds.
- For major incursions towards land, only a limited number of squadrons, equipped with Spitfires, will be deployed against enemy fighters. Our primary purpose is to attack the enemy bombers, especially those who fly in under the cloud base.
- If all our squadrons around London are airborne attacking large hostile raids, contact 12 Group and request support to protect the sector stations north and east of London, Debden, North Weald and Hornchurch.
- If a large raid has crossed the coast and is approaching our airfields, send up a squadron, or even the sector's own training group, to patrol over each sector station.[192]

Park, however, did not consider the coastal airfields – Lympne, Hawkinge and Manston – too vulnerable to be evacuated, and this would cost his men dearly in the coming days. Apart from this, Directive No. 4 corrected many of the mistakes that Fighter Command had made since 8 August. Directive No. 4, however, came a little too late. If Park had issued his directive ten days earlier, the fighting between 8 and 18 August would probably have had a better outcome from the British point of view. At the same time Reichsmarschall Göring held a conference with his generals at Karinhall and from there he issued new orders that would reduce the effect of most of Park's Directive No. 4.

Instead of the usually jovial, joking 'Hermann', the German generals found a grim Reichsmarschall. Göring's first instruction was that the Ju 87s would immediately be withdrawn from the campaign against Britain. Instead, they would be saved to support the planned invasion, and possibly used against shipping if the British resumed traffic in the English Channel.

Like Park and Dowding, Göring realized that the Luftwaffe's biggest chance of wiping out RAF Fighter Command was to shoot down its fighters in aerial combat. Therefore, he addressed the question of how to best use the Messerschmitts to inflict some decisive blows against Fighter Command. A common myth claims that at the conference on 19 August Göring gave orders to tie the fighters to close escort missions. In fact, it was the exact opposite – Reichsmarschall Göring gave his commanders a sharp reprimand for not following his instructions to give the Messerschmitt pilots sufficient freedom. It was the generals at the English Channel, not Göring, who wanted close escort to make the bomber fliers feel secure. But Göring realized that it was a false sense of security – the most effective protection was given by the Messerschmitts flying out in advance to take on the British fighters climbing to attack the bombers.

'Only a part of the fighters may be used for direct escort for the bombers', said Göring. 'We must dispatch as many fighters as possible on free hunting, which allows them to provide the bombers with an indirect cover since they then operate under the most ideal conditions to combat enemy fighters.'

From now on, Göring decided, the Messerschmitts would play the lead role in the offensive against the RAF. It was clear that the long flight across the English Channel from Luftflotte 3's bases on the Cotentin Peninsula made it easier for the British defenders to organise countermeasures. This had led to particularly severe losses for Luftflotte 3. In consequence, Göring decided to transfer the majority of the fighter units in Luftflotte 3 to Jafü 2 at Pas de Calais. Luftflotte 3 would then change strategy and mainly devote itself to night bombing of British industrial targets and airfields. Interesting to note is that Bomber Command's repeated 'pinpricks' against Germany had had the effect that a large part of the German night raids were directed specifically against British bomber bases, and thereby diverted efforts from attacks on Fighter Command's ground installations.

The bombers of Luftflotte 2 would continue to be deployed against the RAF ground organisation in daylight, but in small groups each time. To provoke the opposing fighters into air combat, the attacks would now be extended to ground targets and aviation industries around London. Smaller bomber formations with an overwhelming escort of Bf 109s and Bf 110s would continue to arrive over the British Isles with the smallest possible intervals. 11 Group ended up right in the line of fire – and they had just received tougher orders from Park to avoid fighter combat. It seems as if Göring had guessed his opponent's intentions.

One problem for German fighter operations over the British Isles was that they often ended with the fighters having to carry out a half-hour long return flight without ammunition and with too little fuel to allow any major evasive manoeuvring if they were attacked by British fighters. Göring therefore gave his Jagdfliegerführer (Jafüs) a mandate to organise 'reception' of returning fighter units: For each major fighter operation over the British Isles they would hold back some fighter units that would be sent out to cover the main force's retreat. It is this order that has been misinterpreted as Göring giving orders that Bf 109s would be escorting Bf 110s.

With these directives, Göring laid the foundation for the phase of the Battle of Britain that the British later would call 'the critical period'.

24 August 1940

After a few days of tranquility because of adverse weather conditions, the German storm broke out again on 24 August. For the first time in almost a week the British radar screens at the stations along the south coast began to fill with echoes of incoming aircraft.

At eight in the morning no less than eleven squadrons were ordered into the air to meet the incoming German raid.[193] At 4,000 metres above the Strait of Dover some of these encountered three formations of German bombers as well as a large number of Bf 109s. In accordance with Park's new directives, the Spitfires attacked the German

On 24 August 1940, the Defiant fighter was reinstated in the battle, now with 264 Squadron. In two hectic days – 24 and 26 August – this unit amassed 14 air victories against eight own losses. The picture shows some of the unit's airmen. Sixth from the left is the unit commander, Squadron Leader Philip Hunter. (Photo: Goss.)

fighter escort while the Hurricane pilots steered towards the bombers. However theory is one thing, and practice is something quite different. No. 610 Squadron's Sergeant Ronnie Hamlyn turned his Spitfire in behind a Ju 88, which he managed to destroy with only a two-second burst that hit the port motor.[194]

'There was no dogfight in the true meaning of the word', recalled 610 Squadron's Sergeant Cyril Bamberger, 'but rather a confused chaos of swirling aircraft, where everyone was firing at everyone and chasing everyone for maybe thirty hectic seconds. Then all of the individual airplanes had scattered to the winds, and most pilots had lost

This Hurricane, 'VY-K', P3408, was flown by 85 Squadron's Pilot Officer Geoffrey 'Sammy' Allard. Allard already had eight air victories when the Battle of Britain began. When 85 Squadron was turned into a night fighter unit in October 1940, his score stood at 19 individual and five shared victories. Allard was awarded with the Distinguished Flying Cross (DFC). He died in a plane crash on 13 March 1941.

contact with all other aircraft, so the combat, so to speak died out.'[195] 610 Squadron's war diary recorded that 'the rest of the unit scattered, and neither saw nor attacked any enemy aircraft.'[196] Sergeant Stanley Arnfield, however, was attacked and shot down by Oberleutnant Josef Fözö from II./JG 51. In return, Ronnie Hamlyn attacked one of Fözö's comrades. Hamlyn came in from behind and fired a short burst from 150 metres, aiming at the centre of the fuselage, where the large fuel tank was located. It was sufficient for the Bf 109 to crash into the Channel. The pilot was picked up by German air-sea rescue. Another Bf 109 from II./JG 51 was shot down by 85 Squadron's Pilot Officer Geoffrey Allard. Moreover, the violent British fighter attack scattered the German bomber formation, causing it to return to base with its mission uncompleted.

A little over an hour later the Germans tried again, this time with Major Mölders at the head of the entire JG 51. At 09:35, No. 501 Squadron took off from Gravesend with twelve Hurricanes. Forty-five minutes later, they were on patrol northwest of Dover when the pilots saw about thirty Do 17s escorted by Bf 109s coming in from the southeast. 501 Squadron attacked and the scene from the morning was repeated: the German bombers jettisoned their bombs and turned back towards France.[197] The clash that followed cost each side one loss. Sergeant Antoni Glowacki, a Polish airman in 501 Squadron, was credited with the German loss. It was just the start of Glowacki's feat of arms on this hot summer day.

Mölders landed at St. Inglevert at 11:55 (German time – i.e. one hour before British time).[198] By then the next German formation was already on the way over southern England. Major Adolf Galland brought along his entire JG 26

'Schlageter' on a fighter sweep which, at least initially, was more successful than the one Mölders had led. Above eastern Kent they surprised the Hurricanes of 151 Squadron. In a short but intense encounter, Leutnant Gustav Sprick and Oberleutnant Joachim Müncheberg claimed to have shot down two Hurricanes. In fact, three Hurricanes were hit, but two of these could later be repaired. During the fighter combat the Germans broke formations in the usual way. Half a dozen Bf 109s from III./JG 26, which was now led by Gerhard Schöpfel, promoted to Hauptmann, got into trouble on the way home.

Under the leadership of Squadron Leader John Ellis No. 610 Squadron was tasked to patrol over Gravesend and Dover with twelve Spitfires. They had taken off at 10:35 (British time) and an hour later they spotted six Messerschmitt 109s. One of the German fighters was immediately shot down and the Spitfire pilots then chased the fleeing Messerschmitts all the way to Calais, where they shot down two more.[199] Sergeant Ronnie Hamlyn destroyed one of these with three three-second bursts aimed at the centre of the fuselage.[200] This was Hamlyn's third victory that day. If it had not been for some Bf 109s from I.(J)/LG 2 intervening in defence of their vulnerable colleagues – Oberleutnant Herbert Ihlefeld and his wingman Leutnant Friedrich Geisshardt reported two Spitfires shot down – the three remaining Bf 109s might also have been downed. But the loss of three planes was a bad blow for III./JG 26, even though all pilots survived.

The intensity of the fighting then escalated. The next German bomber unit, II./KG 76, broke through. At 12:45 (British time) its Ju 88s struck the airfield at Manston. In the midst of this attack, something happened that had the attacking German airmen scarcely believing their eyes: between exploding bombs, British fighters rolled out onto the runway – three . . . six . . . nine! Smoke and fire engulfed the entire airfield. Down on the ground the single-engined fighters rolled into the clouds of smoke and the dust and, miraculously, came out the other side again – unharmed!

Squadron Leader Philip Hunter, commander of 264 Squadron's Defiants, had only one thought in his head: Get into the air and beat the Germans! The Boulton Paul Defiant, an anything but conventional fighter, whose armament consisted of four machine guns mounted in an electrically powered dorsal turret, was for obvious reasons his favourite. The machine had really proved itself in the air above Dunkirk in May. But then came the fateful 19 July and the sister unit 141 Squadron lost 60% of its strength in a single battle. It was apparently enough for the high command to give the Defiant the same low status that the Gladiator and Blenheim fighters already had, 'second class fighters'!

But in Philip Hunter's eyes, it was an unfair assessment – 264 was taken out of combat before it had even seen a German aircraft over England. In fact, at that time, the unit was indispensable, or so Hunter and his airmen thought. 264's chance came on 22 August when it was moved South from the remote base at Kirton-in-Lindsey. Twenty-one belligerent Defiant crews left the routine patrols over the East Coast convoys behind and moved to Hornchurch sector airfield – with the vulnerable coastal airfield at Manston as an operational base.

610 Squadron's Ronnie Hamlyn shot down five German aircraft with Spitfire 'DW-Q' on 24 August 1940. Hamlyn achieved a total of 11 air victories. After the war he worked for Save the Children. Hamlyn passed away in 1991, at the age of 77.

The Defiant airmen were full of anticipation when they arrived at Hornchurch. The exhausted Spitfire pilots from 266 Squadron, which had lost seven of their twenty pilots since the unit had moved to Hornchurch ten days before, watched the confident newcomers with a mixture of pity and contempt. In the silent and introverted veterans' eyes could be read: They'll soon learn!

Philip Hunter's death-defying crews charged through the hailstorm of bombs hitting Manston and got into the air. Their throttles were on maximum boost and their gunners had their four Brownings cocked, ready to fire a total of 2,400 rounds from each turret. According to Park's new directive the Defiants, just like the Hurricanes, should concentrate on the German bombers. The German fighter escort, however, had other ideas.

'Bandits! Line astern! Evasive action!' called Pilot Officer Eric Barwell, the pilot of one of the Defiants, when he saw five Bf 109s coming in at full speed. While the Defiants started to turn, Oberleutnant Arnold Lignitz from III./JG 51 scored decisive hits on Pilot Officer Joseph Jones' Defiant and saw it crash in flames.

But the men of 264 Squadron differed from the beginners in their 'sister unit' 141 Squadron – which had suffered such severe losses in July – by their greater experience with the machines, which meant that they had developed better tactics. These Defiant pilots knew to turn in to give the gunners better opportunity to shoot, and in quick succession they knocked down three of III./JG 51's Bf 109s.

This gave the Hurricanes from 501 Squadron a chance to get at the Ju 88s. Major Friedrich Möricke, the commander of II./KG 76, was killed when his Ju 88 crashed in a field just north of Deal. Another machine from his Stabskette crashed nearby. Another two Junkers 88s, both belonging to 4./KG 76, tumbled down in flames from the air south of Manston. One of them was shot down by the British ace Sergeant James 'Ginger' Lacey. This was the eighth confirmed victory for the 23-year-old fighter pilot, who had already been awarded the DFM. Sergeant Antoni Glowacki also bought down a Ju 88 and, shortly afterwards, a Bf 109. Thus Glowacki, just like 610 Squadron's Ronnie Hamlyn, had so far achieved three victories on that day. By pure coincidence this last Bf 109 was flown by Oberfeldwebel Fritz Beeck from II./JG 51 – and was therefore this Gruppe's second loss to the same pilot on 24 August, 1940. Beeck piloted his smoking Messerschmitt down to a field near East Langdon. He belly-landed and climbed out to be met by a police officer with a drawn revolver. 'I surrender, constable', said the young German and put up his hands.

When the Defiant pilots went in to land at Hornchurch three crews were missing, including Squadron Leader Hunter. He was last seen chasing a Ju 88 over the sea. In total the mission to Manston cost II./KG 76 five Ju 88s, one of which was written off when it crashed with severe combat damage after returning to France.

All that could be seen of the airfield at Manston was a huge black cloud of smoke. Buildings, hangars, aircraft on the ground and runways had all been completely destroyed. Violent fires raged, there were unexploded bombs everywhere and all telecommications were broken. And already the next wave was flying in to raid the same airfield again. This formation consisted of the assault planes from Erprobungsgruppe 210. They attacked with their usual precision and then withdrew without having suffered any losses. When yet another German bomber formation flew in over Manston shortly afterwards, these fliers found that the airfield was virtually wiped out. So instead they dropped their bombs on a small sports airfield in Ramsgate. This cost the town 26 dead. After seven large attacks and numerous smaller raids, Fighter Command finally decided to evacuate the airfield at Manston.

More and more German aircraft roared in over the coastline at Dover, Deal, Folkestone, Dungeness, Eastbourne and Brighton. After a tentative start in the morning Göring's new directives had obviously begun to have an effect. In 11 Group's headquarters at Uxbridge they had long since lost control of the situation. The Germans seemed to come from all sides, at all altitudes and in all directions – in wave after wave. Soon it was impossible to distinguish individual formations and their routes. What were their targets? Which formation was approaching what? What should be defended? Which squadrons were to be alerted and at what altitude, in which direction and

towards what should they be vectored? In many units not even the commanding officer knew where his aircraft were – how many were in the air, how many had landed on nearby airfields and how many had crash-landed or been shot down.

Pilot Officer Peter Brothers in 32 Squadron recalled: 'The weather was sunny and clear. We tangled with a bunch of 109Es. All split up and everyone for himself. I got on tail of a 109E, which dived away with me in hot pursuit. I opened fire and he started to smoke, and almost immediately, the pilot baled out and fell into the sea.'

These Bf 109s belonged to III./JG 3, which escorted twenty Ju 88s from Major Erich Bloedorn's III./KG 4. Pilot Officer Karol Pniak, a Polish pilot in 32 Squadron, had his Hurricane shot in flames and bailed out. He hit the ground three miles northwest of Hawkinge and immediately went back to the airfield to take off again. At the same time his equally resolute fellow countryman in 501 Squadron, Sergeant 'Toni' Glowacki, joined the battle. There was also 610 Squadron, which took off from Biggin Hill for the third time in less than eight hours, this time with nine Spitfires. Fighters from III./JG 3 circled the Ju 88s and kept attacking the RAF fighters, who, instead of attacking the bombers were then forced to defend themselves. They carried out the latter, however, with a determination that cost III./JG 3 dearly.

Sergeant Ronnie Hamlyn turned in his Spitfire behind a Bf 109 and placed himself slightly lower than the German aircraft in the pilot's blind spot. There he raised the nose of his plane and fired a burst into the middle of the fuselage – this was his specialty. The German aircraft immediately caught fire and crashed. Hamlyn attacked another '109, adjusted for deflection, and with a well-aimed burst of fire downed the plane.[201] This brought Hamlyn's result for the day to an amazing five confirmed victories. Claiming a Bf 109 and a Ju 88 in the same combat, 'Toni' Glowacki reached the same result.

Two pilots from III./JG 3 were shot down and captured. Three more of its Bf 109s limped off with severe battle damages, and crashed on their return to France. But Major Bloedorn's bombers could not be stopped. While the fighter-versus-fighter combat reached its climax, the Ju 88s flew in towards their target – Hornchurch sector station.

The remaining Defiants of 264 Squadron had just been refuelled and rearmed when the loudspeakers seemed to explode: '264 Squadron scramble, scramble, scramble!' shouted an excited voice through the speakers. 'Personally I blame the panic in the voice for the serious damage to two Defiants – they collided on the ground when taxiing', commented 264 Squadron's Pilot Officer Eric Barwell.[202]

Even if the planes scrambled very quickly, the bombs began to fall while the last Defiants were still jolting across the runway. The Ju 88s swept towards the hangars and the aircraft on the ground. When the rest of 264 Squadron left the ground, two Defiants remained among the craters on the runway. A third was shortly afterwards shot down by a Bf 109 pilot, once again Arnold Lignitz. The others chased the attackers and claimed to have shot down three Ju 88s. In fact, III./KG 4 sustained no losses at all.[203] This was partly due to the German fighter escort, but also to the fact that the new German tactics had made the air controllers of 11 Group lose track of the situation in the air.

Karol Pniak, the belligerent Polish pilot of 32 Squadron who had been shot down less than an hour earlier, was back flying when the unit, led by Squadron Leader Michael Crossley, took off again from Hawkinge. They did not get far. A formation of Bf 109s from I./JG 26 came sweeping in over the coast, and in the combat that followed, four Hurricanes were shot down. But all pilots involved – including Squadron Leader Crossley – survived. Karol Pniak had amazing luck when, for the second time in the space of sixty minutes, he survived being shot down.

While the Ju 88s made full speed back towards France, twenty He 111s from III./KG 53 flew in towards the airfield at North Weald, north of Hornchurch. They were attacked by several squadrons. Eric Clayton, who served as a mechanic in 56 Squadron during the Battle of Britain, witnessed the events from the ground: 'A formation of about 20 He 111s managed to get through. It was a beautiful summer day as we watched the Heinkles approach from the north west at about 15,000 feet. They were about five miles away and in close formation; we could see Hurricanes pressing home attacks but then breaking off, presumably because of the concentrated fire from the bombers.' [204]

What Clayton saw from afar was the Bf 110s of III./ZG 26 'Horst Wessel' keeping the British fighters away from the Heinkel bombers. The British combat report reads: 'Waves of Me 110s stepped up above the bombers and other Me 110s circling the bombers at the same level. The bombers were travelling at 200 m.p.h. and the superior speed of the Me 110s enabled them to perform this circling, weaving evolution which made a concentrated attack on the bombers very difficult. The bombers were able to maintain their close formation and broke through the thin cloud at 15,000 ft to bomb North Weald.' [205]

It was a black day for No. 151 Squadron, which at noon had already lost three Hurricanes to III./JG 26, and now faced III./ZG 26. Pilot Officer Irving Smith, a New Zealander, had just opened fire on a He 111 when he was attacked by the Bf 110 flown by Oberstleutnant Johannes (Hans) Schalk, the commander of III./ZG 26, and a single burst was enough to put Smith's Hurricane out of action. He nevertheless managed to bring the plane down for a landing so that it could be repaired. At the same time Unteroffizier Hans Scheuplein, Schalk's wingman, shot down the British unit leader, Squadron Leader Eric King. But even this Hurricane could be saved since the combat took place right above North Weald's airfield.

It looked as if the Zerstörer airmen's efforts would enable the He 111s to perform a virtually copy-book bombing of North Weald. But they had not reckoned with Wing Commander Victor Beamish, the hot-headed comander of North Weald sector station. Despite his age, he did not hesitate to take off with one of 151 Squadron's Hurricanes. [206] Eric Clayton describes what followed: 'Suddenly a high-pitched whine came from the direction of the approaching bombers and there, high above them, was a single Hurricane hurtling down in a vertical dive, guns firing, and heading for the centre of the German formation. When it was almost on top of them, the formation broke up and the waiting fighters at once pounced on the vulnerable tailenders. The pilot of the diving Hurricane, we were not surprised to learn later, was the fearless Victor Beamish. One can imagine him taking this enemy attack on his station as a personal insult.' [207]

Pilot Officer Andy Mamedoff, American volunteer in 609 Squadron, is posing in front of his damaged Spitfire, obviously glad to have escaped the attack from a Bf 110 of ZG 2 unhurt. (Photo: Vasco.)

Sergeant William Dymond, one of the aces in 111 Squadron, set fire to the engine of a He 111 from 9./KG 53. The pilot of the German plane turned and headed towards a cloud bank but he had no chance. A new attack was carried out by the Defiant crew of Pilot Officer Michael Young/Sergeant Leslie Russell. The four machine guns in the Defiant's rear turret gave the Heinkel a broadside that completely riddled the German plane. The British pilot estimated that about 600 bullets hit the bomber. The pilot in the Heinkel saw his observer, Major Karl Ritscherle, move back in the airplane to help his wounded comrades. A moment later huge flames erupted from both engines and the pilot bailed out. While he was hanging in his parachute, he saw the doomed Heinkel plunge down and crash violently beside a reservoir below. None of the German pilot's crewmates survived.

Pilot Officer John Ellacombe from No. 151 Squadron attacked a He 111 from below, fired and scored hits all over the belly of the bomber. When Ellacombe came up close to the bomber his own plane's spinner was hit either by counter fire or detached parts from the Heinkel, which caused his engine to explode. Both aircraft crash-landed in a field.

When Ellacombe emerged from the wreckage of his Hurricane, he was greeted by a very grim looking farmer with a pitchfork in his hands – he thought Ellacombe was German! Fortunately a British Army sergeant appeared immediately afterwards who could identify Ellacombe's flight uniform. Ellacombe wanted to investigate the He 111 he had shot down, but the Army sergeant advised him against it. 'Don't go and look, they are in a filthy mess' he said. All the crewmen on board were covered in their own blood – the result of the hundreds of bullets Ellacombe had pumped into the belly of the bomber. Instead Ellacombe went and got himself helplessly drunk. . .

Altogether five He 111s were shot down, including four from 9./KG 53. 'However, this brave action could not prevent the inevitable for the bombers were by then too close', Eric Clayton recalled. *Indeed, they had begun to drop their bombs on North Weald village. Our dispersal area was on the far side of the airfield and we decided it was time to take cover. A small slit trench was to hand covered with sandbags with an entrance at each end. About five or six of us dived into it. In the dark we heard the exploding bombs approach relentlessly, at ordered intervals. The words "stick bombing" flashed through my mind and immediately. "Would the intervals match our slit trench or not?" Two thuds away and I was sweating (were my friends?), one thump away and then . . . nothing! That last bomb had landed very close to the trench and we were stunned by the impact of the explosion. I came to in the dark aware of an acrid smell of cordite. There was a glimmer of light above and I clambered towards it, pulling myself up through the soil into the bright sunlight. By now two of the others had "come to" and were following me. I looked at what remained of the trench and, at the other end, there was a pair of legs thrashing the air wildly; then there were muffled shouts. I quickly ran to the waving legs, pulled aside two sandbags – which were riddled with shrapnel – and helped by the others, heaved him out of the ground. A rather pale face with a shock of blond hair appeared; he was a groundcrew colleague, a tall, quiet and friendly Irishman.*

'We had been preoccupied with our own predicament; as I looked about me, I could see that North Weald had received a battering. Immediately before me, the airfield was badly cratered – including a line of craters leading to our slit trench! – though the runway seemed OK. But on the far side where the station buildings were, there was much damage; a pall of dust hung over it and there were fires from which black smoke arose. We could only watch as the station came to life after this pounding – figures appeared out of the dust cloud, the fire tender moved off to deal with the fires, organised group appeared with shovels to fill in the craters – whilst we awaited the returning aircraft. Amazingly, the aircraft hangars, where major repairs and inspections were carried out, were undamaged. However, we later learned that nine soldiers had been killed in a shelter which had received a direct hit. Some of us in B Flight had good reason to be thankful for the "near miss".' [208]

As the Germans' approached North Weald, 11 Group had sent an plea for reinforcments from Air Vice-Marshal Trafford Leigh-Mallory's 12 Group, which had its Duxford Wing based at Duxford and Fowlmere, sixty kilometres north-east of London. This Wing consisted of 19, 66 and 229 squadrons and also the newly arrived 310 Squadron, consisting mainly of Czechoslovak volunteers. Duxford Wing had been instructed to operate in a single compact mass. It was Leigh-Mallory's idea that this would have a greater effect against the German units. It might have looked good in theory, but in practice it did not work. 12 Group's war diary dryly noted: 'Squadrons 19, 66 and 310 were sent to assist No. 11 Group. Of these only 19 Squadron met the enemy. They were helped on to their target by distant A.A. fire and eventually caught up with them over the mouth of the Thames Estuary. They sighted a large formation of enemy bombers and fighters and in the action that followed one Me 110 was destroyed, one probably destroyed and one damaged. Our squadron suffered no damage with the exception of one explosive bullet through a starboard wing.' [209]

In fact 12 Group's contribution was totally ineffective: the only one of its squadrons that managed to get into contact with the enemy, No.19, did so only as these were returning after wreaking havoc on the base at North Weald, and in reality not a single German aircraft was shot down by this squadron. Park, the commander of 11 Group, was furious.

Amidst all the excitement at Bentley Priory, Dowding's underground headquarters, where desperate attempts were made to get an overview of the air situation, a report from the southwest came in: 'Fifty plus spotted east of Cherbourg, another raid approaching from southeast!' These were forty-six Ju 88s from KG 51 and their escort, consisting of both Bf 109s and Bf 110s. It would take a few days before Luftflotte 2 had built a ground organisation to receive the fighter units from Luftflotte 3, and meanwhile Sperrle's air fleet continued to carry out their big raids in daylight. Several squadrons were sent up to repel these invaders, but were themselves stopped by the Messerschmitts. Thirteen Spitfires from 609 Squadron took off between 16:05 and 16:10 hours, only to be attacked by Bf 110s from ZG 2. 609

A Hurricane is hit by a burst of fire from a Bf 110's heavy frontal armament. The picture was taken by a war correspondent who had taken the radio operator's seat in the rear of the Bf 110 cockpit. By shooting down a Hurricane from 151 Squadron on 24 August 1940, the commander of III./26 'Horst Wessel', Oberstleutnant Johann Schalk, achieved his 7th aerial victory. On 11 September Schalk became the first Zerstörer flier to be awarded with the Knight's Cross. On 1 October 1940, when he was appointed to command ZG 26, he had 11 victories to his account.

Squadron's report reads: 'Squadron was ordered to intercept raiders over Ryde, and found themselves 5,000 feet below a large formation of bombers and fighters, right in the middle of our own A/A fire, and down-sun.'[210]

Two Spitfires were put out of action without the British doing any damage to the Germans. Pilot Officer Andy Mamedoff, an American volunteer in 609 Squadron, saw some Bf 110s get onto his tail and in the next moment his Spitfire was shaken by hits. He barely managed to escape and returned to the airfield at Middle Wallop, where he crash-landed his battered fighter.

The Ju 88s of KG 51 meanwhile executed a lightning attack against Home Fleet's installations in Portsmouth and in less than four minutes 50 tonnes of bombs were dropped.[211] Several bombs also fell in the town, where 83 people were killed, 191 injured and 700 were made homeless. An oil depot that was hit burned for 36 hours.

Dowding and Park had good reason to be worried. Between the first raids early in the morning and the attack on Portsmouth in the evening of that fateful Saturday, the German bombers had knocked out four airfields and a large oil depot, and damaged harbour installations in two of the main Channel ports, Dover and Portsmouth.

At Bentley Priory, Dowding tried to form a general picture from the confused reports that poured in during the day. He had just experienced the collapse of the efficient defence system he had helped to build. The Germans had been everywhere at once. The plotting table at the headquarters, which had previously always showed a perfect overview of the air situation, had been filled with markers so that at times it looked as if someone had amused themselves by randomly scattering them in heaps. What previously had been fighter missions controlled in every small detail had dissolved into a scene no more orderly than a gang fight. Against this background, it was hardly surprising that the Luftwaffe was able to neutralise the airfield at Manston and inflict serious damage on North Weald and Hornchurch sector stations.

Despite Park's order that Spitfires should tackle the fighter escort while Hurricanes and Defiants concentrated their efforts against the bombers, it was found that the Spitfire units accounted for only half of the downed Bf 109s. It was both encouraging and worrying for the British at the same time. On the one hand, Hurricane and Defiant airmen proved able to hit back hard even against numerically superior formations of Messerschmitts, but on the other it was found that the Luftwaffe's new tactics thwarted the Spitfire units' efforts to keep the Messerschmitt fighters away from the Hurricanes and Defiants. As a consequence Park issued a new directive: 'We must now drop the practice of detailing a portion of our fighters to go high to engage fighter escort. These squadrons merely get drawn off and permit the bombers with their very close escort to proceed unhindered. All squadrons despatched against raids of thirty or more are to be detailed to engage the bomber formation, i.e. given a height about 2,000 feet above the reported heighth of the enemy bomber formations.'[212]

Park was also furious about what he regarded as 12 Group's failure; he blamed his colleague in 12 Group, Leigh-Mallory, for the devastation at North Weald.

At this airfield Wing Commander Victor Beamish was, if possible, even more upset. He had been told that some of the men under his command had fled from the station during the bombing. Soon his voice roared angrily out of all the speakers on the airfield, 'Any officer, NCO or airman who leaves his post of duty is a coward and a rat – and I shoot rats on sight!'

At Hornchurch, the men of No. 264 Squadron gathered to discuss the day's events. Squadron Leader Hunter and six other airmen were missing. Five Defiants had been downed, but of them one could be repaired, and in return the unit had been credited with seven victories. For 32 Squadron it seemed even worse – the unit had lost five Hurricanes against only three victories.

The fighting on 24 August was a disappointment for both sides. The Germans had tried Göring's new directives for the first time and got mixed results. For II./KG 76 and III./KG 53, it had been anything but a successful day. Nor had the German fighter pilots showed their expected superiority over the RAF. Admittedly, they had reported 48 British fighters shot down – less than half of these would eventually be confirmed – but the price for this had been unexpectedly high: 19 Messerschmitt fighters had also been shot down – 18 Bf 109s and one Bf 110. Actual British air combat losses on 24 August – 19 fighters, including two Blenheims from 235 Squadron which had been accidentally shot down by their own fighters – are surprisingly low, considering the fact that the German fighter formations often had an overwhelming numerical superiority. Once again Göring felt dissatisfied with the results of the Bf 109 units, and not without reason.

To top it all, five Blenheim bombers from Bomber Command's 2 Group had, in broad daylight, carried out hit-and-run attacks on German airfields in the Netherlands. At Schiphol two liaison airplanes were destroyed, and all British aircraft returned to base before any German fighters had had time to take off after them.

Göring's worst headache, however, was caused by a German bomber crew which took part that same evening in a raid on the oil tanks at Thameshaven on the eastern outskirts of London. Luftwaffe bomber units had strict orders to restrict their attacks in the London area to the oil tanks in Thameshaven. Under no circumstances should any bombs fall on London! Due to British interference with the Knickebein radio beams, one aircrew went off course and accidentally dropped the first bombs of the war on London itself.

In Germany there was a violent reaction. Early the next morning all Luftwaffe units that had participated in the raid received a sharp note from the OKL, the Air Force High Command: 'The crews that bombed the prohibited area within London are immediately to be reported. The Commander of the Luftwaffe will personally punish the commanders in question and have them transferred to the infantry.'

The British, who were shocked by the first bombs that fell on residential areas in London, however, could take comfort in the fact that a Blenheim night fighter flown by 29 Squadron's Pilot Officer John Randall 'Bob' Braham had managed to use its A. I. radar to locate and eventually shoot down a He 111 from KG 55.

25 August 1940

On 25 August, the Luftwaffe continued with its new tactic of sending in overwhelming numbers of Messerschmitts over southern England. Despite a constant stream of aircraft from Luftflotte 2 over Kent during the morning hours, Fighter Command nevertheless refused to allow itself to be provoked.

Towards evening, when most of the day had passed without the Luftwaffe managing to pull the RAF into any serious combat, Sperrle launched a large new raid from the Cotentin Peninsula. With memories of the previous day's devastating attack against Portsmouth still fresh, 10 Group sent up its fighters. 11 Group also contributed with 17 and 87 squadrons.

The German attack force consisted of Ju 88s from II./KG 51 and II./KG 54, escorted by 103 Bf 110s from ZG 2, ZG 76 and V.(Z)/LG 1. The British commanders' directive to avoid contact with the German fighters could not prevent the ensuing battle being fought mainly between the fighters on both sides. 'They broke straight at us', said Sergeant Len Bartlett from 17 Squadron. 'I can't really remember what happened from then on, except that the sky seemed full of flaming aircraft.'[213] The Hurricane manned by Bartlett's commander, Squadron Leader Cedric Williams, was seen to go into a spin after a 20mm shell from a Bf 110 shot away all of the left stabiliser.[214]

Squadron Leader Horace Darley's 609 Squadron managed to do the same thing to 1./ZG 2, and was thus able to revenge the losses that No. 609 had suffered at the hands of the Zerstörers the day before. Unteroffizier Siegfried Becker, one of the pilots in 1./ZG 2, said: 'The first I knew that we were under attack was when my Bordfunker started shooting and screamed: "Break left!" and we were attacked from behind and the left. The attack was a complete surprise and had come out of the sun.'[215] This attack cost 1./ZG 2 four '110s.

No. 609 Squadron was noteworthy for the many different nationalities of its pilots. The unit's war diary for 25 August, 1940 notes: 'The squadron was becoming cosmopolitan. One might think that this heterogeneity would interfere with teamwork or morale, but this was not so. Under Squadron Leader Darley's quietly firm and competent leadership the squadron gained steadily in skill and confidence.'[216] 609 Squadron was credited with a total of eight victories against only two of its own aircraft being damaged on 25 August.

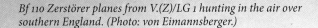
Bf 110 Zerstörer planes from V.(Z)/LG 1 hunting in the air over southern England. (Photo: von Eimannsberger.)

Soon the Messerschmitt 109s arrived on the scene – a total of over two hundred from JG 2, JG 27 and JG 53, and the combat developed into yet another of the large air battles over the central English Channel. Despite their numerical inferiority the British fighter pilots again performed quite well. It was an impressive feat for 17 Squadron to manage to reform and gain height so that they could strike 6./JG 53 with the same devastating effect that 609 Squadron's earlier attack had had on 1./ZG 2. It cost 6./JG 53 four Bf 109s. This Staffel failed to achieve more than a single victory in return.

No. 213 Squadron fought against all of the German aircraft types and was credited with the shooting down of three Ju 88s and two of each Messerschmitt type. Sergeant Reginald Llewellyn contributed with a Bf 110 and Bf 109, his tenth and eleventh victories. This cost 213 Squadron four Hurricanes.

Losses were high on both sides – 10 British and 16 German fighters (including nine Bf 110s). But the Germans were still quite pleased. Generally speaking the Messerschmitt airmen had managed to protect the bomber units, which lost no more than two planes. The bombs dropped over the airfield at Warmwell hit two hangars and knocked out the base's telephone lines. Additionally the German fighters' exagerated claims – 40 victories – helped to raise spirits. Among these was JG 2 'Richthofen's' 250th victory. For this the unit commander, Oberstleutnant Harry von Bülow Bothkamp, was awarded the Knight's Cross.[217] Oberleutnant Helmut Wick, the top ace in I./JG 2, was credited with two new victories, thereby reaching a total of 20. In so doing, he now began to challenge the big aces Mölders and Galland in the German fighters' eternal competition for the top position in the victory race.

Mölders did not fly on 25 August,[218] but that afternoon Major Galland was out over south-east England together with the whole of JG 26 'Schlageter'. 80 fighters of JG 54 also took part. As a small formation of Do 17s were out at the same time, acting, in fact, as decoys, Park sent up a few squadrons. Close to Dover I./JG 26 attacked 32 Squadron and shot down two of its Hurricanes. Shortly afterwards the Spitfire pilots of 54, 610 and 616 squadrons met the vast cloud of Bf 109s. Major Hannes Trautloft, commanding JG 54, said, 'I picked out a Spitfire that was separated from the rest of the formation as the "tail-end Charlie" and attacked

The American volunteer Pilot Officer Eugene Quimby Tobin – called 'Red' by his friends – was credited with the shooting down of two Bf 110s during 609 Squadron's attack on 1./ZG 2 on 25 August 1940. Here he is seen with Pilot Officer Keith Ogilvie (smoking a pipe), a Canadian in the same unit.

RAF Bomber Command's raid on Berlin on the night of 25 August 1940 would have significant consequences for the future course of the Battle of Britain. The image shows a Vickers Wellington, one of the aircraft types that participated in this attack. When the Wellington arrived at the units in October 1938, its so-called geodetic airframe construction, consisting of bent metal beams, was revolutionary. This made the aircraft very durable.

from below. I opened fire at a distance of 80 metres and hit the fuselage. The next salvo hit one wing. Burning, the aircraft spun down towards the Channel. I never saw the impact.'

Trautloft was a veteran of the Spanish Civil War, where he was credited with five victories. The Spitfire pilot he shot down this time was 54 Squadron's 25-year-old Pilot Officer Mick Shand, a New Zealander who had flown his first combat mission just a few hours earlier. Shand had just 20 hours in a Spitfire and had never had any air-to-air firing practice. Being placed second in the Section headed by ace Flight Lieutenant 'Al' Deere did not help him, but he managed to make an emergency landing near Margate.

A British pilot, Sergeant Philip Thomas Wareing, was one of seven pilots from 616 Squadron who were attacked by thirty Bf 109s. Wareing defended himself successfully and then chased a Bf 109 across the Channel and over the French coast before he managed to hit it with a burst of fire. But he failed to notice a '109 behind him. 'My beloved Spitfire was completely riddled with bullets and caught fire and the propeller stopped turning.' said Wareing. Although bullets continued to hammer against the armour plate behind him, Wareing opened fire at four Bf 109s that passed in front of him. The next moment the fuel tank in his Spitfire exploded and blew him out of the cockpit. He opened his parachute and soon afterwards was in German

WAREING'S ADVENTUROUS ESCAPE

After the British pilot Sergeant Philip Thomas Wareing had been shot down in the evening of 25 August, he landed in his parachute in a ploughed field not far from Galland's airfield at Audembert. Soon a German soldier appeared on a motorbike and sidecar, took him prisoner and brought him to the German airfield. There he was received by Adolf Galland and other German fighter pilots. They offered Wareing cigarettes, chocolate and French brandy and apologised for the fact that the stocks of captured British army whiskey (NAAFI) and beer had run out.[1] Before Wareing left the airfield to be transferred to a prison camp, he wrote down his home address on a piece of paper that he asked Oberleutnant Georg Beyer, the adjutant of JG 26, to give to Galland. When Beyer was shot down three days later and taken prisoner, he still had the slip of paper in his pocket. This allowed Wareing's mother to be notified that he was still alive.

But Wareing's mother would see her son again before the war had ended. He was first in the prison camp Oflag XXI-B at Schubin (Szubin in Poland). During a mission to get coal and bread at the railway station on 16 December 1942, Wareing managed to escape. He stole a bicycle and with this he travelled the 200 kilometres to Danzig, where he four days later managed to sneak aboard the Swedish ship *S/S Noreg* from a Gothenburg-based shipping company that was rather aptly named in the circumstances, Rederi AB Fri [Shipping Company Free].[2]

The following morning the ship left the harbour and set course for Halmstad in Sweden. Wareing hid for two days, but at sea he made himself known. In Halmstad, he was handed over to the police and stayed at the police station before getting picked up by a representative from the British Embassy in Stockholm three days later. On 5 January 1943 Wareing was flown with a BOAC courier aircraft to Leuchars in Scotland. For the rest of the war he served as an instructor in the RAF.

Interestingly, even 54 Squadron's Mick Shand – who was also shot down on 25 August 1940 – belonged in the ranks of the British escapees. When he was shot down by a German fighter and taken prisoner on 28 November 1942, he had been promoted to Flight Lieutenant. Shand was one of 76 RAF officers that managed to escape during the 'great escape' from the prison camp Stalag Luft III in Sagan in March 1943. He was however recaptured and was lucky not to be killed. Shand died on 20 December 2007 at the age of 92. Wareing passed away in May 1986.

1. Interview with Adolf Galland.
2. Via Jan-Olof Nilsson.

---

captivity. His Spitfire ended up as number 4 on the victory list of Oberleutnant Kurt Ruppert from I./JG 26.

A total of four Spitfires were shot down by JG 26 on that mission, but at Audembert Galland and his pilots counted up seven victories. One of them was No. 22 on Adolf Galland's personal tally. All JG 26 planes had returned to base. It was clear that there was a slight difference when Galland himself led the unit. The attacks that JG 26 made on 32 Squadron on 24-25 August were nearly fatal for Squadron Leader Crossley's unit. Two days later 32 Squadron was taken out of battle. After 14 victories Michael Crossley, 'The Red Knight', ended his career as a fighter pilot. Awarded a Distinguished Service Order, he was was soon afterwards sent to the USA to test American-made aircraft on Britain's behalf. He returned to England in 1943, but suffered from TB and never went back to front-line service.

Just when things began to look black for Fighter Command, Bomber Command intervened in a way that would eventually prove to be crucial. Churchill had ordered an attack on Berlin in retaliation for the German bombing of London. On the evening of 25 August 81 British bombers took off for the long flight to the German capital. Crews especially skilled at navigation served as pathfinders, yet only 29 bombers ever reached Berlin. They found the area covered by thick clouds and dropped their bombs on what they assumed was the city. Approximately 20 tonnes of bombs struck Berlin's northern suburbs without causing much damage. Seven of the British bombers failed to return from the operation. Compared to the purely material

The officers of Canadian 1 RCAF Squadron immediately after a combat mission. The short statured officer with a moustache, standing in the middle, is the unit commander, Squadron Leader Ernest McNab. No. 1 RCAF Squadron was declared operational on 19 August 1940. In eight weeks the Squadron claimed 31 victories against own losses of three pilots killed and 15 aircraft destroyed in combat.

results of the raid it was a high price but the psychological effect was much greater. Hitler was beside himself with rage, which was exactly what Churchill had hoped. With his sense for psychology the British prime minister hoped repeated bombings of Berlin might provoke the hysterically minded Führer into ill-considered decisions that would benefit the UK.

For Hermann Göring the bombing of Berlin meant a serious loss of prestige. He had previously boasted about the effective fighter defences of Berlin and promised that 'if any single bomb falls on Berlin you can call me Meyer'. Eventually, the RAF's bombing of Berlin would cause a complete reversal of the German strategy against Great Britain but, before that happened, two very difficult weeks were in store for Fighter Command.

26 August 1940

On the morning of 26 August, while hundreds of curious Berliners gathered to view the few houses that had been hit by British bombs – and several new jokes about Hermann Göring were coined – the Luftwaffe commander decided to order his units on the English Channel to attack, despite the increasing rain in that area. At dawn German reconnaisance planes had observed an unusual-

ly large accumulation of British aircraft on the major airfields of Kenley and Biggin Hill and these were the targets when the Do 17 bombers of III./KG 3 took off that same morning.

The commander of 11 Group, Keith Park, was as usual warned in advance by radar and had no difficulty guessing Kesselring's intentions. Orders to take-off went out. First up was Squadron Leader Marcus Robinson's 616 Squadron. Its twelve Spitfires were climbing above Dungeness, when they were discovered by the German fighter escort – about ninety Bf 109s from JG 3 and II./JG 51. Thirty planes from III./JG 3 and II./JG 51 went down to take them on. In a short time seven of 616 Squadron's Spitfires were shot down, two pilots killed and four others severely wounded. Robinson narrowly managed to escape along with the four remaining Spitfires. They had not managed to inflict any losses on the German fighter units. Another squadron appeared above the Thames Estuary. It was the remaining Defiants of 264 Squadron. They made a furious attack on the Do 17 bombers and shot down three from 7./KG 3 before the escorting Messerschmitts forced them to defend themselves.[219]

Pilot Officer Desmond Hughes and his gunner Sergeant Fred Gash claimed to have shot down two Do 17s in this, his first combat. Gunner Sergeant Barrie Baker in Flight Lieutenant John Banham's plane managed to hit a Do 17, but a moment later the Bf 109s from JG 3 came down

on the Defiants. The crew Pilot Officer Harold Goodall/ Sergeant Robert Young deftly parried a Bf 109 attack and managed to shoot down another Do 17. A moment afterwards the cockpit of Flight Lieutenant Banham's plane was hit by a cannon shell which set fire to the aircraft. Both crew members bailed out. John Banham was rescued after half an hour in the water, but there was no trace of his rear gunner. Their aircraft was the eleventh victory for Major Günther Lützow who had taken over command of JG 3 the day before. Shortly afterwards a second Defiant fell to Lützow's guns.

Sergeant Edward Thorn and his rear gunner Sergeant Frederick Barker were the most successful Defiant crew in the RAF, with nine victories to their credit. In this battle they were credited with two more victories – against the Do 17s – and were about to attack a third when Lützow's Bf 109 E went after them. The German hit them with his first burst and bullets smashed the Defiant's oil and glycol pipes. Black and white liquids poured from the nose and covered the entire windshield. Sergeant Thorn realized he had no chance and threw his plane into a spin. Less than 200 metres above the tops of the waves, he took his Defiant up again and set off towards Herne Bay – convinced that he had managed to fool his opponent. He did not know how wrong he was until a series of shell hits smashed into the plane and this time set the Defiant on fire. A minute later it was down in a field north of Canterbury. Thorn and Barker escaped with minor injuries.

A few minutes later Oberleutnant Friedrich-Franz von Cramon from Lützow's Stabsstaffel shot down another of 264 Squadron's machines over the Thames Estuary. The

A formation of Do 17s. One of the Do 17s to be shot down by a Defiant from 264 Squadron on 26 August 1940, was '5K+AR', Werknummer 1160, of 7./KG 3. It crashed into the sea off the English coast. The whole crew managed to save themselves from the sinking aircraft. The pilot, Feldwebel Willi Essmert, and two other crew members spent the rest of the war in British captivity. The observer Gefreiter Heinz Huhn however, died from his injuries shortly after the crash. 73 years later, in June 2013, the aircraft was recovered.

pilot was fished out of the water but his rear gunner was never found.

But by this time the first wave of escorting Bf 109s were low on fuel and turned back and then things began to go badly for the Germans. I./JG 52, which should have arrived to relieve JG 3, was attacked on their way in at Dover by 610 Squadron, and was held up by a fierce battle that cost them two Bf 109s – both from 2./JG 52 – in exchange for three downed Spitfires. II./JG 3 was attacked during its return flight by 56 Squadron and lost three Bf 109s.

When fresh squadrons of British fighters appeared while more and more of the Bf 109s turned back towards the Channel with their last few litres of petrol, the Dornier formations began to break up. Several of the bombers dropped their bombs at random and dived off towards the Channel as fast as they could go. Only a few bombs fell on Kenley and Biggin Hill airfields.

While the disheartened airmen from III./KG 3 returned to their bases at St. Trond, in Epinoy and Cambrai I. and III./KG 2 had been preparing for an operation against 11 Group's sector stations Hornchurch and Debden. After a long, nerve-racking wait, the order to take off finally came.[220]

I./JG 52 was given an opportunity to take revenge for their losses at midday when it was sent on a sweep across Kent[221] but things didn't go any better this time either. Above the Thames Estuary the unit was attacked by a formation of Hurricanes which came diving out of the sun. 'In a dramatically short time three of the '109s were diving down trailing smoke', wrote Ulrich Steinhilper of I./JG 52 in his memoirs. 'I saw this clearly and when the enemy came diving through I managed to push one to the side to get it away from the Chief's tail.'[222]

l./JG 52 thus suffered five losses in a single day. For Oberleutnant Karl-Heinz Leesmann it must have been particularly hard; that same morning he had succeeded Hauptmann Wolfgang Ewald as the commander of 2./JG 52 when the latter was appointed to Gruppenkommandeur as part of Göring's rejuvenation of fighter unit commanders. On Leesmann's first day as Staffelkapitän, his 2./JG 52 lost four pilots. However the fighter pilots were too young and eager for battle to be depressed even by such severe losses; they were obviously more concerned with their own successes. Steinhilper wrote: 'My Rottenhund (Karl Rüttger) took it up, firing with cannons. Kühle got another in front of his guns. Then we beat it, satisfied with two more victories.' I./JG 52 claimed a total of five victories that day, of which Leesmann accounted for one.

While the pilots of I./JG 52 returned home to celebrate their two victories, they met I. and III./KG 2 on their way northwards. Outside the Thames Estuary the bomber formations split up so that III./KG 2, escorted by ZG 26, went to the northwest, towards Debden, while I./KG 2 – with its

escort of Bf 109s from JG 54 – turned westwards towards Hornchurch. Major Hannes Trautloft, the new commander of JG 54, later wrote in his diary: 'We had to reduce the speed of our Messers to adapt to the cruising speed of the bombers. The slowest bomber thus set the pace for the entire unit.'

Ten Hurricanes from Canadian 1 RCAF Squadron attacked the Dornier bombers just as they began their bombing run on Hornchurch. 'The entire I. and II. Gruppen [from JG 54] intervened against the Hurricanes, and in the ensuing combat Oberfeldwebel Hier bagged his fifth enemy aircraft', Trautloft wrote. Canadian Flying Officer Robert Edwards was killed in that action.

Then an unusually large formation of British fighter aircraft appeared – eighteen Spitfires and Hurricanes from 65 and 615 squadrons. One of the pilots from I./KG 2 said: 'I catch sight of a large British fighter formation that flies past us on the right side. Haven't they seen us? I think. But in the same moment they turn and attack us diagonally from the front, and pass through our formation, shooting wildly. The whole thing is over in seconds, but two Do 17s from the leading three-plane formation go down with engines on fire.

'Suddenly our own aircraft is hit. I feel a burning pain in the left thigh. Shortly afterwards there is a muffled bang – and then we have no oxygen. The oxygen tank has been damaged. A cursory glance at the instruments confirms the damage. Luckily the fighters have ceased their attacks, so we can go lower where we don't need the oxygen masks.'[223]

This happened at the same time as the Bf 109s began to depart due to lack of fuel. In one attack two Do 17s from

A pair of Spitfires from 616 Squadron return after a combat mission. The aircraft closest to the camera, 'QJ-G', was flown by 24-year-old Sergeant Ralph Vincent Hogg, who went missing from a fighter patrol on 10 December 1940.

I./KG 2 were shot down, and in one of them the unit lost its Gruppenkommandeur, Major Martin Gutzmann. Three other Do 17s were more or less severely damaged. It was enough to make the remaining Dornier crews from I./KG 2 jettison their bombs and turn back for home at full speed.

III./KG 2, which flew towards Debden, suffered even worse. Park directed four squadrons towards its twenty-one Do 17s. He had also once again asked for support from Leigh-Mallory's 12 Group and its Duxford Wing, which, however, again failed to get all their aircraft there on time. 12 Group's war diary noted: 'Squadrons 310, 66, 19 and 229 were sent to assist No. 11 Group in connection with Raid 3 which came in over the Thames Estuary. Of these only 310 Squadron went into action.' [224]

The first fighter attacks against the German formation were carried out by the Czechoslovak 310 Squadron, which thereby had its baptism of fire. A dozen of the unit's Hurricanes threw themselves upon the Germans southwest of Colchester. Squadron Leader George Blackwood, who had been given command of 310 Squadron, said afterwards: 'The Czechs really did a fine job despite their aggressive attitude. I think their only problem was that as soon as they saw an enemy that would make for a possible target, nothing else mattered.' Blackwood saw how Pilot Officer Emil Fechtner attacked a Bf 110 and opened fire at too great a distance, then continued to fire while holding a straight course towards the 110, and then – when he was within a 100 metres – Fechtner was attacked by other Messerschmitts and was forced to seek sanctuary in the clouds.

The Bf 110s of ZG 26 managed to stave off the initial fighter attacks. '310 Squadron shot down 1 Do 215 and 1 Me 110', established 12 Group's war diary: 'Our casualties were three aircraft Cat. 3.' [225]

Nine Hurricanes from 111 Squadron managed to take advantage of the confused combat between 310 Squadron and ZG 26 and get through to the bombers. Pilot Officer Peter Simpson and Sergeant Thomas Wallace together attacked a Do 17, which they managed to destroy. But then 111 Squadron's further attacks against the bombers were stopped by the German fighter escort – and it is described in the British report: 'The escorting Me 110s dived immediately on to our fighters and the action had to be broken off.' [226]

As more British units turned up, however, an increasing number of RAF fighters managed to reach the bombers. Several bomber crews lost their nerves and turned back. Only three crews from III./KG 2 broke through and dropped their bombs on Debden airbase. The surviving airmen in KG 2 returned to their airfields in the same sorrowful mood as their colleagues in KG 3 earlier. It was different for III./ZG 26 'Horst Wessel', which claimed five victories against two own losses. The day's most successful pilot in 'Geschwader Horst Wessel' was Unteroffizier Richard Heller, who claimed three victories in his first combat.

The British fighters who fought to repel the attacks against Debden and Hornchurch had not even landed when the radar stations in the southwest saw echoes from new German air formations off the Cotentin Peninsula. 10 Group ordered up four squadrons and 11 Group, three.

They clashed with the leading German formations – 48 He 111s from I. and II./KG 55 which tried to get to Portsmouth with an escort of no less than 214 Bf 109s from JG 2, JG 27 and JG 53, and 103 Bf 110s from ZG 2, ZG 76 and V.(Z)/LG 1. [227]

The British fighters attacked with terrible force. When they dived towards their opponents, they could hear excited voices on the German radio frequency in their headphones: 'Acthung Spitfeuer! Spitfeuer!' [228] In the ensuing combat four Bf 109s and Bf 110s crashed in the sea, while only three RAF planes were lost. Then thirty RAF fighters attacked the Heinkel bombers, which jettisoned their bombs and turned back towards the French coast.

Had KG 55 not had the discipline to keep their combat formations together – which made it possible for the gunners to coordinate their fire – the unit could have suffered a real disaster. As it was four He 111s were shot down while three others were damaged. In return the bombers shot down four Hurricanes – all from 43 Squadron. One of those British pilots, Pilot Officer Harold North, wrote in his combat report: 'I was yellow Leader and on the Tally Ho being given I echeloned my Section to port and attacked head-on a formation of six He 111s. They were the lower layer of a much larger mass stepped up. I could only fire the briefest of bursts and broke away below without noticing any results. I was barely hit by some of the shower of bombs that were being jettisoned wholesale into the sea. I climbed back into the attack and got in two long quarter astern bursts (on a He 111). Quantities of smoke were emitted, the undercarriage dropped, one person at least baled out and the enemy was last seen diving, but I got hit by explosive shells which went into my shoulder and arm, and pieces of perspex scratched my face so I could not see very well. I wiped my face, checked over my machine and when I felt better I looked up and saw three Heinkels passing overhead. I turned and attacked one who was lagging behind a bit – expending my ammunition. Smoke belched from one of the engines – and the aircraft was diving steeply in a northerly direction overland when I was forced to bale out, my aircraft having been hit from behind. I landed at Birdham near West Wittering and understand that a Heinkel crashed at Waterlooville.'

While the fighters on both sides retreated with empty ammo drums and dwindling fuel, Sperrle's next attack suddenly appeared. It was thirty-seven Ju 88s from KG 51. These planes rapidly dive-bombed Warmwell airfield and then withdrew without having suffered any losses.

How different viewpoints could be after such extensive air battles at such high speeds is shown by both sides' fighter pilots claiming to have beaten their opponents in the clashes off of Portsmouth on the afternoon of 26 August. I./ JG 2 'Richthofen' returned to base claiming four victories. Two of them raised Oberleutnant Wick's personal score to twenty-two. Morale was high at I./JG 2, despite the fact that one pilot had not returned from the Channel.

'Too bad my poor wingman did not have time to shoot,' said Wick when he landed after the battle: 'But after my work the British ran away as if their tails were on fire.' Among the many enthusiastic airmen who gathered to congratulate Wick on his new victories, was one who had a

The view forward through the glass-covered nose of a He 111.
(Photo: Bätcher.)

theory about why the British broke off the battle so quickly: 'No wonder, Herr Oberleutnant,' he said, 'those Englishmen must have seen the many victory bars on your rudder and didn't want to be added to the row!'

Among the men of II./JG 53, who operated from the Channel Island of Guernsey, things sounded a bit different. This Gruppe had again been hit hard and lost three planes – all from the 5. Staffel – with only one pilot being rescued from the Channel. II./JG 53 had lost thirteen aircraft and eight pilots, about a third of its establishment, in just a dozen operations over the English Channel. Many of the pilots said that it was bad luck to operate from British soil; others had a more rational theory – that agents among the British civilian population telephoned the British mainland and reported when German aircraft took off.[229] It has not been possible to confirm the latter idea.

So ended another day of battle, a day that demonstrated that Fighter Command was far from finished, and that had also taught many lessons. It was as much thanks to British morale as to Air Vice-Marshal Park's skilful command of 11 Group. Although the Germans had initially surprised the British defenders with their new tactic of flying in a never-ending stream of aircraft, most of which consisted of fighters, Fighter Command had succeeded in overcoming even this new situation. The only thing that had not worked on the British side was the interaction between Park and the commander of 12 Group, Air Vice-Marshal Leigh-Mallory, and this Park could not tolerate. The next day he did not hesitate to summon his air controllers and sector commanders, and openly accuse Leigh-Mallory of negligence in front of them. Park rath-

er deviously began by expressing his appreciation for the support from 10 Group: 'Thanks to the friendly cooperation afforded by 10 Group, they are always prepared to detail two to four squadrons.' [230]

Then he got to 12 Group: 'Up to date 12 Group, on the other hand have not shown the same desire to cooperate by dispatching their squadrons to the place requested. The result of this attitude has been that on two occasions recently when 12 Group offered assistance and were requested by us to patrol our aerodromes, their squadrons did not in fact patrol over our aerodromes . . . On both these occasions our aerodromes were heavily bombed.'

After giving additional air to his frustration over 12 Group, Park got to the action he deemed necessary: 'As acceptance of direct offers of assistance from 12 Group have not resulted in their squadrons being placed where we had requested, controllers are from now onwards immediately to put their requests to Controller, Fighter Command.' This was a strong accusation against Leigh-Mallory, and Park rubbed salt in his wounds with the following additional words: 'Such requests via Command will be a little slower in obtaining assistance but they should ensure that the reinforcing squadrons from the North are in fact placed where they can be of greatest assistance.' [231]

It was the beginning of a deepening conflict between Park and Leigh-Mallory, and since the former turned to Dowding, the old commander of Fighter Command was drawn into it. Leigh-Mallory defended himself by saying that 11 Group had called 12 Group too late, which was why the German aircraft were already gone when Leigh-Mallory's fighter pilots had arrived in the area they had been assigned by 11 Group's air controller. To this, Park replied that 12 Group's delay among other things was also due to Leigh-Mallory's 'wrong tactic'of concentrating his fighters into a Big Wing, composed of several squadrons; it simply took too long for all of its aircraft to form up together. Leigh-Mallory countered that the Germans gained the advantage when Park had his fighters engaged them in single squadrons instead of bringing together several of them into Big Wings.

Certainly, several events in recent weeks – the latest being the disaster that hit 616 Squadron on the morning of 26 August – confirm Leigh-Mallory's argument that the numerical inferiority in air combat which was the consequence of Park's tactic was also an important reason for 11 Group's high losses. Against this Park could argue that his method of exposing the Germans to a constant stream of attacks fatigued the German airmen and contributed to their fighter escort rapidly running low on fuel, which was a key to the British success. In addition, 610 Squadron's successful attack against a formation of Bf 109s (I./JG 52) as they approached the coast on 26 August, had forced them to break off, and made it possible to disperse the bomber formations that tried to attack Kenley and Biggin Hill airfields. However, it was clear that it was the combination of two squadrons – Nos. 65 and 615 – which managed to repel the attack against Hornchurch.

On the German side there was a growing crisis of confidence. It was caused by Hermann Göring's growing disappointment in what he thought were meagre results by the Bf 109-equipped fighter units. As usual, he studied the reports of his fighter units with particular interest, and these showed that, contrary to Göring's hopes, the new tactic of concentrating on fighter operations had led to worse results. The past three days' fighter battles had been surprisingly difficult. Moreover, his bomber crews had on several occasions lost their nerves and aborted their attack when British fighters broke through the Messerschmitt

fighter screen – which Göring had hoped would be impenetrable, not least because of its huge numerical superiority. To ex-fighter pilot Göring it was simply humiliating to note that the British fighter pilots, sometimes operating in groups of only a dozen, could give whole Jagdgruppen a thrashing. Although the young hotheads in I./JG 52 felt they had reason to celebrate their five victories, it was obvious that both the unit's operations on 26 August had ended with it taking a beating from Fighter Command. Apparently even greater concentrations of Messerschmitt fighters were needed in the air over southern England!

Irritated, Göring rang his commanders at the Channel coast and wondered why the transfer of fighter units from Luftflotte 3 to Luftflotte 2 was taking so long. Up to then it was just Stab and III./JG 53 that had moved and these had not yet started operations from their new airfield at Pas de Calais. Sperrle and Kesselring promised that the remainder of the fighter units in Luftflotte 3 would be transferred to Pas de Calais next day.

Göring was no happier when Bomber Command the following night repeated their attack on Berlin. Only twelve civilians were killed, but that was of little comfort to the Luftwaffe commander.

28 August 1940

Rain and fog on 27 August gave the pilots on both sides a much needed day's rest. No-one received the news of the transfer to Pas de Calais with greater enthusiasm than the men of II./JG 53, who were then allowed to leave 'unlucky' Guernsey. The battered 5./JG 53 was left behind at the main base of Dinan in Brittany in order to regain its strength.

When 28 August dawned in an almost cloudless sky everyone knew that it was time again. It was no later than about eight and the people in the small English seaside re-

A formation of Spitfires. Guided by radar observations and air surveillance posts, the British fighters often could position themselves at a higher altitude than the incoming German planes.

Messerschmitt Bf 109s on the way in over the English Channel. (Photo: Dahmer.)

sort of Deal had just left their breakfast tables, when the air was filled with the familiar rising and falling roar of hundreds of aircraft engines. It was fifty Heinkel 111s and Dornier 17s from I./KG 3 and KG 53, and above them – so high that they could not be heard from the ground – hundreds of Messerschmitts. They were headed for the air bases at Eastchurch and Rochford.

Almost at the same time as the black-crossed metal birds were seen by the residents of Deal, Keith Park's forces struck – 45 machines from four squadrons. It was just what the Germans had been waiting for. From their altitude of 6,000-7,000 metres Gruppe after Gruppe of Messerschmitt 109s came and drew the British units into separate bitter fights.

While the fighter battles raged at a comfortable distance, the bombers divided themselves up in two columns. The 23 Dorniers of Oberstleutnant Rudolf Gabelmann's I./KG 3 turned towards Eastchurch on the island of Sheppey in the Thames Estuary. At that moment, a new formation of British fighter aircraft took the opportunity to try and sneak up on the other bombers, the IIe 111s of KG 53, which had continued to Rochford on the other side of the estuary. It was 264 Squadron, with its last twelve remaining Defiants, making a self-sacrificing attempt to break up the enemy formation. Unlike operations on 25 August, this time the Germans had more fighters left standing by high up in the clouds. 264 Squadron, now led by Squadron Leader Desmond Garvin, had the misfortune to encounter the Luftwaffe's two best aces majors Werner Mölders and Adolf Galland.

Mölders, who misidentified the Defiants as Curtiss P-40 Warhawks, called his pilots: *'Achtung, Curtiss unten!'* – Look out, Curtiss below!

He then dived at the head of his thirty '109s and shot down one of the Defiants for his 28th victory. At the same time Major Galland picked the same target for his Geschwader's Stabsschwarm. It was a terribly uneven combat.

Galland approached a lone Defiant from behind and below. At 200 metres Galland and the Defiant gunner opened fire simultaneously but the Messerschmitt's heavier armament was decisive. Badly damaged, the Defiant turned left, and was met by a burst of fire from Galland's adjutant, Hauptmann Georg Beyer. Engulfed in flames the British fighter plunged earthwards and crashed east of Canterbury. This was Galland's 24th victory. Two additional Defiants were downed by Galland's wingman, Oberleutnant Walter Horten.

In total seven Defiants were shot down. In return, Mölders' adjutant, Oberleutnant Erich Kircheis, was shot down and bailed out. Even Galland's adjutant Hauptmann Georg Beyer and his wingman, Feldwebel Karl Straub, were also shot down, bailed out and spent the rest of the war in captivity. British records indicate that they were the victims of Pilot Officer Byron Duckenfield, Sergeant Paul Farnes and Sergeant Antoni Glowacki from 501 Squadron.

By that time the Dornier bombers had dropped more than a hundred bombs and spread death and destruction across Eastchurch airfield. The fires and violent explosions destroyed several parked British bombers.

Farther north, things did not go as well for KG 53. Despite what 264 Squadron's report would suggest its Heinkel 111s reached Rochford at full strength, but where the fighters had failed, the anti-aircraft guns succeeded and with the force of desperation created such a barrage that the German formation broke up and their hastily dropped bombs scattered ineffectively across the area.

It was easy enough for the Germans to conclude that the results of the Rochford raid were anything but satisfactory and this led to even greater challenges for the defenders. The exhausted pilots of 11 Group were tied up skirmishing with the last German stragglers when the next alert came: a large hostile force was approaching the Thames Estuary, altitude: 18,000 feet!

By this time resources were almost exhausted; all that Park could muster was a handful of men and machines that were held in reserve. But the British did not give up. Squadron Leader David Pemberton, leading 1 Squadron, made a furious attack on II./KG 3 over Southend and was credited with the shooting down of three Do 17s. Two crashed immediately, and a third returned to France with severe damage. Then the German fighter escort engaged the Spitfires and Hurricanes in fierce air fighting that cost III./JG 3 two Bf 109s for only one British loss.

At 12:35 30 Dornier 17s from II. and III./KG 3 reached Rochford. This time the destruction was almost complete; the air defences at Rochford had used up most of their ammunition in the morning raid. What was left of 264 Squadron's Defiants was turned into scrap in a long series of bomb explosions.

Immediately afterwards, it was time for the next alert: a new German force was approaching from the south and southeast. By this time 11 Group's fighters were refuelled, re-armed and ready to take off again. Park guessed without hesitation that this was a Gerrman follow-up to the airfield raids. Squadron after squadron was scrambled – which was exactly what Göring wanted . . .

This third wave was not in fact bombers, but Messerschmitt fighters; eleven Gruppen with a total of about 300 aircraft. The primary purpose of the morning and midday airfield raids had been to make the British believe that the Germans still were trying to fight the RAF *from* the air rather than *in* the air.

The British discovered too late that that they wouldn't be fighting bombers. Squadron Leader John Ellis, who led No. 610 Squadron, was undaunted by this. His 'B' Flight had taken off from Biggin Hill at 15:30, followed by 'A' Flight 20 minutes later. [232] The air controller led the twelve Spitfire pilots to an enemy formation on its way in over the Strait of Dover. This was I./JG 3 with twenty-two Bf 109s in open formation. [233] Hauptmann Günther Lützow, who commanded that Jagdgruppe, had ordered that several areas on the unit's aircraft – the entire nose, rudder and wing tips – be painted yellow as a recognition signal in order to avoid confusion with the enemy in aerial combat. At that time JG 3 wasn't exactly one of the Luftwaffe's most successful fighter units. Its I. Gruppe was an exception however, and had so far been credited with 11 victories in exchange for only 3 of its own aircraft lost. After Lützow was promoted to Geschwaderkommodore on

▶ *Right: The tension of battle is clearly painted in the face of Feldwebel Erwin Leykauf (III./JG 54), as he climbs out of the cockpit of his Bf 109 after another combat mission over southern England. (Photo: Leykauf.)*

26 August, I./JG 3 got a new commander; Hauptmann Hans von Hahn, a veteran with 10 victories who had hitherto served as Staffelkapitän in III./JG 53. Hahn had taken over Lützow's old Bf 109 E-4 and had his personal emblem of a rooster head painted on it. This was an allusion to his name 'Hahn'/cock, however in that macho environment it also had a risqué double meaning, probably not entirely by accident. This was the first time that I./JG 3 was led by Hauptmann von Hahn on a combat mission, and one can assume that the pilots were excited.

When von Hahn's Messerschmitts swept over the coast at 5,000 metres, they were fired at by the air defences in Dover. It was these puffs of smoke, and not the bright yellow colours of the 109s, which drew John Ellis' attention to the German aircraft. They were coming straight towards 610 Squadron, at a higher altitude. [234] The British unit leader was experienced enough to know what he should do. He had fought in the Battle of France where he shot down five German aircraft. In just five weeks since then he had increased his score to 13, nine of which were Bf 109s. Now he led his pilots past the German formation – which apparently did not see the brown-and-green-painted Spitfires against the fields below – and climbed to a position between the Germans and the sun. 'Our unit was attacked by Spitfires coming straight out of the sun', says the German combat report. [235]

When the British pilots dived to attack, they noted that 'the Me 109s had bright yellow engine cowlings and yellow wing tips.' [236] Sergeant Ronnie Hamlyn, who achieved an amazing five victories on 24 August, aimed for one of the 109s, opened fire and saw his bullets smashing into the German plane. Hauptmann von Hahn was lucky to escape Hamlyn's attention. Instead, the young Spitfire pilot had set his sight on the German unit commander's wingman, Leutnant Hans-Herbert Landry. The British combat report describes this: 'Sergeant Hamlyn fired a couple of bursts against an Me 109 which immediately went down. Sergeant Manton confirmed that he saw it hit the ground further inland and catch fire.'[237]

The Bf 109 plummeted vertically. There were no flames, just a long, narrow trail of leaking petrol. Although Leutnant Landry was bleeding profusely from multiple gunshot wounds, he managed to bail out and opened his parachute. A few thousand metres further down his aircraft crashed in a field at Church Farm, Church Whitfield. On impact the petrol fumes in the aircraft's by then empty fuel tanks exploded, and the machine was torn to pieces.

The Bf 109 formation scattered as the German pilots dived, turned or climbed to get away. Pilot Officer Constantine Pegge gave one '109 a short burst of fire from 50 metres and saw the plane go down in flames, which was confirmed by another RAF pilot. Sergeant Cyril Bamberger swung his 'DW-O' in behind another Messerschmitt. 'I gave him a burst from a distance of around 250 yards and

kept closing in', he afterwards wrote in his combat report. 'After my third burst the Me 109 turned onto its back and black smoke belched from the engine. Since I myself was attacked by another enemy aircraft, I failed to see the impact.'[238]

This is typical of combats with Bf 109s, whose engines emitted such thick, black smoke when pressed hard – when taking evasive action in air combat, for instance – that they could be mistaken for going down in flames. I./JG 3 escaped without further losses. On the other hand, one of its pilots shot down 610 Squadron's Pilot Officer Cox. The 24-year-old Kenneth Cox, who had arrived at the unit in late July directly from flight training, was killed when his Spitfire crashed into a house in Stelling Minnis.

This combat was witnessed by Winston Churchill, who was on an inspection trip to Dover. The British Prime Minister was only too fond of watching air fighting from the ground, but when he shortly afterwards saw the crash site of a downed aircraft, he was quite shaken. 'Good Lord, hope that is not a British aircraft', was all he could say. Churchill was reassured that it was a German aircraft, and the pilot was in captivity, but had been taken to hospital for emergency treatment of his injuries. It wasn't possible to save the life of the German airman who died on 23 September as a result of his injuries.

The RAF fighter pilots had now been given new instructions to help operational control by reporting altitude and position of German formations as soon as they were sighted. Thanks to the report from 610 Squadron, a new Spitfire Squadron, No. 603, was directed towards I./JG 3. This was not as fortunate from the British point of view. 603 Squadron had transferred to Hornchurch the day before and this was the unit's first day of combat in the Battle of Britain; four of its Spitfires were lost fighting a numerically superior force of Bf 109s at around a quarter to five (British time). It seems that these Messerschmitts belonged to both I. and II./JG 3. The latter Jagdgruppe claimed to have shot down eight British fighters, but only two of these were confirmed.

Major Mölders, who took off from St. Inglevert at 18:10, led sixty Bf 109s at high altitude over south-eastern England.[239] Near Canterbury he dived on 151 Squadron and in the space of a minute shot down two of its Hurricanes. Pilot Officer John Alexander bailed out with severe burns over the Thames Estuary and Sergeant Leonard Davies, despite his gunshot wounds, brought his badly mauled Hurricane back to a forced landing at Eastchurch.

54 Squadron ran right into II./JG 54. That day 54 Squadron was led by Squadron Leader Donald Finlay – who took the silver in the 110 metre hurdles in the 1936 Olympics. Its regular commander, James 'Prof' Leathart, had been sent on 'enforced leave'when he had been found to be completely exhausted. In the ensuing scrap, one plane on either side was shot down. The Spitfire that went down in a cloud of smoke and flames was piloted by Squadron Leader Finlay, who, however, bailed out.

Squadron Leader Peter Townsend's 85 Squadron was attacked by, at the very least, II./JG 3 and III./JG 51, but managed to perform much better. It was perhaps lucky for the British that it was just No. 85; this elite unit had done

▶ *Right: A He 111 from Kampfgruppe 100 with the 'X-Gerät' antennas. (Photo: Bätcher.)*

well in several previous encounters with the Jagdwaffe. In the air between Ashford and Lympne its Hurricane pilots defended themselves against the many times superior Messerschmitt formations in an air combat that might almost be called epic. Townsend, Allard and Woods-Scawen – all of whom were prominent aces and highly decorated – kept the Germans occupied and shot down three of them while the other Hurricane pilots pulled away. These victories were recorded as Squadron Leader Townsend's 9th, Flying Officer Patrick Woods Scawens 10th and Pilot Officer Geoffrey 'Sammy' Allard's 15th. But Allard was not satisfied. He flew out over the Strait of Dover. Directly over the German fighter airfield at St. Inglevert, he attacked a formation of returning Bf 109s and shot down III./JG 51's Oberleutnant Arnold Lignitz, who suffered serious injuries when he crashed his Bf 109 E-4. In total 85 Squadron reported six downed Bf 109s without any own losses on 28 August. II./JG 3 lost three and III./JG 51 two Bf 109s.

Thus, the two previous days of combat had cost II./JG 3 a loss of eight fighters. On the British side it looked just as bad in many units. No. 603 Squadron had had a very bad start, and after twenty-one days of combat the veteran 54 Squadron was left with only four experienced pilots remaining. One of 54 Squadron's pilots describes the situation in the unit at that time:

'The strain had almost reached breaking point. The usually good natured George [Gribble] was quiet and irritable; Colin [Gray], by nature thin-faced, was noticeably more hollow-cheeked; Desmond [McMullen], inclined to be weighty, was reduced to manageable proportion . . .'[240]

But the decisive blow against the RAF that Göring had hoped for had still not been achieved. Although the German fighters had flown 576 sorties, they had brought home no more than 32 victories on 28 August, in exchange for 12 Bf 109s lost. One can imagine what Göring would have felt if he had known the actual British fighter losses for 28 August – 15 planes. In the Luftwaffe commander's eyes the Bf 109 units should have been able to do better because of both their numerical superiority and their aircraft being significantly better than the Hurricane fighter, which the majority of Fighter Command was equipped with. Göring put his hopes in the strengthening of the fighter units at Pas de Calais. During the day, the remainder of the fighter units in Luftflotte 3 had urgently flown over to improvised airfields in the Pas de Calais area. This allowed the air fleet to begin its night offensive.

The first attacks on the evening of 28 August were carried out by a handful of bombers on industrial targets in Coventry, but Liverpool – one of the main ports of the British Atlantic convoys – had been designated by Göring as the main target.[241] Eight He 111 crews from KGr 100 led the way using the new navigational aid X-Gerät, and marked the target by dropping incendiary bombs before the main force arrived. In total, 160 sorties to Liverpool took place that night and extensive damage was inflicted.[242]

The British defence was not much to brag about. Liverpool's air defences fired incessantly throughout the night,

X-DEVICE AND PATHFINDERS LED THE GERMAN BOMBERS

During the first air operations against the British Isles the Luftwaffe's most important navigation aid for blind flying was the 'Knickebein' system. This was a simple radio beam that let the navigator on an airplane hear different signals in his headphones if the aircraft deviated to either side of the course that would bring his plane right on target. But when the bomber offensive against London began, the Germans had developed a navigation aid with greater precision. This meant that the large diversive bonfires that the British lit in rural areas far outside of London often failed to mislead the German bombers.

This new navigational device was called, hardly imaginatively, the 'X-device' ('X-Gerät'). As in the case of 'Knickebein', a radio beam of between 66 and 75 MHz was directed towards the target. But the 'X-Gerät's' radio beam – which had a range of 300 kilometres – was crossed by three other rays, called 'Rhen', 'Oder' and 'Elbe'. The first of these indicated that there were 30 kilometres left to the target, the second that 10 kilometres remained to the target. In that situation the navigator would start a pointer in a special clock that resembled a stopwatch. The third intersecting radio beam lay five kilometres from the target, and when the aircraft reached it, the navigator would start the second pointer on the 'stopwatch'. When the two indicators met, a circuit closed and the bombs dropped automatically.

The 'X-Gerät' was introduced for the first time in the evening of 13 August 1940, when a new and specially trained German bomber unit joined the battle – Kampfgruppe KGr 100.

The first target for KGr 100 was the important factory works in Castle Bromwich near Birmingham, where Spitfire planes were built. A few of dozen He 111s took part in the attack, which started at 23:10 hours, UK time. Several bombs hit within 100 metres of the target.

Henceforth Kampfgruppe 100 operated as the Luftwaffe's pathfinder force, to locate the target before any other aircraft and mark it with flares.

but the barrage was scattered and lacked precision; its most important effect was to keep the British night fighters away from the burning city and harbour. In the darkness around the shining fires in Liverpool five squadrons of Blenheim night fighters searched in vain for single Junkers and Heinkels arriving and departing.

29 August 1940

After these raids the German bomber crews were allowed a day's rest on 29 August. Instead, Generalmajor von Döring, Jafü 2, sent out his now significantly strengthened fighter force on free hunting sweeps across southern England. Again, they managed to trick 11 Group into order up a few squadrons. Led by the courageous Squadron Leader Peter Townsend the pilots of 85 Squadron did not let themselves to be deterred by inferiority of numbers and altitude. Instead, they turned their Hurricanes skywards and began the slow climb to get to a formation of over one hundred Bf 109s high above them. It was Major Günther Lützow's JG 3, and the small band of old Hurricanes should have been an easy target when most of JG 3 dived to 'wipe the floor with the Tommies'. Two Hurricanes were hit and their pilots forced to bail out, but for the rest of the clash the RAF pilots quite sensationally gained the upper hand. When JG 3 eventually limped back across the Channel, six of its Bf 109s had been shot down and two more were so battered that they crashed in France. II./ZG 26 'Horst Wessel' performed far better in their engagement with No. 610 Squadron, which led to at least two Spitfires being shot down for no German losses.

As soon as Park realized that there were only German fighters in the air, he called his airmen back. However he felt a growing confidence, so when the next great German fighter sweep was reported a few hours later, he took up the challenge and again 85 Squadron was scrambled, along with 501 and 603 squadrons. But this time the RAF pilots also met significantly more experienced German units – I./JG 26 under Hauptmann Rolf Pingel and I./JG 51 under Oberleutnant Richard Leppla, both prominent aces.

After the initial skirmish, 603 Squadron's Pilot Officer Richard Hillary found to his horror that he had lost the rest of his squadron. Fortunately, shortly afterwards he caught sight of 501 Squadron's Hurricanes and joined their formation. Hillary wrote afterwards:

'I learned within a few seconds the truth of the old warning "Beware of the Hun in the Sun".

I was making pleasant little sweeps from side to side, and peering earnestly into my mirror when, from the sun and dead astern, bullets started appearing along my port wing.' [243]

Hillary managed to bring his bullet-riddled Spitfire down in a belly landing in a cornfield near Lympne. Meanwhile the German fighter pilots shot down four more RAF planes against the loss of two of their own. Hauptmann Pingel himself got two of the German victories. One of those he shot down was Flight Lieutenant John Gibson, 501 Squadron's ace with eight victories, who had recently

had his 24th birthday. He had just brought down one of I./JG 26's Bf 109s when Pingel dived down and set fire to his Hurricane. Gibson bailed out and landed in the water about three kilometres off the coast, where he was picked up by a motorboat. Shortly afterwards, he was awarded with the DFC.

Meanwhile, the men at Hawkinge airfield were witnesses to a duel between a Hurricane and a Bf 109. The British pilot proved himself to be completely superior to the German, who soon had to bail out from his burning machine. He drifted down in a parachute towards the crowd of cheering Britons on the ground. The victorious British pilot was 501 Squadron's Sergeant James 'Ginger' Lacey.

Göring frowned when he received the day's reports on the evening of 29 August. More than 700 fighter sorties had been made, but the number of victories was a paltry 15! The results for several of the Bf 109 units were beneath contempt. Since large-scale air fighting had began on 8 August, for instance, JG 3 had been credited with only 33 victories against 31 Bf 109s lost in action.

It was obvious that for a unit to be successful much depended on the quality of the unit's leader. Worst were II. and III./JG 3 with the very poor results of seven victories for fourteen losses and eight victories for eleven planes and seven pilots lost in battle. It was a dramatic contrast to, for example, I./JG 51, which was credited with 18 victories against an own combat loss of only four planes and a pilot in the same period. I./JG 3 differed from the rest of JG 3; this Gruppe had been led by Major Günther Lützow, who was one of the best pilots in JG 3 and one of the German fighter forces's best unit leaders. As we know, I./JG 3 was now led by Hauptmann von Hahn. A few days later the commander of III./JG 3, Hauptmann Walter Kienitz, was relieved of command and was sent to Germany 'for health reasons'.[244] He was succeeded by Hauptmann Wilhelm Balthasar, a young hothead who had attained 23 victories in the Battle of France – more than any other pilot. Balthasar was, after Mölders, the second German fighter pilot to be awarded with the Knight's Cross.

Squadron Leader Peter Townsend, 85 Squadron, mounts his Hurricane. Townsend is considered as one of the RAF's best squadron leaders during the Battle of Britain as his 85 Squadron recorded 60 air victories against 12 own losses. The Bf 109 that he shot down on 29 August was his tenth and last air victory. Two days later, Townsend was shot down and wounded. Townsend died 80 years old in June 1995.

Göring had already been forced to pull II. and III./JG 52 out of combat. Now, II./JG 51 was also so worn down – both in terms of equipment and the pilots' nerves – that the unit had to be taken out of combat. This Jagdgruppe had been fighting over the English Channel longer than most Bf 109-equipped units, ever since the 'Channel Offensive' had been launched eight weeks earlier. By now its strength was down to fifteen pilots fit for operations and thirteen aircraft – half of its strength compared to mid-July.

By all accounts it was then that the decision was taken to place greater emphasis on the Bf 110 Zerstörers – which had often performed better than the Bf 109 units.

30 August 1940

The sun had barely risen on 30 August, when a formation of Do 17s and Bf 110s appeared and attacked a British convoy outside the Thames Estuary. They were immediately detected by the British air controllers and Spitfires and Hurricanes from two squadrons scrambled to engage. It did not lead to combat, but now that the British machines were airborne, the Germans started phase two in the day's operations: They began this at 10:30 with a formation of 60 Bf 109s flying into Kent from the south. At 11.00 the next group of Luftwaffe planes came – 60 Bf 109s and 30 Bf 110s in the company of 70 Heinkels and Dorniers. Thirty minutes later, the 'back-up' came in the guise of 60 Bf 109s.

The British radar stations reported several formations of German aircraft on the way in, but since most of southeast England was covered by a thick cloud cover at 2,000 metres altitude, the Observer Corp's posts could not tell if they were bombers or fighters. When a convoy in the Thames Estuary was bombed, Park decided to give his units the take-off order.

Near Dover No. 603 Squadron was suddenly attacked by Bf 110s. Oberleutnant Ulrich von Gravenreuth from V.(Z)/LG 1 pushed the control stick of his Messerschmitt 110 forwards to dive and attack. The next moment Squadron Leader George Denholm's Spitfire, 'XT-D', was torn to pieces by direct hits by 20mm shells from von Gravenreuth's cannons. Denholm was fortunate to escape by parachute. Another Spitfire, 'XT-F', was severely damaged by a Bf 110, but the pilot, Sergeant Alfred Sarre, was able to get it back to base. The other pilots from 603 Squadron were spread out over a large area and unable to assemble to attack the German bombers.

During the Zerstörer airmen's continued flight, which led them northwards towards the Thames Estuary, they saw another formation of British fighters – twelve Hurricanes from 151 Squadron, led by Squadron Leader Eric King. V.(Z)/LG 1 immediately went in to attack, and, like 603 Squadron's formation, the twelve Hurricanes of 151 Squadron scattered to the winds. Unteroffizier Alois Pfaffelhuber from 15.(Z)/LG 1 claimed to have shot down two Hurricanes. One of these can be identified in British sources – it was flown by Squadron Leader King. It was the third time in two weeks that he had been shot down by a Bf 110, but this time he did not survive. His dead body was found in the wreckage of the burned-out Hurricane, which had crashed near Rochester.[245] V.(Z)/LG 1 was able to carry out these two successful attacks without losing any of their own planes.[246]

Further west another gaggle of Zerstörers came buzzing in over the English coast, heading north in combat formations stepped up in height. These Bf 110s had shark jaws painted on their noses – it was II./ZG 76 the 'Haifischgruppe', tasked to escort II./KG 1 to the test airfield at Farnborough. One could hardly find a more experienced Luftwaffe unit than II./ZG 76 'Haifischgruppe'. Among the British fighters that took off to meet them was a unit that was just as inexperienced as ill-fated, No. 253 Squadron.

253 Squadron, which was now back in combat for the first time in three months, had had some very demoralising experiences fighting the Luftwaffe – in particular with Bf 110s. The unit had been put in the front line in France on 17 May 1940, and in the very first combat had lost four planes against only one victory. 'Our losses on the first sortie were all caused by 110s', remembered John Greenwood, who flew as a pilot officer with 253 Squadron. After less than a week, what remained of 253 Squadron was pulled out of combat. By then half of the unit's pilots had been lost, including the squadron leader and both flight commanders. The unit was transferred to Kirton-in-Lindsey in Lincolnshire, where they filled the gaps with newly trained pilots. 'When sent up to Kirton-in-Lindsey to reform we were devastated and fearful of being sent back over Dunkirk' John Greenwood told the author. A senior Air Force officer, Squadron Leader Tom Gleave, was given the job of injecting new courage into No. 253. Since Gleave was 32 years old and the RAF's policy was not to give squadrons to Squadron Leaders older than 26 years, Gleave was replaced. 'To our amazement he was replaced as commander by Squadron Leader King'*, commented Greenwood. 'Gleave stayed with us as supernumerary, which was very hard for him, as he told me long after the War.' The unit was moved to Edinburgh, 'and there King was posted away to another squadron to our great relief and Gleave took over once more', Greenwood continued: 'However a week or so later he was replaced by Squadron Leader Starr, who was another inexperienced leader.'

Squadron Leader Harold Starr, who arrived to take over the leadership of 253 Squadron on 23 August, was 25 years old and had just been declared 'air-worthy' again after having been treated for serious injuries that he suffered in a plane crash in 1936.

At 10:50 on 30 August, 253 Squadron took off with fourteen Hurricanes from Kenley for their first combat mission since the Battle of France.[247] That the unit was not really combat-ready is evidenced by the fact that the first reports of German aircraft made the nervous pilots do such violent manoeuvres that their formation broke into several groups which lost contact with each other. The air controller ordered them back to reform over their airfield. Meanwhile, at 11:30, five more Hurricanes took off from Kenley to join them. These were led by Tom Gleave. At 9,000 metres above Redhill the pilots of 253 Squadron spotted three German formations with nine He 111s each, escorted by a total of about thirty Messerschmitts. John

* The same Squadron Leader King who was killed in combat leading No. 151 Squadron on 30 August 1940.

Bf 110s from II./ZG 76 'Haifischgruppe'.

Greenwood remembered clearly how the entire flock of Bf 110s came down on him and the other Hurricane pilots: 'I found one of the '110s coming in head on to me. I knew they had a huge advantage with their 20mm cannons, so I dived steeply underneath it without firing.'

79 Squadron also joined in and was attacked by the Bf 110s. Over the next few minutes four or five Hurricanes were shot down but this could not protect II./KG 1, which, like 253 Squadron also appeared to be an unlucky unit. Just three days earlier its Gruppenkommandeur, Major Willibald Fanelsa, had been lost. This mission, led by Fanelsa's successor, Hauptmann Heinz Fischer, would cost the 5. Staffel of KG 1 dearly. As they continued flying towards Farnborough, II./KG 1 was attacked by the Hurricanes which came singly or in small groups, as they managed to get away from the attacking Bf 110s. It cost a loss of five He 111s, four of them from 5./KG 1. Pilots from at least four RAF squadrons – Nos. 79, 253, 501 and 610 – participated in the attacks on II./KG 1. One of the He 111s ended up on 501 Squadron's Sergeant 'Ginger' Lacey's. This gave him a total of 11½ victories.

The first He 111 to be lost was 'V4+BV', with the commander of 5./KG 1, Hauptmann Rudolf Bäss. According to the German report his He 111 was rammed by a Hurricane.[248] This coincides with the British report on 79 Squadron's Pilot Officer Edward Morris, who bailed out after having rammed an He 111 over Reigate.

Then He 111 'V4+HV' – also from 5./KG 1 – with Feldwebel Schnabel at the controls, was spotted by John Greenwood, who said: 'I came out of the dive to evade the Me 110 at about 12,000 feet and was turning for home base when I spotted the He 111 below me, on its own, making for home. I attacked from above port quarter, shooting out both engines. I followed it down and watched it force-land and aircrew get out; one of the crew was covered in blood.' One of the crew members of the He 111 died of his injuries, but four survived, although Schnabel and another were wounded.

In the furious air fighting it was not so easy to keep count of the number of downed enemy aircraft. 253 Squadron claimed three Bf 110s confirmed, while in fact not a single Bf 110 was lost. II./ZG 76 returned from the mission reporting 18 British fighters shot down – without any own losses. Although these figures are exaggerated, it is clear that 'Haifischgruppe' gained significant success. Four of its pilots – unit commander Hauptmann Erich Groth, and Hauptmann Heinz Nacke, Oberleutnant Wilhelm Herget and Leutnant Siegfried Göbel – each scooped two victories on that mission. Oberleutnant Hans-Joachim Jabs and Leutnant Walter Borchers – both of whom were on their way to becoming élite Luftwaffe aces – also contributed by shooting down one British fighter each. Obviously the Zerstörer units were responsible for most of the 13 RAF fighters shot down in the air fighting around midday on 30 August – nine of which were completely destroyed.

The Messerschmitt 109 units did not do as well. In addition to the results of the Zerstörer units', I./JG 2 and II./JG 27 claimed to have shot down two each of the British fighters without any own losses. II./JG 54 got two more victories, but lost as many Bf 109s. Things did not go better

for II./JG 2, which recorded one victory for the loss of two of its own. For I./JG 27, which was out on its first mission since the unit was transferred to Luftflotte 2, things went simply miserably – to top it all due to a single British fighter pilot.

Immediately after the Bf 110s' attack against No. 253 Squadron, Squadron Leader Tom Gleave – arguably the most experienced airman in 253 Squadron – found that he had a large formation Bf 109s behind him;[249] they belonged to JG 27. Without hesitation, Gleave plunged straight into the mass of Bf 109s, shot down four in rapid succession and bolted out of there at full speed. When he returned to base to report his achievement, he was received with scepticism. Four kills in as many minutes, by a lone Hurricane pilot against 30 Bf 109s, was considered a bit rich. Gleave simply had to settle for four 'probables', but an examination of German reports actually verifies Gleave's victory claims. The four Bf 109 pilots he shot down were:
Oberleutnant Hans Bertram, wounded.
Oberleutnant Erwin Axthelm, captured.
Feldwebel Ernst Arnold, captured.
Feldwebel Georg Lehmann, killed.

With the exception of Lehmann, all belonged to I./JG 27, which since the first 'Channel battles' in July had claimed 10 victories for 15 own losses.

While both sides' fighters fought these battles, the majority of the German bombers got through. Again, the Germans sent in so many different units that British operations rooms lost their overview. It simply could not be deciphered which German formations were intercepted and which slipped through untouched; at noon no less than 48 different air surveillance posts reported that they could hear air fighting taking place above the clouds.

The fate of II./KG 1 was an exception. 11 Group requested reinforcements from 12 Group, but without result. When the bombs fell shortly afterwards on Biggin Hill airfield without 12 Group's fighters making themselves known, Park lost his temper. He rang up 12 Group and hissed: 'Where the hell were your fighters that were supposed to have protected my airfields?' The answer he got – that Leigh-Mallory's pilots had failed to find the Germans – did nothing to mollify the apoplectic commander of 11 Group. 'Listen', he roared, 'your fighter pilots were not supposed to look for the enemy – they should have been above southern London's airfields, waiting for the enemy!'

In addition to Biggin Hill, the airfields at Croydon and Eastchurch were attacked. Kesselring continued to send over wave after wave of his planes. Kenley, Tangmere and Shoreham took more hits. What was worse – a bomb hit on an important electricity station put the radar stations at Beachy Head, Dover, Fairlight, Foreness, Pevensey, Rye and Whitstable out of action.

At airfields throughout north-eastern France and Belgium there was hectic activity as new Luftwaffe units took off all the time. At Lille at half past three (German time) some thirty He 111s from I./KG 53 took off. Their goal was the Vauxhall works in Luton, north of London. At 4,800 metres above Cap Gris Nez, they met their fighter escort – Bf 110s from II./ZG 76 'Haifischgruppe'.[250] From elsewhere came other bombers and other Messerschmitts. 11 Group had thirteen squadrons in the air, but most were involved in hard air fighting with German fighters. 253 Squadron was again in the thick of it and lost two more Hurricanes without succeeding in destroying any German aircraft.

Soon the British radar stations and Observer Corps posts reported about three hundred German aircraft approaching Kent. No. 151 Squadron, which had lost its squadron leader that morning, managed to get up to the bomber formation. Oberfeldwebel Alfred Sticht, who was the observer in the He 111 'A1+LH' of Hauptmann Emil Allmendinger, the commander of 1./KG 53, said: 'We had radio contact with the Zerstörer fliers. Their call-code was "Marabou" and ours was "Owl". Near the Thames Estuary we came under attack from the first Spitfires. The warning blared in the headphones: "Fighters from below!" They looked like mosquitoes down there, but they quickly grew in size. Soon they are close enough to try to attack us from below. The flight engineer and bay gunner meets the assault with repeated short bursts, and even I, the observer, open fire from my glass hood. But the Spitfires of course are superior to us not only in terms of speed and manoeuvrability, but also in firepower. We shout over the radio: "Marabou from Owl! Request fighter cover! Ten Spitfires are attacking us from below!"' [251]

The RAF report reads: 'A large number of Me 110s were above the bombers and on all sides except on the left. [151 Squadron] got in an attack on the bombers before the Me 110s could close up. The Me 110s then chased in all around the bombers circling round in groups of ten.' [252]

II./ZG 76's Hauptmann Heinz Nacke shot down a Hurricane into the cold water of the Thames Estuary. It was Nacke's third kill that day and his 14th in total. The pilot of the Hurricane, Sergeant Feliks Gmur, was a Polish volunteer in 151 Squadron. Shortly afterwards Pilot Officer John Ellacombe went down with severe damage to his Hurricane, but was able to belly-land his aircraft.

222 Squadron then showed up. This was yet another 'green' unit that had arrived in Hornchurch the day before. Three of its Spitfires were shot down by Bf 110s. Hauptmann Groth, the commander of II./ZG 76, shot down one of these. Groth got three victories that day.

Bomber observer Oberfeldwebel Sticht continued his account: 'The contrails in the sky testify to a fierce dogfight. Several aircraft are going down as blazing torches. Whether friend or foe can't be determined. In about fifteen minutes, we should have arrived at our target. Once again I see British and German fighters dive into a cloud bank. The first attack is over. The Zerstörer fliers from the Haifisch Gruppe have protected us well.'

But British reinforcements were on the way. For the second time that day Park had asked Leigh-Mallory for help from 12 Group. This time 12 Group's honour was at stake, and the units were ready.

Thus, No. 242 Squadron, which was to become one of the most renowned in the RAF, got its baptism of fire in the Battle of Britain. Its squadron leader was the renowned Douglas Bader, one of the boldest British air aces. On the ground Bader hobbled on a pair of prosthetic legs – the result of a serious plane crash eight years before the war. But the bulldog-like Englishman had a rare determination. In a situation where others would have given up, he fought on, and shortly after the war broke out he sat again in a fighter aircraft, having defeated both his physical handicap and the RAF's enrolment office.

On his first day of combat, the last day of May 1940, the 'Legless Wonder', as he was known, shot down two German planes over Dunkirk. Bader made such a meteoric career that the very next month he was given the difficult task of leading 242 Squadron, a 'troublesome' Hurricane unit consisting of Canadians who had been demoralized by bad leadership and severe losses. The 30-year-old Bader used all his energy and perseverance in bringing new courage to the unit. When 12 Group in the afternoon of 30 August put some of its forces at 11 Group's disposal, Bader's 242 Squadron was included as the trump card. 12 Group's report reads: 'With so many aircraft about it seemed impossible to order any stereotyped form of attack and Squadron Leader Bader dived into the middle of the formation and broke it up after which a series of dogfights ensued.' [253]

In the fierce combat a few Hurricanes managed to get through and attack the He 111s. 'Suddenly we are attacked by new enemy fighters, coming straight out of the sun,' Oberfeldwebel Sticht continues his account. 'The aircraft on the right hand side of Kette number three starts emitting smoke: the plane is hit and the fuel leaking out! Allmendinger cries in the radio: "Marabou from Owl, requesting assistance!"' [254]

242 Squadron's Pilot Officer Willie McKnight was reported to have shot down two Bf 110s and a He 111 in the clash, increasing his personal score to 13. In his combat report, he described the last victory: 'Was attacked by an Me 110 but succeeded in getting behind and followed him from

Squadron Leader Douglas Bader (left) and Pilot Officer Willie McKnight in front of Douglas Bader's personal emblem painted onto his Hurricane. Douglas Bader was known as 'the Legless Wonder'. He had lost both legs in a plane crash in 1931, but eight years later, he returned to active service as a fighter pilot with two prosthetic legs. With the two downed Bf 110s that Bader recorded on 30 August his track record reached 3½ air victories. On 7 September he added three more victories to this list. When Bader was shot down and ended up in German captivity on 9 August 1941, he had amassed 20 individual and four shared air victories. Douglas Bader passed away in September 1982, aged 72. (Photo: Bader.)

10,000ft to 1,000ft. Enemy aircraft used very steep turns for evasive action but finally straightened out. I opened fire from approximately thirty yards, enemy's starboard engine stopped and port engine burst into flame. Enemy aircraft crashed in flames alongside reservoir.' [255]

Although 242 Squadron's report of twelve downed German aircraft proved to be greatly exaggerated, two of the 'Haifischgruppe's' Messerschmitts crashed. Additionally, Hauptmann Nacke and his radio operator, Stabsfeldwebel Alfred Kühne were wounded when a burst of fire from a Hurricane hit their 'M8+"KM'. Nacke still managed to bring the heavily damaged '110 back to St. Inglevert in France, where it crashed. Thereby one of Germany's best Zerstörer pilots was put of action. Some time later Nacke was awarded with the Knight's Cross.

In addition to 242 Squadron, a Polish Hurricane pilot from 303 Squadron also joined in the action. No. 303 Squadron, which consisted mainly of Polish volunteers – most of whom were far more experienced than the average RAF pilot – had nine days earlier moved from Blackpool to Northolt. There the unit began to train for combat under the guidance of its British squadron leader, Ronald Kellet. On this particular afternoon, a group of the unit's pilots were in the air practising attacks on six Blenheims, when they saw the fight between Bader's Hurricanes and the German planes. Pilot Officer Ludwik Paskiewicz immediately broke out of formation and set off after the Germans. He failed to obey Squadron Leader Kellet's radio call to return, blaming 'faulty radio communication'. The Polish veteran – he had previously flown with the French

Air Force – threw himself into the battle and claimed to have shot down a 'Do 17' (probably a misidentification of a Bf 110). When he returned to base afterwards, he was given a severe reprimand but afterwards it was announced that his efforts had led to the decision to declare 303 Squadron operational. 303 Squadron's combat report on this historic clash for the unit reads: 'In the course of a training interception with six Blenheims in the afternoon "B" flight contacted with some 60 German bombers, 60 fighters and British fighters having a running battle near Hatfield. P/O Paskiewicz brought down one Do 17 (destroyed) while the rest of the fighters escorted the Blenheim safely back to Northolt.' [256]

But the He 111 formation from I./KG 53 was unstoppable. At North Weald airfield the siren sounded as the bombers came in. Eric Clayton, mechanic in 56 Squadron, remembers: 'We nervously watched as it sailed majestically over the station, at great height, without dropping a bomb!' [257] The He 111s continued and came in over Luton in perfect formation. They dropped 194 bombs – the majority over the Vauxhall works, inflicting heavy damage, but also on the airfield and the city itself. A total of 59 people were killed and 141 others injured by the falling bombs.

This was the day Göring's plans worked perfectly. While the He 111s and the other German aircraft in this round of the battle began to return home, swarms of Bf 109s flew in over the English south coast to cover their withdrawal. South of Woodchurch in Kent, Leutnant Heinz Ebeling, one of the aces from III./JG 26, shot down a Hurricane. It was his 12th victory. This plane was flown

A Bf 110 from II./ZG 76 'Haifischgruppe' taxis out to take off. The painted shark jaws on this unit's aircraft inspired RAF 112 Squadron in the spring of 1941 to paint similar shark jaws on their Curtiss P-40s. Pictures of these aircraft in magazines in turn influenced the American volunteer air force in China (AVG) to paint the same predator mouths on their P-40s. Thereby the concept of the Flying Tigers' was born.

by Squadron Leader John Badger of 43 Squadron. Three of Fighter Command's squadron leaders had therefore been shot down during this one day. Badger, who was severely wounded, had taken over command of 43 Squadron on 9 July, after Squadron Leader Lott had been shot down and wounded in combat with ZG 26. Between 14 and 30 August Badger was credited with six victories, but the 30 August sortie was his last. Ten months later he died of his injuries, 29 years old.

During the return flight, which was to the southeast, the He 111s which had bombed Luton were still encountering fighter attacks. 'The British fighter pilots gave proof of great skill and courage', said Oberfeldwebel Sticht. 'They came in between our Ketten so that sometimes it was impossible for us to fire because of the risk of hitting our own planes.' 501 Squadron's Hurricanes carried out a daring frontal assault against the He 111s' rear V-formation.[258] Pilot Officer Stanislaw Skalski – a Polish volunteer who achieved six kills during the fighting over Poland in September 1939 – was credited with shooting down a He 111.

'Near the Thames Estuary, south of Southend on Sea, Feldwebel Sünderhauf's crew reports: "Engine damaged, we switch to single-engine flight. Pilot badly wounded." We immediately call the Zerstörers and request fighter escort for a He 111 lagging behind the formation on one engine.'[259] Some Zerstörer pilots broke away from the fighting with the British fighters and went for 501 Squadron's Hurricanes, which were vulnerable when their pilots pulled up their planes after diving straight through the bomber formation. Sergeant 'Ginger' Lacey's Hurricane shook from hits by a Bf 110's nose armament.*

'Thank God the Me 110s of the Haifisch Gruppe were still with us', Oberfeldwebel Sticht commented, and continued: 'Several He 111s limped back out over the Thames Estuary with severe combat damage, but despite the long return flight and repeated British fighter attacks, the number of aircraft lost during the Luton mission is limited to two.' Sticht finished his account: 'At St. Omer the Haifisch Zerstörers wave their wings in a farewell to us. Via radio we thank them for the excellent fighter escort. Without them it would have been really bad for us.'

Meanwhile the entire JG 54, now under its new Geschwaderkommodore Major Hannes Trautloft, swept across southern England. This unit's mission was to escort the Bf 110 assault planes from Erprobungsgruppe 210 that flew in to follow up the previous attack on the Biggin Hill sector station.[260] One of the air controllers in Park's 11 Group directed the newcomers from Squadron Leader John Hill's 222 Squadron straight towards JG 54. They had no chance against the German veterans.

Oberleutnant Günther Scholz, the commander of 7./ JG 54, saw the Spitfires climbing in line ahead into the air above Kent. Instead of immediately going to attack, Scholz called his men to follow him and led his Staffel in a wide arc so that they could attack with the sun in the back. Three Spitfires fell in flames and the rest were scattered to the winds. A fourth was shot down by JG 26 when Major Galland shortly afterwards led his Geschwader on a fighter sweep over Kent. This meant that No. 222 Squadron had lost eight planes on their first day in combat.

McKnight's personal crest on his 242 Squadron Hurricane. Pilot Officer William 'Willie' McKnight was the top-scoring Canadian fighter pilot in 1940. When 242 Squadron was launched into the Battle of Britain on 30 August, he had already achieved nine victories during the Battle of France. When 242 Squadron was pulled out of combat in early November 1940, he had increased his tally to 16½. McKnight was killed when he was shot down by a Bf 109 of JG 26 on 12 January 1941. (Photo: Bader.)

Under the leadership of its new Gruppenkommandeur, Hauptmann Hans von Boltenstern, Erprobungsgruppe 210 hit the air base Biggin Hill with devastating effect. One of the four remaining hangars was destroyed, as were workshops and several other buildings. In addition most of the telephone lines were cut, as well as gas and water mains and the base's main power cable. A bomb had hit a shelter where airwomen of the WAAF had sought refuge. Historian Dennis Newton describes the situation: 'Everyone outside pitches in and digs furiously to free the trapped women. Ambulance and stretcher parties stand by. One-by-one the women are carried out: some are barely recognizable because of dirt and blood on their faces. Others are dazed and bruised but all, except one, are alive. Lena Button from Tasmania is the only casualty. Altogether, 39 personnel have been killed and 26 injured.'[261]

Biggin Hill had been eliminated as a sector station, at least for now, and sector control had to be moved to Hornchurch. Erprobungsgruppe 210 had had yet another great success, without suffering any losses themselves.

The fighting on 30 August showed for the first time the full impact of Göring's new tactic of sending in an overwhelming number of fighter aircraft. The Messerschmitt units had made 1,265 sorties, which was nearly a record, to escort a total of no more than 80 bombers. For the first time in a long time, Göring was pleased with the fighter formations' results. The Messerschmitt 109 units claimed 28 victories against 12 own losses, while the Zerstörer units had 26 victories in exchange for 7 Bf 110s lost.

On the other side of the Channel things did not look as bright. Certainly Fighter Command claimed 58 victories in exchange for 25 losses. But half a dozen air bases had been bombed and seven radar stations had been knocked off the air. The true German combat losses were 33 aircraft. Air Vice-Marshal Park summoned his sector commanders and air controllers to a conference at 11 Group Headquarters in Uxbridge. He looked unusually grim when the officers arrived. With the help of a graph the commander showed the increase in RAF fighter losses. During the discussion it emerged that the participating parties were in agreement that the increasing losses depended largely on

* The Zerstörer attack was so sudden that Lacey believed that his aircraft had been hit by defensive fire from a He 111, but the damages on his Hurricane proved to have been caused by automatic cannons.

two factors – new squadrons that as yet lacked combat experience had been launched into the battle, and there was an increasing proportion of new and inexperienced pilots in the units. There wasn't much anyone could do about this. On the other hand, Park drew an important conclusion: that the Luftwaffe's new, and clearly successful method of sending aircraft in a never-ending stream, was intended to confuse British combat control. Park therefore ordered his sector commanders to instruct their fighter pilots that as soon as they sighted a German air unit, they were to report its altitude, strength and composition to the Operations Room – thus giving air controllers a better picture of the situation. [262]

When darkness fell, roughly 130 He 111s and Ju 88s from Luftflotte 3 flew towards Liverpool. Meanwhile, Bomber Command was in action over Germany carrying out, among other things, a new attack on Berlin which cost seven bombers. Two of them – a Hampden from 50 Squadron and a Wellington from 214 Squadron – were shot down by a Bf 110 night fighter flown by Oberleutnant Werner Streib from I./NJG 1.

31 August 1940

The battle escalated towards a violent crescendo. The mercilessly beautiful summer weather gave Fighter Command no respite. Göring could taste victory when he ordered a massive operation for the fourth day in a row.

Already at eight o'clock on this Saturday morning Luftwaffe formations were on their way in over the Strait of Dover. They were the Do 17 bombers of KG 2 and KG 3, surrounded by well over two hundred Messerschmitts from JG 2, JG 26, ZG 26 and ZG 76. After intensive repair work the British radar stations were back in service. They reported '200 bandits' approaching, and Park decided to order up no less than thirteen squadrons. This was exactly what Göring and his fighter pilots wanted.

Over the Thames Estuary the Dorniers split up into several small groups. I. and II./KG 3 veered off to the west, towards North Weald and Hornchurch just northeast of London. While the attack on Hornchurch was successful – from the German point of view – the bomber crews who went to North Weald were subjected to furious fighter attacks that forced many of them to jettison their bombs before they reached the target.

The largest British fighter effort was made against the Dornier bombers from KG 2, which continued north-eastwards and flew in over the coast near Harwich. These were II./KG 2 that attacked 12 Group's Duxford airfield and III./KG 2, which had 11 Group's Debden base as its target. II./ZG 76 'Haifischgruppe' escorted the former, while III./ZG 26 'Horst Wessel' had been given the task of protecting III./KG 2.

No. 253 Squadron was at a height disadvantage and broke formation when the Bf 110s from III./ZG 26 'Horst Wessel' came screaming in with tracers pouring from their noses. The first British aircraft to be shot down by the Bf 110s was the Hurricane flown by Squadron Leader Harold Starr of 253 Squadron. The pilot bailed out and opened his parachute, but it did not save him. 'Starr was certainly machine-gunned to death after he baled out', says historian Patrick Bishop. [263]

In the Clacton area the Hurricanes from 257 Squadron were attacked by what was reported as 'fifty Me 110s' which plunged down from 5,500 metres. [264] It is possible that 257 Squadron's Pilot Officer Gerald Maffett encountered the same fate as Squadron Leader Starr. His Hurricane, 'DT-S', was shot down by a Bf 110 and Maffett was seen bailing out. But when the 24-year-old airman reached the ground, he was dead. Flying Officer James Henderson, another pilot in 257 Squadron, was lucky to survive the encounter. He recalled: *'All of a sudden, I saw two Me 110s coming directly at me, full throttle, line astern. Realising that I would present an easy target, I broke away. I flew straight at them and started firing at about 300 yards. I kept up the fire for five seconds. Both enemy aircraft broke away at point blank range, passing straight through my sights. First enemy aircraft must have shot at mine before breaking away as my instruments were shattered. A second or two later, the second Me 110 appeared and there was a great explosion in my aircraft as the fuel tank was hit, presumably by cannon fire. The cockpit immediately became a mass of flames and I baled out, falling into the sea three to four miles off Brightlingsea.'* [265]

Air Vice-Marshal Leigh-Mallory suddenly realized that his 12 Group's airfields were threatened and ordered his units to take off. Among these was 19 Squadron, which went up from Fowlmere with nine pilots led by Flight Lieutenant Wilfrid Clouston. Their cannon-armed Spitfires could not help them when II./ZG 76 'Haifischgruppe' dived and attacked southeast of Cambridge. 'Fighting for their lives,' wrote historians John Vasco and Peter D. Cornwell, 'the Spitfires were only able to claim one Bf 110 probably destroyed and another damaged during this action for the loss of 2 Spitfires. Both British pilots baled out, one of them, Flying Officer Coward, being seriously wounded. Another No. 19 Squadron aircraft dropped out of combat and returned to Fowlmere with its hydraulics shot to pieces only to somersault on landing, burst into flames and kill the pilot, Pilot Officer Aeberhardt.' [266]

Flying Officer Coward was apparently shot down by one of the Dorniers' defensive armament. He escaped with his life thanks to extraordinary presence of mind. He said: *'About thirty miles east of Duxford we spotted fifteen Dorniers at 20,000 feet. Flight Lieutenant Clouston, a New Zealander, ordered a No. 1 attack in which each section of three formed Line Astern and wheeled in behind a section of three bombers. He ordered the last section, led by Flying Officer Brinsden, to continue climbing and try to distract the escorting fighters. As leader of the third Section I turned in behind the Dornier on the right of the third Section. When I opened fire my guns all jammed and I only got off one or perhaps two rounds from each gun. I was told later that to get the large cannons into the thin wing of a Spitfire, they had to be put on their side so that instead of the empty case falling out it had to come out sideways and bounce off a plate into a hole in the wing. This worked on the ground, but at speed the high pressure of air under the wings prevented the case from ejecting and jammed the guns.*

'In breaking away a rear gunner's bullet came through the port side of my aircraft and went through both bones on my left leg. I felt a hard kick on the shin. A glance showed my bare foot sitting on the rudder bar, still attached to the ligaments. The elevator controls failed to stop the aircraft descending so I baled out.

'When my parachute opened I could neither see not hear another aircraft. I baled out at 22,000 feet so it took me about twenty minutes to come down. I was spinning in the air and saw blood shoot out, so I realised I must do something. I used the radio cord from my helmet as a torniquet.

'While I was descending in my parachute, a young lady was waiting outside the Foxtyon Church for her bridegroom. Owing to an air raid he was delayed. When she looked up she saw a man dangling on a parachute. She watched him circle and he seemd to have only one leg (actually I had hooked my left leg up to help stop the blood flow). She sent her wedding bouquet to Addenbrookes Hospital. When I came round from the anaesthetic my wife was sitting by my bed. I naturally thought that she had brought the flowers.

'In 1990 when we came over to the UK for the 50th anniversary of the Battle of Britain, I was speaking at a dinner in Cambridge and recounted the story of my descent. A little grey-haired woman came up to me and said: "Did you get my flowers?"' [267]

Oberleutnant Hermann Weeber, Oberleutnant Erich-Hartmann von Schlotheim and Oberleutnant Wilhelm Herget were each credited with the shooting down of one Spitfire in this engagement, which II./ZG 76 survived without any own losses. The analysis of the battle that the RAF's 11 Group later made gives a good impression of the German escort tactics: 'Waving on each side of this formation, 500 feet higher and overshadowing the last sections of the echelon, were 40 Me 110s equally divided on port and starboard side, and at 25,000 feet were Me 109s. While the attack by our fighters was directed on one section of bombers, the remainder of the Do 17s flew on in the same perfect formation while the Me 110s dived from behind to intercept the Hurricanes. Meanwhile the Me 109s maintained their height and kept vigil and made no efforts to engage. One Me 110 adopted the tactics of diving steeply down apparently out of control and when followed by a Hurricane, the latter was attacked from behind by other Me 110s.' [268]

In the meantime, III./ZG 26 'Horst Wessel' continued to hold off the British fighters far to the east, where these tried to reach the Dornier bombers from III./KG 2. Sergeant Henry Merchant from 1 Squadron had the fuel tank of his Hurricane set on fire by a Bf 110, and barely managed to bail out, albeit with severe burns. No. 56 Squadron took off from North Weald at 08:20. Its war diary describes the mission: 'Near Colchester they became involved with the fighter escort and F/L Weaver was shot down and killed. He had been given the DFC this very day and he was a great loss to the squadron. F/O Westmacott and P/O Mounsdon were also injured but not seriously and their aircraft being lost. Sgt Whitehead was shot down by an unseen aircraft. He bailed out and was unhurt.' [269]

Flight Lieutenant Peter Weaver, who was credited with nine victories, went to his final rest in the Runnymede Memorial, Surrey. Flying Officer Innes Westmacott's Hurricane was probably the second aircraft that Oberleutnant Hans Barschels from III./ZG 26's Stabsschwarm shot down during the fight. [270] Westmacott said afterwards: 'I had a quick look behind and saw a number of '110s belting in from behind on my starboard quarter. I thought I would have time for another attack and turned back in for the Dornier. I think fatigue had affected my judgement, for the enemy had arrived much sooner than I thought fair. I was just pulling up to open fire when, with a tremendous crash, my instrument panel disappeared in fragments, followed immediately by a searing blast of flames as my reserve tank went up in my face.' [271]

19 Squadron's Flying Officer James Coward was an experienced pilot when the Battle of Britain began. He began his fighter pilot career flying a Gloster Gauntlet biplane in 1937. After being shot down on 31 August 1940, Coward was recruited to Winston Churchill's personal staff. Coward, who made a valuable contribution to this book, passed away on 25 July 2012, aged 97. (Photo: Coward.)

When it dawned on Air Vice-Marshal Leigh-Mallory that his own units would not be able to defend 12 Group's bases, he was – for once! – forced to ask Park for help. Park ordered nine Hurricanes from 111 Squadron which were out on patrol towards the formation of Do 17s from II./KG 2, which were headed straight for Duxford airfield. Although these Hurricane pilots were hopelessly outnumbered, they split up into three groups of three aircraft each and these, one after the other, carried out hair-raising head-on attacks right in amongst the Do 17 planes. The attack came suddenly, before the Zerstörer airmen had time to react, and the effect was devastating for the Germans. II./KG 2's formation broke apart as the terrified pilots veered to avoid colliding with the 'mad' British. This affected the results of the subsequent bombing. Bombs were scattered across Essex, Suffolk and Cambridgeshire.[272] However, the British pilots were not able to shoot down more than one Do 17, while they lost a Hurricane; it probably fell to Oberleutnant Hans-Joachim Jabs, who now led 6./ZG 76 since Nacke had been injured.

III./ZG 26 carried out their task with even greater success. The unit was credited with shooting down 13 British fighters in the 20 minutes of furious air combat. This left III./KG 2 free to make its way to its target – the Debden air base – without being disturbed by any fighter attacks. Over one hundred bombs were dropped on the base, the installations were seriously damaged and four Hurricanes were knocked out. On the return flight, the Dornier planes had to contend with renewed attacks by British fighters, but all were driven off by the fighter escort or the Dornier gunners' crossfire.[273]

For III./ZG 26 the price of this success was limited to a single Bf 110 shot down. This was flown by Oberleutnant Erich von Bergen, who was attacked by three British fighters. 'I turned towards the Spitfires and attacked the last one', von Bergen said. 'Shortly after having shot down this one (the pilot bailed out), the first one got me with a full salvo. The oxygen bottles in the rear of the fuselage exploded and the fuselage broke. The plane could not fly any more so I gave the order to [the radio operator Unteroffizier Hans] Becker to jump out and I followed immediately.' [274]

From a great height Major Adolf Galland's Stabsstaffel dived into this jumble of circling, diving and firing aircraft and shot down a fighter – identified as a 'Curtiss P-40' – which became Galland's 25th kill.

By now even more German aircraft were crossing the Channel to cover those returning after using up their ammunition. In the air over Dover Oberleutnant Hans 'Assi' Hahn from 4./JG 2 attacked some Spitfires and two were reported downed. Hahn's companion Oberfeldwebel Erich Rudorffer contributed with the destruction of a third British fighter.

Major Werner Mölders flew his '109 high over the Strait of Dover. He brought with him nearly his entire JG 51, with between 70 and 80 Messerschmitt 109s. White vapour trails streamed backwards from their wing tips in the thin air. Radio silence was ordered.

Park directed two Hurricane squadrons – No. 253 RAF and No. 1 RCAF – towards what he initially thought were bombers. When the Observer Corps identified only single-engined Messerschmitt fighters, the Hurricane pilots were ordered to return. But 1 RCAF's pilots did not get the message and flew straight towards the mass of 109s.

'Hurricanes!' Below and a good bit ahead of him Mölders could see a formation of a dozen Hawker Hurricanes which shot out of the haze and climbed across his Messerschmitts' course. Mölders was calm and restrained: 'Stabsstaffel follows me. Others stay put.' By now the Hurricanes were on the left; they were apparently in a great

hurry. The twelve young men from the Stabsstaffel were seized by the kind of zeal for battle that the Germans called 'hunting fever'. They had the sun behind them as they put the noses of their '109s down, and, feverish with excitement, charged towards the Hurricane formation with all guns ready.

Oberleutnant Karl-Heinz Leesmann, the commander of 2./JG 52 during the Battle of Britain. Leesmann achieved his first air victory on 24 August 1940 and after his triple victory on 31 August he had a total of five. In October 1940 his 14 air victories made him the Staffel's most successful fighter pilot. When Leesmann was shot down and killed in combat with American B-17 bombers on 25 July 1943, he had amassed 37 air victories. (Photo: Broschwitz.)

The cockade-marked machines continued straight ahead showing no sign that the pilots had discovered the horde of Messerschmitts that came diving out of the sun. One of the Hurricanes grew larger and larger in the brilliant crosshairs of Mölders' gunsight. He could clearly make out the red spinner, the three exhaust pipes that spat out little blue flames and left a black stripe of smoke that sprayed backwards and then dissolved far behind the plane, the birdcage-like cockpit hood. His thumb and index finger squeezed the two firing buttons. Small bright yellow streaks hurled from the muzzles of the Messerschmitt's guns, and four parallel lines tore through the air and disappeared into the enemy fighter plane a hundred metres away. Direct hit! The Hurricane made a violent jerk in the air and then disappeared downwards in a cloud of smoke and fire. Perhaps a thousand metres further down a parachute opened like a huge flower in the middle of the sky.

A Hurricane from 601 Squadron. The aircraft in the picture was flown by Australian Pilot Officer Clive Mayer, who scored his fifth air victory by shooting down a Do 17 on 31 August 1940. (Photo: Riddle via Ivers.)

Mölders had bagged his thirtieth victory – the first pilot of the war to do so. Ten minutes later three Hurricanes had fallen to his guns. The German report reads: 'Major Mölders shot down three Hurricanes between Folkstone and Dover – his victories numbers 30, 31 and 32 – and Obltn. [Georg] Claus shot down a Hurricane for his ninth victory. They attacked the formation from behind and Mölders shot down the two first British aircraft and Obltn. Claus a third, whereupon Major Mölders shot down the fourth.' [275] This was quite correct, 1 RCAF Squadron lost four Hurricanes.

Meanwhile thirty Messerschmitt 109s from I./JG 52 took the chance to sneak in from the south and plaster the airfield at Detling with machine gun fire in a surprise low-level attack; then they quickly turned south again and attacked Dover's balloon barrage and shot down 50 blimps.

An hour's violent clashes in the air cost the RAF 19 fighters, plus the four that had been destroyed on the ground. For the rest of the morning Jafü 2's units did their best to wear the Britons out with incessant fighter sweeps. Park sent out a repeat of his order prohibiting fighter attacks on any formation that was mostly Messerschmitts. At eleven (German time), after the Germans had failed to lure the British into combat, they sent a Staffel of Do 17s – 2./KG 76 – to attack Eastchurch airfield. The 'Flying Pencils' were met by JG 54, and the whole armada formed up at 4,500 metres above Calais before moving off across the Channel.[276]

The Germans were met by anti-aircraft fire at Dover, and near Eastchurch eight Hurricanes from 151 Squadron made a death-defying attack against the bombers. They managed to shoot down a Dornier, which cost them a plane – flown by the Polish Volunteer Pilot Officer Franciszek Czajkowski. In the general confusion as dozens of Messerschmitt pilots hurled themselves at the small band of Hurricanes, the Germans thought that they had shot down four Hurricanes. Oberleutnant Hans-Ekkehard Bob from 9./JG 54 – the so-called 'Devil's Staffel' – was even credited with two victories.

Shortly after noon Kesselring again dispatched his bombers in larger formations. This time it was both Do 17s and He 111s and they went against Biggin Hill, Hornchurch and Croydon airfields. As before, the bombers were provided with an overwhelming number of escort fighters. On this 31 August, 1940 more than eight German fighters were in the air for every bomber that was sent across the English Channel.

The sector station at Biggin Hill, which had suffered three attacks the day before, recived another battering. This time it was He 111s that rained down bombs from 3,800 metres. The long-suffering men on the airfield were by then convinced that Biggin Hill was the main target for the entire Luftwaffe! [277]

Park has no choice but to send his weary units into the air again. The RAF pilots were met by numerous Messerschmitts which flew in over the coast at high altitude. Squadron Leader Tom Gleave, who the day before spread terror in JG 27, took off in front of seven Hurricanes from 253 Squadron. He failed to see the Messerschmitt that simply flew up behind and below him.

'Flames roared over him as he tried to tear himself loose of his radio and oxygen connections. He saw his skin bubble and crisp, and felt the pain from his burning clothes as he undid the harness and slid back the hood. An explosion threw him out of the cockpit, and he managed to pull the ripcord of his parachute. By the time he landed in a farm, his burned flesh had swollen to close his eyes to thin slits.' [278]

At Hornchurch 54 Squadron attempted to take off in the middle of the bombing, with the result that three Spitfires were destroyed on the runway. Flight Lieutenant 'Al' Deere and the other two pilots of these aircraft were lucky to escape with their lives.

Squadron Leader Peter Townsend, who took off from Croydon along with the other Hurricane pilots in his 85 Squadron, nearly met the same fate. He said: 'As Dornier bombers swept over Croydon, demolishing hangars and technical buildings, I led my squadron off through the smoke and dust against the attackers. Twenty minutes later, after a sharp cut and thrust combat with a swarm of escorting Messerschmitts, my Hurricane was hit. So was I. Once again my parachute saved me.'

It is impossible to determine exactly who shot down Townsend and Gleave, since such a large number of German fighter pilots reported shoot-downs in the same area – 27 in all. In reality these air combats cost the RAF a loss of 10 fighters. Meanwhile, German fighter pilots once again paid an high price for the slow close escort missions. For I./JG 77, this was its first day of combat. [279] Its Messerschmitt pilots crawled along next to the bombers at just 1,000 metres above the Thames Estuary. At 13:30 (British time) the Hurricanes from 601 Squadron and Spitfires from 603 Squadron dived down on them. It was a massacre. One of the five pilots from I./JG 77 to be shot down over the Thames Estuary was Leutnant Bruno Petrenko. He recalled: 'All around me several of my comrades were shot down – a fate that I too met.' [280]

Feldwebel Günther Kramer escaped the British attack and tried to escape by flying low over the British coun-

Spitfires at the Hornchurch base in early September 1940. 'XT-W' was flown by 603 Squadron's Pilot Officer Brian Carbury. Twenty-two year old Carbury belonged to the élite among the fighter aces during the Battle of Britain, on both sides. Before the Battle of Britain, he had made himself known by shooting down the first German aircraft in British airspace since 1918, on 16 October 1939. In late 1940 his 15½ air victories made him one of the RAF's top aces. His feat of shooting down five aircraft in a single day was shared with only two other pilots in the RAF during the Battle of Britain, Archie McKellar and Antoni Glowacki. Carbury died in 1961, only 43 years old. The aircraft closest to the camera, 'ZD-D', X4278, was flown by 222 Squadron's Flying Officer John Cutts, who was shot down and killed on 4 September 1940.

tryside, but was chased by a Hurricane from 601 Squadron flown by Sergeant Norman Taylor. After a wild chase Taylor destroyed the radiator of Kramer's 'White 5'. The German pilot crash-landed at Fort Shornemead at Gravesend, where he was taken prisoner. Today the clock from the dashboard of his Bf 109 E-1 is in the Kent Battle of Britain Museum. Ten minutes after he shot down Kramer, Taylor himself was shot down by another '109, but likewise escaped unharmed.

Immediately afterwards, III./JG 51 – which was out free hunting – attacked 601 Squadron and shot down three Hurricanes, one of which was chalked up as Oberleutnant Arnold Lignitz' thirteenth victory. All of III./JG 51's planes returned safe from the mission, while four Hurricanes went missing from 601 Squadron. No. 603 Squadron survived without any own losses. In that squadron the New Zealander Pilot Officer Brian Carbury claimed two '109s – his second and third victories (the fifth and sixth for the squadron) on that day, since he had shot down another '109 in the morning.

This was the day that Carbury, amazingly, shot down five Messerschmitt 109s. 31 August, 1940 ended in the evening with a massive German fighter incursion together with a raid by KG 76 on Hornchurch. The fighter pilots of JG 3 had the misfortune to be tasked with close escort. The war diary of I./JG 3 reads: 'Oberleutnant Keller leads our Gruppe. East of London combat with ten Spitfires. The Spitfire is very manoeuvrable even at high altitudes, exceeding the Bf 109 in this regard.'[281] 603 Squadron's Spitfires came down from 8,500 metres and shot down six pilots from JG 3 for the loss of two of their own. Two of the victories were Carbury's.

Meanwhile, Major Adolf Galland led his Stabsstaffel and III. Gruppe of JG 26 in a fighter sweep to pave the way for II./KG 76, which flew towards Hornchurch. The bombers had I. and II./JG 26 as close escort. It resulted in a whole series of clashes with various British fighter units. Galland shot down a Spitfire above Gravesend and ten minutes later attacked a group of Hurricanes from 79 Squadron near Maidstone and shot down one of them in flames. Like Mölders and 'Assi' Hahn, he got three victories that day. Altogether JG 26 claimed to have shot down nine British fighters in exchange for the loss of three of their own during this mission. Presumably the three Bf 109s from JG 26 were shot down by Polish 303 Squadron, which claimed to have destroyed six Bf 109s.

One of Fighter Command's last losses this 31 August occurred at seven o'clock in the evening when a Hurricane was shot down as 79 Squadron attacked the Do 17 bombers from II./KG 76 above Biggin Hill. Pilot Officer Edward Morris escaped with severe injuries; he was the same pilot who the day before had rammed the He 111 of Hauptmann Bäss from II./KG 1. Morris was probably shot down by Oberleutnant Karl-Heinz Leesmann from I./JG 52, who at that time was out on a fighter sweep over Biggin Hill.[282]

The German fighter units that were out over southern England in the evening of 31 August reported having shot down a total of 13 British fighter aircraft. These correspond to British reports of six destroyed and six damaged RAF fighters.

When darkness fell, Dowding and Park realized that the crisis was deepening. This single day's air fighting had cost Fighter Command nine dead and eleven wounded pilots, as well as 42 fighter planes. A further 19 had recieved

Pilots from 303 (Polish) Squadron: From the left Pilot Officer Miroslaw Feric, Flight Lieutenant John Kent, Pilot Officer Bohdan Grzeszczak, Pilot Officer Jerzy Radomski and Pilot Officer Jan Zumbach in the background, Pilot Officer Witold Lokuciewski, Flying Officer Zdzislaw Henneberg, Sergeant January Rogowski and Sergeant Eugeniusz Szaposznikow. (Photo: Jacek Kutzner by Tomasz Szlagor.)

severe damage, and several of them had survived only because they did not have to fight over the enemy controlled territory. This total of 61 destroyed or damaged British fighters can be compared with the German combat losses – 36 destroyed and 7 damaged aircraft.

Aside from heavy losses in air combat, bombs had fallen on the radar stations at Beachy Head, Whitstable, Foreness, Dunkirk, Rye and Pevensey, and airbase after airbase had been devastated – Debden, Duxford, Eastchurch, Detling, Croydon, North Weald, Biggin Hill and Hornchurch. The worst hit was Biggin Hill. There the air controller's operations room had been put out of action, as well as all hangars, messes and barracks. Telephone and telegraph connections were broken, and a courier sent to Biggin Hill from Kenley, returned with the shocking report: 'It looks like a slaughter house!'

But things looked just as bad on the other airfields that had been bombed. Wing Commander Laurence Fuller-Good, commanding Debden sector station, reported eighteen killed or wounded, and four Hurricanes hit on the ground, plus the heavy casualties inflicted on 601 Squadron in the air – five more Hurricanes. Wing Commander Victor Beamish, the commander of North Weald sector station, found that two of his squadrons were in shambles. After losing eleven aircraft in six days, 56 Squadron was down to seven Hurricanes. No. 151 Squadron had only ten aircraft and twelve pilots left. The next day both of these units were withdrawn from first-line service.

The battles of August 1940 cost the RAF, in total, 496 aircraft, of which 389 were from Fighter Command, 103 from Bomber Command and four from Coastal Command and the Fleet Air Arm. Most serious for the British, however, were the pilot losses in Fighter Command. 'Our losses were of such magnitude that the rested squadrons were decimated at a higher rate than it took the run-down units to be rehabilitated in order to be reinstated in the battle', wrote Dowding. During the month of August, 148 RAF fighter pilots had been killed or written off as missing, and 156 others had been wounded. The worst thing was that the irreplaceable veterans were disappearing in increasing numbers. Of the 46 squadron leaders and 97 flight lieutenants who took part in the August fighting, 11 of the former and 46 of the latter were gone. At the same time, admittedly, a small group of above-average pilots had been able to gain experience. We have seen Pilot Officer Brian Carbury's outstanding achievement on 31 August, the same day No. 85 Squadron Sergeant Geoffrey Allard got his 19th victory, but at the same time prominent aces such as Townsend, Gleave and Flight Lieutenant Weaver had also been lost.

On the other hand, Fighter Command was reported to have shot down 986 German aircraft during the month of August, of which 11 Group claimed 707. In addition there were unconfirmed claims of 352, of which 11 Group's share was 265.[283]

The real German combat losses for the month of August were just slightly more than half of the British estimates – 585 planes.[284]

The Luftwaffe looked to the future with confidence, and the Messerschmitt pilots, eager for new victories, prepared to harvest what was expected to be the war's last successes in the coming weeks. Results looked very different between the various German fighter units. For instance, II. and III./JG 52 had been badly beaten and taken out of action – which also had to be done with II./JG 51, although this unit had also had some successes. In contrast, I./JG 2 had been credited with 40 victories against only 5 combat losses. II./JG 3 had a significantly worse result. Although the Bf 109 equipped Jagdgruppe had been launched into the fighting over the Channel as late as middle of August, it had lost 16 fighters and 9 pilots, in exchange for only 7 confirmed kills. Nor had III./JG 3 much to be proud of – with 12 aircraft lost in combat and 15 confirmed victories since early July.

The hardest hit Zerstörer units were II. and III./ZG 76, each having sustained thirteen combat losses since the battle over the Channel began. However, they were part of one of the Luftwaffe's most successful Geschwader and II./ZG 76 'Haifischgruppe' had a ratio of at least five kills for each own loss. The German Fighter Aviation's hitherto most successful Gruppe in the air fighting with the RAF was another Zerstörergruppe – III./ZG 26 'Horst Wessel', one of the few fighter units that had been constantly in action over the English Channel since 'the Channel Offensive' started in early July. Since then, III./ZG 26 had achieved about 70 victories against only 6 own combat losses. Even III./JG 26 'Schlageter' had claimed some 70 victories in July and August 1940, albeit at a price of 15 own combat losses.

1 September 1940

The month of August ended with a new raid against Liverpool – for the fourth night in a row. During those four nights the Luftwaffe made a total of 629 sorties to Liverpool – guided by the experts of KGr 100 – and dropped 455 tonnes of high-explosive bombs and 1,029 containers of incendiary bombs. In all, 160 major fires were started and extensive damage was done to the port facilities, docks and oil tanks in the port. Civilian casualties, however, were no more than 23 dead and 86 injured.[285]

These attacks compelled Dowding to order the shifting of the two Defiant-equipped squadrons, Nos. 141 and 264, to night operations. By shooting down 15 German aircraft in less than a week in late August, 264 Squadron had demonstrated that the Defiant was an excellent 'killer', but it couldn't stand up to the German Messerschmitt fighters.

During the last two days of August the British had been under greater pressure than ever before. The already exhausted fighter pilots had to carry out altogether more than 2,000 sorties in the space of 36 hours. The effect of the increasing pressure on the young pilots clearly showed in the air battles during the first days of September, when

Göring for the most part repeated the ideas he had tried so successfully in the last days of August.

1 September 1940 was a dark day for the RAF. It began in the morning, when hundreds Bf 109s and Bf 110s flew in over Kent to protect several small formations of German bombers. Park sent up fourteen squadrons. One of these, 54 Squadron, managed to force its way through to the He 111s of KG 1, and Pilot Officer Colin Gray hit one of the German bombers so hard that it turned back and shortly afterwards crashed in France. The crew escaped unharmed, however. But then the Bf 110s fell upon 54 Squadron. Gray had his Spitfire badly damaged but managed to escape with a quick evasive manoeuvre, after which the rest of 54 Squadron chose to break off the uneven combat.

The He 111s from KG 1 flew on and were met by the Hurricanes from 1 Squadron and Spitfires from 72 Squadron, which came in from the west. The German fighter escort was immediately there to intercept them. I./JG 52 had been sent out free hunting ahead of the other German planes.[286] Now their Bf 109s gathered to attack, led by Hauptmann Wolfgang Ewald. No. 1 Squadron took the first blow.

Flight Sergeant Frederick George Berry was one of the most experienced pilots of Fighter Command, and had been awarded with the NCOs' medal for bravery, the DFM. He had been a fighter pilot since 1936 and during the Battle of France had fought under the command of the legendary Squadron Leader 'Bull' Halahan in No. 1 Squadron. Berry had become famous by shooting down German bombers which tried to attack the troop transport ship *Lancastrian*, which was fully loaded with British and French soldiers in St. Nazaire's harbour on 17 June 1940. None of this helped him when the Bf 109s now came from above. Leutnant Hans Nestler shot Berry's Hurricane to pieces. Presumably Berry was killed instantly. He was still in the cockpit when the aircraft crashed at Brisley Farm near Ruckinge.

Flight Sergeant Frederick George Berry (left). (Photo: Elkington.)

With 1 Squadron's Hurricanes scattered to the winds, the German fighter pilots went on to attack the next British formation – from 72 Squadron. The first Spitfire fell before the guns of Oberleutnant Helmut Bennemann's '109, and immediately afterwards Oberleutnant Karl-Heinz Leesmann shot down a second. Two more Spitfires crashed after being seriously damaged by gunfire from pilots in I./JG 52. With five kills for the loss of only one, I./JG 52 had paid back their defeat on 26 August, when the unit had lost five pilots.

In the meantime the He 111s from KG 1 had reached their target, the Tilbury Docks, east of London, and dropped their bombs in perfect formation. The railway station was hit and the lines in both directions were blocked. Gas and water mains were cut. The Harland & Wolff shipyard was badly damaged; several of the dry docks being hit by bombs. 'Following the air attacks against the Tilbury docks on 1 September', noted a German report, 'a huge black column of smoke rose to 4,000 metres' altitude, where the smoke drifted far out over the North Sea. This was a sight that met us during our mission to England for several days afterwards.' [287]

Other German formations attacked the airfields at Kenley, Gravesend, North Weald, Hornchurch and Biggin Hill. All this cost the German bomber units no more than one plane. When the bomber pilots from KG 1 returned from their successful mission, they could report: 'Weak fighter defence, which was effectively taken care of by our fighter escort.' [288]

These scenes were repeated a few hours later, when Luftflotte 2 sent out the next series of raids, escorted by many more fighters. Again Biggin Hill and Kenley were the bombers' targets. Outnumbered British fighter units made brave but desperate attempts to get past the covering Messerschmitts to attack the Do 17 bombers from KG 76, which flew towards Kenley. It cost them dearly.

Led by the ace Oberleutnant Hans-Joachim Jabs, the Zerstörer airmen from 6. Staffel of II./ZG 76 'Haifischgruppe' were once again out on a free hunting sweep and scored the greatest success on the German side. Once again Oberleutnant Jabs and Oberleutnant Wilhelm Herget stood out by scoring three kills each. 6./ZG 76 was credited with, in all, eight victories with no loss to themselves. Seven of these can be identified in British reports – four Hurricanes from 85 Squadron, a Hurricane from 253 Squadron and two Hurricanes from 1 RCAF Squadron were shot down by these Zerstörer airmen. [289]

It is possible that the Zerstörers' eighth kill actually was a Messerschmitt 109 – Leutnant Josef Bürschgens from 7./JG 26 'Schlageter'. He had shot down a Spitfire – his 10th victory – when he happened to end up between a Bf 110 and a Spitfire that the Zerstörer was just about to shoot at. With his Bf 109 shot to pieces by shells from the Zerstörer, Bürschgens had no choice but to go down and make an emergency landing. Judging from a photograph taken immediately after his capture, it does not seem to have bothered Bürschgens that much; he was quite convinced that the Germans would soon be in England.

Oberleutnant Hans-Joachim Jabs posing in front of his Bf 110 from II./ZG 76 'Haifischgruppe'. Jabs was one of the Luftwaffe's most skilled fighter pilots during the Battle of Britain. On 1 October 1940 he was awarded the Knight's Cross for 17 air victories. Jabs was a master in the use of the Bf 110's benefits. He said: 'With a Messerschmitt 110 on free hunting you could strike down on the British and destroy them with the aircraft's heavy armament. Then we could use the speed accumulated during the diving to climb to a higher altitude again. If we were attacked by British fighters when we had such a high speed, we could easily outclimb them. Then we could use our dive speed for a renewed attack to shoot down another one of them who was not careful enough.' Jabs continued his successes as a night fighter pilot and had 50 air victories when the war ended. Jabs passed away on 26 October 2003, at the age of 85.

In total, the Luftwaffe's combat losses on 1 September amounted to no more than five Bf 109s, two bombers and a single Bf 110, while Fighter Command lost fourteen fighters.

The next day 85 Squadron was taken out of first-line service. Of the eighteen pilots in the squadron that had arrived at Croydon thirteen days earlier, fourteen had been shot down – some of them twice – and three had been killed while five had been wounded.

Spirits were high on the other side of the Channel. With the 'Haifischgruppe's' performance on 1 September, Major Walter Grabmann's ZG 76 – the Luftwaffe's most successful fighter unit – had reached a total of 483 kills. Every man in this Geschwader now looked forward with great anticipation to the next day, when they hoped to reach the magic number of 500 victories.

2 September 1940

Monday 2 September continued at the same murderous pace. The airfields of Biggin Hill, Detling and Eastchurch, Short Brothers' aeroplane works at Rochester and the Vickers factories at Brooklands were bombed while the English late summer skies were literally darkened by vast numbers of Messerschmitt 109s and 110s. While some Geschwaders on the German side, such as KG 2 and JG 26, were allowed a day's rest, other units carried out a total of 872 fighter and 88 bomber sorties.

Shortly before nine in the morning (German time), two small Do 17 formations from KG 3, with 50 Bf 110s of ZG 26 as close escort and Bf 109s of JG 51 flying top cover, crossed the coast between Dover and Lympne. The targets for the bombers were the airfields at Eastchurch, North Weald and Biggin Hill, but the main aim was to draw the RAF into air combat.

Fighter Command scrambled eleven squadrons. But not everyone on the British side seemed to realize how serious the situation was. At North Weald the hardened ground staff watched with amazement at how the over-confident pilots of 249 Squadron behaved! 'The groundcrew were dismayed to witness the nonchalant attitude of 249 pilots when ordered to scramble', said Eric Clayton of the ground personnel at North Weald. 'They strolled casually out to the aircraft whilst groundcrew stood by them, engines running, waiting with disbelief. They seemed unaware of the critical need for urgency.' [290]

No. 249 Squadron, which had arrived from 10 Group to replace the worn-out 56 and 151 squadrons, had so far had impressive results – an average of four kills for each own loss. But that had been in 10 Group, where the distance that the German aircraft had to travel from their bases had made it possible for the British fighter units to take off in good time. The unit's pilots would soon learn that things were different in 11 Group. Its Hurricane pilots sighted the Do 17s from III./KG 3 and what followed is described in an RAF report: '[The Dorniers were escorted by] large numbers of Me 110s stepped up behind in wide vics of three. Our fighters carried out a beam attack in line astern on the leading bombers before the enemy fighters could close round the bombers. Another attack was attempted but this time the fighters had closed round and individual combats with them took place.' [291]

The encounter with II./ZG 26 cost 249 Squadron three planes. But Fighter Command took revenge on the Bf 109 units. The 'wild' Hurricane pilots of 501 Squadron clashed with I./JG 53's Bf 109s and destroyed four of these – two by Pilot Officer Stalislaw Skalski and one each by Sergeant 'Ginger' Lacey and Pilot Officer Hugh Adams. A fifth Bf 109 was so badly shot up that it had to belly-land on the French coast near Boulogne. 501 Squadron sustained no other losses than Skalski's belly-landed Hurricane.

Meanwhile JG 51 was badly mauled by two Spitfire squadrons. First it lost two Bf 109s against no own victories in a scrap with 54 Squadron. Then it was chased back across the Strait of Dover to France by 603 Squadron, which cost the unit two more '109s, again without any loss to the British. 603 Squadron's Pilot Officer Richard Hillary described how he pursued a Bf 109 which 'darted about in front like a startled rabbit, and finally plunged into the sea about three miles off the French coast.' [292]

Pilot officers Brian Carbury and Roland Berry of the same squadron also claimed one Bf 109 each. These increased Carbury's tally to 9½ kills and Berry's to five (three individual and two shared).

One of the pilots who was shot down into the Channel by 603 Squadron was the future 220-victory ace Heinz Bär, who now was a Feldwebel. He was picked up out of the Channel by the German Seenotdienst. Bär's morale nevertheless seems to have been unshaken – at least according to what he said when Reichsmarschall Göring inspected JG 51 a few days later. Major Werner Mölders told the story: 'Göring summoned the recently rescued Bär and asked how he had managed the parachute jump and the salvation from the Channel. The Reichsmarschall asked: "Well, Bär, what were you thinking while you were swimming around there in the Channel before your saviour appeared?" Alluding to the Reichsmarschall's statement that "England no longer is an island", Bär replied in his broad Saxonian dialect: "For each stroke, I thought of your words: England no longer is an island!"'

At noon on 2 September (German time), two Gruppen of He 111s from KG 53 were sent out for another raid against the airfield at Eastchurch. They were accompanied by Bf 110s of ZG 2 flying as close escort and Bf 109s of JG 2, JG 3 and JG 54 as top cover. Shortly afterwards, Erprobungsgruppe 210, escorted by I./JG 52, was dispatched against the airfield at Detling, just 20 km further to the southwest.

Again Fighter Command met them in force. The Spitfires of 72 Squadron were first to intercept. They dived down on the Heinkels and their close escort. One Bf 110 was shot down in flames, but in the continuing combat the Zerstörers shot down two Spitfires and damaged a third. Squadron Leader Anthony Collins was shot down for a second time, and this time he was badly wounded in his knee and hand; he never returned to the squadron. [293]

No. 111 Squadron also joined the fight with the '110s but two of its Hurricanes were shot down. With one of

Bf 110s from ZG 76 on a fighter sweep over southern England. This Zerstörergeschwader was the Luftwaffe's most successful fighter unit during 1940. On 2 September 1940, ZG 76 achieved its 500th air victory. Two weeks later, JG 51 was the Luftwaffe's second Geschwader to reach 500 air victories.

them, Fighter Command lost one more of its precious veterans, 11-victory ace Sergeant William Dymond. When ZG 2 returned to base afterwards, it was found that three aircraft were missing, but the unit also had achieved its 257th aerial victory.[294] The cost for this was 38 combat losses since the war began. Of these, 20 had been sustained during the Battle of Britain.

While the Zerstörers managed to save the bombers from any losses in the skies over Kent in the early afternoon on 2 September, the Bf 109 top cover came hurtling down on the RAF fighters, which in turn soon received reinforcements. However, no great results were achieved on either side. 603 Squadron fought more or less alone against over 70 Bf 109s from JG 3, JG 52 and JG 54, but managed to shoot down two Bf 109s – one of them by Pilot Officer Hillary again – while the Germans failed to do any harm to the British other than to force a Spitfire to belly-land. JG 54 returned from that mission with four fewer Bf 109s; two had collided and crashed in England.

Meanwhile, No. 43 Squadron was bounced by a large gaggle of Bf 109s from JG 2 and lost three Hurricanes but managed to shoot down just as many Bf 109s. One of 43 Squadron's pilots was killed – Pilot Officer Charles 'Wombat' Woods-Scawen, who after six victories finally met his fate when he now was shot down for the fourth time. An extra dimension of tragedy was added by the fact that his brother Patrick Woods-Scawen had died the day before, in what appeared to be similar circumstances; both brothers

had bailed out of their bullet-riddled Hurricanes but none of them managed to open their parachutes.

The air fighting on 2 September had been fairly inconclusive when Kesselring later in the afternoon dispatched ZG 76 and a bomber Gruppe up to London. Their Geschwaderkommodore, Major Walter Grabmann, had given his airmen a pep-talk before take-off: 'Now the 500th victory-mark must be reached!'

Park sent up as many as 85 Spitfires and Hurricanes in an attempt to stave off. *'Jäger von vorn!'* – Fighters ahead! – sounded the enthusiastic cry on the Zerstörer airmen's radio frequency when the first British fighters emerged from the haze above the Thames Estuary. What followed next, from ZG 76's point of view, is described in a German narrative:

'Major Grabmann leads the first Gruppe of ZG 76 in a diving attack right down among the British fighters, while all our aircraft open up with their nose guns. The British formation is immediately dispersed and the individual airplanes dive to escape our attack, without having managed to attack our bombers.

'But the Spitfire pilots won't give up. Even though they now fly individually, they come climbing back and try to form up again. The Zerstörer fliers immediately attack them. Grabmann himself attacks the leading British fighter head-on. Both pilots open fire simultaneously. Next second the Spitfire bursts into fire and goes down in spirals. Shortly afterwards another one falls prey to Grabmann's greater skill

This Hurricane, P2946, was one of 24 British fighters that were shot down on 2 September. The pilot, Sergeant James Metham from 253 Squadron, survived slightly wounded. The picture shows the aircraft after a crash landing a few weeks earlier.

and superior armament. *This Spitfire turned into a veritable ball of fire and drops vertically. A third one makes an effort to attack the adjutant, but fails and instead becomes shot down himself.*

'It is obvious that our Zerstörers have the upper hand, but our British opponents also are quite tough. Again and again they challenge our Angriffskreis – but each time with the same result: A Zerstörer detaches itself from the circuit, a short burst of fire, and the next Spitfire plummets, fatally hit. The combat rages without interruption for nearly thirty minutes. As soon as the Tommies try to attack – individually or in pairs – several Me 110s swoop down on their tails. Before the enemies are able to open fire, they are torn to pieces by our guns. By now, this has cost them seven Spitfires, and eventually the courage of the remainder begins to falter. One by one, they leave the scene, and soon only German aircraft are visible in the air.*

'Meanwhile, the bomber unit, covered by the two other Gruppen in our Zerstörergeschwader, has reached its target: an air base near London. Just as the bombers initiate their bomb run, a squadron of Hurricanes pops out of the clouds above and dives to attack. Apparently, their aim is to disperse the bomber formation. But our Zerstörers intercept them on their way down, and the bombers are able to carry out their attack without being disturbed by enemy fighters.*

'When the bombers head out from the target area, the British assembled for a renewed attack. They try to avoid our Zerstörer planes, but in vain. A Hurricane pilot is a bit too bold. Several "sharks" [aircraft from II./ZG 76] are immediately in position behind him, and a few seconds later the Hurricane goes down, enveloped by flames. The British follow us to the coast – but without making any new attempts to attack – before finally departing.'[295]

Spirits were high when the airmen of ZG 76 returned to base. The two Spitfires that Major Grabmann had shot down raised his personal tally to 13, but he was mostly concerned about his Zerstörergeschwader's total results. Grabmann hurried to the command post. There Hauptmann Erich Groth, the commander of II./ZG 76 'Haifischgruppe', was already waiting on the phone: his report meant that the Geschwader's total number of victories stood at 496. A few minutes later Hauptmann Rolf Kaldrack rang to submit his report. Twenty-seven-year-old Kaldrack was a veteran of the Spanish Civil War, where he attained three kills. In early 1939, he had become world famous for a flight around the coast of Africa. He had been chosen for the new Zerstörer aircraft shortly before the outbreak of the war, and when the commander of III./ZG 76, Hauptmann Dickoré, was lost, he had taken over this Zerstörergruppe. Like Grabmann, Kaldrack had been credited with a total of 13 victories. Everyone in Grabmann's command post pricked up their ears when Kaldrack announced his Gruppe's results, and then a wild cheering broke out: with four victories from III. Gruppe, ZG 76 had reached a total of 500 victories – the first Geschwader of the war to do so.

The only price paid for the Geschwader's success on 2 September was the Bf 110 flown by Oberleutnant Karl Wrede, technical officer of II./ZG 76: this aircraft crashed near Billericay, and both crew members were killed.

When Major Grabmann phoned Generalmajor von Döring, Jafü 2, to report the day's results, he could not resist adding: 'Soon there will be nothing left on the other side of the Channel!' Twelve days later, Grabmann, now promoted to Oberstleutnant, was awarded the Knight's Cross.

On the whole, 2 September was taken up by violent air fighting between RAF Spitfires and Hurricanes and Luftwaffe Messerschmitts. On the German side 2 September was one of the worst days for the Bf 109 units: that day's actions resulted in a loss of no less than 21 Bf 109s, with four more returning to base with severe combat damage. ZG 76 was not only the Luftwaffe's most successful fighter unit overall – its 17 victories against only one loss on 2 September also was the best result among the German fighter units that day.* The other Zerstörer units' losses amounted to three planes each in ZG 2 and ZG 26.

At the same time 24 British fighters were shot down, but 10 of those could be repaired. However, the fact that the RAF failed to shoot down more than two German bombers that day – a very low price for the bombing of seven airfields and aircraft works. On two of these airfields, nine fighters were destroyed on the ground, in Eastchurch the bomb dump exploded and 2.5 square kilometres of the airfield were devastated, and at Brooklands great damage was inflicted on the Vickers works – where the Wellington bomber was produced. Among the Luftwaffe units which contributed to this destruction was one that had only just joined the battle. This was Bf 109-equipped II.(S)/LG 2, commanded by Hauptmann Otto Weiss. This unit had been founded as a trial unit for assault and fighter-bomber missions, and thus preceded e.g. Erprobungsgruppe 210. It was based on the experience drawn by Galland's close-support unit 3./J 88 in the Spanish Civil War, and had participated in the invasions of Poland and France with Hs 123 assault biplanes. In the summer of 1940, the unit was re-equiped with Messerschmitt 109s of both E-4 and E-7 versions – which had been fitted in the factories already with a hard point for a bomb under the fuselage.

During the hours of darkness, 120 of Sperrle's night bombers were out spreading death and destruction over a number of cities across the country. Three bombers were lost. At the same time, Bomber Command sent 84 bombers to, among other places, Ludwigshafen and Hamm in Germany and Genoa in Italy. It cost them four aircraft, one of which was shot down by Feldwebel Paul Gildner, I./NJG 1, from a German night fighter force that was gaining proficiency.

3 September 1940

'3 September dawned dark and overcast, with a slight breeze ruffling the waters of the Estuary. Hornchurch aerodrome, twelve miles east of London, wore its usual morn-ing pallor of yellow fog, lending an added air of grimness to the dimly silhouetted Spitfires around the boundary.' [296]

Thus Pilot Officer Richard Hillary of 603 Squadron described the dawn on 3 September 1940 at Hornchurch. It would be the 21-year-old pilot's last day of combat in the Battle of Britain. A few hours later, he was shot down and badly wounded. No. 603 Squadron had been ordered up from Hornchurch at 10:15 and was climbing when the Spitfires were attacked by a horde of Bf 109s. 'They came straight on like a swarm of locusts', remembered Hillary. 603 Squadron fought desperately against great odds and managed to shoot down two Bf 109s for the loss of two of their own.

Meanwhile around thirty Do 17s from II./KG 2 and eighty Bf 110s from ZG 2 and ZG 26 roared across the Thames Estuary. Park guessed that they were heading towards the air base at North Weald, northwest of London, and ordered all available fighters to intercept this force. Once more he asked for reinforcements from 12 Group, and once again Leigh-Mallory failed to give 11 Group the support it needed. It was only 17 Squadron that was in time to intervene before the Dorniers reached their target. The appearance of its Hurricanes was a complete surprise for the Germans. Before the Zerstörer pilots had time to react, the three pilots of 17 Squadron's Green Section had shot a Dornier in flames. It fell vertically into the sea. Only one man survived by bailing out.

Then the '110s from III./ZG 26 counterattacked. Two British fighters fell to Oberleutnant Sophus Baagoe's cannons. They were the Zerstörer ace's 11th and 12th kills. Leutnant Alfred Wehmeyer shot down a third British plane. No. 17 Squadron's war diary reads: 'F/O Czernin destroyed one Me 110 and probably another. Sgt Fopp went down with his aircraft on fire, and baled out near Brentwood. He was badly burnt and is in Brentwood hospital; but is reported not on the danger list. S/Ldr Miller was attacked by a Me 110 and force-landed in a field near North Weald. He was unhurt and rejoined the Squadron. F/O Hanson was missing, and has since been reported killed.' [297]

Without having sustained any further losses, the Dorniers flew in over North Weald in perfect formation and dropped over 200 bombs on the airfield from a height of 4,500 metres. All the hangars were hit, as well as canteens, administrative buildings and the Operations Room.

As the bombers and Zerstörers turned away from the burning air base, they were attacked by the the greater part of a force of of no less than 122 Spitfires and Hurricanes that had been sent after them. This time the situation was the opposite of what it had been during the past few weeks: Now it was the British attacking with a numerical superiority of fighters – and it was the Germans who deftly parried the fighter attacks. Most heavily engaged was III./ZG 26, which was flying top cover and thus had more opportunities to manoeuver than ZG 2, which was tied up as close escort. III./ZG 26 exacted a terrible toll on the attacking Hurricanes. No. 46 Squadron, which just two days earlier moved from a quiet corner in 12 Group's area to 11 Group, lost three Hurricanes in a matter of minutes. No. 257 Squadron also lost three Hurricanes to the Bf 110s – for only one unconfirmed kill in return – and the unit's

---

* A comparison with British records however reveals that no more than five of those 17 victory claims can be substantiated.

High up in the English skies can be seen the silhouetted condensation trails of Bf 110s in an 'Angriffskreis'. An air combat with British fighters takes place, and some Bf 110s are seen to dive out of the circle to strike down on RAF planes.

war diary bears clear testimony to the fierce clash with the Zerstörers: 'The whole squadron took off from Martlesham under the command of S/Ldr Harkness and was involved in a combat with enemy raiders in the Chelmsford area. In the combat P/O Bonseigneur was shot down and killed after baling out at Ingatestone. P/O Hunt was also shot down. He succeeded in baling out when his cockpit was on fire. He was taken to Billericay Hospital suffering from severe burns. P/O Grundy landed at Martlesham after his port tail had been shot off by an explosive shell. Sgt. Nutter's main starboard plane and petrol tank were shot by explosive cannon of which he received small splinters in his legs.' [298]

Squadron Leader Philip Pinkham, at the head of eight aircraft from 19 Squadron, was doubly frustrated in that the cannon-armed Spitfires once again proved their inadequacy. After having fired only ten shells from each gun he had a blockage and was forced to break off from the combat. After this it was decided that the unit's Spitfires would be rearmed to carry only machine guns.

No less than 21 British fighters – i.e. one in six of the RAF aircraft that took part in the combat – were shot down. Of these, 12 were written off while 9 would eventually be repaired. For once the German victory claims were consistent with actual British losses. The Germans reported 19 victories, with III./ZG 26 accounting for 12. At the same time the Germans escaped with much milder losses than the day before. That said, I./ZG 2 suffered badly: Three of their Bf 110s were shot down, and two other planes col-

lided in the violent manoeuvres of air fighting. II./ZG 76 lost one of its best pilots, Leutnant Walter Manhart, with 13 kills. He spent the rest of the war in British captivity.

That afternoon Göring treated his tired pilots to a short rest. It was a welcome respite also for the hard-pressed British. The next German sortie to the British Isles was not made until 16:35 (British time), and then only by a lone reconnaissance aircraft. Between 17:30 and 17:50 a number of German formations, each consisting of between two and six aircraft, crossed the Channel in order to to keep the British nerves on edge.

4–6 September 1940

Both sides were equally exhausted after a week of daily, large-scale operations. Historian Tony Holmes describes the situation in 601 Squadron: 'By now the handful of seasoned pilots that remained on the squadron were suffering from chronic fatigue, and with the rest of No 601 Sqn staffed by combat novices, the outfit was hardly fit to remain in the frontline. However, with the Luftwaffe seemingly gaining the upper hand in the battle, all available squadrons had to be thrown into the fray, and that included No 601 Sqn.'[299]

There was, however, a limit to how much a military unit was capable of, and by this time the RAF squadrons were being worn down at such a murderous pace that a

On 6 September 1940, 603 Squadron's Pilot Officer Caister was shot down by Hauptmann Hubertus von Bonin from I./JG 54 and was forced to belly-land on the airfield at Campagne-lès-Guines in France. Caister was captured and was invited to dinner in Hauptmann von Bonin's tent. (Photo: Trautloft.)

Fighter Command squadron was taken out of action after an average of five to six weeks – this despite the fact that Dowding needed every available unit. To better organise the rotation of his units Dowding introduced three categories:

Category A: Units that were in the first line.
Category B: Units that were fully combatworthy, ready to be shifted to the first line.
Category C: Worn out units removed from combat, and which had most of their veteran pilots transferred to an A-unit. The Category C units' main task was to train new pilots.

To have their squadron demoted to a 'C unit' was a blow to many men of Fighter Command. On 3 September, 54 Squadron was pulled out of combat, with only four pilots surviving who had been serving in the unit in early July 1940. Still, these four found it difficult to accept that 54 Squadron was completely exhausted. Flight Lieutenant 'Al' Deere was one of the four. 'That 54 Squadron should be singled out to suffer such an ignoble fate, seemed to us a peculiar form of gratitude', he said. [300] It probably felt particularly bad given that 54 Squadron's total of 92 victories made it Fighter Command's most successful squadron at the time. However, this categorization was the result of a harsh reality, Dowding managed in this way to slowly rebuild the British fighter strength.

Although the opposite has sometimes been argued, Göring also pulled his air units from combat when they were worn out and needed to be rebuilt. It was not just

the high losses, but also the intense tempo of combat that broke the spirit of many German airmen. In addition there was the strain of flying over open sea – which always creates a feeling of uncertainty in airmen. Gerhard Schöpfel, who led III./JG 26 during the Battle of Britain, said:

'After a few weeks of fighting over the Channel a new phenomenon became known. We called it *Kanalkrankheit*, Channel disease. It had various symtoms – either as various psychosomatic disorders or excessive irritability. In some cases the disorder manifested itself in "technical faults" on the aircraft when it was time for a new combat mission over the Channel. Pilots reported technical faults on the aircraft and canceled the mission. Back at the base the technician was unable to find anything wrong with the aircraft, which seemed to have repaired itself in the meantime.' [301]

Within the Zerstörer units, morale seems to have been higher than in many other Luftwaffe units at the Channel. When Kesselring on 4 September was about to strike at the Vickers-Armstrong works in Brooklands near Weybridge, in the south-west outskirts of London – where two-thirds of the Wellington bombers were made – he chose to use only Bf 110s for the mission. Fourteen Bf 110s from Erprobungsgruppe 210 would be responsible for the bombing, and about fifty planes from ZG 2, III./ZG 76 and V.(Z)/LG 1 would escort them. Although Schöpfel (quoted above) was referring to fictional technical problems, there were many aircraft in the Zerstörer units that by now were quite worn. When the adjutant of ZG 2, Oberleutnant Wilhelm Schäfer, flew Messerschmitt 110 C-4 Werknummer 2116 ('3M+AA') – which was nor-

The Germans repaired Caister's Spitfire. (Photo: Leykauf.)

Another picture of Pilot Officer Caister's German-repaired Spitfire. (Photo: Leykauf.)

mally flown by Geschwaderkommodore Oberstleutnant Friedrich Vollbracht – he discovered that the engines were so worn that they could barely reach half the regular maximum speed.

The mission went badly for the Germans from the beginning. Already during the flight across the English Channel, the commander of Erprobungsgruppe 210, Hauptmann Hans von Boltenstern, inexplicably dived into the sea and perished.

The Bf 110s flew low, to avoid detection by the radar. This they managed, but because some eighty He 111s and Do 17s, and two hundred Bf 109s simultaneously flew in over the British coast between Dover and Littlehampton, at 7,000 metres, Fighter Command was soon alerted. Fourteen squadrons were ordered up. The idea behind the bombers' approach was to divert Fighter Command and lure its fighters into combat so that the Bf 110s could slip through to Brooklands undisturbed. Instead the effect was that the British were prepared when the '110s came in over the coast. It started with twelve Spitfires from 234 Squadron diving to attack from behind. The Bf 110s had been given strict and idiotic orders to stay on course at all cost. Unteroffizier Adolf Käser, a radio operator in Leutnant Hans Münch's Bf 110, '2N+CN', from 7./ZG 76, said: 'The enemy was so quickly above us and soon Willy, my Staffelkamerad, had one on his tail. I told my pilot at once and alerted him to the Englishman's attack. He did not react but held his course, flew straight on and after a short while, I did not see neither friend nor foe.' [302]

When 234 Squadron's pilots later returned to base they counted up an amazing fifteen downed Bf 110s – at a cost of only one Spitfire damaged! The two aces Flying Officer Paterson Clarence Hughes and Pilot Officer Robert Doe were credited with three each.

Meanwhile the Hurricanes from 1 RCAF, 43, 253 and 601 squadrons and Spitfires from 72 and 79 squadrons dived down on the Messerschmitt 110s from above. A few lines from 72 Squadron's Operations Record Book gives a clear image of the devastating force with which the British fighters struck the Bf 110s (which in some cases were misidentified as 'Ju 86s'): 'At 1320 hours the enemy was sighted in the Tenterton – Tunbridge Wells area, consisting of Ju 86 and Me 110s flying at 15,000 feet. An attack was made by quarter attack, and as result 6 Me 110 and 3 Ju 86 were destroyed, 2 Me 110 probable, 1 Me 110 damaged.' [303]

One of the RAF pilots that took part in the attack on the Zerstörers was Pilot Officer Clive Mayers, the Australian from 601 Squadron who on 13 August had escaped by a hairsbreadth when a Bf 110 pilot attempted to shoot him as he hung in his parachute. Now he got his revenge and was credited with one 'probable' Bf 110.

The Messerschmitt 110s were forced to run a terrible gauntlet all the way to the target. When they eventually reached Brooklands, they were met by concentrated anti-aircraft fire which shot down two of the escorting aircraft and damaged several others. Yet the assault planes conducted their attack with Erprobungsgruppe 210's customary efficiency. Eighty-eight workers were killed, more than 600 were wounded and production at the Vickers works was completely stopped. According to British estimates, this caused a production loss of 125 Wellington bombers. [304]

Outside the target area the British fighters were lying in wait for the Germans, who continued to endure fighter attacks during the entire return flight to the Channel. The participating RAF units reaped great success, but exaggerated their results by more than 300%.

In fact, the Zerstörer crews managed to protect Erprobungsgruppe 210 from suffering any losses from fighter attacks, but they themselves paid a high price for this success. V.(Z)/LG 1 lost four crews, including Oberleutnant Michel Junge, the commander of 14. Staffel. III./ZG 76 was even worse hit and lost six crews, while ZG 2 escaped with a single loss. If it had not been for II./ZG 76 'Haifischgruppe', which arrived to meet the fighter-bombers and their embattled escort during the return flight, the German losses could have been even higher.

In a fierce battle south of London the 'Haifischgruppe' claimed to have shot down 20 Spitfires and Hurricanes. In return the unit lost three machines, all of which were flown by experienced crews. The adjutant, Oberleutnant Hermann Weeber, an ace with five victories, was forced to make an emergency landing with his damaged 'M8+IM'. He and his radio operator Unteroffizier Michael Max were both wounded and were taken to Kent and Sussex Hospital in Tunbridge Wells. Oberleutnant Ernst-Hartmann Freiherr von Schlotheim, an ace with five kills, also had his '110 damaged and on the way back to base had to ditch in the Channel. He and his radio operator escaped in the aeroplane's inflatable boat, but were carried by the currents to the English coast, where they too were captured. Crew-mates Oberleutnant Günther Piduhn/Gefreiter Rudolf Condne were less lucky. Both perished when their Bf 110 'M8+CP' exploded after its fuel tanks had been hit by a machine gun burst from Flying Officer Ross Smither of 1 RCAF Squadron. Piduhn had been credited with two victories and his rear gunner with one.

But II./ZG 76 had still been successful. Unit commander Hauptmann Erich Groth was credited with the shooting down of no less than four British fighters in eight minutes – his 8th to 11th victories. Oberleutnant Hans-Joachim Jabs had shot down three, his 15th to 17th, as had Oberleutnant Walter Borchers, who thus got his 7th to 9th. A comparison with British reports indicates that II./ZG 76 'Haifischgruppe' appears to have accounted for the majority of the 15 British fighters that were shot down in the air battle in the early afternoon of 4 September.* The already badly mauled 222 Squadron lost a further three Spitfires. Things went even worse for 66 Squadron, which had six of its Spitfires downed over the course of two missions on this 4 September.

Lord Beaverbrook, in charge of British aircraft production, had reason to be worried. The devastating bomb attack on the Short Brothers' factory in Rochester on 13 August, and the latest attack against the Vickers-Armstrong works in Brooklands had highlighted the vulnerability of the British aircraft industry. The very next day Beaverbrook gave orders to move production out from Vickers-Armstrong's premises to a number of smaller, private houses in the surrounding area that were simply confiscated. Pro-

---

*Of these, however, half could be saved and repaired.

Polish Flying Officer Juliusz Topolnicki was one of four pilots from 601 Squadron who was shot down on 6 September 1940. Topolnicki survived and continued to fly the Hurricane seen in the picture. He died in a plane crash on 21 September 1940. (Photo: Riddle via Ivers)

duction of Wellington bombers could just be maintained, but it would still be eight months before it was up to the same level as before Erprobungsgruppe 210's attack.

The following night was one of the worst in terms of bombing raids on the British Isles. Nearly 200 German bombers took part, and the main target once again was the port city of Liverpool.

But the Luftwaffe handed out the worst blows in the daytime over southern England. On the morning of 5 September the airfields at Lympne, Biggin Hill, Eastchurch, Detling and North Weald were raided by the Germans. The war diary of I./JG 3 reads: '10:15 hrs: Seventeen aircraft from our Gruppe take off to escort a bomber unit (Do 17s, 22 aircraft). Our task is: "Cover the entire bomber formation with our Rotten." Following the bomb drop at London's southern outskirts, we meet around 15-20 Spitfires that dive down individually against the escort fighters or bombers. They execute their attacks from behind and then dive away. Oberleutnant Reumschüssel shoots down two Spitfires; Hauptmann von Hahn, Feldwebel Ehlers and Feldwebel Vollmer one Spitfire each, and Leutnant Bock a Hurricane. When an alien '109 unit passes between us and the bombers, Leutnant Busch loses sight of his Rotten-flieger, Oberleutnant Lammers, who is missing since then. Leutnant Schnabel failed to return from this mission. Unteroffizier Grabow from the 3. Staffel was very upset when his aircraft was hit by the British, and he screamed so terribly over the radio that one could barely hear what he said. He too failed to return from this mission.' [305]

Among the Spitfires that I./JG 3 met were eleven machines from 19 Squadron that had been sent up from Fowlmere at 09:47 to patrol Hornchurch at 15,000 feet. With the inoperable cannons in their Spitfires replaced with machine guns, 19 Squadron gave a much better account of itself and shot down at least two Bf 109s, but it cost them badly – Squadron Leader Pinkham was shot down and killed.

This was Fighter Command's worst crisis, and it really looked as if Göring was about to succeed in bringing Fighter Command to its knees. 'Fighter Command was now approaching the point at which nervous and physical exhaustion among the squadrons could no longer be offset adequately by replacements of men and machines', Francis K. Mason noted in his classic *Battle over Britain*. [306]

At least as severe were the effects of German air attacks on the RAF's ground organisation during the preceding days. As we know, sector stations were Fighter Command's 'nerve centres': it was from these that it was decided which units would be deployed, where they would be deployed in battle, how they would attack and from what height. Without these sector stations, Fighter Command was like a short-sighted boxer who can just hit out randomly in different directions and hope that the opponent is there somewhere.

During the so-called 'critical period', Park's 11 Group, responsible for the area between Southampton and the coast at Dover, had to defend Fighter Command's very existence virtually alone. In the area under 11 Group's control, there were seven sector stations. In daylight the entire struggle was led from these seven sector stations. Up until 6 September, German bombs had wholly or partly wrecked six of these seven nerve centres; the most important sector station, Biggin Hill, was so damaged that it only had resources left to control a single squadron; the remaining twenty squadrons in 11 Group were shared between one fully functional and five half wrecked sector stations. The repeated attacks on Biggin Hill left the sector commander there, Wing Commander Richard Grice, so demoralised that he had the last remaining hangar blown up in a desperate attempt to protect the base from more German air raids. Of course Grice was court-martialed for this, but he was aquitted. Forty-one-year-old Grice was a popular war hero from the First World War; in April 1918, he had participated in the air combat in which Manfred von Richthofen, the 'Red Baron', was shot down and killed.

As a result of the new German tactic of sending a constant stream of aircraft over southern England the sector commanders and air controllers of 11 Group were by now quite exhausted and often demoralized. Badly led units often ended up at the wrong altitude in the wrong place and became easy prey for the hordes of hunting Messerschmitts – which meant a heavy burden for the men in charge on the ground.

At 15:00 on 5 September Squadron Leader Hilary Richard Hood was instructed to take twelve of 41 Squadron's Spitfires up from Hornchurch for a patrol at 4,500 metres over Maidstone. A large number of bombers and fighters had been reported on their way in over the coast, but 41 Squadron met them at a height disadvantage. Pilot Officer Wally Wallens from 41 Squadron describes the following combat: 'As usual I was flying Number 2 on "Robin" Hood leading "B" Flight and, being unable to gain height advantage and position in time, "Robin" put us in line-astern and open echelon port and attacked head-on, a desperate manoeuvre that could age one very prematurely. Within seconds all hell broke loose and, as the action developed, "B" Flight was overwhelmingly attacked by the '109s. Four Spitfires from 41 Squadron failed to return from this engagement. Pilot Officer Tony Lovell had parachuted out of

In spite of heavy combat damage, this 238 Squadron aircraft managed to land at the air base at Middle Wallop, testifying to the Hurricane's ruggedness. (Foto via Goss.)

his burning aircraft over South Benfleet and returned to Hornchurch. Pilot Officer Wallens had force-landed, near Orsett, with a cannon shell through his leg and had been taken to hospital. One pilot was confirmed killed in action. His body was identified as that of Flight Lieutenant [John Terence] Webster, DFC.* Squadron Leader Hood was officially recorded as missing.' [307]

I./JG 2 'Richthofen' returned from the clash with four kills and no losses. Oberleutnant Helmut Wick scored his 23rd kill. On the same day he was transferred to II./JG 2 where he took over the command of 6. Staffel. After the severe losses of 4 September Kesselring had allowed the Zerstörer units a few days of rest, so on this day all German fighter efforts were carried out by Bf 109s alone. III./JG 53 'Pik As' was credited with five victories and I./JG 3 with two.[308]

The next day, 6 September, Major Galland's Stabsstaffel from JG 26 'Schlageter' and I. Gruppe from JG 26 and II./JG 27 attacked 601 Squadron under similar circumstances. 'In a matter of seconds four Hurricanes were hurtling earthward in flames. Two wounded pilots succeeded in bailing out of their stricken fighters, but the remaining pair slammed into the ground still strapped into their respective aircraft.' [309] The fallen pilots were both well known aces: American Flight Lieutenant Carl Davis had been credited with 9½ victories, and Flying Officer 'Willie' Rhodes-Moorhouse had nine victories on his account. The German pilots claimed five kills in the battle – one of which was Galland's 29th.

But the RAF could still hit back. No. 601 Squadron reported six Bf 109s shot down on 6 September – of which Flight Lieutenant Peter Robinson accounted for three and Flying Officer Tom Grier for two. The day before, one British pilot, 23-year-old Pilot Officer Eric Lock, had managed to take some revenge for 41 Squadron's bitter losses. After 41 Squadron had ended up fighting at a height disadvantage, Lock forced his way through and attacked a formation of He 111s from III./KG 53. He chased a diving He 111 until he saw that it would not survive and was going down into the Thames. It was Eric Lock's first victory. He then climbed back to 2,400 metres and attacked a He 111 which was lagging behind the main formation. Without much difficulty Lock shot down this one as well. At that moment Lock was himself attacked by a Bf 109 which hit his Spitfire with a burst of fire that wounded the young Englishman in one leg. But undeterred, Lock attacked as the German veered off, fired and blew up the petrol tank of the '109.

On 6 September, 41 Squadron continued to exact revenge, when the unit's Spitfires surprised JG 27 over the Thames Estuary. While Red and Yellow sections dived to attack the Germans, Blue Section remained at a higher altitude to cover them. Several '109s crashed in flames, and then it was time for the Blue Section to intervene. Pilot Officer George 'Ben' Bennion shot down two Bf 109s. In one of them sat Hauptmann Joachim Schlichting, the commander of III./JG 27, who ended up with severe burns in British captivity. Even the adjutant of II./JG 3, Oberleutnant Franz von Werra, who had eight victories, was shot down and captured.

* Flight Lieutenant Webster was the pilot who had wounded the German ace Mölders in air combat on 28 July 1940.

Flight Lieutenant Peter Robinson of 601 Squadron was recorded to have shot down three Bf 109s on 6 September 1940. One of them he forced to belly-land, and then he threw a pack of cigarettes to the German pilot. Later Robinson looked up his defeated opponent and to his surprise, found that it was a German whom he had met in Augsburg before the war. Here we see Robinson posing next to his damaged Hurricane on another occasion. Robinson was killed in action on 10 April 1942. (Photo: Riddle via Ivers.)

Altogether 15 RAF fighters and 12 Bf 109s were downed in fighter combat on 5 September. One of the latter fell prey to one of the first Hurricane fighters that had had its eight 7.7mm machine guns exchanged for four 20mm cannons. The plane was flown by 46 Squadron's Flight Lieutenant Alexander 'Sandy' Rabagliati, who afterwards wrote in his combat report: 'I spotted a '109 on the tail of a Spitfire; I gave this enemy aircraft a three-second burst and he blew up in the air.' The next day 17 fighters from the RAF and 15 from the Luftwaffe were shot down in encounters between Fighter Command and the Bf 109 units. A Schwarm from 7./JG 26 was attacked by Spitfires on the morning of 6 September and lost three planes. These Spitfires came from 234 Squadron, which had achieved an amazing success against the Bf 110s two days earlier. When they landed at ten o'clock in the morning in Middle Wallop, they reported an equally great victory against the Bf 109s: eleven shot down. After debriefing, eight of those were confirmed, two of which were granted to Squadron Leader Joseph O'Brien, and another ended up on Flight Lieutenant Hughes' tally. Australian Paterson Clarence Hughes was one of Fighter Command's most effective fighter pilots at that time; by shooting down three Bf 110s on 4 September, two Bf 109s on the 5th and now this 109 on 6 September, he reached a total of 13 victories. Only one of the Bf 109s in the four-plane group from 7./JG 26 got away from 234 Squadron's attack on 6 September. This was manned by Oberleutnant Joachim Müncheberg, who shot down a British fighter, while 8. Staffel's Leutnant Gustav Sprick accounted for 234 Squadron's second loss in that engagement. These two German pilots belonged to the élite of JG 26, and with these victories Müncheberg reached a total of 17, and Sprick 16.

Despite such successes, Fighter Command's 'critical period' was at its height. Between 24 August and 6 Sep-

tember, in just two weeks, the RAF lost over 250 fighter aircraft.* During the same period more than 230 fighter pilots were stricken from the rosters – 103 dead and 128 wounded. In purely numerical terms, it meant a fall-out of almost a quarter of the entire British fighter force's establishment of pilots – and this within a period of 14 days! New arrivals from flight schools had only been able to cover a small portion of these huge losses; the RAF could not produce more than 65 new pilots a week at this time. Inevitably this led to a drastic reduction in the number of pilots available to Fighter Command – from 1,430 at the end of July to 1,020 in late August and after the first September week just 840!

Squadron Leader Edward Donaldson, whose 151 Squadron was withdrawn from the frontline on 1 September, remembered: 'I was convinced that we were beaten, that we had lost the battle. I was fantastically tired and utterly depressed.'[310]

Wing Commander Laurence Fuller-Good, the commander of Debden sector station, reported that one of his subordinate units, 257 Squadron, was in particularly bad shape. 'They had simply lost faith in themselves, which is the worst thing that can happen to a fighter pilot' said Robert Stanford Tuck, who was assigned to lead No. 257 Squadron. Historian Larry Forrester describes the pilots in this unit at the beginning of September 1940: 'They were a sorry-looking lot. Scruffy, listless and leaderless, they were quarrelling among themselves over trivialities, drinking hard but entirely without zest. Over the last few weeks they had taken a severe mauling. [. . .] Two of the sergeants were bad "twitch" cases, regularly reporting sick to avoid flying. They complained of stomach aches, back aches, stiff necks and other ailments which the M.O. could not dismiss because they didn't necessarily produce visible symptoms. One of these men had some excuses for his ediginess: only

---

* According to *Battle of Britain Then & Now*, Vol 5, p. 707, Fighter Command's losses during this period amounted to 264 aircraft. Wood's and Dempster's *The Narrow Margin*, p. 287, gives even higher figures: 287. To these various numbers of aircraft destroyed in combat should be added 156 badly damaged aircraft (Category 2). Thus, the total for the so-called 'critical period' might be as high as 440 shot down RAF fighters.

▼ *A group of pilots from 610 Squadron in July 1940. Pilot Officer Frederick Gardiner, standing to the right, was shot down and wounded on 25 August 1940. Next to him is the ace Sergeant Ronnie Hamlyn. Next is Flight Lieutenant William Warner, who was shot down and listed as missing on 16 August. Lying in the middle is Pilot Officer Constantine Pegge, who was shot down on 18 August. Lying on the far right is Sergeant Douglas Corfe, who was shot down on 22 August. In early August 1940, 610 Squadron had eighteen pilots. A month later, eleven had been killed and seven wounded, and the unit was withdrawn from combat. (Photo: Foster.)*

▲ *Spitfires on standby in their revetments. (Photo: Goss.)*

a few weeks ago he had been clobbered by a '110's cannon and got the backs of both legs peppered with shrapnel.' [311]

No. 257 Squadron's statistics were not very encouraging, as is seen in the unit's Operations Record Book: '257 Squadrons result up to the end of August were 9 enemy aircraft destroyed, 9 probable. Squadron losses: F/L [Noel] Hall, F/O [Brian] D'Arcy-Irvine, Sgt [Kenneth] Smith, P/O [John] Chomley, P/O [Gerald] Maffett killed or missing. P/O [David Arthur] Coke, Sgt [Alexander] Girdwood, P/O [James] Henderson wounded. Sgt [Ronald] Forward sent for a rest after suffering from shock.' [312]

With his tactic of always keeping about a quarter of the units in the northern parts of the British Isles, far beyond the battle, Dowding always had rested and aggressive units available that were eager to do battle with the Germans. One of these was 92 Squadron, which had been 'in reserve'

since the fighting over Dunkirk in late May/early June. This unit arrived at Biggin Hill on 8 September. With it came veterans such as Don Kingaby and Brian Kingcombe. No. 92 Squadron's top ace was Flight Lieutenant Robert Stanford Tuck, who had a score of fourteen. He was asked to take over the magnificent 257 Squadron and get the unit back on its feet. Instead of letting themselves be intimidated by the more experienced pilots' often bleak perception of the battle, the new arrivals helped give new courage to the tired veterans. Twenty-year-old Pilot Officer Robert Foster was one of nineteen pilots from 605 Squadron who arrived at Croydon airfield south of London on 7 September, after a long time in Scotland. In Croydon, they joined together with 72 Squadron, which had lost sixteen Spitfires and seven pilots during the first seven days of September – which should be compared to the fifteen operational aircraft and twenty pilots that the unit had on the morning of 1 September. The pilots of 605 Squadron came as a shot in the arm. Foster recalled: 'We were highly motivated. Our morale was always high. We could not imagine that we could be beaten. People got tired and irritable, but we never had low morale. The only thing we wanted was to get up and give the Germans what they could take!' [313]

CHAPTER 7
'LONDON'S BURNING!'

The Battle of Britain has been the subject of much counterfactual guesswork – what would have happened if . . .

If Göring had used his tactics from the 'critical period' from the very beginning of the Battle – would the Battle of Britain then have been fought on the ground, on British soil, by the beginning of September 1940?

Few dates in history have been the subject of so much counterfactual reasoning as 7 September 1940:

If the Luftwaffe had continued to concentrate on Fighter Command's ground organisation even after 6 September – would Fighter Command and the entire RAF then have been beaten? If that had happened – would there have been a German invasion, an implementation of 'Seelöwe'?

If Churchill's bombers had not begun to disrupt the Berliners' sleep that Sunday evening in late August 1940 – would Hitler and Göring still have turned their air armada on London?

This counterfactual reasoning is nourished by the fact that the 'plot' is like something dreamed up by a playwright: in the moment where Fighter Command wavered on the verge of incipient collapse, the Luftwaffe turned around and lost its last chance to destroy the RAF. One can easily summarize the turning point in four main factors:

25 August: On Churchill's order RAF Bomber Command initiated a series of nocturnal raids against Berlin. This had, as the British prime minister guessed, a huge psychological effect, not least among the German High Command.

4 September: Hitler gave a speech in Berlin, venting his fury at the RAF attacks on the Third Reich's capital: 'The British will see that we shall now pay back a hundredfold!'

7 September: Just before the autumn weather began to hinder the continued German air-offensive, the Luftwaffe halted its offensive against Fighter Command's ground organisation, instead directing their operations against the British capital. This, combined with a few days of bad weather that prevented large-scale air operations, gave Fighter Command the respite it needed to recover its strength.

15 September: During the next major daylight attack against London, the Germans were met by a reinforced and rested defence, which inflicted heavy losses on them and forced them to stop regular bombing raids against London in daylight. By then there could no longer be any talk of destroying the RAF – which was the condition for the invasion to take place and the original reason for the air offensive over the English Channel. A few days later Operation 'Seelöwe' was postponed 'indefinitely'.

Five days after the Luftwaffe offensive against Fighter Command's ground organisation ceased, on 12 September 1940, Keith Park, in a report to Dowding, summed up the situation as it appeared for 11 Group on 6 September 1940: 'Contrary to general belief and official reports, the enemy's bombing attacks by day had done extensive damage to five forward aerodromes and also to six out of seven sector stations. The damage to forward aerodromes was so severe that Manston and Lympne were for several days quite unfit for fighters. Biggin Hill was so severely damaged that only one squadron could operate from the airfield and the remaining two squadrons had to be placed under the control of adjacent sectors for over a week. [. . .] Had the enemy continued his heavy attacks to the adjacent sectors, knocked out their operations rooms or telephone communications, the fighter defences of London would have been in a powerless state during the last critical phase, and the unopposed heavy attacks would have been directed against the capital.'[314]

It is said that the victor writes history, and that is certainly true. But there is also a story written by representatives of the losing side, and this is often characterized by a hunt for scapegoats. This is especially true of the history written by some of the most colourful commanders on the German side in the decades immediately following the Second World War. This historiography 'from the other side of the hill', as we saw earlier, created the myth of Hermann Göring's almost totally incompetent leadership of the Luftwaffe. The Battle of Britain constitutes the very foundation of this myth. As with so much else that has turned into 'established truths' about Göring's role in the Battle of Britain, the notion that Göring was behind the decision to switch from airfield attacks to terror bombing of London also needs to be modified.

It is quite correct that on 6 September Göring arrived in Holland to personally take command of the air offensive against Britain, and the next day he stood on the cliffs of Cap Blanc Nez at the English Channel coast and watched the armadas he had sent out towards London passing in the air above. But the path to his decision was not as straight as it is often alleged.

During the weeks leading up to 7 September 1940, there had been many voices on the German side arguing that the Luftwaffe should concentrate its resources on bombing London, but Göring had not been one of them. Among those who most strongly advocated a shift to attacks on London was General Alfred Jodl, who as head of the Wehrmachtführungsstab had almost daily contact with Hitler. At a meeting with Hitler on 13 August 1940, Jodl proposed the launching of 'ruthless air raids on London'. But Göring was of an entirely different opinion. 'The main task is to continue to strike against the enemy fighter force in southern England,' he said.[315]

4 September 1940. Generalfeldmarschall Kesselring visits ZG 76 and V.(Z)/LG 1. Lined up in front of an aircraft of II./ZG 76 'Haifischgruppe', four airmen from V.(Z)/LG 1 are awarded with the Iron Cross, first class. From the left: Leutnant Hugo Adametz, Unteroffizier Albert Köpge (radio operator in Hauptmann Liensberger's aircraft), Unteroffizier Horst Brüggow and Unteroffizier Seufert. Leutnant Adametz, credited with 10 air victories, was killed in action on 15 September 1940. (Photo: Eimannsberger.)

Göring did not belong to those who imagined that British morale would collapse. As Fighter Command destroyed their illusions, those who were of that opinion began to increasingly lean towards the idea of a devastating blow to British morale by mass bombing of London. These included not only Generalfeldmarschall Albert Kesselring, the commander of Luftflotte 2, and General Wolfram Freiherr von Richthofen, commanding Fliegerkorps VIII, but also General Hans Jeschonnek, Chief of the Luftwaffe General Staff. Göring was under growing pressure to shift to attacks on London, but he fought back.

When Jeschonnek pointed out that another general had stated that 'everything would be over in six weeks' if the Luftwaffe began bombing London, Göring asked the question: 'Do you think that Germany would collapse if Berlin was destroyed?' 'Of course not!' replied Jeschonnek. 'The British morale is not as good as the German.'

Göring looked at his Chief of Staff with a concerned expression and replied laconically: 'I'm afraid you are mistaken.' As it turned out, Göring was right.

On 3 September, Göring travelled to The Hague for a conference with Kesselring and Sperrle, and the subject was then raised again. Kesselring referred to what Major Walter Grabmann, the commander of the ZG 76, had said the day before – 'On the other side of the Channel there soon won't be anything left!' – and to the reports from the bomber units: 'Weak fighter defence, which was effectively taken care of by our fighter escort.' In fact, during the pre-

vious two days (1-2 September) Kesselring's bomber units had been able to carry out all operations with no more than four of their aircraft getting shot down.

At the same time, a report came from Oberst Josef 'Beppo' Schmid, the commander of the Luftwaffe's intelligence service, which seemed to provide evidence for the notion that Fighter Command really did stand on the brink of annihilation. According to the latest estimates, the RAF had lost 1,115 fighters and 92 bombers since 8 August. The report continued: 'Eighteen airfields have been wiped out and another 26 are damaged. 10 % of the ground organisation is destroyed.' Even if the overly optimistic estimates from mid-August were revised, it was concluded that Fighter Command's strength had gone down from 900 aircraft, plus 250 in reserve on 1 July to 'slightly more than 600 fighters, plus 100 newly manufactured, including 420 serviceable' on 1 September.[316]

In fact this time Oberst Schmid's estimate of Fighter Command's numerical strength was surprisingly good. In reality, Fighter Command had over 701 operational fighters on 1 September, 1940 – of which 405 were Hurricanes and 208 Spitfires. What misled the Germans was that they thought this was a decline from 1 July. In fact, Fighter Command had only about half as many fighters as the Germans believed on 1 July, 1940. Although Fighter Command was in crisis after the first September week, Kesselring jumped to conclusions. He assumed that Fighter Command's crisis had already reached the point of no return, and he therefore now found new arguments for his old view that the attack should be directed towards London.

Invoking all these figures and reports Kesslering claimed that Fighter Command was about to withdraw its forces to airfields north of London in order to save them from heavy losses, and that only heavy attacks on London would force the British to fight. Moreover, he explained, it was pointless to continue attacking the airfields 'because there are no more British aircraft there'.

'When we've killed a couple of thousand Cockneys the British will beg for peace!' Kesselring blurted out.

The commander of Luftflotte 3, Hugo Sperrle, a scowling old Prussian, was of a different opinion. He was skeptical of reports of British losses and said that he had seen the same thing in Spain during the Civil War. Sperrle doubted that Fighter Command was finished and claimed that if the attacks on Fighter Command's ground organisation ceased, the British would be given the opportunity to build up their fighter force again. Göring agreed with Sperrle.

There was another, less factual argument against air raids on London. Luftwaffe Service Regulation 64/2 forbade any attack on residential districts. In addition, the Führer himself in his Directive No. 17 underlined in particular that the ban on 'terror raids' against English civilians and 'bombing aimed at causing mass panic' still applied. This was something that concerned the UK in general and London in particular, 'I have no intention of waging war against women and children. I have ordered my Air Force to confine its attacks solely against military objectives.'

The issue was finally decided by Hitler. Initially he had been on Göring's side on this issue. We have already seen the Führer's both ambivalent and unrealistic attitudes towards Britain. His strong resistance to air strikes against civilian targets in the British Isles was, like so much else, influenced by his confused 'racial thinking' rather than military considerations. Hitler was above all an ideologue trapped by the power of his own often uncontrolled emotional outbursts.

It is said that the first British bombing of Berlin affected Göring badly. Certainly the Reichsmarschall, had half-jokingly said that 'if any single bomb falls on Berlin you can call me Meyer', and it was of course a blow to Göring's prestige when Berlin was subjected to a series of British bombings from the night of 25 August onwards. But the one who reacted most strongly was Hitler, with his bizarre 'love affair' with his twisted image of 'the German people'.

While Göring summoned the commanders of the air fleets to the Hague, a large funeral ceremony took place in Berlin in honour of the twelve people killed in the latest British bombing raid. Werner Girbig writes in his documentation of the bombing war against Berlin: 'At the Jakobi cemetery on 3 September, in the presence of many

residents and a large group of Nazi party members, vice-Mayor Görlitzer holds the funeral speech for the victims from Kottbuser Strasse. The City President and Berlin's Mayor, Dr. Lippert, are also present.'[317]

William Shirer was an American reporter in Berlin at this time. After the bombing on 29 August he wrote: 'If the British keep this up, it will have a tremendous effect upon the morale of the people here. Goebbels today suddenly changed his tactics. His orders after the first big bombing were to play the story down in the press. Today he orders the newspapers to cry out at the "brutality" of the British fliers in attacking the defenceless women and children of Berlin.'[318]

On 1 September, the German authorities sealed off the area hit by the recent bombings to prevent people from seeing the extent of the damage. Shirer wrote in his diary: 'The main effect of a week of constant British night bombings has been to spread great disillusionment among the people here and sow doubt in their minds. One said to me today : "I'll never believe another thing they say. If they've lied about the raids in the rest of Germany as they have about the ones on Berlin, then it must have been pretty bad there."'[319] On 3 September, the Wehrmacht's War Diary noted that the residents of Berlin 'have spent a total of eight and a half hours in the shelters during the week 25 August to 1 September.'[320]

By directing their attacks against Berlin Bomber Command actually contributed almost immediately to the relief of the hard-pressed Fighter Command. Although ZG 76 was the Luftwaffe's most successful fighter unit, its I. Gruppe was, on 7 September, shifted from the Channel area to be reorganised into a night fighter unit. The unit was stationed at the Deelen base near Arnhem and given the new designation II./NJG 1.

But it did not stop at that. In the end, the bombing of Berlin was too much for the emotionally unstable Führer. On 4 September, he shouted in a radio speech broadcast from Berlin's Sportpalast: 'It is a wonderful thing to see our nation at war, in its fully disciplined state. This is exactly what we are experiencing at this time, as Mr Churchill is demonstrating to us the aerial night attacks he has concocted. He is not doing this because these air raids might be particularly effective, but because his Air Force cannot fly over German territory in daylight.'

'While German fliers are over England day after day, Churchill's night raiders indiscriminately drop their bombs over towns and villages and farms wherever a light is showing.

Six officers from 601 Squadron have lined up in front of the unit's Hurricane 'UF-N'. From left to right: Polish Flying Officer Juliusz Topolnicki, Flight Lieutenant Robinson, American Flight Lieutenant Carl Davis, Polish Flying Officer Jerzy Jankiewicz and American Pilot Officer Clive Mayers. All of these claimed to have shot down one Bf 110 each in the combat on 4 September 1940. The pilot to the right of Mayers in the picture is an unidentified flight sergeant. (Photo: Riddle via Ivers.)

'For three months I have been holding back the order to retaliate, but Churchill mistook that for a sign of weakness.

'We are going to give them their answer night after night from now on. When the British Air Force drops two or three or four thousand kilograms of bombs, then we will in one night drop 150-, 230-, 300- or 400,000 kilograms. When they declare that they will increase their attacks on our cities, then we will raze their cities to the ground. We will stop the handiwork of those night air pirates, so help us God!'

The following night William Shirer opened up his diary and wrote: 'The British came over again tonight, arriving punctually at fifteen minutes before midnight, which is their usual time. The fact that the searchlights rarely pick up a plane has given rise to whispers among the people of Berlin that the British planes are coated with an invisible paint. Tonight the bombers cruised over the city at intervals for two hours. The flak guns thundered away like mad, but without effect. Another bomb drop in the Tiergarten killed a policeman.' [321]

Now there was no turning back. But Göring was still hesitant to interrupt the offensive against Fighter Command's gound organisation, which, among others, Oberst 'Beppo' Schmid observed. Göring continued to be against it when Hitler on 6 September announced that he had decided to lift the ban on assaults on London. But the proponents of London raids felt increasingly self-assured, and that same day General von Richthofen wrote in his diary: 'This afternoon, the decision to attack London will be made. Let's hope that the Reichsmarschall stands fast. I have my doubts in this respect.'

It was precisely in order to make sure that nothing went wrong now that London was to be the main target that Göring decided to travel to the Channel and personally take command of the air operations.

Göring devoted a good part of the night of 7 September to creating very careful plans for the large scale attack on London. The operation orders went out to Luftflotte 2 early on 7 September with the following instructions:

1. On the evening of 7 September, Luftflotte 2 will carry out a major operation against target 'A' Loge (the codename for London).

2. The attack will take place in the following stages:
   18:00: initial attack to be carried out by Fliegerkorps II using one Kampfgeschwader;
   18:40: main attack to be carried out by Fliegerkorps II, using the remaining Kampfgeschwaders;
   19:00: Fliegerkorps I shall attack, using KG 30;
   21:00: 9. Fliegerdivision shall attack, using all available aircraft.

3. Fighters and escort:
a) The initial attack will draw most of the British fighters into the air, so that they will have left the area when the main attack takes place
b) Jafü 2 is responsible for the escort, using one Jagdgeschwader per Kampfgeschwader.

c) From 18:40 ZG 76 will clear the air of British fighters in the target areas assigned to Fliegerkorps I, and shall protect the bomber formations' approach and return flights
d) Jafü 2 shall assign two Jagdgeschwader to meet the units from I. and II. Fliegerkorps when they return from their attacks.

4. Implementation:
a) Bomber units will meet the fighters pilots during flight over the coast. The fighters shall avoid weaving unnecessarily.
b) The approach route is to be determined in consultation between the air corps and Jafü 2.
c) Regarding the escort of units subordinate to Jafü 2: As the fighter aircraft are flying to the limit of their range, every detour is to be avoided and the approach must be done at the highest possible airspeed.
d) Flight altitude after meeting with fighter aircraft: between 5,000 and 6,500 metres. By using vertical separation, the length of formations is to be kept down as much as possible. The return flight shall be carried out in a shallow dive, so that the English coast is passed at about 4,000 metres altitude.

This tactic would, as we shall see, put the defence in a difficult position.

7 September 1940

On the afternoon of 7 September Göring stood with his entire staff on the cliffs near Cap Blanc Nez and looked up towards the sky, his face flushed with excitement. High above his head the swastika-marked aircraft passed minute by minute. There were almost one thousand aircraft – 343 bombers and 642 fighters. It was the largest air armada ever seen; it came as a huge black cloud and filled an airspace of 2,000 cubic kilometres – 50 kilometres long and 30 kilometres wide.

Göring stood for a long while looking after the many hundreds of aircraft as they disappeared off in the distance on their way to strike London.

'We were elated' said one of the German fighter pilots who flew in the armada on this Saturday afternoon. 'Now the moment finally seemed to have come when we would smoke the last British reserves out of their holes.'

That they flew much higher than usual – between 5,000 and 6,500 metres – helped to further increase Fighter Command's difficulties.

15:54: Fighter Command's headquarters in Bentley Priory received the first indications of the start of a German raid. Twenty minutes later reports began to pour in from the observation posts: The front of the German raid had reached Maidstone while hundreds of German aircraft continued to pour in westwards over the coast between Ramsgate and Deal.

16:17: While the German bomber crews began trying to find their vulnerable targets – the docks below the Tower

On the afternoon of 7 September 1940, Göring and his staff stood at the cliffs at the French Channel coast near Cap Blanc Nez and watched how the armadas of Luftwaffe planes passed overhead on the way to London.

Squadron in an attack on a numerically superior formation of German aircraft. The British report states: '43 Squadron encountered three enemy formations roughly 20 miles apart. Each formation consisted of 20-25 Do 17 at 15,000 feet with 12-15 Me 110s circling over them at 17,000 feet and 25 Me 109s, Me 110s and possibly He 113s stepped up to 22,000 feet. In the ensuing dogfight it was noticed that when attacked the bombers kept straight on their course whilst the Me 110s dived down to keep off the attacking fighters.'[322]

It cost 43 Squadron three aircraft. Caesar Hull was killed, as well as Flight Lieutenant Richard Reynell. The Australian Reynell was the Hawker Works' most famous test pilot. Not long before, the British Air Ministry had agreed to allow a number of test pilots to take part in air combat for a short time to gain better understanding of the demands made on the aircraft in combat. Reynell was one of them.

Twelve Hurricane pilots from 249 Squadron managed to reach and attack a formation of He 111s, and reported one of these shot down and one damaged, but it cost them five Hurricanes when German fighters intervened.

The leading three-plane formation from II./KG 1, led by Oberst Benno Kosch, was the target of vigorous attacks by several Hurricanes that had managed to break through. Oberst Kosch saw one Heinkel going down with a burning engine – it was the aircraft of the commander of 4./KG 1, Hauptmann Rolf-Paul von Neumann. A He 111 on Kosch's other side was also badly hit. A moment afterwards a burst of fire slammed into Kosch's own Heinkel, and the German unit commander was wounded by two bullets in the shoulder and a third that scored his face. 'One engine is smoking', reported the observer. But Kosch had no intention of aborting the attack. While the Messerschmitt fighters arrived and drove away the Hurricane, he continued the attack and shortly after flew in over London, where he dropped his bombs directly over the target area. Kosch even succeeded in getting his damaged aircraft back to the base.[323]

17:15: The first wave dropped its bombs on Woolwich Arsenal and two large factories. The bombers then turned to the right, away from the fires that started down below where their deadly cargoes exploded.

The following waves continued further west and dropped their bombs on both sides of the Thames just where it forms two large loops – in other words, where the docks were concentrated. Here the Germans for the first time used 1.5-ton sea mines against the city, as a kind of blockbusters.

The greater part of the 300 tonnes of high-explosive bombs and thousands of incendiary bombs that fell on London that afternoon, was directed against four specific targets: the Victoria and Albert docks, the West India docks and the impressively sized Surrey Commercial docks. This most vigorous and concentrated air strike of the war so far, lasted exactly 90 minutes. During those 90

Bridge, the arsenal in Woolwich and the oil tanks further down the river – the commander of 11 Group ordered up his first eleven squadrons.

16:23: All units of 11 Group were either airborne, about to take off, or on standby.

16:30: All units around London – twenty-one squadrons of Spitfires and Hurricanes – had been scrambled. One of them was Douglas Bader's Duxford Wing.

The British air controllers guessed that the Germans would, as so often before, cross the Thames and attack the Hornchurch, North Weald and Debden sector stations; strictly speaking it was Leigh-Mallory's 12 Group that was responsible for defending the latter. Park therefore concentrated most of his fighters north of the capital. This gave the British good time to prepare for action.

The hour had come for Bader and Leigh-Mallory, the foremost advocates for interception with Big Wings instead of in the traditional way with single squadrons.

The first British fighter attack occurred just east of London a few minutes after five o'clock. At first it was just a few Hurricanes, engaging the enemy over the Thames Estuary.

Squadron Leader Caesar Hull, one of Fighter Command's largest personalities, led nine Hurricanes from 43

minutes over three hundred German bombers unloaded their bombs and veered away so as to not get in the way for the next wave. Everything was done in the shortest possible time, and therefore the bombs not only fell on the docks but also on the workers' houses, packed together in narrow alleyways right in the target area. The slum areas of London's East End were badly hit. 400 Londoners were killed and many thousand were wounded.

It was only when the main German force dropped its bombs that the British air controllers realized that London was the target, and in a panic sent all their fighters southwards. Most got tied up in bitter fighting with the overwhelming German fighter escort and were unable to get to the bombers. At the same time the next German wave arrived over the capital from the south and southwest. This time it was the bombers from Luftflotte 3.

When the German aircraft formations began to split up and flew away from London to the north, west and south, the air combats spread out over an area of 25,000 square kilometres. It was a frightening and at the same time fascinating sight for spectators down on the ground. High up among the light clouds in the blue sky – between five and six kilometres up in the air – hundreds of white condensation trails formed grotesque patterns as the warring planes, turned, twisted, rose and fell in every possible direction. Every now and then something gleamed and seconds afterwards a black plume of smoke appeared with an aeroplane in front of it that dropped towards the ground. There would be an eruption of flame in a distant field and then maybe a bang was heard. A minute later the next burning aircraft tumbled down, bringing death to its pilot. Another twenty-year-old man sat trapped while murderous flames of high octane gasoline mercilessly enveloped his whole body. The skin of his face was burning. He grabbed the cockpit hood and screamed in pain when the white-hot metal cut into his hands. His face swelled up in the flames and his eyes shrank, while life vanished from his scorched body.

The air battles on 7 September were a real defeat for the RAF. Firstly: all the German bombers had managed to drop their bombs on their targets without being significantly disturbed by either fighter or anti-aircraft fire. Secondly: the air fighting had also been a new hard blow to Fighter Command. No German formations had been driven back and the British had suffered severe losses. Of the 268 Spitfires and Hurricanes in contact with the enemy, 44 had been shot down, i.e. every sixth plane. Of these, 25 were total losses. Among the pilots lost were two of the aces in 234 Squadron – Squadron Leader Joseph O'Brien, with five kills and Australian Flight Lieutenant Paterson Clarence Hughes with 14 kills.

Of the German aircraft that took part in the attack, 26 were lost, which is less than three per cent.[324] Those who fared the very best were the German bomber units – their average losses amounted to a mere two per cent, or a total of seven aircraft. Göring was in a splendid mood, and he was particularly pleased with his fighter force, whose first success reports added up to 75 victories. Hauptmann Wolfgang Ewald's I./JG 52 had managed to escort the initial attack force bombers to and from London without a single bomber being lost. 'For this admirably executed escort mission, we received a special commendation by the Reichsmarschall' the unit's war diary noted with pride.[325]

'This is the historic moment when our Air Force has struck directly against the enemy's heart' Göring proclaimed in a radio speech.

Meanwhile London burned more and more fiercely. All the wood in the houses that had been exposed by exploding bombs gave plenty of nourishment to the flames started by the incendiary bombs. By the time the sun went down the fires were colossal; the sea of fire in the East End was reflected against the night sky like an artificial sunset; the light from the flames was visible for miles away and was a perfect guide for Göring's next band of attackers.

At eight o'clock on the evening of 7 September the next German attack force began to take off from their airfields. This time it was night bombers. Between 20:10 and 04:30 hours, 320 planes flew in over London and dropped another 330 tonnes of high-explosive bombs along with 440 containers of incendiary bombs. Just around the Surrey docks an area of 100 acres was in flames. The entire Woolwich Arsenal exploded.

Whole working class areas were reduced to ashes. Across the East End fires raged unchecked. From flaming rubber stocks poured clouds of black toxic smoke that threatened to suffocate the survivors. Melting, burning wheat, flour and sugar flowed like a sticky mass along the streets. An enormous amount of lumber turned into huge bonfires.

In the space of ten hours more than 1,000 Londoners lost their lives. It was only the first of 65 consecutive days when London would have to endure Hitler's fury. In just the next seven days, 2,000 more Londoners were killed while over 10,000 were injured.

These violent attacks on London, and air reconnaissance reports of the large number of barges and other sea-going vessels that the Germans had pulled together in the ports along the French and Belgian Channel coast, caused

A Do 17 drops its bombs. The bomb bay of this aircraft could be loaded with either twenty 50-kilo bombs or four 250-kilo bombs, or a mix of these, up to a total payload of 1,000 kilos.

A wounded man is gently pulled out of the rubble of a house after a bombing raid on London.

the British to fear that an invasion was imminent. Church-ill even sent out the password 'Cromwell' on the evening of 7 September – which was the signal for the highest state of readiness for an imminent invasion.

8 September 1940

On the morning of 8 September, German news broadcasts boastfully declared that London had ceased to exist as a port city – a huge exaggeration. The city and the port had been dealt some deep wounds, but London was still the world's biggest and busiest port.

At Fighter Command's headquarters in Bentley Priory and in 11 Group's staff bunker in Uxbridge, there was great activity and notably mixed feelings. At long last Fighter Command's ground organisation had had a quiet day, and every effort was now made to start repairing the damage received during the 'critical period'. Fighter Command's optimists were proved right – the 'tranquil day' for the air bases became undisturbed weeks.

The day after the bombing of the British capital the sky was covered by merciful clouds that made the Ger-mans postpone the raid on London that had been sched-uled for the morning of 8 September. At midday the Do 17s from II. and III./KG 2 finally took off to attack a power station and a major pumping station in London. Several fighter units took off to escort the next operation against London. One of these units was JG 54, whose Geschwad-erkommodore noted in his diary: 'The take-off order ar-rives only towards noon. Our Geschwader is tasked to carry out "extended fighter escort" for Kampfgeschwader 3. We take off at 12:45. The rendezvous point is set at 5,000 metres over Cap Gris Nez. But we wait in vain for KG 3. In order not to waste more fuel, we join another Kampf-geschwader.' [326]

'Our unit was escorted by three full Jagdgeschwader' said Oberfeldwebel Borner from II./KG 2. 'It is an impres-sive force that makes us feel pretty safe. By all accounts the enemy's defence has also weakened.' [327]

Park sent up four squadrons, but these had no chance against the overwhelming mass of Bf 109s. In 11 Group's typical style the British units went in to attack one by one. Already over Dover No. 41 Squadron was the first to make contact, and was pounced on by the entire II./JG 2 'Rich-thofen'. Shortly afterwards 46, 222 and 605 squadrons also appeared – only to be attacked by JG 3 and JG 51. It was so obvious that the German fighter escort's strength was fully sufficient to hold 11 Group's battered forces in check that Trautloft's JG 54 was soon recalled to base. Six British fighters were shot down. Oberleutnant Helmut Wick from 6./JG 2 was credited with shooting down three Hurricanes, thereby reaching a total of 28 victories.

Not surprisingly, the German bomber crews hardly saw any British fighters. Oberfeldwebel Borner from II./KG 2 says: 'Over London a lonely British fighter pops up behind us, but keeps at a safe distance.' [328]

A Bf 109 from I./JG 2 on its way in over England. This aircraft, 'Yellow 14', was flown by Leutnant Franz Fiby. (Photo: Mombeek.)

The participating German fighter units managed this while losing only one of their own aircraft. II./KG 2 however lost three Do 17s to anti-aircraft fire.

Göring began to wonder if Kesselring had been right in his assessment of the effect of bombing London – at least regarding the notion that Fighter Command was more or less finished. The Reichsmarschall now issued an order to continue the attacks on London, which had been divided into two target areas: Area 'A' was the eastern districts with the port facilities and area 'B' was the western part with the large power and supply facilities.

At 20:30 in the evening on 8 September the air raid sirens sounded across London again, and over the next nine hours, 170 German bombers were in action over the capital and dropped their bombs. This time, the city's power plants and railway lines were targets for a total of 1,700 high-explosive bombs with a total weight of 207 tonnes, supplemented by several thousand incendiary bombs. When 9 September dawned fires once again raged in London. All rail lines to and from from the city to the south and the southeast had been cut and a further 1,150 people had been killed or wounded.

Initially, the British were virtually defenceless against the night raids. Usually the German bombers flew in at altitudes of between 4,500 and 4,800 metres – which made it extremely difficult for the defenders. The British anti-aircraft searchlights were not strong enough to reach the matt black aircraft at altitudes above 2,000-3,000 metres in the dark. Nor were the Air Defence's acoustic instruments of much use. Their range was often as low as 8,000 metres,

which means that an aircraft flying at an altitude of 4,500 metres could be detected at a distance of only 6.5 kilometres, which the plane would cover in slightly more than a minute at a cruising speed of 320 km/h, which was normal for the He 111. But these instruments soon became of no use at all when the pilots began to turn off their engines before they reached London, and then glide in over the target. In addition the crews manning the British air defence guns used a tactic that wasn't very successful: instead of meeting the Germans with an intense barrage of fire, each gun only fired single shots and then only against aircraft that could be clearly identified as hostile – in order not to risk hitting one of the RAF night fighter aircraft which prowled the skies above the capital.

The British night-fighters achieved very little with their very much improvised equipment.The night fighter force, consisting of Hurricanes, Defiants and Blenheims, did their best but without much success as they were directed from the ground with a completed system of optical signals. In fact, the English night fighter pilots flew around blindly hoping to get a glimpse of a German bomber flying in at 300 km/h in the pitch black darkness. 'Most nights we could hear the bombers pass over the airfields before we even caught up in our plan to start', said British night fighters pilot John Cunningham. 'Once we had taken off and reached altitude, we could rarely or never see them. The radar was not sufficiently effective to lead us into contact. On the few occasions when the searchlights lit up an enemy aircraft, we usually were in the wrong position or not high enough, and if we managed to get close to the target the searchlights lost it, or the bomber had flown out of their reach. We felt almost completely helpless.' Statistics for the German KG 55 bomber squadron show that during eight months of nocturnal air operations over the British Isles only ten of its aircraft were even discovered by RAF night fighters![329]

Darkness did not however cause the Germans any difficulty finding their way – on every night attack they were guided to London by the huge fires; the glow from these was visible all the way to the coast of France!

It was not as easy for the British during their nocturnal attacks against Germany. The British tabloid press, however, was just as sensationalist then as now, and even then they weren't much concerned with the truth. So after the attack on Hamburg during the night between 8 and 9 September these newspapers trumpeted out that the huge city had been 'pulverized'.

The Germans responded by showing some foreign journalists around Hamburg. The American radio reporter William Shirer wrote: 'Even if the Germans hadn't kept their promise to show me the things I asked for, it was plain from what little we saw that slight damage had been done. [. . .] It was depressing, too, to think that perhaps British propaganda had exaggerated the effects of their raids in other places in Germany.' In fact, no more than 96 high-explosive bombs and 69 incendiaries fell on Hamburg on the evening of 8 September, 1940, killing one person and injuring twelve.[330]

One reason for Bomber Command's meagre returns over Germany on the night of 8/9 September was of course that the bulk of its operations that night were carried out against the German-occupied Channel ports, where the invasion fleet was assembled. The British lost ten bombers. One of them was shot down by a German night fighter from I./NJG 2 (formerly II./NJG 1 until I./ZG 76 was converted to the new II./NJG 1).

9 September 1940

Just as Göring›s airmen seemed to have had gained a decisive advantage, autumn weather began to put obstacles in the way of the German plans. 'This morning the cloud level is so low that any mission before noon seems to be out of question,' wrote Major Hannes Trautloft in his diary on 9 september.[331] It was not until late in the afternoon that it cleared up so that the Luftwaffe could begin the next big attack on London. KG 1, KG 2, KG 30 and KG 53 took off, escorted by nearly all the German fighter aircraft, both Bf 109s and Bf 110s.

This time Fighter Command met them with a powerful force – nine whole squadrons. The Duxford Wing managed to form up for a massive attack on the Ju 88s of KG 30, which took the route along the Thames Estuary to attack from the east. The Big Wing formation flew so close together that two Hurricanes collided during the attack, one plunged straight into a Ju 88 and all three planes crashed. Three more Ju 88s were shot down by the Duxford Wing pilots before they were engaged by the escorting Zerstörers from III./ZG 76 and V.(Z)/LG 1. Further south, just above the English coast at Beachy Head, the Hurricanes from 1 RCAF and 303 RAF (Polish) squadrons attacked a formation of He 111s from KG 1 escorted by Bf 109s. Here also the RAF pilots ended up battling the German fighter escort and managed to shoot down no more than one He 111.

The day's greatest individual feat on the British side was reported in from 605 Squadron: In an attack against the He 111s from KG 53 that attacked the Vickers-Armstrong works in Brooklands, in London's south-western outskirts, Flight Lieutenant Archie McKellar was credited with shooting down three He 111s and one of the escorting Bf 109s. However, this was an obvious exaggeration. The only He 111 that the Germans lost from the formation was Oberleutnant Kurt Meineckes 'A1+ZD' which crashed after it had been rammed by Pilot Officer George Mathwin Forrester's Hurricane. It was Forrester's first air combat, and he never managed to get out of his descending Hurricane.

The British reported that their fighter attacks had created such confusion among the German formations that the bombing was widely dispersed and didn't cause particularly serious damage. But German sources claim that after the initial surprise they held off most of the British fighter attacks, and that it was the heavy cloud cover instead that saved the British capital. The fact is that the majority of the air fighting once again took place between the fighter planes of both sides, with RAF Fighter Command losing 17 aircraft – with 6 more crash-landing – while 12 Bf 109s and 4 Bf 110s were shot down. Pilot Officer Jim Humphreys from 605 Squadron described one of the day's many combats: 'We were bounced by the Me 110s, which I had not seen. Probably they were on free range. My aircraft was hit three or four times, one being a 20mm high explosive right beside the throttle quadrant. I went down in an aileron turn for 2,000 ft to 3,000 ft and took stock. There was a sizeable hole in the cockpit wall, the throttle quadrant was gone, the cockpit was full of smoke and petrol fumes and I was feeling mighty sick. It seemed that she was about to burn so I baled out. This would be about 12,000 ft. I did not want to stay in that area so I did a free fall down to cloud level (about 3,000ft) and opened my 'chute. My hand was a mess – blood, flesh, bone and glove all mixed up together – so for the rest of the descent, I was hanging grimly onto the pressure point.'[332]

The fires in London showed the way for the German airmen who flew in to continue the attack as soon as darkness fell on 9 September. The beams from the British searchlights also helped them. In all 195 German bombers flew over the British capital far into the small hours of the 10th and dropped 230 tonnes of high-explosive bombs and 290 containers of incendiary bombs. One of the bombs struck the River Thames at Hungerford Bridge, producing a column of water that sprayed straight up for 30 seconds, followed by a huge wave. The bomb had struck a railway tunnel under the Thames, a tunnel which still, to this day, 75 years later remains unusable. The night's attack cost 370 Londoners their lives. An additional 1,400 were badly injured.[333] It cost the Germans only one downed bomber.

The same night, Berlin was once again the target for Bomber Command and some bombs hit the Arts Academy and a hospital in the city.

10 September 1940

'Bad weather all day', a frustrated Hannes Trautloft wrote in his diary on 10 September. 'Incessant rain. From one hour to the other, the planned operation against London is postponed, until it is finally cancelled late in the afternoon. This waiting is unbearable! A day like this puts a severe strain on your nerves. I would prefer three combat flights with take-off times that are kept.'[334]

Hermann Göring was equally impatient. He realized that the RAF would take advantage of the respite that the bad weather offered to rebuild its forces. The Reichs-marschall therefore issued a new order to his forces: 'If the weather does not permit the operation of large forces from Luftflotte 2 and 3 against England, the air fleets shall carry out small-scale attacks against the aviation industry.'

By nightfall most clouds cleared, however, and 148 German bombers flew in over the British Isles, the major-ity headed for London. But now the British had a surprise in store for the Germans. The commander of the British Anti-Aircraft Command, General Frederick Pile, worked energetically to strengthen the defence of London. On the afternoon of 10 September, he summoned anti-aircraft commanders at all levels to the Signal Corps' drill hall on Brompton Road in London and issued new instructions: 'All guns are to maintain a continous fire until the bombers have left. All barrels shall be held in the same direction and the same elevation and fire a barrage!'

Pile had arranged for the British night-fighters to stay away from London. In addition, significant reinforce-ments had been brought into the capital. During the first three nights of the attack there had been no more than 92 heavy anti-aircraft guns in London. (In addition, there were a large number of light and medium anti-aircraft guns, but these didn't have the range necessary to engage the high-flying bombers.) By the evening of 10 Septem-ber, the number of heavy anti-aircraft guns in London had increased to nearly 200. The barrage they created forced the Germans higher up, making it more difficult to con-centrate the bombing. When they met the blazing wall of exploding AA shells several German airmen turned away and dropped their bombs on London's southern suburbs. Crews that braved the barrage ended up so high up that it was impossible to find their exact target. Of the total of 230 tonnes of bombs dropped on the factories along the Thames, only a small proportion fell within the target area. The vast majority of the bombs were spread over an area from Bromley in the south to Edmonton in the north, and from Hornchurch in the east to Kingston in the west.

The air defences did not actually shoot down any more aircraft than before – the night between 10 and 11 Septem-ber not a single German bomber was lost – but the barrage had a demoralizing effect on the attackers and saved the lives of far more Londoners than just shooting down planes would have done. Furthermore the work of the London Fire Brigade was less difficult than in the previous days and nights; they now had to deal with smaller fires that were easier to tackle instead of the immense fires from before.

A visibly tired RAF pilot climbs out of his Spitfire after a combat mission during the Battle of Britain.

The number of Londoners killed or injured was less than 300 on the night of 10/11 September.[335] That same night, RAF Bomber Command attacked Bremen, Hamburg and Berlin. The next day, the Brits announced that 'extensive damage' had been caused in the German capital; among other things the Potsdamer Bahnhof main railway station had been completely ruined by the bombs. Once again the Germans showed foreign journalists around the bombed city, and William Shirer found that the Potsdamer Bahnhof was as unscathed as ever. Four British bombers failed to return from that night's operation. Again, one fell prey to a German night fighter from I./NJG 2.

For a while after that the frequency of Bomber Command's attacks on Germany declined. Instead a new emphasis was placed on attacks on the fleet of barges in German-occupied ports of the English Channel. It was about time! The date Hitler had set for Operation Sealion, 18 September 1940, was rapidly approaching.

11 September 1940

Hannes Trautloft's diary entries for 11 September begin as follows: 'During the night just past the weather cleared. Again, several British bombers have flown against the Reich area [Germany]. But early in the morning the entire area again is covered with thick fog that prevents any air operations. It seems that the British work in cooperation with the weather gods!'[336] No one could have imagined that it would become one of the most intense days of combat in the Battle of Britain.

On the other side of the Channel, Park summoned his air controllers and sector commanders for a new conference. Until then, Park's tactic had been to deploy a squadron at a time against the German units flying across the UK. The purpose of this was to force the German fighters into an uninterrupted series of combats, which in a relatively short period of time would force them to abort the mission as their ammunition was exhausted or their fuel ran out. But Park could now confirm that the German tactic of deploying large concentrations of Messerschmitt fighter aircraft – according to Göring's instructions from 19 August – thwarted the British tactic, simply because the British attacking formations were so small that large parts of the German fighter escort could ignore them. Park therefore now issued Directive No. 16, which required sector commanders as often as possible to order up squadrons in pairs, i.e. two squadrons would operate together. These would preferably be a squadron of Hurricanes, which would take care of the bombers, and a squadron of Spitfires to attack the German fighter escort. In addition, sector commanders should prepare for a greater effort, with two additional pairs of squadrons being deployed at 15 minutes intervals.[337]

Towards noon on 11 September the fog dispersed and the clouds began to lift above the French, Belgian and Dutch airfields. Weather reconnaissance promised clear weather for the rest of the day, so orders went out to KG 1 and KG 26 for a major attack on London!

At around a quarter to four a dense collection of white spots was seen on British radar screens. From each radar station observations were routinely telephoned to the Filter Room at Bentley Priory, Dowding's Headquarters. From there the reports went on to Park's headquarters and the sector stations' operations rooms. Keith Park immediately gave his sector commanders the order to set pairs of squadrons on standby. The first units from 11 Group were sent into the air.

Meanwhile, 12 Group and its Duxford Wing were also put on standby. This Wing had now been extended from three to five squadrons. No. 616 Squadron had left Duxford, but instead 74 and 611 squadrons had arrived to join 19, 242 and 310 squadrons. 74 and 611 squadrons had been the first to be equipped with the latest Spitfire version, Mk IIA. This had the new 1,175-horsepower Rolls-Royce Merlin XII engine that could be cooled with dilute glycol. This was an improvement compared with the Merlin III engine of the Spitfire Mk I, which needed pure glycol for its cooling – which made the engine more prone to catching fire.

No. 74 'Tiger' Squadron also was one of Fighter Command's best fighter units and was led by the legendary 'Sailor' Malan. After several weeks of rest and recuperation in Lincolnshire, Malan and his young men were eager for battle.

At five past four, the Bf 109s from Major Galland's Stabsstaffel JG 26 passed over the British coast at Folkestone at an altitude of 4,000 metres. When Galland flew on in over England, he could see that the overcast had dispersed so that only a few small fluffy clouds remained drifting about two thousand metres further down. Above, the sky was blue, and high up there could be seen what appeared to be a swarm of gnats. There were about twenty-five Bf 109s from II./JG 2, and in one of them sat Oberleutnant 'Assi' Hahn looking around excitedly, as he himself said, for British planes to shoot down.[338]

The German planes were immediately reported by the Observer Corps on the ground. A few minutes later, even more white dots appeared on the British radar screens. It was the fighter escort taking off from its airfields in the Pas de Calais area. At 16:13 Major Mölders lifted his Bf 109 from the airfield at St Inglevert/Pihen.[339] He assembled his JG 51, and the Bf 109s from I.(J)/LG 2, and then began to orbit in the air while waiting for the bombers, He 111s from KG 26. While Mölders circled around in the brilliant sunshine, he saw several other units of Messerschmitts climbing from various airfields in the vicinity. At 16:16 Oberleutnant Hans-Ekkehard Bob, who recently had become commander of 7./JG 54, took off from the airfield at Guines. He was part of the Geschwader under the leadership of Major Trautloft that had been ordered to escort KG 1. Bob remembers the 'completely overwhelming sight of hundreds of Messerschmitts that slowly began to fill the sky'.[340]

As well as the majority of the Bf 109s in the Pas de Calais area, even ZG 26 'Horst Wessel' and II./ZG 76 'Haifischgruppe' went up to escort the bombers towards London. The élite 'Haifischgruppe' split up into two formations, with one covering the operation against London

A Bf 110 from II./ZG 76 with its typical shark jaw painting.

and one being assigned for a special mission further to the west.

Soon, telephones shrilled in alerts shacks at airfields all over Kent and Sussex and the area north of London. Terse orders were quickly given: 'Plus 300 bandits approaching. Take off immediately. Further instructions in the air.' 'Scramble! Scramble!' The electrifying order sounded like a trumpet blast. At airfields throughout southeast England the British, Polish, New Zealand, Canadian and Czech pilots came rushing to their Spitfires and Hurricanes where mechanics waited to help them up.

At 15:15 (British time) came reports of the first contacts with the enemy. 'Bandits ahead, slightly higher', the RAF airmen heard the air controllers warn. There, straight ahead to the southeast, a cloud of tiny dots appeared that quickly grew in size . . . Messerschmitts! The British unit commander led his Hurricanes in a climb right up towards the 'Huns'. Ten against twenty! That was bad enough but what the pilots from 46 Squadron didn't know, was that they had challenged some of the war's most renowned German fighter pilots. . .

Up there the German pilots waggled their wings nervously, and then – as if by magic the German formation split up and ten Messerschmitt 109s dropped their starboard-wings and came plunging downwards. Sergeant William Peacock died in his bullet-riddled Hurricane. The clock on the dashboard of Oberleutnant 'Assi' Hahn's Bf 109 showed 16:15 as the German ace recorded his 16th kill.

46 Squadron's formation was scattered to the winds by the violent attack and became easy prey for several German fighters. A Bf 110 swooped down into position behind a Hurricane. 46 Squadron's Sergeant Roger de Cannart d'Hamale had been the first Belgian pilot to reach the UK after his country's defeat in May 1940. Now his Hurricane was torn to pieces by shells from the Bf 110's 20mm cannons and the young Belgian bailed out.

Then it was Major Galland's turn. He swept in at a lower altitude and attacked the British at the head of his 'Schlageter' pilots. Together with his Stabsschwarm he picked out a lone Hurricane, which soon fell to the ground leaving a thick cloud of smoke behind. Badly wounded in the cockpit of his bullet-riddled Hurricane, Pilot Officer Peter McGregor still succeeded in crash-landing in a field near Staple Cross, northwest of Dungeness.

The fighting spread as more RAF fighter units arrived and further German fighter units came in over the coast. Unteroffizier Kurt Bühlingen from 6./JG 2 shot and set fire to another Hurricane. It was Bühlingen's second victory – a number that would rise to 112 before the war had ended. Still, it was just the two sides' fighters fighting each other. The Heinkels of KG 26 kept a respectful distance when they flew in over the Thames Estuary.

Now things started happening even further to the west. Thirteen assuault planes belonging to Erprobungsgruppe 210 – nine Bf 110s and four Bf 109s – took off from Cherbourg at 16:30. Erprobungsgruppe 210 had been hastily moved to Cherbourg for an attack on the Supermarine works at Woolston in Southampton, where Spitfire fighter aircraft were manufactured. The unit's new Gruppenkommandeur – the third in a month – was Hauptmann Martin Lutz, a veteran who had previously led 1. Staffel in 'the 210th'. When the bomb-loaded Messerschmitts flew north-

A Hawker Hurricane above the clouds.

wards they were joined by their escort – twenty-six Bf 109s from JG 2, I. and II./JG 27 and III./JG 53, and sixteen Bf 110s from ZG 2, II. and III./ZG 76 and V.(Z)/LG 1.[341] The target was the Spitfire factory in Eastleigh near Southampton. Three squadrons from the RAF's 10 Group tried to intercept them, but failed to prevent the lightning attack. Erprobungsgruppe 210 carried out a complete demolition job, but at the Cunliffe-Owen works, not the Supermarine plant. After that the crews from Erprobungsgruppe 210 were able to withdraw without suffering any losses. This was thanks to the Zerstörers which engaged the British fighters over the sea off the Isle of Wight.

The Spitfire pilots from 602 Squadron, who were meant to cover the Hurricanes, did not do particularly well and had three planes downed by the Zerstörer escort. Two of them were later repaired. Sergeant Antoni Wójcick from 213 Squadron was still in the cockpit of his burning Hurricane, 'AK-P', when it struck the water. Another Polish pilot had been killed in the Battle of Britain. Almost at the same time as Wójcick was shot down, 'AK-A' also crashed after having been shot to pieces by a Bf 110. The pilot of the Hurricane, Flight Lieutenant 'Jackie' Sing, managed to get out in time and pulled the rip-cord on his parachute. Shortly afterwards a British air-sea rescue boat pulled him out of the English Channel. With his six kills, he was one of 213 Squadron's top aces at that time. In October 1940, he was awarded the DFC. Sing was surpassed, however, by another airman from 213 Squadron, Sergeant Reginald Llewellyn, who claimed to have shot down two Bf 110s in this engagement. This gave him 13 ½ confirmed victories, plus one unconfirmed, one "probable" and two damaged.

To what extent Llewellyn's success reports corresponded to actual German losses is hard to determine, but apparently his claims on 11 September were exaggerated as German losses were confined to one plane, from I./ZG 2.

Farther to the northeast the fight continued to rage between 11 Group's aircraft and the Messerschmitts from Luftflotte 2. The pilots from 41 Squadron made desperate attempts to get at the German bombers, but didn't manage to do more than damage one of them, while the Bf 110s shot down three Spitfires, two of which were written off.

The 'pair' 229 and 303 squadrons fared no better. A flock of Messerschmitt fighters came diving from on high and the Hurricanes set off in all directions doing wild evasive manoeuvres. Five completely bullet-riddled Hurricanes crashed to the ground, three of them with Polish pilots. One of them crashed into two villas in Hartland Way, one of London's fashionable southern suburbs. Burning high-octane petrol from the wreck sprayed into a provisional shelter, where there were two women and two children. In the air high above a Messerschmitt 109 climbed back to attack height. Major Werner Mölders had achieved his 36th victory. If his kills in the Spanish Civil War are included, his overall score now stood at 50. The commander of 1./JG 51, Oberleutnant Hermann Friedrich Joppien, one of Mölders' most promising officers, meanwhile claimed to have shot down two British fighters and reached his 19th victory.

In return, Hauptmann Ernst Wiggers, commander of 2./JG 51 and an ace with 13 victories, was killed. Additionally a young Fähnrich from I.(J)/LG 2 brought his plane back across the Channel after it has been badly damaged by gunfire from a Hurricane. His name was Hans-Joachim Marseille, and over the next two years he would develop into perhaps the most skilled fighter pilot in the Luftwaffe, with a final score of 158 victories.

Chaos and confusion characterized the air battle this Wednesday afternoon. Some British air controllers, such as those in Northolt and Hornchurch, made the mistake of placing their fighters at too low an altitude. Because of this several RAF units had the incoming Bf 109s high above them when the combat began. That cost many Spitfire and Hurricane pilots dearly. In this way 1 RCAF Squadron was surprised by the Germans in the area of Tunbridge Wells. Flying Officer Thomas Little, one of the most experienced pilots in the Canadian unit, ended up in hospital with serious leg injuries; of his Hurricane only a burned steel skeleton remained. His compatriot Flying Officer Peter Lochnan crashed in a field near Romney.

On the plotting table in 11 Group's command centre it looked bad. More German formations were coming. From all sides came reports of fierce fighting with superior enemy fighter units. Fighter Command had lost over a dozen fighters without having managed to get to the German main attack force. All of this despite the fact that almost the entirety of 11 Group, plus the Duxford Wing, was in action. It seemed that nowhere had they been able to deal the bomber streams a hard blow. Only a few bombers had been shot down. Park was very dissatisfied.

But suddenly the entire picture was transformed! The fighter combats began to break up. The fighter pilots and Observer Corps started reporting 'The '109s are leaving!' From Rochford, Reigate, Rochester and Sheppey the leading German fighter units turned and dived back towards the south coast. 'The Germans are withdrawing towards the coast at treetop level! More and more German fighter units left the battlefield and flew home. What had happened? – It was fuel shortage: the protracted dogfighting, usually being fought at full throttle, had drained away at the Bf 109s' limited fuel load faster than the Germans had anticipated. Or rather – the Germans had not expected to face such vigorous and prolonged resistance. And now dozens of German fighter pilots hurried home with the red warning lights winking on the dashboards. Göring's planning had failed; there were no new fighters to fill the void left by all those who now broke off. In the space of ten minutes the entire battle picture changed.

Park was the first to react: 'Never mind the fighters. Let them flee. Concentrate on bombers over the Thames Estuary!'

The only German fighters that were left to protect the bombers were the Zerstörer units. These dived on the British fighters like hawks, and soon even the veterans of 74 'Tiger' squadron were engaged in a wild fighter combat. The hot-head 'Sailor' Malan made repeated attempts against a bomber formation, but was constantly busy hav-

Air base Gravesend, September 1940: A Spitfire from 66 Squadron comes in to land while others are ready to engage in combat.

ing to defend himself against the fiercely attacking German fighter pilots. Only after a long while did he manage to get so close that he could open fire on a bomber. The bomber descended with its left engine in flames and one crew member jumped out. By then Malan was up at 6,000 metres altitude, far away from the rest of his squadron. Two seconds later he got a new Messerschmitt behind him. Malan dived steeply to get away. Down at 3,000 metres, he made a sharp left turn, which gave him a blackout but also shook off his pursuer. Away from the main combat Malan found it best to return to base and replenish his ammunition before getting quickly back into the fight. Only after a few minutes did it occurr to him that he had just achieved his 10th victory.

74 Squadron's Pilot Officer Peter St John hit another German bomber, but before he could see the effect of his firing, he had a whole mob of Messerschmitts after him, and they chased him all the way back to the base at Duxford. Pilot Officer Douglas Hastings, also from 74 Squadron, reported: 'I attacked a Ju 88 and white smoke poured out of it as it dived with its undercarriage down. I then attacked a Me 110 from abeam and saw smoke pouring from its rear after pieces had broken off. I gave him another burst, but had to break away as two were diving on my tail. I did a steep climbing turn to the left and shook them off. They had yellow wingtips and camouflage made up largely of yellow.' [342]

Oberleutnant Walter Borchers (II./ZG 76), who achieved his 10th victory on that mission, describes the scene from the perspective of a Zerstörer pilot: 'I saw a Spitfire latch onto the tail of my Kommandeur, who flew right in front of me. What a beautiful picture, flashed through my head. Both aircraft were illuminated by the bright sunlight: The Spitfire gleamed in grey-green and brown on top and light blue on the underside, its two cockades glittered like the eyes of a beautiful butterfly. All this, I subconsciously noticed, while I pushed the control stick slightly to gain speed so that I could quickly get into a better shooting position. Just then my headphones seemed to explode: "Damn! Spitfire to the left!" And immediately afterwards: "Another Spitfire to the right!" This will be tough, I thought, but it would be a shame if the Chief gets shot down right in front of my nose!

'All this flashed through my head in the fraction of a second, and I had already made my decision: Attack the Spitfires to the left and to the right and save the Chief! I was in a favourable position. The Spitfire was already in my gunsight. I pressed the firing button and tracers gushed out and slammed into its target. The Spitfire trembled, turned over and fell onto its back, all within a moment. I gave it another burst, and it went down steeply and disappeared into the clouds below. And I'll be damned if good deeds aren't sometimes rewarded! Indeed so, at least this time, for while I shot down the Spitfire, my comrades further back shot down the other one too.' [343]

The war's first Spitfire Mk II to get shot down was Sergeant Frederick Shepherd's plane from 611 Squadron. The pilot bailed out, but his parachute had been burned, so he fell to certain death. A few minutes later, a second Spitfire II

from 611 Squadron was shot down, but this time the pilot survived. While 73 Squadron's Sergeant Herbert Webster had to bail out of his burning Hurricane after it had been set on fire by a Bf 110 over Sheppey, his comrade Sergeant Ronald Ellis managed to bring his plane – which had also been hit by a Bf 110 – back to base.

Still protected by the Bf 110s the Heinkels moved in over London where their bombs inflicted serious damage on Surrey's trade docks and caused large fires.

When the bombers left London, they were again attacked by RAF fighters. Oberleutnant Borchers continues his description: 'For a while it was fairly quiet. The enemy fighters were somewhere else. But soon they returned! We struck back hard and barely gave them an opportunity to shoot. I wasn't able to see much of what was going on, because all the time I kept focused on our Kommandeur's aircraft. Something had happened to it. For each turn, it lost speed, it trembled and seemed as if it would descend. What was wrong? Engine trouble! I saw that the right propeller was rotating slower and slower until it stopped altogether. The right engine had been hit – and this above London, right in the lion's den, in the middle of a combat with a numerically superior enemy who attacked us from all sides! Hardly a desirable state! The damaged aircraft naturally was slower and not as manoeuvrable anymore, so we had to defend it. This influenced the whole unit's manoeuvrability and combat capability. But our Kommandeur was an experienced Lufthansa pilot so he managed to keep his machine flying.'

'We shot down three Spitfires before we finally slowly disengaged from the enemy and headed for home. This is always a critical moment as it often happens that the aircraft flying at the rear ends up in trouble. The dogs always bite the last one! But fear not – in this case the Sharks, and no dogs, were the ones biting! We reached the coast without having sustained any losses. We held our Kommandeur in the middle of our formation to avoid any unpleasant surprises, crossed the English coastline and flew out over the Channel.

'We still were at a fairly high altitude. We were cold and needed oxygen. Then it happened! One last surprise on this mission, which certainly hadn't been uneventful! The second engine on our Kommandeur's aircraft also seized! Right above the Channel, far from our own coast. I must admit that I felt scared. What could our Kommandeur do? Bail out? Hardly conceivable! Glide, then? In the right hands, our Me 110s were excellent gliders. And as I said, the Chief really knew how to fly! Luckily, we found ourselves at such a high altitude. I was unsure of the ratio between height and glide ability of a Me 110, that is, how far it can glide horizontally while it drops a certain number of metres. But everything went well. Slowly, painfully slowly, the French coast grew increasingly clear in the distance, and after a while I could make out the broad, yellowish-brown beach. At that point, we were no longer that high up, because our Kommandeur lost much altitude during the glide flight. Suddenly, he made an unexpected turn and flew parallel to the coast. What was he up to? His new course pointed in the direction of the airfield at Boulogne, but he didn't seem to be heading there. Instead he continued to glide along the beach.

A crashed He 111. (Photo: Balss.)

'Now things really looked critical. It appeared as though the aircraft would crash at the last minute. But then it became clear what a skilled pilot our Kommandeur was. He discovered the danger and reset the course. Shortly afterwards the aircraft made an emergency landing. With an unknown surface and dead engines, a belly-landing was the only option. It was low tide, and the glittering beach was very wide. Our Kommandeur put down his plane just where land and water met. For a few seconds the aircraft disappeared in spouting water, and then when I looked down again I saw the aircraft lay in calm, shallow water with the Chief standing on one wing.' [344]

Thirteen He 111s from KG 26 came back to base with various degrees of damage. Two dead and eight wounded crew members were lifted out of these damaged planes. Seven others had been shot down. One of these He 111s ditched in the sea, and air-sea rescue was able to pick up four crew members, two of whom were wounded. On top of this a war reporter, Sonderführer Wilhelm Trapp, had joined a He 111 as a passenger to report on the mission to London. His He 111 was one of those which was riddled by gunfire from Browning machine guns, and Trapp and two of the plane's crew members were wounded.

KG 1 fared slightly better, but still lost three crews. In addition, two He 111s were so badly damaged that they had to be written off upon returning to France. Even ZG 26 'Horst Wessel' had been suffered heavy casualties. When the last plane from the unit landed, Geschwaderkommodore Oberstleutnant Joachim-Friedrich Huth found that

five planes were missing. In addition, a sixth made an emergency landing in France with a dead rear gunner in the shattered cockpit. Worst hit was Hauptmann Ralph von Rettberg's II. Gruppe, which lost three Bf 110s. II./ZG 76 'Haifischgruppe' had one Bf 110 that had to forced-land; it was 'M8+KC', flown by Gruppenkommandeur, Major Erich Groth. He survived with minor wounds and was soon back in the thick of it.

The Germans reported that they had shot down 67 British fighters. With two of these the commander of I.(J)/LG 2, Oberleutnant Herbert Ihlefeld, reached a total score of 21 victories. Two days later he joined the growing number of German fighter pilots who had been decorated with the Knight's Cross. In exchange for Ihlefeld's victories on 11 September, two of the unit's pilots had been shot down.

As usual, the Germans victory claims were exaggerated. But even if the air fighting on 11 September cost the RAF a loss of 30 fighters – which after all represented more than one-tenth of the aircraft that had joined battle – the Britons could look at the coming days with confidence. Park's new method of subjecting the German formations to incessant attacks by squadrons that operated in pairs had finally paid off. The Germans should have been able to take this as a warning of what to expect for their next major attack.

The RAF was also exaggerating its successes. 24 German aircraft genuinely shot down on 11 September were transformed into 89 victories by optimistic RAF pilots and anti-aircraft gun crews. Fighter Command claimed 80 of them. In Northolt the Poles celebrated. They claimed to have shot down 16 German planes – seven Bf 109s, four He 111s, three Do 17s and two Bf 110s. 'Sailor' Malan's 74 'Tiger' Squadron reported five victories without any own losses.

But while Fighter Command was busy defending London, the Junkers 87s made a temporary reappearance on the stage. When the British coastal convoy CW.11 moved out from the Thames Estuary with six merchant ships escorted by two destroyers and a group of anti-submarine ships, the Stukagruppe II./StG 1 was deployed, escorted by Bf 110s.[345] Nine of the twenty-one Ju 87s attacked the escort destroyer *Atherstone*, which was hit by three bombs and had five near misses. Two others turned on the anti-submarine trawler *HMS Bay*, which was also damaged. *Atherstone* was so badly damaged that repairs took three months. Throughout the entire aerial attack the convoy commander repeatedly requested help from the RAF, but no British aircraft showed up. All the Ju 87s returned to the base.[346] Even the British were sending out aircraft against German maritime targets. On the evening of 11 September 100 RAF aircraft, divided into several small formations, flew towards the ports of Le Havre, Boulogne, Calais and Dunkirk. They dropped about 80 tonnes of bombs and succeeded in destroying close to one hundred barges. Additionally six torpedo planes – Fairey Albacore biplanes from Fleet Air Arm's 826 Squadron – as well as eleven Blenheims from Bomber Command's 53 and 59 squadrons attacked a German convoy off the coast at Calais. They were escorted by twelve Blenheim fighters from 235 Squadron. Bf 109 pilots from I./JG 52 and III./JG 53 reported shooting down five Albacores and four Blenheims without any own losses. The actual British losses were limited to two Blenheims and one shot down and three damaged Albacores.

12–14 September 1940

'Again bad weather. Thick clouds hang low over the Channel coast. Our Geschwader is granted a day off.'[347] These lines from Hannes Trautloft's diary on 12 September 1940 highlight the Luftwaffe's growing difficulties with the autumn weather. It was not just the poor visibility which made flight operations difficult or impossible, but many of the provisional airfields the Germans had constructed in fields in the Pas de Calais area were turned into marshland by the persistent rain. This was particularly the case regarding the airfields that had been hurriedly made for the fighter units arriving from Luftflotte 3 in late August. For example, because of the the soggy runway at Fiennes, II./JG 27 failed to get a single plane into the air for several days. The unit's war diary reads: 'As soon as possible, the transfer will take place from Fiennes to St. Inglevert, an airfield that at least *has a grass field*, but unfortunately is visible from Dover.' (Author's italics.)

PEACE OVERTURES

While Hitler had bombs raining down on London, he made a last desperate effort to end the war with Britain. His 'secret' representative in Stockholm, Ludwig Weissauer, told the Swedish President of the Court of Appeal, Birger Ekeberg, that he wished to meet with the British Ambassador Victor Mallet for peace talks. Weissauer announced that it was Hitler's view that 'for the white race there must be two great economic units – Germany, the continental unit, and the British Empire and America.' Basically, it was a repetition of Hitler's peace invitation from July 1940.[1] Mallet's reply came on 11 September, transmitted to Weissauer via Ekeberg: 'His Majesty's Government did not enter this war for selfish aims, but for large and general purposes affecting the freedom and independence of many States in Europe. [. . .] The intention of all the peoples of the British Empire to prosecute the war has been strengthened by the many horrible crimes committed by the rulers of Nazi Germany against the smaller States on her borders, and by the indiscriminate bombing of London without the slightest relation to military objectives.'[2]

The following night the Luftwaffe sent 217 bombers for a violent attack against London, resulting in 235 dead and 1,000 injured.[3]

1. National Archives, Kew. FO 371/24408.
2. National Archives, Kew. CAB 65/15/3.
3. National Archives, Kew. CAB 66/12/12.

501 Squadron's James Harry Lacey, best known as 'Ginger', was one of the RAF's most successful fighter aces during the Battle of Britain. In November 1940, he had 23 air victories, but by that time he had also himself been shot down no less than nine times. In August 1941, when Lacey was withdrawn from the front service, he had 28 air victories. Lacey passed away in May 1989, aged 72.

On the other side of the Channel the Spitfires stood in hangars that had been repaired one week previously. Damaged aircraft were restored, losses were replaced and the calm was used to train the inexperienced newcomers from flight schools. The weather did not affect the state of the British airfields – they were all constructed before the war, on land that was properly drained.

There were so few German aircraft that disturbed the calm of the stormy period that if any did appear on one of these rainy days, the RAF unit commanders could afford the luxury of sending up volunteers to meet them.

And then came 13 September – Friday 13th. When low cloud, rain and fog had covered the area for the second day in a row, Göring decided to send some crews trained in instrument flying to carry out nuisance raids on London and

a number of British fighter airbases. Hornchurch, North Weald and Debden were included in the list of targets. According to a well-known story, 501 Squadron's Sergeant 'Ginger' Lacey is meant to have shot down, at 12:40, the He 111 which bombed Buckingham Palace. A few German bombs did fall on Buckingham Palace on 13 September. There is no German record that says that any bomber was shot down on this day, but of the thirteen Ju 88s from LG 1 that took off towards London at midday (British time), one was badly damaged by a British fighter.[348]

In the duel between Lacey and the gunner on the Ju 88, Unteroffizier Werner Gottlieb, Gottlieb was wounded but managed to get in some bad hits on his opponent. Lacey was forced to abandon his mauled Hurricane. He bailed out and got stuck in some tree branches. As he hung there, an elderly man in a Home Guard uniform came and pointed a double-barrelled shotgun at the young aviator. 'For God's sake!' Lacey roared terrified and added a long list of Anglo-Saxon fire and brimstone profanities. 'That's fine', the old man replied: 'Anyone who can swear like that can't possibly be German.'

'Ginger' Lacey had been in combat almost continuously since May 1940. He was known to never avoid a fight – however unfavourable the odds may have been. This meant that he was shot down several times, but he miraculously survived each time and was usually back in the midst of it the day after, hurt or not. Several of his combat reports show the most incredible breaches of all of the tactical instructions the flight schools gave, and he shot down German aircraft in a most unprecedented manner. Up until this Friday the thirteenth Lacey had broght down 15 German aircraft. In August 1941, when he was taken out of combat in order to serve as a flight instructor of new fighter pilots, his 28 victories gave him third place among the RAF aces and he had twice been awarded with the Distinguished Flying Medal (DFM). He did three tours as a fighter pilot in the Second World War and was fortunate to survive. After the war, Lacey continued his career in the RAF. 'Ginger' Lacey died in May 1989, aged 72.

The bombing of Buckingham Palace came as a godsend for the British authorities. They had been worried by the political implications of the poor in the shoddily-built workers' houses in the East End having to bear the heaviest burden of the German bombings. Soon, large quantities of postcards depicting the king and queen in front of their bombed palace were in circulation in the whole of Britain.

Hitler was furious about the effects that these bombs had. Propaganda Minister Goebbels called an emergency meeting for the Propaganda Department and gave orders to the Luftwaffe liaison officer in Goebbels' Ministry, Oberst Rudolf Wodarg, to immediately find out if there were any military targets in the vicinity of the British royal palace. 'If not,' said Goebbels, 'we must maintain that secret military stores were hidden in its immediate vicinity.' By now the German leadership began to grow impatient. Since the large scale attacks against London had begun, Luftwaffe operations had been completely or partially foiled by the weather five days out of seven. Things didn't go much better at night. On the nights of 12/13 and 13/14 no more than 71 people were killed in bombing raids on London.[349]

When Saturday the 14th dawned with the same miserable weather, Göring knew that he could not afford to wait any longer. Because Hitler had called him to Berlin for a conference with the commanders of the three Wehrmacht branches, he ordered a new daylight attack against the British capital – bad weather or not. First especially selected bomber crews were to knock out the radar stations on the English south coast, after which the Bf 109 fighter-bombers of II.(S)/LG 2 would openly fly over London with a large number of fighters. The aim was again to lure large parts of Fighter Command into battle. Meanwhile, single planes or bombers in smaller formations would attack the coastal towns of Brighton and Eastbourne in order to drag the defence westwards and leave passage for the main force which would head for London – accompanied by large numbers of escort fighters.

But this was not Göring's day. The information the Führer gave came as a shock for the Air Force Commander: Operation 'Seelöwe' was to be postponed. It was certainly necessary – Hitler stressed that 'The Luftwaffe's operations are more than commendable', and that that it was mainly the unstable weather that prevented the Germans from acquiring total domination in the air. But Hitler could not say when the new date for 'Seelöwe' would be; he wanted to wait another three days before he announced the new date. The worst thing was that General Alfred Jodl, Chief of the Wehrmachtführungsstab, afterwards confided to the assembly that Hitler had actually decided the day before to give up operation 'Seelöwe' altogether![350]

Göring, however, is thought to have have hoped that Hitler would still set an invasion date as he set out on his long return journey back to the Channel on the afternoon of 14 September. On his arrival he was met by sombre reports.

Events had not gone according to Göring's plans. For the entire day the weather had caused problems for his airmen. During the attacks against the radar stations visibility had been too poor to allow for effective bombing.

At half past five (German time), the bomb-laden machines of Hauptmann Otto Weiss' II.(S)/LG 2 had moved off towards England with fighters from JG 26, JG 27, JG 51, JG 54 and JG 77 – a total of about 150 Bf 109s. They flew towards London at an altitude of 5,000 metres and managed to provoke the British into sending up a large number of fighters – no less than twenty-two squadrons from 11 Group and five from 12 Group. But even if the British had met the Germans in combat, things had not gone as Göring had hoped; as soon as the Brits realized that there were no bombers, they disengaged from the clashes and disappeared into the clouds on their way back to their bases. Only a handful of British fighters were shot down. Among the German losses was the adjutant of I./JG 26, Oberleutnant Kurt Dähne. He fell prey to Sergeant Allen Dredge from 253 Squadron. On the other side, Major Adolf Galland could report his 31st victory on his return to France, and in his old III./JG 26, one of his protégés, Oberleutnant Joachim Müncheberg, had got his 20th. But overall the results were meagre.

The Messerschmitts landed at a quarter to six. The planes ware refuelled, ammunition was refilled, new bombs were hung under the bellies of the planes in II.(S)/LG 2, and an hour later they went back for a similar operation. This was, in almost all respects, a repeat of the first. Again the German penetration initially resulted in quite extensive air fighting, but soon the boys of Fighter Command broke off and dived towards their own bases again. Although the day's result – 25 victories against four own fighters lost – was an impressive yield, Göring was far from happy. It would take more than 25 downed British fighters to break the back of Fighter Command! He would certainly not have been more satisfied if he had known that the real British losses on 14 September were only about half of the German reports – 12 fighters destroyed and another five making force-landings.

15 September 1940: 'Battle of Britain Day'

Although no one on the German side was aware of the actual figures for the RAF's strength and losses, they could figure out that the British Air Force was becoming stronger with every 'quiet' day that passed. Despite several devastating attacks on the British aircraft industry, Britain's total fighter production was only slightly affected. The supply of new British fighter aircraft was reduced from 1,261 during the five weeks 7 July to 10 August, to 1,154 in the following five-week period (11 August–14 September). In the latter figure are also included 26 Brewster Buffalo fighters that came from the USA. Like other US fighters at this time, however, the Buffalo was hopelessly inferior to the Germans' Messerschmitts, and the British palmed some of them off on the Fleet Air Arm and sent the rest to the Far East – far beyond the reach of German fighters in both cases. It is unlikely that any Buffalo ever fought in the Battle of Britain, although it has been popular among some German writers to speculate that the difference between German victory claims and British loss statistics can partly be explained by unreported Buffaloes.

In any event, it was clear that the Germans needed a quick decisive victory. When Sunday 15 September dawned with bright sunshine on a nearly cloudless sky – for the first time since 7 September the weather forecast appeared to promise excellent 'attack weather' for the entire day – no one doubted that the decisive moment had come.

It was time for the final showdown between the Luftwaffe and Dowding's rested and reinforced Fighter Command that was up to full strength. This was the day that has gone down in British history as the 'Battle of Britain Day', the day the battle was decided.

Göring's plan was to pull Fighter Command into a crucial clash through two major operations against London, one in the morning and one in the afternoon. The morning attack would be carried out by only 27 Do 17s from I. and III./KG 76, but these were to be accompanied by more than four times as many fighters, 120 Bf 109s from JG 3, JG 27, JG 52 and JG 53 and all available Zerstörers. 'Our instructions read: "Assemble at 6,000 metres over Cap Gris

Hurricane fighters are being prepared for a new combat mission.

Nez, where you will rendezvous with the bombers'", said Feldwebel Hermann Neuhoff from III./JG 53.[351] Additionally twenty-two fighter-bombers from II.(S)/LG 2 were sent in at high altitude.

The German bomber pilots had been given strict instructions to keep the formation as tight as possible. This would improve the firepower of the defensive machine guns, but it also meant that the entire formation adjusted its speed to that of the slowest bomber. An even less successful consequence of this was that it made the Bf 109s use up far too much of their small fuel load while orbiting above the bombers while they slowly crawled along 5,000 metres over the Strait of Dover. Moreover, the Dorniers met an increasing headwind which further reduced their speed.

That day, Winston Churchill had decided to pay a visit to Keith Park's headquarters at the Uxbridge bunker. He arrived just in time to see how the orders to take off went out. A request was also sent to 10 Group to dispatch the fighters at Middle Wallop. Shortly afterwards the commander of 12 Group, Leigh-Mallory, was asked if he could have the entire Duxford Wing patrol at 20,000 feet (6,000 metres) over Hornchurch. He ordered up five squadrons – 19, 242, 302, 310 and 611. The new Polish 302 Squadron had replaced No. 74 'Tiger' Squadron, whose more individualistic warriors had not been able to accept the thought of operating in a Big Wing.

At 11:50 (British time) the Biggin Hill Spitfires of 72 and 92 squadrons slid and sled in the thin air 8,000 metres high above Canterbury. This beautiful autumn Sunday it was bitterly cold at this high altitude, and the pilots of the small Spitfires did not know if they were shaking from the cold or the excitement. Suddenly they saw far ahead, and approximately one thousand metres below, a cloud of tiny dots. As they got closer they saw even more of them two thousand metres further down.

'Tally-ho right, here they come!' – called Flight Lieutenant Brian Kingcombe, one of 92 Squadron's pilots. He felt the frenzy of battle taking hold of him. They had managed to climb high above the highest German fighters! Now they were about to give them what they deserved!

'Okay, boys, let's go!'

The order had an electrifying effect. The Spitfires rolled and dived while the pilots uncocked their guns.

'Achtung! Indianer von oben!' – Watch out! Enemy fighters from above! – sounded the cry in the headphones of the Messerschmitt pilots from JG 53, which was the German formation's top cover. Though the Germans were cruising at 7,000 metres, the damned Spitfires were coming from above!

The first blow hit I./JG 53, and the first plane to go down in flames belonged to Feldwebel Herbert Tzschoppe.[352] As he threw himself out of the cockpit of his doomed 109, two other airmen in the same unit were also leaving their plunging machines. Although he had been wounded by British bullets, Oberfeldwebel Alfred "Molinero" Müller managed to bail out and float down to captivity. Oberleutnant Julius Haase, the commander of 2./JG 53, was not so lucky; his parachute refused to open. For more than a minute he tumbled helplessly through the air before vio-

A Do 17 from 2./KG 76.

lently hitting the ground. Unteroffizier Hans Schersand died in the flames of his burning Bf 109.

No. 72 Squadron's Flight Lieutenant John Wolferstan Villa, commonly known as 'Pancho Villa', scored two of these victories. The Messerschmitt formation was scattered by the devastating attack from above. 'We were met by a superior number of British fighters, and our formations dispersed into individual dogfights', Hauptmann Hans-Karl Mayer, the commander of I./JG 53, later wrote in his report.[353] In the confused combat that ensued, Mayer claimed to have shot down a Spitfire, while Unteroffizier Willi Ghesla reported that he had saved a comrade by destroying a Spitfire that was pursuing his 109. The pilots of III./JG 53, who rushed to the rescue claimed to have shot down another three Spitfires. In fact not one Spitfire was shot down during the mission – a sign as good as any of the confusion that the British caused by their attack.

After attacking I./JG 53, Nos. 72 and 92 squadrons continued on towards the Dornier bombers, which came cruising along further down in the company of the Bf 109s from JG 3. 'Pancho' Villa claimed to have shot down one of the Dorniers, but then the intense defensive fire from the tightly packed bombers forced the British to break off. The Spitfire pilots left the scene in a steep dive.

While 72 and 92 Squadrons returned to base, three new squadrons appeared. Spitfires from 603 Squadron attacked the Messerschmitt 109s. Squadron Leader 'Uncle' George Denholm and Pilot Officer McPhail were credited with shooting down one Bf 109 each without the unit losing any of its own aircraft.

When the Hurricanes from the 'pair' 253 and 501 squadrons appeared on the scene, they were slightly lower than the Dorniers, but they managed to make their way up to the bombers and shoot down a Do 17 without being spotted by the German fighters. Then they too were dragged into combat with the numerically superior Messerschmitt escort. This also applied to No. 605 Squadron.

The Dornier bombers continued along the Thames Estuary towards London. Up till then, only one Do 17 had been lost. In contrast, several burning Hurricanes had tumbled from the sky, but only a few German fighters. The RAF pilots even had a problem with one lonely Do 17, 'F1+FH', which due to an engine failure limped on one kilometre behind the others. Several British airmen made repeated attacks on this Dornier and finally the crew bailed out of the bullet-riddled machine. But the pilot, Oberleutnant Robert Zehbe, had switched on the autopilot, so the plane carried on dead ahead like a flying zombie, and in the following minutes drew the attention of even more Hurricanes. According to historian Stephen Bungay it was reported as shot down no less than nine times.[354]

Unteroffizier Hans Zonderlind, who sat in the cramped cabin of a Do 17 from III./KG 76 in the air over the Thames during those long minutes, recalled: 'From the time that we came in over Maidstone until we reached the outskirts of London, we had been under extreme pressure. The British fighters had been with us since we had first crossed the English coast and their attacks grew in intensity all the time. Our escort had been doing a grand job with the Spitfires at keeping them away from us, and we thought

A formation of He 111s. (Photo: Waiss.)

Pilot Officer Jan Malinski from the new 302 Squadron. This unit had its first major clash with the Luftwaffe on 15 September 1940 and was recorded for ten victories against one own loss. (Photo: Jacek Kutzner by Tomasz Szlagor.)

that would things remain like this, then this bombing run would be an easy one.'[355]

But with ever more new formations of Spitfires and Hurricanes appearing in the sky ahead of them, an increasing number of German fighter pilots lost contact with the bombers. To the Dornier airmen's horror they saw that there were fewer and fewer '109s left as they neared London. So far, they had managed to ward off attacks by single Hurricanes. Perhaps they started hoping that they had seen everything that the RAF had?

The target now spread out in front of them. At that moment several crews shouted together: In front of them the whole sky full of dots. *Mein Gott!* What was this? The British had another entire air force on standby?

It was the Duxford Wing, led by Squadron Leader Bader. The effect was terrible as four squadrons attacked together.

Bader saw the '109s as 'little grey sharks' high up. He called Squadron Leader 'Sandy' Lane, who led the Spitfires of No. 19 Squadron:

'Sandy, watch those '109s!'

'OK, chum, I can see them!' came the reply.

Lane's Spitfires climbed to meet the '109s while the Hurricanes pounced on the bombers. Several Do 17s were hit and began trailing smoke. Unteroffizier Hans Zonderlind remembers the impression the Duxford Wing made: 'We saw the Hurricanes coming towards us and it seemed that the whole of the RAF was there, we had never seen so many British fighters coming at us at once. I saw a couple of our comrades go down, and we got hit once but it did no great damage. All around us were dogfights as the fighters went after each other, then as we were getting ready for our approach to the target, we saw what must have been a hundred RAF fighters coming at us. We thought that this must have been all the RAF planes up at once, but where were they coming from, as we had been told that the RAF fighters were very close to extinction.'[356]

The remaining Dorniers continued and turned in over central London – where they were met by the barrage from General Pile's anti-aircraft guns.

Last of all came the stray Do 17 'F1+FH'. Sergeant Ray Holmes from 501 Squadron aimed his Hurricane at this Dornier. Afterwards Holmes could not tell if he rammed it on purpose or if he simply became hypnotized by the bomber which so stubbornly kept on dead ahead. 'I just went straight ahead and hit the Dornier' he said. Although Bader chased another Do 17, he saw clearly how the Hurricane flew into the German plane, whose tail section was torn off in the collision, then the whole plane seemed to fold up. Both wings broke off outboard of the engines and it fell with such force that its bombs exploded. It smashed down into Victoria Station with a series of violent explosion. Meanwhile Holmes dragged himself out of his spinning Hurricane and pulled his parachute's rip-cord.

Twenty-five Do 17s were now being harried by no less than 160 British fighters. Do 17 'F1+FS' from 8./KG 76 was hit by three bursts that smashed both engines and the glass-covered cockpit. With Feldwebel Stephan Schmidt hanging dead in his straps and another man wounded, the injured pilot fought the slipstream as he took the plane down. An emergency landing was his least bad option. 'We managed to get between two cumulus clouds and had to force-land in a field which sloped uphill', said Feldwebel Rolf Heitsch, the only crew member aboard 'F1+FS' who escaped being hit by British bullets.[357]

Six Do 17s had been lost – almost every fourth plane – when a new large group of fighters showed up against the sky to the south. This time it was Messerschmitts that swept in in order to cover their return. It was in the nick of time! The British fighters saw fit to break off action instead of challenging these Messerschmitts, which had arrived with full ammunition belts.

Four damaged Do 17s barely got back across the Channel. One of them, with Oberleutnant Martin Florian bleeding from gunshot wounds, crashed near Poix. Another crash-landed near Boulogne. Three wounded airmen were extracted from the wrecked machine. One of them died shortly afterwards.

Meanwhile, those among the downed airmen that had the good fortune to survive tried to regain contact with reality. Near Shoreham four young German airmen were trapped in the belly-landed Do 17 'F1+FS'. One of them, Feldwebel Stephan Schmidt, was dead, and two others were bleeding from gunshot wounds. 'We could not get out because the exits had been so badly damaged by gunfire' recalled Feldwebel Rolf Heitsch, the only one not wounded.[358] Shortly afterwards a group of British Home-Guardsmen arrived and freed them from the wreckage to take them prisoner. Feldwebel Pfeiffer and Feldwebel Sauter were taken to a nearby hospital while the shocked Feldwebel Heitsch was taken to the local police station for interrogation. The war was now over for him, and he had almost eight years of war captivity in front of him.

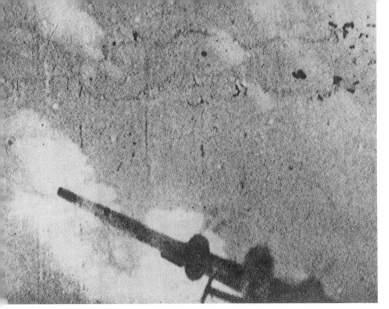

A camera mounted to the machine guns on a British fighter registers the attack on a Bf 110 during the afternoon battle on 15 September 1940.

For Oberleutnant Robert Zehbe, the 24-year-old pilot who had jumped out of Do 17 'F1+FH', which was later rammed by Sergeant Ray Holmes, the end arrived sooner. While Zehbe floated down in his parachute towards Kensington a large crowd of people gathered on the street below. Zehbe's parachute got caught on the top of a telegraph pole leaving him hanging half a metre above the ground surrounded by a furious crowd consisting mainly of women. A reporter from the *Daily Herald* wrote afterwards that Zehbe had desperately appealed to him, 'Kamerad, Kamerad. I am an officer, I am an officer!' When a policeman arrived shortly afterwards, Zehbe was still hanging in his parachute cords, badly injured. The German airman was transferred to Millbank Military Hospital, where he died the next day from his injuries.

At that time, no one could even begin to imagine that this day would go down in history as the turning point of the Battle of Britain. Fighter Command had dispatched 254 Spitfires and Hurricanes against 120 Bf 109s and 27 Do 17s. The result of such an effort was undeniably relatively lean. 6 German bombers and 7 fighters were shot down. In exchange, the RAF had lost 12 Hurricanes and Spitfires. At that time no one on the British side knew that the ratio was so bad. After returning to base excited RAF pilots reported that they had shot down 87 German aircraft. 80 of them were even confirmed!

On the German side the situation was seen as considerably more serious. Certainly the fighter escort had yet again done a very good job, which seemed to be the norm since Göring had arrived at the Channel area to personally take command of operations. But the very large number of British fighters that the Germans had been confronted with came as a shock to them. 'The men and the NCOs were very critical when we returned to base. Had this been "the last fifty Spitfires" that our commanders had been talking about?' said Hermann Neuhoff, who served as a Feldwebel in III./JG 53.

On the other hand this first attack was just the vanguard intended to soften up the British forces before the main attack. This was launched at two in the afternoon, British time. The force that now took off to attack London was much bigger than the noon formation – 114 bombers and 360 fighters. The bombers were divided into four waves, with 43 Do 17s from II. and III./KG 2 in the lead,

followed by, in turn, 24 He 111s from I. and II./KG 53, 19 Do 17s from II./KG 3 and finally 28 He 111s from I. and II./KG 26. Galland's JG 26 and Mölders' JG 51 went out first of all, free hunting between Dover and London. Major Günther Lützow led his entire JG 3 on the top cover mission, to which also II./JG 2, I./JG 52, III./JG 53 and I.(J)/LG 2 were assigned. Major Trautloft led his Stabsstaffel and I./JG 54 on the close escort mission, which was shared with 20 Bf 110s from II./ZG 76 'Haifischgruppe' and V.(Z)/LG 1. Feldwebel Hermann Neuhoff from III./JG 53 recalled: 'Once again the instruction reads: "Assemble at 6,000 metres over Cap Gris Nez, where you will rendezvous with the bombers." This time we flew together with He 111s, which really were "lame ducks" compared to our fast '109s.' [359]

They were met by eleven squadrons from 11 Group, several units from 10 Group and the entire Duxford Wing. As with earlier that day Fighter Command's response began with an attack on the Bf 109s by Spitfires coming from much higher up where they had been guided by the air controllers – with the assistance of regular information from the Observer Corps posts. Again No. 92 Squadron was in the lead, this time with 41 and 222 squadrons. They came down on the Bf 109s of the top cover and spread disorder in their ranks.

Yet the two sides appear to have been able to defend themselves quite well during these initial fighter clashes. Only 222 Squadron's Flying Officer Desmond McMullen succeeded in shooting down a Bf 109 from 7./JG 51 during the quick attack. The German pilot, Leutnant Kurt Bildau, bailed out.

Several Spitfires and Hurricanes engaged Major Galland's JG 26 in a swirling battle, without any planes being shot down. At the same time other squadrons got past the German fighters, and when the German bombers flew over the coast they were subjected to furious attacks. This time the RAF fighter pilots did a lot of frontal attacks but the gunners aboard the German planes managed to hold them off.

Nineteen-year-old Pilot Officer 'Mike' Cooper-Slipper (605 Squadron) managed to get through to the Do 17 formation from II./KG 3 and was about to attack when 20mm shells from a Messerschmitt set his own Hurricane on fire. He may have been hit by Gefreiter Hans Swietlik, a pilot in V.(Z)/LG 1, who shot down the first British fighter during the afternoon operation. But Cooper-Slipper refused to be distracted from his target! He flew at full speed straight into the starboard wing of Do 17 '5K+YN', belonging to 5./KG 3. Both aircraft lost a wing and fell in a cloud of debris before the eyes of the other shocked airmen of II./KG 3. Four parachutes opened. They carried Cooper-Slipper and three of the Germans towards the ground. One of the German pilots remained in the descending plane. On the ground Cooper-Slipper had a possibly even more upsetting experience when a group of civilians mistook him for a German and he came close to being lynched.

Further ahead in the stream of German bombers, the He 111s from KG 53 warded off most of the British fighter attacks. Flying Officer Arthur Yuile from 1 RCAF Squadron was wounded in the shoulder and steered his damaged Hurricane back to Northolt, where it was classified as 'Damaged Category 2'. Even Pilot Officer Keith Lofts from 249 Squadron had his Hurricane put out of action by the Heinkel gunners, and he crashed at West Malling.

From KG 2, which led the German attack formation, a Do 17 airman said: 'We are escorted by one fighter and one Zerstörer Geschwader. Our escort takes good care of the British.' [360]

Major Trautloft in JG 54 described the sight that greeted him as he approached London: 'At the same height as I was flying, but far away to the right, I saw Zerstörer planes shoot down two British fighters. Both of these fell burning to the ground. A little further down an Me 109 approached a Spitfire from behind. Shortly afterwards the enemy aircraft made a half roll and went into a nosedive. Just before it reached the clouds below, an object detached from the aircraft. It was the pilot. A few seconds later he hung like a small dot underneath his white parachute and then disappeared into the thick overcast.' [361]

Sergeant Reginald Llewellyn (213 Squadron), who, with 13½ victories belonged to the élite of Fighter Command, was shot down and badly wounded by a Bf 110. Ironically Llewellyn was counted as one of Fighter Command's best 'Messerschmitt 110 killers', and had six of these on his tally.

Major Galland disengaged from the first unsuccessful combat with the Spitfires and headed northwards with his Stabsschwarm. By then Park had ordered up his last available units. Park's greatest hope rested with the Duxford Wing, which had performed miracles in the last raid. He could see it on the plotting table approaching the German formations. But there was also a German formation heading towards the Duxford Wing!

While the Duxford Wing led by Squadron Leader Bader climbed to reach an attack position east of London, Galland and the yellow-nosed Messerschmitt 109s of his JG 26 'Schlageter' flew in above them. The sight of the mass of British fighters reminded Galland, an enthusiastic hunter, of a flock of pheasants. He immediately gave his pilots the attack orders and shoved his control stick forward. His Bf 109, embellished with a painting of Mickey Mouse beneath the cockpit, went into a dive towards Bader's Wing.

Douglas Bader cursed when he saw Galland's Messerschmitts come hurtling down. His biographer Paul Brickhill recreates the combat from Bader's perspective: 'Over his shoulder the yellow spinners were diving on them and he yelled as he steep-turned, "Break up!" Around him the sky was full of wheeling Hurricanes and 109's. A yellow spinner was sitting behind his tail, and as he yanked harder back on the stick an aeroplane shot by, feet away. Bader hit its slipstream and the Hurricane shuddered, stalled and spun off the turn. He let it spin a few turns to shake off the 109 and came out of it at 5,000 feet.' [362]

While Bader dived away to save himself, Galland pushed his control stick forwards and surprised two Hurricanes from Czech 310 Squadron. These were flown by Pilot Officer Alexander Hess and Sergeant Josef Hubáček. Before the Czechs had realized the danger Galland and his wingman, Oberleutnant Walter Horten, were on them.

Hubáček said afterwards: 'I had the impression that I heard machine gun fire behind me. I looked back several times but I did not see anything. I retrimmed the aircraft, but at that moment I was hit – I do not know by what.' [363]

To attack without being seen was the hallmark of a prominent ace and Galland mastered that skill to perfection. Hubáček's 'NN-X' (R4087) fell before Galland's guns and Hess' 'NN-A' (R4085) was torn to pieces by Horten's guns. Hubáček immediately threw himself out of the burning plane and opened his parachute. Hess managed to steer his shattered plane away from some buildings below before he also bailed out. Adolf Galland's combat report reads: 'After an inconclusive combat with about 8 Hurricanes where I lost a lot of height, I went along with my Stabsschwarm to attack two Hurricanes 800 metres below. I took advantage of the element of surprise and approached the British wingman. When he made a gentle turn to the left, I gave him a burst of fire from a distance of 120 metres. The enemy aircraft reeled as my rounds struck the nose from below, and pieces were torn off the left wing and fuselage. The left side of the fuselage caught fire. The enemy leader was shot down in fire by my wingman, Oberleutnant Horten.' [364]

After both Czech pilots bailed out, Galland and his men quickly set off back to France with the red warning light on the instrument panel winking – showing that their fuel was running out.

While the Hurricanes' Wing formation dissolved, 'Sandy' Lane again led his Spitfires from 19 Squadron against the overwhelming mass of Bf 109s. Major Günther Lützow, the commander of JG 3, saw them coming but could not prevent the nimble Spitfires from shooting down three Messerschmitt 109s, all from I./JG 3. The unit's war diary noted: 'During the attack of the nine Spitfires, Oberfeldwebel Oljenik lost sight of his Rottenführer, Oberleutnant Reumschlüssel – who was recorded as missing after that mission. Oberfeldwebel Hessel also lost contact with his comrades. He was heard calling his unit on the radio, but we never saw him again. Oberfeldwebel Bucholz got a radiator hit and had to ditch in the sea.' [365]

19 Squadron's Flight Sergeant George 'Grumpy' Unwin shot down another two Bf 109s to add to the one that he bagged in the morning. In the meantime, Polish 303 Squadron – which only had nine operational planes after the unit's efforts earlier that day – was able to get at the Do 17s from KG 2 while these flew towards London, and went in to the attack with throttles on maximum. But as on several occasions in the past the effect of their attack was reduced by bad formation discipline. The unit's Operations Record Book reads:

'S/L Kellett was ordered to patrol Northolt at 20,000 ft. and took off with the nine serviceable machines. The other Squadrons had left sometime previously and 303 operated throughout alone. On reaching a height of 6000 ft. the Squadron was vectored 100 degrees and climbed over the I.A.Z. When still 2,000 ft below their patrol level, they sighted coming head on from the southeast a very large formation of bombers and fighters. The Bombers were in vics of three sections line astern with Me110s in sq formation between

Flight Sergeant George 'Grumpy' Unwin, 19 Squadron. In 1936 the coal miner's son Unwin arrived as a newly trained pilot at 19 Squadron, which two years later became the first unit to be equipped with Spitfires. Therefore, he had more experience than most others on the Spitfire when the Battle of Britain began. Unwin attained 14 air victories in 1940 and was awarded the DFM twice in the space of two months. He passed away on 28 June 2006, at 93 years of age.

the vics of Bombers. To the flanks and stepped up above to 25,000 ft. were many formations of Me109s. Blue Section had got rather in front of the others, and wheeling round to let them come up. S/L Kellett had to deliver a quarter frontal attack instead of head on. This he did initially with only the other two members of Blue Section – Sgt. [Miroslaw] Wojciechowski and P/O [Walerian] Zak. Probably as there were a lot of clouds about, the enemy imagined that this was the advance guard of a large force and began to wheel towards the east, and when the other two sections came in they turned completely to the east. After the first rush the Me110s and the 109s fell upon the nine Hurricanes which were compelled to defend themselves individually as best they could, and escaped destruction in the clouds.' [366]

Squadron Leader Witold Urbanowicz, Polish unit commander with Kellett as co-commander, made a frontal attack against a Do 17 and opened fire with the glass-covered cabin in his gunsight. With its pilot lying dead at the controls and one engine on fire, Do 17 'U5+JT' from 9./KG 2 entered its final dive. Only one man escaped – radio operator Unteroffizier Jacob Sehrt floated down in his parachute. Urbanowicz immediately attacked the next bomber. He said 'I attacked another ¾ from the rear, and after a long burst, one engine stopped working, aircraft lost speed, and began to lose height. Having satisfied myself that no enemy fighter was on my tail, I again attacked the bomber, and fir-

ing from a distance of 150 yards, saw him burst into flames and fall into the sea.' [367]

Two men from the crew on Do 17 'U5+FT', also from 9./KG 2, bailed out while this plane crashed again with a dead pilot at the controls. But then the German fighter escort arrived on the scene. Urbanowicz continued his account: 'Suddenly I see that the fighters are diving towards us. A bit too late. Alas, one pilot from my flight is mortally hit, he never bales out, his plane bursts into flames. One more is trailing black smoke, something separates from the plane, a parachute opens up. Thank God, at least the pilot is safe! There are only three of us left, we keep on chasing the bombers.' [368]

Back at the bunker in Uxbridge, Churchill noticed that Park grew tense. At the wall where the state of the squadrons was indicated, all the light bulbs were glowing red.

'What other reserves have we?' Churchill asked.

Park turned around.

'None!' he snapped.

But by that time, the German fighters had been engaged in bitter fighting with scores of RAF planes for 20 minutes. And now – when it really 'mattered' – the petrol in the Messerschmitt 109s began running out. Despite the fact that the red warning lights had been on long ago, the German fighter pilots stayed for another few minutes and tried to help the hard-pressed bombers. But in the end they had to leave for their own side of the Channel. Oberleutnant Friedrich-Karl Müller, an ace from III./JG 53, was forced to ditch his Bf 109 in the Channel with empty fuel tanks. Some other pilots managed to glide their Bf 109s – with stationary propellers – to the French Channel coast. Two of them were seriously injured in the emergency landings that followed. [369]

The Bf 110s did their best to defend the bombers, but they were only twenty to many more Spitfires and Hurricanes. Squadron Leader Ronald Kellett of 303 Squadron said: *'I fired at a Do 215 [Do 17] from very close range – I saw pieces fly off both engines and front of the fuselage. I could not stay to see what happened as I was immediately attacked by four yellow-nosed Me 110s from all sides and had to dive to get out of it. I reached cloud and shook off the Me 110s by doing a series of turns. I climbed back where I could see streamers to the East. As I climbed I was again attacked, but by a single Me 110. I had no difficulty in evading him, and got on to his tail. I gave him two good bursts into his starboard engine from the quarter. The engine stopped and smoked, and flames burst from the wings. Enemy aircraft fell flaming into the clouds.'* [370]

V.(Z)/LG 1 lost three Bf 110s, and from one of them Oberleutnant Helmut Müller, the commander of 14. Staffel fell into captivity.

Exposed to the fury of the great mass of RAF pilots, the remaining German bombers quickly dropped their loads and dived off at full speed towards the English Channel. No. 607 Squadron came in on the German bombers' right flank and reported six downed. The Spitfires in 92 Squadron appeared again and Pilot Officer Howard Hill saw how the first Heinkel bomber he fired at caught fire while a crew member bailed out. He immediately attacked a second He

A shot down He 111.

111 and soon afterwards saw it crash in a wood by a beach on the Thames Estuary. Next he hit a third bomber, which was reported to have crashed near Rochester. Then he co-operated with other RAF pilots to shoot down a fourth and a fifth bomber! If only that morning's claim of a Messerschmitt 109 had been confirmed, Hill would have got the Battle of Britain's highest score for one day, six victories, unprecedented on either side.

Pilot Officer Crelin 'Bogle' Bodie, a Spitfire pilot from 66 Squadron, was cedited with shooting down three Do 17s. Scottish Flight Lieutenant Archie McKellar from 605 Squadron destroyed a Do 17; this together with two Bf 109s which he had claimed in the morning gave him a day's result of three. Another of the hundreds of RAF fighter pilots who chased the German bombers was 501 Squadron's Sergeant 'Ginger' Lacey; he reported that he had shot down a He 111 and a Bf 109 – which made his score for the day three victories. Horst Zander, observer aboard a Dornier 17 from II./KG 3, recalled: 'Our Gruppe had scattered. Each crew sought its own safety in a powered gliding race down over the sea and for home. [. . .] Suddenly our Dornier was struck hard. The cabin was full of blood. Our pilot was hit. In the intercom I heard him say feebly: "Heinz [Laube], you have to fly us home!"'

When the traumatised German crews that were lucky enough to escape had returned to their bases, every fifth aircraft was missing. KG 2 had sustained the heaviest losses – eight of its Do 17s had been shot down and another seven returned damaged. KG 53 lost six He 111s, which was 25 % of those sent out. Worst hit, however, was II./KG 3 – the six

crews that this Gruppe lost represented a frightening 30 % loss rate. Of the nineteen Do 17s from II./KG 3 which took off from Antwerp-Deurne, less than half got away without combat damage.

But in Uxbridge and Bentley Priory, Park and Dowding still had no clear picture of the victory they had just won. Just as the formations from Luftflotte 2 left British airspace, reports came in from the radar station at Ventnor on the Isle of Wight of German aircraft approaching from the Cotentin Peninsula. Sperrle had been instructed to dispatch a Gruppe of bombers against Portsmouth's harbour, and twenty-seven He 111 crews from KG 55 were given the assignment. But 10 Group was fully occupied fighting Luftflotte 2 further to the east. The defence had nothing but the Spitfire planes of 152 Squadron to defend Portsmouth. This failed, and bombs fell over the port facilities, with only one He 111 getting shot down.

Fighter Command succeeded no better two hours later, when thirteen Bf 110s from Erprobungsgruppe 210 again swooped down on the Supermarine Works in Woolston, Southampton. Although 10 and 11 Group scrambled seven squadrons, they failed to shoot down even one of the attacking aircraft – mainly because the air controllers erroneously directed the RAF pilots to too high an altitude. This was compensated for by Southampton's anti-aircraft guns, which alone were able to avert the attack.

When Churchill left Park at Uxbridge, 11 Group's tired commander told him:

'During the last twenty minutes we were so choked with information that we couldn't handle it. This shows you the limitation of our present resources. They have been strained far beyond their limits today.'

Indeed this was no exaggeration. On 15 September 1940 the RAF pilots gave proof of a fighting stamina that completely overwhelmed the Luftwaffe. This delivered a terrible blow to the morale of the German airmen, who until then had believed that the RAF was at the end of its tether. And now this proved to be completely false. The victory on 15 September was equally a result of the heroism of the RAF pilots and Park's modified tactics of constantly intercepting the German formations with pairs of squadrons. This was what had made the Bf 109s run out of fuel before the combat was over.

The great battle on 15 September was also decided by quantity. Fighter Command had not launched more fighters on 15 September than on any other day. The total of 709 sorties on 15 September had been surpassed several times – most recently the day before with 860. Since the 8 August, Fighter Command had made numerically larger daily efforts no less than fourteen times, including twice – 15 and 30 August – with more than a thousand fighters a day. But the record set in this regard was the number of British fighter pilots who *made contact* with the enemy on 15 September. With 550 contacts Fighter Command surpassed its own previous record by a wide margin – the previous best figures were 396 on 15 August, 390 on 31 August and 333 on 18 August. All other days the Germans had encountered fewer than 300 RAF fighter planes in combat. But the feat on 15 September was even more about qualitative measures; specifically the improved ability of the air controllers to bring the fighters into contact with the enemy. No less than 77 % of the British fighters that took off on 15 September engaged the enemy – which compares with just over 30 % on 15 August and 26 % on 30 August.

But Keith Park was still not satisfied. He knew how many British fighters had attacked the Germans, and yet they had not been able to prevent the bombing of London! When he received the victory reports he became furious; he dismissed as utter nonsense claims that 185* German aircraft had been shot down – in that case the Germans would not have been able to get through to London! Most of all Park was irritated by the information he received from his rival Leigh-Mallory who claimed that the Duxford Wing had definitely shot down 105 German aircraft and probably another 40, with another 18 damaged. Instead of letting himself be carried away by the euphoria, Park set out to analyse the shortcomings and mistakes that had been made: 'There are too many inexperienced leaders in the squadrons, interceptions were being missed and the pilots spent too much time on stragglers and lame ducks which were no military threat.' Park's attitude is characterized by a devoted professionalism; the only motive he had for his harsh criticism was to further sharpen the defence's efficiency – which he suceeded in doing. Politicians and others who were not in direct control of Fighter Command could by all means celebrate big victories, but Park did not have time for that. In that sense, he was like the commander of Fighter Command, Hugh Dowding, whose harsh humourlessness earned him the nickname 'Stuffy'.

The fact that the Germans claimed that 79 British and 43 German aircraft were shot down, while the British reported the losses as 25 British and 185* German aircraft, was an embarrassment to the British government. But they received no help from Dowding when Archibald Sinclair, Secretary of State for Air, asked him to comment on it. 'He was anxious about the effect on the American people of the wide divergence between the claims of the two sides', Dowding wrote after the war. Tiredly, Dowding replied: 'I'm not very interested in propaganda. The Americans will soon find out the truth. If the German figures are accurate they will be in London in a week, otherwise they will not.' Then he hung up. [371]

This attitude, which some regarded as haughty, probably contributed in no small measure to both Dowding and Park being dismissed from their posts as soon as the worst crisis in the Battle of Britain was over. It was also this uncompromising focus on professional management of Fighter Command that made it possible for Britain to resist the Luftwaffe assault which culminated on 15 September, 1940.

Churchill, a politician, of course reacted differently. The next day he triumphantly went onto the BBC and proclaimed – and unable to refrain from having a dig at the German propaganda : 'Aided by Czech and Polish squadrons, and using *only a small proportion* of their total strength, the Royal Air Force cut to rags and tatters separate waves of murderous assault upon the civil population of their native land.' Goebbels' German propaganda ministry responded with a lame comment: 'The effects of the last attack against London were probably so great that the British population must be calmed with such lies.'

Park was obviously right when he concluded that claims to have shot down nearly two hundred German aircraft were hugely exaggerated. Counting all operations that day – including a number of missions with much smaller forces – Luftwaffe combat losses on 15 September 1940 amounted to 57 aircraft. It was not the highest daily loss that the Luftwaffe suffered during the Battle of Britain. More were lost on 15 and 18 August, with 77 and 71 downed planes. But the loss ratio, that is losses in relation to the number of participating aircraft, reached a very serious level on 15 September. While the loss ratio was 4.5 per cent on 15 August and just over six per cent on 18 August, it reached seven per cent on 15 September.

Fighter Command had indeed, as we have seen, also had to pay a pretty high price for their success, but its 31 combat losses were still only half as high as the German – even with regard to loss ratio.

With hindsight, the communiqué from the German Wehrmacht headquarters appears slightly bizarre: 'Retaliation attacks were made against London despite difficult weather conditions . . . The enemy's total losses amounted to 79 aircraft.' [372]

Despite the exaggerated British reports on the number of destroyed enemy aircraft, Churchill was right – Fighter Command had achieved a fabulous victory. No one knew this better than the German leadership.

---

* The figure 185 is given here because this is the most common figure of British claims on 15 September 1940 in post-war accounts. Actually, the figure given in British press on 16 September was 175 (Daily Herald, Monday September 16, 1940), and at the meeting of the War Cabinet at noon on 16 September, Chief of the Air Staff, Air Chief Marshal Newall gave the figures 186 destroyed, 46 probable and 72 damaged.

CHAPTER 8

A CHANGE OF DIRECTION

16–20 September: New directives

'Herr Reichsmarschall, the British are bombing our Channel ports!'

A visibly shaken Reichsmarschall Göring sat absorbed in the reports of the day's combat results when a new message came in late on the evening of 15 September.

Undoubtedly, the RAF bomber crews displayed the same high fighting spirits as their colleagues in Fighter Command during the daytime. No target was more popular among Bomber Command's airmen than the Channel ports where the German invasion fleet gathered. Historian Alastair Revie notes that the bomber pilots had a sense of 'being with Drake against the Armada or with Nelson against Napoleon's forces at Boulogne'.[373]

During operations on the night of 15 September a twin-engined Handley Page Hampden from 83 Squadron was hit by anti-aircraft fire. An 88mm shell smashed into one wing tank, which exploded in a cloud of fire. It was pure luck that the whole wing was not torn off, but the flames spread and soon burned the inside of the aircraft. The rear gunner and the navigator both bailed out. As the heat from the flames began to make the cabin floor melt, the radio operator, 18-year-old Sergeant John Hannah, seized a fire extinguisher and managed, although half blinded and nearly unconscious from the smoke and the high temperature, to eventually extinguish the fire. With his uniform and the thick fur jacket scorched into rags and with his face and hands swollen from burns, he crawled forwards in the smoke-filled cabin, took a seat next to the pilot and helped him to navigate the aircraft back to England again. He became the fifth RAF airman to receive the Victoria Cross.

When Göring next day, 16 September, summoned his commanders to a conference in Boulogne, he was serious. He began by giving orders for a stronger defence of

the Channel ports. Then he summed up the great battle on 15 September. The German analysis underlined the British pilots' embittered resistance: 'The British have used the breathing space [because of bad weather] to strengthen their fighter force with pilots from flight schools and new material from their factories, including aircraft that have not yet even been painted. Thus, the enemy air force was greatly reinforced. The British engaged the German bomber units with less well trained fighter squadrons, with several cases of deliberate ramming taking place as a last resort. Meanwhile the German fighters came under attack from better trained British fighter pilots.'[374]

Göring was, in spite of everything, still optimistic. The weak resistance that the two attacks against Portsmouth and Southampton had met on the afternoon on 15 September undeniably seemed to suggest that the British had scraped together everything to defend London. From the German perspective, it looked as if 15 September has been Fighter Command's death spasm.

Although many of the statements that have been ascribed to Hermann Göring since the war have turned out to be inaccurate it is nevertheless clear that he was unhappy with the fighter pilots, who normally were his favourites. Göring indeed was usually much more prone to praise the fighter pilots than was the surly Park, but there were limits even for the jovial Reichsmarschall. As we have seen, the severe bomber losses on 15 September occurred when the Bf 109s had to leave the scene because their fuel was running low. The Luftwaffe Commander's criticism of the fighter pilots can be summarised in two points: they had failed to get the next wave of fighters in place at the right time, and they should have been able to shoot down more British aircraft. The objection from one of his commanders that the British surprised the Germans by sending in their fighters 'en masse' did not impress a warrior like Göring.

'Now that's good', he thundered. 'If they attack en masse, we should also be able to shoot them down in large numbers!'

At the same time Göring acknowledged that one important explanation for the fighter aircraft not performing according to expectations was the fatigue many pilots felt after the intense combat missions over England. He now demanded a last great effort by his men.

'We need only four or five such days, and that will be the end of the British fighter aviation', he said.

A Handley Page Hampden bomber from RAF Bomber Command's 144 Squadron. The Hampden, with a crew of four, entered service in 1938. By then, its top speed of 395 km/h made it the fastest among the RAF's three medium-heavy bombers (the other two were the Wellington and the Whitley). The armament consisted of six .303 machine guns, and the aircraft could carry a bomb load of 1,800 kg.

Göring's new directives, based on the analysis of 15 September, meant a certain change of direction. Admittedly attacks on London would continue – Fighter Command's record-breaking effort to defend its capital on the 15th showed that the Germans had found out how to force the British to take on the German fighters – but at the same time the RAF's ongoing reinforcement would be countered with a new air offensive against the British aviation industry. The Filton works in Bristol was singled out as a particularly important target.

Shortly afterwards Göring left the Channel area on board his special train 'Asia'.

While the generals met, the Luftwaffe unit commanders also used the bad-weather day of 16 September to analyse what went wrong on 15 September. In Compagne-les-Guines, Major Hannes Trautloft gathered his three Gruppenkommandeurs in JG 54 and he did not mince the words. The first thing he brought up was the notoriously poor radio discipline, which constituted a serious obstacle to the rational management of forces in combat: 'The radio discipline among the pilots must improve! There is far too much babbling on the radio, particularly during return flights!'

Then Trautloft addressed the subject of victory reports. It was not only on the British side that there was reason to question the size of the fighter pilots' claims. 'The victory reports reports must be more accurate', Trautloft demanded. 'Only indubitable reports are to be submitted!'

He was also keen to bolster the fighting spirits among the men in the units that had less 'glamorous', but no less important tasks – the ground personnel: 'Even the Gruppen commanders have to show themselves among the technical staff on the airfields. Make sure that you pay attention to and promote qualified mechanics, arms technicians, radio operators, truck drivers and so on!' Eventually Trautloft touched on the complaints he heard from his pilots: 'The nightly anti-aircraft gunfire disrupts the pilots' important sleep. Explore the possibilities to accommodate pilots further inland. Possibly it must be done even at the cost of longer routes to the airfields!'

By constantly keeping his eyes open for such details, large and small, Trautloft managed to create one of the most efficient Jagdgeschwader in the whole Luftwaffe.

But he had no control over the weather. 'Rain and low cloud level', he wrote in his diary on September 17: 'This miserable weather is a big problem. What if this bad weather lasts? If so, it will be impossible to finish the air war against England during this year.' [375]

It was exactly the same thoughts that inspired Adolf Hitler when he decided on the same day – in response to a weather report that predicted bad weather for the remainder of the week – how long he was going to postpone operation 'Seelöwe': 'Until further notice', in other words, indefinitely. In fact, it was the death blow for the planned invasion of England.

For Göring and his generals it undeniably meant a change of direction. Until then, they had planned their operations with regard to the imminent invasion. (As late as 17 September Luftflottenkommando 2 had modified the orders for tactical air operations during the invasion.) Now they were instead instructed to maintain maximum pressure on Britain, not knowing what timetable the Führer intended.

Despite the bad weather the fighter pilots of III./JG 26, JG 27 and III./JG 53 went out on a free hunting sweep over southern England in the afternoon of 17 September. I./JG 27 attacked 607 Squadron near Gatwick, and the German Gruppenkommandeur, Hauptmann Eduard Neumann, shot down two Hurricanes in a surprise attack. In the vicinity of Gravesend the ace of 8./JG 26, Leutnant Gustav 'Micky' Sprick attacked No. 1 Squadron and shot down Flying Officer Carl Briese.

Things went significantly worse for III./JG 53 when it attacked 41 Squadron's Spitfires at 8,000 metres over Chatham. In the initial attack, out of the sun, the Germans succeeded in shooting down two Spitfires, but then 41 Squadron's top cover got into the game. The British report reads: 'The rearguard pilots turned and attacked a formation of seven Me 109s which immediately turned for home in such disorder that two of the enemy aircraft collided and crashed.' 9./JG 53 lost three Bf 109s. In one of them died the unit's Staffelkapitän, Oberleutnant Jacob Stoll. The loss of Stoll was particularly severe for III./JG 53, as he was the unit's top ace with 13 victories.

During the battered German formation's return flight, they were attacked by a lone Hurricane near Ashford. This was flown by 501 Squadron's reckless Sergeant James Harry 'Ginger' Lacey. He had previously been credited with 18 victories and was now trying to reach number 20. However, Lacey may have been a bit too eager. The Germans blocked his attack, and immediately afterwards Hauptmann Wolf-Dietrich Wilcke, commander of III./JG 53, got into position behind Lacey's Hurricane and set it on fire. When Lacey jumped out of his burning Hurricane and pulled the rip-cord to his parachute it was the third time in less than three weeks that he had been shot down. It was Wilcke's his ninth victory.

Increasing mental exhaustion was making itself felt among the pilots. Hermann Neuhoff describes the condition of several of the pilots from III./JG 53 at the time: 'We were completely exhausted. This was no normal fatigue, but the result of too much tension. I saw pilots walk to the command post and light a cigarette, take two puffs, throw it away, pick up another cigarette, take two puffs, throw it away, take up a new . . . Completely absent-minded because their nerves were finished!' [376]

Neuhoff achieved his last victory in the Battle of Britain on 18 September 1940. Shortly afterwards his Gruppenkommandeur, Hauptmann Wolf-Dietrich Wilcke, sent him on 'obligatory leave' – against Neuhoff's will. 'Although we were exhausted, we didn't notice it ourselves', explained Neuhoff. When he returned to the unit after a month of rest at home, his chief mechanic said that Neuhoff had been close to having a change of personality.

On Wednesday 18 September people on both sides of the English Channel woke to a bright blue sky. As usual, there had been a terrible night of bombing. London had been attacked by 268 German bombers, and up north a lone German aircraft managed to hit the cruiser

Major Hannes Trautloft (left) and Major Günther Lützow (right). In August 1940, Trautloft was appointed commander of JG 54 and Lützow of JG 3, as part of Göring's rejuvenation of the fighter unit commanders. Both belonged to the German fighter aviation's most famous command personalities during the Second World War. On 18 September 1940 Lützow was awarded the Knight's Cross for 15 air victories. Thirteen months later, he became the second German fighter pilot, after Werner Mölders, to reach 100 air victories. In 1942–1945 Lützow served in various staff positions, but because of his explicit criticism of Göring, he was placed in Galland's jet fighter unit JV 44 towards the end of the war. On 24 April 1945 he went missing after a mission with an Me 262. Trautloft led JG 54 until 1943 and subsequently held various staff positions. He passed away in January 1995. (Photo: Trautloft.)

HMS Sussex in Glasgow's harbour so badly that the ship burned for 23 hours and finally had to be beached. The German-occupied Channel ports had been subjected to Bomber Command's attacks, with the result that eighty barges and a torpedo-boat were sunk. Also, a train loaded with 500 tonnes of ammunition was hit and blew up with a terrible explosion.[377]

At nine in the morning on 18 September the radar stations along the English south coast reported German aircraft assembling in the skies over Pas de Calais. These were the fighter-bombers from II.(S)/LG 2, which together with JG 54 flew at high altitude towards London. Park allowed himself to be fooled into sending up fifteen squadrons, of which six had time to engage the enemy before it became clear that it was only Messerschmitt 109s. It cost five RAF fighters but its main effect was wear and tear on the nerves of the British fighter pilots.

The British airmen had barely landed before the sector stations were alerted again. This time it was twelve He 111s from I./KG 53 that flew towards the British capital, again surrounded by a large number of Bf 109s. Twelve squadrons scrambled only to be attacked from above by free hunting Bf 109s. Adolf Galland's Stabsschwarm JG 26 attacked 46 Squadron near Rochester, and Galland

himself shot down three of its Hurricanes – these were the German ace's 33rd, 34th and 35th victories. The He 111s dropped their bombs on the City of London and all of them returned to base.

The Germans felt encouraged by this success when the largest operation of the day set off. A completely new and refreshed Kampfgeschwader had just moved to France to take part in the fighting. It was Oberstleutnant Johann Raithel's KG 77. This unit would now have its baptism of fire in the Battle of Britain. First off this Wednesday afternoon was II./KG 77 under Major Max Kless, with London as the target. Several Jagdgeschwaders were deployed to escort their eighteen Ju 88s. When the Germans came in over the south of England there was thick overcast at between 5,500 and 7,000 metres. JG 51, assigned to fly close escort, lost the bombers in the clouds. Fighter Command, however, which was guided by radar, did not.

To tackle the bombers, Fighter Command sent up fourteen squadrons, including the Duxford Wing. It is easy to imagine what the 'green' crews of the eighteen unescorted Ju 88s felt when they saw more than one hundred Spitfires and Hurricanes coming in to attack. It was a terrible massacre, worse than any of the clashes that took place on 15 September.

Amidst all of this hatred and killing, a young New Zealander in 92 Squadron, 20-year-old Pilot Officer Howard Hill, demonstrated an increasingly rare decency. Hill, who had shot down four German bombers on 15 September, participated in the attack on III./KG 77 on 18 September and chased Ju 88 '3Z+BS' from 8./KG 77 through a cloud and out over the Thames Estuary, where he destroyed both the Ju 88's engines. The German pilot ditched in the water, seventy kilometres from the coast, and Hill saw how the crew got out. Instead of immediately flying away, Hill circled in the air above while he used his radio to report the impact site. Guided there by the orbiting Spitfire a British rescue boat appeared shortly after and picked up the German airmen.

In the turmoil where several British fighters often attacked one and the same bomber the RAF pilots claimed they had shot down 41 German bombers – more than twice as many as the Ju 88s that took part in the mission. In the Duxford Wing Bader's 242 Squadron claimed to have shot down 12 German bombers, while the new Polish 302 Squadron was credited with shooting down nine.[378]

The actual German losses – nine crews, including Major Max Kless – were bad enough.[379] It only cost the RAF one Spitfire shot down.

After returning to France, the German fighter pilots had great difficulty explaining how they had lost the bombers, with such a disaster as a result. The next day the Jagdgeschwader commanders concerned were summoned to the Jafü 2 Headquarters, where Generalfeldmarschall Kesselring and the commander of KG 77, Oberstleutnant Raithel, were waiting. 'We received a hail of abuse' said Hannes Trautloft. 'Kesselring now requires us to fly even closer to the bombers during our close escort missions.'[380]

Leutnant Max-Hellmuth Ostermann from III./JG 54 wrote: 'Now we began to feel the effect of the strain on the nerves caused by our missions over England. For the first time since the campaign started, pilots were heard saying that they looked forward to being relieved and sent to a quieter section. More than our own losses, the losses among the bombers brought down the mood.'[381]

The outlines of the German strategy were now becoming clearer and clearer. During a meeting with the commanders of the three Wehrmacht branches in Berlin on 19 September, Hitler gave the order to cancel the assembly of the invasion fleet, and to disperse the ships which had previously been concentrated in the Channel ports. It was a clear recognition of the strength of Bomber Command, which by that time had destroyed about one-eighth of the 1,900 barges gathered in the Channel ports. As a reason for dispersing the ships to more ports, Hitler declared: 'To render them less vulnerable to air attacks.'[382] The Führer was now increasingly busy with his coming war of aggression against the Soviet Union. The transfer of troops to the East, 'Aufbau Ost', had been going on since August. In September 1940, there was already an outline for a plan of attack against the Soviet Union, and on 12 September Hitler reached an agreement with Finland on German troop transits to the area from which the offensive against Soviet Murmansk would be launched. The day after his decision

to disperse the invasion fleet in the West, Hitler gave the order to send German army and air units to Romania.

While it seems as if the Nazi dictator increasingly lost interest in trying to reach a quick conclusion to the war with Britain, there could of course be no interruption of Luftwaffe activities as that might indicate that the Germans were assembling their forces elsewhere. During the night of 18 September the worst German night attack on London to date was carried out. Three hundred bombers attacked in a continuous stream which went on from half past seven in the evening to half past five in the morning. A total of 350 tonnes of high-explosive bombs and 268 containers of incendiaries were dropped.[383] Dawn the next day revealed havoc in the city. Piccadilly, Regent Street, Bond Street, North Audley Street and Park Lane were blocked by rubble from collapsed buildings. By that time, far more than 30,000 Londoners had lost their homes.

Meanwhile, RAF Bomber Command fought back by attacking the German-occupied Channel ports. They were met by terrific resistance, including the German night fighter force – which had now been strengthened by the addition of I./ZG 76, the new II./NJG 1. Of 41 British bomber crews that were sent out on that night, nine failed to return.[384] Two were shot down by Feldwebel Paul Gildner from I./NJG 1.

On 20 September, after a day of torrential rain and storms, the German fighter airmen took the opportunity to carry out a large fighter sweep over southern England to rehabilitate themselves after the blunder two days earlier. All Jagdgeschwaders under Jafü 2 took off between a quarter to and quarter past twelve.

Park initially thought that this was the vanguard of a major new raid on London, and ordered fifteen squadrons to take-off. But when the Observer Corps reported that they could not see anything other than Messerschmitt 109s through the gaps in the clouds, the RAF pilots were called back to their bases. They had just got down to low altitude when twenty-two fighter-bombers from II.(S)/LG 2 appeared over London and dropped a 250-kg bomb each through the clouds.[385] 'London is being attacked!' So there were bombers! Park again changed his orders to the airborne fighter pilots; now they had to turn back and intercept the German 'bombers'! In this way, they ended up right under the noses of the much higher-flying German fighter pilots.

'Abschuss!' – I got one! – The first kill was claimed by Oberleutnant Erbo Graf von Kageneck, the commander of 9./JG 27. His victory, however, was not confirmed, and in fact Pilot Officer Witold Glowacki managed to bring his mauled 605 Squadron Hurricane back to Croydon. A few minutes later, Major Galland of JG 26 caught sight of 222 Squadron's Spitfires. 'The JG 26 formation leaders went hunting for targets, and soon found them among the squadrons apparently milling about aimlessly below. Most Fighter Command squadrons still flew in their tight pre-war formations that forced the pilots to concentrate on stationkeeping rather than looking out for the enemy. Such formations could usually be attacked with impunity; it was only after their formations split up and combat became individual that the British fighters' superiority in turning

A group of pilots from Polish 302 Squadron in front of the unit's Hurricane, 'WX-A'. From left to right: Sergeant Eugeniusz Nowak-iewicz, Pilot Officer Władysłav Kaminski, Sergeant Antoni Łysek, Pilot Officer Jan Malinski, Warrant Officer Ziemiara Leon, Pilot Officer Zbigniew Wroblewski and Pilot Officer Stanislaw Lapka. (Photo: Jacek Kutzner via Tomasz Szlagor.)

combat became relevant, and the RAF pilots had a chance to score.

'Major Galland spotted a Spitfire formation below him at 14,000 feet and dived at full speed as soon as it turned away from him. Not a single British pilot had a clear view of the Messerschmitt as it fired a burst at the right-hand aircraft in the leading Vee and dived past the formation. The Spitfire fell away and crashed near Rochester, its pilot dead.' [386]

South of London both I./JG 26 and III./JG 27 attacked a formation of Hurricanes and shot down three. Pilot Officer Alan Barton, Sergeant Robert Innes and another of 253 Squadron's pilots were all fortunate to survive when their Hurricanes were shot down. Hauptmann Johannes Seifert, commanding 3./JG 26, was credited with two of these, while the young Gefreiter Viktor Gruber from III./ JG 27 brought home his first victory. Barton set another, rather unpleasant record – it was the fourth time in eight weeks that he had been shot down! This time his luck ran out; he was badly wounded and did not return to service until two years later – only to be killed in a plane crash in 1943.

The only German losses on this big fighter sweep were two Bf 109s. One of them fell prey to 41 Squadron's top ace, Pilot Officer Eric Lock. Lock reported two victories, which put his personal score up to fourteen – all within a matter of fifteen days! This clash put another British fighter unit, 92 Squadron in great danger. Nos. 41 and 92 squadrons had taken off from Biggin Hill to operate as a pair, but when 41 Squadron failed to show up at the agreed place, the ten Spitfires of No. 92 were left on their own. They climbed to 6,000 metres and were still climbing north of Dungeness when the German ace Werner Mölders dived on them.

Mölders was over the Channel on his way in when he suddenly heard his wingman, Oberleutnant Georg Claus, call over the radio: *'Hinten links unter uns fünf Spitfires!'* – Behind us below on the left – five Spitfires! [387] While the unsuspecting Spitfire pilots swung left, Mölders and Claus dived and placed themselves behind their formation. The British had still not discovered them. Mölders approached until Claus feared that he would ram the rearmost Spitfire, and then he opened fire. A short burst was enough.

92 Squadron's Pilot Officer Howard Hill had accomplished the astounding feat of shooting down five German bombers in a row on 15 September, and a few days later he had behaved chivalrously towards a Ju 88 crew that he had shot down into the sea, but nothing of this helped him when Werner Mölders dived with Hill's Spitfire in his sights. While Hill's burning aircraft went down in its last dive, Mölders turned, lightning fast, to the next Spitfire. Sergeant Peter Eyles never had time to detect the danger before the shells from Mölders' Bf 109 E's wing cannons tore chunks from his aircraft. When the Spitfire plunged into the water off Dungeness, Werner Mölders had become the first fighter pilot of the war to reach a score of 40 victories. (Including his performance in the Spanish Civil War the total was 54.)

Eyles never got out of the burning plane. Howard Hill was recorded as missing. A month later the remains of his Spitfire were discovered by pure chance – the wreck hung in the canopy of a thick wood, thirteen metres above the ground. In the cockpit the rescue crew found the thirty-day-old, half-mummified corpse of the pilot.

That same evening Werner Mölders was called to Hitler's headquarters and there received the newly instituted highest award for gallantry, the Oak Leaves to the Knight's Cross. He was the second man in Germany (after General Eduard Dietl, the conqueror of Narvik) to receive the award. The German fighter pilots felt that they had double cause to celebrate: Mölders' Oak Leaves and their victories on 20 September. 'Vati' Mölders' greatest significance for the pilots in JG 51 was, as we have seen the positive role he played in their personal development as fighter pilots. On the other hand, it was not always the case that a particularly successful pilot had an inspirational effect on the other pilots in a unit. Sergeant Cyril Bamberger, who arrived at 41 Squadron from 610 Squadron in mid-September 1940, said: 'Eric Lock certainly was a very good and experienced pilot. But it didn't always feel well when he returned from one mission after another, reporting one or two shot down. Eventually it made many of us less prominent pilots feel inferior.' [388]

Although Göring was in high spirits when he received Mölders, he realized that the German strategy against Britain lay in ruins – not least after Hitler gave the order to disperse the invasion fleet. The heavy bomber losses on 15 September had also convinced Göring that the Royal Air Force had grown too strong. Therefore, on 20 September, the Reichsmarschall issued new directives which marked the beginning of a significant strategic rethink:

1. From now on, major attacks in daylight will only be carried out by small formations of bombers, not more

Adolf Galland in the cockpit of his Bf 109 during the Battle of Britain. Galland took the Mickey Mouse symbol as his personal emblem from the attack unit with which he had served during the invasion of Poland. (Photo: Galland.)

than the size one Gruppe, escorted by strong forma-tions of fighters and Zerstörer units.

2. Individual bomber crews shall carry out nuisance raids using clouds as protection from fighter attacks. The targets of these nuisance raids are London and in-dustrial targets in other cities.

3. The bomber war on England is to be mainly shifted to the hours of darkness.

It was an implicit recognition that the Battle of Britain had been lost. While Luftwaffe daylight operations on 20 September were carried out exclusively by fighters and fighter-bombers – except for some reconnaissance aircraft – during the following night 109 bombers were sent to London and dropped 154 tonnes of bombs, which caused widespread fires.

A stronger RAF

When Major Trautloft, the commander of JG 54, met Jafü 2, Generalmajor Kurt-Bertram von Döring, on 21 Septem-ber, he noticed that the general was 'utterly pessimistic'. A dismayed Trautloft wrote in his diary: 'He talks about high bomber losses during the repeated day operations. Von Döring is obviously depressed.' [389]

That day heavy, dark clouds were again hanging low over the Channel and prevented the Luftwaffe from car-rying out any major operations over England. When the weather improved slightly towards the evening, Luftflotte 2 conducted a fighter sweep similar to the one the day before. A total of 175 Bf 109s flew high above the Channel. Park ordered up twenty squadrons, but most were warned that it was only Bf 109s and pulled off. The only positive result for the Germans was that Major Galland shot down Pilot Of-ficer Tom Sherrington from 92 Squadron. While Galland recorded his 38th victory, Sherrington nursed down his smoking Spitfire and managed to perform an emergency landing at Manston.

The following night 113 German bombers dropped 164 tonnes of bombs on London, while Bomber Command raided Boulogne and Dunkirk, where port facilities were severely damaged and 76 civilians were killed and about 200 injured.[390]

Despite increasingly dark nights Bomber Command's attacks on the Channel ports were becoming more effec-tive. On the night of 22 September, 27 barges were de-stroyed in a raid against the port of Ostend, while four smaller boats were sunk in Boulogne's harbour and eight barges were destroyed in Calais. On the adjacent Marck airfield a Bf 109 from I.(J)/LG 2 was damaged during an-other British bombing. But worst of all from the German point of view was that Berlin was bombed again. At Lüne-burgerstrasse 27 in the district of Moabit, nine people were killed and fourteen wounded by a direct hit in an air-raid shelter. American reporter William Shirer commented on the air raid on Berlin in his diary: 'After a week's absence

the British bombers came over last night and kept the pop-ulace in their cellars for two hours and twenty minutes in the middle of the night. This was a little shock for most people, for they had been told all week that for several nights the British had been trying to get through but had always been turned back by the anti-aircraft defences.' [391]

The German reaction did not take long. During day-light hours on 23 September more than 400 fighters were over England to exact revenge. But things did not go as the Germans had planned. Fighter Command ordered up fourteen squadrons. The air controller directed 92 Squadron to the highest possible altitude, from where it pounced on the mass of Bf 109s as these came in over the coast at high altitude. Flight Lieutenant Kingcombe and Pilot Officer Drummond shot down one Bf 109 each. Both pilots, belonging to III./JG 26, ended up in British captivi-ty. Then the Spitfires from 41 Squadron attacked and shot down four Bf 109s from I.(J)/LG 2 (one of which, however, could be repaired after an emergency landing at its own airfield) without any losses to themselves. Pilot Officer George 'Ben' Bennions, an ace from 41 Squadron with 11 victories, said: 'I eventually sighted enemy aircraft slight-ly below on our starboard side. I ordered line astern and turned in to attack and a series of dogfights ensued in the course of which I succeeded in shooting down one Me 109 which landed on the sea N. of Dover; about one mile from the shore, and nosed in – the tail remained visible for ap-proximately 3 minutes and had a yellow strip down the rudder at its extremity.'

This Messerschmitt was flown by twenty-year old Fähnrich Hans-Joachim Marseille, who after 20 minutes in the cold water was rescued by a He 59.*

But one group of three Hurricane-equipped squadrons did not fare as well as the Spitfire units. One of these, No. 73 Squadron, had a bad start to the day, as its unofficial war diary describes: 'Inspite of the bright sunny morning our spirits sagged – and our stomachs revolted – when we had our breakfast placed before us. It purported to be mince, but it gave us all many unpleasant thoughts and even the most hardened stomachs decided to go breakfastless. If our breakfast was bad, worse and infinitely more tragic hours awaited us. At 0920 hours 12 of our machines, lead-ing 257 took off, and were to be covered by 17 Squadron from Debden. 17 Squadron failed badly in their necessary task, and aided by what can only be described as class stu-pidity of the part of Ops. the Squadrons were broken up by Me109s. While patrolling at 20,000 feet the Squadron was ordered to 10,000 feet. Smithy, who was leading, promptly and wisely questioned this, but the order was confirmed, so being left no option he began to go down. Disaster then came among us. At 12,000 feet when 17 Squadron had left the tail completely uncovered, Me109s and He113s hurtled down from the sun and the formations went over like nine pins.'

It was Adolf Galland at the head of his JG 26 who dived onto the Hurricanes and sent two of them down in the space of a single minute – his 38th and 39th victories. He described this combat: 'I attacked from behind, from a po-sition 800 metres higher up. I approached the three-plane formation on the far left with pretty much maximum speed

---

* This was not the first time that Marseille was shot down. But he immediately was back in action and four days later shot down a Hurricane for his sixth victory. This number would increase to 158 (including 17 Allied fighters in a single day) before he was killed in a flight accident in September 1942.

and opened fire against one of the British until I almost collided with him. Large metal chunks flew off from the Hurricane. When I pulled the control stick and whizzed past above him, I found myself in the midst of the enemy formation, which was stepped up in height. I immediately made a side-attack against the aircraft on the right hand side of the leading three-plane formation, which was almost upon me. Once again large pieces of metal sheet flew off from the Hurricane, which crashed in flames. All the other Hurricane pilots were so surprised and terrified that none of them came round to attack me from behind. Instead, the whole bunch scattered and went diving off. Two pilots opened their parachutes about 500 metres further down.'

73 Squadron's Sergeant Maurice Leng and Sergeant Frederick Perkin survived by parachuting. In the continuing combat, pilots from II./JG 26 reported the shooting down of five RAF fighters. 73 Squadron lost two more planes: Pilot Officer Neville Langham-Hobart ended up badly burned in the Thames Estuary near Lightship 93 and drifted around there until a boat spotted him; Pilot Officer Douglas Kinder was rescued from the Channel severely burned.

No. 257 Squadron was also hit by Galland and his pilots. Sergeant Donald Aslin had to leave his bullet-riddled Hurricane and floated badly burned down towards the Channel by parachute – he had arrived at 257 Squadron the day before. Squadron Leader Robert Stanford Tuck – who after the war became one of Galland's best friends – described afterwards how he had to weave for dear life until he was exhausted, but still a pursuing Bf 109 scored more hits on his Hurricane. When Tuck afterwards returned to the airfield at Debden, he was in a furious mood. Two of the pilots in his Flight had simply turned and fled from the scene when the Bf 109s appeared, leaving Tuck and another pilot in his Flight in the lurch.**

From the Thames Estuary and all the way to the French coast a fierce combat took place between two veterans. On the German side, it was III./JG 3's commander, Hauptmann Wilhelm Balthasar, the most successful German ace in the Battle of France. On the British side, it was Pilot Officer Terence Kane, who had served in the RAF since July 1938, and now flew a Spitfire from 234 Squadron. They clashed when Balthasar shot down a Spitfire over the Thames Estuary. Wilhelm Balthasar said afterwards: 'Over London my Schwarm met a formation of Brits, around sixty fighters. I made a head-on attack on a Spitfire. The enemy tracers flew past my canopy, but the Englishman went spinning down in flames. Perhaps he had lost his nerve. Now a wild dogfight began. It was best to break away. Suddenly I had four Spitfires on my tail. I was at 1,8000 metres, and I pushed the stick forward and dived away at full speed, pulling out at ground level with my wings fluttering. No British fighter could have followed my wild dive. I looked behind. Damn! There were two Spits on my tail again. There was no time to draw breath. My only chance of escape lay in my flying ability at low level, hedgehopping to the Channel over houses and around trees. It was no use, one of them was always there and I couldn't shake him off. He hung a hundred metres behind me. Then we were over Dover. I thought: He can't keep

Robert Stanford Tuck developed into one of the RAF's top aces during the war. This image shows him in the cockpit of his Hurricane, adorned with 23 swastikas – each one symbolising a shot down German aircraft. After the war Galland and Robert Stanford Tuck developed a personal friendship. A plaque from a dual wild game hunting trip that hung in Galland's hobby room after the war carried both men's signatures and the text: 'It is much nicer to meet here than in 1940 over the Channel.' (Photo: Tuck.)

this up as I fled out over the wavetops but the Spitfire stayed behind. I jinked to right and left as the pilot opened fire and the bullets splashed into the water in front of me. I blinked the sweat out of my eyes. The French coast was now in sight. My fuel was getting low. I kept squinting behind so as not to miss the moment when he broke away. Wait, my friend, I thought, you must return soon, and then I will be the hunter. Cap Gris Nez loomed up in front, and I skimmed over it one metre above. Suddenly the Tommy pulled up steeply and slowed down. . . . At once I turned my Me 109 and zoomed up in a tight bank, engine howling, straight at him. I fired one burst from close range, I nearly rammed him and the Spitfire went straight into the sea. He flew fantastically!'

Terence Kane himself continues the story: 'I turned the aircraft on its back, jettisoned the hood and started to climb out. Then I realised the radio unit and oxygen supply were still fastened to the plane and to me, so I climbed back in and unfastened them. The aircraft decided it didn't like being on its back and went on its side, so I had to turn it on its back again and climb out. I reached for the parachute ripcord – and couldn't find it. Panic began to set in. I was falling through cloud and at the very moment I got the chute open I broke cloud and there was the Channel 500 feet below. If I had been three seconds later pulling the ripcord I would not be here now. The Germans fished me out and I spent the rest of the War as a prisoner of war.' [392]

A little further west across the Channel the RAF lost another of its aces, 152 Squadron's Pilot Officer William Beaumont, who had a tally of seven victories. Pilot Officer Eric Marrs from the same unit said: 'He went up to chase a lone Hun that was making a condensation trail along the

---

* It is possible that Tuck was the pilot who shot down the future German ace Marseille, but it is more probable that the '109 that he scored for his 15th victory off Cap Gris Nez is identical with the one flown by Oberleutnant Walter Radlick, III./JG 53's Gruppen-adjutant, who crashed on the French coast near Wissant. In his logbook, Tuck noted: 'Ran into 40 Me 109s over London. Shot down 1 Me 109. Slightly shot up myself.'

coast. The last that was heard of him was an R.T. message to say that he was on fire.' [393]

A comparison with German documents shows that Beaumont probably was killed in combat with a Ju 88 flown by Leutnant Elmar Hauer from the reconnaissance unit 3.(F)/123, which was also recorded as missing over the English Channel.

But the attempt to inflict a severe defeat on Fighter Command backfired on the Germans. Eleven fighters on each side had been shot down when I./JG 54 came in to cover the first wave of '109s as these returned across the Channel, often with dwindling fuel and ammunition. This was the unit's last mission before it was withdrawn from the Channel Front. The 3. Staffel in particular had been quite badly mauled, without shooting down more than two enemy aircraft themselves since the beginning of August. Geschwaderkommodore Major Trautloft noted in his diary: 'It was a sad exit. The 3. Staffel was surprised by 20–30 Spitfires and Oberfeldwebel Helmut Knippscher was shot down. At least he managed to save himself by bailing out but ended up in British captivity. The 3. Staffel begun its operations against England with 17 pilots. Since then, 15 of them have been killed, written off as missing, ended up in captivity or wounded.'

It was clear to the Germans that their opponents rather than getting weaker were, on the contrary, becoming stronger. That 261 German bombers dropped 300 tonnes of bombs on London during the night of 23 September was of little comfort to Hitler when RAF Bomber Command raided Berlin at the same time, for the second night in a row. This time it was a record-breaking force of 119 Whitleys, Wellingtons and Hampden bombers that attacked the German capital. Although poor visibility, combined with the lack of proper navigational instruments, meant that only 48 crews found their way to the target, the impact of the attack was pretty extensive. Incendiary and high-explosive bombs that again fell on the residential district of Moabit killed 22 civilians and wounded 83. It was the heaviest Berlin raid so far.

The respite that the German civilian population had received while Bomber Command flew against the invasion fleet in the Channel ports was now over. When the All Clear siren sounded in Berlin in the morning of 26 September the German capital had endured bombings four nights in a row. The next day, William Shirer noted in his diary:

'We had the longest air-raid of the war last night, from eleven p.m. to four o'clock this morning. If you had a job to get to at seven or eight a.m., as hundreds of thousands of people had, you got very little sleep. The British ought to do this every night. No matter if not much is destroyed. The damage last night was not great. But the psychological effect was tremendous.' [394]

The demands on the German night fighter force grew. As we have seen, it had been shown that the Messerschmitt 110 was superior to the Bf 109 as a night fighter. The problem for the Germans was that they had invested in the Bf 110 too late. At the end of September 1940, there was a total of no more than 181 Bf 110s, of which 114 were in operational condition. Therefore, Göring had no choice but

transform more Zerstörer units into night fighter units. On 27 September, ZG 2 was ordered to dissolve; the greater part of the aircraft and crews were transferred to the Night Fighter Corps, where they formed the nucleus of the new units II./NJG 2 and II./NJG 3.

It has been assumed that the decision to dissolve ZG 2 and use it to strengthen the German night fighter force was based on exceptionally high losses of that unit. However, this is not correct. ZG 2 certainly had sustained heavy casualties, but not to an extent that differed from the average German fighter unit. During August and September 1940 combat losses in I./ZG 2 and II./ZG 2 were 21 and 19 aircraft respectivley. In the same period, III./JG 26 for example lost 22 Bf 109s in combat. If we compare with JG 27, which like ZG 2 operated under Luftflotte 3 for most of August, we find that the I. and II. Gruppen lost 22 and 19 aircraft in combat during the period August–September 1940. [395] Meanwhile, ZG 2's total tally of air victories stood at around 300 – against 52 combat losses since the war began. Of particular pride to ZG 2 was the fact that the Luftwaffe's first top ace, Hauptmann Hannes Gentzen – previously the Gruppenkommandeur of I./ZG 2 – was counted among the unit's pilots. When Gentzen was killed in a take-off accident in late May 1940, he had a score of 18 kills, higher than anyone on either side by that time. The most successful pilot in ZG 2 by the time it was dissolved was Leutnant Hans Schmid of II. Gruppe, who had a score of 15 victories, eight of those in the Battle of Britain.

In fact at this time the night fighter force was Göring's big hope for putting an end to the humiliating British raids against the German capital, and the German night fighters were certainly improving their efficiency. In the Bf 110 they had a much better night fighter than the RAF possessed, and they had already begun to emulate Fighter Command's air control system. The first night fighter tactic – simply to search for bombers caught by searchlights from the ground – was supplemented in September 1940 by the so-called 'Dunkelnachtjagd', dark night fighting. According to this, a night fighter crew was guided by an air controller who had radar observations available. Another new method was to connect radars to searchlights – which enabled Oberleutnant Werner Streib from I./NJG 1 to shoot down three British bombers on a single sortie in the evening of 30 September. The first victories of the 'dark night fighter' system were achieved on 2 October.

Before more Zerstörer units could be retrained for night fighting however, one important mission remained for the Bf 110s on the English Channel. In the days after Hitler's announcement that 'Seelöwe' was postponed indefinitely, German air operations conducted against the British Isles undeniably give the impression of lacking any real objective. Although it turned out that it was not possible to lure Fighter Command into any large and decisive air battles as the Germans hoped, the extensive German free hunting sorties were repeated over southern England. But from 24 September a change occurred. That day a series of coordinated daylight strikes against both London and the British aircraft industry began, and there the Zerstörers would play a very important role. Thus began another phase of the Battle of Britain.

The offensive against the British aircraft industry

When Oberstleutnant Raithel's KG 77 set off for London early in the morning on Tuesday 24 September, the crews had been given an absolute guarantee by the fighter units' commanders that there would be no repetition of the mistake six days earlier. When Major Hannes Trautloft took off at the head of his JG 54 at 09:05, he knew that the Fighter Aviation's honour was at stake. Nearly 200 Bf 109s from JG 2, JG 26, JG 54, I./JG 77 and I.(J)/LG 2 were responsible for the bombers' security.

Park decided to scramble eleven squadrons, but only three of them located the German planes in the haze. They managed to damage three Ju 88s before they were driven off by the German fighter escort which shot down three British fighters. When 17 Squadron's Pilot Officer Harold Bird-Wilson – an ace with six victories – bailed out of his burning Hurricane, 'YB-W', Major Galland's 40th victory was a fact. Galland gives this account of the combat:

'We were out on a bomber escort mission towards London and I peered keenly in every direction searching for British fighters, but it was only on the return flight that I sighted some. Near Southend, Spitfires and a couple of Hurricanes approached in dense formations. There were around thirty of them, a couple of hundred metres higher than us, but they seemed to have another target in mind. I called my wingmen and gave instructions. Then I pulled up steeply towards the British, with my wingmen covering me on both sides. In the next moment the British formation broke. I selected a Hurricane which flew slightly higher than the rest. I closed in from behind while climbing and delivered two short bursts from 60 metres. A sheet of fire shot out from the Hurricane, which briefly continued straight ahead before it went into a spin. I thought the pilot had been killed until suddenly a black dot was detached from the flames and then I saw a parachute open.' [396]

Bird-Wilson described how it looked from the perspective of the one that was shot down: 'Ground control vectored our 17 Squadron to the Thames Estuary, but as we arrived we were attacked by a couple of Me 109s. Before I had time to make any evasive manoeuvres, my Hurricane shook under hits from cannon shells. The aircraft immediately was on fire. I only had time to shout "Mayday, Green 1 on fire", and then the hot flames came into the cockpit. I baled out, landing in the Thames where I was rescued by an MTB of the Royal Navy. I was already scarred by the burns I got in a plane crash before the war, and now I was more burned. I also was injured by shrapnel from the German shells. I was brought to the hospital in Haywards Heath, where received the news that I had been awarded the DFC.'

It was even worse for Pilot Officer Witold Jozef Glowacki, a Polish pilot from 605 Squadron who chased the returning Germans back across the Channel. He was apparently so concentrated on the bomber he pursued that he failed to notice the danger above him. Two Bf 109s from II./JG 51 pounced on the British fighter and scored some serious hits on wings and fuselage. A few minutes later the Hurricane staggered over the airfield at Guines and crash-landed on a meadow right next to it. The German fighter pilots hurried over, helped the wounded Polish pilot from his cockpit and took him to the infirmary, but his life could not be saved.

Two hours later, the He 111s from KG 27 went out to repeat the entire operation, but soon enough had to return as the south-east of England was found to be completely covered in fog. The German fighters continued in over England and were engaged by the Spitfires from 41, 66 and 92 squadrons. It was hardly ideal weather for air combat. Fighter pilots weaved around with each other in the fog, but kept losing their opponents because of the poor visibility. The Germans claimed to have shot down eight British fighters, but a Spitfire from 41 Squadron was the only loss on either side in the confused scrap.

The gun camera in Adolf Galland's Bf 109 E-4/N captured Pilot Officer Harold Bird-Wilson's Hurricane P3878, 'YB-W', as it is hit by Galland's fire. (Photo: Galland.)

But this was just the beginning. The main German target for the day was the Supermarine works in Woolston near Southampton. Erprobungsgruppe 210, which by now was permanently based at Cherbourg, was tasked to carry out the first attack. The unit started at 14:05 with eleven Bf 110s. Nine of these had each been loaded with a 500-kilo SC 500-explosive bomb, and three with a large 250-kilo incendiary bomb each. Their escort was six Bf 110s from the 'Haifischgruppe's' fourth Staffel (4./ZG 76), led by Oberleutnant Walter Borchers. At the same time twenty-six Bf 109s from JG 2, eleven from JG 27 and five from JG 53 conducted a sweep of the area as a further protective measure. The British fighter interception became a total failure. Not one of the pilots from the six squadrons that were sent up to meet the raid managed to catch sight of the Germans before they hit the Woolston works. It was a typical surprise attack by Erprobungsgruppe 210. Alexander McKee, who lived in Southampton during the war, said: 'No-one from Woolston reached the shelters before the bombs struck . . . The bombs whistled over the top of the Woolston works and pitched further down the road, opposite the Itchen works, onto the shelters, onto the crowds running for shelter, and onto the railway arch – which collapsed on top of the men and women struggling through below.' [397]

A close-up of the personal emblem on Pilot Officer Harold Bird-Wilson's Hurricane. This aircraft, P3878, 'YB-W' ended up as number 40 on the list of Adolf Galland's air victories. Bird-Wilson survived the war as an ace with nine air victories. He passed away in December 2000, at the age of 81.

As soon as the German unit returned to base, the Bf 110s were readied for a follow-up raid. That time the assault planes received heavier loads; altogether they carried twenty 500-kg SC 500s high-explosive bombs and two 250-kg incendiary bombs when the eleven '110s took off at 17:00. Seven fighter squadrons took off to ward off the attack, but just got embroiled in fighting with the German fighter escort. When the assault planes reached Woolston, the anti-aircraft guns were ready and hit five Bf 110s, three of which crashed.

The Woolston works however, were already seriously damaged after the first raid earlier that afternoon. Two-thirds of the factory was completely destroyed. 'The final effect on output of the disaster will probably be a loss of six weeks' Spitfires', the troubled British War Office stated.[398] (Spitfire production was reduced, but not to as great an extent as the War Office feared – from 112 between 8 and 28 September to 88 the following three weeks.) A few days later the commander of Erprobungsgruppe 210, Hauptmann Lutz, was awarded the Knight's Cross.

In the evening of 24 September, at JG 26 'Schlageter's' Headquarters in Audembert, a telegram rattled in, announcing that Major Galland had been awarded the Oak Leaves to the Knight's Cross. He was the third man in the Wehrmacht to receive this award. Galland was instructed to proceed immediately to Berlin, where he would receive the award from Hitler.

The next aircraft works to be targeted in a daylight attack was the Bristol Works in Filton, in the northern outskirts of Bristol. Located nearly 100 kilometres north of the coast at Portsmouth this was an operation that could not be escorted by any other aircraft than the Bf 110. It was a risky long-range mission, but aerial reconnaissance on 23 and 24 September had noted that there were no fighters on the airfield at Filton. In addition, both a diversionary attack and a fighter sweep by Bf 109s were planned in support of the operation.

At exactly 12:00 (German time) on 25 September, eleven Bf 110s from Erprobungsgruppe 210 carried out the diversionary attack against Portsmouth. The defenders were not fooled, however. The British radar had picked up a larger force that was coming in just behind the twin-engined assault planes, so Erprobungsgruppe 210 was left in peace. The main German force consisted of 58 Heinkel 111s from KG 55, escorted by fifty Bf 110s from ZG 26 and II./ZG 76. Robert Götz, the gunner aboard one of the He 111s, afterwards wrote down his impressions when the aircraft set off out over the English Channel: 'We are assigned three full Zerstörer Gruppen as fighter escort! Above Cherbourg, they suddenly appear, high above us. It is reassuring to see so many twin-engined fighters up there, with their shark jaws and other similar symbols painted on the planes. These are able to follow us much further inland than the single-engined '109s, and they also have terrific firepower.'

The approach flight to the British coast was covered by about fifty Bf 109s from JG 2 and JG 53 – which had returned from the Pas de Calais to the Cotentin Peninsula. The main German formation came in over the coast at Weymouth and headed due north ten minutes after the bombs fell on Portsmouth. The commander of 10 Group, Air Vice-Marshal Christopher Brand, first wrongly judged that the Germans were heading for the Westland works in Yeovil, 75 kilometres from Filton. When he realized his mistake it was too late to try to avert the raid.

The twin-engined German aircraft slipped past the assembled British fighters by a wide margin and sighted Filton's fuming smokestacks fifteen minutes before the workers in the factories were due to go to lunch. Just then the British fighters appeared. Pilot Officer Eric Marrs from 152 Squadron wrote: 'We climbed up to 16,000 ft and saw a tremendous cloud of aircraft just round Yeovil way going North. There were two large groups of bombers consisting of about 40 bombers each. Milling around and above and behind them were numerous Me 110s acting as guard. Well the two of us proceeded North, passed the enemy and came round in front of them. We waited just South of Bristol for them. Then we attacked. We went head-on straight for the middle of the foremost group of bombers firing as we went, we cut through the heart of them like a knife through cheese; but they wouldn't break. They were good, those Jerry bombers!'[399]

In spite of both fighter attacks and anti-aircraft fire, the Heinkel machines roared towards the target area. At 12:45 (German time) the bombs fell. A total of 100 tonnes of bombs rained over the factory, which disappeared in a sea of explosions, flames and black clouds of smoke. The entire facility was destroyed.

Two He 111s and one Bf 110 crashed after being hit by anti-aircraft fire, and when the others turned away from the target area, the British fighters attacked again.

This aircraft from 1./KG 55, flown by Feldwebel Fritz Jürges, was one of only two He 111s that the RAF managed to shoot down during the raid against Filton on 25 September 1940.

But the Bf 110s struck back hard. Eric Marrs continues his account: 'On coming through the first group I ran into some Me 110s. I milled around with those for a bit trying to get on the tail of one of them, but there was always another to get on to my tail. Things became a bit hot, and seeing a 110 very close to getting a lovely shot in on me, I pulled the stick back hard and pushed on full left rudder. I did three smart lick rolls and span. I came out of the spin below everything. I climbed up to sunwards of everything to have another crack at the bombers, climbed to the same height and slightly in front of them on their starboard side. I saw a Heinkel lagging behind the formation and dived to attack it from the starboard quarter. I put a long burst into it and it also streamed glycol from its starboard engine. My attention was then occupied by a Me 110 which came to the help of the Heinkel. A steep turn was enough to get behind it as it did not seem very anxious to stay and fight. I came in from the starboard quarter again and kept my finger on the firing button, turning in behind it. Its starboard engine streamed glycol. Suddenly there was an almighty bang and I broke away quickly. I looked around glanced at my engine and oil tanks and positioned myself for another attack, this time going for the port engine. I just began to fire when my ammunition petered out. I broke away and dived below cloud, throttled back, heaved a deep sigh and looked around to see where I was. I steered South, came to the aerodrome and landed. I had a look at my machine and counted 11 bullet holes in it. The one that made a bang in my cockpit had come along from the rear, nipped in the right-hand side of the fuselage and smashed the socket into which the R.T.is plugged.' [400]

At a cost of only two Bf 110s and two He 111s – and a third 110 that made an emergency landing in France – the Bf 110s shot down six RAF fighters (four of which could be repaired) and damaged three more. With one of the lost Bf 110s, however, one of the aces from III./ZG 26 ended up in captivity. He was Feldwebel Walter Scherer with a score of 10.

The attack on the Bristol Works in Filton was in all respects a great success for the Germans. Twenty newly built night fighters were destroyed by fire, the important rail link between Cornwall and Wales was cut and over 350 workers became casualties. 'This was another heavy blow' wrote Lord Beaverbrook, the British Minister for Aircraft Production. 'We lost the Rodney works, with complete stoppage of engine output for one week. The effect on airframe production at the plant represents a loss of two or three weeks' output of Beauforts and Beaufighters.' [401]

On the night of 25 September London was attacked by 219 German bombers, and the following day the Woolston works in Southampton were again the target of a German day attack. Once again, Oberstleutnant Hans Kortes' KG 55 'Greifengeschwader' and ZG 26 'Horst Wessel' played the main role. Fifty-nine He 111s moved out over the

303 Squadron's Pilot Officer Jan Eugeniusz Zumbach on stand-by. Note that the start charger is plugged in. Polish-Swiss Jan Zumbach was a Swiss citizen, but served in the Polish Air Force in 1938–1939. In 1940, he flew for the French Air Force, fled to England and was transferred to 303 Squadron in August 1940. Zumbach ended the war with 12 individual and two shared air victories. After an adventurous life as a fighter pilot in various African conflicts, he died in 1986. (Photo: Jacek Kutzner by Tomasz Szlagor.)

Channel, escorted by seventy Bf 110s from ZG 26. Twelve RAF squadrons went up to meet the Germans, but again they ended up in the wrong place.

Meanwhile the Heinkels reached their target. Close to three hundred 250-kg high-explosive bombs fell square on the Woolston Works, where around 25 newly built Spitfires were destroyed or damaged.

Eight squadrons of RAF fighters then tried to cut off the bombers' retreat, but were involved in combat with the German fighter escort and failed to shoot down more than a single He 111. Several Zerstörer aces played a prominent role in the air combat: Oberstleutnant Johannes Schalk achieved his 10th victory, Oberleutnant Sophus Baagoe recorded his 12th, Oberfähnrich Alfred Wehmeyer and Unteroffizier Richard Heller their 5th, and Feldwebel Helmut Haugk his 6th. The RAF units did indeed suffer some very heavy losses through III./ZG 26 on this mission. Sergeant Sidney Merrywater from 229 Squadron had his Hurricane shot to pieces and crashed at Hambledon. 238 Squadron was severely mauled: Squadron Leader Harold Fenton, Pilot Officer Robert Austin King and Sergeant Vladimir Horsky were all shot down. King managed to bail out and Squadron Leader Fenton emergency-landed at the naval air base Lee-on-Solent, but the Czech pilot Horsky was recorded as missing. Another Czech pilot from 238 Squadron, Sergeant Jiri Kucera, had his Hurricane badly damaged by 20mm shells but still managed to nurse the plane back to base. The same thing happened to

Polish Sergeant Jozef Jeka. All of these losses were caused by Messerschmitt 110s.[403] In addition, 152 Squadron lost two Spitfires and 607 Squadron a Hurricane, added to which five other fighters from 303, 602 and 609 squadrons were severely damaged. Bf 109 pilots from JG 2 and JG 53 were deployed to cover the twin-engined aircraft as these withdrew, but even with these reporting several victories, the RAF units appeared once again to have had most of their losses caused by the Zerstörers. Of the RAF's losses in the combat against KG 55 on 26 September it was just the two Spitfires from 152 Squadron that were reported to have been caused by Bf 109s.*

For ZG 26 the price for these successes was only two Bf 110s. In addition to these two aircraft, the operation only cost the Germans the single He 111 previously mentioned. The RAF units involved, however, submitted some of the most exaggerated victory claims of the entire Battle of Britain: Their victory reports were thirteen times higher than the actual German losses! Of the thirty-nine reported kills only seven were not confirmed. The greatest successes were attributed to 303 Squadron, which accounted for one third of the victory claims (all of which were confirmed) – including two each by the Czech Sergeant Josef František and Flying Officer Jan Zumbach. One possible explanation for the hugely inflated claims may be that King George VI happened to visit 303 Squadron's airfield at Northolt that day; he was there when the pilots received the take-off order, he listened to their radio communications during the combat, and he was still there to receive the pilots when they returned and listened eagerly to their battle reports. Group Captain Stanley Vincent, station commander at Northolt, afterwards wrote down the following interesting comment: 'The visit of the King was a most inspiring day. Everything went off as if faked for the occasion!'[404]

*A shot down Spitfire is salvaged.
(Photo: Goss.)*

---

* According to available loss records of the RAF units at the National Archives in Kew, eight fighters were destroyed in combat. However, British Air Ministry received reports of ten total losses. (National Archives, Kew. CAB 65/9/22.) Three more fighters force-landed.

A Hurricane from 1 RCAF Squadron at Northolt in September 1940.

27–30 September: Catastrophe for the Luftwaffe

When Adolf Galland was in Germany to receive the Oak Leaves to the Knight's Cross, he got an interesting insight into the way the air campaign was run. From Berlin he flew to Göring's 'Hunting Castle' on Romintherheide in East Prussia, where he would be the Reichsmarschall's guest for some wild game hunting.

On the steps to the splendid palace, he met his 'scoring rival' Mölders, who had stayed with Göring after he was decorated with the Knight's Cross the Saturday before. 'Vati' Mölders was in a hurry to get back to his unit and catch up with Galland's score.

'Fatty has promised me that he will keep you for as long as he held me', he shouted after Galland: 'By the way – good luck with the hunt with the stag; I missed him!'

Adolf Galland said: 'Göring appeared in splendid white uniform and was in great spirits. His earlier critical stance was gone. The Reichsmarschall had just initiated the offensive against the British aircraft industry, and the first results had an encouraging effect on him.' [405]

On 27 September, the Luftwaffe carried out its largest daylight operation against England since 15 September. But everything went wrong from the start. A Ju 88 reconnaissance plane from 2.(F)/123 which had been sent out to reconnoitre before the main attack was intercepted and shot down by a Spitfire. The pilot, Oberleutnant Willi

Rude and another two men from the Junkers' crew was captured, but seemed nevertheless to be in quite good spirits – as the victorious British pilot, Eric Marrs, could testify: 'I set the ball rolling by finding a lone Ju 88 at 23,000 ft. I had a long running fight during which we came down to 50ft and skimmed the hills of Devon. I did continuous quarter attacks aiming at his engines and was able to hit both of them. Glycol streamed forth and I hovered around waiting. As I expected, both engines soon stopped. He made for the South coast of the Bristol Channel and landed about 20 yds from the beach in the water, running his machine up on to the beach. I circled around and watched the crew get out. They waved to me and I waved back and then hordes of civilians came rushing up. I watched the crew taken prisoner, beat up the beach and then climbed away. The place he came down at was Porlock and no doubt you heard that little engagement mentioned over the wireless on the news that night. Well, his rear gunner had landed a few bullets in my machine. One had penetrated the leading edge of my machine, going through the well into which the wheel was retracted and puncturing the tyre. One other had landed in the fuselage about 6 ins from my left knee. When I landed at the aerodrome I could feel the aeroplane slewing and swinging and tending to tip forward on its nose, but was able to pull off the landing O.K. in spite of a burst tyre. The pilot of the German Ju 88 shot down this morning sent a message of congratulation on a very fine fight. He would like to meet me.' [406]

-234-

A German Junkers Ju 88 taxis out to take off.

In the morning the Germans dispatched twenty-nine bombers against London, divided into several smaller bomber formations – Ju 88s from II./KG 76, escorted by JG 52 and JG 54, Ju 88s of KG 77 and He 111s from KG 53. Fighter Command countered them with twenty squadrons with over two hundred Spitfires and Hurricanes. The majority of these were concentrated against the fifteen Ju 88s from I./KG 77. These had been provided with a close escort of twenty-three Bf 110s from V.(Z)/LG 1 and ZG 76. Moreover, forty Bf 109s from JG 27 flew 'extended escort'.

Twelve Hurricanes from 213 Squadron were the first to attack. They got past the Bf 109s and went for the Ju 88s at full speed. The Bf 110s, however, caught them and shot down one of the British machines. In the confusion that arose, the ten Bf 110s from V.(Z)/LG 1 lost contact with the bombers and the other Zerstörers and flew north-west instead of towards London. This had disastrous consequences. V.(Z)/LG 1 immediately drew the attention of the RAF air controllers who ordered several squadrons against them.

Unteroffizier Hans Berchthold, one of the pilots from V.(Z)/LG 1, said: 'Hans reported two more attackers. This time they attacked simultaneously from below and above. My radio operator fired steadily at both. I hauled the machine around and took aim at one attacker. Hit, he veered off. But my machine had also been hit in this attack.'[407] Berchthold was in the air over Horam, north of Hailsham, five kilometres north of the coast at Eastbourne, when he bailed out from his burning '110 where the rear gunner,

Unteroffizier Hans Koch, was sitting, dead. No. 303 Squadron's Witold Urbanowicz saw how the pilot of the '110 that he just had shot down escaped by bailing out. Meanwhile, however, three of 303 Squadron's Hurricanes also crashed in the same area.

ZG 76, heading towards London further east, was attacked by twenty-three Spitfires from 72 and 92 squadrons but shot down one of those without any own losses. Then the Spitfire pilots got into a difficult battle with the Bf 109s from JG 27 and JG 54 and lost five more planes. Oberleutnant Roloff von Aspern from 4./JG 54 claimed to have shot down three.

At the same time V.(Z)/LG 1, with nine remaining Bf 110s, found themselves in an increasingly difficult situation. 253 and 602 squadrons, each with ten Hurricanes and Spitfires, also had joined the attacks on this formation when a second Bf 110 from V.(Z)/LG 1 was shot down. At Redhill, twenty-four more Hurricanes from 17 and 249 squadrons came in to attack the Bf 110s. Despite a numerical inferiority of one to three, the Zerstörer airmen damaged two Hurricanes from 249 Squadron. 23-year-old South African Pilot Officer Percy Burton from 249 Squadron, had a really bad experience of Bf 110s. He had been shot down by one on 2 September, and now he was determined to pay back, but he had difficulty in getting any decent hits. In the end, he seems to have become quite frustrated. 249 Squadron's war diary noted: 'From reports from the Hailsham district Observer Corps, it appears that PO Burton has been attacking an Me110 for some time and was seen to climb above it and dive down on to it, he rammed it and cut its tail off and both aircraft crashed.'

Shortly afterwards, near Biggin Hill, another two dozen Spitfires and Hurricanes from 66 and 605 squadrons turned on the last seven Bf 110s of V.(Z)/LG 1. Several of them chased the Bf 110 which was flown by the commander of 15./LG 1, Oberleutnant Ulrich Freiherr von Gravenreuth. The German pilot flew low to escape his pursuers, and did not notice he was coming in over Gatwick airfield – where several anti-aircraft guns and machine guns hit the '110 with devastating effect. The Messerschmitt exploded, and the burning wreckage rained over the airfield.

Oberleutnant Otto Weckeiser from the same Staffel fought alone against eight Spitfires. He claimed to have shot down one, but was forced to perform an emergency landing with his bullet-riddled Messerschmitt and was captured. He was probably shot down by Pilot Officer Albert 'Zulu' Lewis, another South African in 249 Squadron, which reported four Bf 110s downed.

By that time, the Bf 109s had to turn for home with dwindling fuel loads, and there was not much that II./ZG 76 could do to rescue the remaining crews from V.(Z)/LG 1. Oberstleutnant Walter Grabmann, the commander of ZG 76, said: 'Over London we came under concentrated attacks by superior numbers of enemy fighters, which separated us from the bombers. The thirteen aircraft in ZG 76 –

I led the formation – flew in a defensive circle over London for more than twenty minutes.' [408]

The aircraft of ZG 76 were pinned down by twenty-four Hurricanes from 73 and 501 squadrons which reported combat with '30-40 Me 110s flying in circles at 18,000ft over London'.[409] In this protracted clash three Hurricanes and a Bf 110 were downed, with a fourth Hurricane getting badly damaged.

303 Squadron's pilots launched a furious attack on the bombers, which then broke off and turned southwards.[410] Two of them were brought down by Flight Lieutenant Atholl Forbes. Another two were shot down by Pilot Officer Miroslaw Feric and Sergeant Josef František, who shortly afterwards also shot down a Bf 110. Subsequently ten Spitfire pilots from 602 Squadron who had taken off from Westhampnett, joined in and attacked the bombers.

But none of the German units was in such trouble as V.(Z)/LG 1 which finally turned and fled back towards the coast with only three Bf 110s remaining. One of the pilots, Unteroffizier Peter Voelskow said: 'I did the only possible thing: low-level flight at a few metres over willows, hedges and the occasional houses. As I did so I made repeated quick, steep turns very near the ground in order to give my pursuers a more difficult target. Once one of them went too high and lost sight of us under his engine cowling. My radio operator Kurt Schwarz fired at him. The Hurricane rolled to the right and I almost rammed it as I had also

Ground personnel posing in front of a Spitfire during the Battle of Britain. The RAF's ground personnel accomplished great deeds during the Battle of Britain. They were affectionately called 'erks', which probably derives from a popular song in the 1920s. 'One of the Aires' (short for 'Aircraftman'). (Photo: Goss.)

A Hurricane from 238 Squadron. (Photo: Vasco.)

just made a right turn and was flying roughly parallel to a slope. Then my other two pursuers lost sight of me, they fired over the crest of the hill. I continued to stay low at maximum speed until the middle of the Channel, when Kurt Schwarz pounded on my shoulders with his fist and screamed: "Let up!" The Hurricanes had not followed us any further.' [411]

In addition to Voelskow's/Schwarzs' plane just two other Bf 110s from V.(Z)/LG 1 returned from the fateful mission. Among the missing airmen was the unit commander, Hauptmann Horst Liensberger. The last that was heard from him was a radio message: 'Both engines hit, trying to turn back. . . It's impossible. . . I'm trying to land!' It seems as though his aircraft was the one rammed by Pilot Officer Burton from 249 Squadron.

After this hard blow V.(Z)/LG 1 joined the German units that were taken out of combat. Additionally I./KG 77 lost four Ju 88s and II./ZG 76 one Bf 110. But the combat was not as one-sided as it has often been portrayed. While this took place, between 09.30 and 10.00 in the morning, no less than 19 British fighters were shot down, 11 of which were total losses. It seems that at least seven of these were shot down by V.(Z)/LG 1, with two more damaged. V.(Z)/LG 1 reported six victories in this its last epic fight.

A few hours later, the next formation of German aircraft was on its way to England, this time from Luftflotte 3. Thirty He 111s from I. and II./KG 55 and nineteen Messerschmitt 110 fighter-bombers from Erprobungsgruppe 210, escorted by I. and II./ZG 26. The RAF's 10 Group met up

with five squadrons, and when they landed at their bases an hour later, they had achieved one of Fighter Command's single greatest victories of the Battle of Britain.

To begin with, they made such a violent attack that the Heinkel formation was torn to pieces. The bomber pilots jettisoned their bombs in the Sherbourne area and fled back towards the Channel. This saved the Bristol Works in Filton from another airstrike. The air controllers then ordered the Spitfire and Hurricane pilots to go after the Bf 110s which were on their way towards Bristol.

The Observer Corps posts reported the movements of the Bf 110s for the entire 80 kilometres to Bristol. The target for Erprobungsgruppe 210 was the Parnall works at Yate, five kilometres north-east of Bristol. The German report reads: 'Five kilometres before the target we were attacked by fifteen Hurricanes in a closed formation, which interfered with the accuracy of the bombing.' [412] These Hurricanes belonged to No. 504 Squadron, and despite the twenty Zerstörers that escorted Erprobungsgruppe 210 having the advantage of both height and numbers, the Hurricane pilots quickly managed to gain the upper hand.

They shot down four Bf 110s without any own losses. Then twelve Hurricanes from 56 Squadron joined in and shot down two more – also without any own losses. I. and II./ZG 26 not only lost three of their Bf 110s, but they also failed completely to protect the assault planes. Of the nineteen crews in Erprobungsgruppe 210, four were lost. The Gruppenkommandeur, Hauptmann Martin Lutz, fell in the air over Bristol. A little further north, the ace Ober-

Bf 110 assault planes of Erprobungsgruppe 210. 'S9+DH' was the aircraft in which the Gruppenkommandeur, Hauptmann Martin Lutz, was shot down on 27 September 1940. (Photo: Vasco.)

leutnant Wilhelm Richard Rössiger perished in the flames of his burning Bf 110. Both were posthumously awarded the Knight's Cross four days later.

According to the German plans the élite unit III./ZG 26 'Horst Wessel' would meet the returning Bf 110s when they flew back out over the English coast off Swanage. About twenty Zerstörers from III./ZG 26 were orbiting at 8,000 metres altitude off the English coast when 609 Squadron's Spitfires suddenly appeared. It was some of the best fighter pilots on each side that clashed high up in the air above the Channel. The Australian Pilot Officer Roger Miller led Yellow Section in a frontal attack on the Bf 110 that was manned by Gefreiter Georg Jakstadt. Neither of the two pilots shied away, and the Spitfire and Messerschmitt dissolved in a cloud of flaming petrol and ammunition. 609 Squadron's Operations Record Book notes: 'For the second time in three days No. 10 Group Control positioned the squadron so badly that they had little or no chance of catching any of the bombers over the coast. Both Flight Commanders' R/T having failed, Yellow Leader, P/O [Roger] Miller led the squadron into an attack on the escort fighters that were seen circling over Warmwell, losing his life in a collision with an Me 110, in which both aircraft appeared to explode in mid-air.' [402] Miller, who arrived at 609 Squadron on 26 June, had been credited with three individual, one half and one-third victory. After that, a fighter was shot down on each side. Yet both sides reported six victories each. Among the pilots from 609 Squadron, the aces Flying Officer John Dundas

and Pilot Officer David Crook were credited with new victories, and in III./ZG 26 Leutnant Botho Sommer and Oberfähnrich Alfred Wehmeyer, among others, increased their tallies.

During the ninety days that Erprobungsgruppe 210 had been in combat, the unit made more than sixty air strikes, mostly in the form of swift attacks on small but important and heavily defended targets. The unit's tallies of both successes and losses had always been notably high; that four of its pilots received the Knight's Cross during the Battle of Britain says a great deal about its successes; that 40 of the Gruppe's crew members – including its last three Gruppenkommandeurs (Rubensdörffer, von Boltenstern and Lutz) and four Staffel commanders – had not returned in the last thirteen weeks of effort, also speaks for itself.

At about the same time as Erprobungsgruppe 210 bled to death in the air over Dorset, Luftflotte 2 started its other operation on this 27 September. The target was London. It would be the first daylight raid on the British capital since the great defeat on 15 September, and this time the Germans succeeded far better than in the morning. This was not least due to the fact that the 30 He 111 bombers from II./KG 53 which would carry out the attack were covered by no less than 200 Bf 109s and Bf 110s. Park responded by ordering up twenty squadrons. While the fighters on both sides clashed, the Heinkels were able to reach London and drop their deadly cargo. JG 52 was responsible for most of the German successes, with seven victories for the loss of two. On the RAF's side Pilot Officer Albert 'Zulu' Lewis, the South African from 249 Squadron who shot down two Bf 110s in the morning, destroyed two Bf 109s. But overall, this operation was a significant success for the Luftwaffe. Twelve British and only half as many German fighters were shot down, and all Heinkels returned to their bases.

A few hours later Luftflotte 2 carried out its next big mission. Now the Messerschmitt units were the first to arrive over England. They were under orders to meet and escort a large formation of Do 17s and Ju 88s to London. But this time nothing seemed to go right for the Germans. Their fighter pilots climbed to high altitude above the agreed rendezvous point to wait for the bombers. The minutes passed but no bombers appeared. The pilots in the little 109s began to get nervous. What had happened? Where were the bombers?

What they did not know was this: When the bomber units, the inexperienced I. and II./KG 77 took off from their bases the weather forecast had promised clear weather. But the first machines had barely got into the air when huge banks of cloud towered up ahead of them. There was no turning back! The aircraft had to go through the clouds. It was then the trouble started – most of the newly trained pilots in KG 77 had not been given any training in instrument flying! The formations split up. Some crews tried to climb above the clouds, some tried to take a detour around them, others lost orientation in the fog and mist. On the other side of the clouds the unit commanders desperately tried long and hard to assemble their crews in the dense formations that would enable them to meet the British fighter attacks with concentrated crossfire. When KG 77 eventually moved off towards England, the unit was stretched out in a long 'stream' that allowed fighter attacks from all angles.

When the 55 bombers finally got in touch with the fighters, the Bf 109s' fuel was running out. In that moment, a couple of hundred Spitfires and Hurricanes struck. Complete chaos broke out in the German formations. Bomber pilots panicked and forgot everything they had learned about meeting an attack. With the fuel warning lights shining the Messerschmitt pilots went down to rescue the Junkers, but after a few minutes, lack of fuel forced them to hurry back towards the Channel. All the way back to the French coast the defenceless German fighter pilots were harassed by swarms of British fighters.

Fighter Command won a great victory. 'Zulu' Lewis was now credited with shooting down two more Bf 109s and one Ju 88. He set a record for both sides during the Battle of Britain: Six confirmed and three probable victories in a single day! This gave him a total score of 18 victories. Another pilot from 249 Squadron, Pilot Officer Tom Neil, reported three victories on 27 September; so did Sergeant John Beard from the same unit, as did Flying Officer Blair Russell for 1 RCAF Squadron. Flying Officer Witold Urbanowicz from 303 Squadron, added two Ju 88s to the Bf 109 and Bf 110 he had shot down at noon. In total, 303 Squadron reported fourteen victories. The unit's top ace, Sergeant Josef František, reached a total of 27 with his two new victories.

On the German side Oberleutnant Hans Philipp, the commander of 4./JG 54, was credited with four victories on 27 September – his 12th to 15th. But it could not compensate for the heavy losses the Luftwaffe was dealt. For KG 77 this day was a bitter repetition of 18 September: out of 55 Ju 88s, eight were shot down. This brought the unit's total losses on 27 September to twelve aircraft. In six hours – between 10.00 and 16.00 on 27 September – the Luftwaffe lost 54 fighter aircraft over England. Although 42 British fighters had been shot down – of which 14 could be repaired – it was a brilliant victory for the defence.

In total the Luftwaffe carried out 1,173 sorties over England in daylight on 27 September, but the only reasonably successful operation was the daring solo attack that the commander of 7./KG 53, Oberleutnant Irmfried Leonhardi, carried out towards the evening with his He 111 against the Morris Works in Birmingham. Despite a heavy anti-aircraft fire, Leonhardi's crew attacked from low altitude and reported a direct hit with a 1,000-kilo SC 1000 bomb.[413] This got the German crew a mention in the German Armed Force's daily communiqué the next day. In fact, it was Dunlop's rubber factory that had been attacked, and the resulting damage was moderate.

Far away from all of this, Adolf Galland was still at Göring's estate on Romintherheden in East Prussia. In the afternoon of 27 September when he and Göring returned to the hunting lodge after a successful hunt in the forests, Göring explained that he had to use his office for a while to study the reports received from the operations over England. Neither of the two suspected anything about the disaster at the English Channel. Galland said: 'Two hours later, an Unteroffizier came and took me to the Reichsmarschall's study. Instead of my jovial host from the breakfast table, I saw before me a broken man. With a tired gesture he showed me the latest reports. It was disastrous news. Deeply shaken, Göring asked me to tell him the truth without any euphemisms. He couldn't understand why our bomber losses kept increasing. I told him about the same as I told Hitler. . . my admiration for the opponent and what I thought of exaggerated reports in the press and radio.'

Winston Churchill was right when he stated that '27 September ranks with 15 September and 15 August as the third great and victorious day of the Fighter Command during the course of the Battle of Britain'. Just as 15 September, the success on the 27th was to a large extent thanks to the British air controllers. On this day they managed to lead 513 fighter pilots into combat with the enemy – the second highest figure since the record of 550 on 15 September. It should be emphasized that the Germans carried out almost twice as many fighter sorties on 27 September – a total of 998. This time they were simply defeated by the RAF. No less than 36 Messerschmitt fighters had been shot down (excluding the losses in Erprobungsgruppe 210). Two Gruppes had suffered a loss of seven fighters each – V.(Z)/LG 1 and II./JG 52.

That the losses on 27 September meant the death knell for V.(Z)/LG 1 is well known. This unit, which had been in the front line the whole time, had lost no less than 42 Bf 110s in combat since the beginning of July 1940 – including 18 in September – and was taken out of combat.[414]

But V.(Z)/LG 1 could nevertheless show quite good results during the Battle of Britain; the unit was credited with at least 59 victories. II./JG 52, however, could not. They had returned to the 'Channel Front' just a few days previously, after having been withdrawn from combat in mid-August because of high losses. In less than ten combat missions over the English Channel, in not more than five days, II./JG 52 suffered a loss of 13 aircraft and as many pilots – against only two confirmed victories. Johannes Steinhoff, who at the time served as Oberleutnant and Staffelkapitän of 4./JG 52, explained in a letter to the author how this affected the mood of II./JG 52: 'It had a great impact on the pilots' strength. Our morale was badly affected and many simply couldn't take it psychologically. We felt helpless and confused.' [415]

On the whole, many on the German side felt perplexed and confused regarding the continued campaign against Britain. Ulrich Steinhilper from I./JG 52 – the only Gruppe in JG 52 that performed fairly well during operations over the Channel – wrote in a letter to his mother: 'It seems that you don't think it will be over by Christmas. I believe there is still a chance. If not, then all of our missions which have hit the British fighter defences really hard will have been for nothing.' [416]

For many of the German airmen the motivation to keep on fighting hard was a desire that the sacrifices of the past few weeks should not have been in vain. On 27 September even I./JG 54 was withdrawn from the Channel area and relocated to Jever in north-western Germany. The men of that unit reacted with mixed feelings, as the unit chronicle describes: 'On the one hand it was a delight to go home to Germany again, but on the other hand, we wanted to be part of the great effort against England and the invasion, which we all still thought was imminent.' [417]

In the evening on 27 September the commanders of all German Jagdgeschwaders at the Channel were again summoned to a meeting with Generalfeldmarschall Kesselring and General Loerzer. Kesselring explained in very clear terms that Göring was furious about the high bomber losses. His instructions from 20 September that airstrikes performed in daylight would only be carried out by small formations of bombers, a maximum of one Gruppe's size, escorted by very strong formations of fighters and Zerstörer units had obviously not been followed. The 60 Bf 109s and Bf 110s sent to escort 15 Ju 88s on the morning of 27 September were far too few. In contrast, the mission had gone much better when 200 fighters had been dispatched to escort 30 He 111s. Göring reiterated the importance of sending out quite overwhelming formations of fighters along with only small groups of bombers, which would actually work best as decoys.

These stern instructions were followed to the letter the following day, with much better results than the 27th. Between half past ten and two in the afternoon, Luftflotte 2 conducted two major operations with 120 fighters and only half a dozen bombers at a time. On both occasions both the British radar and air observers gave too low altitude for the intruders, with the result that the British fighter pilots ended up at a height disadvantage. Among the RAF pilots that were shot down was 'Zulu' Lewis. When he left his burning 'GN-R' to bail out Major Mölders had scored his 42nd victory. Lewis survived, albeit with severe burns.

Twelve British and only two German fighters – and not a single bomber – had been shot down when the British radar detected what appeared to be 100 German aircraft on their way towards the Portsmouth area. With the devastating bombing of the Bristol Works in Filton and the Woolston Works in Southampton fresh in memory, the commander of 10 Group, Air Vice-Marshal Brand, didn't dare not send up his fighter aircraft to meet the enemy. It was exactly what the Germans had anticipated. This time, they came in without any bombers; it was a pure fighter intrusion by 42 Bf 110s from ZG 26 and 53 Bf 109s from JG 2 and JG 53.[418] The result of the ensuing clash was disappointing for the Brits: with only three reported own victories, seven Hurricanes were shot down. Air Vice-Marshal Brand would likely have been even more unhappy if he had known that the Germans, in fact, had not lost a single aircraft.

Obviously ZG 26 was responsible for most, if not all, of the British losses:*

'The final attack came in the 10 Group area, when a formation approached Southampton. These proved to be Bf 110s, which were engaged off Selsey Bill by three squadrons of Hurricanes. The big "twins" proved, on this occasion, to be a match for the Hurricanes. Despite claims of three destroyed and one damaged, not a single Messerschmitt was lost. The German crews succeeded in downing no less than six Hurricanes with the loss of five pilots.' [419]

Göring was in a slightly better mood when 30 September dawned. The two previous nights London had been attacked by 249 and 246 German bombers respectively, and there had been no more bombs on Berlin. The night of the 28th the RAF had made an attempt, but it had been averted by the air defences with the result that all the bombers missed their target. The following night Göring's night fighters had again managed to shoot down a British bomber.

Göring gave his airmen a day's rest from any major operations because of bad weather – thick, dense clouds and continuous rain – but when the weather cleared up on Monday 30 September, he order a new large attack. Things initially went well. Led by Major Galland the entire JG 26 'Schlageter' conducted a large free hunting sweep at half past ten (German time). They attacked 229 Squadron and shot down five of its Hur-

---

* According to *The Battle of Britain Then and Now*, two aircraft from 213 Squadron were shot down by Bf 110s while five aircraft from 238 and 607 squadrons were lost in combat with Bf 109s during this engagement on 28 September. However, it is hard to see on what grounds these assessments are made. The Operations Record Book of 607 Squadrons does not specify the type of aircraft that shot down its Hurricanes. (ORB 607 Squadron. National Archive, AIR 27/2093.) According to historian Robert Gretzyngier, 238 Squadron engaged 'a German formation consisting mainly of Bf 110s'. (Gretzyngier, p. 119.) This is repeated by, e.g., the combat report of 238 Squadron's Pilot Officer Wladyslaw Rozycki, who claimed the destruction of a Bf 110: 'I saw Me 110s flying in a defensive circle at about 20,000 ft.' (Combat Report Wladyslaw Rozycki, National Arcive. AIR/50/91.) 11 Group's report on this combat mentions only Bf 110s. Neither JG 2 nor JG 53 sustained any losses or damaged aircraft, and the participating RAF squadrons foiled no claims for even a damaged Bf 109, while four Bf 110s were reported destroyed or damaged.

Feldwebel Alfred Warrelmann from V.(Z)/LG 1 has marked his victories on the rudder of his Bf 110. The first four represent Polish aircraft he shot down in September 1939, and the four next represent RAF fighters. The picture was taken shortly after this Zerstörergruppe was converted into I./NJG 3. (Photo: von Eimannsberger.)

ricanes – of which, however, three were repairable. JG 2 and Hauptmann Helmut Wick fared less well during a fighter intrusion over Portland at lunchtime. Air Vice-Marshal Brand ordered up a single squadron, No. 609, but that proved to be sufficient. Guided by radar and the Observer Corps the Spitfire pilots pounced on the German formation over Portland. The entire German formation broke up and the Bf 109 pilots dived desperately to escape the British. 'A few of our Spitfires were chasing Messerschmitts all over the place and obviously a very nice little massacre was in progress', Pilot Officer David Crook wrote afterwards.[420] When 609 Squadron afterwards landed at full strength, its pilots could report five downed Bf 109s, two of them by Crook. Without a doubt, it was a humiliating setback for JG 2, which lost two Bf 109s – with a third damaged – without even managing to damage a single British aircraft. Interestingly, however, JG 2 reported the shooting down of five Spitfires – two of them as Helmut Wick's 33rd and 34th victories.

In the afternoon, when Kesselring, the commander of Luftflotte 2, sent 150 Bf 109s and a handful of Do 17 bombers from III./KG 3 towards London, Park had also adapted his tactics. He decided to accept the challenge and ordered up no less than sixteen squadrons, ten of which made contact with the enemy. For the loss of only three of their own, 11 Group's pilots shot down eight Bf 109s and a Do 17. Polish 303 Squadron recorded another great success with five victories for one own loss. Flying Officer Witold Urbanowicz contributed with three of these successes. No. 222 Squadron's Sergeant Iain Hutchinson was successful in a slightly different way: when he crawled unharmed out of the wreckage of his Spitfire near Denham, he had survived being shot down for the third time in a month.

After these aircraft returned a short pause followed while the Germans prepared their units for the day's most extensive operation: a complex operation against the Westland Works in Yeovil that included a contribution by KG 55 from Luftflotte 3. The operation would be preceded by a diversionary attack against Portland by eleven Ju 88s from I./KG 51. At the same time Luftflotte 2 sent I./KG 77 towards London.

I./KG 51 was fortunate enough to be attacked by only eleven Spitfires, which cost the Germans no more than one aircraft. The He 111s from KG 55 on the other hand attracted the attention of nine whole squadrons. But the Heinkels had a powerful escort, consisting of 40 Bf 110s from ZG 26 and 52 Bf 109s from JG 2 and JG 53. The most effective resistance against the British fighter attacks seemed once again to have come from the Zerstörer airmen. The chronicle of KG 55 notes that 'ZG 26 fought hard to defend Kampfgeschwader 55'.[421] While ZG 26 and II./JG 53 claimed to have shot down four and two British fighters repectively without any own losses, JG 2 reportedly bagged eight in exchange for one own plane that failed to return. Interestingly, it appears as though the Zerstörer airmen underestimated the number of aircraft they shot down, while the Bf 109 pilots from JG 2 again appear to have exaggerated their success. 56 Squadron, which on this day was deployed in combat for the first time since the unit was taken out of combat in early September, had a severe blow inflicted on them by the Bf 110s. Eric Clayton, a mechanic in the squadron, explains: 'The squadron started operating by day from Warmwell, a forward satellite airfield and on the 30th September, it was scrambled to intercept a large force bound for the Westland factory at Yeovil. It climbed to attack some escorting Bf 110s and in the encounter, seven Hurricanes were shot down – though none of the pilots were killed. Only P/O [Frederick] Higginson (recently commissioned) was able to claim a Bf 110 probably destroyed. This was the squadron's last major encounter with the enemy during the Battle.' [422]

In addition, five Spitfires from 152 Squadron were hit by gunfire from the Bf 110s – which resulted in one total loss, three damaged Category 2 and one slightly damaged. Pilot Officer Eric Marrs from this unit survived an attack by a Bf 110 by a hairsbreadth. He describes this himself: 'Soon we saw a large formation of enemy bombers arriving with a large number of Me 110s as guard. We were just going in to attack when somebody yelled "Messerschmitts!" over the R.T. and the whole squadron split up. Actually it was a false alarm. Anyway, being on my own I debated what to do. The bombers were my object, I swooped in under the '110s and attacked the bombers (about 40-50 Heinkel He 111s) from the starboard beam. I got in a burst of about three seconds when – crash! – the whole world seemed to be tumbling in on me. I pushed the stick forward hard, went into vertical dive and held it until I was below cloud. I had a look round. The chief trouble was that petrol was gushing into the cockpit at the rate of gallons all over my feet, and there was a sort of lake of petrol in the bottom of the cockpit. My knee and leg were tingling all over as if I had pushed them into a bed of nettles. There was a bullet hole in my windscreen where a bullet had come in and entered the dashboard, knocking away the starter button. Another bullet, I think an explosive one, had knocked away one of my petrol taps in front of the joystick, spattering my leg with little splinters and sending a chunk of something through the backside of my petrol tank near the bottom.' [423]

Although the Zerstörers shot down 11 RAF fighters without any own loss other than a 110 which was so badly damaged that it later crashed back at base, the bomber raid came to nothing. When the bomber pilots found the entire target area hidden under a thick blanket of clouds and were also subjected to repeated attacks by RAF fighters – which cost a loss of three He 111s – they decided to abort the mission. With eleven British fighters, five bombers and one Bf 109 shot down, the commander of Luftflotte 3, Sperrle, could nevertheless describe the operation as quite successful – especially as his pilots claimed to have shot down 16 British fighters.

But further east the simultaneous operation against London by I./KG77 from Luftflotte 2 ended in a disaster. All available fighters in Luftflotte 2 were employed to escort the bombers, but here they were mostly Bf 109s – which was fatal for the Germans. Again the lack of experience of the airmen in KG 77 showed itself. When they flew towards England, they had difficulty orienting themselves as they flew above a perfectly unbroken cloud cover. Only when they made landfall too far west across the English Channel did they discover their mistake and turned north. In Uxbridge, Park was surprised to see that the Germans, when they reached a point south of London, turned westwards again and continued all the way to Reading, then turned 180 degrees and followed the Thames downstream until they came in over London, where they dropped their bombs through the clouds.

KG 77 escaped with only one loss – caused by anti-aircraft fire – but when the bombers and their escorts left the London area, they were subjected to repeated attacks by RAF fighters. Although many of the Bf 109s had by then used up two-thirds of their fuel, the constant RAF fighter interceptions made it impossible for them to leave the bombers. But instead of taking the shortest route back to France – that is, to the southeast, towards Pas de Calais – I./KG 77 turned to the southwest. Without anyone really having an idea exactly where they were, the Ju 88 unit commanders brought the Bf 109s along in a wide arc to the west and southwest, over Farnborough and Winchester. The war diary of 7./JG 54 reads: 'Time passes and our fuel reserves are getting dangerously low. In the 62nd flight minute we get embroiled in a dogfight near Brighton.' [424]

'We ran a pure gauntlet', Oberleutnant Hans-Ekkehard Bob from III./JG 54 remarked. The Bf 109s became easy meat for the British; the remaining fuel reserves gave no room for evasive manoeuvres. On this day, Adolf Galland flew his first three sorties since he returned from the meeting with Hitler and Göring. He was in a very bad mood as he led his Geschwader back towards the Channel. He attacked a lone Hurricane.

'I opened fire when I was so close that I almost rammed my opponent, and in the next moment my windshield was covered with black oil, while a small piece of metal from the British plane blocked my engine intake.' [425]

Galland had managed to surprise the Polish Sergeant Marian Belc, who left his formation in 303 Squadron's 'B' Flight to protect what he thought appeared to be an RAF

This Bf 109 from 2./JG 26 'Schlageter' barely made it to the French Channel coast where it bellied in with empty fuel tanks.

pilot in a parachute who was being attacked by German fighters. Belc made it down safe and sound in his parachute and was soon back with his comrades again.

But Galland didn't have long to rejoice over his new victory. A moment afterwards he saw to his horror how his wingman's Bf 109 E-4/N was turned into a fireball. It was with great relief he soon afterwards spotted a parachute. Oberleutnant Walter Kienzle floated down with captivity awaiting. He was the second wingman that Galland lost during the Battle of Britain. 92 Squadron's Spitfires that had attacked, and Flying Officer John Drummond was credited with a Bf 109 probably destroyed while Sergeant Don Kingaby had to put up with having his claim being reduced to a damaged. This is quite remarkable, because two of the pilots from JG 26 actually survived and were taken prisoner. In addition to Kienzle it was Unteroffizier Horst Perez from 4./JG 26. He managed to belly-land his damaged 'White 4' at East Dean near Eastbourne. (Today it is on exhibition at the Imperial War Museum in Duxford.)

At the same time 303 Squadron's Flying Officer Witold Urbanowicz shot down a Bf 109 near Brooklands, which raised his day's tally to four victories.

A comparison between British and German documents shows that the RAF managed to shoot down fourteen Bf 109s while only three of its own planes were lost. Hardest hit was JG 26 'Schlageter', which lost five pilots to British fighter attacks – and two more Bf 109s so badly damaged that they had to make emergency landings in France.

At last the Ju 88s – along with their entire Bf 109 escort – flew out across the English Channel near the Isle of Wight! Oberleutnant Johannes Steinhoff from II./JG 52 describes the anguished return flight: 'In the end we had to leave the bombers behind us. Come what may! Soon the fighters began to run out of fuel. For an hour we had been flying without any orientation. There was a risk that we, the entire fighter force, would never reach the French coast.' For half an hour the desperate cries were heard over the German fighter pilots' radio frequency: 'My red light is on!'

On one Bf 109 belonging to III./JG 51 the fuel ran out over the Channel. The other airmen watched anxiously as the pilot left his falling plane. Leutnant Gerhard von Carnier had recorded his first victory earlier in the mission. Now he drifted down in his parachute into the clouds and disappeared. A few days later, his dead body washed ashore on one of the Channel beaches.

When they finally saw the grey cliffs at the French Channel coast rise out of the mist in front of them, one of the German fighter pilots could not contain himself.

'Cape Horn ahead!' came as a relieved shout over the radio.

Several Bf 109s navigated in over the coast just a few metres up and with stationary propeller blades. Several of them forced-landed just inland of the coast. 'Only two aircraft from our Staffel manage to reach the airfield' noted the war diary for 7./JG 54. 'Two others force-land on the last drops of petrol at Boulogne after 105 flight minutes. Feldwebel Oeltjen and Unteroffizier Schweser return to our

A boat from 3. Seenotflotille of the German Seenotdienst (sea rescue service). The Luftwaffe's Seenotdienst was formed as early as in 1935 and was thev first organised air-sea rescue service. (Photo: Trautloft.)

Staffel after two days. They made emergency landings with empty fuel tanks at Dieppe. After this, our Staffel is down to only four operational aircraft.' [426]

Altogether, the operations on 30 September meant a new major setback for the Luftwaffe. Göring had every reason to be dissatisfied with the fighters. 25 Bf 109s and one Bf 110 were lost in the air battles. In addition, five Bf 109s were lost when their fuel ran out during the day's final mission. Including accidents, 36 German fighters were written off on this day. Fighter Command's aircraft losses on 30 September were 20 destroyed and 13 that made emergency landings.[427]

Although the Luftwaffe fighters had managed to ward off most British attempts to attack the bombers, the bomber losses of nine planes still corresponded to 5.5 % of the task force.

That morale was deteriorating in more than one Luftwaffe unit became obvious to Generalfeldmarschall Erhard Milch, the Luftwaffe general inspector, as he carried out an inspection tour of German air bases in the Netherlands a few days later. He visited III./KG 4 and III./KG 30. The first unit was found to be in very good condition, but Milch's disappointing conclusion after visiting III./KG 30 was that no more than five of the unit's twenty-six crews could be classed as 'fully combat-ready'. The result was that III./KG 30 was immediately taken out of combat to be reorganised into a reserve force, Ergänzungskampfgruppe 6. III./KG 4

on the other hand, was incorporated into KG 30 as its new III. Gruppe.

The war diary of 9./JG 54 notes for 30 September, 1940: 'Lately, our aircraft have been incessantly in action and it has not been possible to maintain them well enough. Therefore, several are in a totally unreliable condition. On our first mission today three of eight aircraft had to make emergency landings immediately after take-off.' [428]

That RAF Bomber Command again struck Berlin the following night – albeit on a small scale – was additional salt in the wounds of the distressed Reichsmarschall. On 3 October, he was forced to stop thinking about the Battle of Britain to hold a conference on organising anti-aircraft defences and air raid shelters in Berlin. At the same time the Luftwaffe's own bomber offensive was hindered by an extensive low pressure area with solid cloud cover. On the night of 2 October, only 105 bombers reached London, and the following night merely 44.

CHAPTER 9
THE TIME OF THE FIGHTER ACES

Fighter-bombers

There were only shattered remnants left of several Luftwaffe units when September came to an end. As we have seen, no unit had been harder hit than V.(Z)/LG 1. This Gruppe was transferred to Germany, where it became the nucleus of the new I./NJG 3. II./JG 27 was also withdrawn from the Channel area on 1 October. With the losses on 30 September, this Gruppe had lost 26 Bf 109s and 19 pilots in combat since late July. For the whole of JG 27, combat losses amounted to 29 Bf 109s during September 1940. During the same period, ZG 26 'Horst Wessel' had suffered almost as many combat losses – 25 Bf 110s. The Messerschmitt unit that had suffered most during the battles of September 1940 was JG 53, which had 33 of its Bf 109s shot down in that month alone. Combat losses for some other Messerschmitt units in September 1940 were 24 for JG 3, 20 for JG 51, 18 for ZG 76, 17 for JG 26 'Schlageter' and 16 for ZG 2. Among the German bomber units, KG 77 was hardest hit, losing 25 crews in combat during the last half of September alone. Even KG 26 was badly mauled with 20 combat losses during September.[429]

A measure of the RAF fighter pilots' tenacious resistance against the Luftwaffe is the fact that things looked even worse in several of Fighter Command's units. We have seen how the newcomers of 222 Squadron were hit hard on their first day of combat on 30 August, but those who survived continued to put up a stiff fight; of the 19 pilots from 222 Squadron who were sent into first-line service on 30 August, 15 were either dead or wounded a month later. Of the 20 pilots in 46 Squadron on 1 September, 8 were killed and 6 wounded during the month of September. No. 72 Squadron lost 25 aircraft in less than four weeks in September, and of its 20 pilots, 14 were killed or wounded. No. 73 Squadron lost 14 aircraft and 9 of its 19 pilots in just three weeks.

The actual Battle of Britain was over, but the heavy air fighting over the Channel would last for another couple of weeks. For the Germans it was now mostly about 'keeping up appearances'– maintaining the illusion that the Luftwaffe was close to bringing Britain to its knees. It was important for Hitler, not least for diplomatic reasons. The Führer was in the midst of intense diplomatic activity; he intended to try to convince the Spanish dictator Franco to

A mechanic posing in front of Oberleutnant Hans-Ekkehard Bob's Bf 109, equipped with a 250-kg bomb for a fighter-bomber mission. (Photo by Bob.)

join him in the war, and he worked on the governments in the Balkans and in Finland in order to make them sympathetic to the upcoming invasion of the Soviet Union. Additionally Hitler watched with growing concern how his ally Mussolini, Italy's 'Il Duce', met serious difficulties in his warfare against the British in the Mediterranean.

October began with reasonable weather and on the first day of the month the Luftwaffe sent out about 350 Messerschmitts and 73 bombers on at least two dozen operations over England. The largest operation took place around noon when ZG 26 'Horst Wessel' dispatched 32 Bf 110s on a free hunt in the Swanage area, along with 40 Bf 109s from JG 2 'Richthofen' and 8 from JG 53 'Pik As'. 10 Group ordered three squadrons to meet them, and in the ensuing combat the Germans claimed to have shot down 12 – six each by JG 2 and ZG 26 – and the British that they had shot down two enemy aircraft. In reality four Hurricanes were shot down – including at least two by Bf 110s and one by Bf 109s – while the German losses were limited to a Bf 110 that crashed due to combat damage upon its return to base.[430] Among the German pilots, Hauptmann Helmut Wick claimed two air victories, thus increasing his score to 36.

But the day's most important event for the air war over the Channel was the visit that Generalmajor von Döring, Jafü 2, made to some of his Geschwaderkommodores. These were now instructed to assign one Staffel per Jagdgruppe to fighter-bomber attacks. Adolf Galland said: 'Von Döring explained that Fighter Command, after their heavy losses in September, was now estimated to be down at a strength of just over 300 serviceable fighters, and that now we were to lure them into combat. We could hardly believe our ears! For too long we had heard the phrase "the last three hundred Spitfires", and in the end there was no longer anyone who believed in this. The result was just that we lost even more of our already low confidence in the leadership. But the strategy was decided. Von Döring announced that Göring no longer wanted to use the bomber units as "decoys" – the losses it had already cost them were too high. We could concede he was right in that, but the new directives from the Reichsmarschall were just too much: One third of the entire fighter aviation would be converted to Jabos, fighter-bombers!'[431]

In the circle of friends around the young Geschwaderkommodores Mölders, Galland, Lützow and Trautloft, this new order was received with sharp criticism. 'Fighter-bomber operations might harrass the British, perhaps even demoralize them', said Mölders, 'but they will never be of any decisive importance. Worse, these fighter-bomber missions may lead to our own morale getting undermined.'[432]

Galland had extensive personal experience of fighter-bomber missions. He had begun his career as a fighter pilot in what he developed into a fighter-bomber unit, and had carried out 280 fighter-bomber or assault missions during the Spanish Civil War and another 50 during the invasion of Poland, before he was transferred to fighters in the spring of 1940. Indeed, many German fighter pilots disliked any fighter-bomber mission anywhere, because a 250-kg bomb made their aircraft slow and hence a fairly easy target for enemy fighters. Galland did not belong to them. His well-known criticism of Göring's orders to switch the fighter aircraft to fighter bombing missions primarily had other reasons behind it. He compared it to 'a fool who when he discovers that his sword had been blunted in battle, instead of grinding it, grabs it in the blade and swings the handle against his opponents'.[433] In an interview with the author Galland clarified what he meant: 'Fighter-bombers in itself can be a quite effective weapon. This had been demonstrated by us in Spain and Poland, and through the repeated missions by Erprobungsgruppe 210 during the Battle of Britain. But the directive that one third of the fighter aircraft would be converted to fighter-bombers, while the other two thirds would support them, was wrong on two main grounds. First, it was a tired fighter arm with many dejected pilots that were affected by this directive, and many perceived it as a "punishment" for the "failure" that Göring accused us of. Second, at such a late stage of the Battle, in October 1940, it could not not meet the supposed military aims. It is quite possible that the "fighter-bomber offensive" that now began was primarily politically motivated, namely to show that we could still drop bombs over London.'

The main target for the German 'Jabo offensive' was London, and the attacks would be carried out from an altitude of 5,000–6,000 metres. Therefore, they could not build on the experience of Erprobungsgruppe 210, which mainly carried out precision attacks at low altitude against ships, radar installations, airfields and industrial facilities. Pilots in II.(S)/LG 2, however, could contribute with important experience, but the fighter pilots had to perfect their bombing methods by themselves. The task was particularly difficult because the Bf 109s lacked any bomb sight. The commander of JG 54, Major Hannes Trautloft, chose four of his most suitable pilots to test the best fighter-bombing methods – Oberleutnant Hans-Ekkehard Bob, Oberleutnant Günther Scholz, Oberleutnant Heinz Lange and Leutnant Waldemar Wübke. The hard line Hans-Ekkehard Bob, who unlike many other fighter pilots did not shy away from fighter-bombing missions, went to work with enthusiasm. He said: 'We selected a small uninhabited spit of land near Dungeness, where we conducted our test bombings. The first time we tried was a failure. But after a while we honed our methods. Eventually we came to the conclusion that the best results were achieved when we dropped our bombs from a shallow dive at a certain angle. Many years after the war, I met an old fighter pilot from the RAF who had taken part in the Battle of Britain. He told me about one question he had brooded on for years. He said: "The most remarkable thing throughout the Battle of Britain was that you Germans subjected a small deserted spit of land at Dungeness to intensive bombings. We could not understand what on earth you were doing. There were no military installations, nothing!" I was able to solve one of the biggest mysteries of his life.'[434]

Hans-Ekkehard Bob's experience led to the obligatory painting of a thin red line at an angle of 47 degrees on the side panels of the Messerschmitt 109s' canopies. When bombing, the pilots dived until the line was parallel to the

Bf 110s in an 'Angriffskreis' over southern England.
(Photo: Galland.)

horizon; then the aircraft was at an angle where it was easiest to calculate the trajectory of the dropped bomb.

While the German fighter force switched to fighter-bomber missions, most of the bomber units' activity was to be during the dark hours, when industrial targets and ports in British cities – particularly London – would be attacked. During the night between 1 and 2 October, 269 German bomber crews took off towards these targets. Most of them bombed London, while Liverpool and Manchester were raided by twenty-five bombers. In the latter city extensive fires were started that devastated large parts of the western and southern districts.

During daytime the German bomber units conducted nuisance raids with either single aircraft or groups of three. These were usually left alone by the RAF's fighters, and those that were intercepted could often take advantage of the cloudy autumn weather. The clouds played a key role for the German nuisance bombers' ability to escape fighter attacks. It was not unusual that the planned nuisance raids over the British Isles were cancelled when the weather turned out better than expected.[435] Fighter-bombing strategy – or at least its supposed strategy – was based on two false premises. One was that Fighter Command was down to only three hundred serviceable fighters. True, the fighting on 30 September temporarily reduced the number of operational Spitfires and Hurricanes from 621 to 593, but it was still twice as many as the Germans thought. Secondly, the Germans assumed that if Fighter Command was drawn into combat with the German fighters, it would in some way automatically lead to the RAF coming off worst. As we have repeatedly seen, this was not the case – the fighter-versus-fighter combats would instead suggest that both sides were fairly evenly matched.

The Luftwaffe's fighter-bomber offensive began on 2 October. First up were the veterans of II.(S)/LG 2. One of its Staffels took off at nine in the morning to fly to London, escorted by about forty Bf 109s from JG 54. Since the Bf 109s climbed to 6,000 metres before they flew out over the Channel, they were quickly detected by the British radar. Eight squadrons went up against them. When the Germans came in over England, the Spitfire units were ready to attack even higher up. The RAF fighter pilots reported that it was only Bf 109s, and received orders from the air controller not to attack. Some thirty Bf 109s from JG 54 stayed and began to orbit over Dover, while the fighter-bombers and the rest of the fighter escort continued towards London. Shortly afterwards, Dowding in Bentley Priory received a report that bombs were falling on London. He sent the information to Park, who forwarded it to his air controller.

The air controller called the airborne RAF pilots: 'Bandits over London! Bombs are dropped!' Back came the answer: 'Those are no bombers, they are just Me 109s!' It was too late to intervene when it finally dawned on the British that the Germans were using fighter-bombers against the capital. At 10:20 (German time) the fighter-bombers flew out over the Strait of Dover again, heading back to their bases.

This exchange of words was later interpreted by historians to imply that the British at that time were not unaware of the existence of bomb-carrying Bf 109s. British archival sources show, however, that the RAF had been aware of this since at least 9 September, when a British report concluded that the presence of bomb-carrying Bf 109s 'now can be confirmed'.[436]

At the next Jabo raid Fighter Command was ready. Here, for the first time, an actual fighter unit took part as Jabos.

III./JG 53 had appointed Oberleutnant Ernst-Günther Heintze's 8./JG 53 to 'Jabo Staffel'. Escorted by forty other Bf 109s from JG 53, its bomb-laden planes passed the coast at Dungeness at 7,000 metres, about half an hour after II.(S)/LG 2 had flown back to France. The Jabo airmen split up so that some attacked Lympne airfield – where a bomb-shelter and a truck were hit by bombs – while the main force raided London.

The RAF fighter pilots had no difficulty in identifying which of the German formations that were fighter-bombers. The Germans had placed their fighter escort up at 9,000 metres. The fighter-bombers could not reach that high because of their heavy load. On 2 October 1940 the weather was clear and almost cloudless, and under such circumstances it is very difficult for pilots who are high up to identify aircraft that are almost directly below them at a much lower altitude; their camouflage simply merged with the ground below. This was what occurred on 8./JG 53's first fighter-bomber mission. No. 603 Squadron was able to sneak up on the fighter-bombers unnoticed and deliver an attack that cost the Germans four Bf 109s before the despairing radio calls from the remaining Jabo pilots got their escort to react.

At the same time, a total of 109 German bomber crews were out over the British Isles in different nuisance raids. Among other targets, the airfields at Penrhos, Rochester and Cleave were attacked. The main purpose of these operations was to draw Fighter Command's fighters up into the air. But the British did not as a rule send up any fighters against single enemy aircraft. Therefore, most of the German bomber pilots who participated in the attacks on 2 October could also get away unscathed, despite the lack of clouds to hide in. The crew of Oberleutnant Hans Seidel's 'A1+CH' from I./KG 53 had bad luck however. In the afternoon Pilot Officer Irving Smith from 151 Squadron got wind of Seidel's He 111, which had bombed the Rolls Royce Works in Derby. At 16:34 the headquarters of I./KG 53 received a radio message from the radio-operator aboard Seidel's plane: 'Aircraft hit, must force-land!'[437] When the He 111 crashed, Pilot Officer Smith's sixth air victory was a fact.

The majority of the German bomber pilots rested during the day, to be sent up when darkness fell. London was the main target, but Manchester, Glasgow and many other cities also received German bombs during the night between 2 and 3 October 1940.

Weather conditions on 3 October were the exact opposite to those of the previous day. The Germans took advantage of poor visibility, pouring rain, low cloud base and fog to dispatch a few dozen bomber crews specialised in instrument flight to attack airfields and industrial targets across England. Fifteen airbases received German bombs. In most places the damage was limited, but at St. Eval two hangars were hit and two Spitfires from 222 Squadron and an Avro Anson were destroyed by two Do 17s from KGr 606.

Even greater devastation was caused by a Ju 88 flown by Leutnant Otto Bischoff from 4./KG 77. At half past eleven (British time) Bischoff swept in toward the Havilland works at Hatfield in Hertfordshire at just 50 metres altitude and dropped four 250-kg bombs that bounced off the wet grass and went straight into the production halls. The attack cost twenty-two dead and seventy people injured, besides which the rolling-mill was destroyed. The bombs also destroyed 80 per cent of the stored material for the brand new Mosquito bomber. The Mosquito prototype's maiden flight was at that time still six weeks in the future.[438]

Following a day of mist, rain and poor visibility throughout the day and fog at night, the Germans dis-

patched 480 Messerschmitts for five Jabo operations on 5 October. The largest operation was made early in the afternoon with about 200 Messerschmitts from Luftflotte 2 flying towards London and various targets in Kent, while at the same time Luftflotte 3 sent thirty-eight Bf 110s from ZG 26 along with forty Bf 109s from JG 2 and seven from JG 53 on a fighter sweep up towards the Isle of Wight area. The former drew the attention of most of the seven RAF squadrons that were scrambled, and in fierce dogfights eight Messerschmitts – including two Bf 110s from Erprobungsgruppe 210 – were shot down, with another three crash-landing in France, against a loss of no more than four RAF fighters.

Meanwhile a mere nine Hurricanes of No. 607 Squadron encountered the entire collection of Luftflotte 3 fighters alone. Led by Flight Lieutenant Francis Blackadder, No. 607 patrolled the air above Swanage with when suddenly Flight Lieutenant James Bazin was heard on the radio: 'What's that up there?'

The next moment Pilot Officer John Sulman screamed: 'Break hard! Bandits to the rear coming down hard!' While the Messerschmitts came diving from 1,000 metres higher up, the nine Hurricanes scattered.

In the cockpit of one of the Messerschmitts that came hurtling down on these unfortunate Hurricanes sat one of the Luftwaffe's greatest aces, Hauptmann Helmut Wick, who had led I./JG 2 'Richthofen'since 7 September. He was, as we have seen, right on the heels of Mölders and Galland in the 'competition of the aces'. When he started the mission in the afternoon on 5 October, he had a total of 36 air victories on his account, five behind Galland and six behind Mölders. Now he was eager to catch up. Wick describes the ensuing combat from his perspective: 'Once again we met a lower flying formation Hurricane . . . They turned abruptly, which was a mistake. We managed to shoot down four of them in a very short space of time. One of them ended up on my account. The other Hurricanes tried to escape in a dive, but shortly afterwards came climbing up again. This gave me the opportunity to shoot down the plane that flew on their far right side. Then the Hurricanes put their noses down again and dived away.'[439]

Flight lieutenants Blackadder and Bazin, Pilot Officer David Evans and Sergeant Richard Spyer were all shot down. None of the nine Hurricanes escaped undamaged. The pilots of JG 2 optimistically reported eleven (!) shot down, including three by 1. Staffel's Oberfeldwebel Rudolf Täschner (his 9th through 11th victories) and two by Wick – his 37th and 38th. Not a single German plane was even damaged in the combat.

Officer pilots from 74 'Tiger' Squadron in the alert room at the Biggin Hill base in October 1940. From the left: Flying Officer Roger Boulding, Flying Officer John Freeborn (with a deck of cards at the table), Pilot Officer Henryk Szczesny, Pilot Officer Harbourne Mackay Stephen, Flight Lieutenant Dillon Kelly, Pilot Officer Peter Stevenson, Pilot Officer Alan Ricalton and Flying Officer Walter Franklin. Ricalton was killed on 17 October 1940 when he was shot down by a Bf 109 from JG 53. (Photo: Tidy.)

German pilots often spent the time between combat missions in loungers near the aircraft. (Photo: Leykauf.)

What according to Wick's depiction then followed, is interesting. Wick said: 'I don't know what came over me – if I simply was not in the right mood or if it was that my nerves were exhausted – but when I had shot down the second Englishman, I just wanted to fly home. I had certainly fuel for another few minutes, but I was overpowered by a strong will to fly back home. Perhaps there was not so much more to be done in the flight minutes that we had left. Having turned towards the base, I suddenly spotted three Spitfires above myself. They seemed to come from the sea. I saw them first, attacked, and soon I had shot down the first one. [. . .] I gritted my teeth and made a new attack. Number two also plunged into the sea after just a few rounds. Now only one was left. Unfortunately, by then I had run out of cannon shells, so I was left with only the machine guns. After a while, he left a white trail behind, which presaged gasoline fire. By all accounts, the pilot was also hit, since the aircraft swerved off uncontrollably. However, after a while the pilot seemed to have regained control over the machine, so I have to give him the coup de grace. The Spitfire reeled over and splashed into the sea. Now it was high time to fly home. Because the gasoline could end at any moment I dared not even make my five victory wagglings with the wings.' [440]

With these five victories in a single air combat – a record on the German side during the Battle of Britain – Hauptmann Wick passed the 'magic' level of 40 victories and reached a total of 41. However, it has not been possible to find any evidence on the British side of the three Spitfires which Wick

reported that he encountered when he flew back after the clash with the Hurricane unit.

During the following night, 177 Luftwaffe bombers were in action against the British capital, dropping 242 tonnes of bombs and 176 containers with incendiaries, which caused a particularly large fire at the West India Docks on the Isle of Dogs in London.

The events of 5 October show the pattern of the air war in October 1940. During the remainder of the month it was mainly in the form of Jabos – and their fighter escorts – and the occasional 'nuisance bomber' that the Luftwaffe showed itself over England in daylight. In parallel with this the intensity of the Luftwaffe's nightly bombardment of London and other British cities escalated.

One exception was 7 October, when Luftflotte 3 dispatched twenty Ju 88s of II./KG 51 to attack the Westland Works in Yeovil in daylight. Thirty-nine Bf 110s from ZG 26 'Horst Wessel' was mainly responsible for the escort but even JG 2 'Richthofen' and JG 53 'Pik As' participated with a total of fifty nine Bf 109s. It seems that this time the Bf 109s only participated to a limited extent; they were likely forced to return to France due to lack of fuel before the ensuing combat reached its peak.

The last major air battle during the Battle of Britain took place between the Isle of Wight and Portland in the afternoon on 7 October. 238 and 609 squadrons were the first RAF units to reach the German formations – only to be attacked from above by the Bf 110s, similar to what 607 Squadron had experienced two days before. No. 609 Squadron's Operations Record Book reads: 'Both 609 and

238 squadrons (the latter on our flank) suffered attack from enemy fighters coming from unusual heights with the sun in their favour. The Squadron destroyed 4 Me 110s plus 2 Me 110s probable and 1 Me 109 damaged, at the expense of four Spitfires and one very good pilot, Sergeant A. N. Feary being killed. [. . .] Staples was shot in the knee, and his cockpit having caught fire, he bailed out safely from 21,000 feet. Dundas' Spitfire was hit by explosive shell, and the pilot received many small pieces in his leg, but landed safely and soon recovered. Howell's engine seized up on his way back to base, necessitating a successful wheels-up landing in a field.' [441]

Alan Feary had been credited with five and one-third air victories since he arrived at 609 Squadron on 26 June. The loss of this ace was obviously hard for the unit. But contrary to the clash on 5 October, the defenders soon received reinforcements – 56, 152, 601 and 607 squadrons arrived, and the combat developed into a large melee. Pilot Officer Eric Marrs' depiction of the fight provides an excellent picture of how the Zerstörer planes applied their Angriffskreis – 'attack circle' – as the escort for the bombers: 'This raid consisted of about 40–50 Junkers Ju 88's and an equal number of Me 110's. Some people say that there were also Me 109's about, but I saw none. They crossed the coast and went North just to the East of Warmwell and then turned North-West and made for Yeovil. We attacked them just about as they turned North-West. The bombers were in loose formation at about 16,000ft with their guard of Me 110's behind and above them. We were at 20,000ft and to one side of the bombers.

'We all dived down on the latter to try to split them up thoroughly. I was not able to get in a good shot at them and pulled away to the right and up again. I then took stock of the position. I was in a bad position to go for the bombers again, so I thought I would have a crack at the fighters. These I found were going about in strings of about 10 aircraft sneaking along behind the bombers. From time to time the leader of each string would come round behind the last man in the ring to form a defensive circle. The leader would then break the circle again to catch up the bombers.

'After one or two attempts I found I was able to sneak up behind one of these strings and attach myself to the end of it for a short spell, shooting at the end machine in the line. Every time the leader came round to form a defensive circle I had to break away and wait till the circle broke up again. I was however, able to tack myself on again. In this way I was to make the end one of one of these lines stream glycol from one of its engines. I was not able to finish it off as the leader of this particular string was forming one of the defensive circles and was coming round behind me . . . I then drew away for a bit to take stock of the position.

'The Huns were now making for the coast again, and I saw a straggler all by himself. I swooped up on him from the starboard rear quarter. He saw me coming and opened up, but I was able to catch him up quite easily. I opened fire and his starboard engine streamed glycol. I switched on to the fuselage and then over to the port engine. I was by now overtaking him somewhat fast, so I drew out to his left. Suddenly the back half of his cockpit flew off and out

jumped two men. Their parachutes streamed and opened and they began drifting slowly earthwards. Their aeroplane, left to itself, dived vertically into the sea, making a most wonderful sight and an enormous splash . . .

'I had not finished my ammunition and looked around for something else to shoot at, but everything seemed to have cleared off, so I circled round the two Hun's, now floating earthwards. They took an awful long time to come down, as they baled out at about 15,000ft they came down on land and I watched the Army rush up and capture them.

'I then returned to the aerodrome and landed to see what had happened to the rest of the squadron.....The squadron's score was three confirmed and one probable that day. We unfortunately had one chap shot down. He was very badly burnt and died of his burns next day. This was a most unfortunate case. The man was a Sergeant Pilot and he had just received his commission. He was due to go on leave that morning, but was not able to owing to the fact that there were no spare pilots in our flight. The flight-commander had gone ill the day before and I, being the next senior officer in the flight, was acting flight-commander.' [442]

While most British fighters were kept busy by the fighter escort, the Ju 88s made their way to the Westland Works which was hit by eighty bombs. [443] An air-raid shelter received a direct hit and caved in, killing more than one hundred workers.

Nine British fighters, seven Bf 110s and only two Ju 88s were shot down during the operation of Luftflotte 3 in the afternoon on 7 October. The worst affected units were 609 Squadron and III./ZG 26, which each had four planes shot down. In contrast to the German unit, two of the British pilots survived as they fought over their own territory. One of them was the ace Flying Officer John Dundas, who was hit in the leg by shrapnel from a 20mm shell when he was attacked by a Bf 110 and crashed his Spitfire 'PR-O' at Warmwell.

For 601 Squadron's Pilot Officer Clive Mayers it was the second time in less than two months that he had been shot down – both times by Bf 110s. The first time had been on 13 August, in an otherwise fairly successful engagement with V.(Z)/LG 1. On that occasion he just escaped being killed when a Zerstörer pilot tried target-practice at the young RAF pilot who hung and dangled in his parachute. Despite the shrapnel in his leg he was soon back in the battle, and recorded five air victories before he was again shot down by a Bf 110 on this 7 October, but survived, albeit wounded.

The raid against the Westland Works in Yeovil on 7 October, was however the Luftwaffe's last major bomber daylight operation against targets in the British Isles. In the future, Luftwaffe operations over England in daylight consisted exclusively of fighter-bombing and small nuisance flights by bombers. This reduced the need for Bf 110s as Zerstörers over the British Isles – at the same time that the night fighter force had a desperate need for more Bf 110s. The Messerschmitt 109 now conclusively took the lead role in Luftwaffe operations during the daytime across the British Isles.

When KG 51 attacked the Westland Works late in the afternoon on 7 October, Luftflotte 2 had already been in

601 Squadron's Pilot Officer Clive Mayers was shot down by a Bf 110 while flying this Hurricane on 7 October 1940.

action all day with a whole series of fighter-bomber operations that again cost quite severe losses. At 10.45 Major Mölders had taken off from St. Inglevert to take part in an escort mission for the fighter-bomber Staffel in his squadron, 2./JG 51. This was led by Werner Mölders' little brother Victor, who he had transferred to JG 51 three months earlier. Werner Mölders said himself: 'The little guy was so frivolous. We flew to England to drop bombs and I flew with his Gruppe. All released their "eggs" over London without being attacked. But while the rest of us flew homewards, Victor took a "detour" to see what effect the bombs had had – which was totally unnecessary. It was not long before he and Leutnant Meyer had a couple of Spitfires on their tails, and that was the last we saw of them.' [444]

Oberleutnant Victor Mölders crashed near Guestling and was captured. His wingman, Leutnant Erich Meyer, was chased out over the Channel by Pilot Officer Kenneth Mackenzie in a Hurricane from 501 Squadron. Mackenzie can well be seen as personifying the British determination to fight in the summer and autumn 1940. He had learned to fly before the war and further trained as a fighter pilot during the summer of 1940. On 21 September 1940, he was transferred to 43 Squadron, and on the 29th to 501 Squadron. When Mackenzie chased a lone Bf 109 over the Channel at noon this 7 October, his machine guns scattered their bullets over a wide area without succeeding in getting any decisive hit on the German. When he finally realised that this German would be able to return to his base, he became so enraged that he opened up full throttle and rammed the German. One wing on his Hurricane struck the tail fin of the 109, which immediately dived into the grey waves below. Mackenzie managed to turn his battered Hurricane around and emergency-landed in a field outside Folkestone.

In total the fighter-bombing mission on 7 October cost 2./JG 51 a loss of three Bf 109s. But it would be worse in the afternoon, when JG 27 was sent to escort II.(S)/LG 2 against London and Biggin Hill airfield. The fighter-bombers managed to carry out their attack undisturbed, but when the Germans turned back towards the coast, Hurricanes from 1 RCAF and 303 RAF (Polish) squadrons attacked. This time, however, it was the Germans that had set a trap. As soon as the Hurricanes dived down behind the main German formation, they were themselves attacked by Bf 109s from II./JG 27, which had been lurking higher up. Oberleutnant Ernst Düllberg set fire to a Hurricane. The pilot, Canadian Flying Officer Deane Nesbitt, barely managed to escape and then nursed his damaged plane to Biggin Hill. But this was a game that two could play! Another formation of Hurricanes now appeared. These came from 605 Squadron. Their Scottish commander, Squadron Leader Archie McKellar, had the situation completely under control. Two Bf 109s crashed during his first attack. Then he made a sharp turn and sent down a third 109. The Germans did not know what had hit them! When the distressed Messerschmitt pilots later landed at their bases, seven '109s were missing. Four of these had been downed by Archie McKellar – in the space of three minutes! The other three Bf 109s were shot down by 303 Polish Squadron's pilots. The RAF's total losses in the clash were confined to one damaged and one destroyed Hurricane.

In fact, McKellar claimed a fifth victory that day – later in the afternoon, when some 30 Bf 109s made a third Jabo operation against London – but this cannot be confirmed from German loss reports.

The great fighter combats

The German Jabo offensive marked the beginning of a period of great fighter combats, and here a handful of aces on both sides made themselves notable. The largest individual successes were achieved by the leading aces on the German side. A major reason for this was that the Luftwaffe usually kept its airmen in action for longer periods. The three leading German aces at this time – Mölders, Galland and Wick – had been more or less continuously in action at the English Channel since the end of July 1940. Although few in number, there were also RAF pilots who had equally long and uninterrupted front line service. One of them was 501 Squadron's Sergeant 'Ginger' Lacey, who by early October 1940 had a score of 18½ air victories. Of critical importance was the very strong emphasis that the German side put on individual performance in air combat. As with Mölders and Galland, Wick was awarded the Oak Leaves to the Knight's Cross for his 40th victory. At the same time he was promoted to Major. Wick had now come level with Galland and was just one kill behind Mölders. In the RAF there were certainly those who fought for personal success, but team spirit was more common, as demonstrated by the attitude of the ace in 92 Squadron, Flight Lieutenant Brian Kingcombe: 'Kingcombe was not interested in the "ace" conception fostered by the press; anyone who wasted time trying to confirm a "kill" or hung on unnecessarily to a damaged bomber was quite simply not doing his job. Split them up with a quick head-on attack from a high position was his method.'[445]

This phase of the Battle of Britain also meant that an 'altitude race' began between the fighter pilots on both sides. Since accuracy in bomb dropping no longer played such an important role as previously, while shooting down enemy planes instead was the most important thing, flight altitudes grew higher during the fighter-bomber offensive. 'Because we always tried to stay above the opponent, air fighting took place at ever higher altitudes', Adolf Galland said. 'My personal record was 8,200 metres, but you could see Me 109s and Spitfires engaged in dogfights at over 9,000 metres, close to the stratosphere's lower limit. You could see their vapor trails against the dark blue sky.'[446]

Park, for his part, gave orders to, 'when time permits', allow the fighter planes to climb to high altitudes – Spitfires to 30,000 to 35,000 feet (about 9,000–10,500 metres), individual Hurricane squadrons to 20,000–25,000 feet (6,000–7,500 metres) and Hurricane squadrons which operated in pairs to 18,000–22,000 feet (5,500–6,700 metres) – before they were sent against the German flight formations.[447] In addition, he had a special 'scouting unit' formed, 421 Flight. Its mission was to patrol at high altitude along the south coast and report incoming German units and their altitude. This was obviously a very dangerous mission, and therefore Flight 421 was equipped with the latest Spitfire model, Mk II. Under the leadership of the South African veteran Flight Lieutenant Charles Green, Flight 421 immediately began its missions – called 'Jim Crow'.

Tuesday 8 October was marked by the top fighter aces. In the morning, Major Galland escorted the fighter-bombers in LG 2 to the British capital. It was just one of several fighter-bomber formations with escort that flew to London. Park detailed eleven squadrons to intercept this raid. At 09:15 (British time) bombs on the British capital were reported. 'As usual, the British fighters were waiting for us

high above London', said Oberleutnant Werner Voigt, who commanded 4./JG 3. 'Our bomb-Staffel dropped its little "eggs" on London with the usual feeling of hopelessness, and then the Englishmen attacked. I tried to count how many they were, but gave up when I arrived at twenty, because time was becoming sparse. Then we all dived at the Kommandeur's order towards a cloud cover at 3,000 metres' altitude over London.'[448]

Apparently the RAF fighters disappeared in search of the first wave of fighter-bombers; to Galland's disappointment, there were no enemy planes in sight when he flew towards London. He was hunting for his 42nd air victory.

At Hawkinge on the English south coast 21-year-old Canadian Pilot Officer George Corbett took off with his Spitfire R 6779, 'LZ-X', from 66 Squadron. He flew as Blue 2 in 'B' Flight, and the mission was: 'Patrol over a convoy off Herne Bay.' The Spitfires flew across Kent and climbed. At 7,000 metres over the Isle of Sheppey a group of Bf 109s surprisingly appeared out of the sun. One of the German fighters quickly got behind Corbett's Spitfire and gave a well-aimed burst of fire. The Spitfire rolled and fell burning while all the other British fighters disappeared from the scene. Adolf Galland's logbook for 8 October reads: 'Direct escort of an attack on London. 42nd victory, a Spitfire, at 10:20 hrs, 6,800 metres' altitude, east of Eastchurch.'[449]

George Corbett's Spitfire crashed in Bayford Marsh, about one kilometre north of Upchurch. In the remains of the wrecked cockpit the dead pilot's body was found, completely shattered by bullets. Next to him was the gold watch that Corbett recently received from his family for his 21st birthday. Corbett still rests in the cemetery at St. Mary the Virgin, Upchurch. The propeller from his downed Spitfire was dug up in 1982 and is exhibited today at Tangmere Military Aviation Museum.

When Galland triumphantly landed at Audembert, another of the great aces took off – it was 303 Squadron's Sergeant Josef František, the most successful pilot in the RAF at the time. He had scored 17 victories in the RAF, plus possibly ten or eleven more during his time in the French Air Force. He climbed into the sky in his Hurricane when 303 Squadron went up from Northolt for a patrol south of London at 09:50 (British time). The unit never made contact with the enemy, despite another thirty German planes flying over Lympne at 10:25, heading towards London. The latter were from III./JG 54 – Oberleutnant Hans-Ekkehard Bob and his fighter-bombers, escorted by the other Messerschmitts in the unit.[450]

Twenty minutes later, III./JG 54 clashed with RAF fighters. Leutnant Max-Hellmuth Ostermann, Oberfeldwebel Max Clerico and Feldwebel Fritz Oeltjen claimed to have shot down three of these with no own losses. At about the same time and in the same area a Hurricane crashed. The pilot, who was thrown out of the cockpit and was killed, was identified as Josef František. For unknown reasons he had disappeared from 303 Squadron's formation during the patrol, and now he also crashed for reasons that have never been clarified.

On 10 October, 92 Squadron lost two of its top aces, Pilot Officer Desmond Williams and Flying Officer John Drummond, when one of them was shot down by the rear

Josef František (right) had served in the Czechoslovak Air Force for four years when Hitler marched into his country. He fled to Poland and flew for the Polish Air Force during the German invasion of that country in 1939. After fleeing this country, he made his way to England and in August 1940 was placed in the newly formed 303 (Polish) Squadron. Sergeant František was regarded as notoriously undisciplined and wilful during flights, but he was a brilliant fighter pilot. He often performed solo missions, and after his 27th victory on 30 September 1940, he was awarded the Distinguished Flying Medal. He died the day after his 26th birthday. With 17 victories – attained in just a month – František was the RAF's top ace during the Battle of Britain, between July and October 1940.

Spitfires from 66 Squadron take off from Gravesend. The rightmost aircraft is R 6779, 'LZ-X'. Canadian Pilot Officer George Corbett died when he was shot in this aircraft by the German ace Adolf Galland on 8 October 1940.

gunner in Lieutenant Walter Dilcher's Do 17 from I./KG 2, and then collided with his comrade. John Drummond had nine victories, and Desmond Williams was credited with eight. A third Spitfire from 92 Squadron was also shot down by the clearly accurate gunners in the Do 17 and crashed, but the pilot survived.

After Galland had been on a par with Mölders in the number of victories for three days, he took the lead again – and kept it for five hours. By coincidence, it was again No. 66 Squadron that had to pay with one of its planes. Pilot Officer Hubert Allen, a veteran from 66 Squadron, was fortunate enough to escape with his life when Mölders shot down his Spitfire on 11 October.*

Meanwhile Galland was in a hurry to catch up with Mölders. He flew two sorties over southern England without seeing a single British aircraft. But during final missions of the day, towards the evening, he and the pilots from II./JG 26 came upon a lone Spitfire. It was a Mark IIA from 421 Flight, and its pilot, Sergeant Charles Ayling, became the unit's first casualty when Galland sent the aircraft to the ground in a fireball to get his 43rd kill.

Obviously Ayling did not have time to report the German aircraft, as Galland and his airmen a while later managed to surprise 41 and 92 squadrons, which operated in 'pairs'. John Lecky was nineteen and a pilot officer when he arrived at 41 Squadron as a rookie fighter pilot on 2 October. He did not get much older. At approximately half past five (British time) in the afternoon of 11 Octo-

ber, his Spitfire was shot to pieces by a Bf 109 from JG 26. Lecky attempted to bail out, but failed. Another two Spitfires crashed – the result of a collision, according to British records. Galland was credited with the first of these Spitfires (probably Lecky's machine). Hauptmann Walter Adolph – who recently arrived from JG 27 to take command of II./JG 26 – was credited with shooting down the last two, to be chalked up as Adolph's 10th and 11th victories. On the British side, two Bf 109s were claimed shot down by the two aces Flight Lieutenant Brian Kingcombe (92 Squadron) and Pilot Officer Eric Lock (41 Squadron). This brought Lock to 15½ and Kingcombe to seven (two shared) victories.

When Galland returned to France after the final mission on 11 October, there was a high spirited atmosphere at the airfield at Audembert. By listening to the radio communication between the pilots everyone knew that their Geschwaderkommodore by scoring his 44th victory had taken the lead in the competition between the aces. But Galland did not maintain his lead for long.

At 09:50 the following day, 12 October, Mölders took off from St. Inglevert. Along with twenty Bf 109s he swept in over the coast at Dungeness. A few minutes later Pilot Officer Herbert Case (72 Squadron) dived to his death in the cockpit of the Spitfire that Mölders shot down. The German fighter aircraft continued north, in the direction of the Thames Estuary. When Flight Lieutenant George Perrin, a French volunteer in 249 Squadron, bailed out of his burn-

* When Allen several years later was informed that he was recorded as Mölders' 43rd victory, he said to have been quite upset.
  (Foreman, p. 64.)

Incendiary bombs are loaded onto a He 111 from KGr 100. (Photo: Bätcher.)

ing Hurricane, Mölders had his 45th victory confirmed. The German ace landed in St. Inglevert at eleven o'clock. After lunch with his men, he climbed into the cockpit of his Bf 109 again and sped along the runway. Overall, there were about fifty Bf 109s that flew over southern England. Sergeant Peter McIntosh, a 20-year Hurricane pilot from 605 Squadron, lost his life so that Mölders could increase his number of victories to 46.

Retaliation

Thick autumn fog that swept in over the English Channel kept daytime air activity down for a few days, but did not affect the nightly operations, which now intensified during the period of the full moon. It began on the evening of 13 October when 211 German bombers flew towards London.[451] 24 hours later the British capital was hit by one of its hitherto worst air raids when 242 German bombers dropped, among other things, 1,800-kg high-explosive bombs. One of these penetrated into the Balham underground station, where many people had sought refuge. It caused 66 casualties. A large number of incendiary bombs – including some of 500 kilograms – caused widespread fires. In central London several fires united until they covered an area of almost a square kilometre. According to the returning German airmen they had never seen such a large 'fire effect' in the British capital.[452]

This attack caused 500 deaths and 2,000 people were seriously injured, while not a single German bomber was shot down during the nights of 13/14 and 14/15 October. By that time, the bomb raids had deprived a million Londoners of their gas supply.[453] At the British War Cabinet's meeting on 15 October there was concerned discussion that: 'The civilian population in London were beginning to wonder whether we were hitting back hard enough at Germany in our bombing operations'.[454]

Bomber Command tried to retaliate to the best of its ability, but did less well. Of the 78 aircraft which attacked Berlin on the night of 14/15 October, eight failed to return to their bases. German night fighter pilots accounted for three of those losses, but two German night fighters were also shot down. The damage in Berlin this night was of rather limited extent. Up to then, the British air strikes against the German capital had cost a total of 200 casualties among the city's population. The following night British losses were even worse – thirteen out of seventy-three bombers. The results were anything but good. The Leuna-Merseburg oil-refinery, which was one of the main objectives, was hit by only three bombs.[455]

When the weather cleared on 15 October, all of the three German top aces were out over the south of England. That day the Luftwaffe carried out 500 fighter and 304 bomber sorties over England, and Fighter Command responded with a total of 598 fighter sorties, of which more than two hundred made contact with the enemy. High in the skies over the county of Kent and above the Thames

Estuary the sky filled with coiling condensation trails that marked the violent combats.

At 09:15 (German time) Major Mölders shot down a Hurricane. The pilot escaped by bailing out. It was Squadron Leader John Banham, who previously had flown a Defiant in 264 Squadron until he was shot down by Major Günther Lützow on 26 August. On 7 September, he was appointed commander of 229 Squadron, and now he was shot down by Lützow's friend Mölders.

Galland was at an altitude of 6,500 metres just south of the Thames Estuary when he spotted a formation of British fighters. Afterwards he wrote this combat report: 'Mission: Extended escort of II./LG 2 and own fighter-bombers towards London. During the approach flight I and my Staffel shielded II./LG 2 against an attack from behind by a squadron of Spitfires. Coming from below, I attacked a lone Spitfire which had become separated from the others.

'I opened fire from 150-200 metres and could see my bullets hitting. The aircraft levelled off. My wingman and I made one pass each against the Spitfire, which at that time was flying very slowly and without taking any evasive action. Suddenly, we saw the pilot bail out. He fell freely at least 1,000 metres before his parachute opened.' [456]

A comparison with British reports indicates that the Spitfire which ended up as Adolf Galland's 45th victory belonged to 92 Squadron. The pilot who Galland saw bail out was none other than the famous Brian Kingcombe.

Major Helmut Wick participated in a large fighter sweep by both JG 2 and ZG 26 over the Isle of Wight. They were met by four squadrons from 10 Group, and after the ensuing combat, JG 2 again gave proof of some wild exaggerations: Its ten victory claims were matched by only two British fighter losses. (However, JG 2 lost three Bf 109s, while the British claimed to have shot down four.) One of these ten victories was chalked up as number 42 on Major Wick's tally.

One of the two RAF pilots who were shot down by JG 2 was Pilot Officer Jiří Macháček, a Czech volunteer; he had flown as 'Tail End Charlie' for 145 Squadron and became easy prey for the attacking '109s. Macháček managed to bail out and escaped with shrapnel in his leg.

Another German fighter ace who reaped successes on 15 October was Oberleutnant Josef Priller, the commander of 6./JG 51. In the vicinity of Dover he scored two of the three victories that the Germans claimed in the clash, which raised his total to 19. Before the war was over, he had amassed a total of 101 victories. Priller got one of them – number 34 – on 8 July, 1941, and it is likely that the plane he shot down then was flown by Jiří Macháček, who did not make it out alive that time.

The Germans had now learned from their initial mistakes during the Jabo-offensive, and now had fighter escort flying together with fighter-bombers, which also yielded results in the form of increased British losses. Between 10 and 15 October the air fighting in connection with Jabo missions and 'nuisance flights' by German bombers resulted in a loss of 40 fighters on the British side, while only 19 Bf 109s and three German bombers were shot down. No one could be more concerned about this than Park. On 15 October, he issued new instructions to his air controllers

and sector commanders. He noted that the recent German tactic allowed the opponent to be above London at height only 20 minutes after his formations had been detected by radar. For his fighters to have time to climb higher than their opponents, Park decided to abandon the tactic of letting his squadrons operate in pairs, or even in Wings. 'Controllers will see the importance of ordering pairs or Wings to rendezvous over a point at operating height in order that they can climb quickly, singly, and not hold one another back by trying to climb in an unwieldy mass', Park wrote. 'Bitter experience has proved time and again that it is better to intercept the enemy with one squadron above him than by a whole wing crawling up below, probably after the enemy has dropped his bombs.' [457]

During daytime on 17 October the Germans dispatched 110 fighter-bombers against London, divided into four different raiding groups. The first two, involving, among others, III./ZG 76, hardly led to any air combat. The third raid against London – just after three in the afternoon (British time) – was met by no less than fourteen British squadrons. Now Park's new tactic was put into action, and with good results. 41, 66, 74 and 222 squadrons engaged the Bf 109s. Aces on each side clashed – the RAF's Squadron Leader 'Sailor' Malan (74 Squadron) and Flying Officer Desmond McMullen (222 Squadron), and the Luftwaffe's Major 'Vati' Mölders (JG 51) and Hauptmann Hans-Karl Mayer (JG 53). 'Sailor' Malan was quick to attack:

'We suddenly saw some yellow-noses (Me 109s) crossing our bows, and surprised them from the sun. I gave the right-hand one a two-second burst with quarter deflection from 200 yards and closed to 150 yards astern and delivered another two-second burst. I then closed to 100 yards and delivered a four-second burst which appears to damage elevator controls, as his nose went vertically downwards very suddenly instead of the usual half-roll. My engine naturally stopped when I followed suit, but it picked up again and I closed to 150 yards on half-roll and gave another four-second burst. I found myself doing an aileron turn to keep direction and delivered another four-second burst. He then started to smoke, but I blacked out completely and lost consciousness for a couple of seconds.' [458]

That combat cost the attackers three Bf 109s, all from JG 53, and all with unit commanders at the controls. Hauptmann Hans-Karl Mayer, who led I./JG 53, crashed in the Thames Estuary. The combat report Pilot Officer Edward Wells from 41 Squadron wrote, seems to describe the shooting down of Mayer: 'I noticed a single Me 109 returning from the London area and heading towards the Channel. I immediately gave chase; as my height was only about 2,000 feet more he took some time to overtake. He seemed unaware of my presence and took no evasive action, so I closed until he exactly filled the sight bar, range 250 yards. I gave what I considered a preliminary burst of about 2 sec-

◄ *Oberleutnant Victor Mölders (to the right in photo) was the younger brother by one year of Werner Mölders (centre). Victor Mölders flew with I./ZG 1 in the Battle of Poland and during the invasion of France. Subsequently, he was briefly trained as a night fighter pilot in I./NJG 1 before his brother had him transferred in August 1940 to JG 51, where he took command of the 2. Staffel on 12 September. When he was shot down and taken prisoner on 7 October 1940, he had claimed seven air victories. Victor Mölders, who contributed with interviews and footage for this book, passed away on 3 July 2010, aged 93. (Photo: Mölders.)*

onds and glycol smoke imnmediately poured away in large quantities and the machine started a shallow dive which he continued until about 7,000 feet, when he suddenly dived very sharply straight down into the sea. No pilot attempted to leave the machine at any time. I circled over the spot on the sea at 500 feet. Nothing came to the surface.' Hauptmann Mayer's dead body washed ashore ten days later. With 30 victories in in the Second World War and another nine in the Spanish Civil War, he was the most successful fighter pilot to be killed in the war so far.

While this took place, 'Vati' Mölders and two pilots from JG 53 claimed to have shot down a Spitfire apiece. Two Spitfires were, in fact, downed, and neither of the pilots survived. Pilot Officer Hugh Reilley, an American volunteer, was killed when his Section was attacked at height by Major Mölders' Schwarm. His Spitfire – R6800, 'LZ-N' – was recorded as Mölders' 48th victory.

In London the Messerschmitts' bombs fell at random, as usual. Five bombs struck Wilkins Street, killing three people, wounding ten and burying dozens of others in the collapsed houses.

Fritz von Forell describes the scene at the airfield at St. Inglevert when Mölders landed twenty minutes later to report his forty-eighth victory in the Second World War: 'His plane roars over the airfield with wings waving to indicate a new victory. As always, the entire ground staff rushes to surround his aircraft when it taxiis in after landing. His men are eager to hear the details, and if he is happy with their work on his aircraft. So he opens the cockpit hood – and laughs! His face still is marked with the strain from the combat, but he is laughing! He shakes hands with all the men who enabled this victory through their hard work. To Mölders, it is natural that the first he shakes hands with are the men of his ground crew. "In London", he says, "there is hardly a single windowpane left. One wonders how long the British will be able to stand these bombing raids day and night!"' [459]

The remark about window panes was hardly an overstatement. On the night of 15 October the Luftwaffe dispatched a record 410 bombers that dropped 538 tonnes of bombs on London, where no less than nine hundred fires were started, 400 people were killed and 800 were injured. The following night there were 280 bombers, and on 17/18 October 254 which again caused widespread fires in the city. But at the same time London's air defences strengthened. During these three nights, 18 German night bombers were downed – one of them by a Defiant from 264 Squadron.

Bomber pilot Leutnant Sven Schulte from KG 54 wrote in his diary: 'The strange thing is that the defence of London has grown stronger. Tonight I was caught by the light beams from ten of searchlights simultaneously. But our newspapers tell us that there are no more searchlights in London.' [460]

It got even worse the following night. The 129 German bombers that in spite of bad weather flew to London on the night of 18/19 October encountered a stronger air defence than ever. Sven Schulte wrote: 'Once again we encountered searchlights, barrage balloons and heavy anti-aircraft fire. On the return flight my air base and

Spitfires from 66 Squadron. The airplane closest to the camera is 'LZ-N'. Pilot Officer Hugh Reilley flew this plane when he was shot down on 17 October 1940 by German ace Werner Mölders.

the entire surrounding area was covered by thick clouds. For over two and a half hours, I tried to find a gap in the clouds, while my radio operator called various aerodromes to inquire about landing opportunities. After five hours in the air, I found a suitable location. Several other crews from my air base had to bail out because their aircraft ran out of petrol.'[461]

Bomber Command, after a night's rest, sent in 28 Whitley and Hampden bombers against various targets in Germany and also to Milan the night of 18/19 October. Only 19 of them returned to their bases, while the night's bombing claimed one person's life in Germany. The following night, the 19/20, Bomber Command limited its actions to three bombers that flew against Germany, while 282 and 298 German bombers attacked London during this and the following night. Because both the anti-aircraft gun and night fighters were hindered by a thick cloud cover over England no German bomber was lost. This was reflected in the atmosphere in London, which during the meeting of the war cabinet on 21 October was described as 'somewhat pessimistic'.[462]

Bomber Command continued unabated its almost suicidal operations against Germany. Of the thirty Hampdens that flew to Berlin during the night of the 20th, three were shot down. At the same time eleven Whitley bombers from 58 Squadron were sent to the Skoda works in Czech Pilsen, but failed to locate the target and lost three machines. One of them was destroyed by a German night fighter who pursued the British planes in over England.

But despite the high losses and a terribly poor accuracy, the British bombings were maintained because of the encouragement they gave the British people. In the last attack on Berlin a bomb hit a bomb shelter with the result that over 40 people were killed or injured. Such incidents eroded the Germans' belief in an early end to the war.

A heavy downpour combined with thick fog gave a relatively quiet day on 21 October. Still, this date came to be a milestone in Fighter Command's history. The Germans decided to take advantage of the bad weather to send out a few bombers on nuisance raids over the British Isles. Meanwhile Thomas Fitzgerald, a test pilot, took off with his armed Hurricane II prototype. By chance, he came across a Do 17, which he attacked and shot down. Leutnant Heinz Wildhagen's crew from 8./KG 76 is probably the only Luftwaffe crew to fall victim to a civilian.

In the afternoon Oberleutnant Maximilian Fabian's Ju 88 '9K+BH' from I./KG 51 flew in over Portsmouth and continued all the way to Gloucester. There, he turned south and made a low-level attack against the RAF base at Old Sarum. At the same time two Spitfires from 609 Squadron were approaching. Flight Lieutenant Frank Howell and Pilot Officer Sydney Hill received orders from the air controller to fly to Salisbury, and they arrived at Old Sarum just in time to see Oberleutnant Fabian's Ju 88 leave. The two British fighter pilots took up the chase. Oberleutnant Fabian's mistake was to try to escape at low altitude instead of climbing up into the low clouds. Fatally hit by bullets

FOREIGN PILOTS AMONG 'THE FEW'

The role played by foreign fighter pilots in the Battle of Britain is well known. The RAF Roll of Honour recognises 574 foreign pilots who flew at least one authorized, operational sortie with an eligible unit during the period 10 July–31 October 1940, alongside 2,353 British pilots.

The mentioning of an 'Israeli' pilot among 'the Few' in some sources has caused some confusion, since Israel did not exist in 1940. The pilot in question was actually a British citizen, Pilot Officer George Ernest Goodman. He served with No. 1 Squadron, and was credited with three victories in the Battle of France and another five in the Battle of Britain until he was shot down and injured by a Bf 110 on 6 September 1940.

NATION	NUMBER
Poland	145
New Zealand	127
Canada	112
Czechoslovakia	84
Belgium	30
Australia	26
South Africa	22
France	14
Ireland	10
USA	11
Southern Rhodesia	4
Jamaica	1
Barbados	1
Newfoundland	1
Northern Rhodesia	1

The Swedish voluntary pilot Ralf Häggberg was admitted to the RAF in 1940 and flew twin-engined Westland Whirlwind fighters with Fighter Command in 1941–1942. In this picture Ralf Häggberg is seen, third from the left, along with comrades from No.137 Squadron in front of a Whirlwind. (Photo: Mary Farron via Barbro Holmbäck.)

One of fourteen French fighter pilots in the Battle of Britain. Jean Demozay (far right) was a French liaison officer at RAF in France in 1939–1940 and flew to England in June 1940. In October 1940 he joined No. 1 Squadron RAF. Demozay developed into one of the most experienced Allied fighter pilots during the Second World War, flying over 400 combat missions. His 21 victories made him the third highest scoring French ace during the war. He was killed in a flight accident on 19th December 1945.

from both Spitfires the Junkers crashed near Lymington. No one in the crew survived.

With this victory, No. 609 Squadron became the first fighter unit in the RAF to achieve 100 victories in the war – and this was celebrated grandiosely. 'We trooped into the writing-room and there found a couple of waiters behind the bar and almost hidden by the large stock of champagne and brandy that had been installed for the occasion. [. . .] We toasted practically everything we could think of, in round after round of champagne cocktails', said Flight Lieutenant David Crook. [463] Although the RAF did not emphasise individual victories in the same way as the Luftwaffe, there were many RAF pilots who hunted for victories with the same zeal as the German aces.

Next day it was on a German air base that there was a celebration. Shortly after three in the afternoon on 22 October Major Mölders took off from St. Inglevert. For two days now he had been flying combat missions with an entirely new aircraft, a Messerschmitt Bf 109 F-1. In early October a plane of the new Messerschmitt 109 version, the F-1, had been delivered to Major Mölders' Stabsstaffel JG 51. With this aircraft, the Messerschmitt designer had achieved considerable aerodynamic improvements, making it more manoeuvrable and faster – the Bf 109 F-1 could reach nearly 600 km/h in level flight. A weakness of the new '109, however, was the armament; the two 20mm MG FF cannons in the wings had been replaced with a single cannon firing through the propeller hub. For a marksman like Werner Mölders this constituted no problem. He took up his Bf 109 F-1 for a first flight on 9 October, but it took until 20 October before he used the new F-1 on any combat mission. By that time, another couple of Bf 109 F-1s had also been delivered to I./JG 51.

When Mölders ventured out over the Channel on the afternoon of 22 October, the mission was again to escort fighter-bombers towards London. In Biggin Hill the alarm sounded and 74 'Tiger' Squadron went up to meet Mölders and his men. Mölders led his airmen up to almost 9,000 metres, and in the frigid air at that height, he hoped to avoid being attacked from above. But the British radar and air surveillance provided 11 Group's command centre with accurate information about the German altitude, and from there the information went on to Wing Commander Grice, sector commander at Biggin Hill, who ordered 74 Squadron's Spitfires up to over 9,000 metres. Flight Lieutenant John Mungo-Park lay in wait 300 metres higher than the Germans when he led 'Tiger Squadron' to attack.

'Achtung, Spitfire!' cried Mölders and swerved to fend off the attack, but he could not prevent Mungo-Park from getting behind a Bf 109 flown by Fähnrich Kurt Müller, a 19-year-old newcomer in I./JG 51. Müller dived in desperation, but could not escape the British ace who shot down the German fighter six thousand metres further down.

Werner Mölders (left) and Hauptmann Heinz Bretnütz, the commander of II./JG 53. Bretnütz achieved his 20th air victory on 20 October 1940 and two days later was awarded with the Knight's Cross, which he carries in this picture. Bretnütz, a veteran of the Spanish Civil War, reached a total of 35 victories before he was shot down and badly wounded on the Eastern Front on 22 June 1941. Five days later he died from his injuries. (Photo: Trautloft.)

To dive after them would have been crazy, so Mölders instead turned his attention to the other British fighters. Three times in the space of two minutes his voice sounded over the radio – 'Abschuss!' – proclaiming a new victory. Pilot Officer Peter St John died in the flames in the cockpit of his burning Spitfire and his comrade Pilot Officer Robert Spurdle was fortunate to survive by bailing out.

According to South African Squadron Leader Douglas Tidy, Spurdle was attacked by a Bf 109 while he sank down defenceless in his parachute dome, but was saved by his friend Harbourne Stephen who drove off the German. [464]

It has proved impossible to identify the pilot of this Messerschmitt 109, whether it was Mölders himself or someone else. However, among the German veteran airman no one was better known for his attitude of fair play to the opponent than Werner Mölders. There are known instances in which Mölders became very upset about subordinates who committed acts that violated the 'rules of war' – for example, when Hauptmann Joppien fired on a civilian train during a flight over England. A short time afterwards Mölders defied the Nazi police state by giving his support to the German Bishop Clemens August Graf von Galen who raised his voice against the Nazis' first mass murder, the so-called 'euthanasia program'.

With the three victories – attained between 15:40 and 15:42 – Mölders became the first pilot in the war to exceed 50 victories. His nearest rival Galland was only four victories behind.

In fact, it cannot be excluded that Galland – without knowing about it! – may have shot down three British fighters shortly afterwards. At half past six in the evening

(German time), he led a formation of 18 Bf 109s at high altitude over the English coast at Dungeness and saw 'eight Spitfires and a Hurricane' at 4,000 metres, with an additional squadron of Hurricanes higher up. It was the Hurricanes from 46 Squadron, with 257 Squadron as top cover. Galland divided his formation and led half in a diving attack on the lower of the two Hurricane formations while the rest were assigned to take care of the British top cover.

One of the British pilots involved was 257 Squadron's Flight Lieutenant The Honourable David Arthur Coke.[465] If anyone resembled the standard image of the English fighter pilot as a young nobleman, it was this 24-year-old son of the fourth Earl of Leicester and godson to the previous British King Edward VIII. He was now back in the thick of combat again after he had been shot down and had a finger shot off by a Bf 110 over Portland on 12 August, and he was determined to get revenge. Coke's combat report reads: 'I was flying Yellow 1 doing rear section lookout to 257 Squadron who were escorting 46 Squadron. At 22,000 feet above New Romney I saw about nine Me 109s above and behind, manoeuvering to up sun of us. I warned 257 Sqdn leader, turned towards the enemy aircraft and saw two of them come down at us. I got in one short burst from quarter ahead at the second one, but observed no result. I then saw a dogfight in progress south of me over the sea and below, and flew west and then turned and flew towards it down sun. However at 19,000 feet I sighted 7 Me 109s in wide Vic slightly below and flying straight towards me. I don't think they saw me. I carried out a ¾ head-on attack on the right-hand Me 109 of the Vic; I could see my bullets hitting him from the engine right through to the tail. I passed about 50 yards from him and turned, but lost them in the sun.' [466]

Messerschmitt 109 E-4 'Black 10' flown by Galland's wingman, Feldwebel Heinz Arp, exploded in the air. Its shattered parts floated down from 6,000 metres' altitude over the sea just east of the Dungeness. The 24-year-old pilot had no chance of survival.

When the pilots from JG 26 later landed in Audembert, no one reported any victory. But the fact is that a Hurricane with 257 Squadron's Pilot Officer Norman Heywood had been shot down and crashed into the sea. The Germans also saw two other damaged Hurricanes flying towards land with glycol spouting out of their punctured radiators.[467] None of the German pilots saw it, but at Newchurch, ten kilometres north of Dungeness, the Hurricane flown by 46 Squadron's Sergeant Joseph Morrison crashed. Shortly afterwards the other damaged machine, from 257 Squadron, crashed five kilometres further inland and caught fire on impact. The pilot, 20-year-old Sergeant Robert Fraser, died.

None of the three Hurricane pilots survived. Morrison and Heywood were 'green' – they had only served a few weeks.*

On Sunday 25 October, in bright sunshine, the Luftwaffe dispatched 634 fighters – including 186 fighter-bombers – most of them towards London. It was the highest number in three weeks, but Fighter Command responded with a total of 776 fighters. Most of the Germans came in four different waves. At nine o'clock in the morning (British time) fierce air battles were raging and five British and one German fighter were shot down. JG 26 attacked 603 Squadron, which was on patrol above Maidstone, and shot down three of its Spitfires. The two pilot officers Frank Soden and Peter Olver survived by bailing out. The third pilot, Pilot Officer Ludwik Martel, lost consciousness when his Spitfire Mk IIa ('XT-W'), P7350 was hit – possibly by bullets from the Bf 109 flown by Hauptmann Walter Adolph, commander of II./JG 26, who thus claimed his 13th kill. When Martel came to, he discovered that he was flying upside down and just came out of a cloud. A large hole gaped in one wing and the engine was dead, but he still managed to take the plane down to a crash-landing.**

At the same time Mölders achieved his 52nd victory by shooting down a Spitfire flown by 66 Squadron's ace Flying Officer Robert Oxspring. The latter, credited with eight victories (of which three were shared), survived by bailing out. On the next mission, at noon, another Spitfire fell before Mölders' guns. On the day's final mission, JG 51 clashed with No. 501 Squadron, with four Hurricanes and two Bf 109s getting shot down. One of the latter was Major Mölders' plane – a Bf 109 E-4 with staff markings. The pilot bailed out and ended up in captivity. However the man who had flown the plane that day was Hauptmann Hans Asmus. Mölders himself flew the new Bf 109 F-1.

On this day Galland had flown three sorties without managing to increase his number of victories. Eager to catch up with Mölders he decided on the evening of the next day – 26 October – to brave the bad weather and fly across England with 3./JG 26. Up at 8,000 metres he spotted a solitary Hurricane which boldly climbed towards the Bf 109s. Galland immediately went to attack. New Zealander James Hayter, who was then a 23-year-old Flying Officer in 605 Squadron, remembers: 'In 605 Squadron's Hurricane "UP-D" – a borrowed aircraft – I was flying over Kent, Gravesend. We had attacked a bunch of '109s. I got separated on my own, and saw a formation of eight or nine '109s in tight formation above me. I was creeping up behind them, hoping to take them by surprise. Then I myself got shot down by a '109 behind me – he had crept up on me – at about 15,000 feet. My rudder controls were shot away from my feet – leaving a big hole – and something hit the armour plate behind my seat as I got shrapnel in my head and in my side. I opened my hood and tested my ailerons and I was flicked out when it turned over suddenly. I opened my parachute and was spinning as I was hit on the way out.' [468]

While Galland returned to Audembert to celebrate his 46th victory, Hayter involuntarily ended up in another

---

* Another Hurricane from 257 Squadron was damaged and force-landed at Gatwick. The pilot, Sergeant Reginald Nutter, survived however and passed away only recently, nearly 95 years old.
** The aircraft could be repaired and still exists, being the oldest Spitfire in airworthy condition, although re-painted and presented as 41 Squadron's Spitfire Mk Ia N3162, 'EB-G', depicting the one flown by Eric Lock during the Battle of Britain. As such it is part of the Battle of Britain memorial Flight.

celebration. He landed in Mayor Victor Castlet's garden in Staplehurst where a cocktail party was going on! With typical British calm the partygoers offered the shot down RAF pilot refreshments, while someone called a doctor who bandaged the pilot's wounds. Then Hayter called his fiancée – who lived not far from there – and asked her to come by and pick him up with her car!

The air combats on 25–26 October saw 14 German and 24 British fighters get shot down; among the latter, however, five could be repaired. Both sides were now fighting on the brink of exhaustion. But by now, Park's new directives had begun to pay off. On the morning of 27 October, 74 Squadron was ordered up against a new German raid. The Spitfires climbed to 9,000 metres. Above Maidstone they saw the Germans – 'a number of Me 109s at about 23,000 feet'.[469] These were eight Bf 109s from I./JG 52 escorting the fighter-bombers from I.(J)/LG 2, which flew lower.

'Raven calling! Raven calling! Eleven o'clock high! Condensation trails, same course!' crackled in the German fighters' headphones. The tense Messerschmitt pilots followed the condensation trails with their eyes. After a while, it was obvious that the British up there were preparing to attack.

'Achtung, sie kommen! Sie kommen!' – They're coming, they're coming!

The British had split up into several groups, and two of them managed to evade detection while the Germans watched the sharp condensation trails that looped against the clear blue sky above. Suddenly there was a shrill scream over the German radio: 'Out of the sun! Out of the sun!'

Oberleutnant Ulrich Steinhilper recalled: 'I made a steep turn, full throttle, rudder bar hard round and the stick against my leg, the engine turning at 2800 rpm – 400 too many! We had to make as much speed as possible – the British fighters were diving towards us.'[470]

Gefreiter Karl Bott's Bf 109 was hit and went into a spin. The pilot bailed out. Pursued by several Spitfires, Oberleutnant Steinhilper and his wingman Feldwebel Lothar Schieverhöfer, veered towards the sun. Flying Officer William Nelson, an American in 74 'Tiger' Squadron, explained: 'Two of the '109s came across my bows, heading into the sun. I followed and closed to 150 yards on the port side of the enemy and opened fire with a three-second burst which caused the '109 to smoke badly and half-roll down.'[471]

'The first Spitfire already had red flames dancing along the leading edge of his wings as his guns fired' Steinhilper continued. 'I dived away and saw that the engine was now turning at 3300 rpm, the throttle fully open. I couldn't risk the engine blowing up, so at 7,000 metres I levelled out.'

'I followed easily', said Nelson, 'and the enemy, after a sharp dive, pulled steeply into the sun. I could only follow him with the smoke trail. After two minutes I closed once more in the climb and gave a continuous burst of fire at point-blank range. The '109 shed bits of machine which hit my aircraft and damaged the spinner and propeller.'

'Bang! There was an explosion at the left side of my fighter, near to the front. The control column shook as something hit the elevators in the tail' – that is what Steinhilper experienced. 'The enemy then wallowed in a shallow dive, and I formatted on it down through the clouds', continued Nelson – or with Steinhilpers words: 'I put the nose down and glided down towards the cloud layer below.'

The war was over for Steinhilper. He survived by bailing out, and so did his wingman and Gefreiter Karl Bott. 74 Squadron's Sergeant John Alan Scott was not so lucky. His Spitfire crashed in a fireball, killing the pilot.

For I./JG 52 too the Battle of Britain was then over. Its war diary notes: 'In mid-October, the combat strength of our Gruppe had dropped so much that we flew our missions with an average of ten aircraft. After those three losses on 27 October, seven pilots is all that remains of the unit.'[472] A few days later, I./JG 52 was pulled out from combat and was transferred to Krefeld in Germany.

On 29 October, Park's new tactics brought about a brilliant victory over the fighter-bombers and their escorts. At 11:58 hours, Nos. 229 and 615 squadrons were ordered to take off. Two German formations with a total of fifty Messerschmitts had been sighted heading towards Dover. The first clashes cost one fighter on each side. But that was only the beginning. When the fighter-bombers from I. and II./LG 2 and 3./Erprobungsgruppe 210, and their escort from Stab, I. and II./JG 51 came in over Kent, they spotted a Spitfire section which reported their altitude. Four squadrons were by then already airborne, so the controller could set a trap for the Germans. While the Hurricanes from two squadrons attracted the attention of the Germans by climbing a bit in front of them, 222 Squadron's Spitfires came in from behind. Meanwhile, twelve Spitfires from 602 Squadron lay at 9,000 metres, right on the edge of the altitude where they would start leaving revealing contrails behind. Slowly they began to wheel over and plunged straight down on the Messerschmitts while Flight Lieutenant Christopher 'Mickey' Mount shouted over the radio: 'Okay Villa Squadron, Tally Ho! Let's get them!'[473]

Major Mölders saw how the German formations scattered as the pilots panicked, and suddenly burning Messerschmitt 109s were going down everywhere in the sky. No less than 11 Bf 109s were shot down in the space of six minutes.[474] All were bagged by 602 Squadron, which reported 11 Bf 109s shot down – of which the ace Sergeant Andrew McDowall accounted for two, his 9th and 10th victories. No. 602 Squadron suffered only some slight damage to a Spitfire.

Then 222 Squadron's Flight Lieutenant Eric Thomas and Sergeant John Burgess joined the game. They spotted a Bf 109 that dived towards the ground and then levelled off. Both of the British pilots went after the '109 and after two or three minutes of searching they saw it again. Thomas opened fire and hit the radiators under the German plane's wings. In the cockpit of the shot-up Bf 109 the the pilot saw how the engine temperature rose rapidly. It was Oberleutnant Otto Hintze, the commander of 3./Erprobungsgruppe 210 – the Luftwaffe's first single-engined Jabo-unit. Until then, Hintze had carried out about 200 combat missions, including fifty-four Jabo flights over England. But now he knew that there would be no more.

A 609 Squadron Spitfire over the English south coast. On 21 October 1940, this unit became the RAF's first squadron to achieve 100 air victories. (Photo: Goss.)

Flight Lieutenant Thomas also knew it, so when he saw the Messerschmitt leaving a white trail of coolant behind, he stopped his attack to give the German a chance to bail out to awaiting captivity. But Sergeant Burgess was of a different opinion. When Thomas turned aside, Burgess pushed his control stick forward and slid in behind the '109. After a while, the German plane stopped leaking glycol. The coolant was out, and the cramped cockpit of the doomed plane was filled with a grinding and cutting noise that made it difficult for Hintze to collect his thoughts – would he bail out or risk a belly landing?

Hintze had still not decided which when there was a violent explosion in the engine. Three hundred yards behind the Messerschmitt, Sergeant Burgess pressed the firing button on the control stick, and continued firing until the ammunition was exhausted. Then he was just fifty metres away. The armour plate behind Hintze's neck saved the life of the German fighter-bomber veteran, but Hintze knew that he no longer had any choice. He pulled the trigger that blew off the pilot's canopy and waited until the Englishman stopped shooting. Then he unstrapped, threw himself out, felt a hard blow when one shoulder bumped against the tail fin, and opened his parachute. Otto Hintze had seven years of captivity ahead of him.[475] Major Mölders came too late to save Hintze, but he could at least shoot down his enemy. With the glycol system in his Spitfire shattered, Sergeant Burgess dived to the ground and crashed near Lanham. Unlike Hintze, he was soon back in action again.

After returning to France the extent of the defeat was clear for Major Mölders. His JG 51 had lost five pilots – including aces Leutnant Heinz Tornow (10 victories) and Oberleutnant Ernst Terry (8 victories), who also was adjutant of I./JG 51. The loss of fighter-bomber veteran Oberleutnant Hintze weighed even heavier. Finally a report came from II.(S)/LG 2 that three pilots were missing, including Oberleutnant Bruno von Schenck, the commander of the 5./LG 2, and from 6./JG 52 Leutnant Gerhard Barkhorn was forced to ditch in the Channel.*

All this the British had achieved from a numerical disadvantage of one to five, and with no greater losses than two damaged planes. The key was superior altitude, and there the controllers' guidance and Park's new directive played a key role.

But the day was not yet over. While Mölders and his men gathered to review the causes of the setback on the last mission, the pilots from JG 2 'Richthofen' at Beaumont-le-Roger's airfield got ready to embark on a fighter sweep. For nine days now, the famous 'Richthofen Geschwader' had been commanded by Major Helmut Wick. He summoned his pilots for a final briefing, and then they were off to the waiting Messerschmitt 109s.

The Ventnor radar station on the Isle of Wight reported 'fifty plus'. In Tangmere the hated emergency phone rang

---

* Barkhorn however was rescued and continued an amazing career with the Luftwaffe, ending the war with a total of 301 victories. During the next fortnight, Mölders was sick and made no combat flights. [476]

Sergeant John Burgess, 222 Squadron. 20-year-old Burgess arrived as a rookie pilot to 222 Squadron on 29 July 1940. When his Spitfire became number 54 on Werner Mölders' victory list on 29 October 1940, he had been credited with 3½ air victories. In November 1942 Burgess was shot down again, this time over Sicily, and spent the rest of the war in captivity. He passed away in 1988, 68 years old. (Photo: Vasco.)

and a short order was called out. A few minutes later the Hurricanes from 145 and 213 squadrons climbed to engage the enemy. In the ensuing clash the Germans claimed to have shot down six British fighters. Major Wick's Schwarm accounted for four of them – two by Wick (his 43rd and 44th victories) and one each by Oberleutnants Erich Leie and Rudi Pflanz. Historian John Foreman has compared this with British documents, and writes: 'Pilot Officer Peter Dunning-White of 145 Squadron [had his] aircraft slightly damaged due to being overstressed in a dive. 213 Squadron was hit hard. Pilot Officer [Richard] Hutley abandoned his shot-up fighter near Tangmere, but fell dead. A second aircraft is reported by Fighter Command to have been a "write-off" and a third crashed near Fort Wallington.' [477] In return, the Germans lost one pilot, who however appears to have been shot down by anti-aircraft guns.

Towards the evening on 29 October Generalmajor Theo Osterkamp – the new Jafü 2 – sent out several of his fighter units to pay back for the humiliating defeat earlier that day. The Bf 109s of III./JG 3 took off from Desvres and swept across the south-east of England. Led by Hauptmann Wilhelm Balthasar – the great ace from the Battle of France, who, however, had significant difficulties in following up his success during the Battle of Britain – they searched for British fighters. But instead, they were themselves attacked by 'Sailor' Malan's 74 'Tiger' Squadron. Flying Officer John Colin Mungo-Park and the American volunteer pilot Flight Lieutenant William Nelson shot down two Bf 109s. With one of them the commander of 9./JG 3, Oberleutnant Egon Troha – an ace with five victories – ended up in British captivity.

Jafü 2 was really in need of something that could even out the score when he sent out more units towards the evening. This cost II./JG 51 a loss of three aircraft. The unit had just returned, revitalised, to the Channel after being removed from the battle in late August.

At the same time, the entire JG 26 'Schlageter' was out, with Major Galland in the lead, along with II.(S)/LG 2. In order to truly ensure that the RAF sent up some of their fighters so that Galland and his pilots could shoot them down, Osterkamp gave orders that a unit of Ju 87 Stukas would conduct a diversionary attack on Folkestone. This was a new approach, and as of that date the Stukas would be used regularly as decoys. Osterkamp had been given command of the Stuka units which had been inactive for two months, and II./StG 1 took off on its first decoy mission at 17:25 on 29 October.

Fighter-bomber pilots from II.(S)/LG 2 made an exemplary dive-bombing attack against North Weald's airfield. They struck just as the aircraft from 249 and 257 squadrons rolled out for take-off, and destroyed two Hurricanes. Then they followed up with several strafing runs over the airfield, killing nineteen and wounding forty-two people on the ground. The British fighters that managed to get up in the air were attacked by Messerschmitt 109s and scattered in wild flight. Hauptmann Gerhard Schöpfel still managed to shoot down one of them, but when Galland himself was looking for a suitable victim the sky was empty of British aircraft. The whole Stuka force landed in St Pol at 18:30.

The result of the air fighting on 29 October confirmed the correctness of Park's tactics: sixteen Bf 109s and only eight British fighters were shot down.

The next day the Germans wanted revenge. 'As the Tommies proved quite aggressive towards our Jabos the past few days, we take off without any bombs for a real free hunting mission', Major Trautloft wrote in his diary. Of the 150 Bf 109s from JG 26 and JG 54 which flew in over England at noon, only ten were carrying bombs.

Park had ten squadrons scrambled. Southeast of London six Spitfires from No. 222 Squadron's 'A' Flight dived on Galland's thirty Messerschmitts. Six other Spitfires from 'B' Flight remained higher up, and even higher up

The rudder of Werner Mölders' Bf 109 after 29 October, embellished with 54 victory bars.

41 Squadron lay and waited. While a Bf 109 was hit and exploded, Galland turned after a Spitfire flown by Pilot Officer Alfred Davies from 222 Squadron. Twenty-three-year-old Davies had arrived in early September to 610 Squadron as a rookie pilot. Just then 610 Squadron was resting in a quiet corner of Britain after participating in the hard August fighting. On 28 September, Davies transferred to 222 Squadron and had not therefore been in the front-line for more than a month. Without great difficulty Galland was able to get into position behind Davies, and fired a devastating salvo. The Spitfire crashed and exploded on impact, and the pilot was killed. But Galland had no time to reflect on his 47th victory; he got himself attacked by a Spitfire which came diving out of the sun. Galland immediately pulled up his '109 in a climbing turn while his wingman chased away the Spitfire pilot, 41 Squadron's Flying Officer Dennis Adams.

Three-quarters of an hour later III./JG 51 clashed with 249 Squadron, resulting in the Australian ace Pilot Officer William Millington – with 10 victories on his account – being shot down and killed by Feldwebel Werner Bielefeld. In the afternoon Jafü 2 made a similar intrusion, again with about 150 Bf 109s. This time No. 602 Squadron was in the way of Major Galland's hunt. Pilot Officer Douglas Gage's and Canadian Sergeant William Smith's aircraft ended up as Galland's 48th and 49th victories. Both pilots, however, survived.

Sending out more fighters and fewer fighter-bombers proved to be a good tactic – the result was eight British and four German fighters shot down on 30 October.

After a day when flight operations were limited by a raging autumn storm, a change in the weather occurred during the night of 31 October. Next day dawned with breaking cloud cover. At noon Major Galland took off at the head of JG 26. The mission was: 'Escort fighter-bombers!' Everyone was waiting for Galland to get his fiftieth victory, and the fighter-bombers' purpose was to lure up some suitable victims. But during the entire approach flight, not a single British aircraft appeared. The fighter-bombers swept across London and dropped their loads. They could even afford the luxury of taking an extra turn over the British capital to study the effect of their attack.

When the Bf 109s flew out from London's airspace, Galland called his men and ordered a free hunt over south-eastern England. He himself set out with only a wingman, Leutnant Heinz Heinemann. The idea was that if they were only two, it would be easier to sneak up on a British fighter unit without being detected. The plan worked. After about ten minutes Galland caught sight of a formation of Spitfires at a lower altitude. It was 'Sailor' Malan's 74 'Tiger' Squadron which had taken off with their new Spitfire Mk IIs to intercept the Germans as these returned to France. But the 'Tigers' failed to spot two small Messerschmitts that were sliding into position from out of the sun.

Galland called his wingman and gave him instructions for the attack. They picked out a Spitfire each. Flight Lieutenant William Nelson and Sergeant Harold Soars were sitting in the planes selected. The two Germans dived down and opened fire almost simultaneously. Galland saw large chunks torn away from 'his' Spitfire as shells hammered into the fragile little fuselage. Because the effect of the first burst of fire was not enough, Galland pressed the firing buttons again. At that moment there was a terrible explosion and the British fighter plane disappeared in a fireball. William Nelson was killed instantly.[478] At the same time Sergeant Soars bailed out from his bullet-riddled Spitfire. While he sank to the ground in his parachute, the other Spitfires disappeared diving in all directions. Galland and his wingman turned away, pleased.

Back at base Galland was received with great enthusiasm. When he took off for his next sortie an hour later, the rudder on his Messerschmitt 109 was adorned with a new black victory bar – the fiftieth.

Fatigue

The search for new victories – in which the Germans were by no means alone – often led to disastrous consequences for the aces themselves. This was the case for the RAF's by then top ace, Squadron Leader Archie McKellar of 605 Squadron, on 1 November. Robert Foster, a pilot officer in the same unit, recalled: *'We were on patrol over Kent. Archie led the attack on Me 109s under us. The controller had reported a formation of Messerschmitt 109s coming in, and we hurried to intercept them. We managed to get into position above them, and Archie said "Come on, here we go down", so we went down but we were much too fast, and* the '109s saw us and we overshot them on the way down. In the next moment our entire formation had scattered, as did the German formation. There were aircraft flying in all directions. We were ordered back to base, but Archie wouldn't listen to that. He went on, on his own, didn't look around, chasing a Messerschmitt 109. But the Germans always operated in pairs, and we heard that this Messerschmitt's companion had attacked Archie from above and shot him down. It took until the evening before we were informed that Archie's Hurricane had been found shot down and the pilot was dead. It was a severe shock. To have such a skilled pilot as Archie among us meant a lot to the unit's morale. Some of the pilots felt that his death was completely unnecessary. He shouldn't have chased that German alone. But towards the end, we noticed how Archie became increasingly careless. Perhaps it was his personal ambition to increase his victory account that caused him to finally take excessive risks.'* [479]

McKellar, credited with 21 victories, was apparently shot down by Hauptmann Wolfgang Lippert, commander of II./JG 27, as his 16th victory. The following day, Lippert's Gruppe conducted its last combat mission over the Channel. After that the unit was sent for much-needed 'winter holidays'. The entirety of JG 27 was then out of the battle.

Meanwhile II./JG 52 was again at breaking point – for the second time since August when the unit first joined the battles over the Channel. The unit's own combat losses were by this time more than twice as high as their own confirmed victories. At eight in the morning on 2 November, 1940, thirty Bf 109s from II./JG 52 took off, led

Hermann Göring and Ernst Udet during an inspection tour at the English Channel in 1940. Both Göring and Udet appear to have been affected by depression as a result of the RAF's victory over the Luftwaffe in the autumn of 1940. (Photo: Trautloft.)

by Hauptmann Wilhelm Ensslen, to escort fifteen fighter-bombers. Over Ramsgate the Spitfires from 92 Squadron attacked the fighter escort. Squadron Leader Johnny Kent reported two victories – Feldwebel Otto Junge fell into captivity, while another Messerschmitt pilot managed to get back across the Strait of Dover and crash in France. Squadron Leader Kent then attacked Hauptmann Ensslen's Bf 109. After a ten minute long duel, the combat was settled in the RAF pilot's favour. Ensslen threw himself out of his falling 109, but for some reason his parachute never opened. The airman fell to his inevitable death. It was the last time II./JG 52 was sent into action during the Battle of Britain. 'The losses were so high that this Gruppe could hardly be regarded as fit for combat anymore', says Bernd Barbas in the chronicle of II./JG 52. Because of this the entire JG 52 was pulled out of combat.

The air war had by then degenerated into a game of tit-for-tat – and, on the German side, a competition between the most prominent air aces. Fighting spirits among the Germans reached a new low. Generalmajor von Döring, Jafü 2, left France without further ado for a home leave that gave rise to rumours that he was 'finished' and in disgrace with the high command. Major Günther Lützow could not accept this, but took up his pen and wrote a letter to von Döring to express his support: 'Our hunter's instinct is certainly trained to meet surprises, and now we have to face a new fait accompli that one would be able to meet with a shrug. Personally, I have got used to this state of affairs ever since my best Gruppenkommandeur, Hauptmann von Selle, was removed without my knowledge. I can only wholeheartedly wish Herr General all the luck in the future. The knowledge that you have led a force of crucial importance to results exceeding all expectations in unfavourable circumstances, will help Herr General through discouragement and many disappointments.'[480]

This was the beginning of a growing rebelliousness in Lützow, which towards the end of the war would have Göring threatening him with a firing squad.

Mölders was on sick leave and flew no more combat missions. 'The flu' was Mölders' official reason, but that did not stop him from, among other things, meeting with his colleagues among the young Jagdgeschwader commanders in Pihen on 3 November, in Wissant the following day, in Marck on 6 November and in Pihen on the 7th.[481] On the latter day, Mölders, Galland, Lützow, Trautloft and Oberstleutnant Carl Vieck (the former commander JG 3) met for an 'exchange of ideas'. Hannes Trautloft wrote in his diary: 'We are all disappointed with the development of the air battle of the British Isles, but we are particularly annoyed that Göring, who has already said that he could have the fighter aviation disbanded, now puts all the blame for the failure on the fighter pilots. The air campaign lacks thoughtful planning. The incessant changes of operational tactics, from the first massive day attacks by the entire Luftwaffe to the small pinprick attacks by Jabos, which is costing us high losses, has resulted in widespread doubts in our high command out on the airfields. We all say that there have been too many cooks. Although no one says it bluntly, we feel that our optimism, our élan and our fighting spirit has waned. Something has really gone wrong . . . Towards midnight we break up, saddened and filled with serious thoughts.'[482]

Of course, the root of the malaise was the defeat the Luftwaffe had suffered at the hands of Fighter Command. The Germans were simply shocked at not winning, and this resulted in a psychological crisis. 'We quarreled with the high command, with the bomber fliers, with the dive-bomber fliers, with the Zerstörer fliers, and finally also among ourselves', wrote Adolf Galland.[483]

Reichsmarschall Göring was also in the midst of a personal crisis, which explains his bad judgement at that time. In a letter to his Swedish brother-in-law Count Eric von Rosen, he spoke of his 'exhaustion'. However, it seems to have been clear to Göring that the fighter-bomber offensive had degenerated into mutual 'face slapping' without any real importance for the further conduct of the war. On 30 October, Göring met with the commanders of the air fleets and air corps in Deauville, where he announced his decision to send the entire fighter force on a 'winter vacation', four Jagdgeschwaders at a time. In practice this meant that the fighter-bomber offensive was cancelled. Göring himself took a 'leave' on 14 November and appointed Generalfeldmarschall Milch acting Luftwaffe Commander. A few days later the Swedish Count von Rosen received a letter from Göring that showed just how bad things were with the Luftwaffe commander's mental condition: 'Right now I am taking a couple of weeks of sick leave because I could not take any more.'

Generaloberst Ernst Udet – whom Göring had appointed Quartermaster-General of the Luftwaffe, and in that capacity was responsible for German aircraft production – was also sick. He suffered an acute infection with high fever and was admitted to hospital.

Although the RAF's units had often suffered even worse losses than those of the Luftwaffe, the mood on the British side was, for quite understandable reasons, the opposite to that which prevailed in the Luftwaffe at this time. Robert Foster, Pilot Officer in 605 Squadron in 1940, said: 'Morale was always high in our unit. Of course we

A shot down Hurricane.

Vereint
gegen
England

Formationen der italienischen Luftwaffe werden gemeinsam mit den
deutschen Verbänden zum Kampf
gegen die britische Insel eingesetzt

Aufn.: AP(2), PK-Schwarz-Presse-Hoffmann(2)

So wie das deutsche Fliegerkorps an der Seite der italienischen Luftwaffe im Mittelmeer, kämpfen italienis[che]
Flieger Schulter an Schulter mit den deutschen gegen den gemeinsamen Feind. Eine Abteilung des Co[rpo]
Aeronautico Italiano kehrt nach erfolgreichem Feindflug zu ihrem Einsatzhafen zurück

Der gemeinsame Kampf gegen England hat das Band der Kameradschaft zwischen d[en]
Fliegern der Achsenmächte noch fester geschmiedet. Ein italienischer Staffelkapitän bespri[cht]
mit seinem deutschen Kameraden den bevorstehenden Einsatz. — Rege Tätigkeit herr[scht]
beim italienischen Bodenpersonal (Bild unten), das Bomben schweren Kalibers für d[en]
Feindflug vorbereitet

„In bocca al lupo — Hals- und Beinbruch!" Ein kameradschaftlicher
Händedruck vor dem Feindflug gegen England

This article from the Luftwaffe magazine Der Adler gave a quite euphemistic image of the Italian Air Force's participation in the Battle of Britain. The picture at the top shows a formation of Fiat BR.20M, Italy's standard medium bomber at the beginning of the war. The BR.20 had a fairly high top speed for a bomber, 440 km/h, and could carry 1,600 kg of bombs. But the armament was rather weak, only three 12.7mm Breda-SAFAT machine guns. The photo bottom left shows Tenente Pier Antonio Poggi (43° Stormo) wearing a cap. He was killed when his BR.20 was shot down on 11 November 1940.

lost many pilots, but they always were replaced. I remember that the enthusiasm and morale increased even more during October and November 1940. We felt, quite rightly, as the victors, and that always has a positive effect on morale.' [484]

'It seems as if our leaders no longer know what they want'

A theatrical dimension was added to the tragedy when Italy's pompous dictator Benito Mussolini decided to come to his beleaguered German ally's help. On airfields in Belgium a strange armada of aircraft landed – Italian Fiat planes. It was eighty Fiat BR.20 bombers, fifty Fiat CR. 42 biplane fighters and forty-eight Fiat G.50 monoplane fighters. They constituted the flight strength of the Italian air corps Corpo Aereo Italiano (CAI) under the command of Generale Rino Corso Fougier who arrived to 'help Hitler win the Battle of Britain'.

The Germans could do nothing but shake their heads. None of these aircraft could be described as modern, and they were judged not to stand a chance against the Royal Air Force! One can really ask oneself what purpose this Italian air force could fill – apart from satisfying Mussolini's vanity.

The first Italian air operation against the British Isles was carried out during the night between 24 and 25 October, when eighteen of the twin-engined BR.20-bombers attacked Felixstowe and Harwich. Four of the participating aircraft crashed for various reasons.

On the afternoon of 29 October, fifteen BR.20s from 43° Stormo took off, led by Maggiore Mario Tenti, to attack Ramsgate's harbour. Three of the Italian bombers were forced to abort due to engine failure, and one of them made an emergency landing at Ostend. But the twelve remaining met an overwhelming escort – thirty-nine fighters of both Fiat types as well as Bf 109s from II. and III./JG 54 – and flew over the south-east of England. As if it was an air show the Italians roared in at low altitude over Ramsgate, wing tip to wing tip. When they dropped their bombs the entire formation made a new sweep over the target area again, to let the accompanying photographers from Italian newspapers get some good pictures. They were lucky to escape Fighter Command's attention. Three days later 39 Fiat CR.42s from 18° Gruppo and 26 Fiat G.50s from 20° Gruppo swept in over Canterbury in an equally theatrical manner, still without encountering any British fighters.

Of course, the Italian aircraft were hopelessly inferior to the British fighters, but the idea that the Italian airmen lacked motivation or skill is unfounded. Among the fighter pilots from the CAI were very experienced pilots such as Sottotenente Franco Bordoni-Bisleri and Sergente Maggiore Luigi Gorrini – both of whom would become successful aces, each with 19 victories. The German fighter pilot Oberleutnant Hans-Ekkehard Bob from III./JG 54 frequently met the Italian airmen in 'The Pilot's Bar' in Lille and flew several missions along with them. He was impressed both by their combat spirits and their skill. Bob said, 'I remember once when some Italian biplane were attacked by Spitfires. I was so amazed that I forgot to intervene; for the next few minutes I witnessed a most amazing air show: rolls, loopings, Immelmann-turns, sharp turns – indeed it surpassed even the greatest aerobatic show. It is perhaps superfluous to mention that finally the British gave up and left the scene without having been able to achieve any result.' [485]

On 11 November, 99° Gruppo dispatched ten BR.20Ms for a daylight attack on Harwich, escorted by forty Fiat CR.42s from 18° Gruppo. The Italians were met by the RAF's 41, 46, 249 and 257 squadrons, and this time the Italian fighter aircraft could not manoeuvre out of danger but were forced to fight to defend the bombers. A lone Spitfire pilot decided to first challenge the Italian fighter escort to pull them away from the bombers. The British stratagem succeeded and the bold Spitfire pilot survived thanks to his airplane's superior performance and made it without much difficulty away from the entire mass of biplanes. The British pilot's report is quite illuminating: 'The Italian aircraft came over in small formations of 2-3 at various heights between 5,000 and 10,000ft. [. . .] Several pairs and threes of the CR.42s then dived on the single Spitfire which gained height and succeeded in getting clear of most of them. No doubt this operation delayed their making contact with the Hurricanes of 46 and 257 squadrons who were attacking the bombers. In attacks on the CR.42s which followed the enemy are reported to have half rolled very tightly, and to have easily out-turned the Spitfire. In two cases as they came out of their rolls, they were able to turn up sharply enough without stalling to allow them to open fire on the Spitfire, but did not damage. Their speed and climb was much inferior.' [486]

The British optimistically reported the shooting down of 14 Italian aircraft – nine bombers and five fighters – without any own losses. This was an exaggeration, but the Italian losses were severe enough. Three bombers and three fighters were shot down. Another four bombers and 19 Fiat CR.42s emergency-landed in France or Belgium – however, most of the latter did so because of fuel shortage. The Italian fighter airmen however did not let themselves to be discouraged, but happily reported that they had shot down nine Hurricanes!

The following day, the British tabloid press invented a name for the victory over the Italian Air Force – the 'Spaghetti Party'. Winston Churchill appeared most of all to feel sorry for the Italians when he let slip: 'Those aircraft might have found better employment defending the fleet at Taranto.' The same day, British torpedo planes had struck at the Italian fleet in Taranto, sinking a battleship and damaging another two, plus a cruiser – all without losing more than two own aircraft. Shortly afterwards, Hitler decided to send a Flying Corps from the Luftwaffe to help the Italians in the Mediterranean. . .

On the German side perplexity turned to discouragement. No one knew what would happen next. Only the High Command knew that Hitler was in the midst of planning

21-year-old Pilot Officer Eric Lock from 41 Squadron was one of the leading RAF aces in 1940. He scored his first two air victories on 15 August 1940, and on 20 October that number had increased to 19. When Lock went missing on a fighter mission over France on 3 August 1941, he had 26½ victories.

his invasion of the Soviet Union. On 12 November an Atlantic storm kept air operations over the Channel down. The young Jagdgeschwader commanders Mölders, Galland, Lützow and Trautloft instead took the opportunity of engaging in a day hunting wild game, and carried on their destructive criticism of Göring as they did so. 'It seems as if our leaders no longer know what they want', Trautloft wrote in his diary.[487]

While Mölders still did not participate in any combat missions, Galland and Wick continued their competition for the lead position in the 'victory race'. It almost seemed as if they escaped military realities by hunting trophies in the air more fervently than ever.

On 6 November Sperrle helped by sending out a few bombers as decoys while Wick led his JG 2 'Richthofen' out towards the Isle of Wight. Wick's airmen clashed with six RAF squadrons and reported eight aircraft shot down against only one own loss. Of this number, Wick himself was responsible for five – and this in the space of thirteen minutes. The engaged RAF forces in fact lost five fighters; Wick's claims seem essentially to have been correct. Wick now surpassed his rival Galland and placed himself, with 52 victories, just one step behind Mölders.

On 7 November, a group of Stukas was used as decoys when Major Wick conducted his next free hunt over the Isle of Wight area. 145 Squadron fell into the trap, which cost four Hurricanes without a single German plane being shot down. The Germans reported exactly twice as many victories as the actual British losses. One of these ended up on Wick's tally.

Another of the high-scoring aces in the RAF was a whisker away being killed on 8 November. No. 41 Squadron's Pilot Officer Eric Lock, with a score of 19 victories, had his Spitfire shot to pieces by a burst of fire from a Bf 109. He succeeded, however, in getting away and then brought his damaged plane down to an emergency landing at Beachy Head. It is likely that Lock's Spitfire was the ninth kill for Oberfeldwebel Willy Roth from III./JG 26. Hurricane pilots from 17 Squadron were guilty of perhaps the greatest exaggeration of shot down enemy aircraft in a single engagement during the entire Battle of Britain when they reported twenty Ju 87s shot down. Of these claims, fifteen were confirmed, of which three each ended up on Pilot Officer David Leary's and Sergeant Glyn Griffiths' respective tallys. In fact not one Ju 87 was lost.[488]

On 10 November Wick claimed to have shot down yet another Spitfire. It was his personal number 54, which meant that he now was in the lead. That same day Galland returned from a weeklong leave, in connection with having been promoted to Oberstleutnant, very eager to regain the lead in the 'victory race'. 'I admit', Galland said after the war, 'that we strove to achieve as many victories and awards as possible. As for myself, however, I always tried to make sure that my personal ambitions didn't take prec-

edence over the responsibility for my unit.' Still the impression remains that at least some of those around Galland were prepared to go to excess in order to help him to new successes.

On 11 November, Galland flew two sorties over Britain, both unsuccessful. After a day's break because of the weather – when he went game hunting with his comrades, as we have seen above – other fruitless flights followed.

One of Galland's supporters was his superior, the new Jafü 2, Generalmajor Theo Osterkamp. At eleven in the morning on 14 November Osterkamp contacted III./StG 1 in St. Pol and ordered the unit to take off to tackle 'an enemy convoy' off Dover. The operations officer in III./StG 1 thought that the information he received was suspiciously vague, and the commander of III./StG 1, Hauptmann Helmut Mahlke, agreed. 'It was the strangest mission order I had ever heard', said Mahlke, 'Could it really be intended that we be the target of the entire British air defence on such a lunatic parade flight?'[489]

But orders are orders, and at 14:22 Hauptmann Mahlke took off from St. Pol, and after him came twenty Ju 87s. They climbed in spirals and when they had assembled in their combat formation, they flew towards the coast where the fighter escort would meet them. At 14:45 Galland took off from Audembert at the head of JG 26 and III./JG 51.[490] Mahlke said: *'The fighters meet us at the agreed rendezvous point. They will escort us while we fly north, until we can see the whole sea area all the way to Margate. As I thought, no ships can be seen. We turn to the south and scan the sea all the way to the opposite coast: Nothing! Not even a rowboat! Just an old wreck that sticks out of the water ...*

German airmen listen intently to the radio traffic from their airborne comrades in combat over southern England. (Photo: Broschwitz.)

'We change direction again and fly westwards, towards Dover, which we know is well defended. At 3,500 metres there is a closed cloud cover, so we have to go down below the clouds. That will make us prime targets of the powerful air defence at Dover! I guess our escort had the same thought, for they stopped over the middle of the Channel, out of range of the anti-aircraft guns. Well, they are probably waiting to see what the fireworks look like from a distance.' [491]

Five squadrons of RAF fighters meanwhile closed in on the Stukas. Among these was 74 'Tiger' Squadron, with twelve Spitfire Mk. IIs, from Biggin Hill. Galland and his Bf 109s were flying around above the clouds over the Channel when the first RAF fighters struck.

When the Stukas flew in over Dover without the anti-aircraft guns opening fire, Mahlke was filled with foreboding. He called his rear-gunner, Unteroffizier Fritz Baudsich on the Ju 87's intercom: 'There ought to be fighters here soon, so keep a watchful eye!'

He had scarcely said this when his fears came true: 'There they are: Right in front of us, on the opposite course, a Spitfire unit in tightly closed formations emerge from the clouds, coming straight towards us. As the Spitfires approach us, we open fire with our two fixed machine guns each, but the British planes pass completely unperturbed above us, and calmly go into position behind us. We must attack our target, now or never! Although we had not yet reached the target, I give the signal to commence the diving attack. We dive at an angle of almost 70 degrees, but the fighters attack us already when we enter the dive. How they are able to handle it with their fast Spitfires I cannot understand. But they succeed in creating such disarray to our formation that only

few bombs hit within the target area, with a terrible accuracy. Several bombs go down in the surrounding fields while our aircraft make wild evasive manoeuvres to avoid the fighter attacks.'

74 'Tiger' Squadron's chronicler wrote: 'The Tigers attacked the port flank. Mungo-Park went for one Ju 87, giving it a three-second burst at 75 yards' range. It blew up and burst into flames. H. M. Stephen engaged a section of three Junkers. After firing a five-second burst into one of them, he was amazed to see it roll into the aircraft flying next to it. The wing of one of the pair came off. The other went down out of control, starting to disintegrate as it fell. Stephen then attacked a third machine, which was last seen flopping towards the Channel in a blaze of glory.'

'Pilot Officer Draper experienced ten memorable minutes. First he took a deflection shot at a Ju 87. Parts of the left wing root and engine cover were torn off and the plane crashed vertically near Dover. Next, Draper's machine guns took out another Junkers, which caught fire after a short volley, and then he went on to a third bomber, which was seen plunging into the Channel. . .

'The day's most exciting adventures were experienced by Pilot Officer Armstrong. To begin with a Ju 87, which Armstrong had picked out, dropped its bombs before he even had time to open fire. The rear gunner opened fire at him, but without effect, and Armstrong silenced him with a four-second burst from 300 metres. Yet another burst at 100 metres tore off parts of the German plane, which rolled on its back and dived into the Channel. Another Junkers soon followed.' [492]

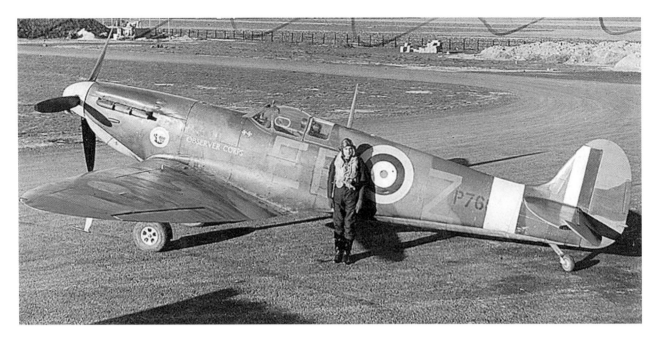

Squadron Leader Donald Finlay, 41 Squadron, posing proudly in front of his new Spitfire Mk IIA, which was delivered in November 1940. With this aircraft Finlay shot down two Bf 109s on 23 and 27 November 1940. This Spitfire version, which first arrived at 74 and 611 squadrons in August 1940, was provided with a 1,175-horsepower Rolls-Royce Merlin XII engine, using a dilute glycol (30/70% glycol/water mixture) coolant, making it less flammable than the pure glycol coolant of the Spitfire Mk I's Merlin III engine.

For Stuka pilot Mahlke it was at least as 'exciting', albeit from a different perspective. He continues his story: 'A Ju 87 goes down in flames. The crew bails out and sinks to the ground in their parachutes. The Spitfires are many more than us, and each of us is attacked by at least two or three Spitfires. I count to as many as five attacking me at the same time . . . I use every trick in the hat: tight turns at low speed, sometimes even with the dive brakes extended, climbs, dives, anything that prevents the Spitfires with their higher speed from shooting with deflection. But it can't be helped that I receive quite a few hits. This goes on for more than ten minutes – or is it just as it seems? – before our escort fighters turn up. At last! Without them it would have been the end of us. But this time they let us take a beating for quite some time.'

Among the German fighter pilots, Oberstleutnant Galland was first to arrive at the scene, and at 15:28 a Spitfire plunged into the Channel as his 51st victory. 'Attempting to rejoin the squadron', wrote 74 Squadron's chronicler, 'Armstrong's Spitfire was unlucky enough to receive a hit from a cannon shell, and later an explosion in the engine caused flames to pour from the exhaust manifold. Armstrong had to take to his parachute, returning eventually to join the other Tigers who were celebrating their joyful fighting day.'

On their return to Biggin Hill 74 Squadron counted the results and came to the amazing sum of 15 downed German planes. In fact, several British fighter pilots had fired at the same plane, but in the heat of combat each of them had reported it as their own victory. It is also likely that Stukas that dived steeply to escape their pursuers were regarded by mistake as shot down by eager Spitfire

pilots. Mahlke continues: 'I put down our badly damaged aircraft at St. Pol at 15:31. Two of our aircraft have been shot down over the British Isles. Three others force-land in France with severe combat damage. Almost all our aircraft are sieved through by bullet hits. Only Oberleutnant Schairer, the commander of the 7. Staffel, returns with a completely undamaged aircraft. Although he also was chased around by two to three Spitfires, he was able to avoid all attacks by constantly sideslipping in different directions.'

Mahlke was furious when he contacted his Geschwaderkommodore, Oberstleutnant Walter Hagen for debriefing. 'This was completely outrageous', were his word, which went on to Jafü 2. The next day Mahlke and Hagen went to Osterkamp's headquarters. 'I agree', admitted Osterkamp, 'I made a mistake.'

Nevertheless, the German fighter aces continued their hunt for victories. On 15 November, JG 26 and II./JG 54 escorted fighter-bombers from 3./JG 26 towards London. They were attacked by 92, 501 and 605 squadrons and lost three Bf 109s while Galland feverishly chased a really 'slippery' Hurricane across half of Kent. At 10:28, he could finally report it as shot down, and back at Audembert his 52nd victory was entered into the logbook. Although it was the only German victory recorded for the mission, the RAF actually lost two Hurricanes – both from 605 Squadron. Pilot Officer Czeslaw Gauze was killed while his companion Pilot Officer Eric Jones survived by bailing out – for the second time in exactly two months.

The next day Galland conducted his 150th combat sortie, with no results. On 17 November, 210 Erprobungsgruppe 210 was called in to attack the airfield at Wattisham. It would give the RAF reason to send up some fighters, and Galland had high hopes when he climbed out over the Channel along with the entire JG 26. Robert Michulec and Donald Caldwell wrote in their biography about Adolf Galland: *'Galland displayed a true fighter's skill on 17 November when, while escorting twin-engined Messerschmitts of ErprGr 210, he claimed three Hurricanes of 17 and 257 Squadrons, shot down almost one after another. In spite of the success, it has to be stressed that the escort failed in its task, by being tied up by the pilots of 257 Sqd. As a result the formation from 17 Squadron performed an effective attack against the Bf 110s. British pilots claimed 4 victories, while in fact they destroyed three machines. At the same time 257 Squadron pilots claimed 2-1-0 successes, but they only downed a single Bf 109 E-7, although this was flown by a better than average pilot. W.Nr. 5967 was piloted by Oblt. [Eberhard] Henrici, commander of 1. Staffel and an ace with 7 kills to his credit. It is possible that the victor was P/O P. A. Mortimer who was then hit by Galland. . .*

'After this initial clash, the combat continued to rage over the Suffolk coast for at least five minutes. The fight between JG 26 and 257 Squadron did not stop until 17 Squadron's Hurricanes ended their attack against the Bf 110s. When they noticed what was going on, the escort fighters immediately went to counterattack, and managed to get into position behind the aircraft in 17 Squadron, whose formation scattered by this attack. Galland took advantage of this favourable situation and was able to gain his next victory with his first attack. This time he shot down one of the most colourful aces in the RAF, Count Manfred Beckett Czernin,* who by then had 15 victories to his credit.

'While Czernin hauled himself out of the cockpit to save himself by parachute, Galland aimed at the next aircraft, and soon afterwards hit it. This time it was a Hurricane flown by Sergeant Bernard Henson from 257 Squadron. His aircraft survived the attack and crashed when it was attacked east of Harwich by another ace in JG 26, the commander of the 8. Staffel, Oberleutnant Sprick.' [493]

Two of these victims were claimed by Galland as his 53rd and 54th kills. Although he chased victories with a bit too much eagerness, Galland appears not to have succumbed to the temptation of overestimating his own results to any great extent. Having scrutinized Galland's first 94 victories, attained in the West 1940 and 1941, the author has arrived at the conclusion that 44 can with certainty be verified with Allied loss records. Five could not be verified with Allied sources. This gives an almost unsurpassed accuracy rate of 90 %. It has been impossible to make any assessment on Galland's 45 other victories in this period, owing to the fact that too many German pilots on those occasions filed claims at the same time. On at least four occasions, it seems as though Galland could have actually shot down enemy aircraft without noting them as destroyed. The conclusion is that Galland might well in fact have shot down 94 enemy aircraft in 1940 and 1941.

41 Squadron's Spitfires also participated in the combat, and its top ace, Pilot Officer Eric Lock, claimed to have shot down two Bf 109s – which raised his total to 21.

Immediately afterwards Lock was himself attacked by a Bf 109 which sent a burst of bullets and shells into the Spitfire's cockpit and wounded Lock in the right arm and both legs. Another bullet hit the throttle so that the engine was locked at full speed. It may have saved the dazed Lock, who was scarcely able to take any quick evasive action; his plane now automatically removed itself from the hazardous environment at maximum speed.

But when Lock wanted to bail out, he discovered that the release handle that would jettison the canopy had also been shot off. Trying to push back the hood was not possible with his right arm paralyzed by the gunshot wound, so Lock grabbed the control stick with his left hand and carefully descended while taking a course to the southwest. At 600 metres, he switched off the engine and glided in smooth curves to reduce the speed. Eventually the young airman took his plane down for an emergency landing in a grass field that appeared to be flat enough.

When the plane had stopped, Lock collapsed from the shock. For two hours he sat bleeding in the cockpit of his Spitfire before a couple of soldiers came by and discovered his plight. They made a makeshift stretcher with two rifles and a fatigue-jacket and then carried away the injured airman. Eric Lock woke up in a hospital and found out that he had been awarded the DSO.

In the next three months Lock went through no less than fifteen operations to remove all the shrapnel that he received during the air combat on 17 November. It is conceivable that Lock's plane was one of the three that Galland claimed to have shot down that day.

On 23 November, the Italian air force suddenly decided to become active again. Under the command of Maggiore Feruccio Vosilla, 19 Fiat CR.42 biplanes from 18° Gruppo conducted a new fighter sweep. The Italian biplanes, which really should have been in a museum, moved out over the Strait of Dover – almost wingtip to wingtip. They had planned to fly in a wide arc from Dunkirk to Margate, from thence in over the Thames Estuary and finally back to the coast at Folkestone. They did not make it further than out over the Channel before the Spitfires from 603 Squadron attacked from behind. Tenente Guido Mazza and Sergente Maggiore Giacomo Grillo were immediately shot down, while Maresciallo Felice Sozzi, Sergente Maggiore Franco Campanile and Sergente Pietro Melano managed to bring their damaged CR.42s back to the French coast, where they crashed. With one of these Pilot Officer Ronald Berrie scored his 9th victory. 18° Gruppo claimed to have shot down five Spitfires, but it turns out that the worst damage they managed to inflict on their opponents was to put a few bullets through the canopy of a Spitfire. [494]

However, something even worse happened to Bf 109 -equipped I./JG 51 during a fighter-bomber mission four days later, on 27 November. Oberstleutnant Galland led a fighter sweep to support the fighter-bombers, but three squadrons of Spitfires managed to slip past Galland's formation. Squadron Leader 'Sailor' Malan led his 74 'Tiger' Squadron to attack the fighter-bombers and fired at two '109s with devastating effect. One crashed into the sea, and the other swerved off, leaving a thick trail of smoke behind. 'To judge by its gyrations, either the machine was badly damaged or the pilot was badly frightened', Malan commented afterwards. He decided, however, to refrain

---

* Count Manfred Beckett Czernin indeed was an 'international' fighter pilot in the RAF, born in Berlin as the son of an Austrian diplomat and a British woman. A couple of years after the Battle of Britain he participated in secret operations behind enemy lines in Italy.

Adolf Galland in the cockpit of his Bf 109 E-4/N. Note the telescope gun sight, which was a special piece of equipment that Galland tested, not however with great success. (Photo: Galland.)

from administering the coup-de-grace, and instead let Squadron Leader Wilson – who was temporarily attached to 74 Squadron to gain combat experience – put an end to the German. Then 41 Squadron went to attack and was reported to have shot down five '109s. I./JG 51 lost six aircraft without being able to shoot down even one of the British. Adolf Galland arrived on the scene too late to avert the massacre, but he could at least put his 20mm shells into one of 74 Squadron's Spitfires.

Pilot Officer Peter Chesters could not see the plane that attacked him. 'During this dogfight over Chatham,' wrote historian Simon Muggleton, 'Peter Chester's Spitfire P7306 was hit, badly damaging his controls, and suffering wounds and burns to his legs. Despite this P/O Chesters remained with the crippled aircraft until he was clear of the built-up areas, finally taking to his parachute over open countryside below, the aircraft crashing on the mud at Blacketts Marshes, Essex.' [495]

The end

28 November marks in a dramatic way the end of the great air battles over the English Channel in 1940. When the day dawned Oberstleutnant Galland was, with his 55 victories, in the lead of Wick, but the 25-year-old Major Wick was going to change that. At three in the afternoon

his Stabsschwarm and I./JG 2 attacked 213 and 602 squadrons in the air over the Isle of Wight. Without suffering any losses the Germans claimed to have shot down three Spitfires – the successful pilots being Wick, Oberleutnant Erich Leie and Unteroffizier Günther Seeger. 213 and 602 squadrons lost one pilot each.

When Wick returned to Beaumont-le-Roger to celebrate his 55th victory, he received a message that Galland had just returned from a fighter sweep where he had shot down a Hurricane. When South African Flying Officer Pat Wells from 249 Squadron left his fiercely burning Hurricane to bail out, Oberstleutnant Adolf Galland's 56th victory was a fact.

Wick immediately decided to fly out over the Channel again, in search of new victories. He brought his Stabsschwarm and all of I. and II./JG 2 'Richthofen'. In this sector, the English Channel is about 150 kilometres wide, and since the Messerschmitts had climbed to 7,000 metres, they were soon detected by the British radar – which at such high altitudes reached all the way to Beaumont-le-Roger. The commander of 10 Group decided to put several squadrons on standby, and to order up two in the air. The sector commander at Middle Wallop scrambled two Spitfire squadrons for a patrol over Portland: 609 Squadron from Middle Wallop and 152 Squadron from Warmwell.

Suddenly, Squadron Leader Denis Robinson from 152 Squadron caught sight of white condensation trails against the blue sky high above.

'Bandits at 12 o'clock high!' – was heard over the British fighter aircraft radios.

At about the same time the German airmen caught sight of the Spitfires.

Wick immediately attacked. One of the wings of his '109 pointed downwards and then the aircraft descended into a fairly steep dive while turning to position itself with the sun in the back.

One of 609 Squadron'spilots from was Paul Baillon, a French volunteer who had recently completed his fighter training and had been promoted to pilot officer. Although he had arrived at the unit as late as mid-October 1940, he had already been shot down once – on 27 October, by a machine gunner aboard a Ju 88 bomber. We will never know what Baillon thought or felt during those seconds when the '109s swept around the Spitfire formation and came down behind them. Did he see them coming in the rear-view mirror? Was he starting evasive action, or did the Messerschmitts' rapid manoeuvre make it hard for him to decide what was best to do? Suddenly, they were almost upon him, just behind his own Spitfire. And the one who aimed precisely at Baillon's plane was Major Helmut Wick. The young Frenchman had no chance.

Canadian Pilot Officer Keith Ogilvie, who flew beside Baillon, would never forget the lightning attack that he and his comrades were subjected to. That night he wrote in his diary:

'I was Yellow 3 and was weaving merrily behind, keeping an eagle eye above, when I caught a glimpse of 3 "yellow noses" in my mirror. They were obviously crack pilots by their tight formation and strategy. I gave the warning and dove as the centre "Johnny" opened fire on me, and I was speeded on my way by a cannon shell up the fuselage and a second through my prop.' [496]

While Ogilvie hurled his already damaged Spitfire into violent evasive manoeuvres, Baillon's plane was hit and caught fire. The Canadian saw how the Frenchman bailed out about thirty kilometres south of Bournemouth, but also saw that he showed no signs of life when he reached the water. Baillon was probably dead when he landed in the water. On 5 January 1941, his body was washed ashore at St. Martin de Varoville in Normandy, and he is buried in St. Marcouf.

Helmut Wick's first diving attack had a huge effect. In a split second the formations of both sides had scattered as if they had exploded, and the various aircraft flew at full speed with roaring engines in every possible direction, and spread out over a volume of roughly fifty cubic kilometres of air. This was what the British called a 'mixup', a totally confused mess of fighter aircraft which scattered in a sort of Big Bang in miniature, so that after half a minute a lot of lone pilots were flying around in what they felt was a completely empty sky. But before the fight reached that stage, in the first chaotic minutes, Wick turned tightly to place himself in firing position behind another Spitfire. Pilot Officer Eric Marrs from 152 Squadron said: *'On looking over my right shoulder, I saw one of those beastly yellow-nosed blighters about a hundred yards on my right. It had obviously dived down and had a pot at somebody in our formation and I must have first seen*

him just after he had finished shooting. My instinctive reaction was to pull up sharply to the right to see if anything was coming down on my tail. As I did this, the Me 109 slid across under me to my left and dived full speed for France. I flipped over to the left and dived flat out after him. The 109 was very keen to get home, and was a fool of over-confident, for he never looked round once to see whether he was being pursued or not.

'It took me time to catch up, especially as I was not such a fool and weaved slightly to keep a look out behind my tail. I was very angry with him for having surprised us and I knew that one of us must have been shot up by him. I distinctly remember muttering to myself as I flipped over and dived after him: "You dirty b. . .! This is where you get yours!"

'I crept up on him slowly, keeping beneath him in his blindest spot. Slowly he got bigger in my sights – then he was in range, but I did not open fire; I was going to make absolutely sure of him, so I waited till I was within about 100 yards. Then aiming carefully I fire a one second burst.

Helmut Wick began his career as fighter pilot before the war. He scored 14 air victories during the Battle of France and during the Battle of Britain he advanced to the position of one of the Luftwaffe's three top aces, alongside Mölders and Galland. After claiming five British fighters on the same day, 5 October 1940, he was awarded the Oak Leaves to the Knight's Cross and was promoted to the Wehrmacht's youngest major, only 25 years old. On 6 November 1940, Wick repeated the feat of claiming five victories in a single day. Wick's death on 28 November 1940 was a heavy blow to morale within the Luftwaffe.

152 Squadron in November 1940. Pilot Officer Eric Marrs is fifth from right in the front row. (Photo: Vasco.)

That was enough. Black smoke belched forth and oil spattered over my windscreen. He half-rolled and dived away. I followed in a steep spiral to see what was going to happen but my speed became so great I pulled away and my wing hid him for a bit.'[497]

It was probably at the same moment that 609 Squadron's ace Pilot Officer John Dundas turned and fired a burst after Wick's already damaged Messerschmitt. Flight Lieutenant Field, the ground controller who had led the British fighters to the Germans, heard Dundas shouting: 'I finished a 109 – Whoopee!'[498] It was Dundas' 13th victory. When Squadron Leader Robinson asked Dundas to answer his radio call, Dundas had already been shot down by Oberleutnant Rudi Pflanz. Neither Wick, nor John Dundas were seen again.

Pflanz had not really kept up with Wick's fast manoeuvres, and when he discovered two planes, one behind the other, he thought at first that it was Wick and his wingman, Leutnant Franz Fiby. But in the next instant he saw how one fired at the other. Pflantz increased speed and approached, and then recognised to his horror Wick's plane with its commander's markings. He saw that it was badly damaged, and he identified the rearmost plane as a Spitfire. Pflanz immediately shot down the Spitfire and then turned around and saw Wick dangling in his parachute. He called for the air-sea rescue.

'When I looked again', recounted Eric Marrs, 'there was a large number of flaming fragments waffling down to the sea. One large black lump, which was not on fire,

trailed a white plume which snapped open and became a parachute. This was the pilot and he must have baled out just before the petrol tank blew up.'[499]

In the continuing combat, two of 152 Squadron's pilots were shot down. Neither of them survived. One was the Polish Sergeant Zygmunt Klein. Pilot Officer Janusz Zurakowski's Spitfire also was badly damaged. Eric Marrs recalled: 'I went home in great spirits but this joy soon evaporated, for when I landed I heard of the death of the chap who had been flying just behind me. The 109 had shot at him, hitting his glycol system. Streaming smoke, he made for land and then tried to bale out. He bungled up his baling out and tore his parachute in doing so, with the result that his descent to earth was somewhat swift. His parachute streamed out behind him but owing to the tears did not open. We lost one other pilot that day, one of the Polish sergeants. He just disappeared and must have become involved with a large number of enemy fighters. So we lost two for two and that is not very satisfactory.'[500]

For 609 Squadron the loss of the talented and popular airman John Dundas was a heavy blow. The atmosphere was decidedly worse at JG 2. When the 'Richthofen' pilots returned to base, they could report six victories – which corresponded to the four downed and one badly damaged Spitfire. But it certainly could not offset the loss of Helmut Wick. Oberleutnant Rudi Pflanz had seen how the downed Helmut Wick climbed up into an inflatable rubber raft in the cold water. After that there is no trace of the Luftwaffe's top ace.

Helmut Wick starts his Messerschmitt Bf 109.

In his memoirs, Julius Meimberg wrote: 'Next day, in bad weather, we systematically scanned the sea area between Cherbourg and the Isle of Wight to try to find Wick. When I went out over the Channel for the second time, I quite surprisingly came across a Bristol Blenheim which I shot down at 16:35 hrs. This twin-engined aircraft is the first bomber that I shot down. In doing so, I kill Flying Officer Arthur P. Hovenier, Sergeant James B. Scotchmere and Sergeant Lewis E. Magee, all of whom follow their machine down into the Channel. Several decades later, I find out who my victims were, and held photographs of them in my hands. Three young men in their early twenties – pilots like me, like Helmut Wick, the victor in 56 aerial combats who never was seen again.' [501]

The death of Wick quickly became known even on the British side. Interestingly, Sergeant Klein was for some reason credited with the shooting down of a Bf 109. The war diary of 609 Squadron – where Dundas was almost officially proclaimed as Wick's slayer – generously gave its support to the claim of a victory for the fallen Klein: '152 Squadron was also engaged at the same time and place, and it is considered possible that either one of their pilots, Sgt Klein (Polish) or Dundas may have been responsible for bringing down the German ace.' [502] But this finds no support in the Operations Record Book of Klein's own unit, 152 Squadron, which states: 'Sgt Klein, one of our Polish pilots is missing. Nothing has been heard of him since he took off with the squadron except that P/O [Fredrick] Holmes during the battle caught sight of a Spitfire upon which he saw

what appeared to be a bright spark. This plane spun three or four times. F/O Holmes then lost sight of the plane as he was hotly engaged with enemy aircraft.' [503]

It seems pretty clear that 152 Squadron's Pilot Officer Eric Marrs was the one who shot down Helmut Wick. Unaware that he had shot down the Luftwaffe's top ace, Marrs wrote in a letter home: 'I found that I had shot down my 109 with 440 rounds, that is 55 rounds from each gun. This is the easiest victory I've had and fulfilled a long-felt ambition to shoot down one of those damned yellow-nosed blighters.' Then he added: 'My total score is now six and a third confirmed, one unconfirmed and four damaged and is made up as follows: Destroyed confirmed: A half Dornier 17, one Ju 87, one and a half and a one-third Ju 88, one Me 109, two Me 110s. Probably destroyed: One He 111. Damaged: Two He 111s, two Me 110s. . .' [504]

'White 10' from I./JG 2 'Richthofen' taxis out to take off. (Photo: Mombeek.)

A shot down Ju 88.

CHAPTER 10
THE VICTORS AND THE DEFEATED

During the following days most of the German fighter units were away from the battle – for 'winter holidays' as Göring called it. Until the end of the year Fighter Command lost no more than twelve aircraft in combat. The German fighters recorded the last victories of the year over England on 5 December. One of these was Adolf Galland's 57th victory.

Even if some, in particular, German writers, have made attempts to downplay the impact of the Battle of Britain after the war, it is perfectly clear that the RAF won a decisive victory at that time, and that Göring's Luftwaffe had suffered a major defeat. The South African pilot in the RAF, Squadron Leader Douglas Tidy, expressed the mood of triumph that was prevalent among the airmen on the British Isles: 'For we who stood alone in 1940 our victory meant that we were invincible, come what may. That was our victory. We had won something at last after Dunkirk, Norway, and all the other frustrations. We all basked in the reflected glory of "The Few" – the term derived from the speech of the then Prime Minister of Britain on 20 August 1940.'

For obvious reasons, things looked quite different on the German side. 'We were defeated, and that's it', commented Johannes Steinhoff, who belonged to II./JG 52 – one of the German fighter units that had received the worst beating by Fighter Command. Several attempts have been made of late to downplay the significance of the British airmen's efforts on the outcome of the Battle. The widespread perception that Göring's supposedly incompetent leadership played a decisive negative role for the Luftwaffe during the Battle of Britain must be rejected as this viewpoint is mainly based on myths and half-truths constructed after the war. Certainly, Göring lost his grip towards the end of the Battle – in which he certainly was not alone in on the German side – but that was only after it was obvious to the more perceptive on the German side, and Göring must be counted as one of them, that the Battle of Britain was lost.

The two Bf 109s from JG 26 that Adolf Galland alternated between in the autumn of 1940. The rudder on the aircraft closest to the camera shows Galland's tally on 28 November 1940 – 56 victories. (Photo: Galland.)

The badly thought-out directives that Göring issued after the end of September 1940 – apparently under the duress of stress caused by the defeat – cannot explain the German defeat, which by then was already a fact.

The decision to halt the air base offensive in favour of attacks on London gave – at least according to what Air Vice-Marshal Park thought – Fighter Command an important breathing space, but by that time the RAF had already won enough time to hold out until the deteriorating autumn weather hampered Luftwaffe operations. The crucial role played by the young RAF fighter pilots' inexorable struggle against a vastly superior enemy during the summer of 1940 stands beyond all doubt. War History is full of exaggeration and empty slogans; Churchill's famous statement about 'The Few' – 'Never in the field of human conflict was so much owed by so many to so few'– does not belong there.

The RAF's fighter pilots waged a tenacious struggle against overwhelming odds and defeated the most powerful air force in the world, at that time, including its confident fighter pilots. The outcome of the battle was decided neither by radar, nor alleged German mistakes, but above all by the superb fighting spirits of the RAF fighter pilots. There is a plethora of examples of self-sacrificing efforts by pilots in the RAF during the Battle of Britain – airmen in small formations of fighters crawling slowly upwards towards many more German aircraft, in order to 'give the bastards what they deserve'; pilots that rammed German aircraft when the result of their gunfire was not enough; and above all pilots who remained in the combat until all possibilities of destroying more German aircraft were definitely exhausted. Certainly there are plenty of examples also to the contrary – even for those young men who start out well motivated, stamina and nerves can run out – but the RAF's contribution during the Battle of Britain is characterized by a particularly stubborn will to resist.

The equally self-sacrificing efforts made by the crews of RAF Bomber Command must also be emphasized. Despite the lack of appropriate equipment for night operations, they made a very important psychological contribution to the battle. Despite losses which at the end of October 1940 amounted to 75% of the strength they had started with four months earlier, they maintained an uninterrupted activity over Germany and the occupied countries. By doing so they strengthened British morale – including that of Fighter Command – and created concerns in Germany's leaders that eventually led to the strategic mistake of starting to bomb London instead of Fighter Command's ground organisation.

'The Few' could also be boiled down to two people who both were of decisive importance to the British victory. For fighting spirits, Britain could hardly have had a better leader than Winston Churchill, whose flair for mass psychology did wonders for morale in the isolated island. As he correctly predicted, the US would begin increasingly to actively support the UK as long as the British could prove that that they could hold out. For this they needed a will to resist that – at least from a strictly military strategic point of view – seemed fairly 'irrational' in June 1940, at the time of the capitulation of France.

In the military field, Air Vice-Marshal Keith Park played an equally important role. It was he who organised and led the majority of Fighter Command's defensive battles against the Luftwaffe. Although Park has also been criticised for making some mistakes – e.g. the insistence on using certain airfields quite close to the English south coast which resulted in unnecessarily high losses – his leadership of the battle represents without doubt one of the most important factors in the British victory. Lord Arthur Tedder, who was appointed Chief of the British Air Staff after the war, said in 1947 that 'if ever any one man won the Battle of Britain, he did. I don't believe it is recognised how much this one man, with his leadership, his calm judgement and his skill, did to save not only this country, but the world.'

The gun camera in Adolf Galland's Bf 109 E-4/N recorded the German ace's 57th air victory on 5 December 1940. The British pilot, Sergeant George Stroud from 249 Squadron, bailed out with severe burns from his Hurricane V7677, 'GN-N'. (Photo: Galland.)

The outcome of the Battle of Britain is often measured in terms of the number of shot down aircraft. This is a tradition that goes back to both Hermann Göring and the German propaganda's fixation on victories, and the British tabloid press' daily reports on 'today's shoot down results' in a way that not by coincidence resembled football results. It is a well-known fact that both sides exaggerated the opponent's losses. Between 10 July and 31 October, 1940 – the period that British historiography has chosen to locate the Battle of Britain to – Fighter Command reported the shooting down of a total of 2,692 German planes.[505] The actual German combat losses – i.e. even to ground fire – was only about half as many. During the same period, the Germans reported that they had shot down about 3,600 British aircraft, which is nearly two and a half times higher than the actual British losses.

Before we study the statistics of the aircraft lost in combat during the Battle of Britain, it is important to keep in mind that exact figures can hardly be calculated. This is due to several reasons, one of which is the human factor that created errors in the reporting of losses – losses have been recorded on the wrong date, an incorrect cause of loss may have been given, or a loss report has disappeared. In addition, it may in many cases be a purely subjective assessment if the loss of an aircraft is considered as a combat loss or not. A collision during air combat could, for instance, be judged in various ways.

For a long time the dominating image of the Battle of Britain was the one presented by Winston Churchill in his war memoirs, published in 1949. According to these, 1,733 German aircraft and 915 British fighters were lost during the period 10 July to 31 October 1940.[506] These figures – which are the basis for the widespread belief that the Germans lost two aircraft for each downed British fighter – have been corrected by modern research in British and German archives.

According to the Luftwaffe's own carefully made accounting for the period July–October 1940, a total of 2,069 aircraft were written off as total losses, and of these, 1,385 were recognised as 'caused by enemy action'.[507] The analysis that the author made of each individual German loss report during this period has, however, led to the conclusion that the latter figure is slightly too low. The author has identified 1,411 German aircraft that during the period 1 July–31 October 1940 should be considered as lost in combat (of which 1,369 from 10 July). These are distributed as follows:

July	186 (144 from 10 July)
August	585
September	446
October	194

Fighter Command's losses were recorded accurately, though not with the same care as the Luftwaffe catalogued their losses. Therefore, an accurate calculation of the RAF's fighter losses is harder to do. According to historians Derek Wood and Derek Dempster, Fighter Command lost 1,135 fighters in combat during the period from 4 July to 2 November 1940. (603 Hurricanes, 394 Spitfires, 115 Blenheims and 23 Defiants).[508] These are distributed as follows:*

4–31 July	142
1–29 August	367
30 August–26 September	389
27 September–31 October	284

* These sums are not in accordance with the loss figures when divided between various aircraft types.

The Battle of Britain Then and Now gives somewhat different figures:

10–31 July	91
August	389
September	358
October	185
Total	**1,023**

The detailed study that the author made of British records has found that in addition to these overall losses at least 289 RAF fighters were shot down but could be repaired:

July	27
August	86
September	134
October	42

This indicates that the number of RAF fighters shot down during the Battle of Britain is about twelve hundred (not including aircraft destroyed on the ground). A study of British loss reports indicates that about 12% of these were victims of German bomber gunners, of which follows that approximately 1,050 were shot down by German fighters. As we have seen, even RAF Bomber Command made a significant contribution to the British victory. Bomber Command's combat losses amounted to 72 aircraft in July, 103 in August and 87 each in September and October 1940 – a total of 349.[509] Additionally, RAF Coastal Command and Fleet Air Arm – which amongst other things were responsible for some air strikes against the German 'invasion ports' – lost 148 aircraft.

The total combat losses were therefore higher on the British side. If all the shot down aircraft are counted – i.e. even those that afterwards could be repaired – the numbers are just over 1,800 British and 1,400 German. This certainly gives a completely different image of the Battle of Britain than the one that has long been prevalent.

What should have become fairly clear by now is that the main combats in daylight were between Fighter Command and the Luftwaffe. Blenheim planes participated in this only to a very limited extent, so the 1,020 losses of Hurricanes, Spitfires and Defiants should be set against the 1,400 German combat losses. Calculated from the aircraft Fighter Command lost on the ground and the Luftwaffe lost to the British AA defence, Fighter Command's fighter pilots shot down an average of about 1.3 German aircraft for each own loss. If the downed British fighters which could be repaired are included, the ratio is more even.

The Battle of Britain, like other major clashes in the history of warfare, is surrounded by many myths, some old and tenacious and others of more recent origin. The latter, especially from German writers, includes the more common perception that the German Bf 109 units were after all significantly superior to their opponents in Fighter Command. As we have already seen, the training levels of the RAF and the Luftwaffe were not different to any appreciable degree, and although the Germans had a core of airmen with more combat experience than the RAF's

pilots, RAF fighter pilots with many years of experience as fighter pilots were relatively numerous. In addition, Fighter Command was significantly supplemented by volunteer pilots from German-occupied countries, airmen who were both trained and had combat experience. Here the Polish volunteers should be particularly emphasized. The average level of training and combat experience of the pilots of the all-Polish 303 Squadron was probably higher than in any other of RAF fighter unit in the autumn of 1940. And 303 Squadron was also, in terms of the number of victories, Fighter Command's most successful unit during the Battle of Britain. It should be added, however, that the pilots of No. 303 also appear to have overestimated their own successes to a greater degree than any other unit. Historian John Alcorn has made a comprehensive analysis of the RAF's victory claims during the Battle of Britain and compared these with German losses. Even if he cannot claim a hundred percent accuracy, it is interesting to note that he has only been able to verify 44 of 303 Squadron's 130 victory claims with German losses, which is a greater so-called 'overclaim factor' than any other RAF units in Alcorn's investigation.[510] However, 303 Squadron still deserves to be mentioned as Fighter Command's most successful unit during the Battle of Britain, underlining the importance of the foreign pilots for the British defence. Dowding characterized the Polish pilots of 303 Squadron as 'very dashing but totally undisciplined', and at the same time 'magnificent fighters'.[511]

A detailed analysis of aerial combat during the Battle of Britain provides little support for the view that the Bf 109 units were superior to Fighter Command. There are numerous examples where RAF fighter pilots engaged numerically superior German fighter formations and defeated them – and it is not even unusual that that happened when RAF pilots flew Hurricane planes, which were decidedly inferior to both the German Messerschmitt fighters. However, the Germans could often use their overwhelming numerical superiority, coupled with a tactical advantage (height advantage over the RAF aircraft that were only just in the air) to inflict severe losses on their opponents. The RAF only lost relatively few fighters to the German bombers' defensive firepower, but the German fighter pilots had the advantage of being able to attack and 'finish off' the Spitfires or Hurricanes that had been damaged by fire from machine gunners aboard the German bombers.

Between 1 July and 31 October 1940 the German fighter and Zerstörer airmen claimed to have shot down at least 2,426 British aircraft. Available statistics confirm the thesis that the twin-engined Bf 110 fighter has been grossly underestimated in historiography. Of these 2,426 victory claims, the Bf 109 units were responsible for 1,752 and the Bf 110 equipped Zerstörer units for 674. Thereby the share of the Bf 110s was 27.8%, which is remarkable, given that the aircraft in the Zerstörer units represented only 20% of the number of German fighters on 13 August, 1940.

A comparison between victory claims and combat losses for the two German fighters in the Battle of Britain shows the following relationship:

Bf 109 fighter units   1,752 victories
                               534 combat losses
Bf 110 fighter units*   674 victories
                               196 combat losses

* Means Zerstörer units.

Thus the Zerstörer, with an average of 3.40 victories for every loss in battle, even had a slightly better ratio than the average of 3.28:1 of the Bf 109 units. It would be premature from these figures to conclude that the Bf 110 was the better aircraft of the two German fighters. In fact, at the beginning of the war the Luftwaffe picked some of its best fighter pilots for the newly formed Zerstörer units. Moreover, it seems the Zerstörer units often had better fighting spirits than many of the Bf 109 units – although there certainly were many Bf 109 units that also had quite high fighting spirits. From the end of July 1940, several Bf 109 units had to be removed from combat because high losses reduced the fighting spirit of the surviving pilots to nothing. One can possibly say that V.(Z)/LG 1 ended up in this situation – with its heavy losses on 27 September 1940, including the unit commander, being the decisive cause – but then only after this Gruppe had been in continuous combat activity since the beginning of July (longer than most German fighter units at the time); if so, this is the only such case among the Zerstörer units.

Nevertheless the Bf 109's alleged superiority over the Bf 110 apparently finds no support in the statistics above. That the Spitfire, on the other hand, was better than the much older Hurricane is also apparent from the statistics on both sides. A phenomenon that clearly manifests itself in the German victory reports is the misidentification of enemy aircraft. Remarkably often the Germans reported Spitfires when in reality Hurricanes were concerned. Possibly it was an expression of the greater respect the Germans felt for the Spitfire. The Hurricane units were responsible for most of the Luftwaffe losses, however, simply because there more of them – the ratio of Hurricane and Spitfire numbers in Fighter Command actually increased from 1.4:1 to 1.75:1 during the Battle of Britain. Of Fighter Command's victory claims between 10 July and 31 October, 1940, the Hurricane units were responsible for 55% and the Spitfire units for 43%.

If we accept Wood's and Dempster's figures of 603 Hurricanes and 394 Spitfires lost in combat between 4 July and 2 November 1940, we get an average relationship between the reported successes and losses of 2.6:1 for Hurricanes and 3.6:1 for Spitfires. The RAF units that produced the most advantageous loss ratio during the Battle of Britain were 19 Squadron, who in fifteen days of action recorded 60 ½ victories against seven combat losses (8.6:1) and 611 Squadron, with 18 victories against only two losses during six days of action. Both squadrons were equipped with Spitfires. Polish 303 Squadron was able to achieve the best ratio among the Hurricane-equipped units – 130 victories against 16 losses (8.1:1). Next came 17 Squadron with 42 ½ victories against nine combat losses (4.7:1).

An estimate based on the respective fighter's victory claims according to the tables above, and actual combat losses of each side, gives the following results for the period July to October 1940*:

	Authentic shootdowns	Own combat losses*	Ratio
Spitfire	c. 560	394	1.4 : 1
Hurricane	c. 715	603	1.2 : 1
Bf 109	c. 760	534	1.4 : 1
Bf 110	c. 290	196	1.5 : 1

* Concerning own combat losses, only aircraft totally destroyed are included.

In the RAF loss reports, a slightly different relationship is reflected. In many cases, it was unclear what caused the shooting down of a British fighter, but of the 333 cases during the period from 8 August to 7 September where the lost plane was recorded in British records shot down by a specified German fighter, the Bf 110s' share was 23%. If this is equivalent to an average, it would indicate that the Zerstörer units during this period in fact shot down around 150 British fighters against own combat losses of 134 Bf 110s. (In the same period the Zerstörer units claimed to have shot down 477 British aircraft.) As the author has found however, the specified loss cause in British records is often inaccurate because the pilot who was shot down often did not see the airplane that shot him down – which can testify to the Bf 110s' advantage, given their tactics of rapid attacks from above directed against British fighters which often at the same time could be involved in a more prolonged 'dogfight' with Bf 109s.

Both sides suffered quite severe losses. In addition to the more than one thousand British fighter aircraft which were completely destroyed in combat between July and October 1940, the number of aircraft severely damaged in combat (Category 2) in Fighter Command amounted to 731 for the period from 27 June to 2 November 1940.[512] In addition, of course, to the losses caused by accidents. When one considers that Fighter Command had only 446 operational fighters on 4 June 1940 when the Battle of Dunkirk ended, it is clear that losses at these levels could very well have had catastrophic results. It shows the immense importance of Lord Beaverbrook's effort to raise British aircraft production. On 17 December 1940, Lord Beaverbrook gave a radio speech where he expressed his appreciation for the workers of the British aircraft industry: 'For what has already been done I ask you to give the praise to the men and women of the aircraft factories. They have suffered and endured the bombing. And, thanks to their labour and their courage, we can say that in the past seven months we have increased our strength in aircraft of each type – fighters, bombers, reconnaissance machines, and trainers. In every type there is an increase. We have done this job in the face of all our losses in battle.'[513]

On 26 October 1940, Fighter Command could muster 746 operational fighter aircraft. The picture on the German side was much darker. The bloodletting the Luftwaffe had sustained during the Battle of Britain is evident from a comparison between the units' strength returns on 29 June and 28 December 1940: during this time the number of operational fighters went down from 1,117 to 755, while the number of operational bombers dropped from 841 to 722.[514] To top it all the Germans were compelled to send parts of their already battered air forces to new areas of crisis. In his speech on 17 December 1940, Lord Beaverbrook also said: 'And while we have supplied these fighters and bombers to the squadrons, we have, at the same time, equipped our Air Force in the Middle East.'[515] The importance of the latter cannot be underestimated – the fact that the British air forces in the Mediterranean had grown so strong that they could deprive the Italians of air superiority. In the winter of 1940/41 this compelled Hitler to relocate the entire Fliegerkorps X from the campaign against the British Isles to the Mediterranean theatre.

These Messerschmitt 109s have flown for the last time.

The German response to Fighter Command's victory was to unleash the Luftwaffe in a hitherto unheard of bombardment of British cities. On the night of 14 November Coventry was subjected to one of the war's most concentrated bombings so far. Guided by Kampfgruppe 100, 450 German bombers dropped 503 tonnes of high-explosive bombs and 881 incendiary bomb containers, which turned large parts of the city into a sea of fire. It cost 554 dead, and another 881 wounded among the city's inhabitants. The bombing of Coventry became an important symbol, and later on the image of the devastation in the city helped to define Bomber Command's increasingly harsh warfare.

From mid-November 1940 the mutual nightly bombing raids came to dominate the air war in the West right up until the US entered actively into the war two years later. In retaliation for the attack on Coventry the RAF dispatched a record number of 127 bombers against a German city – Hamburg, where 121 people were killed or injured. The Luftwaffe responded with 369 bombers against Birmingham on the night of 19 November 1940. The bombing of Birmingham lasted three nights in a row and resulted in 900 civilian deaths. On the evening of 7 December, Bomber Command carried out a relatively large air strike against Düsseldorf, with close to four thousand fire-bombs being dropped. The Luftwaffe responded the following night with 413 bomber sorties to London, and dropped 378 tonnes of high-explosive bombs and close to 100,000 incendiary bombs. In inner London forty 'vast fires' were caused. Among others, Coventry, Birmingham, Sheffield, Liverpool and Manchester were subjected to large-scale nocturnal attacks in December 1940, but the worst raid was directed against London during the night between 29 and 30 December. At that time the Germans changed tactics and loaded their bombers mainly with incendiary bombs. The result was 1,500 fires in the British capital. This was more than the already heavily strained fire department could deal with, and over the course of the night several fires joined into two giant fires – one that included half a square kilometre, and one that covered almost twice as large an area within the urban districts. The city continued to burn until well into the next day. London had not seen such devastation since the Great Fire of 1666. The Germans were able to accomplish this with only 130 bombers.

At the turn of the year, the number of deaths within the British civilian population had risen to 23,000. Although the targets directly attacked were 'legitimate targets' such as industrial installations and ports, the aim was to crack the British will to resist. But the Germans never came even close to this. Instead their assaults helped to add a burning hatred to the already strong will to resist. Eventually, when Bomber Command had better equipment and another leadership, they would pay a heavy price for this.

Ironically these nightly airstrikes – which never posed any threat to Britain's ability to continue the war – contributed to defeating the two men that symbolised the victory over the Luftwaffe: Hugh Dowding and, indirectly, Keith Park.

As we have seen, the intensity of the bitter feud between the commanders of 11 and 12 Groups, Keith Park and Trafford Leigh-Mallory, intensified during September 1940. As far as Park was concerned, it was all about Leigh-Mallory's alleged inability – or unwillingness – to give 11 Group support.

Park was not known for diplomatic tact, and on 29 September he dispatched a PM to Dowding where he repeated his earlier sharp criticism of his colleague in the North and demanded that Dowding, in his capacity as commander of Fighter Command, intervene to force Leigh-Mallory to cooperate and on request and without delay send two or three squadrons to 11 Group's area 'instead of wasting time forming up into a mass of five squadrons'. The question of Big Wings – which was Leigh-Mallory's hobby horse – versus operations of the size of single or pairs of squadrons, which was Park's main tactic, became the great

The victors' group photo. Pilots from RAF 234 Squadron pose proudly in front of one of their Spitfires. Between July and October 1940 this unit recorded 69 air victories against 17 own losses.

casus belli. Although Dowding tried to calm them down, two rival camps were soon formed. It may have been Park that made the most noise in the beginning, but the camp that stood against Park and Dowding that was the most aggressive, the one that was on the offensive. This camp received significant support from a group of Conservative MPs who wanted to attack the Chief of the British Air Staff, Air Chief Marshal Cyril Newall. Historian Richard Overy establishes:

'Throughout the battle a backstairs intrigue was conducted against Newall and Dowding, involving among others, the veteran airman Lord Trenchard and the Minister of Aircraft Production, Lord Beaverbrook. A whispering campaign against Newall's alleged imcompetence,

begun by a junior officer in the Air Ministry, reached [Secretary of State for Air] Sinclair and Churchill.' [516]

As Dowding and Park were close, these politicians joined forces with the group of high-ranking air officers who were plotting against Park. One ingredient in Leigh-Mallory's criticism of Park was possibly the jealousy he may have felt that Dowding promoted Park over his head to the prestigious post of Commander of 11 Group.

Leigh-Mallory was supported by Air Vice-Marshal Sholto Douglas, Assistant Chief of the Air Staff. Moreover, he had a faithful supporter in the combative ace pilot Squadron Leader Douglas Bader, the commander of 242 Squadron and an uncompromising advocate of the

Big Wing tactics. Bader's adjutant, Flight Lieutenant Peter Macdonald, also happened to be the Conservative Party representative for the Isle of Wight in the British Parliament, and in that position he was able to gain an audience with Winston Churchill. Macdonald made no secret of his strong support for Leigh-Mallory and negative attitude towards Park.

On 17 October, Sholto Douglas called a conference with the alleged purpose of discussing fighter tactics. By that time Newall's fate had already been decided: on 4 October the political decision was made to take effect from 24 October to replace him with Sir Charles Portal, up to then commander of Bomber Command. Significantly, Churchill's works in several volumes on the Second World War give no clue to the reason why Newall, despite his merits,

had to leave and instead was sent to New Zealand as its governor.

When Dowding and Park arrived at the conference on 17 October, they found to their dismay that not only was Newall absent, Leigh-Mallory had been allowed to bring along the young Squadron Leader Bader. He gave a speech about the benefits of the Big Wing, and what a mistake it was not to let 11 Group operate Big Wings. For high-ranking Dowding and Park it was a tremendous humiliation being more or less lectured by a young squadron leader in this way. The notes from the conference show 'Park defending himself against overwhelming odds and Dowding appearing to be mildly unconcerned'. [517] Leigh-Mallory could not have chosen a more appropriate spokesperson than the young, stubborn and aggressive Bader.

On 26 October – two days after Newall went – Air Minister Sir Archibald Sinclair made a visit to the Duxford base where he met Bader and the other pilots from the Duxford Wing. A week later Duxford was visited by Harold Balfour, the Conservative Undersecretary for Aviation and a close friend of Air Vice-Marshal Sholto Douglas. Balfour listened to Bader and the other pilots and then authored a report in which he concluded that a serious 'personal conflict' had developed where the pilots of 12 Group had become averse to both Park and 11 Group. 'There had been no improvements as a result of the conference [on 17 October] and the Duxford Wing was still called in too late [by Park and 11 Group].'[518] According to historian Stephen Bungay without asking the men in the 11 Group, Balfour argued that the pilots of 11 Group opposed the '"poaching" on their territory' and that their morale was being 'unnecessarily shaken' because they constantly found themselves numerically inferior.[519]

The latter undeniably seems a bit rich, because it was those pilots who – rightly – just at that time felt like proud victors. Copies of the report were sent to Air Minister Sinclair, to Portal, the new Chief of the Air Staff, and to Air Vice-Marshal Sholto Douglas. The latter forwarded it to Dowding and urged him to intervene to induce Park to better use the Duxford Wing.

It appears that it was only now that the reserved commander of Fighter Command understood what was going on. He responded emphatically, dismissed every point in the report, and announced his intention to personally take control of the cooperation between 11 and 12 Groups. He had some special words to say about the young Squadron Leader Bader, whom he found to be, regardless of his merits in air combat, 'suffering from an over-development of the

critical faculties' and felt that it was mainly his 'amazing gallantry [in combat]' that prevented him from subjecting Bader to disciplinary action. Dowding suggested, however, the transfer of 'the young Bader to another station where he could be kept better in control'.[520]

Strengthened by this Park handed Dowding a new report on the Duxford Wing on 7 November. In this, he pointed out that in ten missions during the second half of October the Duxford Wing managed to find the enemy only once, which resulted in the shooting down of only a single German aircraft. Dowding, who always supported Park in his view of the Big Wing tactic, sent the report on to Portal's Air Staff on 15 November, but there no one was interested. It turned out that the conflict had not really been about Big Wings.

While Dowding and Park discussed Big Wings, Dowding's critics had gathered arguments against Dowding's alleged slowness when it came to building an effective night fighter force. Air Vice-Marshal Douglas, Portal's assistant, had long believed that Dowding had failed to develop the night fighters.

In fact, Dowding encouraged the installation of radar on night fighters – which Fighter Command was the first in the world to do – and the development of the world's first aeroplane designed and built as a night fighter. As we have seen, Britain went to war without a long-range fighter like the Luftwaffe's Bf 110. But based on the torpedo bomber Beaufort and inspired by the Bf 110 the aircraft manufacturer Bristol developed in near record time a twin-engined fighter called Beaufighter. This received Dowding's full support, and when it was put into service with night fighter unit 29 Squadron, Fighter Command had one of the world's best night fighter aircraft. The Beaufighter was not as fast as the Bf 110 perhaps – but it had, with its four cannons and six machine guns, a devastating armament. In addition, Dowding had already in early September issued a directive on the so-called 'Kenley experiment' which was to connect the radar with anti-aircraft searchlights, and then establish liaison with the air controllers that guided the radar-equipped night fighters.

Yet Sir John Salmond – Director of Armament Production at the Ministry of Aircraft Production – had in mid-September 1940 authored a very critical report on Dowding's role in the development of British night fighter aircraft. When he submitted it to Lord Beaverbrook, a personal note was added: 'Dowding has to go.'

Of course it was disturbing to see that the German night fighters developed into a more efficient force than that of Fighter Command. Statistics for October 1940 speak for themselves: of the total of 5,900 sorties made by German bombers over the British Isles at night, the Britons only managed to shoot down twenty-three, i.e., a loss ratio to the Luftwaffe of 0.4%. At the same time Bomber Command conducted 2,200 sorties over enemy territory

An image of London after the so-called 'Blitz', which lasted until May 1941. By that time the German bombings had cost 43,000 British lives and about 46,000 people had been injured. London had been worst affected, with 28,000 dead and 26,000 injured.

and lost 87 bombers – a ten times higher loss ratio – twelve of which fell victim to German night fighters. But the belated start of night fighter development was a sin of omission that many shared responsibility for.

In all events, the Air Ministry was busy with events other than the controversy about Big Wings when Dowding submitted his report on 15 November 1940. The previous night the Luftwaffe had nearly erased Coventry.

That the first kill by a radar-equipped Beaufighter night fighter was achieved on the night of 19 November, seems not to have affected perceptions of Dowding's role in British night fighter development.

On 25 November 1940, Dowding was deposed as commander of Fighter Command.

It has been claimed that he really just retired. In fact, he would have retired earlier that year, and had been asked by Churchill to remain. But the circumstances surrounding the change of command at Fighter Command and, not least, Dowding's own reaction, suggest that the background was different. When the British Information Ministry at the beginning of 1941 published the first official account of the Battle of Britain, Dowding was not even mentioned by name![521]

Dowding was succeeded by Air Vice-Marshal Sholto Douglas, Leigh-Mallory's staunch supporter.

On 18 December Keith Park was deposed from the post of commander for 11 Group, and nine days later was appointed to command 23 Group, a training unit. He was replaced by – Leigh-Mallory.

'To my dying day', Park said many years later, 'I shall feel bitter at the base intrigue which was used to remove Dowding and myself as soon as we had won the Battle of Britain.'[522]

The leaderships of the RAF, the Air Ministry and Fighter Command had never built up the same almost personal relationships with their pilots that the Luftwaffe's charismatic and very popular commander Göring did. Therefore, it was possible to dismiss Dowding and Park without it having a significant impact on morale or confidence in the leaders of Fighter Command. Robert Foster, who was pilot officer in 605 Squadron, said: 'Of course we thought it was a shame that Dowding and Park had to go. We couldn't understand it, but it didn't make any difference, it didn't effect us. Although both were very popular, they were distant figures. Park had visited our Squadron twice, but it had been rather short visits, and we never had seen Dowding.'[523]

With this, the proponents of Big Wing tactics had prevailed in Fighter Command. Not surprisingly, Douglas Bader's military career took off substantially. He was promoted to Wing Commander and appointed to commander of the new Tangmere Wing.

For 75 years, the debate has raged over the issue of Leigh-Mallory's Big Wing tactics – which also meant that the the German aircraft formations would be allowed in over England before a more concerted attack would be made against them. Keith Park never had a doubt. After the war, he wrote that 'we should have lost the Battle of Britain if I had adopted the "withholding" tactics of No. 12 Group'.[524]

Air Vice-Marshal Sir Trafford Leigh-Mallory led Fighter Command's 12 Group during the Battle of Britain until he succeeded Park to command 11 Group.

In June 1941, most of the German Air Force was moved to the East, and was used in Hitler's invasion of the Soviet Union, which began on 22 June. Thus, the Luftwaffe definitely went over to the defensive in the West. Only a fraction of the German fighter force – JG 2 'Richthofen', JG 26 'Schlageter' and I./JG 52 – were left to defend the airspace above the occupied territories in the West against the RAF's daytime intrusions. Sholto Douglas and Leigh-Mallory took the opportunity to mobilise Fighter Command – along with the bombers of Bomber Command's 2 Group – in a 'reverse Battle of Britain'. Between June and December 1941 the RAF conducted 20,495 fighter sorties and 1,406 bomber sorties over the English Channel during daytime. Fighter Command made full scale use of Big Wing tactics. The German fighter units copied in turn the methodology Park had used against them so successfully during the Battle of Britain, exposing the large formations of Spitfires to series of attacks of Schwarm or Staffel size. The statistics speak for themselves: These operations cost Fighter Command a loss of 411 fighters. Meanwhile Sholto Douglas' and Leigh-Mallory's pilots – those who so convincingly had defeated the Luftwaffe a year earlier – did not succeed in shooting down more than 119 German fighters: 57 from JG 2, 55 from JG 26, five from I./JG 52 and two from other units. Among the British pilots who were lost during this time was Douglas Bader. He spent the remainder of the war in German captivity.

The Spitfire stands as a symbol of the Battle of Britain, but the main burden was borne by the Hawker Hurricane, which accounted for the majority of the German aircraft losses. The picture shows a Hurricane Mk I with the 18-inch wide recognition tape in 'Sky Blue' (light blue), introduced in Fighter Command in December 1940 to indicate that it was a friendly day fighter. (Photo: Svensk Flyghistorisk Förening archives.)

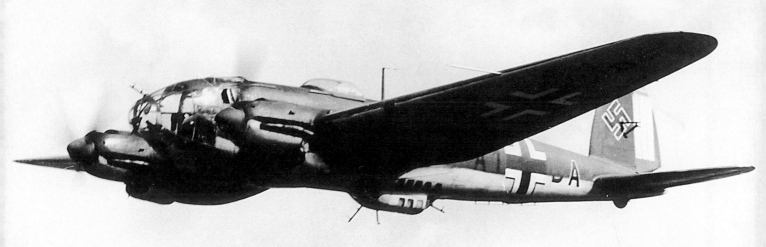

1.

2.

3.

4.

The men and women of the battle

Photo 1.
Bird of death over England – a He 111.

Photo 2.
Sergeant 'Ginger' Lacey, the British top ace during the Battle of Britain. The red-haired Lacey received his nick-name from the likewise red-haired and freckled character in W. E. Johns' Biggles books. The Yorkshireman Lacey was infamous for his outspoken attitude towards officers, who often came to dislike him strongly, but this made him very popular among the rank-and-file. The daring Lacey was shot down no less than nine times, but survived the war. He passed away in 1989.

Photo 3.
This woman has just been rescued from her bombed house in London in September 1940.

Photo 4.
One of the aces in V.(Z)/LG 1, Oberleutnant Helmut Müller, demonstrates in classic manner how he shot down an enemy aircraft. In the centre, with arms crossed, stands the unit commander, Hauptmann Horst Liensberger, and next to Müller is Oberleutnant Ernst Zobel. Müller scored 12 victories before he himself was shot down and captured on 15 September 1940. Ernst Zobel survived the war but was killed in a car accident on 13 April 1972. (Photo: Von Eimannsberger.)

Photo 5.
Feldwebel Erwin Leykauf of III./JG 54 in the cockpit of his Bf 109 E during the Battle of Britain. (Photo: Leykauf.)

Photo 6.
The RAF's 601 Squadron was, not without reason, called 'the Millionaires' Mob'. The unit was formed by a group of wealthy aristocrats who after a meeting at White's – London's oldest gentleman's club – in 1925 decided to form their own squadron within the RAF. The young upper class boys of 601 distinguished themselves in various ways. They often owned their aircraft privately, drove fast sport cars and played 'polo' with motor cycles. They carried uniforms lined in red silk and wore blue ties instead of the prescribed black.
One of the upper class officers of 601 was Flight Lieutenant William Henry Rhodes-Moorhouse, posing in the image above. He was the grandson of William Barnard Rhodes – one of New Zealand's wealthiest men in the 19th Century– and the son of First World War's famous combat pilot William Barnard Rhodes-Moorhouse, who was awarded the Victoria Cross post-humously after a daring air raid in April 1915. William Henry followed his father's footsteps and achieved 8 ½ victories before he was killed in action on 6 September 1940.

APPENDIX 1
LUFTWAFFE ORDER OF BATTLE ON 13 AUGUST 1940

Oberbefehlshaber der Luftwaffe (ObdL), Berlin

Reichsmarschall Hermann Göring

Unit	Airfield	Commander	Aircraft	Number of aircraft	Operational
AufklObdL	Neufchâteau	Obstlt Rowehl			
1.(F)/AufklObdL	Neufchâteau	Hptm Förster	Ju 86 P	2	2
			He 116	4	3
			Do 215	2	1
			Bf 110	2	2
			BV 142	2	2
			He 111 P	7	6
			He 111 H	2	1
			Do 217	3	2
			Ju 88	3	1
2.(F)/AufklObdL	Neufchâteau	Hptm Pritzel	Do 215	8	4
			He 111 P	1	1
Wekusta 1./AufklObdL	Oldenburg	Oblt Jonas	Do 17 Z-2	3	3
			He 111 H	2	2
Wekusta 2./AufklObdL	Lanveoc-Poulmic/ Brest	Oblt Prasse	He 111 H	5	2
Wekusta 26	Brussels-Grimberghen	Hptm von Rotberg	Do 17 Z-2	5	3
			Bf 110	1	1
			He 111 H	4	4

Luftflotte 2, Brussels

Generalfeldmarschall Albert Kesselring

Fliegerkorps I, Beauvais
Generaloberst Ulrich Grauert

Unit	Airfield	Commander	Aircraft	Number of aircraft	Operational
Stab/KG 1	Amiens-Glisy	Oberst Exss	He 111 H	4	4
I./KG 1	Montdidier	Major Maier	He 111 H	27	23
II./KG 1	Amiens-Glisy	Major Kosch	He 111 H	31	29
III./KG 1	Rosières-en-Santerre	Major Fanelsa	He 111 H	32	15
Stab/KG 76	Cormeilles-en-Vexin	Oberst Fröhlich	Do 17 Z-2	5	5
I./KG 76	Beauvais-Tille	Hptm Lindeiner	Do 17 Z-2	29	29
II./KG 76	Creil	Major Möricke	Ju 88	36	28
III./KG 76	Cormeilles-en-Vexin	Obstlt Genth	Do 17 Z-2	32	19
Lehrstaffel/KG 76	Beaumont-le-Roger	Hptm Kröchel	Do 17 Z-2	11	7
Stab/KG 77	Laon	Generalmajor von Stutterheim	Ju 88		
I./KG 77	Laon	Major Balcke	Ju 88	33	0
II./KG 77	Asch-Nord	Major Behrendt	Ju 88	38	0
III./KG 77	Laon	Major Kless	Ju 88	35	0
III./KG 26 'Löwengeschwader'	Poix	Major Wolfien			
5.(F)/122	Haute-Fontaine	Hptm Böhm	Ju 88	3	1
			Do 17 P	6	4
			He 111 H	–	–
3.(H)/32		Hptm Ehlers	Hs 126	8	7
4.(H)/32		Hptm Sell	Hs 126	9	8

(Note: KG 77 not operative)

Fliegerkorps II, Ghent
General der Flieger Bruno Loerzer

Unit	Airfield	Commander	Aircraft	Number of aircraft	Operational
Stab/KG 2 'Holzhammer'	St. Lèger	Oberst Fink	Do 17 Z-2	7	4
I./KG 2 'Holzhammer'	Epinoy	Maj Gutzmann	Do 17 Z-2	43	27
II./KG 2 'Holzhammer'	St Lèger	Obstlt Weitkus	Do 17 Z-2	35	31
III./KG 2 'Holzhammer'	Cambrai-South	Maj Fuchs	Do 17 Z-2	34	32
Stab/KG 3 'Blitz'	Le Culot	Oberst von Chamier-Glisczinski	Do 17 Z-2	7	3
I./KG 3 'Blitz'	Le Culot	Obstlt Gabelmann	Do 17 Z-2	36	28
II./KG 3 'Blitz'	Antwerp-Deurne	Hptm Pilger	Do 17 Z-2	35	32
III./KG 3 'Blitz'	St. Trond	Hptm Rathmann	Do 17 Z-2	30	25
Stab/KG 53 'Legion Condor'	Lille-North	Oberst Stahl	He 111 H	5	1
I./KG 53 'Legion Condor'	Lille-North	Major Kaufmann	He 111 H	28	27
II./KG 53 'Legion Condor'	Lille-North	Oblt Kohlbach	He 111 H	28	15
III./KG 53 'Legion Condor'	Lille-North	Major Edler von Braun	He 111 H	33	24
II./StG 1	Pas-de-Calais	Hptm Keil	Ju 87 B	38	30
IV.(St)/LG 1	Tramecourt	Hptm von Brauchitsch	Ju 87 B	36	28
Erpr. Gr. 210	Calais-Marck	Hptm Rubensdörffer	Bf 109 E-4B	10	9
			Bf 110 C-6	5	4
			Bf 110 D-0	21	17
Stab (H)/30	Woensdrecht	Major Berger			
4.(H)/31	Woensdrecht	Major Sorge	Hs 126	9	8
5.(H)/32		Hptm Sieckenius	Hs 126	9	9

9. Fliegerdivision, Soesterberg
Generalleutnant Coeler

Unit	Airfield	Commander	Aircraft	Number of aircraft	Operational
Stab/KG 4 "General Wever"	Soesterberg	Oberst Rath	He 111 P	6	5
I./KG 4 "General Wever"	Soesterberg	Hptm Meissner	He 111 H	30	12
II./KG 4 "General Wever"	Eindhoven	Maj Dr. Wolff	He 111 P	31	25
III./KG 4 "General Wever"	Amsterdam-Schiphol	Hptm Bloedorn	Ju 88	35	23
Stab/KG 40	Brest-Guipavas	Obstlt Geisse	Ju 88	1	1
I./KG 40	Brest-Guipavas	Hptm Petersen	Fw 200 C	9	3
KGr 100	Vannes-Meucon	Hptm Aschenbrenner	He 111 H	41	19
KGr 126	Nantes	Maj Schulz	He 111 H	34	8
3.(F)/122	Eindhoven	Obstlt Koehler	Ju 88	4	3
			He 111 H	7	6

Nachtjagddivision 1, Oldenburg
Oberst Josef Kammhuber

Unit	Airfield	Commander	Aircraft	Number of aircraft	Operational
Stab/NJG 1	Düsseldorf and Deelen	Hptm Falck	Bf 110 B	3	3
I./NJG 1	Bönninghardt	Hptm Radusch	Bf 110 B	4	3
			Bf 110 C	30	19
II./NJG 1	Düsseldorf	Hptm Heyse	Ju 88 C	11	4
			Do 17 Z	7	6
			Do 17 Z	3	3
III./NJG 1	Cologne-Ostheim	Hptm von Bothmer	Bf 110 C	13	4
			Bf 109 D	3	1
			Bf 109 E	17	16

Jagdfliegerführer 2, Wissant
Oberst Kurt-Bertram von Döring

Unit	Airfield	Commander	Aircraft	Number of aircraft	Operational
Stab/JG 3	Wierre au Bois	Obstlt Vieck	Bf 109 E	3	3
I./JG 3	Grandvillers	Hptm Lützow	Bf 109 E	33	32
II./JG 3	Samer	Hptm von Selle	Bf 109 E	29	22
III./JG 3	Desvres and Le Touquet	Hptm Kienitz	Bf 109 E	29	29
Stab/JG 26 'Schlageter'	Audembert	Major Handrick	Bf 109 E	4	4
I./JG 26 'Schlageter'	Audembert	Hptm Fischer	Bf 109 E	38	34
II./JG 26 'Schlageter'	Marquise	Hptm Ebbighausen	Bf 109 E	39	35
III./JG 26 'Schlageter'	Caffiers	Major Galland	Bf 109 E	40	38
Stab/JG 51	Wissant	Major Mölders	Bf 109 E	4	4
I./JG 51	Pihen	Hptm Brustellin	Bf 109 E	32	32
II./JG 51	Marquise-West	Hptm Matthes	Bf 109 E	33	33
III./JG 51	St. Omer-Claimarais	Hptm Trautloft	Bf 109 E	32	30
Stab/JG 52	Coquelles	Major von Bernegg	Bf 109 E	2	1
I./JG 52	Coquelles	Hptm von Eschwege	Bf 109 E	40	33
II./JG 52	Peuplingues	Hptm von Kornatzki	Bf 109 E	39	32
III./JG 52	Zerbst	Hptm von Winterfeldt	Bf 109 E	31	11
Stab/JG 54	Campagne-les-Guines	Maj Mettig	Bf 109 E	4	2
I./JG 54	Guines	Hptm von Bonin	Bf 109 E	34	24
II./JG 54	Hermelingen	Hptm Bode	Bf 109 E	36	32
III./JG 54	Guines	Hptm Ultsch	Bf 109 E	42	40
Stab/ZG 26 'Horst Wessel'	Lille	Obstlt Huth	Bf 110 C	3	3
I./ZG 26 'Horst Wessel'	Yvrench and St. Omer	Hptm Makrocki	Bf 110 C	39	33
II./ZG 26 'Horst Wessel'	Crécy and St. Omer	Hptm von Rettberg	Bf 110 C	37	32
III./ZG 26 'Horst Wessel'	Barly-Arques	Hptm Schalk	Bf 110 C	35	24
Stab/ZG 76	Laval	Major Grabmann	Bf 110 C		
II. /ZG 76 'Haifischgruppe'	Abbéville	Hptm Groth	Bf 110 C		
III./ZG 76	Laval	Hptm Dickoré	Bf 110 C		

Luftflotte 3, Paris

Generalfeldmarschall Hugo Sperrle

Unit	Airfield	Commander	Aircraft	Number of aircraft	Operational
Wekusta 51	Buc, Versailles	Oblt Kreowski	Do 17 U	1	1
			He 111 H	5	2

Fliegerkorps VIII, Deauville
General der Flieger Wolfram Freiherr von Richthofen

Unit	Airfield	Commander	Aircraft	Number of aircraft	Operational
Stab/StG 1	Angers	Maj Hagen	Ju 87 B	3	2
			Do 17 M	2	1
I./StG 1	Angers	Maj Hozzel	Ju 87 R	39	27
III./StG 1	Angers	Hptm Mahlke	Ju 87 B	38	26
Stab/StG 2 'Immelmann'	St. Malo	Major Dinort	Ju 87 B	4	3
I./StG 2 'Immelmann'	St. Malo	Hptm Hitschhold	Ju 87 B	35	29
II./StG 2 'Immelmann'	Lannion	Hptm Enneccerus	Ju 87 R	37	31
			Ju 87 B	2	2
Stab/StG 77	Caen	Major von Schönborn-Wiesentheid	Ju 87 B	4	3
			Do 17 M	4	1
I./StG 77	Caen	Hptm Meisel	Ju 87 B	36	33
II./StG 77	Caen	Hptm Orthofer	Ju 87 B	37	25
III./StG 77	Caen	Hptm Bode	Ju 87 B	38	37
II.(S)/LG 2	Böblingen	Major Weiss	Bf 109 E-7	39	31
V.(Z)/LG 1	Caen	Hptm Liensberger	Bf 110 C	32	21
			Bf 110 D	11	8
2.(F)/11	Bernay	Maj Paulitsch	Do 17 P	5	2
			Bf 110	4	4
2.(F)/123	Cherbourg-West	Hptm Hurlin	Do 17 P	6	4
Aufklärungsgruppe(H)/21	Bergen op Zoom	Major von Franzius	Hs 126	21	16

(Note: II./LG 2 not operative)

Fliegerkorps V, Villacoublay
General der Flieger Robert Ritter von Greim

Unit	Airfield	Commander	Aircraft	Number of aircraft	Operational
Stab/KG 51 'Edelweiss'	Paris-Orly	Major Schulz-Heyn	Ju 88	1	1
I./KG 51 'Edelweiss'	Melun-Villaroche	Hptm von Greiff	Ju 88	30	21
II./KG 51 'Edelweiss'	Etampes-Mondèsir	Major Winkler	Ju 88	34	24
III./KG 51 'Edelweiss'	Etampes-Mondésir	Major Marienfeld	Ju 88	32	25
Stab/KG 54 'Totenkopf'	Evreux	Obstlt Höhne	Ju 88	–	–
I./KG 54 'Totenkopf'	Evreux	Hptm Heydebreck	Ju 88	35	29
II./KG 54 'Totenkopf'	St. André	Hptm Schlaeger	Ju 88	31	23
Stab/KG 55 'Greif'	Villacoublay	Oberst Stoeckl	He 111 P	4	1
I./KG 55 'Greif'	Dreux	Major Korte	He 111 P	18	17
			He 111 H	21	18
II./KG 55 'Greif'	Chartres	Major Kless	He 111 P	38	28
III./KG 55 'Greif'	Villacoublay	Major Schemmell	He 111 P	38	33
4.(F)/14	Cherbourg	Hptm von Dewitz	Do 17M	3	–
			Do 17 P	7	7
			Bf 110	3	2
4.(F)/121	Villacoublay	Hptm Kerber	Ju 88	4	4
			Do 17 P	4	3

Fliegerkorps IV, Dinard
Generalmajor Alfred Keller

Unit	Airfield	Commander	Aircraft	Number of aircraft	Operational
Stab/LG 1	Orléans-Bricy	Oberst Bülowius	Ju 88	2	1
I./LG 1	Orléans-Bricy	Hptm Kern	Ju 88	33	23
			He 111 H	2	1
II./LG 1	Orléans-Bricy	Major Dobratz	Ju 88	34	24
III./LG 1	Chateaudun	Major Bormann	Ju 88	34	23
Stab/KG 27 'Boelcke'	Tours	Oberst Behrendt	He 111 P	5	1
I./KG 27 'Boelcke'	Tours	Major Ulbricht	He 111 P	15	12
			He 111 H	18	10
II./KG 27 'Boelcke'	Dinard-Bourges	Major Schlichting	He 111 P	26	18
			He 111 H	8	3
III./KG 27 'Boelcke'	Rennes	Major Speck von Sternburg	He 111 P	30	22
			He 111 D	1	1
KGr 806	Nantes and Caen-Carpiquet	Hptm Linke	Ju 88	33	22
Stab/StG 3	Bretigny	Oberst Angerstein	Ju 87 B	–	–
			He 111 H	2	1
			Do 17 M	1	–
			Do 17 Z-2	4	3
3.(F)/31	St. Brieux	Hptm Sieckemus	Bf 110 C	3	1
			Do 17 P	7	5
Stab(H)/31					
2.(H)/12		Hptm Samwer	Hs 126	9	9
4.(H)/22		Hptm Kötzing	Hs 126	9	9
2.(H)/31		Oblt Herbig	Hs 126	7	6
Stab(H)/41/ Kommandeur der Luftwaffe Armee-Oberkommando 8		Oberst Kettembeil			
2.(H)/13		Hptm Herbig	Hs 126	7	5
1.(H)/41		Maj Stein	Hs 126	8	5
2.(H)/41		Hptm Girke	Hs 126	7	5

Jagdfliegerführer 3, Deauville
Oberst von Massow

Unit	Airfield	Commander	Aircraft	Number of aircraft	Operational
Stab/JG 2 'Richthofen'	Beaumont-le-Roger	Obstlt von Bülow	Bf 109 E	3	3
I./JG 2 'Richthofen'	Beaumont-le-Roger	Hptm Strümpell	Bf 109 E	34	32
II./JG 2 'Richthofen'	Beaumont-le-Roger	Hptm Schellmann	Bf 109 E	36	28
III./JG 2 'Richthofen'	Le Havre	Major Dr. Mix	Bf 109 E	32	28
Stab/JG 27	Cherbourg-West	Obstlt Ibel	Bf 109 E	5	4
I./JG 27	Plumentot	Hptm Neumann	Bf 109 E	37	32
II./JG 27	Crépon	Hptm Andres	Bf 109 E	40	32
III./JG 27	Arcques	Hptm Schlichting	Bf 109 E	39	32
Stab/JG 53 'Pik As'	Cherbourg	Major von Cramon	Bf 109 E	6	6
I./JG 53 'Pik As'	Rennes and Guernsey	Hptm Blumensaat	Bf 109 E	39	37
II./JG 53 'Pik As'	Dinan and Guernsey	Hptm von Maltzahn	Bf 109 E	38	34
III./JG 53 'Pik As'	Brest and Sempy	Hptm Wilcke	Bf 109 E	38	35
Stab/ZG 2	Toussus-le-Noble	Obstlt Vollbracht	Bf 110 C	4	3
I./ZG 2	Caen-Carpiquet	Hptm Heinlein	Bf 110 C	41	35
II./ZG 2	Guyancourt	Major Carl	Bf 110 C	18	14
			Bf 110 D	23	20

Luftflotte 5, Oslo

Generaloberst Hans-Jürgen Stumpff

Fliegerkorps X, Oslo
General der Flieger Kurt Geisler

Unit	Airfield	Commander	Aircraft	Number of aircraft	Operational
Stab/KG 26 'Löwengeschwader'	Aalborg	Oberst Fuchs	He 111 P	6	6
I./KG 26 'Löwengeschwader'	Aalborg	Major Busch	He 111 H	30	29
II./KG 26 'Löwengeschwader'	Stavanger-Sola	Major Vetter	He 111 H	26	26
Stab/KG 30 'Adler'	Aalborg	Obstlt Loebel	Ju 88	1	1
I./KG 30 'Adler'	Aalborg	Maj Doench	Ju 88	40	34
II./KG 30 'Adler'	Aalborg		Ju 88		
III./KG 30 'Adler'	Aalborg	Hptm Kollewe	Ju 88	35	27
I./ZG 76	Stavanger-Forus	Hptm Restemeyer	Bf 110 C	34	32
II./JG 77	Stavanger-Sola (4./JG 77 at Måndal, 5./JG 77 at Aalborg)	Hptm Hentschel	Bf 109 E	43	38
KüFlGr 506	Stavanger-Sola	Major Eisenbeck	He 115 B	8	7
			He 115 C	18	14
3.(F)/AufklObdL	Stavanger-Sola	Oblt Rothenberg	Do 215 B	7	5
			Bf 110 C	2	1
			He 111 P	2	1
1.(F)/120	Stavanger-Sola	Maj Schub	Do 17 P	3	2
			He 111 H	1	1
1.(F)/121	Stavanger-Sola	Hptm Klinkicht	He 111 H	6	4
			Ju 88	3	2
Stab(F)/22	Trondheim-Vaernes	Oblt Thomas	Do 17 P	5	4
2.(F)/22	Aalborg		Do 17 M	1	1
			Do 17 P	5	3
3.(F)/22	Stavanger-Sola		Do 17 M	1	1
Wekusta-Kette Fliegerkorps X	Stavanger-Sola	Lt Zöllner	He 111 H	4	2

Stab and III./JG77 at Döberitz, and I./JG77 at Wyk auf Föhr.

General der Luftwaffe beim Oberbefehlshaber der Marine, Berlin

Generalmajor Hans Ritter

and

Führer der Seestreitkräfte

Generalmajor Hermann Bruch

Unit	Airfield	Commander	Aircraft	Number of aircraft	Operational
Stab/KüFlGr 406	Hörnum	Major Stockmann	Do 18		
3./KüFlGr 406	Hörnum	Hptm Holte	Do 18	10	10
2./KüFlGr 106	Rantum	Hptm Schrieck	Do 18	10	6
2./KüFlGr 906	Hörnum	Hptm Fliessbach	Do 18	9	8
Stab/KüFlGr 706	Stavanger	Obstlt Lessing	He 115 BV138		
1./KüFlGr 406	Stavanger	Hptm Kayser	Do 18	10	8
2./KüFlGr 406	Stavanger	Hptm Tantzen	Do 18	7	7
Stab/KüFlGr 606	Brest	Major Hahn	Do 17Z Ju 88A		
1./KüFlGr 606	Brest	Hptm Lenschow	Do 17 Z-2	11	11
2./KüFlGr 606	Brest	Hptm Lassmann	Do 17 Z-2	11	11
3./KüFlGr 606	Brest	Hptm Golcher	Do 17 Z-2	11	10
1./BFGr.196	Wilhelmshaven	Hptm Wiegmink	Ar 196 A	21	20
Transozeanstaffel	Brest	Hptm Brockmann	Do 26	2	1
1./KüFlGr 106	Norderney	Major Emonds	He 115 C	12	12

APPENDIX 2
RAF FIGHTER COMMAND ON 1 AUGUST 1940

Unit	Airfield	Commander	Aircraft	Number of aircraft	Operational
Fighter Command					
Fighter Commands Headquarters	Bentley Priory, Stanmore	Air Chief Marshal Sir Hugh Dowding			
No. 10 Group	Headquarters	Air Vice-Marshal Sir Christopher Brand			
Pembrey Sector		Wing Commander J. H. Hutchinson			
No. 92 Squadron	Pembrey	S/Ldr P. J. Sanders	Spitfire	16	12
Filton Sector		Group Captain R. Hanmer			
No. 87 Squadron	Exeter	S/Ldr T. G. Lovell-Gregg	Hurricane	18	13
No. 213 Squadron	Exeter	S/Ldr H. D. McGregor	Hurricane	17	12
St. Eval Sector (Coastal Command) Headquarters		Group Captain L. G. le B. Croke S/Ldr J. S. O'Brien			
No. 234 Squadron	St. Eval	Flight Lieutenant	Spitfire	16	10
No. 247 Squadron		H. A. Chater	Gladiator	(6)	
Middle Wallop Sector		Wing Commander D. Roberts			
No. 152 Squadron	Warmwell	S/Ldr P. Devitt	Spitfire	15	10
No. 238 Squadron	Middle Wallop	S/Ldr H. Fenton	Hurricane	15	12
No. 604 Squadron	Middle Wallop	S/Ldr M. Anderson	Blenheim	16	11
No. 609 Squadron	Middle Wallop	S/Ldr H. Darley	Spitfire	16	10
No. 11 Group	Headquarters Uxbridge	Air Vice-Marshal Keith Park			
Debden Sector		Wing Commander L. Fuller-Good			
No. 17 Squadron	Debden	S/Ldr C. W. Williams	Hurricane	19	14
No. 85 Squadron	Martlesham	S/Ldr P. Townsend	Hurricane	18	12
North Weald Sector		Wing Commander V. Beamish			
No. 56 Squadron	North Weald	S/Ldr G. A. Manton	Hurricane	17	15
No. 151 Squadron	North Weald	S/Ldr J. A. Gordon	Hurricane	18	13

Unit	Airfield	Commander	Aircraft	Number of aircraft	Operational
No. 11 Group cont.					
Hornchurch Sector		Wing Commander Cecil Bouchier			
No. 41 Squadron		S/Ldr H. Richard Hood	Spitfire	16	10
No. 65 Squadron	Hornchurch	S/Ldr A. L. Holland	Spitfire	16	11
No. 74 Squadron	Hornchurch	S/Ldr F. White	Spitfire	15	12
Biggin Hill Sector		Group Captain R. Grice			
No. 32 Squadron	Biggin Hill	S/Ldr J. Worrall	Hurricane	15	11
No. 501 Squadron	Gravesend	S/Ldr H. Hogan	Hurricane	16	11
No. 600 Squadron	Manston	S/Ldr D. de B. Clark	Blenheim	15	9
No. 610 Squadron	Biggin Hill	S/Ldr J. Ellis	Spitfire	15	12
Kenley Sector		Wing Commander T. Prickman			
No. 64 Squadron	Kenley	S/Ldr A. MacDonell	Spitfire	12	4
No. 111 Squadron	Croydon	S/Ldr J. Thompson	Hurricane	10	2
No. 615 Squadron	Kenley	S/Ldr J. Kayll	Hurricane	14	2
Northolt Sector		Group Captain S. Vincent			
No. 43 Squadron	Northolt	S/Ldr J. Badger	Hurricane	19	18
No. 257 Squadron	Northolt	S/Ldr H. Harkness	Hurricane	10	5
Tangmere Sector		Wing Commander J. Poret			
No. 1 Squadron	Tangmere	S/Ldr D. A. Pemberton	Hurricane	16	13
No. 145 Squadron	Westhampnett	S/Ldr J. Peel	Hurricane	17	10
No. 601 Squadron	Tangmere	S/Ldr W. F. C. Hobson	Hurricane	18	14
No. 12 Group	Headquarters Watnall	Air Vice-Marshal Trafford Leigh-Mallory			
Kirton-in-Lindsey Sector		Wing Commander S. H. Hardy			
No. 222 Squadron	Kirton-in-Lindsey	S/Ldr John Hill	Spitfire	17	14
No. 264 Squadron	Kirton-in-Lindsey	S/Ldr Philip Hunter	Defiant	16	12
Digby Sector		Wing Commander I. Parker			
No. 29 Squadron	Digby	S/Ldr S. C. Widdows	Blenheim	12	8
No. 46 Squadron	Digby	S/Ldr J. R. MacLachlan	Hurricane	17	12
No. 611 Squadron	Digby and Ternhill	S/Ldr J. McComb	Spitfire	13	6
Coltishall Sector		Wing Commander W. K. Beisiegel			
No. 66 Squadron	Coltishall	S/Ldr R. Leigh	Spitfire	16	12
No. 242 Squadron	Coltishall	S/Ldr D. Bader	Hurricane	16	11

Unit	Airfield	Commander	Aircraft	Number of aircraft	Operational
No. 12 Group cont.					
Wittering Sector		Wing Commander H. Broadhurst			
No. 23 Squadron	Colly Weston	S/Ldr G. Heycock	Blenheim	14	9
No. 229 Squadron	Wittering and Bircham Newton	S/Ldr H. J. Maguire	Hurricane	18	14
No. 266 Squadron	Wittering	S/Ldr R. L. Wilkinson	Spitfire	18	13
Duxford Sector		Wing Commander A. B. Woodhall			
No. 19 Squadron	Fowlmere	S/Ldr P. Pinkham	Spitfire	15	9
No. 13 Group	Headquarters Newcastle-on-Tyne	Air Vice-Marshal Richard Saul			
Catterick Sector		Wing Commander G. L. Carter			
No. 219 Squadron	Leeming	S/Ldr J. H. Little	Blenheim	15	10
No. 54 Squadron	Catterick	S/Ldr J. Leathart	Spitfire	14	11
Usworth Sector		Wing Commander B. Thynne			
No. 72 Squadron	Acklington	S/Ldr A. R. Collins	Spitfire	15	10
No. 79 Squadron	Acklington	S/Ldr J. Harvey Hayworth	Hurricane	12	10
No. 607 Squadron	Usworth	S/Ldr J. Vick	Hurricane	16	12
Wick Sector		Wing Commander G. Ambler			
No. 3 Squadron	Wick	S/Ldr S. F. Godden	Hurricane	12	10
No. 232 Squadron	Sumburgh	S/Ldr M. M. Stephens	Hurricane	10	6
No. 504 Squadron	Castletown	S/Ldr J. Sample	Hurricane	17	13
No. 804 Squadron	Wick	Lieutenant Commander J. C. Cockburn (Royal Navy)	Gladiator	14	8
Dyce Sector		Group Captain F. Crerar			
263 Squadron	Grangemouth	S/Ldr H. Eeles	Hurricane	6	4
Turnhouse Sector		Wing Commander Duke of Hamilton and Bradon			
No. 141 Squadron	Prestwick	S/Ldr W. A. Richardson	Defiant	12	8
No. 253 Squadron	Turnhouse	S/Ldr T. Cleave	Hurricane	16	12
No. 602 Squadron	Drem	S/Ldr A. V. R. Johnstone	Spitfire	15	11
No. 603 Squadron	Turnhouse	(vacant)	Spitfire	15	11
No. 605 Squadron		S/Ldr W. Churchill	Hurricane	18	14
Church Fenton Sector		Group Captain C. F. Horsley			
No. 73 Squadron	Church Fenton	S/Ldr M. W. Robinson	Hurricane	16	11
No. 249 Squadron	Church Fenton	S/Ldr E. King	Hurricane	16	11
No. 616 Squadron	Leconfield	S/Ldr M. Robinson	Spitfire	16	12
Aldergrove Sector					
No. 245 Squadron	Aldergrove	S/Ldr F. W. Whitley	Hurricane	10	8

APPENDIX 3
THE HIGHEST MILITARY AWARDS DURING THE BATTLE OF BRITAIN

British

• **Victoria Cross.** The highest British award was the Victoria Cross. It was instituted in 1856, and until 1942 Victoria Crosses were cast of Russian bronze cannons that had been captured during the Crimean War. During the Battle of Britain (July–October 1940) three pilots received this award: Flight Lieutenant Roderick Learoyd and Sergeant John Hannah of Bomber Command, and Flight Lieutenant James B. Nicolson of Fighter Command.

• **Distinguished Service Order** (DSO) was instituted in 1886 for officers who distinguished themselves particularly well in battle. The DSO could be awarded to the same individual up to four times. In such cases these were designated as the DSOs with bar(s). During the Second World War, 870 officers of the RAF and the Commonwealth air forces were awarded with the DSO. Of these, 62 received one bar, eight a second bar and two a third bar. (The corresponding award for NCOs and rank and file, the CGM – Conspicuous Gallantry Medal – became available for service in the RAF only in 1942.)

• **Distinguished Flying Cross** (DFC) was established in 1918 for officers of the RAF and the Commonwealth air forces who distinguished themselves particularly well in combat. The DFC was lower in rank than the DSO. This award could also be received several times, marked by one or more bars. During the Second World War 20,354 officers in the RAF and the Commonwealth air forces were awarded with the DFC, of whom 1,550 received one bar and 42 a second bar.

• **Distinguished Flying Medal** (DFM) established in 1918 correspondence to the DFC for NCOs and rank and file. During the Second World War, 6,637 servicemen received the DFM, including 60 as a bar.

German

Based on the famous Iron Cross, which was instituted by the Prussian King Frederick William III in 1813, the Third Reich developed a comprehensive flora of military awards. The Iron Cross was issued in two denominations:
• **The Iron Cross of first class** (*Eisernes Kreuz 1. Klasse, EK I*)
• **The Iron Cross of the second** class (*Eisernes Kreuz 2. Klasse, EK II*), which was marked with a black-white-red ribbon.

Already during the First World War, the large number of awarded iron crosses caused a certain inflation of its value. During the First World War an estimated five million EK IIs and 218,000 EK Is were awarded. During the Second World War II an estimated three million EK IIs and 450,000 EK Is were awarded.

The highest German military award during the First World War was the *Pour le Mérite*, the so-called 'Blue Max'. During the Second World War, this was substituted by the Knight's Cross, the *Ritterkreuz*:

• **The Knight's Cross** – or, as it was actually called, the Knight's Cross of the Iron Cross, *Ritterkreuz des eisernen Kreuzes* – was a particularly high award, and assumed that the receiver first had been awarded with the two Iron crosses. During the Second World War, 7,200 persons received the Knight's Cross out. A higher grade was instituted on 3 June 1940:

• **The Oak Leaves to the Knight's Cross,** *Eichenlaub zum Ritterkreuz des Eisernen Kreuzes.* Of four Oak leaves to the Knight's Cross that were awarded until October 1940, three went to the fighter aces Werner Mölders, Adolf Galland and Helmut Wick.

• **The Oak Leaves with Swords to the Knight's Cross** – *Eichenlaub mit Schwertern zum Ritterkreuz des Eisernen Kreuzes* – was established in September 1940, but the first two 'Swords' were not awarded until in June 1941, once again to the fighter aces Adolf Galland and Werner Mölders.

Later on in the war even higher grades of the Knight's Cross were instituted.

In addition, after the victory over France in 1940, Hitler instituted what would remain the highest military award throughout the war, **the Grand Cross of the Iron Cross** (*Grosskreuz des Eisernen Kreuzes*). Hermann Göring was awarded with this on 19 July 1940, and he would remain the single recipient.

SOURCES

Archives

Archiv JG 52 – Alfons Altmeyer and Mannfred Wägenbaur.
Archiv JG 54 – Hans-Ekkehard Bob.
Archiv JG 54 – Günther Rosipal.
Deutsches Museum, Munich and Schleissheim.
The Battle of Britain Historical Society.
Bundesarchiv/Militärarchiv, Koblenz.
Imperial War Museum, London and Duxford.
Kent Battle of Britain Museum, Hawkinge.
Krigsarkivet, Stockholm.
Luftfahrtmuseum, Hannover-Laatzen.
The Museum of Army Flying, Middle Wallop.
National Archive, Kew.
National Archives and Records Administration, Washington, D.C.
RAF Museum, Hendon.
Suchgruppe 45.
Svensk flyghistorisk förening, Stockholm.
Technikmuseum, Speyer and Sinsheim.
Traditionsgemeinschaft JG 26.
Traditionsgemeinschaft JG 51.
Traditionsgemeinschaft JG 52.
Traditionsgemeinschaft JG 54.
Traditionsgemeinschaft des Stukageschwaders 2 Immelmann Traditionsverband Boelcke.
WASt Deutsche Dienststelle, Berlin.

Other unpublished material from private archives etc.

52er Nachrichtenblatt.
Abschussberichte 1940 from various German pilots.
Chronik der I./JG 54.
Various combat reports (ref.notes)
Varipous log books (ref. notes)
Kampfgeschwader 1 'Hindenburg': Geschwadergeschichte in Kurzfassung. By Oberst a.D. Gerhard Baeker.
KTB I./JG 52. Traditionsgeschichte der I./Jagdgeschwader 52.
Kriegstagebuch 9./JG 54.
Luftwaffe losses – archive Matti Salonen.
Martin Mettig, written memoirs from I./JG 21 – III./JG 54 15 July 1939–31 January 1940.
Staffel-Chronik der III. Jagdgeschwader 54 7. Staffel.
Trautloft, Hannes – Diary July–November 1940.
ZG 26 documents via Günther Rosipal.

Periodicals

Der Adler. (1940)
Aeroplane. (1940)
Aeroplane Monthly.
Airlife.
AvStop Magazine Online.
Jägerblatt.
Kleine Kriegshefte. (1940)

The Mail on Sunday.
The New Zealand Herald.
Scramble! Official Newsletter of the Battle of Britain Historical Society.
South African Military History Journal.

Books

Allen, Wing Commander Dizzy, *Fighter Squadron,* Granada, London 1982.
Balke, Ulf, *Kampfgeschwader 100 'Wiking',* Motorbuch Verlag, Stuttgart 1981.
Balke, Ulf, *Der Luftkrieg in Europa 1939–1941,* Bechtermünz Verlag, Augsburg 1997.
Barbas, Bernd, *Die Geschichte der II. Gruppe des Jagdgeschwaders 52,* Traditionsgemeinschaft JG 52, Überlingen 2005.
Bartley, Tony, *Smoke Trails in the Sky: The Journals of a Battle of Britain Fighter Pilot,* Crécy Publishing, 1997.
Bergström, Christer, *Hans-Ekkehard Bob,* AirPower Editions, Crowborough 2007.
Bergström, Christer, *Max-Hellmuth Ostermann,* AirPower Editions, Crowborough 2007.
Bishop, Patrick, *Fighter Boys,* Viking Penguin, New York 2003.
Bob, Hans-Ekkehard, *Verratener Idealismus: Erinnerungen eines Jagdfliegers,* private edition, Bob, Freiburg 2000.
Bohlander, Knud Graah, *Englands väg,* Bonniers, Stockholm 1941.
Brew, Alex, *The Turret Fighters: Defiant and Roc,* Ramsbury, Marlborough, Wiltshire: Crowood Press, 2002.
Brickhill, Paul, *Reach for the Sky: The True Story of Douglas Bader,* Ballantine Books, New York, 1967.
Brunswig, Hans, *Feuersturm über Hamburg,* Motorbuch Verlag, Stuttgart 1982.
Bungay, Stephen, *The Most Dangerous Enemy: A History of the Battle of Britain,* Aurum Press, London 2001.
Burns, Michael G., *Bader – the Man and his Men,* Arms & Armour Press, London 1990.
Caldwell, Donald, *JG 26 War Diary Volume 1 1939-1942,* Grub Street, London 1996.
Cameron, Ian, *Wings of the Morning: the Story of the Fleet Air Arm in the Second World War,* Hodder & Stoughton, London 1962.
Chorley, W. R., *Royal Air Force Bomber Command Losses of the Second World War, Vol. 1,* Midland Publishing, Hinckley 2005.
Churchill, Winston, *Andra världskriget, Första bandet: Stormolnen hopas,* Skoglunds bokförlag, Stockholm 1948.
Churchill, Winston, *Andra världskriget, Andra bandet: Englands stoltaste stund,* Skoglunds bokförlag, Stockholm 1949.
Clark, Ronald W., *Battle for Britain,* George G. Harrap, London 1965.
Collier, Basil, *The Battle of Britain,* Berkeley Medallion Books, New York 1969.
Collier, Richard, *Eagle Day: The Battle of Britain,* Cassel Military Classics 1999.

Cossey, Bob, *A Tiger's Tale: the Story of Battle of Britain Fighter Ace Wing Commander John Connell Freeborn,* J & KH Publishing, Hailsham 2002.

Deere, Alan, *Nine Lives,* Wingham Press, Canterbury 1991.

Deighton, Len, *Fighter: The True Story of the Battle of Britain,* Castle Books, Dison, NJ 1993.

Dickfeld, Adolf, *Footsteps of the Hunter,* J. J. Fedorowicz Publishing, Winnipeg 1993.

Dierich, Wolfgang, *Kampfgeschwader 51 'Edelweiss',* Motorbuch Verlag, Stuttgart 1975.

Dierich, Wolfgang, *Kampfgeschwader 55 'Greif',* Motorbuch Verlag, Stuttgart 1975.

Dixon, Jack, *Dowding & Churchill: The Dark Side of the Battle of Britain,* Pen & Sword, Barnsley 2008.

Doe, Bob, *Bob Doe – Fighter Pilot,* CCB Aviation Books, Cambridge 1999.

Donnelly, Larry, *The Other Few,* Red Kite Books, Walton on Thames 2004.

von Eimannsberger, Ludwig, *Zerstörergruppe: A History of V.(Z)/LG 1 – I./NJG 3 1939–1941,* Schiffer Publishing, Atglen 1998.

Fahrten und Flüge gegen England, Zeitgeschichte Verlag, Berlin 1941.

Falck, Wolfgang, *Wolfgang Falck: the Happy Falcon,* Eagle Editions, Hamilton 2002.

Fast, Niko, *Das Jagdgeschwader 52,* Bensberger Buch-Verlag, Bergisch Gladbach 1988–1992.

Fiedler, Arkady, *Squadron 303: the Story of the Polish Fighter Squadron with the RAF,* Roy Publishers, New York 1943.

FitzGibbon, Constantine, *London's Burning,* Ballantine Books, New York 1970.

Flint, Peter, *Dowding and Headquarters Fighter Command,* Airlife Publishing, Ramsbury 1996.

von Forell, Fritz, *Mölders und seine Männer,* Steirische Verlagsanstalt, Graz 1941.

Foreman, John, *Fighter Command War Diaries. Volume 2: September 1940 to December 1941,* Air Research Publications, Walton-on-Thames 1998.

Foreman, John, *RAF Fighter Command Victory Claims of World War Two, Part One, 1939–1940,* Red Kite Walton-on-Thames 2003.

Forrester, Larry, *Fly for your Life: the Thrilling Story of Wartime Air Ace R. Stanford Tuck,* Granada Publishing Ltd., Frogmore 1979.

Franks, Norman L., *Royal Air Force Fighter Command Losses of the Second World War, vol. 1,* Midland Publishing, Leicester 1997.

Frayn Turner, John, *The Battle of Britain,* Airlife Publishing 1998.

Galland, Adolf, *Die Ersten und die Letzten,* Schneekluth Verlag, München 1953.

Galland, Adolf, *The Luftwaffe Fighter Force: the View from the Cockpit,* Greenhill Books, London 1998.

Girbig, Werner, *Im Anflug auf die Reichshauptstadt,* Motorbuch Verlag, Stuttgart 1977.

Goss, Chris, *The Luftwaffe Bombers' Battle of Britain,* Crécy Publishing Ltd., Manchester 2000.

Goss, Chris, *The Luftwaffe Fighters' Battle of Britain,* Crécy Publishing Ltd., Manchester 2000.

Goss, Chris, *Brothers in Arms.* Crécy Publishing Ltd., Manchester, 2004.

Gretzyngier, Robert, *Poles in Defence of Britain,* Grub Street, London 2001.

Griese, Friedrich, *Oesau,* Hanns Arens Verlag, Berlin 1943.

Gundelach, Karl, *Kampfgeschwader 4 General Wever,* Motorbuch Verlag, Stuttgart 1978.

Halley, James J., *Royal Air Force Aircraft L1000–N9999,* Air Britain, Tunbridge Wells 1996.

Halley, James J., *Royal Air Force Aircraft P1000–R9999,* Air Britain, Tunbridge Wells 1996.

Halley, James J., *Royal Air Force Aircraft W1000–Z9999,* Air Britain, Tunbridge Wells 1998.

Helmut Wick, Adler-Bücherei, Verlag Scherl, Berlin 1943.

Herrmann, Hajo, *Bewegtes Leben: Kampf- und Jagdflieger 1935–1945,* Motorbuch Verlag, Stuttgart 1986.

Hillary, Richard, *The Last Enemy,* Michael O'Mara Books Limited, London 2014.

Hinchliffe, Peter, *The Other Battle,* Castle Books, Edison 2001.

Holmes, Tony, *American Eagles: American Volunteers in the RAF 1937–1943,* Classic Publications, Crowborough 2001.

Irving, David, *Göring: A Biography,* William Morrow & Co, New York, 1989.

Irving, David, *Hitler's War,* Focal Point, London 2002.

van Ishoven, Armand, *The Luftwaffe in the Battle of Britain,* Ian Allan Publishing, 1998.

Johnson, James E., *Full Circle: the Story of Air Fighting,* Chatto & Windus, London 1964.

Johnson, Air Vice-Marshal J. E. and Wing Commander P. B. Lucas, *Glorious Summer: The Story of the Battle of Britain,* Stanley Paul, London 1990.

Jones, Ira, *Tiger Squadron,* Award Books, New York, 1954.

Jähnert, Erhard, *Mal oben – mal unten: ein Sturzkampfpilot erzählt 1935–1945,* Verlag Remer Heipke, Bad Kissingen 1992.

Kent, John, *One of the Few,* Kimber, London 1971.

Kershaw, Alex, *The Few: The American Knights of the Air Who Risked Everything to Save Britain in the Summer of 1940,* Da Capo Press, Philadelphia 2007.

Kesselring, Albert, *The Memoirs of Field Marshal Kesselring,* Greenhill Books 1988.

Kiehl, Heinz, *Kampfgeschwader 53 'Legion Condor',* Motorbuch Verlag, Stuttgart 1996.

Klee, Karl, *Das Unternehmen 'Seelöwe',* Musterschmidt Verlag, Göttingen 1958.

Knight, Dennis, *A Harvest of Messerschmitts,* Frederick Warne, London, 1981.

Kohl, Hermann, *Volltreffer: Einsatz der Luftwaffe 1940.* Reutlingen: Ensslin & Laiblin, 1941.

Kriegstagebuch des Oberkommandos der Wehrmacht, vol. 1. Red. Percy E. Schramm, Hans-Adolf Jacobsen, Bernard & Graefe Verlag, München 1982.

Mahlke, Helmut, *Stuka: Angriff: Sturzflug,* Verlag E. S. Mittler & Sohn, Berlin 1993.

Mason, Francis K., *Battle over Britain,* McWhirter Twins Ltd., London 1969.

Matloff, Maurice and Edwin M. Snell, *Strategic Planning for Coalition Warfare 1941–1942,* Center of Military History, United States Army, Washington, D. C., 1990.

McIntosh, Dave, *High Blue Battle: the War Diary of No. 1 (401) Fighter Squadron RCAF,* Spa Books, Stevenage 1990.

McKee, Alexander, *Strike from the Sky: the Story of the Battle of Britain,* Souvenir Press, London 1989.

Meimberg, Julius, *Feindflug,* Kurt Braatz – NeunundzwanzigSechs, Moosburg 2002.

Michie, Alan and Walter Graebner, *Their Finest Hour,* Harcourt, Brace and Company, New York 1941.

Michulec, Robert and Donald Caldwell, *Adolf Galland,* Stratus, Sandomierz 2003.

Mobeeck, Erik and Jean-Louis Roba with Chris Goss, *In the Skies of France: A Chronicle of JG 2 'Richthofen', Volume 1: 1934–1940,* A.S.B.L. La Porte d'Hoves, Linkebeek n.d.

Mosley, Leonard, *Battle of Britain,* Time-Life Books, Alexandria, Virginia 1977.

Nauroth, Holger, *Stukageschwader 2 Immelmann,* Verlag K. W. Schütz, Preussisch Oldendorf 1988.

Newton, Dennis, *A Few of the Few,* Australian War Memorial 1990.

Nilsson, Jan-Olof, *Lucky Strike,* Carlssons Bokförlag, Stockholm 2013.

Osterkamp, Theo, *Durch Höhen und Tiefen jagt ein Herz,* Kurt Vowinckel Verlag, Neckargemünd 1952.

Ostermann, Max-Hellmuth, *Vom Häschen zum As,* Ludwig Voggenreiter Verlag, Potsdam 1944.

Overy, Richard, *The Battle of Britain: the Myth and the Reality,* W. W. Norton & Company, New York 2002.

Price, Alfred, Battle of Britain, Arms and Armour Press, London 1990.

Price, Alfred, The Spitfire Story, Arms and Armour, London 1995.

Price, Alfred, The Hardest Day: the Battle of Britain 18 August 1940, Cassell Military Classics 1998.

Price, Alfred, Battle of Britain Day, Greenhill Books 1999.

Prien, Jochen, Geschichte des Jagdgeschwaders 77, Struve Druck, Eutin 1992.

Prien, Jochen and Gerhard Stemmer, Messerschmitt Bf 109 im Einsatz bei der II./Jagdgeschwader 3, Struve Druck, Eutin n.d.

Prien, Jochen, *Jagdgeschwader 53: A History of the 'Pik As' Geschwader March 1937–May 1942,* Schiffer Publishing, Atglen 2000.

Prien, Jochen, Gerhard Stemmer, Peter Rodeike and Winfried Bock, *Die Jagdfliegerverbände der Deutschen Luftwaffe 1934 bis 1945, Teil 4/I – Einsatz am Kanal und über England 26.6.1940 bis 21.6.1941,* Struve Druck, Eutin 2004.

Prien, Jochen, Gerhard Stemmer, Peter Rodeike and Winfried Bock, *Die Jagdfliegerverbände der Deutschen Luftwaffe 1934 bis 1945, Teil 4/II – Einsatz am Kanal und über England 26.6.1940 bis 21.6.1941,* Struve Druck, Eutin 2004.

Priller, Josef, *J.G. 26: Geschichte eines Jagdgeschwaders,* Motorbuch Verlag, Stuttgart 1980.

Radtke, Siegfried, Kampfgeschwader 54, Schild Verlag, München 1990.

Rall, Günther, *Mein Flugbuch,* Kurt Braatz – NeunundzwanzigSechs, Moosburg 2004.

Ray, John, *The Battle of Britain – New Perspectives,* Arms & Armour Press, London 1994.

Revie, Alastair, *Bomber Command: The Courageous Men who fought the Longest Battle of World War II,* Ballantine Books, New York 1972.

Richards, Denis, *Royal Air Force 1939–45, Volume 1: The Fight at Odds,* Her Majesty's Stationery Office, London 1953.

Ring and Girbig, *Jagdgeschwader 27,* Motorbuch Verlag, Stuttgart 1972.

Ross, David M. S., Squadron Leader J. Bruce Blanche and William Simpson, *The Greatest Squadron of Them All: The Definitive History of 603 (City of Edinburgh) Squadron, Vol 1,* Grub Street Publishing, London 2003.

Sarkar, Dilip, *Bader's Duxford Fighters,* Ramrod Publications, Worcester 1997.

Shirer, William, *Berlin Diary,* Alfred A. Knopf, New York 1942.

Schmidt, Rudi, *Achtung! Torpedos Los: der strategische und operative Einsatz des Kampfgeschwaders 26,* Bernard & Graefe Verlag, Bonn n.d.

Schulte, Eduard, *Flieger Sven: ein deutsch-schwedisches Lebensbild 1917 bis 1940,* Selbstverlag, Wöbbel, Kreis Detmold 1957.

Steinhilper, Ulrich and Peter Osborne, *Spitfire on my Tail,* Independent Books, Keston 1990.

Stokes, Dough, *Wings Aflame: the Biography of G/Cpt. Victor Beamish,* Crécy Publishing Ltd., Manchester 1991.

Strohmeyer, Curt, *Stukas!,* Verlag die Heimbücherei, Berlin 1941.

Taghon, Peter, *Die Geschichte des Lehrgeschwaders 1, Band 1 1936–1942,* VDM Heinz Nickel, Zweibrücken 2004.

The Battle of Britain Then and Now. Mk. V, Winston G. Ramsey (red.), After the Battle, London 1989.

The Ministry of Information, *The Battle of Britain August–October 1940: An Air Ministry Account of the Great Days from 8th August–31st October 1940,* His Majesty's Stationery Office, London 1941.

Toliver, Colonel Raymond F. and Trevor J. Constable, *Fighter General: the Life of Adolf Galland,* AmPress Publishing, Zephyr Cove 1990.

Townsend, Peter, *Duel in the Dark: A Fighter Pilot's Story of the Blitz,* Arrow Books, London 1986.

Townsend, Peter, *Duel of Eagles,* Weidenfeld & Nicolson, London 1990.

Townshend-Bickers, Richard, The Battle of Britain, Salamander Press, London 1990.

Vajda, Ferenc A. and Peter Dancey, *German Aircraft Industry and Production 1933–1945,* Airlife, Shrewsbury 1998.

Vasco, John, *Messerschmitt Bf 110 Bombsights over England: Erprobungsgruppe 210 in the Battle of Britain,* Schiffer Publications, Atglen 2002.

Vasco, John J., *Zerstörer, Volume One,* Classic Publications, Crowborough 2005.

Vasco, John J. and Peter D. Cornwell, *Zerstörer: the Messerschmitt 110 and its Units,* JAC Publications, Drayton 1995.

Waiss, Walter, *Boelcke-Archiv, Band II: Chronik Kampfgeschwader Nr. 27 Boelcke: Teil 1: 1934–31.12.1940,* Walter Waiss, Neuss 2000.

Walker, Oliver, *Sailor Malan,* Cassell, London 1953.

Die Wehrmachtsberichte 1939–1945. Band 1 – 1. September 1939 bis 31. Dezember 1941, Gesellschaft für Literatur und Bildung, Köln 1989.

Williams, David P., *Day Fighters,* Cerberus Publishing Ltd., Bristol 2002.

Winterbotham, F. W., *The Ultra Secret,* Harper & Row, New York 1974.

Wood, Derek and Derek Dempster, *The Narrow Margin,* Pen & Sword Military Classics, Barnsley 2003.

Wright, Robert, *Dowding and the Battle of Britain,* MacDonald, London 1969.

Wundshammer, Benno, *Bomben auf Engeland. Kleine Kriegshefte Nr. 8,* Zentralverlag, München 1940.

Wykeham, Peter, *Fighter Command,* Putnam, London 1960.

NOTES

1   Bungay, The Most dangerous Enemy, p. 219.
2   Richards, Royal Air Force, 1939–1945, vol. I: The Fight at Odds, p. 150.
3   Matloff and Snell, Strategic Planning for Coalition Warfare 1941–1942, p. 22.
4   Irving, Hitler's War, p. 314.
5   Ibid.
6   Vajda and Dancey, German Aircraft Industry and Production 1933-1945, p. 144.
7   Royal Air Force Operations Record Book. Form 540: No. 10 Group 1940–1943. National Archives, AIR 25/182.
8   Winterbotham, The Ultra Secret, p. 50.
9   Interview with Cyril Bamberger.
10   Interview with Robert Foster.
11   Deere, Nine Lives, p. 106.
12   Ernst Kühl in Dierich, Kampfgeschwader 55 'Greif', pp. 67–68.
13   Interview with John Elkington.
14   Alfred Grislawski's logbook.
15   Interview with Robert Foster.
16   Interview with Cyril Bamberger.
17   Interview with James E. Johnson.
18   Ibid.
19   Irving, Göring, pp. 140–141.
20   Deighton, Fighter, pp. 42f.
21   Bungay, p. 132.
22   Interview with Erwin Leykauf.
23   Price, The Spitfire Story, p. 78.
24   Interview with Hermann Neuhoff.
25   Vord. II. L. Genst.Gen.Qu./6 Abt.Nr. 4008. Bundesarchiv/Militärarchiv.
26   Prien et al, Die Jagdfliegerverbände, Teil 4/II, p. 427.
27   Royal Air Force Operations Record Book. 11 Group Operations Record Book September 1939–September 1940: 11 Group Intelligence Bulletin No. 34, Part II. 22/8/40. National Archives, Kew. AIR 25/197.
28   Price, p. 78.
29   Interview with Adolf Galland.
30   Allen, Fighter Squadron, p. 57.
31   Interview with Robert Stanford Tuck.
32   von Eimannsberger, Zerstörergruppe, p. 101.
33   Western Plan W.A. 5 (a): The Attack of German War Industry. National Archives, Kew. AIR 20/280.
34   Irving, p. 322.
35   Bundesarchiv/Militärarchiv. RL 2 II/27.
36   Interview with Hajo Herrmann.
37   Geheim-Akten über Lagebericht (Lw) vom 7.7. 1940 bis 1.8. 1940.
38   Deere, p. 88.
39   Osterkamp, Durch Höhen und Tiefen jagt ein Herz, pp. 318ff.
40   Vasco and Cornwell, Zerstörer, p. 79.
41   Deere, p. 89.
42   Ibid.
43   R.A.F. Form 540: Operations Record Book of No. 54 Squadron. National Archives, Kew. AIR 27/511.

44   R.A.F. Form 540: Operations Record Book of No. 609 Squadron. National Archives, Kew. AIR 27/2102.
45   Royal Air Force Operations Record Book. Appendices B, Bomber Command Operations June–August 1940. II M/A1/1A. National Archives, Kew. AIR 24/220.
46   Generalquartiermeister der Luftwaffe.
47   Geheim-Akten über Lagebericht (Lw) vom 7.7. 1940 bis 1.8. 1940.
48   Donnelly, The Other Few, p. 27.
49   Geheim-Akten über Lagebericht (Lw) vom 7.7. 1940 bis 1.8. 1940.
50   R.A.F. Form 540: Operations Record Book of No. 54 Squadron. National Archives, Kew. AIR 27/511.
51   John Freeborn, letter to the author.
52   Hannes Trautloft, diary, 10 July 1940.
53   Jones, Tiger Squadron, p. 249.
54   Griese, Oesau, p. 30.
55   R.A.F. Form 540: Operations Record Book of No. 111 Squadron. National Archives, Kew. AIR 27/866.
56   Balke, Der Luftkrieg in Europa 1939–1941, p. 135.
57   Winterbotham, p. 41.
58   Vasco and Cornwell, p. 88.
59   Interview with Erhard Jähnert.
60   Erhard Jähnert's logbook.
61   Interview with Erhard Jähnert.
62   Bundesarchiv/Militärarchiv. RL 10/116.
63   Geheim-Akten über Lagebericht (Lw) vom 7.7. 1940 bis 1.8. 1940.
64   National Archives, Kew. AIR 50/22/657. Combat Report J.H. Coghlan.
65   Kohl, Volltreffer, p. 95.
66   Royal Air Force Operations Record Book. 11 Group Operations Record Book September 1939–September 1940: 11 Group Intelligence Bulletin No. 8. 19.7. to 20.7.40. National Archives, Kew. AIR 25/197.
67   Kohl, p. 96.
68   R.A.F. Form 541: Operations Record Book of No. 141 Squadron. National Archives, Kew. AIR 27/969.
69   Brew, The Turret Fighters, p. 56.
70   Generalquartiermeister der Luftwaffe.
71   Mason, Battle over Britain, p. 182.
72   Dierich, Kampfgeschwader 51 'Edelweiss', p. 82.
73   Bundesarchiv/Militärarchiv. RL 2 II/30.
74   Winterbotham, p. 41.
75   Royal Air Force Operations Record Book. 11 Group Operations Record Book September 1939–September 1940: 11 Group Intelligence Bulletin No. 12. 24/7/40. National Archives, Kew. AIR 25/197.
76   Caldwell, JG 26 War Diary, vol. 1, p. 47.
77   Interview with Edmund Rossmann.
78   Rall, Mein Flugbuch, p. 52.
79   Deere, p. 97.
80   Rall, p. 52.
81   R.A.F. Form 541: Operations Record Book of No. 54 Squadron. National Archives, Kew. AIR 27/511.
82   Michie and Graebner, Their Finest Hour, p. 29.

83 R.A.F. Form 541: Operations Record Book of No. 65 Squadron. National Archives, Kew. AIR 27/592.

84 Interview with Günther Rall.

85 Interview with Edmund Rossmann.

86 Günter Rall's logbook.

87 Deere, p. 101.

88 Ibid, p. 99.

89 Interview with Edmund Rossmann.

90 Deere, p. 99.

91 Werner Mölders' logbook.

92 Royal Air Force Operations Record Book. 11 Group Operations Record Book September 1939–September 1940: 11 Group Intelligence Bulletin No. 12, 24/7/40. National Archives, Kew. AIR 25/197.

93 von Forell, Mölders und seine Männer, p. 154.

94 Jones, p. 235.

95 Ibid, p. 259.

96 Vasco and Cornwell, p. 93.

97 Johannes Steinhoff in letter to the author.

98 NARA, T971 R4. Von Rohden, 'Der Luftkrieg gegen England 1940–41', Vortrag gehalten am 4. Juli 1944 auf Grund der Unterlagen im Gefechtskalender 'Luftkrieg gegen England mit Anlagen'.

99 R.A.F. Form 541: Operations Record Book of No. 609 Squadron. National Archives, Kew. AIR 27/2102.

100 R.A.F. Form 540: Operations Record Book of No. 257 Squadron. National Archives, Kew. AIR 27/1526.

101 Michie and Graebner, p. 81.

102 Royal Air Force Operations Record Book. Form 540: No. 10 Group 1940–1943. National Archives, Kew. AIR 25/182.

103 Generalquartiermeister der Luftwaffe.

104 Vasco, Zerstörer, Volume One, p. 55.

105 Royal Air Force Operations Record Book. Form 540: No. 10 Group 1940–1943. National Archives, Kew. AIR 25/182.

106 Balke, p. 147.

107 Goss, The Luftwaffe Fighters' Battle of Britain, pp. 40–41.

108 A. G. Malan, Combat Report, 11 August 1940. National Archives, Kew. AIR 27.

109 Hans-Ekkehard Bobs logbook.

110 KTB 9./JG 54. Via Hans-Ekkehard Bob.

111 Deere, p. 105-106.

112 Ibid., p. 107.

113 Ostermann, Vom Häschen zum As, p. 50.

114 Ibid., p. 51.

115 Interview with Hermann Neuhoff.

116 Balke, p. 148.

117 Holmes, American Eagles, p. 43.

118 Ostermann, p. 52.

119 Deere, p. 107.

120 Werner Mölders' logbook.

121 R.A.F. Form 541: Operations Record Book of No. 151 Squadron. National Archives, Kew. AIR 27/1018.

122 Jones, p. 269.

123 Bundesarchiv/Militärarchiv. RL 7/89.

124 Royal Air Force Operations Record Book. 11 Group Operations Record Book September 1939–September 1940: 11 Group Intelligence Bulletin No. 26. 13/8/40. National Archives, Kew. AIR 25/197.

125 Interview with Thomas Dalton-Morgan.

126 Bundesarchiv/Militärarchiv. RL 7/90.

127 Bundesarchiv/Militärarchiv. RL 2 II/30.

128 Taghon, Die Geschichte des Lehrgeschwaders 1, p. 126–127.

129 Royal Air Force Operations Record Book. Appendices B, Bomber Command Operations September–December 1940. II M/A1/1A. D 981. National Archives, Kew. AIR 24/221.

130 Erhard Jähnert's logbook.

131 Interview with Erhard Jähnert.

132 Vasco and Cornwell, p. 111.

133 Kenneth Gundry, letter to his parents. RAF Museum, Hendon.

134 Interview with Erhard Jähnert.

135 Gretzyngier, Poles in Defence of Britain, p. 18.

136 Strohmeyer, Stukas, pp. 147–149.

137 Ibid., p. 149–152.

138 Royal Air Force Operations Record Book. 11 Group Operations Record Book September 1939–September 1940: 11 Group Intelligence Bulletin No. 26. 13/8/40. National Archives, Kew. AIR 25/197.

139 Royal Air Force Operations Record Book. 11 Group Operations Record Book September 1939–September 1940: 11 Group Intelligence Bulletin No. 26. 13/8/40. National Archives, Kew. AIR 25/197.

140 Caldwell, vol. 1, p. 55.

141 R.A.F. Form 540: Operations Record Book of No. 56 Squadron. National Archives, Kew. AIR 27/528.

142 National Archives, Kew: Ultra Decrypts HW 5/4, CX/JQ/225.

143 Interview with Johannes Steinhoff.

144 Interview with Adolf Galland.

145 Otto Kath's logbook.

146 Kershaw, The Few, p. 117.

147 Bundesarchiv/Militärarchiv. RL 10/100.

148 Robert Stanford Tuck's logbook.

149 Günther Rall's logbook.

150 National Archives, Kew: CAB 65/8/40W.M. (40) 228th Conclusions.

151 Bundesarchiv/Militärarchiv. RL 2, II/30.

152 Price, Battle of Britain, p. 94.

153 Kriegstagebuch 9./JG 54. Via Hans-Ekkehard Bob.

154 Werner Mölders, logbook.

155 Royal Air Force Operations Record Book. 11 Group Operations Record Book September 1939–September 1940: 11 Group Intelligence Bulletin No. 28. National Archives, Kew. AIR 25/197.

156 Generalquartiermeister der Luftwaffe.

157 Deere, p. 110.

158 Interview with Hermann Neuhoff.

159 RAF Acklington. raf-acklington.co.uk/Anecdotes.HTML#FCarey.

160 Schmidt, Achtung! Torpedos Los, p. 70.

161 Royal Air Force Operations Record Book. 12 Group Operations Record Book 1/4 1937–December 1941. AIR 25/219.

162 Fahrten und Flüge gegen England, p. 117.

163 National Archives, Kew. CAB CAB/66/13/7.

164 R. J. Rooker, 151 (Hyderabad) Squadron: Historical Record 1939–1967. http://www.152hyderabad.co.uk/html/flt__c_s_marrs__d_f_c.html. Also published as 152 Squadron: A Personal Diary of the Battle of Britain by Eric Marrs in The Aeroplane, 14 September 1945.

165 Interview with Erhard Jähnert.

166 Goss, The Luftwaffe Fighters' Battle of Britain, p. 65.

167 Fahrte und Flüge gegen England.

168 Goss, The Luftwaffe Fighters' Battle of Britain, p. 65f.

169 Interview with Hans-Ekkehard Bob.

170 John Elkington's logbook.

171 Interview with John Elkington.
172 The Battle of Britain Then and Now, Mk. V, p. 306.
173 Jones, p. 272.
174 Deere, p. 122.
175 Balke, p. 152.
176 KTB I./JG 52. Traditionsgeschichte der I./Jagdgeschwader 52.
177 Deere, p. 129.
178 Interview with Adolf Galland.
179 Martin Mettig, written memoirs. Archiv JG 54. Via Hans-Ekkehard Bob.
180 Ibid.
181 Vasco and Cornwell, p. 134.
182 Interview with Robert Stanford Tuck.
183 Generalquartiermeister der Luftwaffe.
184 Interview with Robert Stanford Tuck.
185 KTB I./JG 52.Traditionsgeschichte der I./Jagdgeschwader 52.
186 Quoted in Gretzyngier, p. 29.
187 Quoted in Price, The Hardest Day: The Battle of Britain 18 August 1940, p. 145.
188 Quoted in Gretzyngier, p. 28.
189 Vasco and Cornwell, p. 139.
190 Price, The Hardest Day: The Battle of Britain 18 August 1940, p. 148.
191 R.A.F. Form 540: Operations Record Book of No. 501 Squadron. National Archives, Kew. AIR 27/1949.
192 National Archives, Kew. AIR 41/16.
193 Royal Air Force Operations Record Book. 11 Group Operations Record Book September 1939–September 1940: 11 Group Intelligence Bulletin No. 35. Part I. 23/8/40 – 24/8/40. National Archives, Kew. AIR 25/197.
194 Royal Air Force Operations Record Book. 11 Group Operations Record Book September 1939–September 1940: 11 Group Intelligence Bulletin No. 38. 27–28/8/40. National Archives, Kew. AIR 25/197.
195 Interview with Cyril Bamberger.
196 R.A.F. Form 541: Operations Record Book of No. 610 Squadron. National Archives, Kew. AIR 27/2106.
197 R.A.F. Form 541: Operations Record Book of No. 501 Squadron. National Archives, Kew. AIR 27/1949.
198 Werner Mölders' logbook.
199 R.A.F. Form 541: Operations Record Book of No. 610 Squadron. National Archives, Kew. AIR 27/2106.
200 Royal Air Force Operations Record Book. 11 Group Operations Record Book September 1939–September 1940: 11 Group Intelligence Bulletin No. 38. 27–28/8/40. National Archives, Kew. AIR 25/197.
201 Royal Air Force Operations Record Book. 11 Group Operations Record Book September 1939–September 1940: 11 Group Intelligence Bulletin No. 38. 27–28/8/40. National Archives, Kew. AIR 25/197.
202 Goss, The Luftwaffe Fighters' Battle of Britain, p. 79.
203 Generalquartiermeister der Luftwaffe.
204 Eric Clayton, What if the Heavens Fall: Reminiscences of 56(F) Squadron in the Battle of Britain. pnc.com.au/~insight/heavens/heavens-000.html.
205 Royal Air Force Operations Record Book. 11 Group Operations Record Book September 1939–September 1940: 11 Group Intelligence Bulletin No. 38. 27–28/8/40. National Archives, Kew. AIR 25/197.
206 R.A.F. Form 541: Operations Record Book of No. 151 Squadron. National Archives, Kew. AIR 27/1018.
207 Clayton, Ibid.
208 Ibid.
209 Royal Air Force Operations Record Book. 12 Group 1 April 1937–December 1941. National Archives, Kew. AIR 25/219.
210 R.A.F. Form 540: Operations Record Book of No. 609 Squadron. National Archives, Kew. AIR 27/2102.
211 Lageberichte Lfl. 3. NARA R 88; Bundesarchiv/Militärarchiv. RL 7/90.
212 Royal Air Force Operations Record Book. 11 Group Operations Record Book September 1939–September 1940: Group Controllers Instruction No. 4. National Archives, Kew. AIR 25/197.
213 Quoted in Vasco and Cornwell, p. 144.
214 R.A.F. Form 540: Operations Record Book of No. 17 Squadron. National Archives, Kew. AIR 27/234.
215 Goss, The Luftwaffe Fighters' Battle of Britain, p. 89.
216 R.A.F. Form 540: Operations Record Book of No. 609 Squadron. National Archives, Kew. AIR 27/2102.
217 Mobeeck and Roba with Goss, p. 223.
218 Werner Mölders' logbook.
219 Generalquartiermeister der Luftwaffe.
220 Balke, p. 160.
221 Traditionsgeschichte der I./Jagdgeschwader 52.
222 Steinhilper, Spitfire on my Tail, p. 281.
223 Balke, p. 161.
224 Royal Air Force Operations Record Book. 12 Group 1 April 1937–December 1941. National Archives, Kew. AIR 25/219.
225 Royal Air Force Operations Record Book. 12 Group 1 April 1937–December 1941. National Archives, Kew. AIR 25/219.
226 Royal Air Force Operations Record Book. 11 Group Operations Record Book September 1939–September 1940: 11 Group Intelligence Bulletin No. 38. 27-28/8/40. National Archives, Kew. AIR 25/197.
227 Lageberichte Lfl. 3. NARA R 88; Bundesarchiv/Militärarchiv. RL 7/90.
228 Via Ronnie Lamont.
229 Interview with Hermann Neuhoff.
230 Royal Air Force Operations Record Book. 11 Group Operations Record Book September 1939–September 1940: Group Controllers Instruction No. 7. Reinforcement from 10 and 12 Groups. National Archives, Kew. AIR 25/197.
231 Ibid.
232 Cyril Bamberger's logbook.
233 Kriegstagebuch der I./JG 3 für den Zeitraum vom 25.8 1939 – 15.1. 1942. Bundesarchiv/Militärarchiv. RL 10/560.
234 RAF Form 'F': Combat Report. Sgt. Bamberger, Squadron No. 610. 28/8/40. Via Cyril Bamberger.
235 Kriegstagebuch der I./JG 3 für den Zeitraum vom 25.8 1939 – 15.1. 1942. RL 10/560, Bundesarchiv/Militärarchiv.
236 F.C.C.R./664/40. RAF Form 'F': Combat Report. Intelligence Report No. 22. 610 Squadron 28.8.40. Via Cyril Bamberger.
237 Ibid.
238 RAF Form 'F': Combat Report. Sgt. Bamberger, Squadron No. 610. 28/8/40. Via Cyril Bamberger.
239 Werner Mölders' logbook.
240 Deere, p. 135.
241 Bundesarchiv/Militärarchiv. RL 7/89.
242 Wood and Dempster, The Narrow Margin, p. 196.
243 Hillary, The Last Enemy, p. 145.
244 Prien and Stemmer, p. 41.
245 R.A.F. Form 541: Operations Record Book of No. 151 Squadron. National Archives, Kew. AIR 27/1018.
246 Generalquartiermeister der Luftwaffe.

247 R.A.F. Form 541: Operations Record Book of No. 253 Squadron. National Archives, Kew. AIR 27.

248 Kampfgeschwader 1 'Hindenburg': Geschwadergeschichte in Kurzfassung. Unpublished. By Oberst a.D. Gerhard Baeker.

249 R.A.F. Form 541: Operations Record Book of No. 253 Squadron. National Archives, Kew. AIR 27.

250 Kiehl, Kampfgeschwader 'Legion Condor' 53, p. 99.

251 Ibid., p. 100.

252 Royal Air Force Operations Record Book. 11 Group Operations Record Book September 1939–September 1940: 11 Group Intelligence Bulletin No. 40. 30/8/40. National Archives, Kew. AIR 25/197.

253 Royal Air Force Operations Record Book. 12 Group Operations Record Book 1/4 1937–December 1941. AIR 25/219.

254 Quoted in Kiehl, p. 100.

255 Goss, The Luftwaffe Fighters' Battle of Britain, p. 99.

256 R.A.F. Form 540: Operations Record Book of No. 303 (Polish) Squadron. National Archives, Kew. AIR 27/1663.

257 Clayton, ibid.

258 R.A.F. Form 540: Operations Record Book of No. 501 Squadron. National Archives, Kew. AIR 27/1949.

259 Quoted in Kiehl, KG 53, p. 101.

260 Hannes Trautloft, diary, 30 August 1940.

261 Newton, A Few of the Few, p. 136.

262 Royal Air Force Operations Record Book. 11 Group Operations Record Book September 1939–September 1940: Notes of Conferences of Sector Commanders Held at Headquarters of No. 11 Group, 30th August 1940. National Archives, Kew. AIR 25/197.

263 Bishop, Fighter Boys, p. 334.

264 R.A.F. Form 540: Operations Record Book of No. 257 Squadron. National Archives, Kew. AIR 27/1526.

265 Goss, The Luftwaffe Fighters' Battle of Britain, p. 103.

266 Vasco and Cornwell, p. 156.

267 Interview with James Coward.

268 Royal Air Force Operations Record Book. 11 Group Operations Record Book September 1939–September 1940: 11 Group Intelligence Bulletin No. 44. 4th September 1940. National Archives, Kew. AIR 25/197.

269 R.A.F. Form 540: Operations Record Book of No. 56 Squadron. National Archives, Kew. AIR 27/528.

270 Vasco and Cornwell, p. 156.

271 Ibid.

272 Collier, The Battle of Britain, p. 99.

273 Balke, p. 162.

274 Goss, The Luftwaffe Fighters' Battle of Britain, p. 103.

275 Werner Mölders' logbook.

276 Hannes Trautloft, diary, 31 August 1940.

277 Wood and Dempster, p. 315.

278 Deighton, p. 203.

279 Bundesarchiv/Militärarchiv. RL 10/302.

280 Prien, Geschichte des Jagdgeschwaders 77, p. 366.

281 Kriegstagebuch der I./JG 3 für den Zeitraum vom 25.8 1939–15.1. 1942. Bundesarchiv/Militärarchiv. RL 10/560.

282 KTB I./JG 52. Traditionsgeschichte der I./Jagdgeschwader 52.

283 Royal Air Force Operations Record Book. 11 Group Operations Record Book September 1939–September 1940: 11 Group Intelligence Bulletin No. 47. 7th September 1940. National Archives, Kew. AIR 25/197.

284 Generalquartiermeister der Luftwaffe.

285 Balke, Kampfgeschwader 100 'Wiking', p. 55.

286 KTB I./JG 52. Traditionsgeschichte der I./Jagdgeschwader 52.

287 KTB 9./JG 54.

288 Bericht K.G. 1 1.9.1940. Via Gerhard Baeker.

289 The Battle of Britain Then and Now. Mk. V, pp. 404 and 406.

290 Clayton, ibid.

291 Royal Air Force Operations Record Book. 11 Group Operations Record Book September 1939–September 1940: 11 Group Intelligence Bulletin No. 44. 4th September 1940. National Archives, Kew. AIR 25/197.

292 Hillary, p. 135.

293 Diary of Pilot Officer Robert Deacon-Elliott, 72 Squadron.

294 National Archives, Kew: Ultra Decrypts HW 5/4, CX/JQ/280.

295 Fahrte und Flüge gegen England, pp. 105–107.

296 Hillary, p. 7.

297 R.A.F. Form 540: Operations Record Book of No. 17 Squadron. National Archives, Kew. AIR 27/234.

298 R.A.F. Form 540: Operations Record Book of No. 257 Squadron. National Archives, Kew. AIR 27/1526.

299 Holmes, pp. 54–55.

300 Deere, p. 158.

301 Interview with Gerhard Schöpfel.

302 Goss, The Luftwaffe Fighters' Battle of Britain, p. 123.

303 National Archives, Kew. AIR 27/624: R.A.F. Form 540: Operations Record Book of No. 72 Squadron.

304 National Archives, Kew. CAB CAB/66/13/7.

305 Kriegstagebuch der I./JG 3 für den Zeitraum vom 25.8 1939–15.1. 1942. Bundesarchiv/Militärarchiv/Freiburg, RL 10/560.

306 Mason, p. 350.

307 hood5940/BBC: WW2 People's War. bbc.co.uk/ww2peopleswar/stories/17/a2045017.shtml.

308 Kriegstagebuch der I./JG 3 für den Zeitraum vom 25.8 1939 – 15.1. 1942. Bundesarchiv/Militärarchiv. RL 10/560.

309 Holmes, p. 55.

310 Mosley, Battle of Britain, p. 99.

311 Forrester, p. 100.

312 R.A.F. Form 540: Operations Record Book of No. 257 Squadron. National Archives, Kew. AIR 27/1526.

313 Interview with Robert Foster.

314 Royal Air Force Operations Record Book. 11 Group Operations Record Book September 1939–September 1940: Report from AVM Park to Fighter Command's Headquarters, 12 September 1940. National Archives, Kew. AIR 25/197.

315 German High Command War Diary, 13 Augusti 1940. Schramm, Kriegstagebuch des Oberkommandos der Wehrmacht, vol. 1, Teil B, p. 30.

316 German High Command War Diary, 3 September 1940. Schramm, vol. 1, Teil B, p. 60.

317 Girbig, Im Anflug auf die Reichshauptstadt, p. 29.

318 Shirer, Berlin Diary, p. 490.

319 Ibid., p. 494.

320 German High Command War Diary, 3 September 1940. Schramm, Kriegstagebuch des Oberkommandos der Wehrmacht, vol. 1, Teil B, p. 59.

321 Shirer, p. 419.

322 Royal Air Force Operations Record Book. 11 Group Operations Record Book September 1939–September 1940: 11 Group Intelligence Bulletin No. 47. 7th September 1940. National Archives, Kew. AIR 25/197.

323 Kampfgeschwader 1 'Hindenburg': Geschwadergeschichte in Kurzfassung.
324 Generalquartiermeister der Luftwaffe.
325 KTB I./JG 52. Traditionsgeschichte der I./Jagdgeschwader 52.
326 Hannes Trautloft, diary, 8 September 1940.
327 Quoted in Balke, p. 170.
328 Ibid.
329 Bundesarchiv/Militärarchiv. RL 10/100.
330 Brunswig, Feuersturm über Hamburg, p. 450.
331 Hannes Trautloft, diary, 9 September 1940.
332 Quoted in Goss, The Luftwaffe Bombers' Battle of Britain, p. 141.
333 National Archives, Kew. CAB 66/12/12.
334 Hannes Trautloft, diary, 10 September 1940.
335 National Archives, Kew. CAB 66/12/12.
336 Hannes Trautloft, diary, 11 September 1940.
337 Group Controllers Instruction No. 16. National Archives, Kew. AIR 25/197.
338 Interview with Hans Hahn.
339 Werner Mölders' logbook.
340 Interview with Hans-Ekkehard Bob.
341 Lageberichte Lfl. 3. NARA R 88; Bundesarchiv/Militärarchiv, RL 7/90.
342 Jones, p. 284.
343 Wundshammer, Bomben auf Engeland, pp. 2–3.
344 Ibid. p. 3ff.
345 Lagebericht Nr. 394. Der Oberbefehlshaber der Luftwaffe Führungsstab Ic Nr. 18550/40 g. H.Qu., den 4. Oktober 1940.
346 National Archives, Kew. ADM 358/3029.
347 Hannes Trautloft, diary, 11 September 1940.
348 Taghon, p. 139.
349 National Archives, Kew. CAB 66/12/12.
350 German High Command, War Diary, 14 September 1940. Schramm, vol. 1B, p. 76.
351 Interview with Hermann Neuhoff.
352 Prien, Jagdgeschwader 53: A History of the 'Pik As' Geschwader March 1937–May 1942, p. 159.
353 Ibid.
354 Bungay, p. 324.
355 Battle of Britain Historical Society: The Battle of Britain 1940. battleofbritain.net/0041.html.
356 Ibid.
357 Goss, The Luftwaffe Bombers' Battle of Britain, p. 151.
358 Ibid.
359 Interview with Hermann Neuhoff.
360 Balke, p. 173.
361 Hannes Trautloft, diary, 15 September 1940.
362 Brickhill, pp. 194f.
363 Price, Battle of Britain, p. 74.
364 Major Adolf Galland, Gefechtsbericht, 15.9.1940. Via Adolf Galland.
365 Kriegstagebuch der I./JG 3 für den Zeitraum vom 25.8 1939–15.1. 1942. Bundesarchiv/Militärarchiv. RL 10/560.
366 R.A.F. Form 540: Operations Record Book of No. 303 Squadron. National Archives, Kew. AIR 27/1663.
367 Gretzyngier, p. 97.
368 AvStop Magazine Online. http://avstop.com/History/AroundTheWorld/Poland/2.html.
369 Gretzyngier, p. 97.
370 National Archives, Kew: Ultra Decrypts HW 5/5, CX/JQ/316.
371 Supplement to the London Gazette, 11 September 1946.
372 Die Wehrmachtsberichte 1939-1945, 16. September 1940.
373 Revie, p. 80.
374 Balke, p. 176.
375 Hannes Trautloft, diary, 17 September 1940.
376 Interview with Hermann Neuhoff.
377 German High Command, War Diary, 19 September 1940. Schramm, vol. 1B, p. 82.
378 R.A.F. Form 540: Operations Record Book of No. 302 Squadron. National Archives, Kew. AIR 27/1661.
379 Generalquartiermeister der Luftwaffe.
380 Hannes Trautloft, diary, 19 September 1940.
381 Ostermann, p. 62.
382 German High Command, War Diary, 19 September 1940. Kriegstagebuch des Oberkommandos der Wehrmacht, vol. 1B, p. 82.
383 Geheim-Akten über Lagebericht (Lw) vom 10.9 1940 bis 2.10 1940.
384 Chorley, Royal Air Force Bomber Command Losses of the Second World War, Vol. 1, p. 111.
385 Geheim-Akten über Lagebericht (Lw) vom 10.9 1940 bis 2.10 1940.
386 Caldwell, vol. 1, pp. 75–76.
387 Kohl, p. 150.
388 Interview with Cyril Bamberger.
389 Hannes Trautloft, diary, 21 September 1940.
390 Geheim-Akten über Lagebericht (Lw) vom 10.9 1940 bis 2.10 1940.
391 Shirer, p. 515.
392 The Mail on Sunday, 14 December 2003.
393 R. J. Rooker, 151 (Hyderabad) Squadron: Historical Record 1939–1967. 152hyderabad.co.uk/html/one_of_the_few_3.html. Also published as 152 Squadron: A personal Diary of the Battle of Britain by Eric Marrs in The Aeroplane, 14 September 1945.
394 Shirer, p. 523.
395 Generalquartiermeister der Luftwaffe.
396 Interview with Adolf Galland.
397 McKee, Strike from the Sky, pp. 262f.
398 National Archives, Kew. CAB CAB/66/13/7.
399 R. J. Rooker, 151 (Hyderabad) Squadron: Historical Record 1939 – 1967.
400 Ibid.
401 National Archives, Kew. CAB CAB/66/13/7.
402 R.A.F. Form 540: Operations Record Book of No. 609 Squadron. National Archives, Kew. AIR 27/2102.
403 The Battle of Britain Then and Now, Mk. V, p. 467.
404 Ibid., p. 244.
405 Interview with Adolf Galland.
406 R. J. Rooker, 151 (Hyderabad) Squadron: Historical Record 1939–1967.
407 von Eimannsberger, p. 145.
408 Ibid., p. 139.
409 R.A.F. Form 540: Operations Record Book of No. 17 Squadron. National Archives, Kew. AIR 27/234.
410 R.A.F. Form 540: Operations Record Book of No. 303 Squadron. National Archives, Kew. AIR 27/1663.
411 von Eimannsberger, p. 149.
412 Lageberichte Lfl. 3. NARA R 88; Bundesarchiv/Militärarchiv, RL 7/90.
413 Bundesarchiv/Militärarchiv. RL 10/88.
414 Generalquartiermeister der Luftwaffe.
415 Johannes Steinhoff, letter to the author.
416 Steinhilper, p. 308.
417 Chronik der I./JG 54. Archiv JG 54 'Grünherz'.
418 Lageberichte Lfl. 3. NARA R 88; Bundesarchiv/Militärarchiv, RL 7/90.

419 Foreman, *Fighter Command War Diaries, Volume 2*, p. 44.
420 Crook, *Spitfire Pilot*, p. 167.
421 Dierich, *Kampfgeschwader 55*, p. 126.
422 Clayton, ibid.
423 R. J. Rooker, *151 (Hyderabad) Squadron: Historical Record 1939–1967*.
424 *Staffel-Chronik der III. Jagdgeschwader 54 7. Staffel*.
425 Interview with Adolf Galland.
426 *Staffel-Chronik der III. Jagdgeschwader 54 7. Staffel*.
427 National Archives, Kew. CAB 65/9/25.
428 KTB 9./JG 54.
429 Generalquartiermeister der Luftwaffe.
430 Lageberichte Lfl. 3. NARA R 88; Bundesarchiv/Militärarchiv, RL 7/90.
431 Interview with Adolf Galland.
432 Hannes Trautloft, diary, 18 October 1940.
433 Galland, *Die Ersten und die Letzten*, p. 109.
434 Interview with Hans-Ekkehard Bob.
435 Bundesarchiv/Militärarchiv. RL 10/88.
436 Royal Air Force Operations Record Book. Appendices B, Bomber Command Operations September–December 1940. II M/A1/1A. D 997. National Archives, Kew. AIR 24/221.
437 Kriegstagebuch der I./K.G. 53. Bundesarchiv/Militärarchiv. RL 10/88.
438 Lagebericht Nr. 394. Der Oberbefehlshaber der Luftwaffe Führungsstab Ic Nr. 18550/40 g. H.Qu., den 4. Oktober 1940; Mason, p. 429.
439 Helmut Wick, pp. 115–116.
440 Ibid.
441 R.A.F. Form 540: Operations Record Book of No. 609 Squadron. National Archives, Kew. AIR 27/2102.
442 R. J. Rooker, *151 (Hyderabad) Squadron: Historical Record 1939–1967*.
443 Royal Air Force Operations Record Book. Form 540: No. 10 Group 1940–1943. National Archives, Kew. AIR 25/182.
444 von Forell, p. 175.
445 McKee, p. 233.
446 Interview with Adolf Galland.
447 Royal Air Force Operations Record Book. 11 Group Operations Record Book October–December 1940. Instruction to Controllers No. 25. 7th October 1940. National Archives, Kew. AIR 25/198.
448 Quoted in Prien and Stemmer, *Messerschmitt Bf 109 im Einsatz bei der II./Jagdgeschwader 3*, p. 29.
449 Adolf Galland's logbook.
450 Bundesarchiv/Militärarchiv. RL 10/546.
451 Lagebericht Nr. 404. Der Oberbefehlshaber der Luftwaffe Führungsstab Ic Nr. 19330/40 g. H.Qu., den 14. Oktober 1940.
452 Lagebericht Nr. 405. Der Oberbefehlshaber der Luftwaffe Führungsstab Ic Nr. 19350/40 g. H.Qu., den 15 Oktober 1940.
453 National Archives, Kew. CAB 65/9/32.
454 National Archives, Kew. CAB 65/9/33.
455 Lagebericht Nr. 407. Der Oberbefehlshaber der Luftwaffe Führungsstab Ic Nr. 19610/40 g. H.Qu., den 17.10. 1940.
456 Major Adolf Galland, Gefechtsbericht, 15.10.1940. Via Adolf Galland.
457 Royal Air Force Operations Record Book. 11 Group Operations Record Book October–December 1940. National Archives, Kew. AIR 25/198.
458 Jones, p. 293.
459 von Forell, p. 180.
460 Schulte, *Flieger Sven: ein deutsch-schwedisches Lebensbild 1917 bis 1940*, p. 182.
461 Ibid, p. 185.
462 National Archives, Kew. CAB CAB/65/9/36.
463 Crook, p. 190.
464 Via Doug Tidy.
465 *The London Gazette*, 5 November 1940, p. 6399.
466 National Archives, Kew. AIR 50/100/101Combat Report Pilot Officer [sic] Coke, 257 Squadron.
467 Lagebericht Nr. 413. Der Oberbefehlshaber der Luftwaffe Führungsstab Ic Nr. 19920/40 g. H.Qu., den 23.10. 1940. Anlage 4.
468 James Hayter, letter to the author.
469 Jones, p. 296.
470 Steinhilper, p. 10.
471 Jones, p. 296.
472 KTB I./JG 52. Traditionsgeschichte der I./Jagdgeschwader 52.
473 Via Ronnie Lamont.
474 Barbas, *Die Geschichte der II. Gruppe des Jagdgeschwader 52*, p. 38.
475 Vasco, *Messerschmitt Bf 110 Bombsights over England: Erprobungsgruppe 210 in the Battle of Britain*, pp. 126-127.
476 von Forell, p. 183; interview with Adolf Galland; Werner Mölders' logbook.
477 Foreman, p. 82.
478 *Scramble! Official Newsletter of the Battle of Britain Historical Society*, March 2006, No. 116.
479 Interview with Robert Foster.
480 Quoted in Braatz, *Gott oder Flugzeug: Leben und sterben des Jagdfliegers Günther Lützow*, p. 233.
481 Hannes Trautloft, diary, 3–7 November 1940.
482 Hannes Trautloft, diary, 7 November 1940.
483 Interview with Adolf Galland.
484 Interview with Robert Foster.
485 Interview with Hans-Ekkehard Bob.
486 Royal Air Force Operations Record Book. Appendices B, Bomber Command Operations September–December 1940. II M/A1/1A. D 1164. Bomber Command Intelligence Report No. 1092. 14 November 1940. National Archives, Kew. AIR 24/221.
487 Hannes Trautloft, diary, 13 November 1940.
488 Generalquartiermeister der Luftwaffe.
489 Mahlke, *Stuka - Angriff: Sturzflug*, p. 96.
490 Adolf Galland's logbook.
491 Mahlke, p. 96.
492 Jones, p. 299.
493 Michulec and Caldwell, *Adolf Galland*, pp. 12–14.
494 Sobski, *Lictorian Fasces over England*, p. 49.
495 *Scramble! Official Newsletter of the Battle of Britain Historical Society*, March 2006, No. 116.
496 Ernie Burton: *Alfred Keith Ogilvie: Battle of Britain Pilot with 609 Squadron*. members.lycos.co.uk/ErnieBurton/Pilots/Ogilvie_Alfred_Keith.
497 R. J. Rooker, *151 (Hyderabad) Squadron: Historical Record 1939–1967*.
498 R.A.F. Form 540: Operations Record Book of No. 609 Squadron. National Archives, Kew. AIR 27/2102.
499 R. J. Rooker, *151 (Hyderabad) Squadron: Historical Record 1939–1967*.
500 Ibid.
501 Meimberg, *Feindberührung*, p. 174.
502 R.A.F. Form 540: Operations Record Book of No. 609 Squadron. National Archives, Kew. AIR 27/2102.

503 R.A.F. Form 540: Operations Record Book of No. 152
     (Hyderabad) Squadron. National Archives, Kew.
     AIR 27/1025.
504 R. J. Rooker, 151 (Hyderabad) Squadron: Historical
     Record 1939–1967.
505 Wood and Dempster, p. 315.
506 Churchill, Andra världskriget, II: Ensamma, p. 362.
507 Generalquartiermeister der Luftwaffe.
508 Wood and Dempster, p. 312.
509 Chorley, pp. 84ff.
510 Aeroplane Monthly, September 1996.
511 London Gazette, 11 September 1946.
512 Wood and Dempster, p. 312.
513 The Aeroplane, 27 December 1940.
514 Vajda and Dancey, p. 144.
515 The Aeroplane, 27 December 1940.
516 Overy, The Battle of Britain; the Myth and the Reality,
     p. 129f.
517 Bungay, p. 357.
518 Ibid.
519 Ibid., p. 358.
520 Ibid.
521 The Ministry of Information, The Battle of Britain
     August–October 1940: An Air Ministry Account of the
     Great Days from 8th August–31st October 1940.
522 Deighton, p. 226.
523 Interview with Robert Foster.
524 New Zealand Herald, 9 September 1952.

INDEX